W9-CLH-163

Reading, Writing, and Rewriting

Writing
Rewriting

J. B. Lippincott Company

Philadelphia New York

Reading and

A RHETORIC READER

William T. Moynihan

University of Connecticut

Donald W. Lee

University of Houston

Herbert Weil, Jr.

University of Connecticut

Library of Congress Catalog Card Number: 64-14848

Printed in the United States of America

Preface

THREE CLOSELY RELATED and practical assumptions underlie this book. Effective writing most frequently stems from intelligent reading. Effective writing also presumes informed self-criticism. And informed self-criticism is best put into practice by learning how to rewrite.

These principles seem to us no radical departure from general principles underlying most college composition courses. As a text, *Reading, Writing, and Rewriting* is new primarily in that it places fresh emphasis on practices long advocated by college composition teachers. As composition teachers, we knew of no text which gave emphasis to reading, self-criticism, and *rewriting* in proportion to their importance. In this book we have tried to redress the balance.

Reading, Writing, and Rewriting has six parts. A general introduction discusses broadly the difficulties facing the average student writer and suggests some of many ways the student may cope with these difficulties. The next five sections of the book deal at length with five aspects of student writing—reading (for writing), language, form, argument, and interpretation.

We have tried to follow a sensible and straightforward procedure regarding introductions, questions, and assignments. In all parts of the book we have attempted to be helpful but unobtrusive. Our policy has been to provide the student and beginning instructor with sufficient commentary, both before and after the selections, to explain one method of approach. We have also provided some questions to guide student reading and to stimulate discussion. With few exceptions, theme topics have been designed for every selection to enable the student to apply the rhetorical techniques he should be learning as he reads.

The readings included have been selected because they lend themselves to analysis, to imitation, to lively discussion. We have not hesitated to use those essays which we had already discovered worked well in the classroom. In order to encourage informed self-criticism we have intentionally included various kinds of writing—contemporary-classical, student-professional, cluttered-uncluttered, creative-analytical. Our experience has shown that students acquire a sense of good writing when they are required to analyze various types of writing—especially the less successful as well as the more successful. Our book also purposely contains a good proportion of creative material to illustrate rhetorical points. Not only did such material seem to us more interesting; it also seemed more appropriate to English teachers who are generally not embryologists or historians.

By *rewriting* we mean both those minor corrections one makes in the process of composition and all the various changes that one can make after finishing an early draft. The book contains four units on rewriting. These units are intended partly as summaries of major points made in previous commentary and readings. The units also contain samples of both student and professional rewriting.

We are indebted to many people at many universities who have helped at various stages in the preparation of this book. Knowingly and sometimes unknowingly they have provided selections and insights scattered throughout the text. We are specifically indebted to Jerome Ellison and John Kouwenhoven for providing us with their own rewritten material, to students at three universities who generously contributed their papers, and to Ruth Moynihan who participated energetically in various phases of production. Finally, we are genuinely indebted to the intelligent and constructive editing provided by Alex Fraser and Thomas Abrams of J. B. Lippincott Company.

WILLIAM T. MOYNIHAN
DONALD W. LEE
HERBERT WEIL, JR.

January, 1964

Contents

Introduction

Part I Reading for Writing

Part II Language

Part IV Argument

Reading, Writing, and Rewriting

Introduction

THE basic fact of any composition course is simple: the student must teach himself how to write. No course, no instructor, no text ever really teaches a student how to write; they only provide the opportunity for him to teach himself. Courses and texts perform the essential function of showing the student where he fails by showing him examples of effective writing. But one becomes a proficient writer only when he himself is reasonably aware of which words, sentences, and paragraphs fail to serve him and how to remedy the situation.

The Student as Critic

Since every writer solves his writing problems somewhat differently, there is no precise formula for good writing. But there are certain factors which remain constant. For example, (1) every writer must become a critic of his own writing. And in order to become critical of his own writing he must have an understanding of what constitutes effective writing. (2) A writer must know how to find a subject and how to prepare that subject for writing. (3) He must realize that his main idea, or in some instances simply point of view, determines the content, the manner, and the order of his composition. In other words, his main idea controls what he says and how he says it. Finally, (4) he must learn that the ability to write well is inseparable from the ability to read well, and also inseparable from the ability to rewrite intelligently.

To emphasize the necessity of the student's teaching himself is not to minimize the role of the instructor. Ideally, the instructor should serve the same function for the student as an editor does for a professional writer. The instructor can point out things to be done and to be avoided, he can point out successes and errors, he can suggest possible ways of improving. But the student must learn a good deal about writing, and about his own abilities in particular, before he can take complete advantage of such assistance.

THE WRITER'S SELF-KNOWLEDGE. At the outset the student can limit his study of writing to those aspects which have immediate relevance. In other words, he need know little or nothing about the history of English prose style or the rise of the essay as a literary form. But he must know the rules of standard written English, and, equally important, he must be aware of his individual strengths and weaknesses. Herbert Read says in his study of prose style (*English Prose Style,* 1928), "All that is necessary for clear reasoning and good style is personal sincerity." While there are countless composition students who would, with justice, reject Read's sweeping statement, nevertheless, personal sincerity is a condition from which good style and clear reasoning may proceed. Much poor writing does result from an elemental dishonesty; namely, a refusal to recognize that words must communicate. The habits of thought and expression that interfere with communication cannot be recognized without a sincere desire to express ourselves in the clearest possible manner. As John Ciardi[1] says,

> . . . the last action every writer must perform for his writing is to become its reader. It is not easy to approach one's own output as if he were coming on it fresh. Yet unless the writer turns that trick any communication that happens will either be by accident or by such genius as transcends the possibility of discussion.
>
> For the writer's relation to his writing is a developing relation. The writing starts as a conceptual buzz. . . . A writer in a really heightened state could jot down telephone numbers and actually believe that he has set down a piece of writing that accurately conveys his original impulse.

ASKING THE RIGHT QUESTIONS. To ask if one's writing makes sense, however, is only a first step. This type of intellectual honesty

[1] From *Dialogue with an Audience* by John Ciardi. Copyright © 1956 by John Ciardi. Published by J. B. Lippincott Company.

must be aided by a knowledge of language and writing techniques in order to be effective. One of the surest signs that a student has neither appraised himself as a writer nor acquired a sufficient knowledge of writing can be seen in the questions he asks, or fails to ask, about his themes.

Uninformed and useless questions usually raise their anguished curlicues shortly after the first batch of graded themes has been returned. The perennial questions are: "How can I improve my grade?" "How can I improve my writing?" Though the former is less mature than the latter, both are equally worthless because both are too vague for any practical answers.

More valuable questions will receive more valuable answers. Such questions and answers are always concerned with specific problems of writing. They are the kind of questions the student may well ask of himself *before* he hands in his paper. When the first draft has been completed, he will not say, "Is this a good description?" but rather, "Do I have enough details, and are they appropriate to the subject and to the point of view I have chosen?" "Is my diction clear?" will become "Is this particular word the best word in this context?" "Is my organization okay?" will become "Does this sentence, and this paragraph, lead to or contribute to my main idea, or do I have just a series of facts and opinions without any main idea?"

Such questions are part of the critical attention the conscientious student owes to his own writing long before the instructor has graded the theme. They enable him not only to teach himself but also to take the best advantage of his objective reader's corrections and advice.

The Body of Knowledge

We have said that a student of writing must become his own critic and that to do so he must find and pay attention to the comments of his "objective readers," he must become aware of his own strengths and weaknesses as a writer, and he must be intellectually honest enough to ask specific questions. In order for any of these three practices to be successful, however, a student must also learn as much as he can about language and writing in general.

The body of knowledge that comprises language and writing extends from the well-defined material of dictionaries, grammars, and handbooks to the almost indefinable areas of tone and style. Obviously, no one can write well without a knowledge of words and customs of usage. College composition courses generally presume a grasp of the fundamentals of expression and a competency in the rules of usage.

Between the black and white rules of vocabulary and grammar and the many-colored ones of tone and style lies the central area of logic (the science of correct thinking) and rhetoric (the art of effective communication). There is no doubt that a knowledge of correct ways of reasoning is indispensable to certain types of writing. Although logic apparently has little to do with the description of a birch tree, it does have a great deal to do with the explanation of a process or with the presentation of a convincing argument. It is just as difficult to appraise the effect of a knowledge of rhetoric. But there are some rhetorical techniques which are found so frequently in good prose that a student can no more ignore these techniques with impunity than a motorist can ignore traffic signs. A knowledge of rhetorical techniques is to the student what a knowledge of basic dance steps is to the dancer or what standard turns and climbing procedures are to skiers. The genius, and even the professional writer, will improvise on the standard patterns, but usually he knows and understands these patterns thoroughly before he modifies them for special reasons.

ENDS AND MEANS. A student might well begin his study of writing with just six familiar terms. Four of these, *description, exposition, argumentation,* and *narration,* name the four chief ends of all writing —to describe, to explain, to prove or persuade, and to tell, that is, to tell a story. The two additional terms, *division* and *expansion,* are the means to those ends.

The division of a subject may be achieved in three ways. A spatial division makes use of word pictures, images, and diagrams. A chronological division proceeds according to time—past, present, and future—or according to steps—one, two, three—of a process. A logical division utilizes classification or cause and effect relationships. The expansion of a subject may be achieved through the use of details and examples, comparison and contrast, or inductive and deductive reasoning.

What complicates any discussion of ends and means is that they are everywhere and in every manner intertwined. Description merges indistinguishably with exposition and exposition with argumentation, and narration uses all the other three as the storyteller's purpose shifts from explaining, to telling, to arguing, to describing. However, we can explain the four basic modes of prose in a few pages, although it will take the whole book to explain and exemplify the chief means of division and expansion available to prose writers.

Description. We have said that each of the four modes of prose defines a purpose; the purpose of description is, as the name implies, to describe. Basically, description is an attempt to render a picture; the writer does with words what the painter does with colors.

The divisions, or parts, of a description are frequently associated with a spatial design. The common remark that a writer has given us a "word picture" implies this kind of division. The writer, like the painter, sees his subject before his eyes and chooses a point of view from which to begin his description. He may work along a straight line—as in a description of a street—or he may begin at the center and work his way out, or work from the outside toward the center. In any case, he keeps a clear spatial arrangement in his mind as he describes.

A more subtle, and usually effective, form of description by spatial means depends upon an image. For example, Washington, D. C., may be described as a wheel because the Capitol lies at the center, or hub, and the streets of the city extend outward from the center like the spokes of a wheel. Victor Hugo's famous depiction in *Les Misérables* of the circumstances of the Battle of Waterloo is an even clearer spatial division superimposed on an image:

> . . . imagine a capital A laid on the ground. The left stroke of the A is the Nivelles road, the right one the Genappe road, while the

cross of the A is the sunken road from Onain to Braine l'Alleud. The top of the A is Mont Saint-Jean, Wellington is there. At the left-hand lower point is Hougemont, Reille is there with Jerome Bonaparte. The right-hand lower point is La Belle Alliance, Napoleon is there. A little below the point where the cross of the A meets the right stroke is La Haye Sainte; in the center of this cross is the precise point where the final battle-word was given. It is here that the lion is placed, the involuntary symbol of the supreme heroism of the ancient Imperial Army. The triangle contained at the top of the A between the two strokes and the cross line is the plateau of Mont Saint-Jean. The whole battle was a contest for this plateau.

Although visual description is the most common mark of effective description, frequent appeal to all the senses—smell, hearing, touch, taste, as well as sight—helps the writer to render his scene. In the following excerpt from *Mary Peters,* by Mary Ellen Chase,[1] the visual outlines are absent, but the odorous boundaries are pungent:

There were smells of soda biscuits, flapjacks, and doughnuts. Breakfasts were thus easily discerned. There were smells of lampwicks and soft soap, homemade sausage and apple butter, baked beans and johnnycake, and buttered popcorn. Colds brought more smells and made one keenly aware of the rigors of rural pharmacopoeia. Flannel chest protectors gave infallible proof of the plasters and poultices they had replaced, plasters of mustard and salt pork, hen's oil and duck's grease, boiled onions and flaxseed. Homemade cough syrups lingered in the warm, close air; and in February and March no child was without his odorous sulphur bag beneath flannel blouses and well-worn woolen frocks.

Exposition. The picture that can be revealed in rich sensuous strokes is the staple of descriptive writing; the diagram, or the abstract ordering of divisions, is the staple of exposition. The more abstract the writing is and the more it tends to outline or diagram, or to

[1] From *Mary Peters* by Mary Ellen Chase. Reprinted by permission of The Macmillan Company.

deal with nonsensuous qualities, the more the writing tends toward exposition.

Exposition is explanation. Rather than trying to make one see, or feel, or hear, or smell a particular room, exposition is designed to make one understand the size of the room, the furnishings, the period of the room. Any piece of writing in which the main purpose is intellectual rather than emotional, explanatory as well as descriptive, is best considered as exposition. We shall discuss the fine points of this distinction when we consider language in Part Two, but for now Edward Gibbon's explanation of the Roman Legion will give a sufficiently clear illustration of what constitutes expository writing:

> . . . The Imperial legion may be described in a few words. The heavy armed infantry, which composed its principal strength, was divided into ten cohorts, and fifty-five companies, under the orders of a correspondent number of tribunes and centurions. The first cohort, which always claimed the post of honour and the custody of the eagle, was formed of eleven hundred and five soldiers, the most approved for valour and fidelity. The remaining nine cohorts consisted each of five hundred and fifty-five; and the whole body of legionary infantry amounted to six thousand one hundred men. Their arms were uniform, and admirably adapted to the nature of their service: an open helmet, with a lofty crest; a breast-plate, or coat of mail; greaves on their legs, and an ample buckler on their left arm. The buckler was of an oblong and concave figure, four feet in length, and two and a half in breadth, framed of a light wood, covered with a bull's hide, and strongly guarded with plates of brass. Besides a lighter spear, the legionary soldier grasped in his right hand the formidable *pilum,* a ponderous javelin, whose utmost length was about six feet, and which was terminated by a massy triangular point of steel of eighteen inches. This instrument was indeed much inferior to our modern fire-arms; since it was exhausted by a single discharge, at the distance of only ten or twelve paces. Yet when it was launched by a firm and skilfull hand, there was not any cavalry that durst venture within its reach, nor any shield or corslet that could sustain the impetuosity of its weight. As soon as the Roman had darted his *pilum,* he

> drew his sword, and rushed forwards to close with the enemy. His sword was a short well-tempered Spanish blade, that carried a double edge, and was alike suited to the purpose of striking or of pushing; but the soldier was always instructed to prefer the latter use of his weapon, as his own body remained less exposed, whilst he inflicted a more dangerous wound on his adversary. The legion was usually drawn up eight deep; and the regular distance of three feet was left between the files as well as ranks. A body of troops, habituated to preserve this open order, in a long front and a rapid charge, found themselves prepared to execute every disposition which the circumstances of war, or the skill of their leader, might suggest. The soldier possessed a free space for his arms and motions, and sufficient intervals were allowed, through which seasonable reinforcements might be introduced to the relief of the exhausted combatants. The tactics of the Greeks and Macedonians were formed on very different principles. The strength of the phalanx depended on sixteen ranks of long pikes, wedged together in the closest array. But it was soon discovered by reflection as well as by the event, that the strength of the phalanx was unable to contend with the activity of the legion.

This paragraph is divided according to spatial design. Gibbon conceived of the Legion as composed of various units, some larger and more important, some smaller and less important. In explaining the nature and composition of the Legion, Gibbon begins with the larger unit and proceeds to the smaller. He moves from the Legion to its largest component, the heavy armed infantry; then he proceeds to the cohort, a smaller unit of organization within the infantry. Finally he concentrates on the individual soldier and proceeds to give a detailed account of his arms and maneuvers. By concluding the paragraph with a comment that places the individual back in the context of the entire Legion, Gibbon is able to proceed logically to another major component of the Legion. His next paragraph, as might be expected, turns to the cavalry, the second largest component.

There is a mid point between exposition and argumentation which may be called analysis. Analysis, strictly speaking, is one kind of exposition. But because analysis, or involved exposition, uses many of the same means as argumentation and similarly seeks to convince the reader, it often merges indistinguishably with exposition and argumentation. We devote considerable space to these means later in the text and will do little more than mention them here. The two methods most common to analysis and argumentation are cause-and-effect and classification, although process, definition, explication, comparison and contrast, and analogy are frequently used. Cause-and-effect asks *why* something happened and shows the results; classification relates its subject matter in terms of parts and groups. John Dewey, in his book *How We Think,* defines reflective thinking by means of classification:

> *Reflective* thinking, in distinction from other operations to which we apply the name of thought, involves (1) a state of doubt, hesitation, perplexity, mental difficulty, in which thinking originates, and (2) an act of searching, hunting, inquiring, to find material that will resolve the doubt, settle and dispose of the perplexity.

Dewey sees "reflective thinking" as one part of the all-embracing mental activity called *thought.* Other members of that class he has described as unreflective thought and belief. In the lines above he is endeavoring to explain how reflective thinking is different from other kinds of thought, and he does this by referring to the distinguishing characteristics of doubt and searching.

ARGUMENTATION. While there are great similarities between analysis and argumentation, argument involves an emphasis on proving or persuading. Admittedly, no writer goes into detailed analysis without a strong desire to convince his reader that his analysis is correct. We simply have to say that whenever the writer's purpose seems to be more a matter of proof or persuasion than of explanation, the writing is argumentative. This is not to call it a formal argument, but that is a special case to be touched on later.

Charles Darwin, in his epochal work *The Origin of Species,* sometimes describes, always explains, and frequently argues. In the following paragraph, he moves quickly from exposition to an argument based on cause and effect:

> Animals remote in the scale of nature are bound together by a web of complex relations. . . . Nearly all our orchidaceous plants absolutely require the visits of insects to remove their pollen-masses and thus to fertilize them. I find from experiment that bumble-bees are almost indispensable to the fertilization of the heartsease (*Viola tricolor*), for other bees do not visit this flower. I have also found that the visits of bees are necessary for the fertilization of some kinds of clover. . . . Hence we may infer . . . , if the whole genus of bumble-bees became extinct or very rare in England, the heartsease and red clover would become very rare, or wholly disappear. The number of bumble-bees in any district depends to a great measure on the number of fieldmice, which destroy their combs and nests; and Col. Newman, who long attended to the habits of bumble-bees, believes that "more than two-thirds of them are thus destroyed all over England." Now, the number of mice is largely dependent, as every one knows, on the number of cats; and Col. Newman says: "Near villages and small towns I have found the nests of bumble-bees more numerous than elsewhere, which I attribute to the number of cats that destroy the mice." Hence it is quite credible that the presence of a feline animal in large numbers in a district might determine, through the intervention first of mice and then of bees, the frequency of certain flowers in that district.

This particular exposition of the interrelatedness of everything in nature aims at demonstrating that the incidence of certain English flowers is dependent on bees. Darwin's detailed explanation of the relationship between animals and insects builds into a convincing cause-effect argument.

NARRATION. A narrative is a story. As with the other modes, a narrative does not exist in isolation. A writer may describe, explain, and argue (and usually does) in the course of his story. What makes a story a story, however, is that the descriptions, expositions, and arguments are subservient to the purpose of telling a story, and they are usually presented by means of dialogue or stream of consciousness. The writer keeps clearly in mind that he wants to tell a story of someone doing something, or of something happening to someone, and he makes everything subordinate to that purpose.

The whole value of understanding the different purposes of description, exposition, argumentation, and narration is that the student may thereby become aware of what he intends to do and of what means he has for doing it. We have indicated only the general characteristics of the four modes of prose, but if you have grasped the essential principle—that writers use different approaches for different purposes—you are prepared to go into these procedures in more detail.

Finding and Recognizing a Subject

Goethe, Germany's Shakespeare, once said, "We see only what we look for; we look only for what we know." The more we reflect on this statement the more we can see its significance for any student of writing. Goethe is considering two aspects of the problem of point of view, perception and knowledge, and the relationship between them. He is telling us that we are able to observe and understand only those things we have trained ourselves to see. A writer must learn to look at his subject in much the same way that a painter looks at a landscape or a detective looks at a room where a crime has been committed. Obviously, such looking requires not only certain techniques of perception, but also knowledge. We must see things both physically and intellectually, with both vision and comprehension. We know, for example, that an amateur archeologist will see things that an untrained layman misses entirely, but, on the other hand, the amateur is generally unable to tell as much as a professional archeologist about the significance of his discoveries. Similarly, good writing depends upon recognizing a subject and understanding its significance.

Learning what to look for and learning how to evaluate what we find are two inseparable parts of the first step in college writing—finding the subject.

Making the Subject Specific. It may seem that finding a subject is the easiest of all procedures involved in writing. It could with practice become relatively simple, but it is usually not simple for the beginner. Although your instructor may give you a topic to write on, the topic which he assigns is not *really* the subject of your theme. An assigned topic is usually either too broad or too narrow. Some students face a long and complicated process of choosing among the many things they want to say; others find themselves in the agonizing position of having "nothing to say."

Consider a traditional assignment: "Write a five-hundred-word theme on your home town." How do we find and recognize a real subject in such an instance? This assignment means, of course, that you are to write about your home town and not about your favorite dessert, or why girls should play football. But a home town is not a subject, it is an unexplored continent. It is as though you were told to write about yourself, or about your family. You would wonder which phase of your life, which quality of your character, or which of your interests should be treated. Or you would wonder what aspect of your family to write on—its members, its origin, its social position, its strangeness, its plans. You must ask the same questions about a subject like "my home town."

Almost everyone can think of countless things to say about his home town. The word alone summons up memories of houses, streets, factories, schools, people, parks, landscapes, and the longer we think the longer the list becomes. Why can we not write a 500-word theme that touches on as many of these features as possible? Quite a few students do just that. The reader is left with the feeling of having been fired at with a shotgun. Read the following student theme with this question in mind: Has the writer recognized and solved the problem of selection; has he really found his subject?

Newtown

(Student Theme # 1)

Newtown is an old community but it has a fast-growing population. The older part of the town is situated on a hill. This is where the first settlers came in the 1600's. The oldest house in the community is located in this part of town. Many stores, Main Street, the town hall are all located on this hill.

The fast-growing parts of Newton are on both sides of this hill. Most of the homes in these parts are project homes and have been built since World War II. The population of Newtown has doubled since these areas of the community were built.

One of the most interesting things about my hometown is that it has very few factories. We are what some people might call a "bedroom town." Most of the people living here work in the larger cities to the north and west. There is only one sizable factory here at present. This is "Newco," the famous plastics corporation which does a great deal of work for the government and has pioneered in the discovery of many well-known plastic products. The "Newco" building is a new one-story factory which nestles into a sloping hillside and is almost invisible except from a position directly in front of it. The architects won an award for the design and plan of this remarkable factory.

Most residents of Newtown have homes of which they are very proud. Beautiful gardens are to be seen everywhere all over town. The interiors of the homes are a pleasure for any visitor to see. The most stately homes are located on "the hill" but many beautiful modern homes have been built in the developments on both sides of the center of town.

The population explosion in Newtown has meant more schools, more stores, more churches, and more homes. When I first came to Newtown two years ago, I immediately noticed the friendliness of the town, especially of the school. I had never seen such school spirit anywhere before. We are all worried that the population increase will mean the loss of school spirit and community friendliness.

The fall is the time to be in Newtown. I miss the enthusiasm of our football games and the weekly dances which had become so much a part of my life. These are the things that mean home town to me: the beautiful homes, the fall, football games, and the school dances. I am glad I moved to Newtown. It is a good place for a man to bring up his family, and I am glad I was able to "grow with Newtown."

This is a poorly written theme. There are many shortcomings we might point out—its sentence structure, its clichés, its paragraph development—but the outstanding failure of the paper is its lack of focus. It tries to touch on everything and, as a result, really touches on nothing. It has no single subject. It gives us a little history, a partial geographical survey, some idea of the homes, some idea of community problems growing out of increased population. It touches on the industrial nature of the community, it tells about its author, and it concludes with a slogan probably taken from a Community Chest drive or the local Chamber of Commerce. In brief, this "500-word theme" might be an outline for a book on Newtown. The writer did not find his subject.

LISTING IDEAS. The writer of this theme has to begin all over again. First he must find his subject, then decide what to do with it. It should be apparent that in 500 words one cannot give a reader a guided tour of streets, houses, factories, football games, and dances. In "My Home Town" there are probably half a dozen true subjects, but the student writer did not recognize them.

We can postulate some of the thought processes that the writer of this theme followed. The words "home town" began a train of ideas and images. This is a good start. Working from just what we have in the theme we can list those ideas:

good place to live	lovely homes
old and new parts of town	beautiful interiors and gardens
friendly community	fall the best season
growing population	school spirit
new schools, stores, churches	football games
only one factory	founded in 1600's
award-winning design	

GROUPING RELATED IDEAS. The second step in finding a subject is to group related ideas. To write on all the ideas and items listed above violates any consistent point of view because the writer has no way of discussing them coherently within the limits of a brief theme. One way to discover what may or may not be handled in one theme is to try grouping your ideas. The ones that go together can be treated in a unified way.

A study of our list reveals that it could be made into several groups, such as historical, architectural, geographical, personal:

historical
founded in 1600's
earliest settlement on hill
subsequent settlements
present mixture of areas
growth indicates future change

geographical
location of town in state
characteristics of land
  hill
  adjacent areas
  boundaries
characteristics of homes

architectural
old and new parts of town
  oldest house
  stately homes
  project homes
  gardens and interiors
new schools, stores, churches
award-winning factory design

personal
what makes Newtown unique
  newness and oldness
  pleasantly residential
what I like best
  school spirit
  friends, dancing
  football
beauty of Newtown in fall

None of these groupings is complete in terms of writing, but each is sufficiently advanced in terms of finding a subject and recognizing it as a subject. It must be remembered that we have traced only the first stage of writing and only in relation to a certain kind of topic—the topic which the student finds unwieldy because it is too broad, because it summons up too many ideas. (Topics which seem to suggest no ideas will be discussed further on.)

DETERMINING A POINT OF VIEW. When a writer has grouped his ideas into natural units, he must decide on his point of view in order to choose his own best topic and to write on it effectively.

The most obvious meaning of the phrase "point of view" is the one dealt with in most composition handbooks as an aspect of grammar. Students are warned not to shift tenses (After he fell, he runs away) and not to shift person or number (New York was an exciting place for me and we all especially enjoyed the night clubs). A rereading of our sample theme shows that the author was guilty of this latter mistake. A recognition of this principle would have enabled him to choose either the objective or the personal viewpoint instead of both. While in a longer piece of writing such shifts may contribute to the understanding of a subject, in a student theme such shifts usually cause confusion.

In a broader sense, point of view refers to the special interests and knowledge through which a writer views his topic and which frame and control his treatment of it. By approaching a general topic from the point of view of special interests and special knowledge, the writer limits his topic to a manageable subject which he can write about informatively and interestingly. Thus the next important consideration is the writer's interest and knowledge. It is a natural assumption that we will be able to write better about what we are interested in and what we know most about. In fact, this is a primary reason for limiting the subject in the first place. Of course, if a writer is deeply interested in a subject about which he knows next to nothing, he must plan to do a great deal of research—or else choose a different subject. In the case of our sample theme, the author indicates both historical and architectural interests, but adequate treatments of his home town from these viewpoints would require names, dates, and details which he most likely does not have, certainly not at his fingertips.

The last paragraph of the theme, however, suggests an avenue of approach which might be more feasible. Since he writes that "the fall is the time to be in Newtown," it is possible that the student's real subject might be found in his personal feelings about his home town. Certainly this subject commands his interest. Secondly, the theme itself and the group listing indicates a unity of thought on the subject. This is the kind of subject the average college freshman knows from experience and can deal with competently. The pleasant places and happy memories of his home town, if handled maturely and from a consistent viewpoint, should provide a satisfactory and sufficiently limited subject.

There are three other aspects of point of view which we should keep in mind: the visual, the intellectual, and the emotional. The visual perspective, the actual physical position of the writer, so to speak, is important to all clear expression, and crucial to descriptive writing. Consider, for example, this description by John Steinbeck from *The Grapes of Wrath:*[1]

> Along 66 the hamburger stands—Al & Susy's Place—Carl's Lunch—Joe & Minnie—Will's Eats. Board-and-bat shacks. Two gasoline pumps in front, a screen door, a long bar, stools, and a foot rail. Near the door three slot machines, showing through glass the wealth in nickels three bars will bring. And beside them, the nickel phonograph with records piled up like pies, ready to swing out to the turn-table and play dance music, "Ti-pi-ti-pi-tin," "Thanks for the Memory," Bing Crosby, Benny Goodman. At one end of the counter a covered case; candy cough drops, caffeine sulphate called Sleepless, No-Doze; candy, cigarettes, razor blades, aspirin, Bromo-Seltzer, Alka-Seltzer. The walls decorated with posters, bathing girls, blondes with big breasts and slender hips and waxen faces, in white bathing suits, and holding a bottle of Coca-Cola and smiling —see what you get with a Coca-Cola. Long bar, and salts, peppers, mustard pots, and paper napkins. Beer taps behind the counter, and in back the coffee urns, shiny and steaming, with glass gauges showing the coffee level. And pies in wire cages and oranges in pyramids of four. And little piles of Post Toasties, corn flakes, stacked up in designs.

Steinbeck's description owes much to cinemagraphic techniques. He describes as a camera would see. First there is the road, the joints along the highway, then a particular shack. We go past the gasoline pumps outside, through the front door, linger near the door, start at one end of the counter, and slowly travel its length. But besides this visual perspective there is the all-important intellectual perspective, the organizing ideas of the writing. Certain ideas frame and control the writing although they are not immediately apparent. Some elements, however, are emphasized more than others, the girls on the

[1] From *The Grapes of Wrath* by John Steinbeck. Reprinted by permission of The Viking Press, Inc.

posters, for example. The reason these things are emphasized cannot be illustrated from this paragraph alone; we would have to go into the unifying ideas of Steinbeck's novel in order to explain this. But we will illustrate the meaning of the term *intellectual framework* when we deal with the organizing principle. For the organizing principle, though controlling both physical and emotional perspectives, is most clearly revealed in the intellectual framework. The visual and intellectual point of view affects, and is affected by, an emotional point of view—what is often referred to as tone. Steinbeck is trying to convey a feeling of crudeness and cheapness which is as significant as the physical description.

An awareness of visual, intellectual, and emotional points of view is essential not only to finding a true subject, but also to recognizing what to do with it, whether to write it as description, exposition, argumentation, or narration. The more conscious we become of our point of view, the more precise our writing should become. Sinclair Lewis in *Main Street*[1] provides a good example of the implications of point of view when he describes the same scene through the eyes of one character and then through the eyes of another. Carol Kennicott, college educated, city-bred, bride of the local doctor, takes a walk down the main street of her new "home town" of Gopher Prairie and finds that

> Main Street with its two-story brick shops, its story-and-a-half wooden residences, its muddy expanse from concrete walk to walk, its huddle of Fords and lumber-wagons, was too small to absorb her. The broad, straight, unenticing gashes of the streets let in the grasping prairie on every side. She realized the vastness and the emptiness of the land. The skeleton iron windmill on the farm a few blocks away, at the north end of Main Street, was like the ribs of a dead cow. She thought of the coming of the Northern winter, when the unprotected houses would crouch together in terror of storms galloping out of that wild waste. They were so small and weak, the little brown houses. They were shelters for sparrows, not homes for warm laughing people. . . .

[1] From *Main Street* by Sinclair Lewis, copyright 1920 by Harcourt, Brace & World, Inc.; renewed 1948 by Sinclair Lewis. Reprinted by permission of the publishers.

She passes a farm girl named Bea, looking for a job as a house cleaner, a girl who has never seen a town with more than seventy-six inhabitants. For Bea, the "roar of the city" is frightening:

> There were five automobiles on the street all at the same time—and one of 'em was a great big car that must of cost two thousand dollars—and the 'bus was starting for a train with five elegant-dressed fellows, and a man was pasting up red bills with lovely pictures of washing-machines on them, and the jeweler was laying out bracelets and wrist-watches and *everything* on real velvet.

Bea sees a drug store

> with a soda fountain that was just huge, awful long, and all lovely marble; and on it there was a great big lamp, with the biggest shade you ever saw—all different kinds of colored glass stuck together; and the soda spouts, they were silver, and they came right out of the bottom of the lampstand! Behind the fountain there were glass shelves, and bottles of new kinds of soft drinks, that nobody ever heard of. Suppose a fella took you *there!* . . .

But Carol sees

> Dyer's Drug Store, a corner building of regular and unreal blocks of artificial stone. Inside the store, a greasy marble soda-fountain with an electric lamp of red and green and curdled-yellow mosaic shade. Pawed-over heaps of toothbrushes and combs and packages of shaving-soap. Shelves of soap-cartons, teething-rings, garden-seeds, and patent medicines in yellow packages—nostrums for consumption, for "women's diseases"—notorious mixtures of opium and alcohol. . . .

In these passages the visual point of view is the same—both women are walking down Main Street. But the intellectual and emotional viewpoints are entirely different. One sees "mosaic" while the other calls it "colored glass stuck together." "Greasy marble" for one is "lovely marble" for the other. Carol's superior knowledge and sense of disgust are vividly contrasted to Bea's ignorance and awe-struck enthusiasm.

The implications of visual perspective, intellectual frame of reference, and emotional attitude, or tone, will become more clear as we deal with these phases of writing throughout the text. Thus perspective will be a crucial aspect of description and exposition, the intellectual frame of reference will be emphasized in analysis and argumentation, and variations in tone will be found in all types of writing.

EXPANDING THE SUBJECT. Generally speaking, the more limited a theme subject is, the better the theme will be. But there is also a tendency among freshman writers to say nothing. They may narrow their sights so well that the target evades their aim. This is one of the weaknesses that the writer of student Theme #1 would have to watch for. In attempting to deal with his personal attitude toward his home town, he might end up by telling the reader little or nothing. The best way to avoid this dilemma is to list ideas thoughtfully in advance and group them logically.

But the writer with "nothing to say" can also make a profitable use of the concept of point of view in order to expand his subject. Some students have too many ideas, some students have too few. Both can write equally weak themes. Some students find they lose their subject when they limit it, others find the assigned topic too limited to begin with. Both types of student need to practice the art of looking at a subject from various angles. Here, for example, is a theme which says almost nothing.

Newark

(Student Theme # 2)

I am very prejudiced in favor of Newark. Undoubtedly, I am prejudiced towards Newark because I have lived there all my life. I am sure the city would seem very different to someone who has not lived there all his life. It is not an easy city to get used to, especially now with all the new factories and the influx of workers from other parts of the country. You just get used to one project and they are starting another.

But I like Newark because it has everything a large city should have. You could travel the world over and you'd find it hard to locate a city that has more than Newark. And if Newark doesn't have it, it can be found across the river in New York.

The opportunities which this town affords are great and help to make it a very favorable place for someone with a college education. This town can provide jobs for anyone with the right ability and the proper training. The brass ring is right here in Newark, and a good education will enable a person to grab the ring and find success.

Everyone has his own opinion and I have stated mine. It is probably not the best opinion but it at least shows how one person feels about his "home town."

This student has almost perfectly concealed his ideas. It would take a major detective job to decide just what he has said about Newark beyond the fact that it has factories, new projects, opportunities for the educated person, and that he is prejudiced in its favor. The emotional point of view is clearly evident, but the ideas supporting that view are almost completely lacking.

In this particular theme the writer is faced with a problem in developing rather than one in limiting. It is not that he is confused by the amount of information he would like to present; instead he fails to show signs of possessing any information. The solution to this problem is the inverse of that of the first theme writer. Where the first writer had to limit his material in order to clarify his viewpoint, the second writer must gather material to support his viewpoint.

There is little question about what kind of approach the second writer wishes to take. He wants to praise his city because it offers him, and people like him, "success" or "opportunity." In order to do this, however, he must show the reader how and why Newark provides the means to achieve these goals. He should have said in effect, "Here's Newark, look at these businesses and industries, look at these intellectual and recreational facilities, look at this pleasant and convenient residential area. These are all the opportunities a man could wish for. They're in Newark. That's why I think Newark is a great city."

Our first theme illustrated the need for selecting and arranging ideas according to a consistent point of view. This example illustrates the need for using multiple perspectives to develop a particular point of view. Once we have found a true subject—in this case, "opportunities offered by Newark"—we must again look at it in detail. That is, each of the opportunities must be explained by citing facts, figures, examples, and all relevant circumstances.

As an instance of understanding a subject in this manner let us look at one of the classic illustrations of the reflective mind in action—Bertrand Russell's consideration of a table. Before reading it, imagine that you have been assigned a very specific essay: "Write a 500-word description of your dining-room table." Think about this and jot down a few notes indicating how you would go about writing such a description. Now see how Russell[1] does it in terms of color, texture, shape, sound:

> . . . it is oblong, brown and shiny, to the touch it is smooth and cool and hard; when I tap it, it gives out a wooden sound. Any one else who sees and feels and hears the table will agree with this description, so that it might seem as if no difficulty would arise; but as soon as we try to be more precise our troubles begin. Although I believe that the table is "really" of the same colour all over, the parts that reflect the light look much brighter than the other parts, and some parts look white because of reflected light. I know that, if I move, the parts that reflect the light will be different, so that the apparent distribution of colours on the table will change. It follows that if several people are looking at the table at the same moment, no two of them will see exactly the same distribution of colours, because no two can see it from exactly the same point of view, and any change in point of view makes some change in the way the light is reflected.
>
> . . . we know that even from a given point of view the colour will seem different by artificial light, or to a colour-blind man, or to

[1] From *The Problems of Philosophy* by Bertrand Russell. Oxford University Press, 1912. Reprinted by permission.

a man wearing blue spectacles, while in the dark there will be no colour at all, though to touch and hearing the table will be unchanged. This colour is not something which is inherent in the table, but something depending upon the table and the spectator and the way the light falls on the table. When, in ordinary life, we speak of *the* colour of the table, we only mean the sort of colour which it will seem to have to a normal spectator from an ordinary point of view under usual conditions of light. But the other colours which appear under other conditions have just as good a right to be considered. . . .

The same thing applies to texture. With the naked eye one can see the grain, but otherwise the table looks smooth and even. If we looked at it through a microscope, we should see roughnesses and hills and valleys, and all sorts of differences that are imperceptible to the naked eye. . . .

The *shape* of the table is no better. We are all in the habit of judging as to the "real" shapes of things, and we do this so unreflectingly that we come to think we actually see the real shapes. But, in fact, as we all have to learn if we try to draw, a given thing looks different in shape from every different point of view. If our table is "really" rectangular, it will look, from almost all points of view, as if it had two acute angles and two obtuse angles. If opposite sides are parallel, they will look as if they converged to a point away from the spectator; if they are of equal length, they will look as if the nearer side were longer. . . .

Similar difficulties arise when we consider the sense of touch. It is true that the table always gives us a sensation of hardness, and we feel that it resists pressure. But the sensation we obtain depends upon how hard we press the table and also upon what part of the body we press with. . . . And the same applies still more obviously to the sounds which can be elicited by rapping the table.

Russell's reflections on a table are *not* a perfect description of a table because his main purpose is expository; he wants to explain the philosophical problem of appearance and reality and the table provides a convenient example. As with most successful combinations of writing techniques, however, this selection shows us the possibilities of looking at a subject from various points of view. The passage demonstrates how a writer can cast light on even the most commonplace of subjects by shifting perspectives and developing unique points of view.

SUMMARY. A writer must do a great deal of thinking before he begins to write. The first step in this thinking is to find a subject. To determine the extent and the nature of his subject there are certain things he must do.

One—List ideas. Think about the assigned topic, or the topic you have chosen, and write down as many ideas, thoughts, feelings, impressions as you can. Let these ideas come at random. Let one idea suggest another. Make no attempt to restrict your list other than in its relevance to the assigned topic.

Two—Group related ideas. Check your first list for ideas which seem to go together. Group them in appropriate categories.

Three—Consider your interest and knowledge. Choose a category which interests you from the groups you have outlined. But, if you find that your interest conflicts with your range of knowledge, do not be led astray by your interest. You may, for example, be chiefly interested in a teenage drinking problem in your town and find on your list several references to "acts of vandalism" or "accidents caused by drinking." But your views may be based on only one isolated experience or even on the secondhand accounts of others. And if your topic is your home town, the drinking problem is probably too tangential to be a valid subject for such a theme. You would be wiser to choose from one of your other groups a subject more closely related to the assigned topic as a whole and about which you have adequate knowledge and information. Let your interests guide you, but do not let them mislead you.

Four—Adopt a point of view. Once you have chosen your own particular subject, making sure that it is consistent with the terms of the assignment, decide on the attitude you will take on that subject. Will your point of view be distant or near, remembering or anticipating, personal or impersonal? Will you speak as a student, as an individual, as a historian, as a scientist, as a sociologist? (Remember, most freshmen are not yet qualified historians, scientists, or sociologists, except in very limited areas.) Is your intellectual framework consistent? Do you move from one idea or image to the next in an orderly, logical way or do you jump from one to the other and back again without any reason? Does the tone of your theme support your real opinion on the subject? Do the words and sentences and images you have chosen reflect your enthusiasm, or your disgust, or your nostalgia? If you can state clearly to yourself in one sentence what is the main idea or purpose of your theme, chances are you have found your true subject.

Five—Expand your subject within its limits. Once you have limited your subject, or if you find it too narrow in the first place, you may use elements of point of view to expand and develop it in a theme. For example, you may have chosen your subject from one of your listed groups, but that group may contain too few ideas. In such an event, you have only one of two choices: (1) find a subject on which you have more ideas; (2) enlarge on your subject by subdividing it and providing specific details for each subdivision.

Using point of view to limit and then to expand are two sides of one operation. It is as if two clocks were put before you and you were to explain the workings of each. Clock A was in pieces, clock B in one piece. To explain A you would sort out the pieces, group them, choose a point to begin with, and start explaining. To explain clock B, you would examine the front, examine the back, expose the parts, experiment with the movements.

In brief, then, there are two phases to the process of selecting and handling a subject: The writer must narrow his subject to workable size. That is, he must write on the workings of a particular clock, not on the history of wrist watches or the current fashions in sundials. Secondly, he must, like Russell, examine his subject from as many relevant perspectives as possible.

Beginning to Write: The Organizing Principle

Writing a theme is not a matter of sudden inspiration. It is a matter of making something, of putting words, sentences, and paragraphs together in such a way that they will best express your ideas and attitudes. Inspiration, of course, can help, but one must learn how to write whether or not he is moved by a flash of insight.

The making of a theme involves using words in a certain manner and a certain order as a means of achieving a particular end. The first step in the process of writing is for the writer to be sure that he knows what particular end he has in mind; in other words, that he knows what his subject really is. He is ready to begin his composition when he can clearly state his main idea, the principle which controls everything he plans to say.

It may be helpful to spell out a little more clearly just how the process of finding a subject leads to an organizing principle and how the organizing principle is related to the rest of the theme. We examined two student themes to see how their authors could arrive at better organizing principles in order to begin new and, we would expect, more proficient themes. We can retrace and complete these steps in the following way:

Student Theme # 1

1. Topic: my home town (Newtown)
2. Reflection on main interest and knowledge: high school days
3. Point of view:
   physical perspective—looking back on a home town after leaving it
   intellectual framework—student in new surroundings
   emotional attitude (tone)—a mature nostalgia
4. Organizing principle: a home town is a place of friends and pleasant memories
5. Compositional purpose: simple exposition
6. Probable means: chronological division, expansion by example, details, comparisons

Student Theme # 2

1. Topic: my home town (Newark)
2. Reflection on main interest and knowledge: future in the business world

3. Point of view:
   physical perspective–looking ahead to employment
   intellectual framework—the idea of "success"
   emotional attitude—pragmatic optimism
4. Organizing principle: my home town offers everything (jobs, recreational facilities, pleasant community) to the college graduate
5. Compositional purpose: simple exposition
6. Probable means: division by classification of opportunities, expansion by details, examples, cause-effect relationships

The student may be wondering if the only subject safe for him to write on is one that comes within the range of immediate student knowledge. Must the writer look back on his community from the viewpoint of the campus, or must he look on his community in terms of what it will offer him as a college graduate? The obvious answer is no. It seems wise for the writers of themes 1 and 2 to adopt these perspectives because their original themes indicated no "adult" knowledge. And in practice this seems to be the general case. College freshmen are better off approaching subjects from the perspectives of college freshmen. It is a common, and usually disastrous, temptation, for example, for college freshmen newly exposed to introductory courses in psychology or sociology or economics to try to write from the point of view of a psychologist or sociologist or economist. But it is possible for students to write mature themes from other perspectives, provided they have the background in experience and knowledge. Here is one such example. Consider the first five points, and then read the theme. Printed along the margin of the theme are running comments related to composition; study these comments carefully.

Student Theme # 3

1. Topic: my home town (Providence)
2. Reflection on main interest and knowledge: the newspaper
3. Point of view:
   physical perspective—recounting events of a summer job

intellectual framework—conviction that the newspaper is an important factor in civilization
emotional attitude–mainly analytical

4. Organizing principle: the life of my city is both revealed and improved by its newspaper
5. Compositional purpose: simple exposition
6. Means: division by cause and effect, expansion by incidents and examples

My City and Its Newspaper

(Student Theme # 3)

Introduction: distinguishing his approach from other approaches

People like their home towns for different reasons. Some like a city that is big, or rich, because it was founded a long time ago, or because it's young and growing. Some like a city because it has a beautiful climate, a baseball team, because it has places to gamble, or the biggest tomatoes, or because it produces heroes—like astronauts. Most people like their cities because they just happen to live there and have a family and friends who live there also. The reason I like my city, Providence, Rhode Island, however, is different from any of these. I like my home town because of a newspaper, the Providence *Journal.*

Statement of main idea

A more precise statement of main idea; division of subject into two parts

The *Journal* has two things to do with my liking Providence. First, it showed me my city; then it made me like my city because it produced and supported such enterprises as the *Journal.*

First part; establishing point of view: time, definition of job

Looking back on it, I can now see that I didn't know very much about Providence before I went to work for the *Journal* last summer as a copy boy. A copy boy performs the same functions for a newspaper as an office boy does for a business office. The copy boy's chief duties are getting coffee, answering

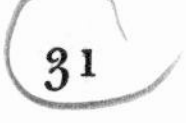

phones, picking up mail, clipping newspapers for stories for the files, and general messenger work.

I learned some short cuts to the Post Office and my way around the railroad station while picking up the mail, but I really got to know the city when I was sent places to pick things up or to bring things back from photographers. I made almost daily trips to the newsroom at the State Capitol. There I picked up photographs to bring back to the newsroom and sometimes I picked up newscopy to bring back to the editor. I often had to wait for the material I had been sent over for, and this gave me the opportunity to watch the state senators and representatives passing bills and debating laws. It gave me a chance to learn a good deal of Rhode Island history as I studied the portraits and statues placed in the hall of the capitol.

Indicating his sources; citing experiences and examples

Occasionally I had the opportunity of riding in one of the press cars and being at the scene of a fire. I was also on hand when the police rescued a man from the seventh story of the Y building. To visit a police station or a fire station as a school boy and to see the police and firemen in action as an older person are two different things. Last summer the men I saw were not aloof and distant figures; they were men often not much older than I, and they were doing a difficult and sometimes unrewarding job. Being close to them, and watching them perform routine and outstanding duties, gave me a sense of community that I had never had before.

Further examples leading to second part; the "sense of community"

It has been more than 10,000 years since men first began to live together in permanent cities, and much of their living together has been painful. But when one watches a large city like Providence going about its business of living, which is essentially the business of making life easier for more people, one can't help but grasp a sense of the

Development of that idea

movement of civilization. For in getting to know a city well one sees life going on with a degree of organization and helpfulness which the world has never known.

Relationship of newspaper to community

Perhaps the most important element in the process of urban civilization is the role of a good newspaper. A good newspaper like the *Journal* allows the city to see itself at its best and at its worst. It holds a mirror up to all the people of the city and says, "this is the crime you committed, this is the act of kindness you performed, this is how you play and this is how you work." And most important of all, on its editorial page a great newspaper says, "this is where you hit the mark, this is where you have fallen short." The newspaper becomes the conscience of the city.

Summary: restatement of subject

This is why I like Providence—because of what the *Journal* showed me, and because of what the *Journal* does.

Questions and Assignments

1. Criticize the above theme. Where is it most successful, least successful? What are some suggestions for improvement? Are there any apparent techniques employed by the writer which you think might prove useful to all theme writers? Why is this theme so much better than the first two student themes?

2. Here is a list of subjects which are too broad for successful themes: a vacation, a summer job, books, relatives, teachers, homes, education, friendship. Following a procedure similar to that used in discussing "My Home Town," narrow down one or more of these subjects, indicate points of view from which it could be written, and then suggest some specific means of dividing and expanding the subject. Outline your proposed theme and then, if your instructor wishes, write it out.

3. For a different theme assignment, use the illustrative paragraphs in this section of the book as models for writing exercises. Write a description using a diagram or image like Victor Hugo's in his description of Waterloo. Study the selection by Mary Ellen Chase and write a description based on one particular form of sensory perception—taste, smell, touch, hearing, sight. Or consider the Sinclair Lewis excerpt and write a one-paragraph description of some particular place from your own point of view and then another paragraph from the point of view of someone else. Or take a subject comparable to Bertrand Russell's table, such as a tree, a car, a dog, a shoe, a hat, a raincoat, and write a brief description based on all the forms of sensory perception.

PART ONE

Reading for Writing

It is impossible to say precisely how much a writer learns from his reading. On the other hand, it is equally impossible to think of any endeavor as useful to the beginning writer as close and critical reading. Thus, although we cannot say exactly how reading is useful in all instances, we can point out its general importance and we can cite specifically some of the more common ways writers may profit from reading.

In general, reading provides two things: forms and ideas. It gives us examples of how to begin, how to develop, and how to conclude; it gives examples of unity, coherence, and emphasis; it enables the student to study *how* a successful writer describes, how he explains, how he persuades, and how he tells a story. In the course of revealing to us how these ends are achieved, what we read also gives us information, new ideas, fresh insights. Sometimes it stimulates us to act, sometimes to react, but always good writing has some effect on the mind and emotions of the reader. Some things we read for form, some for ideas; often we discover both. Occasionally we may find in our reading examples of how not to write or what not to say.

Reading for Form and Idea

Reading for form and idea is a specialized procedure. We must read analytically; that is, we must understand the organization and the ideas of the writing. In addition we must be sensitive to the stylistic merits of what we read and to the techniques and insights that will improve our own writing. Learning how to write from our reading is to a great extent an unconscious process, but there are a few practical procedures that we should know, especially at the outset. Like the mineral assets of the earth, the most useful ideas and techniques of prose are often concealed below the surface.

Mortimer Adler, a distinguished teacher and critic, some time ago devoted an entire book to the problem of reading. The essential point of that book may be plainly stated: Once you have finished reading you should be able to state the writer's main idea and his supporting ideas; and you should be aware of the manner in which these ideas were developed and the means by which these ideas were supported. To put it another way: reading is not a matter of speed. It is a matter of being constantly aware of *what* the writer is saying and of *how* he is saying it.

The process of reading is in some ways the reverse of the process of writing. Reading requires us to abbreviate, writing to expand. The reader must be able to reduce pages to an outline; the writer must be able to take a few key ideas and expand them in a clear and appealing manner. Here is the way Adler[1] summarizes the relationship between writing and reading:

> Writing and reading are reciprocal, as are teaching and being taught. If authors or teachers did not organize their communications, if they failed to unify them and order their parts, there would be no point in directing readers or listeners to search for the unity and uncover the structure of the whole.
>
> Though there are reciprocal rules in the two cases, they are not followed in the same way. The reader tries to *uncover* the skeleton. . . . The author starts with it and tries to *cover it up*. His aim is to conceal the skeleton artistically or, in other words, to put flesh on the bare bones. If he is a good writer, he does not bury a puny skeleton under a mass of fat. The joints should not show through where the flesh is thin, but if flabbiness is avoided, the joints will be detectible and the motion of the parts will reveal the articulation.
>
> I made a mistake several years ago which was instructive on this point. I wrote a book in outline form. I was so obsessed with the importance of structure that I confused the arts of writing and

[1] From *How to Read a Book* by Mortimer Adler. Copyright 1940 by Mortimer J. Adler. Reprinted by permission of Simon and Schuster, Inc.

> reading. I outlined the structure of a book and published it. Naturally, it was repulsive to most self-respecting readers who thought that they could do their job, if I did mine. I learned from their reactions that I had given them a reading of a book I had not written. . . .
>
> Let me summarize all this by reminding you of the old-fashioned maxim that a piece of writing should have unity, clarity, and coherence. That is a basic maxim of good writing. . . . If the writing has unity, we must find it. If the writing has clarity and coherence, we must appreciate it by finding the distinction and order of parts.

Some rhetoricians use the terms unity, coherence, and emphasis rather than Adler's unity, clarity, and coherence. The term unity implies oneness of subject. That is, we do not begin writing about the college preparatory courses in Midtown High, skip over to Midtown's slum clearance project, and then conclude with comments on the success of the soccer team. Coherence means that once we have a unified subject we develop it by moving from paragraph to paragraph smoothly and logically. Emphasis means stressing some things more than other things, knowing how to subordinate minor points to major considerations.

These then would be three of the first questions a critical reader would ask about a selection: Does it possess unity? Is it coherently and logically developed? Does it give proper emphasis to the most significant parts?

Unity is almost guaranteed by a clear main idea. If the writer has a main idea, he has a unifying or organizing concept. If he does not, chances are that his writing will sprawl and be disconcerting and confusing.

Coherence can be recognized in the author's transitions. Words like *moreover, however, and,* the repetition of the same word at crucial points, phrases such as *at the same time* and *on the other hand* are clear signals that the writer is attempting to make his ideas cohere. Of course, the test of coherence is not just in the transitional phrases; it lies finally in the achievement of a smooth and logical progression of thought.

Emphasis, as Adler implies, is a matter of final clarity. It is the end product of unity and coherence. If we are careful and intelligent readers and we are confused at the end of an essay, chances are the writer has failed in terms of emphasis. But emphasis is more than the right ordering of parts. It means also that ideas should be presented in an appealing manner, a manner which induces the reader to pay attention to the thought.

Traditionally, we speak of the introduction, development, and conclusion of an essay. Writing which is properly introduced, developed, and concluded possesses unity. The chief test of coherence lies in the development of the thought, the proper relationship of parts. The final test of emphasis is a conviction of rightness as to order and scale. If the reader feels that the important ideas receive the greatest stress, that the parts are ordered in terms of size and position, that the tone is appropriate, then the writing has emphasis.

There are, to repeat, two things for the writer to keep in mind as he reads: *how* and *what.* He must observe *how* the writing achieves unity, coherence, and emphasis; he must observe *what* the unity, coherence, and emphasis consist of.

The writer makes use of the manner of what he reads, the *how,* by imitating the form directly; he makes use of the content of his reading, the *what,* by quoting, by developing ideas in a new way, by finding similar ideas. The latter method of using what we read should be sufficiently clear; the first method, imitation, probably needs further explanation.

Reading for Imitation

It is one thing to recognize forms and ideas and another thing to apply them to one's writing. It is the difference between understanding the characteristics and techniques, the period, the school of a great painting, and producing a great painting. It is often possible for a student to understand the rhetoric and ideas of a great essay, but it is seldom possible for him to write such an essay himself. In one sense this book has been designed to help you imitate the most useful practices employed in the most effective writing.

Imitation, of course, is something quite different from copying. In a way everything we do as social beings—walking, talking, or playing—is based on unconscious imitation. Boys imitate the gait of their fathers, children imitate the sounds, inflections and accents of their environment, one's method of playing croquet is influenced by the way others play. Such unconscious imitation is always involved in the process of reading and writing. We can take advantage of this, first, by reading a great deal and by reading only the best, and second, by making parts of the process more conscious. It is this direct or conscious imitation that we are here concerned with.

One of the best explanations of imitative writing has been left to us by Benjamin Franklin in his *Autobiography*. Franklin tells us of an occasion when his father criticized the style and clarity of his writing. Franklin determined to improve and did so after obtaining a volume of *The Spectator,* a famous eighteenth-century journal. The method he used to teach himself is explained in the following passage:

> I . . . read it over and over, and was much delighted with it. I thought the writing excellent and wished if possible to imitate it. With this view I took some of the papers and, making short hints of the sentiment in each sentence, laid them by a few days, and then, without looking at the book, tried to complete the papers again by expressing each hinted sentiment at length, and as fully as it had been expressed before, in any suitable words that should come to hand. Then I compared my *Spectator* with the original, discovered some of my faults, and corrected them. But I found I wanted a stock of words, or a readiness in recollecting and using them, which I thought I should have acquired before that time if I had gone on making verses, since the continual occasion for words of the same import but of different length, to suit the measure, or of different sound for the rhyme, would have laid me under a constant necessity of searching for variety and also have tended to fix that variety in my mind and make me master of it. Therefore I took some of the tales and turned them into verse, and after a time, when I had pretty well forgotten the prose, turned them back again. I also sometimes jumbled my collections of hints into confusion and after some weeks endeavored to reduce them into the best order, before

I began to form the full sentences and complete the paper. This was to teach me method in the arrangement of thoughts. By comparing my work afterwards with the original I discovered my faults and amended them; but I sometimes had the pleasure of fancying that, in certain particulars of small import, I had been lucky enough to improve the method or the language, and this encouraged me to think I might possibly in time come to be a tolerable English writer, of which I was extremely ambitious.

Franklin, then, improved his style, language, and organization as a result of his reading of *The Spectator*. It is perhaps not necessary to go to such lengths as Franklin did, but making some practical use of reading is essential to every writer. Here is another account of imitative writing by Professor Winifred Lynskey[1] which may give you a more workable approach to imitating what you read:

In the early nineteenth century Leigh Hunt wrote two companion pieces entitled, "Descriptive of a Hot Day—a 'Now' " and "Descriptive of a Cold Day—a 'Now'." These two studies are based chiefly on sense-impressions. With charm, humor, and informality, they bring nineteenth-century England to life. The repetitive "now" (which few students could or would use of their own accord) is handled with finesse and serves both as emphasis and transition. The cold day begins as follows:

Now the moment people wake in the morning, they perceive the coldness with their faces, though they are warm with their bodies, and exclaim "Here's a day!" and pity the poor little sweep, and the boy with the water-cresses. . . . The breath is visible, issuing from the mouth as we lie. Now we hate getting up, and hate shaving, and hate the empty grate in one's bedroom; and water freezes in ewers, and you may set the towel upright on its own hardness, and the window-panes are frost-whitened; or it is foggy, and the sun sends a dull, brazen beam into one's room; or, if it is fine, the windows outside are stuck with icicles; or a detestable thaw has begun, and they drip; but, at all events, it is horribly cold, and delicate shavers fidget

[1] From "Imitative Writing and a Student's Style" by Winifred Lynskey, *College English,* May 1957. Reprinted with the permission of the National Council of Teachers of English and Winifred Lynskey.

about their chambers looking distressed, and cherish their hard-hearted enemy, the razor, in their bosoms, to warm him a little, and coax him into a consideration of their chins.

A passage from the hot day reads:

Now ladies loiter in baths; and people make presents of flowers; and wine is put into ice; and the after-dinner lounger recreates his head with applications of perfumed water out of long-necked bottles. Now the lounger, who cannot resist riding his new horse, feels his boots burn him. Now buckskins are not the lawn of Cos. Now jockeys, walking in greatcoats to lose flesh, curse inwardly. Now five fat people in a stage-coach hate the sixth fat one who is coming in, and think he has no right to be so large. . . . Now the old-clothesman drops his solitary cry more deeply into the areas on the hot and forsaken side of the street; and bakers look vicious; and cooks are aggravated; and the stream of a tavern-kitchen catches hold of one like the breath of Tartarus.

Having read, studied, and also enjoyed these two essays, my students try to imitate them on an assignment the purpose of which is to evoke sense impressions. The students receive many suggestions but ultimately choose their own subjects. Rare indeed is the student who seeks no further for a subject than a hot or cold day in modern dress. In the first example given below a student tries to create through sense impressions an evening in Chicago spent listening to a concert.

An Evening at Grant Park

Now the retreating sun tints puffs of clouds gold and pink, and the seagulls squawk in rasping complaint of the approaching dusk. Now people in cool linen hurry over the moist green grass and settle themselves on hard, many-slatted benches lined, row upon row, like rows of soldiers, in front of the bandshell. From the east comes the breeze, which hints of fresh water, pleasantly fishy, and we know, with comforting assurance that Lake Michigan's wide blue expanse is within close walking distance.

Now the musicians have crept silently into their seats, and runs and scales, warm-up exercises and sour notes, all reach our ears as one intense, exciting sound. The sun slips further beneath the edge of our world, and Chicago's skyline appears in darkened silhouette below the Evening star, which twinkles with ever-increasing brilliance. Now the huge electric signs lining the sky flash their man-made splendor; they work in time to the soft melody of the music floating out in waves of beauty from the stage before us. Now an airplane at its hangar on the lake's edge, catching the last light from the west on its slick yellow wings, hurtles itself into the air, catches, wavers, and climbs, victorious, into the dusk. . . .

A second example is the concluding paragraph of an imitative theme entitled "Descriptive of September in a College Town—a 'Now' ":

Now the buzzing of electric shavers like a swarm of angry bees invades the halls as would-be lovers prepare for big "dates." Now lucky men pull white shirts from bottom drawers smelling of freshly washed clothes. Now they fasten ties with dexterous flips and those who can tie bow ties are envied. Wistful eyes look up from calculus and physics and follow the young Casanovas down the hall. Now the moon illuminates old brick buildings and makes long shadows of their spires. Millions of stars look down upon a couple walking hand in hand through the moonlight, aware of all the tradition and dreams that surround them. Now God is in his house and all is well.

The student who has once imitated a "Now" by Leigh Hunt understands the difference between generalities and concrete details, between dull and vivid writing as he does from no other assignment I have ever used.

Professor Lynskey's examples should make clear that imitative writing does not mean plagiarism. It means using the form or the technique of what you read—not the content, the words or phrases, or even paraphrases.

In sum, we should read analytically to master the form and ideas. Whenever appropriate, we should apply the techniques we have observed in our reading to our writing. We should not expect to approach every piece of writing in the same way. From some selections we can learn how to develop or unify our thoughts, from others we may be inspired or made angry or curious. It is apparent that students will not learn *how* to write expository prose from reading a poem or a selection from Shakespeare, but it is just as apparent that the poem or Shakespeare may give the student something of importance to say.

Readings: College and Contemporary Life

The readings in this section are all concerned with college life and are designed to provide forms and ideas which are of use to student writers. The readings cover a range of styles, a variety of techniques, and a spectrum of attitudes and ideas. There are strong descriptive elements in the poems, Eric Sevareid's account of college politics combines first-person narrative with exposition, the selection by George Boas is a satire in narrative form, Robert M. Hutchins' essay is a combination of exposition and argument, and Henry Steele Commager's article is almost wholly argumentative.

The first essay, "Why Think?", discusses the failure of collegians to continue thinking after they have graduated from college. It analyzes the problems which confront those who do think and explains why Americans must continue to give all their intelligence to the problems facing the contemporary world. The poem "Campus on the Hill" suggests that the absence of thought is not confined to the post-graduate world but exists in the college classroom as well. The third selection is a good-natured satire on the qualifications and attitudes of some college freshmen. The essay by Eric Sevareid gives a first-hand account of a student's attempt to put his ideas into practice and the resistance this attempt encountered. The last essay is an argument against what the writer feels is one of the most wasteful and irrational activities in college life—big-time football. "The Game" provokes thought about football through humor.

All of the writers represented here are now or have been connected with colleges. Hutchins is former chancellor of the University of Chicago and currently president of the Fund for the Republic. Boas taught philosophy for many years at Johns Hopkins University. Sevareid writes of his own undergraduate days at the University of Minnesota; he is now a CBS news commentator. Snodgrass and Gibson, both prize-winning contemporary poets, teach at Wayne State and New York universities respectively. Commager is Professor of History and American studies at Amherst.

The first of these selections, "Why Think?", is printed with comments before and in the margin of the essay. The same kind of comments will be expected from students as they answer the questions which follow the other selections.

Why Think?

ROBERT M. HUTCHINS

The form of this brief essay is a model of unity, coherence, and emphasis. Hutchins limits the very broad and complicated subject of thinking in the first paragraph by relating it to "common sense." The particular kind of "common sense" that this essay is concerned with is social or public thinking, that is, the intellectual attention devoted to the solution of social or public problems. The essay contains only eighteen paragraphs, which fall into five divisions. Paragraph one introduces the subject, paragraphs two to six deal with the present conditions which seem to have made thinking "painful, unnecessary, and unpopular." Paragraphs seven to eleven seek explanations for this condition and find them in a conspiracy of silence, a "cliché curtain," a prevalence of irrationality, and propaganda. Paragraphs twelve to sixteen form the climax of his essay—if thinking is in such a state, why should we want to do anything about it? Three reasons are provided: for democracy, for peace, and for the improvement of our civilization and ourselves. Paragraph nineteen concludes the essay.

Interesting opening: anecdote catches attention, introduces, implicitly defines subject by suggesting difference between thinking (common sense) and doing a job (the result of technical or vocational education).

My father came home from India about thirty years ago with the story of a British woman who was plagued to death by the questions of her Indian servant. Finally she said to him, "Why don't you use your common sense?" He replied, "Lady, common sense is the gift of God; I have only a technical education."

In college students learn to think. The question is whether they continue to do so upon graduation. We know that whereas a great deal of thinking is required to get through college, none is necessary to get through life. By definition a moron is a person who cannot think, and one of the benefits conferred upon us by the Industrial Revolution is that it has made it possible for morons to be successful. In 1948, Dr. Ruby Jo Reeves Kennedy, sociologist at the Connecticut College for Women, reported to the American Association on Mental Deficiency that the typical male moron earned as much as $3.50 a week more than the average industrial wage and that the female moron uniformly made more money than the normal industrial worker.

Cites facts to support contention that thinking isn't necessary.

These figures should not surprise us, for it is obvious that the aim of mechanization is to get the operation simplified to the point where only his presence, and very little of that, is demanded of the operator. A capacity to think, and still worse, an insistence on doing so, may in such operations be a positive handicap.

Transitional paragraph linking unnecessary and painful aspects of thinking.

We here begin to discern one of the reasons for the prevailing anti-intellectualism in this country. People who think do not fit in easily. The trouble with thinking is that it leads to criticism. A person who thinks is one who dislikes falsehood. And since it is impossible to dislike it and never say anything about it, it is impossible to think and never say anything controversial.

Explanation of painfulness. Anti-intellectualism results from thinking because thinkers criticize and start controversies.

The unpopularity of thinking has a good deal to do with bringing about the alteration in the aims of education that has taken place in the thirty-five years and more that I have been employed by educational institutions. We exhibit a certain shyness now when we talk about those aims, intellectual training and intellectual activity, which were accepted as a matter of course in my youth. The current doctrine is that the aim of education is to adjust the young to the group. Not long ago a young woman at a co-educational college in Oklahoma

Note close texture of thought: unpopularity logically follows from painfulness and lack of necessity. Major example—shift toward adjustment in educational aims.

Effective use of anecdote.

was asked why she was depressed. She replied, "I come here to be went with and I ain't." The failure of education to perform its proper function in her case justified her disappointment with it.

Summarizes first five paragraphs in one sentence. Logical corollary—thinking has also become "next to impossible." All summed up in last sentence for further emphasis.

Thinking is painful, unnecessary, and unpopular. The din of public and private propaganda in which we live, the pressure exerted by the institutions in which we work and have our being, and the tyranny of our neighbor's lifted eyebrow are making thinking next to impossible. Under these circumstances the habit of not thinking, of not caring, of not protesting is the easiest in the world to acquire. The most common statement you can hear today is, "I don't want to get involved."

Defines process of thinking.
Cites causes of current situation. Specific causes named.

Thinking proceeds in the effort to raise and answer questions. The Socratic dialogue is the model of civilized society. Certain technical and economic changes have placed the present generation at a disadvantage. The forum and the general store, which used to be the centers of discussion in this country, are being driven out of business by television and the supermarket. There can't be much conversation when you are watching that little screen or pushing your cart down those unending corridors of cans.

Note transition—"far more serious." More specific examples, this time of current attitudes on the part of public authorities and institutions.
Cites instances of fear of even voicing questions.

Far more serious are the fashions of silence with which we are afflicted. Only the other day the commandants of the Military and Naval Academies thought it dangerous to have their young gentlemen on either side of the question whether Red China should be admitted to the United Nations. Nobody would care to ask today whether our conviction that we need to spend twice or twenty times the amount of money on education that we now devote to it is justified by the quality of education that our children are now receiving or precisely how the quality of education is to be improved by the expenditures proposed. It is now tacitly understood that American education needs nothing but money, that all teachers, all subjects, and all schools and colleges need more money, and it would be rude to ask whether it is absolutely certain that they all deserve it.

If it is possible to ask a question, it may not be possible to get an intelligible answer. The world is hidden from us by the cliché curtain. Just as the question of the actual danger from the Communist Party in America can't be raised because the Party is a treasonable conspiracy, and the question of educational expenditures can't be raised because education is a good thing, so the question of Strontium 90 is disposed of by saying that if leukemia doesn't get us the Russians will, desegregation in the South by saying that everything takes time, inflation by saying that we must reduce Federal expenditures, and the problems of labor organization by referring to the right to work.

Links thought to previous paragraph by pointing out that *even if* questions are raised, clichés prevent intelligible answers. Develops with examples of current clichés in thinking.

According to the law of contradiction, it is impossible to say that the same statement is at the same time in the same respect both true and false. One reason why the Civilization of the Dialogue is so hard to attain is that constant efforts are made to repeal this law. So the great historian of freedom, Lord Acton, had no difficulty in concluding that slavery was necessary to democracy, because, he said, the lower elements in the population would degrade it if they were allowed membership in the political society. According to Acton, slavery is essential if a democratic state is to be free. So, in spite of the fact that Christian love would seem to require that distinctions based on color should never appear in Christian congregations, it has been said that segregation reaches its peak in this country at 11 o'clock on Sunday mornings.

Supports his analysis of situation by citing a universally accepted law as norm for the civilization of the dialogue—the opposite of present situation.

Example of violation of the law.

A more immediate example of violation.

This paragraph is a good example of a technique employed throughout; namely, following an abstract statement with concrete examples.

Consider the possibilities in a local wit's report that the cigarette companies are about to embark

Note coherence: *Consider* is a transition connecting this paragraph with preceding. Reader is asked to reflect on further instances of the violations of fundamental law of logic.

on a national advertising campaign with the slogan, "Cancer is good for you." The more one ponders this suggestion the more probable it sounds. If the cigarette companies did enter upon this campaign, who can doubt that it would succeed? The genius and the devices at the disposal of private and public propaganda have made smooth the pathway to 1984, where slavery is freedom, war is peace, hate is love, and disease is health. We are so used to violations of the law of contradiction that we are startled when the Supreme Court upholds it and rules in civil liberties cases that the Constitution means what it says.

Further instance is advertising, which in turn is connected with propaganda.

Final sentence summarizes previous two paragraphs with allusion to new piece of information.

If thinking is painful, unnecessary, unpopular, and, under present circumstances, next to impossible, why should you do it? Consider what our problems are. They are how to make democracy work, how to survive in the nuclear age, and what to do with ourselves if we do survive.

Emphasis and clarity achieved by repetition of important points. Question introduces last half of essay. Last sentence divides answer into three parts: democracy, peace and survival, civilization after survival.

The first of these questions is how to make democracy work. It is basically the question of how we get the information and intelligence to cope with the totally new economic, social and political situation in which we find ourselves. When it appears likely that $175,000,000 was spent in the last national election, when fewer and fewer voices can be heard through the media of mass communications, when those media are chiefly devoted to mass entertainment, and when the educational system is dedicated largely to adjusting the young to the group, we see that discussion has been replaced by private and public propaganda and that the kind of education we are offering is unlikely to provide a defense against it.

Expands his first point—making democracy work. Note that only one new fact is added here. Method of summary is carried too far. If space had permitted, more specific information would have increased value of this paragraph.

Nor can we suppose that without thought we can survive in the nuclear age. Since we know that the simultaneous explosion of a finite number of bombs can make the world uninhabitable, we must

Paragraphs 13 and 14 linked by implied neither-nor construction: we can neither expect to improve our democracy (par. 13)

recognize that in two hundred years we have moved from polite wars for limited aims fought without disturbing most of the population to the point where we can all go up in one big megabang. To suppose that we can avoid this fate by preparing to make the bang bigger or by talking about the reduction of one or two kinds of forces in one or two kinds of places is as absurd as it was to imagine that the last wars could be avoided by an armament race or by endless conferences about whether the armor plate permitted on a battleship should be reduced by one-quarter or one-eighth of an inch.

nor can we hope to find peace (par. 14) without thought.

Historical analogy underlines reasoning.

And what shall we do with ourselves if we do survive? We have almost reached the 36-hour week, and as automation and atomic energy are brought into industrial use the proportion of our time that we shall have to devote to earning a living will decline still further. In my lifetime the hours of labor have been cut by a third. We don't know what to do with ourselves now. Some think that there is no limit to the capacity and willingness of people to seek and enjoy entertainment, relaxation, and recreation. I do not believe it. It is more likely that the alternatives presented by modern technology are either that we shall all be killed or we shall all be bored to death.

Third point—civilization after survival. What will we do with our newly created leisure if we can't think?

There are two ways to get through life that the educated person cannot permit himself, and they are to fill the time with aimless, and hence thoughtless activity, or to sink into a vegetable torpor. The reasons why these pastimes fail is that neither one is human. Every human being sooner or later has to feel that there is some meaning to his life. He must have a purpose.

Educated person has to think in order to feel like a human being.

You must think for your own sake, and also for your country's. We can be contented with nothing less for this nation than that it should cherish the best things there are. It seems altogether likely that

First sentence—transition, "for your own sake and also." Country needs thought in order to preserve "best things" of civilization.

these are art and education, freedom and justice, courage and compassion—the things the ancients summed up under the three heads of truth, beauty, and goodness. And what are these but the fullest development of man's highest powers in their individual and social aspects?

Concludes and summarizes with appropriate anecdote—despite the "dark days" of the present situation, thinking is the duty of those who have the ability to think.

Let us remember that there have been dark days in the past. There was a famous one in New England in 1780 when the sun scarcely appeared at all. Thousands of people took it for the end of the world. Among them were many in the Connecticut Assembly, in which Colonel Abraham Davenport was sitting. It was proposed that the Assembly adjourn. Colonel Davenport said, "The Day of Judgment is either approaching or it is not. If it is not, there is no cause for adjournment. If it is, I choose to be found doing my duty. I wish therefore that candles may be brought."

The Campus on the Hill

W. D. SNODGRASS

Up the reputable walks of old established trees
They stalk, children of the nouveaux riches; *chimes*
Of the tall Clock Tower drench their heads in blessing:
"I don't wanna play at your house;
I don't like you any more."
My house stands opposite, on the other hill,
Among meadows, with the orchard fences down and falling;
Deer come almost to the door.
You cannot see it, even in this clearest morning.
White birds hang in the air between
Over the garbage landfill and those homes thereto adjacent,
Hovering slowly, turning, settling down

Like the flakes sifting imperceptibly onto the little town
In a waterball of glass.
And yet, this morning, beyond this quiet scene,
The floating birds, the backyards of the poor,
Beyond the shopping plaza, the dead canal, the hillside lying tilted in the air,
Tomorrow has broken out today:
Riot in Algeria, in Cyprus, in Alabama;
Aged in wrong, the empires are declining,
And China gathers, soundlessly, like evidence.
What shall I say to the young on such a morning?—
Mind is the one salvation?—also grammar?—
No; my little ones lean not toward revolt. They
Are the Whites, the vaguely furiously driven, who resist
Their souls with such passivity
As would make Quakers swear. All day, dear Lord, all day
They wear their godhead lightly.
They look out from their hill and say,
To themselves, "We have nowhere to go but down;
The great destination is to stay."
Surely the nations will be reasonable;
They look at the world—don't they?—the world's way?
The clock just now has nothing more to say.

Questions and Assignments

1. What nuances of meaning are conveyed in the first two lines of "The Campus on the Hill" by the words: *reputable, old established, stalk, nouveaux riches*?

2. What is the "waterball of glass" in the fourteenth line? (Hint: the simile has to do with a paperweight.)

3. What does this line mean: "Tomorrow has broken out today"?

4. Discuss the significance of "They wear their godhead lightly" and "Surely the nations will be reasonable."

5. What is "the world's way"? What are the implications of the last line?

6. The general topic of this poem is, as the title indicates, "The Campus on the Hill." But what is its subject—that is, what is the author's main idea or organizing principle?

7. Can this piece of writing be divided into two, three, or more distinct parts or sections in the same way that we divided the preceding essay into five distinct sections? How does the author signal a transition from one part or section to the next?

8. In terms of what special interests and knowledge is the author viewing his topic "The Campus on the Hill"? How do the visual, intellectual, and emotional viewpoints of the author influence his choice of words and his selection and arrangement of details?

Freshman Adviser

GEORGE BOAS

We are sitting pencil in hand, surrounded by college catalogues, rules and regulations, directories, handbooks, mimeographed slips with last-minute changes of courses on them, folders with big cards for the students' records, pads with two carbons on which to write out schedules. We are all washed and clean, fresh from a summer in which we were supposed to rest and which we spent making enough money to fill out the gap between our salaries and a living wage. We are all resigned to the winter that is before us, teaching, coal bills, committee meetings, those tonsils of Susie's, academic freedom, subscription to the Symphony, student activities, what price a decent pair of shoes. . . . We smile at each other and sigh at the mass of paper. We have never learned all the rules. How can anyone learn them? Different ones for students in the college of arts and sciences, pre-meds, engineers. But what are rules anyway?

Here they come. . . .

His name is Rosburgh Van Stiew. One can see he is one of the Van Stiews—and if one can't, he'll let one know soon enough. That suit of fuzzy tweed, that regimental cravat, that custom-made shirt. Right out of *Vanity Fair*. Already he has the Phi Pho Phum pledge button in his buttonhole.

He speaks with a drawl. It is the voice of his mother's *face-à-main*. He has slightly wavy blond hair—his mother still has a crinkly white pompadour, like Queen Mary's. He has weary eyes.

No use to smile.

"Very well, Mr. Van Stiew. Have you any idea of the courses you'd like to take?"

"No . . . aren't there some things you sort of have to take?"

"Freshman English and Gym."

"Well, I may as well take them."

"History?"

"Do you have to?"

"No. You can take Philosophy, Political Science, or Economics instead."

Mr. Van Stiew tightens his cravat.

"Guess I'll take History."

"Ancient or Modern?"

"Well—when do they come?"

"Modern at 8:30, Wednesdays, Thursdays, and Saturdays; Ancient at 9:30, Mondays, Tuesdays, and Wednesdays."

"Oh, Ancient."

Mr. Van Stiew looks shocked that one should have asked.

One shouldn't have.

"Very well, Ancient History."

That leaves three more courses.

"One of the fellows said to take Art Appreciation."

"Yes, you could do that. But sooner or later you are required to take French and German and a laboratory science."

"Couldn't I put them off until next year?"

"You can until you're a senior."

"I think I'll put them off then. I don't want too heavy a schedule."

"Mathematics?"

"Do I have to?"

"It all depends. What are you going to major in?"

"Do I have to major?"

"More or less."

"When do I have to decide?"

"Next year."

So it goes with Mr. Van Stiew. He is using his right of election, his free will. His personality must not be crushed. He will have a Liberal Education, be a member of the Tennis Team, the Dramatic Club, and manager of the Glee Club. And as a prominent alumnus, he will see to it that the Football Team is never oppressed by a fastidious faculty.

Enter Mr. William Hogarth.

Hogarth is from the city Technical High School. Engineer. Red hair, freckles. Ready-made blue serge.

"Math, Physics, Philosophy, German—why can't I take Chemistry too? I'll make up my French this summer. . . . No, can't take any Saturday classes, working at the University Clothing Outlet Saturdays."

"English Literature?"

"Do I have to? . . . All right, Professor, put it down. Where do I get my textbooks? Don't they have any second-hand ones? . . . Classes begin tomorrow? All right. . . . Yes, I know about the Physical Exam. Had it already. . . . No, I guess I know everything now."

"If you need any information, Mr. Hogarth, I'm in my—"

"Thanks, don't believe I will."

He's gone.

Woof! One lights a cigarette.

A presence is before one, grinning. Lots of yellow hair parted in the middle, rising on each side of the part and falling like too ripe wheat. Head slightly to one side. Very red face.

Timidly shoves forward receipted bill from the Treasurer's Office.

Fred Wilkinson.

Mr. Wilkinson doesn't know what he's going to major in as yet—"you see, I may not stay here four years." A glance at his high-school record makes that more than probable.

"English and Physical Training, that is, Gym."

"Can't I be excused from that?"

"Have you a physical disability?"

"I'm not sure . . ."

"Well, we'll put it down anyway and you can talk it over with the doctor. French? German?"

"I'm not very good on languages."

"Mathematics?"

"Heavens, no!"

"Philosophy?"

"What's that?"

"It's—it's part of the business of philosophy to find out, Mr. Wilkinson."

One stops in time.

"I don't believe you'd like Philosophy. Physics? You have to take one science."

"Isn't there one where you take a trip in the spring?"

"Geology?"

"Is that where you study rocks and things?"

"Yes." God forgive me.

"I guess I'll take that."

"History?"

Quick response. The eyes actually grow bright.

"Oh, yes, History. My brother said to take History."

"Good, that's that anyway. . . . Ancient or Modern?"

"A—what?"

"Ancient or Modern?"

Mr. Wilkinson looks as if he were going to cry. His lower lip seems to swell. His eyes blink. But he is only thinking.

"Which do you study Keats and Shelley in?"

"Which History course?"

"Yes. My brother studied Keats and Shelley. That's the course I want. Don't they come in History?"

"They are undoubtedly a part of history" (one grows pontifical) "but I don't believe they usually are discussed in the History courses."

"I'm sure my brother studied them here."

"Maybe it was the History of English Literature."

"Would that have Keats and Shelley?"

"I imagine so."

Mr. Wilkinson is dubious.

"Well, I tell you, Professor. Couldn't you put it down, and then if it isn't all right maybe I could change it afterwards. I could change it, couldn't I, you know, if I didn't like it, if they didn't teach Keats and Shelley in it? I could change it, couldn't I?"

Why not? Mr. Wilkinson will flunk out at mid-term anyway.

So we go.

The pad of the three carbons grows thinner and thinner. The atmosphere grows thicker and thicker. The advisers grow stupider and stupider. The day grows shorter and shorter. By night all schedules are made. Tomorrow classes will begin. And after tomorrow Mr. Van Stiew, Mr. Hogarth, Mr. Wilkinson, and the rest will begin dropping courses, adding courses, shifting courses about until they have left of their original schedules only English Literature and Gym which are required in the Freshman year.

Questions and Assignments

1. What does the first paragraph tell you about the narrator of this incident? What does an expression like "What are rules anyway?" imply?

2. This incident is organized in the most traditional form of narrative fiction. A single focal point is established and a series of characters pass before that point. Many fairy tales are organized this way. Can you remember any? How typical are

the three students who pass before the "freshman adviser"? Is the author fair or unfair? Would you say he has characterized or caricatured?

3. Compare the opening and concluding paragraphs. Is the concluding paragraph necessary? How would its absence affect the account?

4. This selection was written nearly thirty-five years ago. Is it dated? Have collegians changed?

5. Assume that the general topic of this piece of writing is "The Problems of the Freshman Adviser." Can you fill in a six-point plan for this topic, using the same points listed on pages 28-30, which reflects what Boas has done with this general topic?

6. Write a brief narrative exposition using the same technique as Boas. Perhaps you would prefer to take the student's point of view and describe faculty advisers.

7. Write a theme attacking stereotypes, or a theme defending them as an accurate means of describing human character.

8. Write a theme similar to Boas' story about some other aspect of freshman registration and orientation—meeting the other new students in your dorm, fraternity or sorority rushing, trying out for the football team, physical education examinations.

Campus Politics

ERIC SEVAREID

We tried to apply our general ideas about human society to the specific world of the university. I doubt if our families and the public ever realized the deadly earnestness of "campus politics" and the appalling amount of time and energy students put into its practice. As in most state universities the authorities encouraged a modicum of "student government" as a kind of harmless training, always making sure to retain final control themselves. Hitherto, the machinery of student elections to various organizations and the organizations themselves had been the special preserve of the permanent fraternities and sororities, whose real leaders were frequently found among senior students in the law school. A small group of these men usually controlled all nominations by the dominant "party," which was essentially conservative, never dreaming of seriously challenging the university authorities on any real issue. They parceled out the elective honors to the Greek houses as a reward for party loyalty, arbitrarily deciding the class officers, for example, and which girls would have the honors of which places in line for the "grand march" of the class proms and balls. The award of these prerogatives was cause for endless conniving, bitter animosities, and the most acute heartburning imaginable. The most successful exponent of campus politics in years was a law student named Harold Stassen, who had been graduated two or three years previously and whose name was still a byword for political skill. But the coming of the new academic era with its intense concern over economic reform, over the issue of military preparedness and peace, edged our wooden swords with steel, and the battle seemed very real indeed. The Greek houses suddenly discovered that while they had been immersed in such matters as the class proms, other students by some diabolical and mysterious means had overreached them and were controlling the really vital instruments—the daily newspaper, the literary review, the law review, the board of publications, the student council, and so on. At the bottom of all this was the Jacobin Club, formed by ten or twelve of us who were in general revolt against things as they were. The Greek houses first learned of our organized existence when we were included with the regular fraternities in the quarterly list of academic standings, and they found us at the top of the list with a scholastic average higher than any fraternity had established in thirty years. We became suspect among the conventional conformists and very quickly feared by the university administration. We very nearly succeeded—we thought—in making student government truly that, and did succeed in abolishing compulsory military training, the most important issue of all. In the midst of this campaign, the authorities were forced to throw over all pretense of being disinterested advisors of student affairs and clamped a censorship on the daily newspaper. They sent their young stooges from the publications board down to our printery, and the editorial column of the paper carried the heading: "These editorials have been approved by the board of publications." Then followed a series of mock essays on the joys of springtime, the desirability of sprinklers that would throw water in squares instead of circles, and the like. The embarrassed president and the dean of men gave up this form of control, and tried other means, including personal intimidation; but it was too late. We had the Governor of the state on our side, he controlled some appointments to the board of regents, and sixty years of compulsory military training came to an end at that university.

This battle and many others went on, however, and the next year the editor of the paper also was a member of the Jacobin Club. I was to follow him, by right of seniority and general agreement, as editor in my senior year. But the habit of success had relaxed our vigilance. As the election to the editorship drew near, the authorities worked steadily behind us. They had found a weak spot in the wavering convictions of my fellow Jacobin, the incumbent editor. They turned his head with a great deal of flattering attention—the president would call him in for "advice" very frequently—and convinced him that it was his duty to stand again for election and for the good of the university prevent Sevareid from taking over the paper, even though this meant that the boy would have to change his life plan and enter the law school in order to remain on the campus. It was a miniature example of a recognizable political pattern: the liberal, softened by success and propinquity with the rich and powerful, renouncing his comrades in revolt "for the good of all." When we discovered that this lad was "doing a Ramsay MacDonald" on us, the fight became intense and bitter. My friends pleaded with the boy for hours at a time, warning him that his victory would turn to ashes because not only would he lose all his friends but his sponsors would despise him as their tool. It was too late. The military officers, we found, had been working for months on two or three members of the publications board to prevent my election, and the president did something he had never stooped to before—he ordered his own faculty representative on the board to vote as he desired regardless of that gentleman's convictions. After all, he had to keep his job. In sum, the administration in its own behavior betrayed all the principles of political uprightness that it insisted we be taught in our classes. As I later learned from my friends, some of the men and women in the Greek houses, who saw their chance to begin breaking down the power of the Jacobins, deliberately spread a rumor that I needed the editor's salary because I was in trouble and "had to get married." (I was engaged to a girl in the law school, an influential nonconformist herself.) The ferocity and vindictiveness of the campaign reached unbelievable heights. In the election by the board I lost by one vote. Tammany methods, when thus applied, were unbeatable.

Loevinger, who was president of the publications board, broke the news to me in the law review office next morning, and I was stunned. I had worked three years for this position and honor, and by every rule was entitled to it. I had never hidden anything nor worked behind anyone's back. I had assumed the opposition felt as we did: that controversy was controversy, that a man's opinions were his own, and that, however anyone opposed them, he did not resort to calumny nor twist the very lives of his friendly enemies. I was the naïve liberal, still feeling somehow that truth could defeat a Hitler. Dimly I began to perceive the realities of political life. I was unable to speak and walked down the stairs. Sherman Dryer caught up with me, put his arm over my shoulder, and solemnly said: "This changes my whole philosophy."

When the news got out there was an uproar. Although I was doing my major studies in political science and not in the journalism department, all the members of the journalism faculty protested the decision, and about twenty-five of the thirty or so students on the newspaper staff signed an objection. They offered to strike, to refuse to publish, but—still clinging to the liberal's characteristic belief that the persuasion of truth would somehow suffice—I refused this drastic move. A second election was forced, but after an exhausting all-night battle, the board confirmed its vote and we gave up. I became a minor hero and martyr; my opponent was expelled from the Jacobin Club, formally censured for "conduct unbecoming a gentleman" by the journalistic honorary society of which I was president, and continued as editor, a friendless, lonely boy. The pattern of power politics was carried out to its final orthodox step: I was called into the dean's office and with much flattery informed I had been chosen for membership in the senior honor society. This corresponded to a knighthood for an influential but defeated opponent of the ruling system, which uses the glamorous apparatus of royal orders as a political weapon.

After that I buried myself in my books, earning bread and board by rising at five each morning and working in the university post office before classes, handling and distributing bundles of the newspaper which I had cherished and lost. It was many months before the pangs of bitterness left me. I had one last fling. Every four years the students staged a mock political convention, of all parties instead of one, to nominate their choice for the presidency of the United States. As comic relief, I made a nominating speech for one Bernarr MacFadden, elderly exponent of vitamins and setting-up exercises, at that time (1936) seriously trying to get the Republican nomination. I hired a bugler, a girl acrobatic dancer with a fulsome bust, and a football hero with sizable biceps, and paraded with them to the stand carrying a banner that depicted a muscular arm wielding a dumbbell. The speech began: "Fellow Americans, are we men or mice?" and argued the need for a Strong Man in the White House. I was making a sarcastic attack on the preparedness program and warned with mock rhetoric of the imminent danger of the Japanese "invading the California coast in bathing suits." The mass of students in the field house screamed their delight. Sherman, with glittering eye, made an impassioned attack on Governor Landon, "who would sacrifice the youth of the land on the altar of the balanced budget." We nominated Floyd B. Olson. The downtown political writers complimented us on our oratorical mastery and wondered in print why this level of platform brilliance was unattained in state politics.

With this speech, with this message to my fellow students, I ended my university career. It was one year before the battle of Shanghai, two years before the *Anschluss*.

Questions and Assignments

1. This essay is clearly divided according to chronology. Each paragraph, with the exception of the last, introduces a new step in Sevareid's campus battle. (The last paragraph clarifies the significance of the preceding paragraph.) Describe the progression of events in Sevareid's narration.

2. In terms of paragraph structure, what purpose is served by the opening sentence? What were Sevareid's politics? The dates of Sevareid's undergraduate years, which are revealed in the course of the essay, may give you some indication.

3. The first two paragraphs are very long and the third is relatively brief. Can you account for this alteration in length?

4. Sevareid felt that his membership in the honor society was "the final orthodox step" of "power politics." What does this mean? Could there be another interpretation of this action?

5. What is the significance of the final paragraph? Do you think the end to military training and the satire about a Japanese invasion would have been met with "screams of delight" in 1939 or 1941? How does this paragraph change the significance of what has preceded it? What does it reveal about the author's own self-knowledge? What did Sevareid learn from his defeat?

6. The author is writing an account of his undergraduate years, yet he has not covered all aspects of those years. What organizing principle has he used to limit his subject? What particular aspects of his life during those years has he obviously omitted as irrelevant to his main idea?

7. Write an essay about a personal "struggle and defeat," or about a victory, in some aspect of your life in college, high school, fraternity, sorority, family, club, work. Perhaps you can think of an incident in which you later turned out to be wrong, or right.

Give the Games Back to the Students

HENRY STEELE COMMAGER

Almost every year the public is startled by revelations of some new scandal in college athletics—the bribery of basketball players, the open purchase of football players, the flagrant violation of rules by the college authorities themselves.

It is regrettable that these scandals should excite so much attention, for, by dramatizing the ostentatious immoralities of college athletics, they tend to distract attention from the more permanent and pervasive immoralities.

Indignation at the more overt manifestations of corruption is thus a kind of moral catharsis; having expressed it, we then can contemplate with apathy the conditions which almost inevitably produce the corruption.

Thirty years ago a report of the Carnegie Foundation on College Athletics concluded as follows:

"The paid coach, the special training tables, the costly sweaters and extensive journeys in special Pullman cars, the recruiting from the high schools, the demoralizing publicity showered on players, the devotion of an undue proportion of time to training, the devices for putting a desirable athlete, but a weak scholar, across the hurdles of the examinations, these ought to stop and the intramural sports be brought back to a stage in which they can be enjoyed by a large number of students and where they do not involve an expenditure of time and money wholly at variance with any ideal of honest study."

"These ought to stop!" Instead, they have become all but universally accepted and legalized—nay, the malpractices themselves have become respectable, and we can look back upon our old view of them with a certain nostalgia.

For today's malpractices are more extreme and more widespread. Worse yet, they have percolated down to the high school and they have corrupted large segments of our society.

For almost half a century now, educators have talked hopefully about de-emphasizing college athletics. And every year the emphasis has grown greater, not weaker.

The problem is not one of over-emphasis. It is not even one of emphasis. The problem is the enterprise itself—intercollegiate athletics.

If we are going to solve that problem, we must begin by restating principles so elementary and so obvious that they should not have to be stated at all:

The function of colleges and universities is to advance education.

Whatever contributes to education is legitimate. Whatever does not contribute to education is illegitimate.

The only justification, therefore, for games, sports, athletics, is that these do in some way contribute to education.

By education we mean nothing narrow. Clearly, it involves physical and moral as well as intellectual well-being. But these are by-products of education. There are a number of institutions that have responsibility for the physical and moral well-being of the young, but the schools and colleges are the only institutions that have primary responsibility for their intellectual well-being.

Does our current system of intercollegiate or interschool athletics contribute either to the central function of education, or to its by-products?

Clearly, it does not. As now organized and directed in most colleges and in a good many, if not most, high schools as well, athletics contribute nothing whatsoever to education. They simply distract the time, the energy and the attention of the whole community from the main business of education—and from its legitimate by-products.

Our system of athletics does not contribute to the physical fitness of the young. On the contrary, it concentrates on physical training for a mere handful of students—whom it often harms by overtraining—and reduces the great majority of students to the role of passive spectators, or television viewers. Even the facilities provided for physical training are often monopolized by the "teams," to the detriment of most of the student body.

It does not contribute to sportsmanship—which was one of its original purposes. On the contrary, the tremendous emphasis on winning the game has largely destroyed sportsmanship and has corrupted both players and spectators.

It does not contribute to initiative, independence, alertness and other desirable qualities. Instead, by centering authority in paid coaches whose primary interest is winning games, it has gone far to destroy initiative and independence on the part of players.

No impartial student of college and high-school athletics today can doubt that, on balance, these sports—far from making any contribution—actually do immense and irreparable harm. It is not only physical training and sports that are corrupted by the current malpractices; it is the whole educational enterprise. And since the whole community is involved in the educational enterprise, it is the whole community.

Educational institutions themselves are corrupted. They publicly confess that their athletic functions are more important than their academic, and acquiesce in malpractices that they would not tolerate in any other branch of their activities.

Colleges that spend more money on athletics than on the library, that excite more interest in basketball than in music, that cater to the demand for "winning teams" rather than for sportsmanship are faithless to their moral and intellectual obligations.

The community itself is corrupted by being bribed with athletic spectacles to support educational programs which should be supported on their merits.

Perhaps worst of all, the boys and girls of the country are corrupted: here is the real corruption of the innocent. Almost every newspaper, every weekly magazine, every television network makes clear to them that what is most important in education is athletics, and what is most important in athletics is winning.

No newspaper ever celebrates the scholarly achievements of local students in its biggest headlines. Why, then, should we expect the young to believe us when we tell them, on ceremonial occasions, that it is the scholarly achievements that are important? Alumni demand a winning team, and so does the community. Not long ago, a North Carolina coach was quoted as asking, "How can I be proud of a losing team?" Can we, then, expect young people to take us seriously when we tell them that it is the game that counts—not the victory?

What is the explanation of this deep and pervasive corruption of games and sports? What has happened to us?

What has happened is that we have taken games away from the students, to whom they belong, and given them to adults, to whom they do not belong.

We now require of high school and college boys—and, sometimes, girls—that they provide entertainment for the community and bring money to local shopkeepers and restaurants and other business men. (Recently a New York official said of an Army-Syracuse game that "the restaurants reported business to be fabulous . . . the Transit Authority reported 28,000 extra riders that day . . . immensely increased hotel business.") They are expected to provide copy for the local newspapers, for magazines, and for TV and radio.

We do not permit children to work in shops or factories for our profit. Why should they be expected to make money for business interests in the community?

We do not permit our daughters to put on performances in burlesque shows or night clubs for our entertainment. Why should we require our sons to put on gladiatorial spectacles in stadia for our entertainment?

We do not expect the young to pay school taxes, or to support the chemistry department of a university. Why should we expect them to earn money for the athletic programs of the local high school, or to support the athletic departments of our colleges and universities?

The problem is deep and pervasive, but fortunately not complex. The solution is drastic, but fortunately not difficult; all that is needed is the will to apply it. The solution is threefold:

First, give games back to the students.

Second, eliminate all outside pressures to win games.

Third, take the dollar sign entirely out of school and college athletics.

First: Let students manage their own games, as they do at English universities. Let them play their games for the fun of it, not to entertain adults, or make money for the community or win glory for old Pugwash.

An end to games as spectacles. An end to bands in uniforms and drum majorettes and well-trained cheering sections, all of them artificial and all giving a fantastically exaggerated importance to the games. An end to the recruiting of players by coaches or alumni, to coaches who play the games from the side lines and, for that matter, to formal coaching. If there must be coaches, let them depart on the day of the game and permit the players to play their own games. After all, professors do not help the students pass examinations!

Second: Eliminate all outside pressures. Alumni letters about the football team should go into the waste basket, where they belong. An end to pressure from coaches; their jobs should not depend on victories. An end to pressure from newspapers; let them report professional games, and leave students alone to play as well or as badly as they please. An end to pressure from public relations offices of colleges; let them report academic activities or go out of business. An end to pressure from townspeople; they can get their entertainment, find emotional safety valves and get rid of their vicarious sadism elsewhere.

Third: Eliminate money—all the way. No more paid coaches. Let students do their own coaching, or let school teams draw on "old boys," or get such aid as they need from members of the teaching staff who are primarily and legitimately teachers. After all, paid coaches are both new and singular in history: they did not exist until this century, and they do not now exist in England or Europe. An end to all athletic subsidies, direct and indirect; to athletic "scholarships," a contradiction in terms. No student should be encouraged, in high school, to subordinate studies to athletic prowess. No student should be admitted to college on any grounds but those of academic competence; no student should be allowed to stay in college unless he is intellectually competent.

An end to separate athletic budgets; to admission charges for games; to the expectation that football or basketball will somehow "pay for" other parts of physical training. Games should be as much a normal part of school or college as music or drama or the college newspaper, and should no more expect to be self-sustaining.

An end to the building or maintenance of costly stadia. Let us make drastic reductions in expenditures for athletic equipment, for uniforms, for other superfluities. No more travel expenditures for spring training camps, for fall training camps, for airplane junkets to the other end of the country. Let schools play their neighbors in the same town or—at an extreme—in the same state.

Adopt these policies and nine-tenths of the evils that plague intercollegiate athletics would evaporate overnight.

Of course, if they *were* adopted, the games would deteriorate—as spectacles. Those who want to see brilliant performances in football or basketball can then go to professional games, as even now they go to professional rather than to college baseball games.

Let the fans—the subway alumni of Notre Dame or the vicarious old grads of Michigan—organize city or state football and basketball teams, just as the English have city or county soccer teams.

Naturally, student interest in organized athletics will decline; it should. Sensible students already know that if they are going to get on with their education—if they are going to get into a law school or a medical school—they have no time for organized athletics.

European universities have managed to survive for centuries without the benefit of "teams," and doubtless American colleges and universities can learn to do so.

Of course, there will be a falling-off in enthusiasm for old Siwash among certain kinds of alumni. Perhaps, in time, colleges can produce alumni whose interest is in intellectual rather than in athletic programs. In any event, there seems to be a pretty close correlation between high-powered athletics and low-powered finances. It is a sardonic commentary on the current scene that public pressure for winning teams rarely finds expression in lavish gifts or in generous appropriations. Institutions such as M. I. T. and Amherst, at any rate, seem to manage pretty well without the exploitation of athletics, and institutions such as Ohio State, which has yielded to pressure for winning teams, are treated with niggardliness by an ungrateful Legislature.

These are negative consequences which we may anticipate from the elimination of money and of pressures from college athletics and the return of games to the students. The positive consequences which we may confidently anticipate are exhilarating.

This simple program will restore integrity to athletics, making clear once more the blurred distinction between the amateur and the professional. And it will enormously improve programs for physical education for the young people in schools and colleges, an improvement desperately needed.

It will release the energies of educators and students for the primary job of education. The colleges will be freed from improper pressures and influences and permitted to do what they are best equipped to do and what they have a moral responsibility to do: educate the young.

But is all this a counsel of perfection? Can this program of cleansing and restoration be achieved? Well, it has been achieved at Johns Hopkins, at the University of Chicago, and at M. I. T. It has been achieved at Swarthmore and Oberlin and Reed. Somehow, all continue to flourish.

No halfway measures will do. As long as nonacademic organizations have an interest in athletics, as long as games belong to coaches or alumni or townspeople or the business community instead of to the young people who play them, all the evils which have afflicted school and college athletics in the past will continue.

Radical surgery is needed. But it is radical surgery from which the patient is sure to recover and which guarantees good health and good spirits.

Questions and Assignments

1. There are five steps in Commager's argument: (1) Introduction: statement of the problem and failure of previous recommendations; (2) a statement of principle on which his argument rests and evidence that athletics has both fallen short of and corrupted the principle; (3) an analysis of the *causes* of the corruption and the presentation of a proposed solution; (4) a presentation of the negative, then the positive *effects* of his proposed solution; (5) a three-paragraph conclusion pointing out six places where his solution has been successfully tried and reasserting the urgent need for reform. Find these steps in the essay and explain them in detail.

2. Commager's definition of education is crucial to his argument. What is his definition? How valid is his definition? Would it be possible to agree with his definition and disagree with his argument?

3. What does Commager mean by saying "Our system of athletics does not contribute to the physical fitness of the young"? He refers to "athletic spectacles" as bribery. What does he mean?

4. Commager uses several analogies—to child labor, to burlesque shows, to taxation. Are they valid and appropriate to his argument? He also argues from the examples of M.I.T., Swarthmore, and European universities. How convincing are these examples?

5. Drawing upon your own experience or knowledge, write an argumentative essay attacking or defending Commager's position. For example, do you think it is true that "today's malpractices . . . have percolated down to the high school"? Or use facts and figures from your own university about the percentage of scholarships for athletes, whether or not athletics are profitable, and so forth.

6. Using Commager's essay as a model, write about the shortcomings or excesses of some other aspect of your university, such as social life, required subjects, regulations, drinking, cheating.

The Game

WALKER GIBSON

October! Can I stand it one more year?
This Saturday they're playing at the Bowl!
Connecticut's afire with autumn cheer—
There's yellow-red nostalgia in my soul.
Rev up the old convertible, for I'm
Off to New Haven for the thousandth time.

Over and under parkway bridges gliding,
With Thunderbirds and Caddies flitting by,
Again October finds me riding, riding
Into that old familiar autumn sky
Through traffic gay with girls and garish grads,
Blankets, banners, chrysanthemums, and plaids.

Light lunch on someone's lawn—"Park right in here!"—
Ham or egg salad from a plastic basket
(Hammacher-Schlemmer: used it last last year),
Plus little swallows from a pocket flasket
To harden one to hail old friends by name—
"Say Mike!" "Say Mort!" "Say . . . ?" On, on! The Game!

Sluicing through Portal Twelve at two o'clock
(A to the right, B left, C straight ahead),
We reach a roost and perch among that flock,
Each with a pretty feather in its head.
Far far below on geometric green
Infinitesimal figures can be seen.

Running and falling, falling and running, falling,
As in some ritual of holy dance.
With complicated forms of mauling sprawling,
The young rejuvenate arcane romance,
Chasing an egg (the rites of procreation),
Bowed down in mysteries of T-formation.

And every year I manage to forget
How absolutely dull the thing is, too.
That thumping music!—there's that old regret
These fifty thousands number me and you.
But now the first chill of late afternoon
Blows through the Bowl. It will be over soon.

Over and under parkway bridges gliding,
The Thunderbirds and Caddies flitting past,
October night will find us riding, riding

Back to the life we left behind at last.
Every autumn, autumn's a little colder.
Oh every fall I feel a full year older!

Questions and Assignments

1. What is the purpose of the repetition from the second stanza in the last stanza?
2. In what way does the rhythm of this poem correspond to the mood the poet wishes to convey?
3. What is the hidden metaphor in stanza four? In stanza five?
4. What does this poem tell you about the person who is writing it?

Rewriting

There are four views on rewriting. Some pieces of literature have been successful without rewriting, and Shakespeare, for example, is said never to have blotted a line. However, most writers admit that they make minor corrections and improvements as they write. And often writers find it beneficial to expand, to rearrange material, sometimes to reconceive their whole approach. Finally, some writers polish their work repeatedly. Frank O'Connor, for example, says that he rewrites his short stories twelve times, and there are seventy-two distinct versions of one of Dylan Thomas' poems.

We are here concerned with rewriting of the second and third varieties. We admit that it is possible for a writer to have the ability to express himself flawlessly on the first attempt, but we have never seen such a writer in a composition course. If there is such a writer using this book, he need read no further in this section. At the other extreme, most student writers cannot take the time to rewrite twelve times, nor can they seek esthetic perfection in their compositions. This leaves us with just two varieties of rewriting—the corrective and the reconceived.

Both kinds of revision are necessary whenever possible. In an in-class theme or an essay exam, however, the student must confine himself to minor corrections and rewordings. His approach to the subject and his organization must then be especially well thought out beforehand. But even the most carefully thought out essay may be markedly improved by complete revision when time is available. Reflection overnight or for a day or two often provides a fresh perspective which makes complete revision possible and rewarding.

The following selections include both types of revision. The first two examples are by Jerome Ellison, a professional writer; the third example is by the Elizabethan statesman and writer, Francis Bacon. Close study of all three examples should show the student how it is possible to improve by rewriting.

Others See Us

JEROME ELLISON

(Original Version)

"So great has been my lifetime wish to see America," the newly-arrived Frenchman confessed, "that I once pretended it was so. When I was ten years old I falsely told my mistress I had spent my summer vacation there. Now it is for true!"

He was voicing in tourist English (a Frenchman's *"maîtresse"* may also be his teacher) a long-standing, world-wide curiosity. Is America really the land of the free, or are we ground under capitalist greed? Is everybody rich and crazy, as Hollywood movies suggest, or do we have some moderate-income, sane people too?

Spurred by new travel bargains that bring overseas holidays within the reach of working people, foreigners are coming by the hundreds of thousands to see for themselves. The Empire State Building, it turns out, is as great a tourist attraction as the Eiffel Tower. Niagara Falls draws more foreign sightseers than the Matterhorn, The Bowery evokes more shocked gasps than the Left Bank.

The flood of overseas visitors, tourism specialists say, has only begun. More and more travel firms are offering cut-rate fares. The U. S. Department of Commerce, in an effort to recover some of our outflowing gold, has launched a gigantic, world-wide "Visit America" campaign designed to increase tourism from abroad at least eightfold. Already, foreign visitors are up to 602,000 (1960) from the 450,000 of 1957.

I have recently followed the doings of eight typical plane-loads of these holiday-makers—four from France, two from Ireland, one from Germany and one from Peru.

Through the eyes of such visitors one gains a fresh view of America, and it's enough to give the thoughtful American pause. When they go home they'll spread the word about us with the authority of eye-witnesses. They bussed, motored and hitch-hiked throughout the country and spilled over into Canada and Mexico. Almost everything happened—four were jailed without cause, seven were robbed, a score were regally entertained by warm-hearted Americans met casually while travelling. One astonished young Frenchman, by doing nothing more than sitting beside a Florida swimming pool, received a proposal of marriage from a bathing beauty hailing from the American midwest.

The adventures of a French group called *Amis de l'Orient* reveal something of what it's like to go on a bargain junket to the U. S. The tour was organized by a travel agency called Touramerica, at the request of travel-minded employees of several French companies including IBM France. It was a 20-day package, covering hotels, meals, travel and sightseeing, with a week in New York, three days in Washington and five in Miami. It cost $550, time payment over 20 months if desired. To meet Civil Aeronautics Board regulations, which restrict cut-rate group travel to clubs and associations, the trip was also sponsored by a loose-knit organization offering lectures on Hindu art and philosophy and called Friends of the Orient.

The *Amis de l'Orient* had a gay time. On tour they made an attractive group, nattily turned out, brisk, alert, *very* Parisian. They worked through the scheduled sightseeing—boat trips around Manhattan and to the Statue of Liberty; the glass top tour of Chinatown, The Bowery, the UN, the Cathedral of St. John the Divine; the bus ride up the east bank of the Hudson to Poughkeepsie; the visits to museums and art galleries—then made unscheduled sorties of their own. Some went shopping on Fifth Avenue or souvenir-hunting on Broadway, some trekked to a Long Island beach or spent an evening at Broadway's colorful Roseland Ballroom.

Everywhere there were pleasant surprises. The boy who dispensed cokes atop the Rockefeller Center tower had studied French in high school, helped make correct change and said "Thank you" nicely in French. The sightseeing bus was stalled in traffic smack dab against the limousine of Sugar

Ray Robinson, who loves France, took time for autographs, and parted with a hearty "Vive la France."

When Strangers Tour the U.S.A.

JEROME ELLISON

(Rewritten Version)

Is America really the land of the free? Or are most Americans ground under the heel of capitalist greed? Is everybody in America rich and neurotic, as Hollywood movies suggest? Or do we also have some sane people of moderate means?

Lured by new tourist-travel bargains, foreigners by the hundreds of thousands are invading America to find out for themselves. As a result, the Empire State Building has become as great a tourist attraction as the Eiffel Tower; Niagara Falls now draws more international sightseers than the Matterhorn; and the Bowery evokes more shocked gasps than Paris's Bohemian Left Bank.

Tourism specialists say this flood tide of visitors from overseas is just the beginning. More and more travel firms are offering cut-rate fares to America. The United States Department of Commerce has launched a gigantic, world-wide "Visit America" campaign, designed to increase tourism from abroad eightfold. The number of foreign visitors—not counting those from Mexico and Canada—has risen from 450,000 in 1957 to 602,000 in 1960.

Recently I observed and interviewed eight planeloads of these holiday travelers—four from France, two from Ireland, one from Germany and one from Peru. Through their eyes I gained a fresh view of my native land. The perspective they provided is enough to give pause to even the most complacent American. For many of these visitors bused, motored and hitchhiked throughout America and got a close-up view of our triumphs and our tragedies. And when they reach home, they will spread the word about this country with the authority of eyewitnesses.

Last summer, students at the University of Paris organized three round-trip charter flights to America which cost $99 per person the round trip, 118 to a plane. "So many wanted to go," said one flight organizer, Arthur Pilla, "that we could easily have filled half a dozen planes."

The experiences of one French group I talked with reveal what it's like to come on a bargain junket to the U.S. The tour was organized by a travel agency called Touramerica. It was a twenty-day package, covering the cost of hotels, meals, travel fares and sight-seeing expenses. The tour included a week in New York, three days in Washington and five in Miami at a cost of $550 per person.

In New York the French visitors had a gay time. They worked through scheduled sight-seeing—boat trips around Manhattan and to the Statue of Liberty; a glass-top-bus tour of Chinatown, the Bowery, the United Nations and the Cathedral of St. John the Divine; visits to the numerous museums and art galleries. Then they made unscheduled sorties of their own. Some went shopping on Fifth Avenue or souvenir hunting in Times Square. Others visited Jones Beach on Long Island. Several spent an evening at Broadway's colorful Roseland Ballroom.

In many places visitors enjoyed pleasant surprises. The boy who dispenses soft drinks at the Rockefeller Center observation roof had studied French in high school. He spoke briefly to the visitors in their native tongue. One tourists' sight-seeing bus stalled in traffic adjacent to boxer Sugar Ray Robinson's limousine. Sugar Ray gave autographs and drove on with a hearty *"Vive la France!"*

The student will notice several important things in comparing the preceding original and rewritten versions of the Ellison article written for the *Saturday Evening Post* (December 9, 1961). First of all, the title has been changed to "When Strangers Tour the U.S.A." In considering more carefully the readers for whom the article was intended, Ellison decided the original title was too general for a popular magazine. The new title gives a more precise indication of what the piece is about. The anecdote which opened the original version has been deleted from the second. Though the anecdote has some charm, Ellison felt it a little too precious and a little too labored to offer to the kind of hurried reader whom this type of weekly magazine addresses. In paragraph two, Ellison has broken up the pairs of alternatives into short staccato questions. Notice the effect this has in gaining and holding the attention of the reader in the second version. Short sentences call for less effort than long ones and are advisable when the writer is trying to lure the casual reader into a deeper involvement. The same kind of brevity has been achieved throughout the article by cutting and eliminating wordy phrases. Notice that the author has cut and rearranged sentences in paragraphs six, seven, and eight. The full explanations which appear in the original version were not really necessary at this point. They delayed the more important consideration of carrying the reader on into some of the adventures of the travelers before he lost interest.

Austerity Comes to Sunshine U.

JEROME ELLISON

(Original Version)

I have lately been talking with some fraternity men at the University of Miami in Coral Cables, Florida, about their problems. These, as the brothers see them, are acute. The Sigma Alpha Epsilon chaps, for instance, haven't got a single powerboat to tow them at water skiing. A member mourned: "Last year we had three boats in the house. This year the owners had to study and left them home. Now when we want to ski we have to *rent* a boat!"

There are other signs of austerity at "Sunshine U.," once noted for its agreeable program of reading, writing and romping. One of the boys recently asked for an on-campus parking permit. The records showed he already had one. "That was for the hard-top," he explained confidently, "I need another for the sports job." Callously the university said no, there'd be only one car on campus per student.

Skylarking is not as carefree as of yore. Last semester three fraternities were put on probation, a house mother was fired and two fraternity officers were suspended—all for nothing more serious than "having a few drinks" (the brothers' version) at weekend parties. "Things certainly are changing around here," the brothers are grumbling.

They grumble the truth, and the nature of the change should interest all concerned with higher learning. UM is coming to grips with a question that besets all of us to some extent, but particularly our collegians and those who ride herd on them:—how much work should properly be mixed with how much play? UM officials feel the time has come to cut down a little on frolic.

Other schools have entertained similar notions, but few have whoopee problems on quite the same scale. UM has all the party trappings of the standard big-enrollment, coeducational, super-stadium, twirlers-between-halves schools, plus the unparalleled amusement resources of one of the world's great relaxation capitals.

Miami, near the southern tip of the Sunshine State, is a resort city in a land of sand, palms, and warm seas. Its major industry is fun. The tropical glamor of suburban Coral Gables is enhanced by Venetian canals and green lagoons. Hialeah, Tropical Park and Gulfstream racetracks are nearby. . . .

Troubles of Sun-Tan U.

JEROME ELLISON

(Rewritten Version)

I talked lately with some fraternity men at the University of Miami in Coral Gables, Florida, about their problems. These, as the brothers see them, are acute. The Sigma Alpha Epsilon chaps, for instance, haven't a single powerboat for water-skiing. "Last year we had three boats in the house; this year the owners had to study and left them home," a member mourned.

There are other signs of austerity at "Sunshine U.," once noted for its agreeable program of reading, writing and romping. One student recently asked for an on-campus parking permit. The records showed he already had one. "That was for the hard-top," he explained confidently. "I need another for the sports car." Callously the university said no, there'd be only one car on campus per student.

Skylarkers don't get away with what they used to. Last semester three fraternities were put on probation, a house mother was fired, and two fraternity officers were suspended—all for simply "having a few drinks" (the brothers' version) at weekend parties. "Things certainly are changing around here," one brother grumbled.

He spoke the truth, and the nature of the change should interest all concerned with higher learning. University of Miami is coming to grips with a question that bothers all of us to some extent, but particularly our collegians and those who direct them: How much work should be mixed with how much play? U.M. officials think the time has come to cut down a little on frolic.

The crackdown came in August, 1960, in the guise of a routine personnel replacement. U.M.'s executive vice president, Dr. James Godard, had resigned to accept another post. Dr. Robert Johns, director of the Illinois Commission on Higher Education, was hired to replace him. The statement of U.M.'s president, Dr. Jay F. W. Pearson, gave no hint of what was to come. "Doctor Johns's job," President Pearson said, "will be to operate the university under a policy laid down by the Board of Trustees and me."

The "policy laid down," it presently developed, was a tough one. Pearson had become touchy about the reputation of the university which he had helped to found thirty-five years before. He resented the tag "Suntan U.," which he felt unjustly suggested that U.M. was a play school. He was annoyed by jokes about the fact that U.M. once gave university credit for a course in fresh- and salt-water fishing. He intended that everything possible be done to reinforce the school's academic performance and reduce the play-school "smear." He made his intentions known to Johns.

Johns faced a large assignment. Few schools have whoopee problems on quite the scale of those found at the university-under-the-palms. U.M. has all the party trappings of the standard big-enrollment, twirlers-between-halves schools, plus the amusement resources of one of the world's greatest relaxation capitals.

Miami, near the southern tip of Florida, is a resort city in a land of sand, palms and warm seas. Its major industry is fun. Hialeah, Tropical Park, and Gulfstream race tracks are nearby. So are four dog tracks, two auto speedways and a *jai alai* establishment, all presenting opportunities for betting. Such attractions lure Miami's students. One young scholar—"having been told there was blood in his beerstream," as a classmate put it—sold a pint of his blood to finance a go at the Hialeah para-mutual.

Notice again the importance of choosing a good title. "Austerity" is perhaps too fancy a word for use in a general-circulation weekly. The minor adjustments which the author has made in the opening paragraph are aimed at improving clarity and ease of reading. After paragraph four of the original version, Ellison has made a major change by inserting a passage from further on in the article. Since this is mainly a story of educational reform in the face of difficulties, it seemed wise to establish the principal characters earlier in the narrative than first planned. The paragraph on administrative background and dramatis personnae, lifted from a later passage, does the job. The minor rearrangements which appear in the second-to-the-last paragraph of the rewritten version were made for smoother reading. In the following selection, Jerome Ellison himself comments on the importance of rewriting.

Reflections on Rewriting

JEROME ELLISON

Literary composition consists mainly of two operations, writing and rewriting. Writing is the struggle to make the material one's own—to encompass it, subdue it, get it down on paper. Rewriting is the job of making the material somebody else's—attending to those conventions by which, through centuries of usage, anybody who understands English can share one's conquest.

Sometimes, as in the case of the people who "never rewrite," the two processes go forward simultaneously. On other occasions they are distinctly separate. But in all cases the two functions are by nature different.

Well, then, one may reasonably ask, how can one know which is which, and which comes first? Suppose, for instance, I wanted to write a short essay on my summer vacation. At first the job would seem overwhelming—how can I pack into ten minutes of reading something it took weeks to live? By elimination, of course. I hit on the title *Fun and Sorrow Last Summer*. Then I almost panic again—*all* the fun, *all* the sorrow? No, this must be short—only one or two instances of each. But the reliving of these few episodes may give me a fearful emotional bouncing, joy to grief and back again. No matter, I'm going to get this down. Misery be damned, admonitions of a lifetime of remembered teachers be damned, I've got to get it down, never mind in what shape. Now, at last, it's out and it's down—this is writing.

But was it all writing, and no rewriting? Of course not. The instant I was committed to writing an essay I had made a decision about form and style. It was not going to be a sonnet, a play, or a story, but an essay. My outline, whether written down or carried in my head, roughly followed the appropriate form. All through the first-round writing job, everything I had learned about communication in English was being put to work: Have I used this word too often? Try another. Is this a cliché? Say it differently. Is this a repetition? Strike it out. Do you spell the word that way or this way, hook up the sentence like that or like this? Check, decide. What passage should come next? Choose, organize, relate one passage to another.

All this is rewriting, and some of it is going on even while we're still writing. But in writing, the *main thing* is to get it down. Sometimes this is so difficult it requires all our energy; we have none left over for rewriting. Such was the case with Robert Louis Stevenson's *The Strange Case of Dr. Jekyll and Mr. Hyde*. The author got the idea for the tale in a dream. After writing feverishly for three days, he finished the tale—and didn't like it at all. His wife read it. She didn't like it either. So Stevenson made a fresh start and produced a tale of such profundity that even psychiatrists are still writing learned discussions about its insights.

Those who insist they "never rewrite" are usually writers who have learned to manage the writing and rewriting functions simultaneously. Because their attempts are generally not so exhausting as Stevenson's their writing (mastery of content) leaves a margin of energy for rewriting (mastery of form and style) as they go along.

I myself once had the extraordinary experience of writing a full-length short story in a single twenty-four-hour sitting, mailing it to the *Saturday Evening Post* without revision, and having it accepted and printed without alteration—but it happened only once in more than three-quarters of a million words of published writing! The samples of my revisions which preceded this essay are closer to my usual practice. For, along with most other writers, I believe in the accuracy of the well-known adage: "Good pieces of writing are not written, but *re*written."

Of Studies

FRANCIS BACON

(1597 Version)

Studies serve for pastimes, for ornaments, and for abilities. Their chief use for pastime is in privateness and retiring; for ornament is in discourse; and for ability is in judgment. For expert men can execute, but learned men are fittest to judge or censure.

To spend too much time in them is sloth; to use them too much for ornament is affectation; to make judgment wholly by their rules is the humour of a scholar. They perfect Nature, and are perfected by experience. Crafty men contemn them, simple men admire them, wise men use them: for they teach not their own use, but that is a wisdom without them, and above them, won by observation. Read not to contradict, nor to believe, but to weigh and consider. Some books are to be tasted, others to be swallowed, and some few to be chewed and digested: that is, some books are to be read only in parts; others to be read, but cursorily; and some few to be read wholly and with diligence and attention. Reading maketh a full man, conference a ready man, and writing an exact man. And therefore if a man write little, he had need have a great memory; if he confer little, he had need have a present wit; and if he read little, he had need have much cunning, to seem to know that he doth not. Histories make men wise, poets witty; the mathematics subtle, natural philosophy deep; moral grave, logic and rhetoric able to contend.

(1625 Version)

Studies serve for delight, for ornament, and for ability. Their chief use for delight, is in privateness and retiring; for ornament, is in discourse;

and for ability, is in the judgment and disposition of business. For expert men can execute, and perhaps judge of particulars, one by one; but the general counsels, and the plots and marshalling of affairs, come best from those that are learned. To spend too much time in studies is sloth; to use them too much for ornament is affectation; to make judgment wholly by their rules, is the humour of a scholar. They perfect nature, and are perfected by experience: for natural abilities are like natural plants, that need pruning by study; and studies themselves do give forth directions too much at large, except they be bounded in by experience. Crafty men contemn studies, simple men admire them, and wise men use them; for they teach not their own use; but that is a wisdom without them, and above them, won by observation. Read not to contradict and confute; nor to believe and take for granted; nor to find talk and discourse; but to weigh and consider. Some books are to be tasted, others to be swallowed, and some few to be chewed, and digested; that is, some books are to read only in parts; others to be read, but not curiously; and some few to be read wholly, and with diligence and attention. Some books also may be read by deputy, and extracts made of them by others; but that would be only in the less important arguments, and the meaner sort of books; else distilled books are like common distilled waters, flashy things. Reading maketh a full man; conference a ready man; and writing an exact man. And therefore, if a man write little, he had need have a great memory; if he confer little, he had need have a present wit; and if he read little, he had need have much cunning, to seem to know that he doth not. Histories make men wise; poets witty; the mathematics subtle; natural philosophy deep; moral grave; logic and rhetoric able to contend. *Abeunt studia in mores.* Nay, there is no stond or impediment in the wit, but may be wrought out by fit studies: like as diseases of the body may have appropriate exercises. Bowling is good for the stone and reins; shooting for the lungs and breast; gentle walking for the stomach; riding for the head, and the like. So if a man's wit be wandering, let him study the mathematics; for in demonstrations, if his wit be called away ever so little, he must begin again. If his wit be not apt to distinguish and find differences, let him study the schoolmen, for they are *cymini sectores.* If he be not apt to beat over matters, and to call up one thing to prove and illustrate another, let him study the lawyers' cases. So every defect of the mind may have a special receipt.

A CHECKLIST FOR REWRITING

1. Check all mechanical details—for spelling, punctuation, and complete sentences especially. Other common faults are improper references of pronouns, dangling phrases, and omitted apostrophes. A dictionary should be kept at hand at all times and used on every occasion of doubt.

2. Read the theme aloud to yourself. If possible, ask an impartial reader to check any parts about which you are uncertain. If the reader claims he does not understand particular ideas, try to clarify them.

3. Question the means you have chosen to express your idea. Be careful to balance general statements with details and specific examples.

4. Check particularly to determine if your writing has *unity, coherence,* and *emphasis.* For *unity* ask if your essay has an introduction, development, and conclusion, all contributing to a main idea. For *coherence* ask if the thought is clearly and logically developed, if its development is spatial, chronological, or logical, if there are specific details and examples that need clarification, and if there are transitions leading smoothly from one part to the next. For *emphasis* ask if everything in the theme contributes to the understanding of your main idea. Make sure minor points have been subordinated to major points.

5. Check each sentence and paragraph for anemia (saying nothing significant) and its opposite, wordiness and digression.

6. Cut whatever is excess. Add for necessary clarification.

7. If time allows, consider alternative methods for handling your assignment.

PART TWO

Language

Figurative Language: Metaphor and Simile

Rewriting

THIS section deals with clarity, with the problem of how to write clearly without resorting to triteness or oversimplification. Trying to write clearly often develops into an "out of the frying pan into the fire" dilemma. Often when a student succeeds in writing clear, straightforward prose, he does so at the expense of content. Thus it happens that the student who is at first accused of not being clear is later accused of saying nothing. This section, therefore, has as its organizing principle: *Intelligent writing must be made clear and clear writing must remain intelligent.*

"Language" begins with two introductory statements on clarity and style; then moves through discussion and readings concerned with clarity, objective and subjective writing, tone, and figurative language. Finally it summarizes the points made in the readings by demonstrating various ways of rewriting to improve comprehension and style.

Language and Lucidity

Northrop Frye, an outstanding contemporary literary critic, is concerned in the following selection with three obstacles to clear and intelligent prose: the writer's insensibility to the richness of literature, the intrusion of loose, spoken speech rhythms into writing, and the deadening effects of jargon.

The Moral of Manner

NORTHROP FRYE

Ideally, our literary education should begin, not with prose, but with such things as "this little pig went to market"—with verse rhythm reinforced by physical assault. The infant who gets bounced on somebody's knee to the rhythm of "Ride a cock horse" does not need a footnote telling him that Banbury Cross is twenty miles northeast of Oxford. He does not need the information that "cross" and "horse" make (at least in the pronunciation he is most likely to hear) not a rhyme but an assonance. He does not need the value-judgment that the repetition of "horse" in the first two lines indicates a rather thick ear on the part of the composer. All he needs is to get bounced. If he is, he is beginning to develop a response to poetry in the place where it ought to start. For verse is closely related to dance and song; it is also closely related to the child's own speech, which is full of chanting and singing, as well as of primitive verse forms like the war-cry and the taunt-song. At school the study of verse is supplemented by the study of prose, and a good prose style in both speech and writing is supposed to be aimed at. But poetry, the main body of which is verse, is always the central powerhouse of a literary education. It contributes, first, the sense of rhythmical energy, the surge and thunder of epic and the sinewy and springing dialogue of Shakespearean drama. It contributes too, as the obverse of this, the sense of leisure, of expert timing of the swing and fall of cadences. Then there is the sense of wit and heightened intelligence, resulting from seeing disciplined words marching along in metrical patterns and in their inevitably right order. And there is the sense of concreteness that we can get only from the poet's use of metaphor and of visualized imagery. Literary education of this kind, its rhythm and leisure slowly soaking into the body and its wit and concreteness into the mind, can do something to develop a speaking and writing prose style that comes out of the depths of personality and is a genuine expression of it.

As education proceeds, the student finds himself surrounded with what purports to be prose, and naturally gives this rhythm more of his attention. Prose becomes the language of information, and it becomes increasingly also the language of information about poetry, which now tends to recede as a direct experience of words. As a result of colliding with *The Lady of the Lake* in grade nine, I shall associate Scott with unmetrical footnotes all my life:

> *The stag at eve had drunk his fill*
> *Where danced the moon on Monan's, one, rill:*
> *And deep his midnight lair had made*
> *In lone Glenartney's, two, hazel shade.*

I am not disapproving the practice of writing footnotes to the proper names in verse, that being one of the ways by which I make my own living. What I regret is the growth of a tendency to find the footnote easier to read, and which in universities takes the form of dealing with a course in literature by reading books about poetry and skipping the quotations. The process, however, is by no means merely one of transferring literary experience from poetry to prose. What more frequently happens is that, faced with the enormous mass of verbiage on all sides, and having to come to terms with the constant sense of panic that this inspires, the student is taught, or develops by himself, a technique of reading everything quickly and off the top of his head. He no longer responds to the rhythm of the sentence, or to any rhythm at all, but reads with a mechanical express-train efficiency, dealing only with what that kind of efficiency can handle—the main ideas, the gist of the argument, the general point of view, and the like. This means that the process of reading is, like the rhythms of undeveloped speech, becoming purely associative. It is appropriate for a committee's report, or similar expendable document, where there is one essential sentence on page forty-two and the reader wants only to get some notion of its context; but it is inadequate for prose, and impossible for poetry.

Meanwhile, in all the attention put on techniques of teaching students to read, ordinary speech is largely left to original sin. A standard grammatical form of English prose is taught at school, and the student learns to read it after a fashion, but it does not follow that he learns to speak it habitually. Learning to speak on this continent is often associated with "cultivating an accent," and it is generally agreed that anyone who does that is a sissy, a snob, a square, or whatever other abusive term is in vogue at the moment. I am not myself speaking of accent, or of the actual production of the sounds of speech, which is a social convention only. I am speaking of the kind of oral verbal framework that one must develop if one is to convey ideas or communicate any sense of personality. Prose is founded on the sentence, and the sentence is, at least in form, logical, communicable and periodic: it is difficult to use unless one has something to say and means what one says. We notice that associative speakers have a great aversion to the definiteness and full close of the sentence: if they produce a sentence by accident, they will add unnecessary words to the end as an apology for having uttered it, like.

On my desk is the report of a conference transmitted by that sobering register of the spoken word, the tape recorder. The question at issue is the teaching of American literature in foreign countries: *Huckleberry Finn* has been suggested, and the speaker is, I think, warning us that it contains the word "ain't":

> Now, I'm rather more inclined to stick my neck out on things of this sort, therefore, I'm sticking my neck farther than a lot of people here would, in saying that I would also not see any objection to including such a supposedly sub-standard term as ain't in the sense of am not, is not, are not at a relatively early level of work for teaching English, but in this case with a specific indication that this is an extremely frequent form which the learner is very likely to hear in any part of the English speaking world but that he had better be careful about using it himself unless he has more of a feel for the situations in which it is permissible and those in which it "ain't."

This kind of style, once one gets more of a feel for it, is easy to recognize as the quiz programme or buzz session style. Its unit is not the sentence, but the number of words that it is possible to emit before someone else breaks in. A discussion based on such a speech rhythm cannot achieve conversation, but only distributed monologue.

The schools, of course, will be of little help if they have been corrupted by project methods and other anti-verbal perversities. If a standard language is taught in school without conviction, it is unlikely to make much positive impression on the language spoken during recess. I say positive impression, because there does seem to be a negative one. Much of the colloquial language spoken in our society is a curious mixture of associative monologue and childhood resentments. I often revert to a little scene that made a considerable impression on me once: in a grocery store, where the clerk was showing me two things much alike, he remarked: "It doesn't make any difference," then looked me full in the face and instantly corrected himself to: "It don't make no difference." This second form was an improvement on the first, having a higher degree of what literary critics call texture. It meant (a) it doesn't make any difference (b) you look to me like a schoolteacher, and nobody's going to catch me talking like one of them. If he said: "It don't make no difference," it was not because he did not know the accepted form, but because he did know it. His speech was not ungrammatical; it was anti-grammatical. Whatever unconscious resentment may be involved in such rhetoric is not directed against a higher social class: it is directed against eggheads or longhairs or however the people are described who take their education seriously. The language taught at school is taught only there, which is why it is associated with teachers and schoolrooms. It would never have occurred to the student whose ragged speech I have quoted to be anything but clean and well dressed. But no major business is engaged in selling speech, and the example of good speakers is not reinforced by advertising, with its judicious mixture of flattery and threats.

The standard English of schoolrooms is prose, and being prose it can be analyzed grammatically, hence the body of grammatical "rules" which so many students associate with correct English. When anyone starts reflecting, as I am doing, on ordinary habits of speech, it is usually assumed that it is the correctness of one's grammar that is being impugned. But while standard speech is grammatical, it would be silly to judge it solely by its conformity so some alleged grammatical model. For one thing, the strain of constructing prose sentences is clearly marked even in the speech of the most articulate people. That is to say, the point I want to make is, all of us use, sort of, filler phrases to conceal our nervousness, or something, in working out our, you know, sentence structure. Standard English cannot be learned without the study of formal grammar. The little learning of linguistics which prompted some "educators" a few years ago to try to get rid of grammar proved to be a very dangerous thing indeed. Further, those who know language know its logical distinctions and subtle nuances, and have a duty to insist on their usefulness. The notion that the teacher of language has nothing to do but follow "usage" is one of the more miserable forms of academic self-deprecation. But still grammar is the servant and not the master of language, and speech, like handwriting, has to be allowed to find its own rhythm and character.

The hazy general notion that illiteracy is the technical inability to read and write, and that an education which teaches everybody to read and write has overcome illiteracy, is clearly nonsense. One may fully agree with everything that has been said about the futility of teaching dead languages at school. Except for some aspects of scholarly research, dead languages have no place in education. But this does not commit us to making the simple-minded and ill-considered identification of dead languages with the Classical languages. A dead language is a language that one learns to read but never thinks of as spoken. What shows that it is dead is the third factor, the writing of the language. The professor of Latin does not think of Latin as a dead language except when he is marking students' proses. Similarly, a student who has learned to read English prose, and continues to speak only associative jargon, will, when he tries to write English, find himself struggling with a language much more effectively dead than Julius Caesar. Good writing must be based on good speech; it will never come alive if it is based on reading alone.

Many people are puzzled by the fact that only the most disciplined writers are simple writers. Undeveloped writing is not simple, even in the sense of reproducing the associative speech patterns that I have quoted earlier. Writing that did that would achieve, if not simplicity, at least a kind of startling nakedness. Such writing is to be found in examination papers, of the sort that exclude their authors from a university education. Here is an example at random, from a student who was asked to compare Chaucer's Chanticleer with one of the characters in the General Prologue:

> The discription of the cock is like that of the Prioress, for we are told lots about her appearance, just as of the cock. The discription is general, typical of a Prioress, just as the discription is typical of a cock. We are told that she also could sing good, just as the cock. We know she was beautiful and care much about her manners. This is funny, for a prioress should not be concerned with such, but should pay more attention to her religion. It is funny. The discription of the cock being beautiful is also funny, especially the part about his nails compaired to a lilly. He is interested in love, having seven hens, and so is the Prioress . . .

Everybody engaged in teaching has marked bushels of such offerings: my only purpose in quoting it is to call attention to the murmuring, repetitive, asyntactic phrasing of the rhythm of association. But associative speakers are largely unaware of their own speech habits, and unless they are as naive as this student, they do not use them as a basis for writing. Now if we write in a way that we never speak, the first thing that disappears is the rhythm. It is hardly possible to give any spring or bounce to words unless they come out of our own bodies and are, like dancing or singing, an expression of physical as well as mental energy. The second thing that disappears is the color. It is hardly possible to use vivid language unless one is seeing the imagery for oneself: even abstract words, if they are genuinely possessed by the person using them, will still retain something of the concrete metaphor that they originally had. The third thing that disappears is the sense of personality, which only a basis in personal speech can ever supply. These are all, we have said, the results of a literary education centered in poetry. It is natural that associative speakers, for whom even English prose is a dead language, should regard English poetry with the baffled stare of a stranger accosted by a lunatic. I suspect that much of the difficulty complained of in contemporary poetry is really due to its use of simple and concrete language.

I feel, therefore, that there is a close connection among three aspects of language in our society. First is the associative squirrel-chatter that one hears on streets, and even in college halls, jerking along apologetically or defiantly in a series of unshaped phrases, using slang or vogue words for emphasis and punctuation. Second is the poetic illiteracy which regards anything in verse as a verbal puzzle, not even a puzzle to be worked out, but a disdainful and inscrutable puzzle without an answer. Third is the dead, senseless, sentenceless, written pseudo-prose that surrounds us like a boa constrictor, which is said to cover its victims with slime before strangling them. This last, under the names of jargon, gobbledygook, and the like, has often enough been recognized as a disease of contemporary language and ridiculed or deplored as such.

Two features of pseudo-prose seem to me of particular importance. One is that colorless and rhythmless writing is designed to obliterate the sense of personality: we write this way when we want to speak with some kind of impersonal or anonymous voice. It is not a healthy tendency, for, as Kierkegaard reminds us, the impersonal (in this context) is essentially demoralizing. The other is its underlying assumption that the idea is substantial and that the words which express the idea are incidental. This is a fallacy developed from the habit of associative reading. The words used are the form of which the ideas are the content, and until the words have been found, the idea does not fully exist. It seems to me that the fallacy of the substantial idea has a great deal to do with the bewildering woolliness of so much discursive writing today where (as in literary criticism, philosophy and much of the social sciences) the essential conceptions are verbal rather than mathematical, as mathematical language is doubtless used more accurately.

Elsewhere on my desk, which is a very untidy one, I find the following:

> In matters of curriculum, textbooks, or methods of study, variety is the spice of education and decentralization can be even more readily provided than under the small unit system because the resultant stability of teaching personnel means that the central authorities no longer have to keep so tight a grip upon a shifting texture of educational personnel.

The clanging repetition of "personnel" and the huddle of mixed metaphors at the end indicate that the author is writing in his sleep, and there is the usual absence of rhythm and color. But here we notice something else: the cliché or ready-made phrase ("variety is the spice of education") is beginning to make itself felt as a unit of thought and expression. A student of mine recently found herself at a conference of people who write (and talk) like this, and came back muttering a sentence that had, understandably, got stuck in her mind: "Jobwise, are we structured for this activation?" What is striking about this sentence is that it consists entirely of ready-made vogue or jargon words. The cliché is no longer an occasional resource: it has taken over as the only form of expression, and consequently as the only form of thought. A century ago Flaubert explored, with horrified fascination, the cultural life of Bouvard and Pécuchet, whose intellects moved entirely within the orbit of what he drew up as a supplement to his research, the Dictionary of Accepted Ideas. But Bouvard and Pécuchet were still a long way from the verbal automatism, a language based on the conditioned reflex, that we have reached with this sentence. The similar jargon used in Marxist countries looks more philosophical at first glance, but it comes from the same part of the nervous system.

Questions and Assignments

1. What is the point of Frye's opening example of "Ride a cock horse"? How do his remarks about verse apply to good prose?

2. A major point in Frye's essay is his reference to "associative" speech and rhythms. He means by this term the patterns of undeveloped speech. Elsewhere he defines it as a "short phrase of irregular length and primitive syntax." How does

he demonstrate this writing flaw by shifting his own style? Find examples of "associative rhythms" in your own speech and writing. This is one of the first elements you should try to eliminate from your themes.

3. Frye cites one specimen of speech and two of writing which illustrate one of the most basic problems of student language. Study these three examples closely and be prepared to explain Frye's strictures against "repetitive rhythm" and "gobbledygook."

4. List some of the most common phrases and ideas of news media, classroom, dormitory, and cafeteria. From these compose your own "Dictionary of Accepted Ideas." Write a theme based on these clichés and catch phrases. Which are detrimental, which are harmless, which are beneficial? Which prevent thinking? Which are necessary, which unnecessary?

Lucidity

W. SOMERSET MAUGHAM

This selection by W. Somerset Maugham, a widely read modern English novelist, brings to light a basic distinction one must make in discussing clarity—the distinction between ineffective use of language and complexity of subject. Maugham says that although we may not understand the implications of a philosopher's thought, the "meaning" of each sentence should be clear. Curiously, Maugham is himself guilty of a certain lack of clarity in this excerpt, although his main points are well taken.

I have never had much patience with the writers who claim from the reader an effort to understand their meaning. You have only to go to the great philosophers to see that it is possible to express with lucidity the most subtle reflections. You may find it difficult to understand the thought of Hume, and if you have no philosophical training its implications will doubtless escape you; but no one with any education at all can fail to understand exactly what the meaning of each sentence is. Few people have written English with more grace than Berkeley. There are two sorts of obscurity that you find in writers. One is due to negligence and the other to wilfulness. People often write obscurely because they have never taken the trouble to learn to write clearly. This sort of obscurity you find too often in modern philosophers, in men of science, and even in literary critics. Here it is indeed strange. You would have thought that men who passed their lives in the study of the great masters of literature would be sufficiently sensitive to the beauty of language to write if not beautifully at least with perspicuity. Yet you will find in their works sentence after sentence that you must read twice to discover the sense. Often you can only guess at it, for the writers have evidently not said what they intended.

Another cause of obscurity is that the writer is himself not quite sure of his meaning. He has a vague impression of what he wants to say, but has not, either from lack of mental power or from laziness, exactly formulated it in his mind and it is natural enough that he should not find a precise expression for a confused idea. This is due largely to the fact that many writers think, not before, but as they write. The pen originates the thought. The disadvantage of this, and indeed it is a danger against which the author must be always on his guard, is that there is a sort of magic in the written word. The idea acquires substance by taking on a visible nature, and then stands in the way of its own clarification. But this sort of obscurity merges very easily into the wilful. Some writers who do not think clearly are inclined to suppose that their thoughts have a significance greater than at first sight appears. It is flattering to believe that they are too profound to be expressed so clearly that all who run may read, and very naturally it does not occur to such writers that the fault is with their own minds which have not the faculty of precise reflection. Here again the magic of the written word obtains. It is very easy to persuade oneself that a phrase that one does not quite understand may mean a great deal more than one realizes. From this there is only a little way to go to fall into the habit of setting down one's impressions in all their original vagueness. Fools can always be found to discover a hidden sense in them. There is another form of wilful obscurity that masquerades as aristocratic exclusiveness. The author wraps his meaning in mystery so that the vulgar shall not participate in it. His soul is a secret garden into which the elect may penetrate only after overcoming a number of perilous obstacles. But this kind of obscurity is not only pretentious; it is short-sighted. For time plays it an odd trick. If the sense is meagre time reduces it to a meaningless verbiage that no one thinks of reading. This is the fate that has befallen the lucubrations of those French writers who were seduced by the example of Guillaume Apollinaire. But occasionally it throws a sharp cold light on what had seemed profound and thus discloses

the fact that these contortions of language disguised very commonplace notions. There are few of Mallarmé's poems now that are not clear; one cannot fail to notice that his thought singularly lacked originality. Some of his phrases were beautiful; the materials of his verse were the poetic platitudes of his day.

Questions and Assignments

1. You may well have been confused by Maugham's essay on clarity. Reread the essay to see where and how the writer failed to follow his own advice. (A suggestion: Maugham sets up a twofold division in his first paragraph. Does he fail to develop this division, or has he used misleading terms, or is his own thought unclear, or has he simply failed to make paragraphs in the right places?) Be prepared to explain what you would do to make this selection clearer.

2. There is a second kind of obscurity in Maugham—the obscurity inherent in his subject. If, for example, we do not know who Hume, Berkeley, Guillaume Apollinaire, Mallarmé are, we will find the writing unclear. Explain how the sentences containing these names gain in clarity when we know who these people are. In order to do this you will have to look these names up in a reference book.

3. Consider the following phrases from Maugham's selection and be ready to explain their meaning and to identify the cause—if any—of their obscurity: "to express with lucidity the most subtle reflections," "if not beautifully at least with perspicuity," "exactly formulated it in his mind," "the faculty of precise reflection," "wilful obscurity that masquerades as aristocratic exclusiveness," ". . . is not only pretentious; it is short-sighted," "a meaningless verbiage that no one thinks of reading," "the lucubrations of those French writers," "the poetic platitudes of his day." Try to determine whether the phrases deal with matter which is by its nature difficult, or whether the writer was ineffective or confused about what he wanted to say.

Clarity

As far as subject matter is concerned, clarity is relative. It is useless to argue about whether Maugham's reference to Appolinaire is obscure; to some it is, to others it is not. But the manner in which we express ourselves may be clear or obscure. In this regard there are three aspects of clarity it is useful to distinguish—although they usually fade into each other without clearcut lines of demarcation. These three aspects are: clear, straightforward use of grammatical forms—with sufficient variation to avoid monotony; a balance between the specific and the general and between the common and the uncommon expression; use of explanatory techniques to make difficult subject matter more easily understandable. To put these matters another way: relatively simple material must be handled clearly without triteness; relatively complex material must be handled so as not to be confusing.

THE SENTENCE. Faced with the inexorable requirement that four hundred or six hundred words be put on paper in the form of a theme, and unwilling or unable to think out either clear outlines or convincing details, many a student turns out unclear sentences. Rather than "traffic congestion downtown is one of our city's problems," the student is very likely to write "one important phase among the problems of this city about which something should be done is the fact of serious traffic congestion downtown." Instead of "also, many students are now worried and irritated by the increase in the tuition rate," he is likely to produce something like this: "another factor in relation to poor student morale has been the decision that there should be an increase in tuition rates, which causes worry and irritation to be present among the students." "The bite of the East Indian and Burmese krait is extremely venomous" becomes "an important characteristic of the East Indian and Burmese krait is the very venomous nature of the way it bites people." "He answered that he opposed the notion" is likely to be presented as "his reaction on consideration of what he thought about the matter was one of opposition." "This is a wild, thickly forested area" may appear on a student theme as "this area falls into the category of showing a thickly forested condition." This unfortunate style is not unique to student writing, for many sociologists are likely to write "there is incidence of a similar social phenomenon to be observed in Georgia" instead of "much the same thing happens in Georgia," many doctors "an observable imbalance of blood sugar demonstrates that prescribing barbiturates is contraindicated" instead of "don't prescribe barbiturates to patients with a noticeably high or low blood sugar count," many politicians "the practical implementation of this plan would operate as prejudicial to many important interests in Illinois" instead of "this plan would hurt Illinois."

Modern English has a number of words that show a steady weakening and spreading out of meaning. Since these words sound impressive and erudite, they tend to become fashionable. Here is a partial list:

fact	essence	conformity	individual
entity	principle	schedule	enhance
nature	quality	case	factor
state	condition	degree	manifest
category	character	extension	progress
circumstance	phase	indicate	activate
condition	relation	phenomenon	concern
reference	connection	material	requisite
equivalent	characteristic	effect	aspect
reaction	standard	function	agency
influence	tendency	associate	proposition
development	parallel	involve	balance
incident	correlate	policy	judgment
improvement	constitute	relative	system
implement	serious	authority	warranted

This is not at all to say that use of any of these words is unwise or that there is something necessarily wrong or weak about each of them. The point is that they are very likely to be used without maximum force and clarity and that you will often find, after thinking about your wording, that they can be eliminated.

Most English sentences—probably over 95 per cent—conform to a few simple patterns. By the addition of various dependent clauses, phrases, and modifiers, the sentences can be endlessly varied. Consider some of the following examples.

1. Subject—verb (S—V)
The men hooted.
A sentence of this kind may be expanded by addition of co-ordinate elements and by addition of modifiers:
When the speaker said this, the men in the hall who had seen actual

combat service in the North African area hooted and jeered until they were called to order by the commanding officer.

2. Subject—verb—object (S—V—O)
(By *object,* what is commonly called a *direct* object is specified.) *Casey swung his bat.*
Expansion:
With a scowl of resolute determination on his face, mighty Casey, the pride of the Mudville team, swung his bat through the empty air and struck out.

3. Subject—verb—predicate nominative (S—V—PN)
He became president.
Expansion:
Defeated in his previous attempts at the high position, he became president of the organization after a bitter fight with his old friend, James Richardson.

4. Subject—verb—predicate adjective (S—V—PA)
She grew faint.
Expansion:
Reliving that awful moment when she saw her fiance crash to his death, she grew faint again.

5. Subject—verb—adverbial modifier (S—V—AM)
The foremen work Saturdays.
Expansion:
Although there is nothing in their contracts that requires them to do so, the foremen in charge of the busiest departments often work Saturdays.

6. Subject—verb—indirect object—object (S—V—IO—O)
My father told me the news.
Expansion:
Smiling from ear to ear and thoroughly pleased himself, my father then gave me the welcome news that I had been picked to go on this cruise as representative of the Boy Scouts of this area.

7. Subject—verb—object—objective complement (S—V—O—OC)
They made Jennings chairman.
Expansion:
Wanting a reasonably safe and moderate person who would be fair to both sides, they made Senator Jennings chairman of the Ways and Means Committee.

8. Expletive—verb—subject (Ex—V—S)
There was a bus.
Expansion:
Contrary to what we had been told at the railroad station, there was a bus leaving for Echo Glen in about a half an hour.

Following these patterns is easy—in fact, almost inevitable—for any native speaker of English. There are some variations in order that are quite permissible, although they are a little uncommon. But occasionally a writer forgets how he started a sentence and puts various elements together incongruously: "this problem of traffic congestion in the center of the city needs many more parking spaces"; "the reason that I took Chemistry 17 was a requisite for another course I really wanted"; "some turpentine is added to the paint and then applied to the wall."

Nouns and other substantives—which serve as subjects, objects, predicate nominatives, and modifiers—and main sentence verbs usually fall into normal positions in sentences even in amateurish and rather awkward writing. There is usually little problem about placing minor elements like prepositions and articles within the short units containing them. Modifying elements are often less firmly fixed in definite places in sentences. Phrase modifiers—prepositional phrases and phrases beginning with such nonfinite verb forms as participles—may sometimes be placed so that it is possible to misinterpret a sentence and read it with an unintended humorous meaning:

After being sterilized by boiling, the baby may have the milk.
Having been damaged in the stern, the captain halted the ship.
While serving in the army in Europe, his second daughter was born.

He compiled most of his notes at Chicago but actually wrote his textbooks for freshmen at Indiana.

He watched the rhinoceros charging at him with a cool and resolute expression.

He gave the folder to the girl in charge of the storage room wearing a red dress.

She finally received permission to go on a flight with us from her parents.

A little critical thought and some practice at revision usually eliminate most sentences like these.

Today's linguists are making us increasingly aware that many written expressions may be ambiguous if we do not know how they should be said. Consider, for instance, the sentence "they took her baby clothes." With one intonation pattern, this can be read to mean that they took clothes to her baby; with another, it can be read to mean that they took away the baby clothes that belonged to her. "He is a great outdoor lover" seems clear enough, but observe what happens when it is spoken with a noticeable strong stress on both syllables of *outdoor* and a noticeable although slight pause between *outdoor* and *lover.* "He wondered how early passenger planes operated" means one thing if there is a perceptible although slight pause between *how* and *early,* another if that pause comes between *early* and *passenger.*

In some but by no means all situations in which speech would be instantly clear and writing momentarily unclear or ambiguous, punctuation is helpful. It seems especially so when it is used to set off introductory elements that might otherwise be confused. If one writes, "After all this confusion and trouble could have been prevented easily," the reader is very likely to interpret *all* as going with *this confusion and trouble.* If so, he is then puzzled when he meets the verb. The following would prevent that momentary but irritating uncertainty: "After all, this confusion and trouble could have been prevented easily." Notice the following:

Original: After I had won my point no longer seemed very important to me.
Revised: After I had won, my point no longer seemed very important to me.

Original: As I was about to shoot the buck leaped to the right.
Revised: As I was about to shoot, the buck leaped to the right.

Original: After several weeks of drying and curing the fish is ready for packaging.

Revised: After several weeks of drying and curing, the fish is ready for packaging.

In the following passage from *Advise and Consent* by Allen Drury[1] there is an interesting contrast between "beating around the bush" and giving a straight answer. What one man says clearly in three words, the other man takes ten lines to avoid altogether.

> On one big issue, for instance, an expansion of the draft, the press had asked the top contender, the clever young governor of a big eastern state, where he stood.
>
> "In my opinion," he said with a winning, candid smile, "this is a matter of such gravity that it has to be considered in relation to all the relevant factors involved. If an examination of these factors should show it to be desirable to take this course, then it would perhaps be best to do so; if on the other hand such examination should show the better wisdom to lie in some other course, then it is possible that the other course would have to be followed. It will be my intention to study all the pertinent factors before determining whether it should be that course, or the other, which should be followed."
>
> Asked the same question on the same subject Orrin Knox said: "I'm against it."

This passage illustrates a purposeful attempt to achieve vagueness. In general, it is better to learn the art of clear writing before cultivating a knack for vague writing. One of the first rules of rhetoric is to keep the wording as simple as possible.

[1] From *Advise and Consent* by Allen Drury. Copyright © 1959 by Allen Drury. Reprinted by permission of Doubleday and Company, Inc.

Adam Helmer's Run

WALTER D. EDMONDS

Passages like the following from DRUMS ALONG THE MOHAWK *are immediately clear because of their simple diction and sentence pattern. The incident described is from Revolutionary War days in upstate New York. Adam Helmer is a scout of the local militia, and the Indians are allies of the British.*

Adam Helmer had missed all these events while he was traversing a hundred and fifty miles of wilderness, and he felt bitter at having missed the fun. For a month and a half nothing happened. Every time he returned to the flats, Demooth or Bellinger sent him out again at once. He had hardly had time for more than a couple of visits with Polly Bowers; he hadn't been back to McKlennar's for a good meal at all. He hadn't seen Gil; Gil was too busy getting in his wheat. But the wheat would all be in now; and the next trip down they might be able to get up a decent crowd. Joe Boleo was covering the west since the raid on Schuyler in which George Weaver had been taken prisoner. Helmer alone was responsible for the Unadilla trail, unless he included the three men who were supposed to be watching the trail with him. Most likely they were sitting together throwing dice.

Adam combed his hair as he lay in the green filtered sunlight. The woods were dim with the September haze. The August heat was continuing; but it was better to be hot than to lie out in the rain.

His first sight of the Indians came so abruptly that he knew it would be impossible to warn the men beyond him. There were forty Indians, he judged, Mohawks too, coming up the trail at a dogtrot. That many meant surely that there were flankers out. He heard them now. Whatever force it might be, it was coming fast.

At last what everyone had feared had come to pass, and Adam had allowed himself to get caught like a fifteen-year-old boy on his first scout. He knew that there was only one chance of those three fools getting away; and he knew also that someone would have to get away if German Flats were to be warned in time. Adam did not hesitate. He rolled over on his knee and took the leading Indian a clean shot right under the wishbone. Then, while they milled, he charged straight down the slope and over the trail and up the opposite bank. He made it so fast that the first shots the Indians had at him he was dodging through the scrub.

The musket fire crackled like dry sticks, and the stink of black powder reached out in the still air so that he smelled it as he ran. But he paid no attention to the shooting and yelling on the trail. He dodged into some heavier timber, and wheeled down the bank again. He had judged his course exactly. He hit the trail three hundred yards ahead of his first crossing, just beyond a bend.

He ran lightly, listening to the surge of voices behind him. Up at the lodge a sudden feeble burst of three shots sounded, then more yells. The damned fools hadn't had the sense to cut and run when he gave them the diversion. He knew as sure as he knew which end of himself he ate with that the three men were dead. It left him alone to carry the warning into German Flats.

German Flats lay twenty-four miles to north and he knew he had probably the pick of Brant's Indians on his trail, men who could run eighty miles through the woods between sunrise and noon. But Adam knew that he could run himself, and he knew that he would have to run on an open trail and that once the Indians discovered that, they would know he would stick to it. They wouldn't have to be bothered with tracking.

He eased up slightly, listening behind him. The first surge of yelling had overshot the eastern ridge; now it returned. It would be only a minute before they brought his tracks down to the trail. He began to put on a little pressure to make the next bend; but just before he rounded it he heard the war whoop slide up to its unhuman pitch and a wild shot cut the air high over his head.

His wind had come back from that first foolish burst up and down the ridge. He lengthened his stride. His yellow hair, fresh-combed and beautiful, whipped up and down on his shoulders like a short flapping blanket. His mouth opened as he reached his full pace and he took the slight grade with the bursting rush of a running buck deer.

The Indians had stopped yelling. At the end of the next straight stretch Adam flung a look over his shoulder and saw the first brave running bent over, going smooth and quick and soundless. The Indian knew that Helmer had seen him, but he didn't lift his gun. He wasn't carrying a gun. He had only his tomahawk, which was a great deal more deadly if he could pull up within forty feet.

The Indian must have been gaining, Adam thought, or else he was the leader of a group, following the old Mohawk dodge of sprinting to make the fugitive travel at top speed. The others would take a steadier pace; but as soon as the leader tired another man would sprint up. By keeping pressure on the fugitive in this way they could run down any man in four or five hours plain going. Adam would not only have to keep ahead of the press, he would have to run the heart completely out of them.

He sprinted himself now; not blindly, but picking his next easing point beforehand; he knew the trail, every stone and root of it, from Edmeston to German Flats, as well as he knew Polly Bowers. His easing point would be the ford over Licking Brook. A half mile.

At any time it was worth while to see Adam run. He was the biggest man in the flats, six feet five in his moccasins. With his mass of yellow hair he seemed yet taller. He weighed close to two hundred pounds, without an ounce of fat on him.

He began to draw away from the Indian as soon as he started to sprint. Glancing back again, he saw that the Indian had straightened up a little. He got the feeling that the Indian's face was surprised. Probably the Indian fancied himself as quite a runner. Maybe he was champion of some lousy set of lodges somewhere. Adam could have laughed if he had not needed his wind, but the laughter went on in his inside, sending the blood into his hands. His head felt fine and clear. He figured he had gained thirty yards on the Indian when he hit the brook.

He jumped the ford. It was too early to risk wetting his feet and going sore. But as he cleared the water, he threw his rifle from him. It splashed into the pool below the ford and sank. Now that his hands were free, Adam began unlacing his hunting shirt. He got it off. By the time he came to the big butternut tree, he had wrapped his powder flask and bullet pouch in it, and he threw it over a small clump of witch hobble. Then he tightened his belt and stuck his hatchet into the back of his belt where the handle would not keep smacking against his legs.

He was now naked from the waist up. The wind of his running felt good on his chest, cooling the sweat as it trickled down through the short golden mane. He was a wonderful man to see: his skin white as a woman's except for his hands and face, which were deeply tanned. He was feeling fine and going well. He felt so fine he thought he might almost let the leading Indian pull up and maybe chance a throw at him with his tomahawk. He eased a little, enough to see the Indian. When the buck appeared behind him, Adam saw that he was a new man. He was taller, and his face was painted black and white instead of red and yellow as the other's had been. He did not come quite so fast, but Adam's trained eye saw that he had better staying power. Adam decided then and there that he would put all ideas of a quick fight out of his mind. The Indians meant real business.

For the next four miles the chase continued with only a slight variation of the pace, Adam adapting himself to the man behind. He was beginning to feel the pressure, but he was running with greater canniness. He kept his eyes glued to the trail now. He did not dare risk a blind step. His ankles wouldn't hold up as well if he lit on a rolling stone or a slippery root. He had the feeling very definitely that the race was reaching a climax, and though he ran strongly, strong enough to lick any man in the flats at a hundred yards straightway this minute, he knew that these Indians were good.

His breathing was still excellent. He had no fear of giving out; he could run till sundown, he thought; and then it came upon him that it would be a fact, if he managed to clear the Indians, that he would hit the flats just about sundown. Even while he ran, he reasoned it out that Brant must have figured on reaching the valley at dark and striking in the morning. Adam wondered what would happen when Brant knew that the word had gone ahead of him. He doubted whether Brant could get up his main body anyway much before sunset. But it didn't matter much. The only thing in the world Adam could do was to reach the flats. If he got there first some people could get into the forts.

His eyes kept checking in his landmarks and he realized that Andrustown was only a mile, or a little more, ahead. He must have outdistanced most of even the first pursuit. He expected there would not be more than half a dozen who could have held on as long as this, and if that were so they would have to be sending up another man pretty soon. And they would all begin bearing down at the same time.

Adam figured that if he could get through Andrustown clearing he might better take to the woods, for he would have gained as much time as anyone could on the main body.

As he chanced a backward glance, he saw that the Indians were going to try to run him down now. The new man was there and it was evident that he was their best man. He was not tall. He was thickset and had thick short legs. He was entirely naked except for ankle moccasins and breech clout and he was oiled and painted and rather light-colored. He looked like a Mohawk. He wore three feathers. It seemed impossible that he could have kept up with the rest, just to see him at first, for he had a belly that showed out in front. But his belly did not bounce at all. After a minute Adam thought it must be an enlarged place where he kept his wind.

The Indian's legs moved with incredible rapidity. He had already taken his tomahawk from his belt as if he were confident of being able to haul up on the white man. That gesture gave Adam the incentive he needed. He was enraged, and he took his rage out in his running. When the Indian entered the clearing, Adam was already down past the black ruins of the houses and going away with every stride. It was the greatest running the Indian had ever looked at. He knew he was licked, and he started slowing up very gradually. By the time Adam hit the woods, the Indian had stopped and sat down by the roadside.

When Adam looked back from the woods the Indian wasn't even looking at him. He was all alone in the clearing and he was futilely banging the ground between his legs with his tomahawk. Adam knew he had made it. He did not stop, nor even let down quickly on his pace. All he had to race now was time. He would have laughed if he could have got the breath for it. Time? Time, hell!

They saw the runner coming down the long hill, his body glistening with sweat and reflecting red from the low-lying ball of the sun. He was coming hard. The sentry in the spy loft of Fort Herkimer saw men come out of houses as the runner passed. Then the men ran back into the houses. Before the runner was out halfway over the flat land, the family of the first house he had passed had their horse hitched to the family cart in front of the door and were piling their belongings and children into it.

The sentry let out a yell.

"It's Helmer!"

In the yard an officer stopped on his way out.

"Helmer?"

"Yes, Adam Helmer. He's running hard. He ain't got his gun. He ain't got his shirt on." He paused, looked out again, and then bawled down once more. "He looks pretty near played out." His voice flattened. "I reckon its Brant."

"What makes you think so?"

"The people are coming in after him."

Without another word the officer went around the corner of the blockhouse on the run for the church. It was Colonel Bellinger. The sentry heard the whang of his feet on the rungs of the belfry ladder.

Bellinger was now in the steeple. He was yanking the canvas off the swivel. The brass barrel glinted in the sunset. Bellinger stood back, waving the match.

The gun roared. One shot.

All over the valley it brought people outdoors to stare at the church steeple. Before dark they were thronging towards the forts by road and river. Those who had already reached Fort Herkimer stood in front of the church and stared at Helmer's naked chest. It was whipped with branches, the white skin welted and bloody. But Helmer was breathing easily again. He had never, he thought, felt finer in his life.

Questions and Assignments

1. Make a careful examination of the diction and sentence structure of "Adam Helmer's Run." Notice that simple diction really means using the *best* word to express a particular meaning. For example, the author says "the musket fire crackled like dry sticks," "he heard the war whoop slide up to its unhuman pitch," "picking his next easing point beforehand." Find other examples.

2. This selection maintains suspense by its control of information. Recount the vital facts which are successively revealed to the reader and notice where and how they are revealed.

3. Discuss the sentence structure of the first ten paragraphs. Notice the variations in sentence length and organization. Explain the reasons for these variations.

4. Write an account of a suspenseful event using "Adam Helmer's Run" as a model. Note that Adam's run is neatly organized according to chronology—each event as it happened. But since the author is writing from one particular point of view, we learn about other related events only obliquely, as, for example, the death of the other three scouts and the "black ruins of the houses" in Andrustown.

Mick Kelly Dresses for the Party

CARSON McCULLERS

This selection concerns a vastly different subject from "Adam Helmer's Run," one in which adventurous action does not distract from the simplicity of the wording and in which the background is less dramatic. This excerpt describes a young girl getting dressed for her first party. It is written by a contemporary Southern novelist.

The late afternoon had come and the sun made long, yellow slants through the window. If she took two hours over dressing for the party it was time to begin now. When she thought about putting on the fine clothes she couldn't just sit around and wait. Very slowly she went into the bathroom and shucked off her old shorts and shirt and turned on the water. She scrubbed the rough parts of her heels and her knees and especially her elbows. She made the bath take a long time.

She ran naked into the middle room and began to dress. Silk teddies she put on, and silk stockings. She even wore one of Etta's brassières just for the heck of it. Then very carefully she put on the dress and stepped into the pumps. This was the first time she had ever worn an evening dress. She stood for a long time before the mirror. She was so tall that the dress came up two or three inches above her ankles—and the shoes were so short they hurt her. She stood in front of the mirror a long time, and finally decided she either looked like a sap or else she looked very beautiful. One or the other.

Six different ways she tried out her hair. The cowlicks were a little trouble, so she wet her bangs and made three spit curls. Last of all she stuck the rhinestones in her hair and put on plenty of lipstick and paint. When she finished she lifted up her chin and half-closed her eyes like a movie star. Slowly she turned her face from one side to the other. It was beautiful she looked—just beautiful.

She didn't feel like herself at all. She was somebody different from Mick Kelly entirely. Two hours had to pass before the party would begin, and she was ashamed for any of the family to see her dressed so far ahead of time. She went into the bathroom again and locked the door. She couldn't mess up her dress by sitting down, so she stood in the middle of the floor. The close walls around her seemed to press in all the excitement. She felt so different from the old Mick Kelly that she knew this would be better than anything else in her whole life—this party.

Questions and Assignments

1. How does the wording in this selection indicate the character of the girl without actually describing it? What does it tell us about her looks?

2. Examine the sentence structure of the second paragraph. Notice the inverted word order of the second sentence, the last incomplete sentence, the different lengths of sentences, and discuss the purpose they serve and why they enhance the clarity of the passage rather than hinder it.

3. Write a short theme about the preparations for some "first time" of your own: your first date, your first long trip, your first week at college, the day you got your driver's license. Remember that simplicity does not necessarily mean barrenness or lack of variety.

SPECIFIC VERSUS GENERAL. The merits of the types of writing illustrated by the preceding selections are obvious. But attempts to write clear, straightforward prose should be accompanied by safeguards against triteness. The first help against empty or vapid writing is sentence variation, which we have already mentioned. There are three other steps a writer may follow to enrich his prose. First, he should strive for the specific rather than the general, the concrete rather than the abstract. Second, he should, whenever possible, widen his stock of words. Third, he should use figurative language. We will discuss two of these steps in the next few pages; figurative language will be dealt with in detail at the end of the section.

The word *cat* may suggest to a particular writer a bluepoint Siamese pet tomcat aged eleven months and seventeen days in the writer's household. This suggestion of course is very specific; it individualizes one of the infinite number of events in the history of our world. To the writer this specific event has value. It has value and significance to very few others. Notice that, using this particular cat as a starting point, we can evolve a series in which the items are steadily less and less specific. We can put this particular cat into a group of young bluepoint Siamese pet tomcats. When we do so, we will have centered attention on some salient characteristics of the particular cat in question. (What characteristics are necessarily salient in any one classification or at any one time depends on the person doing the classifying and his particular situation.) We have made our wording, and the thought that controls that wording, less specific. In technical terms, we have abstracted out a few of the traits applicable to the particular cat and evolved a classification that includes a number of cats. By abstracting in successive stages, we can readily evolve the following series, in which each item is less specific and more inclusive than the item which precedes it: young bluepoint Siamese pet tomcats—bluepoint Siamese pet tomcats—bluepoint Siamese pet cats—Siamese pet cats—Siamese cats—cats. At this point we understand *cat* to mean *Felis catus,* the common, rather small, carnivorous, domesticated animal. We can, however, continue to go through steps of abstraction, always going away from the specific. We can classify the domesticated cat *(Felis catus)* in the zoological family of Felidae and include it with lions, tigers, jaguars, and cheetahs. Continuing, we can include this whole family with other mammals. Then we can classify mammals as vertebrates and then vertebrates as animals or forms of animal life. We can include animals or forms of animal life under life forms or forms of life. This latter series of abstraction steps may be summarized as follows: cats (*Felis catus*)—cats (Felidae)—mammals—vertebrate animals—forms of animal life—life forms.

We could come out with *life forms* at the end of a number of series—of series beginning with Grover Cleveland, Aunt Minnie's goldfish, the whale that swallowed Jonah, the pine tree at the top of the hill, the fourth tomato plant in the third row in the neighbor's garden. Sometimes—rather frequently—the direction of an abstraction series is more or less consciously guided. We can go more or less plausibly through the following series: this new Lincoln penny—new Lincoln pennies—Lincoln pennies—pennies. At this point we can go on through pennies—coins—currency including coins and bills—currencies—mediums of exchange (including moneys, goods, cattle, women, or whatever else may be used). Or we can evolve the following series: pennies—U. S. coins—U. S. money—U. S. money and stamps—U. S. government issues. Or any of the following: pennies—copper alloy coins—small copper artifacts—copper manufactured articles—metal manufactured articles. Or: pennies—coins—money—wealth—possessions—assets.

An odd thing happens as one works through such series. Very frequently it is possible to picture clearly in one's mind the more specific items; their forms and outlines, sizes and dimensions, colors or tones seem readily apparent and clear; the thought of them, triggered in the mind by appropriate wording, calls up an inner picture. But this picture fades and blurs as we go through steps in abstraction. If we read something like "the gnarled old pine by the water's edge," we can picture rather clearly what the author wishes us to. In any case, there will be more effective communication between him and us with this wording than with something less specific, like "an old tree by the water's edge." With this latter wording some of us may receive mental pictures of pines, some of oaks, and some of palms, and some of us may attempt—unconsciously and momentarily—to picture some sort of growth that expresses general "treeness"—not a pine, not an oak, not a palm, but a tree in general. Probably if we make an attempt to picture the general we won't be very successful.

There are two good reasons for preferring the more specific terms to the more general. One is that specific wording is usually much clearer. If one wishes to communicate facts in objective writing or feelings in subjective writing, he usually does well to be as specific as possible. The second reason is that the specific is likely to be not only more useful to writer and reader but also much more pleasurable to both. It's fun to write and read the specific. Critics of poetry often use the term *imagery*. One good poetry text[1] explains imagery as follows:

> Objects of perception of all our senses may be reproduced as images in the mind. For example, you can at this minute image in

[1] Stageberg and Anderson, *Poetry as Experience* (New York; American Book Company, 1952).

> your mind your classroom building; you can image your favorite tune; you can image the taste of chocolate, the smell of cheese, the cold of a winter wind, the heft of a weight in your hand. And you can conjure up in your mind a medley of images of different sense perceptions, as might occur if you image a hamburger sizzling on a hot griddle; this cluster of images might include the sputtering sound, the fragrant odor, and the luscious sight of a flat, round object, crispy and brown. Such mental reproduction of sense perceptions, when called up by memory or by words, we call imagery.

Good poetry uses a great deal of imagery, but it should not be forgotten that much good prose does too. And often the imagery of a passage is intensified by specific wording.

There is much more to be said about specific wording as contrasted with abstract wording. We have many words that indicate state, condition, process, or association: *arrangement, complexity, duplication, injury, variety, accompaniment, dispersion, mixture, disorder, modification, inclusion, focus, irregularity, deduction, extension, increase, distribution, classification, situation, omission, combination, sequence, conclusion, junction, confusion, activity.* These words are broad and general. Usually their context makes them clear. We have no confusion among such uses of *disorder,* for instance, as "the disorder in the living room after the party," "liver trouble and other abdominal disorders," "civil disorders connected with racist demonstrations." But with these words (and with those mentioned on page 97) we always need a specific qualifying phrase if their meaning and suggestion are not made clear by the context.

Ultimately the general words in our vocabulary are more valuable then the specific ones. In the present state of our thoughts and communications *bird* is more valuable and useful than *wren, robin, sparrow, lark, hawk, owl, gull, eagle,* and *condor.* An entomologist who lacked the general word *insect* would find the process of communication very slow and difficult if he had to mention all or even many of the kinds of insects to communicate the general notion. The single word *cut* we could not do without, although we might dispense with *carve* or *hack.* The development of words with generalized meanings indicates a more advanced civilization. At any rate, linguists and anthropologists tell us of peoples who have names for individual kinds of trees but no general word for *tree,* of far northern people who have different words for newly fallen snow, for snow fit for packing into blocks to make igloos, for snow mushy and half melted, but no word for *snow* in general. The great majority of our communications must be accomplished by use of general terms. Suggestions about use of specific terms are given in this section because almost all writing by beginners uses too many general terms and not enough specific ones. Most college themes say merely "injuries" instead of "shotgun wounds," "laws" instead of "traffic ordinances," "incidental expenses" instead of "costs of movies," "social events" instead of "fraternity dances."

Maugham in the selection on "Lucidity" on pp. 93-95 has suggested one reason for the preference for general rather than specific wording: it is sometimes work to think out the specific items involved. It is easier to say "he was a sloppy dresser" and let it go at that than it is to think of and find words to describe his shirts, their collars, his neckties (if any), his trousers, his shoes, and so on. It is much easier to say "there were many delays" than to list them, "the flood caused much damage" than to start to itemize it. Perhaps unfortunately, we have a number of set phrases that seem to absolve us from being specific —*etc., and so on, and similar things, and others too numerous to mention.* It is a good rule to use these phrases only after four specifics.

The Old Stone House

EDMUND WILSON

Edmund Wilson, a contemporary writer and critic, is the author of AXEL'S CASTLE, TO THE FINLAND STATION, *and* MEMOIRS OF HECATE COUNTY. *In "The Old Stone House" Wilson writes about a relatively uneventful episode—a trip back to his native town. But he manages to be lively and to hold our attention. One of the chief means by which he accomplishes this is precise attention to detail. Clear writing should be as specific as possible.*

As I go north for the first time in years, in the slow, the constantly stopping, milk train—which carries passengers only in the back part of the hind car and has an old stove to heat it in winter—I look out through the dirt-yellowed double pane and remember how once, as a child, I used to feel thwarted in summer till I had got the windows open and there was nothing between me and the widening pastures, the great boulders, the black and white cattle, the rivers, stony and thin, the lone elms like feather-dusters, the high air which sharpens all outlines, makes all colors so breath-takingly vivid, in the clear light of late afternoon.

The little stations again: Barnevald, Stittville, Steuben—a tribute to the Prussian general who helped drill our troops for the Revolution. The woman behind me in the train talks to the conductor with a German accent. They came over here for land and freedom.

Boonville, the pale boxlike building, smooth gray, with three floors of slots that look in on darkness and a roof like a flat overlapping lid—cold dark clear air, fresh water. Like nothing else but upstate New York. Rivers that run quick among stones, or, deeper, stained dark with dead leaves. I used to love to follow them—should still. A fresh breath of water off the Black River, where the blue closed gentians grow. Those forests, those boulder-strewn pastures, those fabulous distant falls!

There was never any train to Talcottville. Our house was the center of the town. It is strange to get back to this now: it seems not quite like anything else that I have ever known. But is this merely the apparent uniqueness of places associated with childhood?

The settlers of this part of New York were a first westward migration from New England. At the end of the eighteenth century, they drove oxteams from Connecticut and Massachusetts over into the wild northern country below Lake Ontario and the St. Lawrence River, and they established here an extension of New England.

Yet an extension that was already something new. I happened last week to be in Ipswich, Mass., the town from which one branch of my family came; and, for all the New England pride of white houses and green blinds, I was oppressed by the ancient crampedness. Even the House of the Seven Gables, which stimulated the imagination of Hawthorne, though it is grim perhaps, is not romantic. It, too, has the tightness and the self-sufficiency of that little provincial merchant society, which at its best produced an intense little culture, quite English in its concreteness and practicality—as the block letters of the signs along the docks made Boston look like Liverpool. But life must have hit its head on those close and low-ceilinged coops. That narrowness, that meagerness, that stinginess, still grips New England today: the drab summer cottages along the shore seem almost as slit-windowed and pinched as the gray twin-houses of a mill town like Lawrence or Fall River. I can feel the relief myself of coming away from Boston to these first uplands of the Adirondacks, where, discarding the New England religion but still speaking the language of New England, the settlers found limitless space. They were a part of the new America, now forever for a century on the move; and they were to move on themselves before they would be able to build here anything comparable to the New England civilization. The country, magnificent and vast, has never really been humanized as New England has: the landscape still overwhelms the people. But this house, one of the few of its kind among later wooden houses and towns, was an attempt to found a civilization. It blends in a peculiar fashion the amenities of the eastern seaboard with the rudeness and toughness of the new frontier.

It was built at the end of the eighteenth century: the first event recorded in connection with it is a memorial service for General Washington. It took four or five years in the building. The stone had to be quarried and brought out of the river. The walls are a foot and a half thick, and the plaster was applied to the stone without any intervening lattice. The beams were secured by enormous nails, made by hand and some of them eighteen inches long. Solid and simple as a fortress, the place has also the charm of something which has been made to order. There is a front porch with white wooden columns which support a white wooden balcony that runs along the second floor. The roof comes down close over the balcony, and the balcony and the porch are draped with vines. Large ferns grow along the porch, and there are stone hitching-posts and curious stone ornaments, cut out of the quarry like the house: on one side, a round-bottomed bowl in which red geraniums bloom, and on the other, an unnamable object, crudely sculptured and vaguely pagoda-like. The front door is especially handsome: the door itself is dark green and equipped with a brass knocker, and the woodwork which frames it is white; it is crowned with a wide fanlight and flanked by two narrow panes of glass, in which a white filigree of ironwork makes a webbing like ice over winter ponds. On one of the broad sides of the building, where the mortar has come off the stone, there is a dappling of dark gray under pale gray like the dappling of light in shallow water, and the feathers of the elms make dapplings of sun among their shadows of large lace on the grass.

The lawn is ungraded and uneven like the pastures, and it merges eventually with the fields. Behind these are great clotted masses of myrtle-beds, lilac-bushes, clumps of pink phlox and other things I cannot identify; pink and white hollyhocks, some of them leaning, fine blue and purple dye of larkspur; a considerable vegetable garden, with long rows of ripe gooseberries and currants, a patch of yellow pumpkin flowers, and bushes of raspberries, both white and red—among which are sprinkled like confetti the little flimsy California poppies, pink, orange, white and red. In an old dark red barn behind, where the hayloft is almost collapsing, I find spinning-wheels, a carder, candle-molds, a patent boot-jack, obsolete implements of carpentry, little clusters of baskets for berry-picking and a gigantic pair of scales such as is nowadays only seen in the hands of allegorical figures.

The house was built by the Talcotts, after whom the town was named. They owned the large farm in front of the house, which stretches down to the river and beyond. They also had a profitable grist mill, but—I learn from the county history—were thought to have "adopted a policy adverse to the building up of the village at the point where natural advantages greatly favored," since they "refused to sell village lots to mechanics, and retained the water power on Sugar River, although parties offered to invest liberally in manufactures." In time, there were only two Talcotts left, an old maid and her widowed sister. My great-grandfather, Thomas Baker, who lived across the street and had been left by the death of his wife with a son and eight daughters, paid court to Miss Talcott and married her. She was kind to the children, and they remembered her with affection. My great-grandfather acquired in this way the house, the farm and the quarry.

All but two of my great-grandfather's daughters, of whom my grandmother was one—"six of them beauties," I understand—got married and went away. Only one of them was left in the house at the time when I first remember Talcottville: my great-aunt Rosalind, a more or less professional invalid and a figure of romantic melancholy, whose fiancé had been lost at sea. When I knew her, she was very old. It was impressive and rather frightening to call on her—you did it only by special arrangement, since she had to prepare herself to be seen. She would be beautifully dressed in a lace cap, a lavender dress and a white crocheted shawl, but she had become so bloodless and shrunken as dreadfully to resemble a mummy and reminded one uncomfortably of Miss Havisham in Dicken's *Great Expectations.* She had a certain high and formal coquetry and was the only person I ever knew who really talked like the characters in old novels. When she had been able to get about, she had habitually treated the townspeople with a condescension almost baronial. According to the family legend, the great-grandmother of great-grandmother Baker had been a daughter of one of the Earls of Essex, who had eloped with a gardener to America.

Another of my Baker great-aunts, who was one of my favorite relatives, had married and lived in the town and had suffered tragic disappointments. Only her strong intellectual interests and a mind capable of philosophic pessimism had maintained her through the wreck of her domestic life. She used to tell me how, a young married woman, she had taught herself French by the dictionary and grammar, sitting up at night alone by the stove through one of their cold and dark winters. She had read a great deal of French, subscribed to French magazines, without ever having learned to pronounce it. She had rejected revealed religion and did not believe in immortality; and when she felt that she had been relieved of the last of her family obligations—though her hair was now turning gray—she came on to New York City and lived there alone for years, occupying herself with the theater, reading, visits to her nephews and nieces—with whom she was extremely popular—and all the spectacle and news of the larger world which she had always loved so much but from which she had spent most of her life removed.

When she died, only the youngest of the family was left, the sole brother, my great-uncle Tom. His mother must have been worn out with childbearing—she died after the birth of this ninth child—and he had not turned out so well as the others. He had been born with no roof to his mouth and was obliged to wear a false gold palate, and it was difficult to understand him. He was not really simple-minded—he had held a small political job under Cleveland, and he usually beat me at checkers—but he was childlike and ill-equipped to deal with life in any very effective way. He sold the farm to a German and the quarry to the town. Then he died, and the house was empty, except when my mother and father would come here to open it up for two or three months in the summer.

I have not been back here in years, and I have never before examined the place carefully. It has become for me something like a remembered dream—unearthly with the powerful impressions of childhood. Even now that I am here again, I find I have to shake off the dream. I keep walking from room to room, inside and outside, upstairs and down, with uneasy sensations of complacency that are always falling through to depression.

These rooms are very well proportioned; the white mantelpieces are elegant and chaste, and the carving on each one is different. The larger of the two living rooms now seems a little bare because the various members of the family have claimed and taken away so many things; and there are some disagreeable curtains and carpets, for which the wife of my great-uncle Tom is to blame. But here are all the things, I take note, that are nowadays sold in antique stores: red Bohemian-glass decanters; a rusty silver snuff-box; a mirror with the American eagle painted at the top of the glass. Little mahogany tables with slim legs; a set of curly-maple furniture, deep seasoned yellow like satin; a yellow comb-backed rocker, with a design of green conch-shells that look like snails. A small bust of Dante with the nose chipped, left behind as defective by one of my cousins when its companion piece, Beethoven, was taken away; a little mahogany melodeon on which my Aunt "Lin" once played. Large engravings of the family of Washington and of the "Reformers Presenting Their Famous Protest before the Diet of Spires"; a later engraving of Dickens. Old tongs and poker, impossibly heavy. A brown mahogany desk inlaid with yellow birdwood, which contains a pair of steel-rimmed spectacles and a thing for shaking sand on wet ink. Daguerreotypes in fancy cases: they seem to last much better than photographs—my grandmother looks fresh and cunning—I remember that I used to hear that the first time my grandfather saw her, she was riding on a load of hay—he came back up here to marry her as soon as he had got out of medical school. An old wooden flute—originally brought over from New England, I remember my great-uncle's telling me, at the time when they traveled by ox-team—he used to get a lonely piping out of it—I try it but cannot make a sound. Two big oval paintings, in tarnished gilt frames, of landscapes romantic and mountainous: they came from the Utica house of my great-grandfather Baker's brother—he married a rich wife and invented excelsior—made out of the northern lumber—and was presented with a solid-silver table service by the grateful city of Utica.

Wallpaper molded by the damp from the stone; uninviting old black haircloth furniture. A bowl of those enormous upcountry sweet peas, incredibly fragrant and bright—they used to awe and trouble me—why?

In the dining room, a mahogany china closet, which originally—in the days when letters were few and great-grandfather Baker was postmaster—was the whole of the village post office. My grandmother's pewter tea-service, with its design of oak-leaves and acorns, which I remember from her house in New Jersey. Black iron cranes, pipkins and kettles for cooking in the fireplace; a kind of flat iron pitchfork for lifting the bread in and out, when they baked at the back of the hearth. On the sideboard, a glass decanter with a gilt black-letter label: "J. Rum." If there were only some rum in the decanter!—if the life of the house were not now all past!—the kitchens that trail out behind are almost too old-smelling, too long deserted, to make them agreeable to visit—in spite of the delightful brown crocks with long-tailed blue birds painted on them, a different kind of bird on each crock.

In the ample hall with its staircase, two large colored pictures of trout, one rising to bait, one leaping. Upstairs, a wooden pestle and mortar; a perforated tin box for hot coals to keep the feet warm in church or on sleigh-rides; a stuffed heron; a horrible bust of my cousin Dorothy Read in her girlhood, which her mother had done of her in Germany. The hair-ribbon and the ruffles are faithfully reproduced in marble, and the eyes have engraved pupils. It stands on a high pedestal, and it used to be possible, by pressing a button, to make it turn around. My cousin Grace, Dorothy's mother, used to show it off and invite comparison with the original, especially calling attention to the nose; but what her mother had never known was that Dorothy had injured her nose in some rather disgraceful row with her sister. One day when the family were making an excursion, Dorothy pleaded indisposition and bribed a man with a truck to take the bust away and drop it into a pond. But Uncle Tom got this out of the man, dredged the statue up and replaced it on its pedestal. An ugly chair with a round rag back; an ugly bed with the head of Columbus sticking out above the pillows like a figurehead. Charming old bedquilts, with patterns of rhomboids in softened browns, greens and pinks, or of blue polka-dotted hearts that ray out on stiff phallic stalks. A footstool covered in white, which, however, when you step on a tab at the side, opens up into a cuspidor—some relic, no doubt, of the times when the house was used for local meetings. (There used to be a musical chair, also brought back from Germany, but it seems to have disappeared.) A jar of hardly odorous dried rose-leaves, and a jar of little pebbles and shells that keep their bright colors in alcohol.

The original old panes up here have wavy lines in the glass. There are cobweb-filthy books, which I try to examine: many religious works, the annals of the state legislature, a book called *The Young Wife, or Duties of Women in the Marriage Relation,* published in Boston in 1838 and containing a warning against tea and coffee, which "loosen the tongue, fire the eye, produce mirth and wit, excite the animal passions, and lead to remarks about ourselves and others, that we should not have made in other circumstances, and which it were better for us and the world, never to have made." But there is also, I noticed downstairs, Grant Allan's *The Woman Who Did* from 1893.

I come upon the *History of Lewis County* and read it with a certain pride. I am glad to say to myself that it is a creditable piece of work—admirably full in its information on geology, flora and fauna, on history and local politics; diversified with anecdotes and biographies never overflattering and often pungent; and written in a sound English style. Could anyone in the county today, I wonder, command such a sound English style? I note with gratification that the bone of a prehistoric cuttlefish, discovered in one of the limestone caves, is the largest of its kind on record, and that a flock of wild swans was seen in 1821. In the eighties, there were still wolves and panthers. There are still bears and deer today.

I also look into the proceedings of the New York State Assembly. My great-grandfather Thomas Baker was primarily a politician and at that time a member of the Assembly. I have heard that he was a Jacksonian Democrat, and that he made a furious scene when my grandmother came back from New Jersey and announced that she had become a Republican: it "spoiled her whole visit." There is a photograph of great-grandfather Baker in an oval gilt frame, with his hair sticking out in three spikes and a wide and declamatory mouth. I look through the Assembly record to see what sort of role he played. It is the forties; the Democrats are still angry over the Bank of the United States. But when I look up Thomas Baker in the index, it turns out that he figures solely as either not being present or as requesting leave of absence. They tell me he used to go West to buy cattle.

That sealed-up space on the second floor which my father had knocked out—who did they tell me was hidden in it? I have just learned from one of the new road-signs which explain historical associations that there are caves somewhere here in which slaves were hidden. Could this have been a part of the underground route for smuggling Negroes over the border into Canada? Is the attic, the "kitchen chamber," which is always so suffocating in summer, still full of those carpetbags and crinolines and bonnets and beaver-hats that we used to get out of the old cowhide trunks and use to dress up for charades?

It was the custom for the married Baker daughters to bring their children back in the summer; and their children in time brought their children. In those days, how I loved coming up here! It was a reunion with cousins from Boston and New York, Ohio and Wisconsin, as well as with the Talcottville and Utica ones: we fished and swam in the rivers, had all sorts of excursions and games. Later on, I got to dislike it: the older generation died, the younger did not much come. I wanted to be elsewhere, too. The very fullness with life of the past, the memory of those many families of cousins and uncles and aunts, made the emptiness of the present more oppressive. Isn't it still?—didn't my gloom come from that, the night of my first arrival? Wasn't it the dread of that that kept me away? I am aware, as I walk through the rooms, of the amplitude and completeness of the place —the home of a big old-fashioned family that had to be a city in itself. And not merely did it house a clan: the whole life of the community passed through it. And now for five sixths of the year it is nothing but an unheated shell, a storehouse of unused antiques, with no intimate relation to the county.

The community itself today is somewhat smaller than the community of those days, and its condition has very much changed. It must seem to the summer traveler merely one of the clusters of houses that he shoots through along the state highway; and there may presently be little left save our house confronting, across the road, the hot-dog stand and the gasoline station.

For years I have had a recurrent dream. I take a road that runs toward the west. It is summer; I pass by a strange summer forest, in which there are mysterious beings, though I know that, on the whole, they are shy and benign. If I am fortunate and find the way, I arrive at a wonderful river, which runs among boulders, with rapids, between alders and high-spread trees, through a countryside fresh, green and wide. We go in swimming; it is miles away from anywhere. We plunge in the smooth flowing pools. We make our way to the middle of the stream and climb up on the pale round gray stones and sit naked in the sun and the air, while the river glides away below us. And I know that it is the place for which I have always longed, the place of wildness and freedom, to find which is the height of what one may hope for—the place of unalloyed delight.

As I walk about Talcottville now, I discover that the being-haunted forest is a big grove which even in daytime used to be lonely and dark and where great white Canadian violets used to grow out of the deep black leaf-mold. Today it is no longer dark, because half the trees have been cut down. The river of my dream, I see, is simply an idealized version of the farther and less frequented and more adventurous bank of Sugar River, which had to be reached by wading. Both river and forest are west of the road that runs through the village, which accounts for my always taking that direction in my dream. I remember how Sugar River—out of the stone of which our house is built—used, in my boyhood, so to fascinate me that I had an enlargement made of one of the photographs I had taken of it—a view of the "the Big Falls"—and kept it in my room all winter. Today the nearer bank has been largely blasted away to get stone for the new state highway, and what we used to call "the Little Falls" is gone.

I visit the house of my favorite great-aunt, and my gloom returns and overwhelms me. The huge root of an elm has split the thick slabs of the pavement so that you have to walk over a hump; and one of the big square stone fence-posts is toppling. Her flowers, with no one to tend them, go on raggedly blooming in their seasons. There has been nobody in her house since she died. It is all too appropriate to her pessimism—that dead end she always foresaw. As I walk around the house, I remember how, once on the back porch there, she sang me old English ballads, including that gruesome one, "Oh, where have you been, Randall, my son?"—about the man who had gone to Pretty Peggy's house and been given snakes to eat:

> *"What had you for supper, Randall, my son?"*
> *"Fresh fish fried in butter. Oh, make my bed soon!*
> *For I'm sick at my heart and I fain would lie down!"*

She was old then—round-shouldered and dumpy—after the year when she had looked so handsome, straight-backed and with the fashionable aigrette in her hair. And the song she sang seemed to have been drawn out of such barbarous reaches of the past, out of something so surprisingly different from the college-women's hotels in New York in which I had always known her as living: that England to which, far though she had come from it, she was yet so much nearer than I—that queer troubling world of legend which I knew from Percy's *Reliques* but with which she had maintained a real contact through centuries of women's voices—for she sang it without a smile, completely possessed by its spirit—that it made my flesh creep, disconcerted me.

My great-aunt is dead, and all her generation are dead—and the new generations of the family have long ago left Talcottville behind and have turned into something quite different. They were already headed for the cities by the middle of the last century, as can be seen by the rapid dispersal of great-grandfather Baker's daughters. Yet there were still, in my childhood, a few who stayed on in this country as farmers. They were very impressive people, the survivors of a sovereign race who had owned their own pastures and fields and governed their own community. Today the descendants of these are performing mainly minor functions in a machine which they do not control. They have most of them become thoroughly urbanized, and they are farther from great-grandfather Baker than my grandmother, his daughter, was when she came back from New Jersey a Republican. One of her children, a retired importer in New York, was complaining to me the other day that the outrageous demands of the farmers were making business recovery impossible, and protesting that if the advocates of the income tax had their way, the best people would no longer be able to live up to their social positions. A cousin, who bears the name of one of his Ipswich ancestors, a mining engineer on the Coast and a classmate and admirer of Hoover, invested and has lost heavily in Mexican real estate and the industrial speculations of the boom. Another, with another of the old local names, is now at the head of an organization whose frankly avowed purpose is to rescue the New York manufacturers from taxation and social legislation. He has seen his native city of Utica decline as a textile center through the removal of its mills to the South, where taxes are lighter and labor is cheaper; and he is honestly convinced that his efforts are directed toward civic betterment.

Thus the family has come imperceptibly to identify its interests with those of what my great-grandfather Baker would have called the "money power." They work for it and acquiesce in it—they are no longer the sovereign race of the first settlers of Lewis County, and in the cities they have achieved no sovereignty. They are much too scrupulous and decent, and their tastes are too comparatively simple for them ever to have rolled up great fortunes during the years of expansion and plunder. They have still the frank accent and the friendly eye of the older American world, and they seem rather taken aback by the turn that things have been taking.

And what about me? As I come back in the train, I find that—other causes contributing—my depression of Talcottville deepens. I did not find the river and the forest of my dream—I did not find the magic of the past. I have been too close to the past: there in that house, in that remote little town which has never known industrial progress since the Talcotts first obstructed the development of the water power of Sugar River, you can see exactly how rural Americans were living a century and a half ago. And who would go back to it? Not I. Let people who have never known country life complain that the farmer has been spoiled by his radio and his Ford. Along with the memory of exaltation at the immensity and freedom of that countryside, I have memories of horror at its loneliness: houses burning down at night, sometimes with people in them, where there was no fire department to save them, and husbands or wives left alone by death—the dark nights and the prisoning winters. I do not grudge the sacrifice of the Sugar River falls for the building of the new state highway, and I do not resent the hot-dog stand. I am at first a little shocked at the sight of a transformer on the road between Talcottville and Boonville, but when I get to the Talcottville house, I am obliged to be thankful for it—no more oil-lamps in the evenings! And I would not go back to that old life if I could: that civilization of northern New York—why should I idealize it?—was too lonely, too poor, too provincial.

I look out across the Hudson and see Newburgh: with the neat-windowed cubes of its dwellings and docks, distinct as if cut by a burin, built so densely up the slope of the bank and pierced by an occasional steeple, undwarfed by tall modern buildings and with only the little old-fashioned ferry to connect it with the opposite bank, it might still be an eighteenth-century city. My father's mother came from there. She was the granddaughter of a carpet-importer from Rotterdam. From him came the thick Spanish coins which the children of my father's family were supposed to cut their teeth on. The business, which had been a considerable one, declined as the sea trade of the Hudson became concentrated in New York. My father and mother went once—a good many years ago—to visit the old store by the docks, and were amazed to find a solitary old clerk still scratching up orders and sales on a slate that hung behind the counter.

And the slate and the Spanish coins, though they symbolize a kind of life somewhat different from that evoked by Talcottville, associate themselves in my mind with such things as the old post office turned china closet. And as I happen to be reading Herndon's *Life of Lincoln,* that, too, goes to flood out the vision with its extension still further west, still further from the civilized seaboard, of the life of the early frontier. Through Herndon's extraordinary memoir, one of the few really great American books of its kind, which America has never accepted, preferring to it the sentimentalities of Sandburg and the ladies who write Christmas stories—the past confronts me even more plainly than through the bootjacks and daguerreotypes of Talcottville, and makes me even more uneasy. Here you are back again amid the crudeness and the poverty of the American frontier, and here is a man of genius coming out of it and perfecting himself. The story is not merely moving, it becomes almost agonizing. The ungainly boorish boy from the settler's clearing, with nobody and nothing behind him, hoping that his grandfather had been a planter as my great-aunt Rosalind hoped that she was a descendant of the Earls of Essex, the morbid young man looking passionately toward the refinement and the training of the East but unable to bring himself to marry the women who represented it for him—rejoining across days in country stores, nights in godforsaken hotels, rejoining by heroic self-discipline the creative intelligence of the race, to find himself the conscious focus of its terrible unconscious parturition—his miseries burden his grandeur. At least they do for me at this moment.

> *Old Abe Lincoln came out of the wilderness,*
> *Out of the wilderness, out of the wilderness—*

The echo of the song in my mind inspires me with a kind of awe—I can hardly bear the thought of Lincoln.

Great-grandfather Baker's politics and the Talcottville general store, in which people sat around and talked before the new chain store took its place—Lincoln's school was not so very much different. And I would not go back to that.

Yet as I walk up the steps of my house in New York, I am forced to recognize, with a sinking, that I have never been able to leave it. This old wooden booth I have taken between First and Second Avenues—what is it but the same old provincial America? And as I open the door with its loose knob and breathe in the musty smell of the stair-carpet, it seems to me that I have not merely stuck in the world where my fathers lived but have actually, in some ways, lost ground in it. This gray paintless clapboarded front, these lumpy and rubbed yellow walls—they were probably once respectable, but they must always have been commonplace. They have never had even the dignity of the house in Lewis County. But I have rented them because, in my youth, I had been used to living in houses and have grown to loathe city apartments.

So here, it seems, is where I must live: in an old cramped and sour frame-house—having failed even worse than my relatives at getting out of the American big-business era the luxuries and the prestige that I unquestionably should very much have enjoyed. Here is where I end by living —among the worst instead of the best of this city that took the trade away from Newburgh—the sordid and unhealthy children of my sordid and unhealthy neighbors, who howl outside my windows night and day. It is this, in the last analysis—there is no doubt about it now!—which has been rankling and causing my gloom: to have left that early world behind yet never to have really succeeded in what was till yesterday the new.

Questions and Assignments

1. Cite some of the details Wilson gives about his trip, the house, the town, and his return. What purpose do these details serve?

2. The author also provides several historical details. What are they, and what purpose do they serve?

3. We know by paragraph six that Wilson is telling us about himself and about life as well as about this particular return visit to his old home. How do we know? What is the value of the comments on New England and how do they relate to the overall theme of this essay?

4. Note the narrowing down and concentration Wilson uses when he reaches the focal point of his essay—the old stone house. Examine closely the use and the relationship of general observation and particular fact. Like almost any other

similar piece of writing, this essay represents a play back and forth between specific and general wording. The first paragraph, for instance, has the following: *north, years, milk train, passengers, old stove, winter, dirt-yellowed double pane, child, summer, great boulders,* and so on. Which of these are general and which specific? How many of these expressions lend themselves to being placed in an abstraction series? Take each of these words one step forward or backward in a series ranging from the very specific to the very broad and inclusive. Treat several other paragraphs in this article in the same way.

5. What method of organization is evident in Wilson's description of the house? You may want to refer back to the discussion of description and methods of organization in the Introduction, pages 7-11. Notice how Wilson blends simple, accurate description with reflections about how these sights and places affect him, as in paragraph nine. What purpose does this serve?

6. What would Wilson want to use and keep of the past, what would he want to forget?

7. Using "The Old Stone House" as a model, write an essay on a visit to some relative, or your former home, or some other place which represents the past for you.

8. Write an essay about the past versus the present, or the present versus the past. Use one focal point such as a house, or use numerous specific details and incidents, to show why one or the other is better, or to show that the present can build on the past.

9. Write an essay based on one of the following quotations:

"The apparent uniqueness of places associated with childhood"

"The very fullness with life of the past, the memory of those many families . . . , made the emptiness of the present more oppressive."

"Let people who have never known country life complain that the farmer has been spoiled by his radio and his Ford."

"the crudeness and the poverty of the American frontier"

THE EXACT WORD. The English language is singularly rich in synonyms. Perhaps it is richer than any other language. For idea after idea we have dozens of synonyms. For *honesty* we have *probity, integrity, rectitude, uprightness, faith, honor, trustworthiness, veracity, scrupulosity.* For *sick* we have *ill, indisposed, ailing, poorly, laid up, under the weather, sickly, infirm, unhealthy,* and others. For *strong* we can work our way through *vigorous, forceful, forcible, robust, sturdy, brawny, husky, stout* to *powerful, puissant* and then on to such really impressive words as *irresistible, invincible, unconquerable, indomitable, overpowering, overwhelming, all-powerful, omnipotent.* Similar lists could be compiled of synonyms for thousands of notions.

A number of books give information about synonyms. Among the best-known of these books is *Roget's Thesaurus,* which, however, is content to list synonyms without telling the consultant about differences among them.[1] The G. & C. Merriam Company's *Webster's Dictionary of Synonyms* contains a great many discussions like the following, in which sets of synonyms are discriminated[2]:

> **imprison. Imprison, incarcerate, jail** (*also* gaol), **immure, intern** agree in meaning to confine closely so that escape is impossible or unlikely. The first three words, *imprison, incarcerate, jail* imply a shutting up in or as if in a prison, *imprison* being the general term, *incarcerate* the bookish or journalistic term, and *jail* the ordinary colloquial word. **Imprison,** however, strictly implies seizure and detention in custody; the term therefore is applicable even when the one confined is not in a prison, or jail, or suffering a penalty; as, "*imprisoned* like a fly in amber" (*Inge*); "the tremendous forces *imprisoned* in minute particles of matter" (*Inge*). **Incarcerate** in precise use implies a shutting up in or as if in a prison cell; as, he easily obtained bail and will, in all probability, not be *incarcerated* before his trial. **Jail** (or gaol in British official use and in some literary use) is often preferred to *incarcerate* in its literal sense as a simpler and more generally intelligible term; as, to be *jailed* for life. Often, however, *jail,* the verb, following *jail,* the noun, in its present accepted sense connotes imprisonment in a building in which persons are held for short periods, either paying the penalty for minor offenses or for the purpose of awaiting legal proceedings. **Immure** (etymologically, to enclose with walls; later, to enclose within walls) is a literary rather than technical term. When it implies punishment for a crime, especially in the type of romantic fiction known as the "Gothic novel (tale or story)," it may connote burial alive within a wall; usually, however, the term suggests imprisonment in closely confined quarters as a captive, a devotee to duty or religion, or the like; as "Constance was now *immured* with her father, it being her 'turn' to nurse" (*Bennett*); "a convent of nuns vowed to contemplation, who were *immured* there for life, and never went outside the convent walls" (*L. P. Smith*). **Intern** is chiefly in military or wartime use; it seldom implies incarceration and usually suggests a keeping within prescribed limits (as in a guarded camp) and under severe restraints; as, to *intern* all enemy aliens for the duration of a war; to *intern* all the war refugees entering a neutral country; to *intern* [i.e., keep in port] a ship carrying contraband. **Ana.** Confine, circumscribe, restrict, *limit, *restrain, curb, snaffle, check.

[1] A convenient modern edition of this book, *Roget's Pocket Thesaurus,* is published by Pocket Books, Inc., by arrangement with Thomas Y. Crowell Company. The Cardinal edition went through almost sixty printings between 1946 and 1963. The usual price for this paperbound book is thirty-five cents.

[2] From *Webster's Dictionary of Synonyms,* copyright 1951 by G. & C. Merriam Co., Publishers of the Merriam-Webster Dictionaries. Reprinted by permission.

There are a number of other books on synonyms; study of these books cannot fail to be at once interesting and informative. Desk dictionaries almost always have synonymy articles, and the G. & C. Merriam Company's *Webster's New Third International Dictionary* contains about a thousand of them.

Synonyms differ from each other in a variety of ways. Sometimes one is part of the everyday language, the other more or less learned or bookish. *Door* is common, *portal* a bit bookish; *favorable* is common, *propitious* definitely learned. *Home* and *domicile, fear* and *trepidation,* and *wealthy* and *affluent* illustrate this difference. Sometimes one synonym belongs to the everyday language and another is noticeably informal. (See pp. 161-177.) *Violin* is an everyday word; *fiddle* is informal. *Good, choice, select, superior,* and *excellent* are everyday words, but *crack, ace, A-1, tops,* and *swell* show degrees of informality.

Effective writing shows well-made choices between synonyms—sometimes, undoubtedly, a measured, considered, thought-out choice, sometimes, again undoubtedly, an unconscious, instinctive choice. Good choices between synonyms is one mark of mature writing.

Consider the following questions: (1) You have invited a stranger to take part in the activities of your group, but he does not do so with much willingness or pleasure. Is he to be described as *indifferent, uninterested, reserved, apathetic, standoffish, aloof,* or *disinterested*? (2) A fireman has entered a burning house to rescue a child. Is he best described as *brave, valiant, valorous, undaunted, dauntless,* or *courageous*? (3) You must make an important decision, but you find yourself unable to make up your mind once and for all. Are you *hesitating, vacillating, wavering,* or *faltering*? (4) You are in a situation in which you cannot help hearing the unwelcome noise of advertisements on a public address system. Is the noise to be described as *harsh, raucous, strident,* or *cacophonous*? (5) You have a professor who occasionally makes remarks that damage your self-esteem and embarrass you a bit. Are his comments best described as *cogent, trenchant, incisive, sarcastic, bitter, mordant,* or *sardonic*?

But don't let your writing show a constant search for the uncommon synonym, for such a search can end with ridiculous results. There are few chances that wording like *a senescent boor* will ever be as good as *an old farmer* or wording like *a saffron mongrel* as *a yellow dog. A peripatetic mendicant* can hardly be interpreted as anything other than polysyllabic humor in expressing the notion of *a wandering beggar.* One might conceivably use *malevolent epistle* for a message of the astringent St. Jerome of the fourth century, but *hateful letter* is likely to fit almost all other situations much better. For a variety of reasons—and we will give two shortly—the maxim that simple wording is to be preferred to bookish should not be lost sight of in making decisions about synonyms. Prefer the more learned synonym only when you are sure that there is a positive gain in so doing. Actually, an analysis of choices made by established writers suggests that they feel the need for the less common synonym only once in fifteen, twenty, or twenty-five possible situations.

One danger in hunting for the bookish synonym is that you may make the ludicrous errors associated with pretentious persons. The English literary critic I. A. Richards, co-author of *The Meaning of Meaning* and author of *Science and Poetry* (1925) and *Basic Rules of Reason* (1933), has written the following in the introduction to the edition of *Roget's Thesaurus* referred to above:

> The great Railway strike in England turned upon the phrase "definitive terms." One side took it to mean "unchangeable"; the other explained too late that they only meant "full and detailed." Well does Peter Mark Roget observe, "A misapplied or misapprehended term is sufficient to give rise to fierce and interminable disputes; a misnomer has turned the tide of popular opinion; a verbal sophism has decided a party question; an artful watchword thrown among combustible materials has kindled the flame of deadly warfare and changed the destiny of an empire."
>
> That is the tragic side. The comic possibilities more concern us here. People who swagger about in borrowed words may, like Porthos in *The Three Musketeers,* impress the inexperienced. They bring the wrong sorts of smiles to the lips of the discerning.
>
> To know the words without the things is perilous indeed. "How often," said the lecturer, "have I dallied by the shores of Lac Leman or strolled on the delightful slopes overlooking Lake Geneva." "Pardon me," said a member of the audience, "but are

> they not synonymous?" "You may think so, Sir," replied the speaker, "but for my part I consider Lac Leman by far the more synonymous of the two." Awful warnings of this sort abound. "I always tell my children to look it up in the dictionary or the encyclopedia," said the Sea Captain. "That is what they are there for. Always be exact . . . No, I don't wear my ribbons in public places. Seems to me they are a bit promiscuous."

The second danger is that you will be misunderstood. Difficulties in understanding the uncommon word have been discussed sufficiently in foregoing sections; it is unnecessary to say much more here. *Fortuitous* is a good synonym for *casual* or *accidental,* but many people connect it with *fortunate*—so many that it is actually coming to have the meaning of "by fortunate chance" instead of merely "by chance." *Militate* and *mitigate* and *affective* and *effective* become confused and color each other's suggestions. A great many people have to think twice before discerning between *perspicacity* and *perspicuity.*

The Death of Leora

SINCLAIR LEWIS

The following selection is by Sinclair Lewis (1885-1951), the first American to receive the Nobel Prize for literature and the author of many novels, among them ARROWSMITH. *This novel, from which the following selection is taken, tells the story of Martin Arrowsmith, nicknamed "Sandy" by his devoted wife Leora. A doctor interested in bacteriological research, he has been sent to a plague-stricken island in the West Indies. His activities in fighting the plague have obliged him to leave Leora at a country estate with only native servants to accompany her.*

Toward dusk, when Leora felt as though a skirmish line were closing in on her, she fled into Martin's laboratory. . . . She kept away from the flasks of plague germs, but she picked up, because it was his, a half-smoked cigarette and lighted it.

Now there was a slight crack in her lips; and that morning, fumbling at dusting—here in the laboratory meant as a fortress against disease—a maid had knocked over a test-tube, which had trickled. The cigarette seemed dry enough, but in it there were enough plague germs to kill a regiment.

Two nights after, when she was so desperately lonely that she thought of walking to Blackwater, finding a motor, and fleeing to Martin, she woke with a fever, a headache, her limbs chilly. When the maids discovered her in the morning, they fled from the house. While lassitude flowed round her, she was left alone in the isolated house, with no telephone.

All day, all night, as her throat crackled with thirst, she lay longing for someone to help her. Once she crawled to the kitchen for water. The floor of the bedroom was an endless heaving sea, the hall a writhing dimness, and by the kitchen door she dropped and lay for an hour, whimpering.

"Got to—got to—can't remember what it was," her voice kept appealing to her cloudy brain.

Aching, fighting the ache, she struggled up, wrapped about her a shabby cloak which one of the maids had abandoned in flight, and in the darkness staggered out to find help. As she came to the highway she stumbled, and lay under the hedge, unmoving, like a hurt animal. On hands and knees she crawled back into the Lodge, and between times, as her brain went dark, she nearly forgot the pain in her longing for Martin.

She was bewildered; she was lonely; she dared not start on her long journey without his hand to comfort her. She listened for him—listened—tense with listening.

"You will come! I know you'll come and help me! I know. You'll come! Martin! Sandy! *Sandy!*" she sobbed.

Then she slipped down into the kindly coma. There was no more pain, and all the shadowy house was quiet but for her hoarse and struggling breath.

Questions and Assignments

1. Lewis wrote "a slight crack in her lips." What effect would he have achieved by using one of the following synonyms for *slight: minor, unimportant, trivial, inconsequential*? Why did Lewis use *fumbling* (in "fumbling at dusting") instead of *blundering, bungling, boggling, botching, floundering, stumbling*? Would "so desperately lonely" have been improved by the substitution for *lonely* of *alone, desolate, forlorn, solitary, lonesome, isolated,* or *deserted*? Why is *lassitude* used rather than *tiredness, fatigue, weariness, exhaustion, drowsiness, languor,* or *lethargy*? "She lay longing for someone to help her." Why did Lewis prefer *longing* to *wishing, desiring, wanting, yearning, pining, craving*? These questions are enough to suggest others similar. Go through this selection carefully, make similar lists of synonyms for fifteen or twenty of Lewis's words, and comment on the effectiveness of his choices.

2. Lewis has written "she kept away," "she picked it up," "meant as a fortress" (rather than "designed (or intended) as a fortress"), "seemed dry," "plague germs." In each of these situations he might have found a less common or more bookish synonym. Throughout this selection how many times does he prefer the simple to the bookish?

The Art and Life of Toulouse-Lautrec

SAM HUNTER

This selection is from MODERN FRENCH PAINTING 1855–1956 *by Sam Hunter, author of books on Miró, Picasso, and others, lecturer on art at Barnard and U.C.L.A., and curator and director of art museums.*

The art and life of Henri de Toulouse-Lautrec reflects a new rapprochement with popular art forms and illustrative conventions—and hopeless personal eccentricity. It is no accident that he has been identified with the development of the poster and the color lithograph or that he invented a style in the graphic arts which still guides commercial artists. He expressed himself in drastic silhouettes, bold outlines and original color, a form of dramatic presentation that put over its message in a single statement. The simplicity and economy of his expression is deceptive, however. Lautrec was an uncannily sharp observer of life as well as a brilliantly succinct and expressive draftsman. His resourcefulness in the graphic media allowed him to set down his subjects with a stylized flatness and still to characterize them in the psychological round. He had a genius for reducing the whole style of a personality to a few gestures and capturing it with a bold silhouette or a single line. His figures are full of life and character no matter how schematized and abstract his pictorial means may appear. He held in a wonderful tension the spectacle of life and pure pictorial values. Like Gauguin and van Gogh he wished the spectator to experience his painting directly through the dynamic operation of his surfaces and with a minimum of interference from pictorial illusion. The spectator is invited to participate in the experience of form and color to a much greater degree than he is, for example, in the paintings of Manet, Degas, and the Impressionists. The elementary potencies of medium and the artist's operations take on an almost independent, abstract importance. This is particularly true in the case of Lautrec's nervous, mobile line, which continually stresses the active presence of the creator in the work of art.

To arrive at his novel style, a style that was vitally of its period,

Lautrec passed first under the influence of Impressionism and then that of Degas and the Japanese print. His painting was also directly connected with the life that he chose for himself in the pleasure-traps of Montmartre and with his physical appearance, which influenced that decision. Lautrec was born a count in a family of provincial aristocrats; his name was Count Henri-Marie-Raymond de Toulouse-Monfa. He was a delicate, rachitic child, and after two falls in early childhood which broke both his legs he never regained normal growth in them. In maturity he was physically grotesque, with a fully developed torso and head and tiny, shrunken legs. His curious appearance cut him off from a normal social life and probably was the factor which led him to choose the demimonde, an underworld of pleasure and vice, as his social and artistic habitat.

Lautrec came to Paris in 1882 to paint and in the next five years attended a number of studios. He had begun to paint and sketch scenes of sporting life at home at the early age of sixteen: horses in motion, tandems being driven along in the Toulouse region at a great clip. Some of these scenes are reminiscent of Constantin Guys's *reportage,* but they have a greater and, for a young boy, remarkable energy. Then he learned to work in a soft Impressionist manner but, unlike Monet and Pissarro, always fixed on the human figure as a center of interest. He later told his biographer and closest friend, Maurice Joyant, "Nothing exists but the figure. Landscape is nothing, and should be nothing but an accessory. Landscape should be used only to make the character of the figure more intelligible." At Cormon's, the last studio in Paris where he worked, he met such independent spirits as van Gogh and Emile Bernard, and he soon began to seek a more original and vital style. In this he was deeply influenced by the Japanese print, which had already played such an important part in supplying new pictorial conventions for the other Post-Impressionists. And he became an admirer and rapt student of the art of Degas, whom he probably met in 1884. So great was his veneration that he is reported to have led a party of fellow-revelers, as a very special treat, on a dawn excursion to Mlle. Dihau's apartment so they could share his rapture over the master's paintings. The elder Dihau was a bassoonist whom Degas had painted in the orchestra pit of the Paris Opéra, and the musician's family collected the artist's work.

Degas supplied Lautrec with forms of composition, which he freely adapted in a simpler and more audacious fashion, and with a whole new repertory of unromantic contemporary subjects. Under the spell of the animated nocturnal life of the Montmartre music halls, cabarets, and brothels Lautrec pushed on even beyond Degas's most controversial subject matter. Degas in his collotypes had depicted inmates of brothels but never with the knowledge and first-hand experience which Lautrec brought to the same themes. Lautrec went to live in the bordellos and became a confidant of prostitutes and pimps, partly no doubt because he wished to defy convention and thereby assuage his own feeling of being socially undesirable. But Lautrec also approached human squalor for the most serious artistic reasons. He refused to be intimidated by taboos on subject matter. For the painter, still working in the spirit of nineteenth-century naturalism, human degradation and the more sordid truths of sexual life in the great city were simply one set of facts among others. Since art had not dealt squarely with them, they were still fair game. Lautrec's unprejudiced observation of sexual matters, neither morally aghast nor sensational in any way, reaffirmed the artist's prerogative to set down the truth of life as he found it.

Sometimes Lautrec, who had a natural instinct for the preposterous, could not help twitting his subjects. In the dress or undress of his models, in their boredom, or in their contrasting characters he found much that lent itself to ironic treatment or outright comedy. Yet his approach was as serious and detached, rather than professionally disenchanted, and as intensely honest as was Degas's attitude towards his little ballet "rats."

While he investigated low life, Lautrec in the early nineties was also developing an expressive style which in song sheet illustrations, posters, and lithographs managed to find public favor. Something of a natural showman, he had a feeling for good visual "copy," as the success of his posters of La Goulue dancing and of various vignettes of cabaret life attested. At the same time he had begun to penetrate the shadier regions of the Paris underworld and to present its subject matter with an uncompromising candor that utterly alienated the public. He was finally as unable to satisfy conventional taste and morality in his own time as were van Gogh and Gauguin.

In his oil paintings Lautrec learned to enrich his surfaces and marry line and color as he mastered technique. Near the end of his career he produced works (they were few, as in the case of Seurat) of remarkable magnitude and power. Perhaps his greatest technical innovations were made in the color lithograph and poster; between 1892 and his death in 1901 he produced some three hundred lithographs and thirty posters which were distinguished by their boldness of attack, freedom of invention, and expressive color. But his precious handful of large paintings were his major effort; they stand with the greatest masterpieces of the modern period.

Among them is the painting, now in the Art Institute of Chicago, *At the Moulin Rouge.* A group of ladies and gentlemen gather around a table; in the right foreground a woman, theatrically illuminated by a greenish light full on her face, is cut off by the picture edge. In the background a figure we recognize as the dancer La Goulue adjusts her hair while nearby pass an incongruous pair, the tall, funereal Dr. Tapié de Céleyran and his cousin, Lautrec himself. The composition burns with electric colors of orange and green; structurally it is organized along the diagonal axis of a handrail, Degas-fashion. The gay-nineties costumes, dresses with leg-of-mutton sleeves, elaborate plumage in the ladies' hats, stovepipes for the gentlemen, have been pushed to the glittering edge of fantasy. The atmosphere is unreal and bizarre; the characterization of personality, brilliantly incisive. Lautrec has endowed a rather shabby music hall setting with barbaric splendor. His figures are described by sinuous, curving contours somewhat in the manner of *Art Nouveau* (although he was openly critical of the new style of decoration which he had had occasion to see first hand on trips to Belgium). While Lautrec's figures are fitted into a decorative ensemble of arabesques and curves, they give an impression of mass and bulk. They break out of their molds and live an intense life of their own both as personages and as vigorous plastic forms.

Lautrec's late lithograph series, called *Elles,* was devoted to women, women who serve sullenly in a world dedicated to carnal pleasures but whose forms have a monumental import and dignity. Like Degas, Lautrec made something legendary and immense out of the stereotypes of naturalistic subject matter. He was perhaps the last modern artist who was able to express a vital interest in life and a curiosity about the human animal without compromising his pictorial values. In the process of doing so he introduced dynamic new elements into his art: irony, fantasy, and an interest in forms and colors as expressive ends in themselves. When he died in 1901 of a stroke produced by alcoholic dissipation, the effort to capture modern life in terms of some realistic convention had been exhausted. The twentieth century took its inspiration instead from Gauguin's advice that "art is an abstraction" and from the formal logic of Cézanne's last compositions.

Questions and Assignments

1. In the first paragraph Hunter uses *rapprochement, eccentricity, drastic, bold, deceptive, uncannily, succinct, capturing, schematized, tension, dynamic, illusion, participate, nervous, mobile, active.* Find synonyms for these words and be prepared to discuss their effect in the same context. Follow the same procedure in other paragraphs in the selection. Why is his wording especially appropriate to art criticism?

2. Note also Hunter's use of the specific and general. Consider these alternations in the first paragraph: "He held in a wonderful tension the spectacle of life and pure pictorial values. Like Gauguin and van Gogh he wished the spectator . . . The spectator is invited to participate in the experience of form and color to a much greater degree than he is, for example, in the paintings of Manet, Degas, and the Impressionists." What effect is achieved by specific reference to other painters? (The effect, of course, is dependent on the reader's familiarity with these other painters.)

3. The overall organization of this selection is chronological. After the introductory first paragraph, Hunter proceeds to account for the origin and growth of Toulouse-Lautrec's art from birth to death. Trace the origin and development of the painter's genius. What were the determining factors, the dominant influences on his life and work?

4. Find some examples of Toulouse-Lautrec's work. Consider the descriptive statements such as: "He expressed himself in drastic silhouettes, bold outlines and original color . . .", a "stylized flatness," personality reduced to a "few gestures," "dynamic operation of . . . surfaces." After studying these and similar expressions used by Hunter, try to describe the paintings in your own words. Try similarly to describe the work of another artist, such as Norman Rockwell, Gauguin, van Gogh, Bruegel, Degas, Manet, Picasso, Jackson Pollock.

CLARIFYING A COMPLEX SUBJECT. In writing on complex, scientific, or esoteric subjects writers must know how to clarify their references and technical wording as much as possible within the context. The better they are able to do this, the wider the audience they will be able to reach and the more effective the ideas which they wish to communicate. In general, there are three ways of achieving such clarification. One way is rather obvious; it is to stop and write a sentence defining or explaining:

First: At that time De Georges was writing feuilletons. *Then*: A feuilleton is a popular novel written to appear in installments.

First: For breakfast they had quantities of hasty pudding. *Then: Hasty pudding,* a New England term, means simply cornmeal mush.

First: Then he first came under the influence of Peter the Hermit. *Then*: The French monk Peter the Hermit was one of the preachers instigating the Crusade that started in 1095.

First: After a while they were able to see Mt. Hood. *Then*: Located somewhat south of straight east about fifty miles from Portland, Mt. Hood is the highest peak in Oregon.

Sometimes such explaining sentences are given in footnotes, sometimes within parentheses, sometimes after a dash followed by *that is,* sometimes with other devices.

Although it is often welcome, the full-sentence explanation is occasionally cumbersome and sometimes interrupts the flow of composition. Accordingly, the explanation is often given in an added explanatory phrase or clause:

First: They were drinking calvados. *Revised*: They were drinking calvados, the dry apple brandy of western France.

First: The cook was making fondant. *Revised*: The cook was making fondant, the sugary cream used inside the soft chocolates.

First: He was joined in this action by Walter Dorr. *Revised:* He was joined in this action by Walter Dorr, agitator for widening the suffrage in Rhode Island.

First: Pago Pago was ceded to the United States in 1878. *Revised:* Pago Pago, a harbor town on Tutuila Island in Samoa, was ceded to the United States in 1878.

If we have the sentence "——————, the second president of the United States, was from Massachusetts," we know that only the name *John Adams* is likely to go into the blank. The context is the determiner. If we have something like " —— his bills, settled his other debts, and re-established his credit," we will be very much surprised if anything other than *paid* or a synonym for it might fit the blank. The context tells us this. In some writing, words accord so well with their contexts that the meanings of those words may be readily inferred from the contexts, with resultant clarity and without the obviousness of the whole-sentence explanation or even the lesser obviousness of the phrase or clause definition or identification. If we have something like "he didn't just scan the letter; he spent some time in perusing it earnestly," then it is hard for us not to know what *peruse* means. If we find in Shakespeare, as we do in Macbeth, a comment about one murderous hand being able to encarnadine multitudinous seas with its guilty blood, then it isn't very hard to conclude that *encarnadine* may mean "make red or bloody." If one reads something like "being swirled about at high speeds, the particles tend to lose their identity and *coalesce,*" it isn't difficult to know what *coalesce* means. If we have only "some modern readers find Dickens' description somewhat mawkish," maybe we won't know what *mawkish* means, but we will probably have a fair idea of its meaning if we have something like "some modern readers find Dickens' description somewhat mawkish because of its sentimental outpouring." Accord between word and context to the point at which context is indicative or defining is the third procedure for making clear the difficult word or reference.

These devices for clarity of wording and reference may be overdone. They may clog a passage and stop its ready flow. They may arouse a reader's fierce resentment if they seem to patronize him and downgrade his intelligence. But they are generally valuable, particularly in writing about complex subjects.

A Discussion of Botulism

BERTON ROUECHÉ

This article deals with a type of food poisoning. Explaining this illness to ordinary readers presents a different problem from the subjects of the preceding essays. The author cannot achieve clarity by avoiding difficult words, but he can use the best possible word for every thought, and he can avoid an overcomplicated sentence structure. He can also include explanations of specialized words and ideas as he goes along. The selection is part of an article called "Family Reunion" which originally appeared in THE NEW YORKER. *Mr. Pappone recovered from the attack of botulism, but a relative who had eaten the same food died.*

Toward dusk on Friday, November 25, 1949, the day after Thanksgiving, a forty-year-old resident of Craryville, Columbia County, New York, whom I will call Charles Pappone, was helped by his wife and their teen-age daughter into the receiving room of the Albany Hospital. Pappone needed help. His head was splitting, his legs were like water, and his vision was blurred and failing. Also, he informed the examining physician in a gravelly croak, there seemed to be something wrong with his throat. It wasn't exactly sore. It just felt stiff and tight. In fact, it was almost impossible for him to speak at all. His wife anxiously took over. The trouble had started the night before, she explained. They had driven down to New York for Thanksgiving dinner with her parents, and on the way back to Craryville her husband had begun to complain about feeling weak. Then his eyes began to bother him. By the time they reached home, everything looked fuzzy. And this morning, all of a sudden, he had started to see double. She had tried to get their doctor, but he was out on calls. Finally, they had become frightened. There had been so much polio going around all fall. The papers said it was the worst epidemic in years. But, of course, it couldn't be that. Or could it? The examining physician shrugged. At the moment, he said, reaching for an admittance form, it was hard to say. He spoke with more compassion than candor. The opinion he was inscribing on the record read, "Suspected poliomyelitis."

Pappone passed a peaceful night in the hospital. The following day, he lay like a log, but he seemed at least no worse. His temperature, which had been normal at the time of his admittance, still held steady, and while neither his voice nor his vision had improved, his mind remained clear and he was altogether free from pain. Even his headache had gone. But on Sunday, at breakfast, a new trouble appeared. After one sip of orange juice, he had to stop. It was more than he could do to swallow. The muscles in his throat felt dead. An hour or two later, he was breathing hard, and choking on his own saliva. The nurse summoned an interne. He arrived on the run with a suction tube. Presently, having drawn off the worst of the congestion, he administered an eruptive dose of ipecac. Pappone's relief was immediate, but it was not of long duration. When the attending physician stopped by on his morning patrol, the patient was again gasping for breath. One good look was all the doctor needed. It showed him a perceptibly progressive paralysis that was beginning to involve the entire upper respiratory system. The doctor's instructions were, under the circumstances, conventional. They included a prompt tracheotomy (the making of an artificial opening in the windpipe), the use of a mechanical respirator, and a regimen of intravenous feeding. He also requested a lumbar puncture. A lumbar puncture is made for the purpose of analyzing the chemical and cellular composition of the cerebrospinal fluid and is, among other things, a generally reliable laboratory aid in establishing a diagnosis of poliomyelitis. Although the attending physician had earlier seen no reason to challenge his colleague's reading of the case, it now struck him as a trifle shaky. Pappone's unexpected decline distorted the clinical picture. In poliomyelitis, the doctor was uncomfortably aware, such violent turns are usually foreshadowed by some degree of pain and fever.

When the attending doctor reached the hospital on Monday morning, the report from the laboratory was on his desk. He read it, reread it, and tossed it aside. The report was negative. Pappone's spinal fluid was normal. This gave the doctor, however, no urge to exult. He had merely escaped from error into doubt. The doctor sat down and reflected. He emerged from his meditations with the feeling that just two possibilities were compatible with the evidence. One of them was epidemic encephalitis. The other was a form of food poisoning called botulism. He looked again at the laboratory report. It didn't precisely support either one, but it rendered the former the more unlikely. Encephalitis, like poliomyelitis, seldom fails to create a minor disturbance in the spinal fluid of its victims. The doctor took a deep breath. Then he picked up the telephone and dialed the laboratory of the State Department of Health. He asked the laboratory to provide him at once with thirty thousand units of therapeutic botulinus antitoxin.

Food poisoning is among the commonest of ailments. It is almost as common as the common cold and, in general, only a little less innocuous. It is also about as widely misunderstood. As a source of wild fears and wilder temerities, it is practically unequalled in the popular mythology of medicine. The most durable delusion in connection with it is that the great majority of acute gastrointestinal upsets are a result of ptomaine poisoning. Even doctors sometimes succumb to this fancy. "In one series of forty-three fatal cases in which the reported diagnosis was ptomaine poisoning, necropsy revealed in every instance some other cause of death," Dr. Walter C. Alvarez, of the Mayo clinic, noted in a recent study. "[These causes included] appendicitis, ruptured ectopic pregnancy, peritonitis, tuberculosis, meningitis, encephalitis, acute alcoholism, carbon-monoxide or metallic poisoning, toxemia of pregnancy, abortion, malaria, diphtheria, fulminating poliomyelitis, bacillary dysentery, coronary disease, pneumonia, and cerebral apoplexy." The diagnosticians involved, as Dr. Alvarez saw no need to add, were doubly deluded. Ptomaine poisoning is a product of the imagination of a nineteenth-century Italian toxicologist named Francesco Selmi. Selmi announced the existence of what he called ptomaines in 1870. They were, he explained to an attentive medical world, noxious substances generated in numerous foods in the natural course of putrefaction. By and large, he added, food poisoning and ptomaine poisoning were synonymous. Selmi was for many years a towering figure in medicine, but his stature has lately shrivelled. About the best that can now be said for his theory is that the name he gave it was an apt one. "Ptomaine" derives from *"ptôma,"* the Greek for "corpse" or "carcass." Modern investigators are far from convinced that any such thing as a ptomaine exists. In any event, they point out, it could have no relation to food poisoning. Age alone has nothing whatever to do with the wholesomeness of food. Its irrelevance has been demonstrated by chemical analysis, by experiments with laboratory animals, and by millions of Chinese lovers of rotten eggs, Eskimo lovers of putrefied fish, and Western lovers of overblown cheese.

The nature of food poisoning has been pretty well riddled since Selmi's time. Clinicians now recognize three major types. Their sources are clearly distinct. One is food contaminated with some pernicious inorganic chemical. Inherently poisonous plants or animals (certain mushrooms, rhubarb leaves, some yams if eaten raw, faba beans, many tropical fish, and, at seasonal intervals, Pacific clams and mussels) are, of course, another. The third is food made toxic by the presence of certain pathogenic bacteria. Of the three, the first is probably the most unreasonably dreaded. Cooks have been known to mistake roach powder (sodium fluoride) for baking soda, or rat poison (barium carbonate) for flour, but such blunders are rare to the point of freakishness. Moreover, even when they occur, the consequences are by no means always catastrophic. Chemical poisoning more often than not provides its own antidote. Usually its victims are at once convulsed by a salubrious fit of vomiting. Most fears of chemical poisoning are wholly hallucinatory. Contrary to nearly universal assumption, there is no conclusive evidence that illness is the invariable result of eating fruit sprayed with lead arsenate or any other conventional insecticide. "Lead arsenate ingested as spray residue [was] not accompanied by . . . the occurrence of any clinical findings," a United States Public Health Service Bulletin recently reported at the end of a three-year study of nearly two hundred and fifty orchard workers who habitually ate unwashed apples and pears. Nor, as many people persist in believing, is the use of aluminum cooking utensils a possible source of illness. Aluminum, far from being a poison, has a respected place on the modern medicine shelf. One form, aluminum hydroxide, is widely considered the drug of choice in the treatment of peptic ulcer. Tin is also prominent in the toxicology of hearsay. Its inclusion is entirely undeserved. "Tin, in the amounts ordinarily found in canned foods and in the quantity which would be ingested in the ordinary individual diet, is for all practical purposes eliminated and is not productive of harmful effects on the consumer of canned foods," the Bureau of Chemistry and Soils of the Department of Agriculture has reported. A hardy corollary of the distrust of canned food, and perhaps the deepest-rooted of all such over-anxieties, is the belief that food should never be left in an opened can. "This [belief] is a myth of long standing," Dr. Gail M. Dack, professor of bacteriology at the University of Chicago and director of its Food Research Institute, has noted in an authoritative monograph. "Spoilage results from bacteria growing in a food, and once the food is contaminated time and suitable temperature will cause spoilage, regardless of whether the food is in a tin can or in a glass or porcelain dish. In fact, contamination is less likely to occur if the food is left in the can." The can, Dr. Dack went on to point out, is more apt to be sterile than the dish.

The usual cause of food poisoning is bacteria. Bacteria of one kind or another are responsible for well over ninety per cent of all outbreaks. The amount of misery these organisms inflict on the human race is incalculable. Everybody has felt their enfeebling touch at least once, and people who frequently eat in restaurants have experienced it numerous times, though not always with clear recognition. One is often only vaguely conscious of their presence. Many epidemiologists believe that most momentary indispositions whose chief characteristic is an uneasy stomach or a spasm of diarrhea are of bacterial origin. The vast majority of attacks are the work of any one of three varieties of bacteria—the staphylococci, the streptococci, and the salmonellae. All are sturdy, prolific, and ubiquitous. Each has its distinguishing traits, but from a practical public-health standpoint staphylococcal, streptococcal, and salmonellal food poisoning are all pretty much the same. They are equally abrupt, equally mild and of equally short duration, and, despite the reassurance of common sense, equally difficult to dodge. Their avoidance is entirely a matter of luck. The presence in a food of even a multitude of such pathogens can be detected solely by laboratory analysis. They in no way alter its appearance, its odor, or its taste. Nor, for the most part, do any of the several other microbes or microbial products that are an occasional cause of food poisoning. The only notable exception to this insidious rule is a toxin elaborated by a bacillus called *Clostridium botulinum.* Botulinus toxin is the cause of botulism. Food into which a lively colony of *Clostridium botulinum* has found its way sometimes emits a disgusting smell. Providentially, it is a distinctively disgusting one. Between 1899 and 1947, according to a compilation by Dr. Karl F. Meyer, director of the George Williams Hooper Foundation for Medical Research at the University of California, only twelve hundred and fifty-three cases of botulism were reported in the whole of the United States and Canada. Of them, however, eight hundred and fifteen, or approximately sixty-five per cent, were fatal.

Botulism is a true but atypical form of food poisoning. Its methodical approach, its excessive lethality, and the predominantly neural cast of its clinical features all are unpleasantly peculiar. Even its history is unusual. Ordinary food poisoning, in common with many other ailments, is probably as old as mankind. Its beginnings go back to the first butcher with an infected finger, the first cook with a streptococcic cough, the first imprudent assumption of the first man rash enough to eat mushrooms. Botulism is of far less fundamental origin. It is, in fact, one of the very few diseases for whose existence man has nobody to blame but himself. Like carbon-monoxide poisoning, and alcoholism, and the bends, botulism is essentially, if inadvertently, a product of human ingenuity. *Clostridium botulinum,* though plethorically abundant throughout the world, is not among man's natural antagonists. The organism is incapable of establishing itself in any living plant or animal. Its home is soil and earthy dust, its food is inanimate matter, and although it is able to exist in a dormant, sporal state almost indefinitely in almost any environment, it can mature and multiply and manufacture its vigorous venom only in the total absence of oxygen. Because of these physiological quirks, the toxin of *Clostridium botulinum,* under normal conditions, is safely out of human reach. It is dissipated deep in the earth. Exactly when botulism seized its first victim is unknown, but it could hardly have been more than eight or ten thousand years ago, when man ceased to subsist exclusively on fresh food. Freshly gathered food, along with everything else on the face of the earth, is exposed to the intrusion of dust-borne botulinus spores, but it is also exposed to the spore-stunting sweep of air. Botulism came into being when man made the otherwise triumphant discovery that prompt deoxidation would make numerous foods more or less permanently resistant to decay.

Despite the profusion of potentially hospitable harbors created by man for wandering *Clostridium botulinum* (canned or pickled fruits and vegetables, and canned, smoked, or pickled meats and fish and poultry), botulism has never been a very broadly urgent problem. There is no good reason why it should be. This is not, as might be supposed, entirely because of the repellent odor that the active organism may impart to its habitat, for the warning reek is not always present. Certain foods may be saturated with botulinus toxin and still smell much as usual. One of the most important determining factors appears to be the *p*H, or relative acidity, of the food. As a rule, the smell is most pronounced in non-acid foods—in meat, for example, and fish. Among acid foods, a category that includes all the more popular fruits and vegetables, it is generally unobtrusive and often wholly absent.

Fortunately, however, a sensitive nose is not the sole defense against an attack of botulism. Since 1895, when the isolation of *Clostridium botulinum* by the Belgian bacteriologist Emilie P. van Ermengem made possible a thorough anatomization of the disease, other, and more dependable, weapons have been worked out. One is an efficient antitoxin serum. Another is heat. Fifteen minutes of boiling (or its thermal equivalent) will destroy any number of adult *Clostridium botulinum* or any quantity of toxin. The spores are less lightly insulated. The amount of heat ordinarily required in the preliminary processing of most preserved foods has no effect whatever on them, and some have been known to survive immersion in boiling water for as long as six hours. Nevertheless, they, too, have their limitations. Even the toughest, as the food industry has been gratefully aware for almost a generation, are bound to perish if subjected for eight or ten minutes to a blast of steam under fifteen pounds of pressure. The discovery of this engaging frailty, by an international army of public and private investigators, has gradually led to the total elimination of commercially processed food as a possible source of botulism. The last outbreak in

Europe involving a commercial packer occurred in 1922, in England. In the United States, the last outbreak was recorded in 1925. All subsequent cases, including, as it turned out, that of Charles Pappone, have been traced to canned, smoked, or otherwise hermetically sealed foods imperfectly processed at home.[1]

Questions and Assignments

1. At first glance the vocabulary of this selection may seem a bit difficult, and the reader may feel that the article is unclear. Analyze the way the following expressions are handled by the author, and, on the basis of the author's handling of them, be prepared to explain them. Notice the devices used in the writing to make them clear: "a suction tube," "the worst of the congestion," "an eruptive dose of ipecac," "a prompt tracheotomy," "a lumbar puncture," "compatible with the evidence," "botulism," "therapeutic botulinus antitoxin," "the most durable delusion," "necropsy revealed," "in the natural course of putrefaction," "overblown cheese." Find other illustrations throughout this selection in which the context makes quite clear the meanings of uncommon words.

2. Comment on the degree to which the context makes clear the meaning of the following: "with more compassion than candor," "the chemical and cellular composition of the cerebrospinal fluid," "epidemic encephalitis," "wild fears and wilder temerities," "fulminating poliomyelitis." Find other expressions which are not defined or explained by their context. Do these expressions detract from the overall clarity of the article? Why or why not? Criticize the author's handling of his necessarily technical and scientific vocabulary.

3. How does Roueché relieve the medical or clinical tone in "A Discussion of Botulism"? How, without sacrificing any impression of medical knowledgability, does he manage by his wording to achieve a smooth and interesting effect in his narration and description?

4. Review the selections previously presented in this section. At the end of the selection called "Adam Helmer's Run," on p. 107, how does Edmonds make clear to you that *swivel* means "small canon"? In the selection called "Mick Kelly Dresses for the Party," on p. 108, why doesn't the wording *shucked off* cause any problem? Why doesn't the author explain *teddies, cowlicks, rhinestones*? What would the effect have been if she had?

5. Write a brief theme about some disease which you or a member of your family has had, such as measles, mumps, pneumonia, hay fever, mononucleosis, chickenpox, flu, or even the common cold. You will probably need to round out your own information with some specific scientific facts and details culled from medical literature and magazine articles in the library. But don't get so embroiled in scientific terminology that you lose your reader.

[1] Since the publication of this article, cases of botulism have been traced to commercially prepared Great Lakes fish. (Editors)

Objective and Subjective

In general, writing that is called *objective* stresses the factual and readily observable; it is likely to deal with materials that lend themselves to being checked by another person; its goal is to impart information to the reader. *Subjective* writing, on the other hand, devotes much attention to impression, feeling, and emotion; it deals with the feelings and emotions of the author, of his characters or subjects, and it attempts to arouse the feelings or emotions of the reader.

Some understanding of objective and subjective styles should help the student in his study and use of language. The following cogent analysis has been written by an English rhetorician and teacher.

Objective and Subjective

MARJORIE BOULTON

When we examine a style we are helped by a realization of how far it is objective or subjective, and it is often necessary to think hard about this. *Objective* in the sense "looking at what is seen and not letting personal feelings come into the picture" and *subjective* in the sense "from the point of view of the observer, coloured by personal feelings" are critical terms that have developed much later than the terms of rhetoric and comparatively late in literary history altogether; they seem to have appeared first in these senses round about the beginning of the eighteenth century, but are not common in eighteenth-century criticism.

A book describing scientific experiments is, or should be, almost completely objective. If we wish to imagine pure objectivity we may think of a proof in geometry. An autobiography is expected to be fairly subjective. Most argumentative prose and fiction will stand somewhere between these two.

A difficulty in making this subdivision is that there are two kinds of subjectivity and objectivity in literary criticism; one is stylistic and easy to

From *The Anatomy of Prose* by Marjorie Boulton, reprinted by permission of Routledge and Kegan Paul, Ltd.

define; the other might be called moral or psychological. Four examples made up for the purpose may illustrate this:

1. *Objective (style)*

"Outside my window there is a grey path, a green lawn and a patch of brown earth in which a number of bushes of different sizes are planted. The bushes are evergreens; the trees behind them have lost their leaves and are therefore bare. There are some more bare trees and a few green bushes, mostly laurels, on the other side of the lawn. A thrush is looking for worms on the lawn."

There is nothing here but a description of what I can see; my eye is on the object. My own feelings are excluded and no adjective or phrase hints in any way at my feelings indirectly. It is possible to treat the same view more subjectively.

2. *Subjective (style)*

"I can see, through my window, a grey path that reminds me of the grey road outside in this dismal weather. The lawn is green, the colour of hope; the trees are bare, stripped like me of most of the hopes of spring. A hungry thrush is looking for worms on the lawn. At present the only comfort for sad eyes is to be found in the evergreen bushes, which prove that winter itself does not defeat all growth, and in the laurels among the evergreens, reminding me that literature may be more lasting than human sufferings."

This description of the same scene is quite different in tone; I am thinking about my own feelings and the scene is merely an excuse for a frank expression of personal conflicts. The subject is important—the one who is looking at the scene.

This is easy. We may, however, have an objective style in which subjective feelings have played a great part, or a style that appears to be subjective when actually the writer is being objective about himself, a detached observer. This kind of paradox of style is much more difficult to discuss.

3. *Subjective (psychological)*

"The view is grey, drab and depressing. Nothing can be seen but a lawn, a path, a few trees and bushes; the only live thing visible is a thrush.

The sky overhead is a slaty grey and the sun is not shining. The path is visibly damp. The leafless trees are grey and motionless."

This sounds like objectivity; there is nothing but a description of the view, with no comment on personal feelings or any "I." Yet if this description is compared with No. 1 the reader will notice how in 3 I have really allowed the description to be affected by my personal feelings of depression, wording the account of the scene in such a way as to stress its drabness. The description 1 is really more accurate.

4. *Objective (psychological)*

"It seems that today I am suffering from a fit of depression. Perhaps this is because I have a slight cold and this is making me feel vaguely unwell. I seem to be unable to take pleasure in what is really quite an agreeable view of a lawn, trees, bushes and a path. Perhaps I shall see it in a different light when my health is better."

This is all about "I," but, as is often found in good autobiographies, especially modern ones,[1] the writer is treating the "I" objectively; I do not assume that my feelings are correct and am trying to look at them as a doctor or psychologist would, in order to understand them. Thus, though the style suggests, at first sight, subjectivity, the psychological atmosphere is one of objectivity.

Thus it is dangerous to assume that everything that omits all mention of personal feelings is entirely objective or that anything full of "I" is wholly subjective. Indeed, I often find it necessary to explain to students, who have been brought up to avoid the "I" in written work as "egotistical," that often "I think the moon is made of green cheese" is much more modest and really much more objective than "Everyone knows that the moon is made of green cheese." It is possible for an intelligent person to state his or her feelings about something with surprising objectivity at times—an honest recognition of personal limitations and possible causes for the feelings, but when we start generalizing recklessly we are more likely to be subjective without even realizing it.

A very common and useful literary device is to use the most objective style possible in order to carry out a purpose of psychological subjectivity;

[1] A recent example is Stephen Spender's *World within World.*

that is, to use what looks like straightforward description in order to share strong feelings with the reader; the air of sincerity and refusal to express an opinion adds to the force of the emotional attack. Any personal comment on this would weaken it:

"All the powder of the *Revenge* to the last barrel was now spent, all her pikes broken, forty of her best men slain, and the most part of the rest hurt. In the beginning of the fight she had but one hundred free from sickness, and fourscore and ten sick, laid in hold upon the ballast. A small troop to man such a ship, and a weak garrison to resist so mighty an army. By those hundred all was sustained, the volleys, boardings, and enterings of fifteen ships of war, besides those which beat her at large. On the contrary, the Spanish were always supplied with soldiers brought from every squadron: all manner of arms and powder at will. Unto ours there remained no comfort at all, no hope, no supply either of ships, men, or weapons; the masts all beaten overboard, all her tackle cut asunder, her upper work altogether razed, and in effect evened she was with the water, but the very foundation or bottom of a ship, nothing being left overhead either for flight or defence. Sir *Richard* finding himself in this distress, and unable any longer to make resistance, having endured in this fifteen hours' fight the assault of fifteen several Armadoes, all by turns aboard him, and by estimation eight hundred shot of great artillery, besides many assaults and entries; and that himself and the ship must needs be possessed by the enemy, who were now all cast in a ring about him; the *Revenge* not able to move one way or another, but as she was moved with the waves and billows of the sea: commanded the master Gunner, whom he knew to be a most resolute man, to split and sink the ship; that thereby nothing might remain of glory or victory to the Spaniards, seeing in so many hours' fight, and with so great a Navy they were not able to take her, having had fifteen hours' time, fifteen thousand men, and fifty and three sail of men-of-war to perform it withal: and persuaded the company, or as many as he could induce, to yield themselves unto God, and to the mercy of none else; but as they had like valiant resolute men repulsed so many enemies, they should not now shorten the honour of their nation, by prolonging their own lives for a few hours, or a few days."

SIR WALTER RALEIGH: *A Report of the Truth of the Fight about the Isle of Azores*

The subjective is not, of course, always weak; the emotions of a strong personality, even when we feel that the speaker is wrong-headed, may be impressive. Nothing can be more objectionable to an educated person of today in England than the view of Nathaniel Ward (1578-1652) that religious toleration was a sin and an error; but certainly the intrusion of personal feeling does not weaken his argument here:

"It is said, though a man have light enough himself to see in the truth, yet if he hath not enough to enlighten others he is bound to tolerate them. I will engage myself that all the devils in Britanie shall see themselves to their shirts to purchase a lease of this position for three of their lives, under the seal of the Parliament.

"It is said that men ought to have liberty of their conscience, and that it is persecution to debar them of it: I can rather stand amazed than reply to this: it is an astonishment to think that the brains of men should be parboiled in such impious ignorance. Let all the wits under the heavens lay their heads together and find an assertion worse than this (one excepted) I will petition to be chosen the universal idiot of the world."

There is really nothing here but personal feeling; yet its vehemence is such that it sounds almost like real argument.

Much apparently objective argument, as in political pamphlets, religious tracts and statements about education, as well as much historical writing, is really prompted by, or coloured by, personal feelings so strong as to give some degree of subjectivity to the work. This is true to a lesser extent even in such fields as science or literary criticism. . . .

It will be clear . . . that anyone who wishes to be a responsible literary critic must also be something of a psychologist. If we are to assess the degree of objectivity—not forgetting that objectivity is not in itself a virtue except in the sciences, but knowing that an accurate appraisal of a style will depend in part on the writer's intentions—we must be skilled in appreciating the use of words as it shows the workings of the mind. No one ever knows enough psychology, but the study of the subject is illuminating in all matters of literary history and criticism.

Sometimes the question of whether or not a piece of writing is objective or subjective in intent conditions the vocabulary used. It is not necessary at this point to say much about the word stock of subjective composition. We do have in the English language a number of what might be called "value judgment" words—words which in effect say to the reader "this is a good (or bad) person or thing, and you should like (or dislike) him or it." Such words include *hearty, cordial, warm, tender, generous, spirited, gentle, winning, charming, warmhearted, pleasant, cheerful, attractive, sunny, bright, gay, beautiful, brilliant, pure, gallant, resolute, noble, modest, friendly, courteous,* and *stingy, caustic, callous, cheap, mean, sordid, greedy, hard, frigid, irritable, hateful, dreary, appalling, grim, revolting, dismal, dull, accursed, odious, vulgar, absurd, stupid, repulsive, vile, clownish, insolent, rude, crusty.* And there are, of course, hundreds of other words like these. It would seem that many of them would be used in subjective writing, especially in simple subjective situations involving conflicts of liked and disliked, or good and bad. Many of them are. But many writers find it good to be sparing in the use of these words; they find that letting the character or situation speak for itself is more effective than telling the reader outright what he should think or feel.

Objective writing can often be accomplished with a very simple vocabulary. But when writing about even the simplest things and concepts, we must sometimes use uncommon wording. Sometimes identifying characteristics and defining criteria can be given only in scientific or technical language. Despite the fact that the definers were abundantly familiar with rhetoricians' advice to keep wording simple, *Webster's Seventh New Collegiate Dictionary* contains the following:

sugar 1 b any of various water-soluble compounds that vary widely in sweetness and comprise the oligosaccharides including sucrose

leaf 1 a (1) a lateral outgrowth from a stem that constitutes a unit of the foliage of a plant and functions primarily in food manufacture by photosynthesis

shale a fissile rock that is formed by the consolidation of clay, mud, or silt, has a finely stratified or laminated structure, and is composed of minerals essentially unaltered since deposition

minnow 1 any of various small fishes; *esp*: a small European cyprinid fish (*Phoxinus phoxinus*) common in gravelly streams and attaining a length of about three inches

Questioned about the wording used, the definer would affirm, quite correctly, that it was admittedly learned and difficult but that it was necessary to scientific or objective accuracy. There can be no rejoinder to this answer. When objective accuracy so demands, directions that simple wording be preferred must be waived.

Attempting to blend the obviously subjective and the obviously objective is likely to produce ridiculous results: "Lightheartedly, Tom raced up the stairs, humming a tune and thinking about Edna. But his racing and humming stopped dead when he reached the third-floor landing. The blow struck above the ear, almost demolishing the right parietal bone. There were severe lacerations of the meninges, followed by a massive subdural hemorrhage. There was deep intercranial bleeding into one of the lateral ventricles."

If you keep in mind what you are trying to do when you write, you will probably avoid any such incongruous blending.

READINGS: OBJECTIVE AND SUBJECTIVE. Consider what is objective and what is subjective—if you can find both characteristics—in each of the four selections that follow. The first is from the entry on reptiles in the *Encyclopedia Americana*. The second selection, a poem by Emily Dickinson, is radically different in tone. The poet makes her crucial point in the last stanza, and this point has to do with her feeling about the subject. The third selection is from *Snakes in Fact and Fiction* by Dr. James A. Oliver. Formerly a member of the faculty of the University of Florida and later Director of the New York Zoological Park, he is now Director of the American Museum of Natural History. W. H. Hudson (1841–1922), the author of the final selection, was born to American parents in Argentina and spent his boyhood there. He moved to England in 1874 and subsequently wrote romantic novels and books devoted to nature study. His best-known books are *The Purple Land That England Lost* (1885), *Green Mansions* (1904), and *Far Away and Long Ago* (1918), from which the present selection has been taken.

Reptiles

(from the *Encyclopedia Americana*)

Reptiles differ from birds in the following characters, which may, therefore, be taken as including the definition of the class *Reptilia*. The covering consists of horny scales or of bony plates (scutes), but never of feathers. The blood is cold and two aortic arches (right and left) exist in living *Reptilia*. The heart is three-chambered in all save the crocodiles, which possess a four-chambered heart. But in all reptiles, without exception, the venous and arterial currents of blood are connected and an impure or mixed blood is thus circulated throughout the body. The lungs do not present the open character of those of birds, but, like those of mammalia, are in modern reptiles almost always closed sacs. The tarsal and metatarsal bones of the hind limbs, which in birds are united to form a single bone, are distinct and separate in the great majority of reptiles. When a sacrum exists it bears sacral ribs, which articulate with the ilia or haunch-bones.

Skeleton. The body in reptiles is generally elongated, the tortoises and their allies presenting the most notable exceptions to this rule. The limbs may be entirely wanting, as in most snakes and in many lizards; or only a pair of limbs may be developed, as in some lizards; while in most other reptiles all four members are present. . . .

Skull. The skull of *Reptilia* possesses but a single occipital condyle, which is sometimes tripartite. The quadrate bone is generally firmly fixed to the skull, joining the squamosal bone, but is freely movable in serpents and only less so in many lizards. Each half or ramus of the lower jaw is composed of dentary, angular, surangular, coronoid, splenial and articular bone. Other regions of the skull are modified in the greatest varieties of ways in the several orders, the most important from a systematic standpoint being in the bones which form the complex roof of the temporal fossa.

A Narrow Fellow in the Grass

EMILY DICKINSON

A narrow fellow in the grass
Occasionally rides;
You may have met him,—did
you not?
His notice sudden is.

The grass divides as with a
comb,
A spotted shaft is seen;
And then it closes at your feet
And opens further on.

He likes a boggy acre,
A floor too cool for corn.
Yet when a child, and barefoot,
I more than once, at morn,

Have passed, I thought, a
whip-lash
Unbraiding in the sun,—
When, stooping to secure it,
It wrinkled, and was gone.

Several of nature's people
I know, and they know me;
I feel for them a transport
Of cordiality;

But never met this fellow,
Attended or alone,
Without a tighter breathing,
And zero at the bone.

The World's Most Dangerous Snake

JAMES A. OLIVER

. . . Twenty-three snakes make up the rogues' gallery of the serpentine world; they are the venomous villains of their respective continents. In any given local region, they may be displaced by a more awesome rival who is usually less abundant in regions of heavy human habitation, but in the larger populated areas they are more important.

Selection of the species that is the most dangerous of all depends not on which has the most toxic venom or which kills the greatest number of human beings, but which has a powerful venom, an effective apparatus for injecting the venom, and an effective method of inflicting a serious bite. This selection is going to favor the larger, more excitable, or more agile species with their relatively longer fangs, larger doses of venom, and more forceful strokes.

Taking them up by continents, I would first narrow the selection in North America to the Western Diamondback Rattlesnake, the Eastern Diamondback Rattlesnake, and the Fer-de-lance. I have collected all three of these species in the wild, and would unquestionably rate the Western Diamondback Rattlesnake as the most dangerous of this trio. In South America, I would tend to favor the Bushmaster as the most dangerous snake on the basis of size and method of striking. Its venom is far weaker than that of the rattler, but the latter is much easier to handle and to avoid. The selection between these two is somewhat like deciding whether you would rather run the risk of being run over by a Cadillac going 30 miles an hour or by a Ford going 50 miles an hour. You *could* recover from either. This is true of any selection among these deadly snakes.

Europe can be bypassed, since none of its venomous snakes is in a class with the others under consideration. Most are small species and their bites are seldom fatal. In Africa a number of species are available for consideration. On the basis of size, agility, and strength of venom, I would unquestionably give my vote to the Black Mamba. However, if I had to choose between being bitten by a ten-foot mamba or a six-foot Gaboon Viper, a flip of the coin would give as good an answer as anyone could. Size has to be emphasized in seeking the "most dangerous snake," and on this basis the King Cobra, the largest of all venomous snakes, appears to be the worst that Asia has to offer. In Australia, the Taipan is the largest venomous species, and merits the designation of most dangerous despite the potent venom of the smaller Tiger Snake and Death Adder.

Making a final decision among this group is extremely difficult, and leaves very little to decide on. We are fortunate in the New World in not having as many really large and terribly deadly snakes as are found in the Old World. Our worst are no match for the Mamba, the Taipan, or the King Cobra. These three have large size, relatively long fangs, and powerful nerve-affecting venoms. Furthermore, all are highly excitable and unpredictable . . . A choice among these three is simply a matter of personal opinion. It is perhaps unfair to the Taipan, which I know only from captive-reared youngsters, but from all reports it is quite similar to the Australian Brown Snake, a species I respect. However, I have more respect for the King Cobra, and whether it's just that I like the name, or whether it is based on something more subtle, I personally think he's "king of the snakes" —the most dangerous of all.

Liaison with a Black Snake

W. H. HUDSON

One hot day in December I had been standing perfectly still for a few minutes among the dry weeds when a slight rustling sound came from near my feet, and glancing down I saw the head and neck of a large black serpent moving slowly past me. In a moment or two the flat head was lost to sight among the close-growing weeds, but the long body continued moving slowly by—so slowly that it hardly appeared to move, and as the creature must have been not less than six feet long, and probably more, it took a very long time, while I stood thrilled with terror, not daring to make the slightest movement, gazing down upon it. Although so long, it was not a thick snake, and as it moved on over the white ground it had the appearance of a coal-black current flowing past me—a current not of water or other liquid but of some such element as quicksilver moving on in a rope-like stream. At last it vanished, and turning I fled from the ground, thinking that never again would I venture into or near that frightfully dangerous spot in spite of its fascination.

Nevertheless I did venture. The image of that black mysterious serpent was always in my mind from the moment of waking in the morning until I fell asleep at night. Yet I never said a word about the snake to anyone: it was my secret, and I knew it was a dangerous secret, but I did not want to be told not to visit that spot again. And I simply could not keep away from it; the desire to look again at that strange being was too strong. I began to visit the place again, day after day, and would hang about the borders of the barren weedy ground watching and listening, and still no black serpent appeared. Then one day I ventured, though in fear and trembling, to go right in among the weeds, and still finding nothing, began to advance step by step until I was right in the middle of the weedy ground and stood there a long time, waiting and watching. All I wanted was just to see it once more, and I had made up my mind that immediately on its appearance, if it did appear, I would take to my heels. It was when standing in this central spot that once again that slight rustling sound, like that of a few days before, reached my straining sense and sent an icy chill down my back. And there, within six inches of my toes, appeared the black head and neck, followed by the long, seemingly endless body. I dared not move, since to have attempted flight might have been fatal. The weeds were thinnest here, and the black head and slow-moving black coil could be followed by the eye for a little distance. About a yard from me there was a hole in the ground about the circumference of a breakfast-cup at the top, and into this hole the serpent put his head and slowly, slowly drew himself in, while I stood waiting until the whole body to the tip of the tail had vanished and all danger was over.

I had seen my wonderful creature, my black serpent unlike any serpent in the land, and the excitement following the first thrill of terror was still on me, but I was conscious of an element of delight in it, and I would not now resolve not to visit the spot again. Still, I was in fear, and kept away three or four days. Thinking about the snake I formed the conclusion that the hole he had taken refuge in was his den, where he lived, that he was often out roaming about in search of prey, and could hear footsteps at a considerable distance, and that when I walked about at that spot my footsteps disturbed him and caused him to go straight to his hole to hide himself from a possible danger. It struck me that if I went to the middle of the ground and stationed myself near the hole, I would be sure to see him. It would indeed be difficult to see him any other way, since one could never know in which direction he had gone out to seek for food. But no, it was too dangerous: the serpent might come upon me unawares and would probably resent always finding a boy hanging about his den. Still, I could not endure to think I had seen the last of him, and day after day I continued to haunt the spot, and going a few yards into the little weedy wilderness would stand and peer, and at the slightest rustling sound of an insect or falling leaf would experience a thrill of fearful joy, and still the black majestical creature failed to appear.

One day in my eagerness and impatience I pushed my way through the crowded weeds right to the middle of the ground and gazed with a mixed delight and fear at the hole: would he find me there, as on a former occasion? Would he come? I held my breath, I strained my sight and hearing in vain, the hope and fear of his appearance gradually died out, and I left the place bitterly disappointed and walked to a spot about fifty yards away, where mulberry trees grew on the slope of the mound inside the moat.

Looking up into the masses of big clustering leaves over my head I spied a bat hanging suspended from a twig. The bats, I must explain, in that part of the world, that illimitable plain where there were no caverns and old buildings and other dark places to hide in by day, are not so intolerant of the bright light as in other lands. They do not come forth until evening, but by day they are content to hitch themselves to the twig of a tree under a thick cluster of leaves and rest there until it is dark.

Gazing up at this bat suspended under a big green leaf, wrapped in his black and buff-colored wings as in a mantle, I forgot my disappointment, forgot the serpent, and was so entirely taken up with the bat that I paid no attention to a sensation like a pressure or a dull pain on the instep of my right foot. Then the feeling of pressure increased and was very curious and was as if I had a heavy object like a crowbar lying across my foot, and at length I looked down at my feet, and to my amazement and horror spied the great black snake slowly drawing his long coil across my instep! I dared not move, but gazed down fascinated with the sight of that glistening black cylindrical body drawn so slowly over my foot. He had come out of the moat, which was riddled at the sides with rat-holes, and had most probably been there hunting for rats when my wandering footsteps disturbed him and sent him home to his den; and making straight for it, as his way was, he came to my foot, and instead of going round drew himself over it. After the first spasm of terror I knew I was perfectly safe, that he would not turn upon me so long as I remained quiescent, and would presently be gone from sight. And that was my last sight of him; in vain I watched and waited for him to appear on many subsequent days; but that last encounter had left in me a sense of a mysterious being, dangerous on occasion as when attacked or insulted, and able in some cases to inflict death with a sudden blow, but harmless and even friendly or beneficent towards those who regarded it with kindly or reverent feelings in place of hatred. It is in part the feeling of the Hindoo with regard to the cobra which inhabits his house and may one day accidentally cause his death, but is not to be persecuted.

Questions and Assignments

1. Although these four selections deal with the same subject, no two are the same in either content or style. Give the theme or purpose of each selection and tell whether each is objective or subjective or both. How does each author's language accord with his purpose and how does he pick and choose his facts to further that purpose? Is Emily Dickinson's poem or Hudson's account any less "true" than the encyclopedia description of reptiles? Why not?

2. Compare the language, especially the adjectives, of the encyclopedia selection and "The World's Most Dangerous Snake." Why is there this difference and what effect does it have? Compare the language and conclusion of Emily Dickinson's poem with the language and conclusion of Hudson's story. What effect does the word *cordiality* have in the poem? Why does Hudson tell us about the bat in such detail?

3. Write a theme on a topic similar to snakes, such as horses, cats, dogs, birds, trees, or perhaps on some other subject which interests you, such as cars, motorcycles, boats, coats, shoes. Decide whether you want your essay to be subjective or objective—that is, whether you want to provide numerous scientific details or put more emphasis on your feeling about the subject—and decide whether you want to discuss the whole subject or just some particular aspect of it. Use one of the selections just read as a model for your theme.

Tone: Levels of Usage

Although there is no way to draw a definite line between them, there are two general classes of words: those that convey only the meanings which common usage has given them, and those that convey their accustomed meanings but also carry additional suggestions and associations. Consider some illustrations taken from words beginning in *ha-*. If we think of *hair, half, hall, hamper* (v.), *hand, hang, happen, hard, harvest, hate,* and *have,* we will realize that these words are part of the vocabulary of practically every speaker of the English language. In general we accept these words simply as indicators of meaning alone; they lack additional suggestiveness.

If, however, we meet with the form *hain't* in speaking or writing, our reaction is different. We know that this form means "am not" (or perhaps "are not" or "is not") or "have not" (or perhaps "has not"). But we are also likely to feel that the speaker is not using "correct" English, upper-class English, prestige-group English. We may call this usage nonstandard English, lower-class English, incorrect English, vulgar English. The form not only communicates its meaning, but suggests to us a background, a context, that we can label as lower-class—a background that may involve poverty, crudeness, lack of refinement, education, or nicety.

On the other hand, we may meet with *habitude, halcyon, hauteur.* If we do, we will probably feel that these words suggest a background or context involving at least some learning, for these words are not part of everybody's vocabulary. Some words—those peculiar to the learned arts and sciences—must suggest a depth of study, information, or training. We are almost bound to associate *hachure* with cartography, *halobiont* with biology, *hamza* with orthography and linguistics, and we are surprised if these words are used by anybody not at least somewhat familiar with these learned matters or anywhere but in a discussion of them.

Some words through their meanings are bound to suggest certain spheres of activity, without, however, being either upper-class or lower-class, learned or unlearned in their effect or color. *Halyard* and especially *hawse* are unlikely to be used other than in a context involving ships, *handcar* other than in one about railroading, *hardbound* other than in one concerning book production. Some words also suggest various specific parts of the English-speaking world, and some others various non-English areas. Many of us feel that *haberdasher* is more English than American; *hacienda* is likely to suggest Southwestern areas in which Spanish influence has been strong. Someone other than a Scotsman might prepare or eat a *haggis,* someone other than a German-American a *hasenpfeffer,* but these comestibles and the words for them are commonly associated with the groups mentioned. An American in Cleveland or Chicago could, one supposes, use *hashish,* go on a *hajj,* employ a private *hamal,* and conduct a *harem,* but these words—*hashish, hajj, hamal,* and *harem*—are usually associated with areas east and south of the Mediterranean. And words can suggest times and eras too. Sometimes they do so through their meanings alone. Mention of a *habergeon* or a *hauberk*—both words mean "chain mail jacket"—is likely to take our thoughts back to the thirteenth century, mention of a *halbert* or a *harquebus* to the sixteenth. Sometimes the words themselves, as separate and distinct from their meanings, are archaic, obsolete, or encountered only in historical writing of one kind or another.

Many of the associations of words—of words, that is, like those just discussed and unlike *hair, half,* and *hall*—concern social or educational level, geographical area, or time division. The associations of many words are concerned with more than one of these divisions. Any mention of the word *haiku* suggests at once an interest in and knowledge of technicalities of poetry and also awareness that a Japanese poetic form is being discussed. In addition to suggesting a learned awareness of early religious rites, the word *haruspex* almost necessarily has to connote the Roman of the classical period. *Habdalah* and *hazan* are bound to suggest a degree of familiarity with the history of Jewish ritual. *Hanky-panky* at once suggests a degree of informality in expression and, when used by an American, a degree of fondness for English expression.

The most important thing about the words cited above and others in their group is that they do have a double effect, not communicating meaning alone but also communicating tone. They have an additional power, an additional capacity, which other words do not have. They can give a tone, hue or color, or mood to a passage in which the other forty-nine or four hundred and ninety-nine words may be colorless and neutral—words that express meaning alone. Perhaps they compare to neutral words without suggestion as very strong medicines or poisons, still effective in a one-to-five-hundred dilution, compare to innocuous materials like common table salt or sugar. They must be used in appropriate situations, in situations in which they help to communicate the tone desired. One word—and one word alone—that suggests an inappropriate tone can make a whole passage ridiculous. Let's illustrate this comment:

> In the first part of World War II the Nazi armies seemed invincible. Poland was overrun and crushed in five weeks in early autumn in 1939. Denmark and Norway were captured by Nazi invaders in April, 1940, and the Netherlands, Belgium, and much of France were occupied in 1940, British field forces narrowly escaping complete defeat and capture on the continent at that time. Greece and the Balkan nations were conquered and occupied during the latter part of 1941 and the first part of 1942. During the summer and fall of the latter year Nazi armies attacked Russian forces and penetrated hundreds of miles into Russian territory. Everywhere Hitler seemed to have at his disposal oodles of experienced, unconquerable soldiers.

Oodles is of course informal, and at least some of us will feel that it is effeminate—a girl's word rather than a man's. Its use here vitiates the whole otherwise serious paragraph.

With many words it is hard to be definite in one's labels. At one time English texts proposed arrangements of "levels," whereby words were called *vulgar, dialectal, colloquial, formal,* and so on. For a number of reasons, these labels, along with various others, are being given up.

Expressions not commonly written—unless for special effect—in serious expository prose should be regarded as substandard, informal, dialectal, or slang. *Substandard* applies to words and wording that would not be used, in speech or writing, by the prestige group of your community. Perhaps *nohow* and *he done it* illustrate. *Informal* may apply to words and wording common and natural in everyday speech but less likely to appear in serious writing. Few of us, however, have at our disposal large-scale recordings of language use, intelligence and judgment enough to evolve criteria for labeling, and steadiness and objectivity enough to apply such criteria in a consistent way. In most discussions of these matters subjectivity enters, and argument becomes futile, agreement impossible. To us, but not necessarily to you or to your instructor, the following words in *ha-* seem informal: *hack* (meaning either "taxicab" or "cabdriver"), *hair-do, half* for *half dollar, half-baked* (in the meaning of "without sufficient thought, judgment, or sense"), *half-cocked* with a similar meaning, *half pint* for "a small person," *ham* for either "radio amateur" or "inept and ostentatious actor or performer," *hand* for either "help" or "applause" (both illustrated by "give him a hand"), *hand-me-downs, hand-out* (n.), *handshaker* ("an ingratiating politician or other opportunist"), *hang* in "to get the hang of it" and in "not to care a hang," *hangover, hanker, harum-scarum,* and *hash mark*. Perhaps this short list will be enough to suggest a feeling for informal words and wording. *Slang* may be thought of as that body of informal words and wordings peculiar to the usage of a special group. Sometimes the group may be narrow and specific, as safe crackers or jazz musicians; sometimes it may be broad and inclusive, as adolescents in general. Dialectal terms are informal or substandard words and turns of speech peculiar to special regions.

Until recently the great majority of teachers warned students against writing anything that could be labeled informal, slang, or dialectal in a theme. For various reasons this practice is less common now. For one thing, in almost all kinds of writing done today by professionals and other persons of influence more and more informal English is used. Examples of this usage are legion; you hardly need an illustration, but you may wish to note what a practiced and popular writer, John Gunther[1], does with *oomph* and *zip* in the following paragraph in the conclusion to his *Roosevelt in Retrospect*:

> This whole book is in the nature of a summary; therefore we need add little further summary now. Roosevelt was a man of his

[1] John Gunther, *Roosevelt in Retrospect* (New York: Harper and Row, 1950).

> times, and what times they were!—chaotic, catastrophic, revolutionary, epochal—he was President during the greatest emergency in the history of mankind, and he never let history—or mankind—down. His very defects reflected the unprecedented strains and stresses of the decades he lived in. But he took history in his stride; he had vision and gallantry enough, oomph and zip and debonair benevolence enough, to foresee the supreme crises of our era, overcome them, and lead the nation out of the worst dangers it has ever faced.

Often wording like this is used to ease tensions in the communication process, to bridge the gap between writer and reader, to insure a warm and easy informality. To a growing extent, professional writers and critics are coming to feel that simple, familiar language may be used in narration and description when the events, situations, or processes being described are not formal or imposing.

The permissiveness of this attitude is, however, deceptive. In accepting permission to use informal, slang, and dialectal words and wording, the writer incurs the responsibility to be reasonably consistent —except in situations in which he wishes to shock or startle by a discordant note—and to make his wording appropriate. He also incurs the obligation to make his wording clear. Slang and dialect by definition are parts of the language peculiar to limited groups and not familiar and readily comprehensible to all. Ready ways of making slang and dialectal terms clear have been suggested before in this section: sometimes one can add a definition or explanation:

> Many of the teen-age delinquents carried zip guns. A zip gun is a homemade pistol capable of firing a small-caliber cartridge with lethal effect at short range.

> After the great storm of 1900 in Galveston some of the survivors found that during the darkness horses or cows had taken refuge on the galleries—to use the local term for front porch—of their houses.

Sometimes care about letting the context define or explain in a less obvious way will insure clarity.

Considerably less needs to be said about wording that is more formal or more learned than the average. Its difficulties and dangers are explicit in themselves, as are the ways of overcoming them. We think that although the following words in *ha-* are neither archaic nor obsolete they do lack vitality and may become so: *habitude, hagride, hail-fellow, halfworld, hallo* or *halloo, halt* (adj., meaning "lame"), *hand* in the sense of "workman, employe," *handmaid, handsel, hang out* ("to live"), *hap, harbinger, hardihood, harlot, harridan, haven, hazard* in many of its senses, and *haze* as a verb. It is a good idea always to make sure that a word that you are thinking of using is really vital in today's language and that it is not lapsing into bookishness.

Vicksburg During the Trouble

MARK TWAIN

Samuel Langhorne Clemens (1835–1910), to use his real name, or Mark Twain, to use his pen name, author of THE ADVENTURES OF TOM SAWYER *and* THE ADVENTURES OF HUCKLEBERRY FINN, *is one of the best-known American authors. From his experiences as a Mississippi River pilot, he wrote* LIFE ON THE MISSISSIPPI *(1883), from which this selection is taken. Held by Confederate forces, Vicksburg underwent a severe siege in the late spring and early summer of 1863, surrendering to General Grant's Union forces on July 4.*

We used to plow past the lofty hill city, Vicksburg, downstream; but we cannot do that now. A cutoff has made a country town of it, like Osceola, St. Genevieve, and several others. There is currentless water—also a big island—in front of Vicksburg now. You come down the river the other side of the island, then turn and come up to the town; that is, in high water: in low water you can't come up, but must land some distance below it.

Signs and scars still remain, as reminder of Vicksburg's tremendous war experiences; earthworks, trees crippled by the cannon balls, cave-refuges in the clay precipices, etc. The caves did good service during the six weeks' bombardment of the city—May 18 to July 4, 1863. They were used by the noncombatants—mainly by the women and children; not to live in constantly, but to fly to for safety on occasion. They were mere holes, tunnels, driven into the perpendicular clay bank, then branched Y shape, within the hill. Life in Vicksburg during the six weeks was perhaps—but wait, here are some materials out of which to reproduce it:

Population, twenty-seven thousand soldiers and three thousand noncombatants; the city utterly cut off from the world—walled solidly in, the frontage by gunboats, the rear by soldiers and batteries; hence, no buying and selling with the outside; no passing to and fro; no God-speeding a parting guest, no welcoming a coming one; no printed acres of world-wide news to be read at breakfast, mornings—a tedious dull absence of such matter, instead; hence, also, no running to see steamboats smoking into view in the distance up or down, and plowing toward the town—for none came, the river lay vacant and undisturbed; no rush and turmoil around the railway station, no struggling over bewildered swarms of passengers by noisy mobs of hackmen—all quiet there; flour two hundred dollars a barrel, sugar thirty, corn ten dollars a bushel, bacon five dollars a pound, rum a hundred dollars a gallon; other things in proportion: consequently, no roar and racket of drays and carriages tearing along the streets; nothing for them to do, among that handful of noncombatants of exhausted means; at three o'clock in the morning, silence; silence so dead that the measured tramp of a sentinel can be heard a seemingly impossible distance; out of hearing of this lonely sound, perhaps the stillness is absolute: all in a moment come ground-shaking thunder-crashes of artillery, the sky is cobwebbed with the crisscrossing red lines streaming from soaring bombshells, and a rain of iron fragments descends upon the city; descends upon the empty streets: streets which are not empty a moment later, but mottled with dim figures of frantic women and children scurrying from home and bed toward the cave dungeons—encouraged by the humorous grim soldiery, who shout "Rats, to your holes!" and laugh.

The cannon thunder rages, shells scream and crash overhead, the iron rain pours down, one hour, two hours, three, possibly six, then stops; silence follows, but the streets are still empty; the silence continues; by and by a head projects from a cave here and there and yonder, and reconnoiters, cautiously; the silence still continuing, bodies follow heads, and jaded, half-smothered creatures group themselves about, stretch their cramped limbs, draw in deep draughts of the grateful fresh air, gossip with the neighbors from the next cave; maybe straggle off home presently, or take a lounge through the town, if the stillness continues; and will scurry to the holes again, by and by, when the war tempest breaks forth once more.

There being but three thousand of these cave-dwellers—merely the population of a village—would they not come to know each other, after a week or two, and familiarly; insomuch that the fortunate or unfortunate experiences of one would be of interest to all?

Those are the materials furnished by history. From them might not almost anybody reproduce for himself the life of that time in Vicksburg? Could you, who did not experience it, come nearer to reproducing it to the imagination of another nonparticipant than could a Vicksburger who *did* experience it? It seems impossible; and yet there are reasons why it might not really be. When one makes his first voyage in a ship, it is an experience which multitudinously bristles with striking novelties; novelties which are in such sharp contrast with all this person's former experiences that they take a seemingly deathless grip upon his imagination and memory. By tongue or pen he can make a landsman live that strange and stirring voyage over with him; make him see it all and feel it all. But if he wait? If he make ten voyages in succession—what then? Why, the thing has lost color, snap, surprise; and has become commonplace. The man would have nothing to tell that would quicken a landsman's pulse.

Years ago, I talked with a couple of the Vicksburg noncombatants—a man and his wife. Left to tell their story in their own way, those people told it without fire, almost without interest.

A week of their wonderful life there would have made their tongues eloquent forever perhaps; but they had six weeks of it, and that wore the novelty all out; they got used to being bombshelled out of home and into the ground; the matter became commonplace. After that, the possibility of their ever being startlingly interesting in their talks about it was gone. What the man said was to this effect:

> It got to be Sunday all the time. Seven Sundays in the week—to us, anyway. We hadn't anything to do, and time hung heavy. Seven Sundays, and all of them broken up at one time or another, in the day or in the night, by a few hours of the awful storm of fire and thunder and iron. At first we used to shin for the holes a good deal faster than we did afterward. The first time, I forgot the children, and Maria fetched them both along. When she was all safe in the cave she fainted. Two or three weeks afterward, when she was running for the holes, one morning, through a shell shower, a big shell

burst near her and covered her all over with dirt, and a piece of the iron carried away her game bag of false hair from the back of her head. Well, she stopped to get that game bag before she shoved along again! Was getting used to things already, you see. We all got so that we could tell a good deal about shells; and after that we didn't always go under shelter if it was a light shower. Us men would loaf around and talk; and a man would say, "There she goes!" and name the kind of shell it was from the sound of it, and go on talking—if there wasn't any danger from it. If a shell was bursting close over us, we stopped talking and stood still; uncomfortable, yes, but it wasn't safe to move. When it let go, we went on talking again, if nobody was hurt—maybe saying, "That was a ripper!" or some such common-place comment before we resumed; or maybe, we would see a shell poising itself away high in the air overhead. In that case, every fellow just whipped out a sudden, "See you again, gents!" and shoved. Often and often I saw gangs of ladies promenading the streets, looking as cheerful as you please, and keeping an eye canted up watching the shells; and I've seen them stop still when they were uncertain about what a shell was going to do, and wait and make certain; and after that they s'antered along again, or lit out for shelter, according to the verdict. Streets in some towns have a litter of pieces of paper, and odds and ends of one sort or another lying around. Ours hadn't; they had *iron* litter. Sometimes a man would gather up all the iron fragments and unbursted shells in his neighborhood, and pile them into a kind of monument in his front yard —a ton of it, sometimes. No glass left; glass couldn't stand such a bombardment; it was all shivered out. Windows of the houses vacant —looked like eyeholes in a skull. *Whole* panes were as scarce as news.

We had church Sundays. Not many there along at first; but by and by pretty good turnouts. I've seen service stop a minute, and everybody sit quiet—no voice heard, pretty funerallike then—and all the more so on account of the awful bomb and crash going on outside and overhead; and pretty soon, when a body could be heard, service would go on again. Organs and church music mixed up with a bombardment is a powerful queer combination—along at first. Coming out of church, one morning, we had an accident—the only one that happened around me on a Sunday. I was just having a hearty handshake with a friend I hadn't seen for a while, and saying, "Drop into our cave tonight, after bombardment; we've got half of a pint of prime wh—." Whisky, I was going to say, you know,

> but a shell interrupted. A chunk of it cut the man's arm off, and left it dangling in my hand. And do you know the thing that is going to stick the longest in my memory, and outlast everything else, little and big, I reckon, is the mean thought I had then? It was "the whisky *is saved*." And yet, don't you know, it was kind of excusable; because it was as scarce as diamonds, and we had only just that little; never had another taste during the siege.
>
> Sometimes the caves were desperately crowded, and always hot and close. Sometimes a cave had twenty or twenty-five people packed into it; no turning room for anybody; air so foul, sometimes, you couldn't have made a candle burn in it. A child was born in one of those caves one night. Think of that; why, it was like having it born in a trunk.
>
> Twice we had sixteen people in our cave; and a number of times we had a dozen. Pretty suffocating in there. We always had eight; eight belonged there. Hunger and misery and sickness and fright and sorrow, and I don't know what all, got so loaded into them that none of them were ever rightly their old selves after the siege. They all died but three of us within a couple of years. One night a shell burst in front of the hole and caved it in and stopped it up. It was lively times, for a while, digging out. Some of us came near smothering. After that we made two openings—ought to have thought of it at first.
>
> Mule meat? No, we only got down to that the last day or two. Of course it was good; anything is good when you are starving.

This man had kept a diary during—six weeks? No, only the first six days. The first day, eight close pages; the second, five; the third, one—loosely written; the fourth, three or four lines; a line or two the fifth and sixth days; seventh day, diary abandoned; life in terrific Vicksburg having now become commonplace and matter of course.

The war history of Vicksburg has more about it to interest the general reader than that of any other of the river towns. It is full of variety, full of incident, full of the picturesque. Vicksburg held out longer than any other important river town, and saw warfare in all its phases, both land and water—the siege, the mine, the assault, the repulse, the bombardment, sickness, captivity, famine.

The most beautiful of all the national cemeteries is here. Over the great gateway is this inscription:

HERE REST IN PEACE 16,600 WHO DIED FOR THEIR COUNTRY IN THE YEARS 1861 TO 1865.

The grounds are nobly situated; being very high and commanding a wide prospect of land and river. They are tastefully laid out in broad terraces, with winding roads and paths; and there is profuse adornment in the way of semitropical shrubs and flowers; and in one part is a piece of native wildwood, left just as it grew, and, therefore, perfect in its charm. Everything about this cemetery suggests the hand of the national Government. The Government's work is always conspicuous for excellence, solidity, thoroughness, neatness. The Government does its work well in the first place, and then takes care of it.

By winding roads—which were often cut to so great a depth between perpendicular walls that they were mere roofless tunnels—we drove out a mile or two and visited the monument which stands upon the scene of the surrender of Vicksburg to General Grant by General Pemberton. Its metal will preserve it from the hackings and chippings which so defaced its predecessor, which was of marble; but the brick foundations are crumbling, and it will tumble down by and by. It overlooks a picturesque region of wooded hills and ravines; and is not unpicturesque itself, being well smothered in flowering weeds. The battered remnant of the marble monument has been removed to the National Cemetery.

On the road, a quarter of a mile townward, an aged colored man showed us, with pride, an unexploded bombshell which has lain in his yard since the day it fell there during the siege.

"I was a-stannin' heah, an' de dog was a-stannin' heah; de dog he went for de shell, gwine to pick a fuss wid it; but I didn't; I says, 'Jes' make youseff at home heah; lay still whah you is, or bust up de place, jes' as you's a mind to, but *I*'s got business out in de woods, I has!' "

Vicksburg is a town of substantial business streets and pleasant residences; it commands the commerce of the Yazoo and Sunflower Rivers; is pushing railways in several directions, through rich agricultural regions, and has a promising future of prosperity and importance.

Questions and Assignments

1. This selection from Twain has been included partly because it shows three different composition tones—Twain's own, that of the Vicksburg citizen beginning on p. 169, and that of the very short next-to-the-last paragraph which is a nine-

teenth-century conventionalized representation of an aged Negro's speech. (It may have been most uncomplimentary and inaccurate.) Analyze the appropriateness and consistency of the wording in each of these three sections. What wording in each section would have been most inappropriate in the other two? Twain's style is of course not heavily or stiffly formal, but what wording used in the Vicksburger's reminiscences would have been inappropriate for Twain? Try to apply descriptive adjectives to the tone of each of these three parts.

2. Discuss, or write a theme on, the following quotes: "A week of their wonderful life there would have made their tongues eloquent forever perhaps; but they had six weeks of it, and that wore the novelty all out. . . ." "Everything about this cemetery suggests the hand of the national Government. The Government's work is always conspicuous for excellence, solidity, thoroughness, neatness. The Government does its work well in the first place, and then takes care of it."

Brown v. Board of Education of Topeka

Before 1954 the established educational pattern throughout the South and in many other areas called for separate schools for white and Negro children. The legality of this arrangement, questioned even in the nineteenth century, rested on a United States Supreme Court decision in the case of Plessy v. Ferguson. *Various cases were taken to the Supreme Court in the early 1950's in attempts to change this pattern. In its decision of May 17, 1954, in the case of* Brown v. Board of Education of Topeka *the Supreme Court reversed the decision of the* Plessy v. Ferguson *case and unanimously declared segregated educational facilities unconstitutional. Few judicial decisions have had such wide social repercussions. Following is a shortened version of that famous decision.*

. . . These cases come to us from the States of Kansas, South Carolina, Virginia, and Delaware. They are premised on different facts and different local conditions, but a common legal question justifies their consideration together in this consolidated opinion.

In each of the cases, minors of the Negro race, through their legal representatives, seek the aid of the courts in obtaining admission to the public schools of their community on a nonsegregated basis. In each instance, they have been denied admission to schools attended by white children under laws requiring or permitting segregation according to race. This

From Harold C. Syrett, *American Historical Documents* (New York: Barnes and Noble, Inc., 1960).

segregation was alleged to deprive the plaintiffs of the equal protection of the laws under the Fourteenth Amendment. . . .

The plaintiffs contend that segregated public schools are not "equal" and cannot be made "equal," and that hence they are deprived of the equal protection of the laws. Because of the obvious importance of the question presented, the Court took jurisdiction. Argument was heard in the 1952 Term, and reargument was heard this Term on certain questions propounded by the Court.

Reargument was largely devoted to the circumstances surrounding the adoption of the Fourteenth Amendment in 1868. It covered exhaustively consideration of the Amendment in Congress, ratification by the states, then existing practices in racial segregation, and the views of proponents and opponents of the Amendment. This discussion and our own investigation convince us that, although these sources cast some light, it is not enough to resolve the problem with which we are faced. At best, they are inconclusive. The most avid proponents of the post-War Amendments undoubtedly intended them to remove all legal distinctions among "all persons born or naturalized in the United States." Their opponents, just as certainly, were antagonistic to both the letter and the spirit of the Amendments and wished them to have the most limited effect. What others in Congress and the state legislatures had in mind cannot be determined with any degree of certainty.

An additional reason for the inconclusive nature of the Amendment's history, with respect to segregated schools, is the status of public education at that time. In the South, the movement toward free common schools, supported by general taxation, had not yet taken hold. Education of white children was largely in the hands of private groups. Education of Negroes was almost nonexistent, and practically all of the race were illiterate. . . . Even in the North, the conditions of public education did not approximate those existing today. The curriculum was usually rudimentary; ungraded schools were common in rural areas; the school term was but three months a year in many states; and compulsory school attendance was virtually unknown. As a consequence, it is not surprising that there should be so little in the history of the Fourteenth Amendment relating to its intended effect on public education.

In the first cases in this Court construing the Fourteenth Amendment, decided shortly after its adoption, the Court interpreted it as proscribing all state-imposed discriminations against the Negro race. The doctrine of "separate but equal" did not make its appearance in this Court until 1896 in the case of Plessy v. Ferguson . . . involving not education but transportation. American courts have since labored with the doctrine for over half a century. . . .

In approaching this problem, we cannot turn the clock back to 1868 when the Amendment was adopted, or even to 1896 when Plessy v. Ferguson was written. We must consider public education in the light of its full development and its present place in American life throughout the Nation. Only in this way can it be determined if segregation in public schools deprives these plaintiffs of the equal protection of the laws.

Today, education is perhaps the most important function of state and local governments. Compulsory school attendance laws and the great expenditures for education both demonstrate the recognition of the importance of education to our democratic society. It is required in the performance of our most basic public responsibilities, even service in the armed forces. It is the very foundation of good citizenship. Today it is a principal instrument in awakening the child to cultural values, in preparing him for later professional training, and in helping him to adjust normally to his environment. In these days, it is doubtful that any child may reasonably be expected to succeed in life if he is denied the opportunity of an education. Such an opportunity, where the state has undertaken to provide it, is a right which must be made available to all on equal terms.

We come then to the question presented: Does segregation of children in public schools solely on the basis of race, even though the physical facilities and other "tangible" factors may be equal, deprive the children of the minority group of equal educational opportunities? We believe that it does.

In Sweatt v. Painter . . . in finding that a segregated law school for Negroes could not provide them equal educational opportunities, this Court relied in large part on "those qualities which are incapable of objective measurement but which make for greatness in a law school." In McLaurin v. Oklahoma State Regents . . . the Court, in requiring that a Negro admitted to a white graduate school be treated like all other students, again resorted to intangible considerations: ". . . his ability to study, to engage in discussions and exchange views with other students, and, in general, to learn his profession." Such considerations apply with added force to children in grade and high schools. To separate them from others of similar age and qualifications solely because of their race generates a feeling of inferiority as to their status in the community that may affect their hearts and minds in a way unlikely ever to be undone. . . .

We conclude that in the field of public education the doctrine of "separate but equal" has no place. Separate educational facilities are inherently unequal. Therefore, we hold that the plaintiffs and others similarly situated for whom the actions have been brought are, by reason of the segregation complained of, deprived of the equal protection of the laws guaranteed by the Fourteenth Amendment. . . .

Because these are class actions, because of the wide applicability of this decision, and because of the great variety of local conditions, the formulation of decrees in these cases presents problems of considerable complexity. On reargument, the consideration of appropriate relief was necessarily subordinated to the primary question—the constitutionality of segregation in public education. We have now announced that such segregation is a denial of the equal protection of the laws. In order that we may have the full assistance of the parties in formulating decrees, the cases will be restored to the docket, and the parties are requested to present further argument on Questions . . . previously propounded by the Court for reargument this Term. The Attorney General of the United States is again invited to participate. The Attorneys General of the states requiring or permitting segregation in public education will also be permitted to appear as *amici curiae* upon request to do so by September 15, 1954, and submission of briefs by October 1, 1954. . . .

Questions and Assignments

1. In what way is the wording of this memorable decision consistent throughout? How would you describe the wording used? Where in this composition would alternative choices have produced an unintended tone?

2. Examine the vocabulary in this selection. Which words are specific, which general, which objective, which subjective? Which type is preponderant? Why?

3. Paraphrase the Court's judgment regarding the significance of the Fourteenth Amendment in the case. What principle did the Court cite in determining the relevance of this amendment and its observance?

4. It is a common contention that precedent plays the dominant role in many legal decisions. (See "Up Popped the Devil," pp. 183-189.) Estimate as well as you can the importance of precedence in the desegregation decision.

5. List the reasons why the Court decided "separate but equal" facilities deprived children of a minority group of fair educational opportunities.

6. In an appropriately objective style and tone write a theme on one phase of one of the crucial issues of contemporary American life: segregation, peace, population problems, conservation, rural-urban political representation, education, migrant workers, political extremism.

Figurative Language: Metaphor and Simile

Literal language often lacks the means for adequate expression. Suppose a parent sees his child killed by a truck. How would one describe such a scene? Would it be adequate to say that he felt "quite sad"? Suppose that a wife who feels that she is loved and that she is secure in her marriage is suddenly asked for a divorce? Could one say that she was "much agitated"? Suppose that, against all probability, you suddenly win some honor or distinction that you had long craved in secret. Would "very happy" be enough to express your feelings? How can anyone adequately express his deepest emotions of love, of faith, of hatred? Figurative language is the only ready means at our disposal to express the inexpressible, the unknown, the conjectural. None of us has seen an atom. Most attempts to explain what one is are likely to find figurative language necessary. Only the operator of an electronic microscope has seen a virus. Figurative language is likely to help in descriptions of this form of life. In fact when we really think about a variety of matters we may find that our human knowledge is inadequate to permit us certain literal expressions and that we must employ figurative language.

Figurative language may be defined as language which expresses a meaning different from the sum of the literal meanings of the words used. For example, we speak of the hands of a clock. The word *hand* literally designates the human organ found as a continuation of the wrist and suited for grasping and a number of other actions. If we were to try to stick to this sense alone, we would have to consider that a clock could have no hands. Similarly with "the heart of the city." Literally, the heart is the hollow muscular organ that pumps blood through the human system. Used in this way, *heart* in "the heart of the city" would not make good sense. The same is true of the eye of a needle, the nose of an airplane, the mouth of a river, the teeth of a saw, the neck of a bottle.

There are many kinds of figurative language. When we say, "He drank the whole bottle," our expression would be ridiculously impossible if we didn't use common sense and expect people to interpret it to mean that he drank the *contents* of the whole bottle. In our expression the word *bottle* designates the liquor or beverage; the word expresses the thing associated with what is meant by the word originally or literally. The word *metonymy* is used to indicate figurative usages of this kind. And sometimes, often with an appropriate vocal intonation, we express a meaning just the opposite from that that our individual words would convey if taken literally. When we list a candidate's liabilities and end by saying, "He would certainly have a fine chance of being elected," we probably mean that he would not have a fine chance. This kind of expression is called *irony*.

It would be possible to list a number of other names for other figures of speech. It seems best here, however, to concentrate on only two figures—the simile and the metaphor.

A *simile* may be defined as a comparison of unlike things accomplished by the use of *like* or *as*. "He went snorting around the room like a bull," "cornered, this alleged coward fought like a lion," "drawing ever smaller and tighter rings around Germany, the Allies overcame Germany as a boa constrictor overcomes its prey"—these are similes. A *metaphor* is a comparison expressed without the use of *like* or *as;* that is, it is a simile without the use of these words. Instead of saying "he was as clumsy as an ox"—a simile—we may say simply "he was a clumsy ox." In so doing, we do not sacrifice clarity—since everyone, however unlettered, is able to understand metaphor. And the expression of identity accomplished by a part of *to be* is often more forceful than the mere expression of similarity.

Very few speakers of English or any other language reach the age of eight without having used a good many similes and metaphors, no matter how intellectually stupid and imaginatively uninventive they may be. A great many of our commonplace informal phrases are metaphors. Consider the following, which again come from the *h* section of a dictionary: *to get in one's hair, to let one's hair down, to split hairs, one's better half, to hammer away at something, to bite the hand that feeds one, to change hands, to eat out of one's hand, to win hands down, to be caught red-handed, to fly off the handle, to settle one's hash, to pass the hat.* Not only do such phrases give us many metaphors; most of our common single words show metaphorical extensions. "A hacking cough" is metaphorical in likening the effect to that of chopping with a hatchet. We may call a person doing dull routine writing a hack; this wording may be interpreted as comparing him to a horse let out for hire. To call a woman a hag is etymologically to compare her to a witch.

If so much of our language is figurative, it necessarily follows that figurative language *in itself* is not in any way necessarily poetic, arty, unusual, different, affected. If you have any doubts about this, observe your own language and that of your friends. You will probably find more metaphors in the sports column of your newspaper or in the financial columns than you will on the literary page.

When a metaphorical phrase is used without either speaker or hearer recognizing that it is metaphorical, we classify it as *dead metaphor.* There is doubtless a paradox in the idea of calling much of our living speech dead metaphor, but this wording is commonly used; when we forget that an expression is a metaphor, we call it a dead metaphor or a cliché. Dead metaphors are common. Here are some overused similes: *as sober as a judge, as high as the sky, as proud as a peacock, as rich as Croesus, as deep as the ocean.* One odd thing about many of these common similes is that they don't make very good sense. One says "as brown as a berry," but a berry is not necessarily extremely brown; most berries are not. One says "as quiet as a church mouse," but why should church mice be more quiet than any other mice? "Dead as a doornail" implies, seemingly, that doornails can more fully illustrate deadness than other nails—an implausible assumption. Students should *always* examine their use of figurative language to make sure it is meaningful and alive.

Below are examples of figurative language drawn from a variety of twentieth-century writers. Examine these selections to determine which most effectively uses metaphoric language. Most rhetoricians would agree that figurative language should have two characteristics:

freshness, and a clear and forceful similarity between the two things compared.

> So one goes from joy to dejection, and hurt to exaltation, and certainty to doubt, as when with some summer storm the whole world is dark and sombre, till suddenly the sun breaks through, almost at its setting, and bathes tree and grass and hill in green and yellow light, the like of which, as the English say, was never seen on land or sea. (Alan Paton)

> After that I was conscious all the time of the dinghy behind us. I can see it still, like a deadly water-beetle crawling after us across the sea, everlastingly following us through an unreal miasma of fog; and I can hear the creak of the rowlocks, the dip and splash of the oars. (Hammond Innes)

> For now [on a night flight] the little towns of Argentina were stringing through the night their golden beads, beneath the paler gold of the star-cities. And at his prow the pilot held within his hands his freight of lives, eyes wide open, full of moonlight, like a shepherd. Already Buenos Aires was dyeing the horizon with pink fires, soon to flaunt its diadem of jewels, like some fairy hoard. (Antoine de St.-Exupéry)

> [On election night] by the time the news systems and the commentators on TV and radio have digested Connecticut, the other big Democratic cities of the East are beginning to flood the wires. First Philadelphia (where polls close at 7:30), then Pittsburgh, then Chicago, then, at nine o'clock, New York City. From nine o'clock, when New York closes its polls, to midnight the Democratic tide reaches its peak as the big cities of Michigan, Illinois, Pennsylvania, Ohio, New Jersey, swamp the vote-gathering facilities of the news networks. (Theodore H. White)

> Nearby some Americans were saying good-by in voices that mimicked the cadence of water running into a large old bathtub. Standing in the station, with Paris in back of them, it seemed as if they were vicariously leaning over the ocean, already undergoing a sea-change, a shifting about of atoms to form the essential molecule of a new people. (F. Scott Fitzgerald)

The crowd was like a cageful of beasts at feeding time. Now, he thought, now's the moment. He swung around to Boyeur. Boyeur had lost control, just as the crowd had done. He only needed the final prick of the goad. Maxwell leant toward him. (Alec Waugh)

At 1100 the first Jap plane came into view. It was a Zero spinning wildly somewhere near the Russells. It flamed and lurched into the sea. The battle was on! For an hour and ten minutes the sky above Guadal and Tulagi was a beautiful misery of streaming fire, retching planes, and pyres flaming out of the sea. The Japanese broke through. Nothing could stop them. (James A. Michener)

Johnny started back to the hotel. He was dripping sweat, dirty, unkempt. He hadn't been out of his clothes for two days. He shut his eyes; the hot sun rained on the lids like fire. (Ross Lockridge, Jr.)

He tried to think of a day different from what today would be. Somehow, deep in him, pale and thin as the groping sprout of a potato forgotten in a dark cellar, hope, or something like hope, probed upward. (Robert Penn Warren)

Briefly, the eighteenth century was in fact an age of enlightenment. It let into Europe a clear, steady daylight, and focused this light on many time-honored prejudices and barbarities, in particular the unreason of political and religious tyranny. It not only diffused knowledge but set up a public standard of truth. (Herbert J. Muller)

Slotin himself appears confident, almost gay. He loves this experiment—"tickling the dragon's tail," he calls it—and he has already performed it at least forty times. Even so, there is a certain tension in the room. Those present are aware that manipulating the guts of an atomic bomb is no child's play. Slotin has his ear cocked to the click of the Geiger counter, and he also glances frequently at an instrument called a "neutron monitor," which is recording on a roll of paper, in a thin, wavy line of red ink, the radiation emitted by the lumps of metal. As Slotin slowly moves the lumps, the red line staggers upward and the Geiger counter clicks erratically, always a little faster, like a deranged clock. Suddenly the Geiger counter begins to click insanely, and then stops dead. All in a moment, the people in the room sense rather than see a strange blue glow, stronger than the spring sunlight. (Stewart Alsop and Ralph E. Lapp)

The New Class is not exclusive. . . . Any individual whose adolescent situation is such that sufficient time and money is invested in his preparation, and who has at least the talents to carry him through the formal academic routine, can be a member. There is a hierarchy within the class. The son of the factory worker who becomes an electrical engineer is on the lower edge; his son who does graduate work and becomes a university physicist moves to the higher echelons; but opportunity for education is, in either case, the open sesame. (John Kenneth Galbraith)

For the Majority Leader was aware from the President's tone that he was not, as he had said, about to abandon his commitment without a struggle; and it had been quite apparent from the iron in his voice the kind of struggle it would be. Occasionally in the past Bob Munson had seen the normally equable temper—equable as long as things were going his way—flare up; he had watched the force of that personality lash out at obstacles in its path, and he had known of actions taken with complete ruthlessness that had for all practical political and national purposes completely destroyed some of the men who had gotten in his way. (Allen Drury)

Zamenhofa Street, from a peephole of the stronghold. A dim light of pre-dawn. Emptiness. Across the way, the house fronts, with doorways boarded over and windows shuttered or papered, looked like the faces of wise and taciturn men, casual masks that hinted (to the acquainted) at interesting activities within the skulls: what subterfuges were behind the foreheads of those faces, in the attic-minds, what plans and early-morning stirrings in the recesses just back of the cornice-hairlines? (John Hersey)

But they were married. Then for the next five years what his uncle called that whole broad generation of spinster aunts who, still alive seventy-five years after the Civil War, are the backbone of the South's social and political and economic solidarity too, watched it as you watch the unfolding story in the magazine installments. (William Faulkner)

Up Popped the Devil

JAMES THURBER

James Thurber (1894—1961) was one of America's foremost humorous essayists and cartoonists. Here Thurber writes about Harold Ross, the editor of the NEW YORKER *magazine from its start in 1925 to his death in 1951. This selection is taken from Thurber's book* THE YEARS WITH ROSS.

If it wasn't one thing it was another, at the *New Yorker,* and sometimes both. There was the day, twenty-five years ago, when two New York detectives called on Ross. They wanted to ask questions about, and then of, one E. B. White, a writer and, the dicks half suspected, the brain guy behind the daring robbery of a bank in Ardsley, New York, not far from Tarrytown. Andy at that time owned a Buick sedan, which he kept in a garage in Turtle Bay, on New York's upper East Side; it had been stolen from the garage one night and used in the robbery by a group of bandits. After a wild chase by state cops the robbers had abandoned the automobile with a few bullet holes in it. The car was then taken to the state police barracks at Hawthorne. They wouldn't let White have it for almost a month.

Ross, who was always at ease with cops, in uniform or in plain clothes, had a wonderful time about it all. He said to the detectives on their first visit. "I think you're on the right track all right. White has been silent and brooding—he's definitely got something on his mind that's worrying the hell out of him." He took the men to White's office, grinning widely, made a big gesture with his right hand and said, "There's your man, officers."

"The detectives paid two or three visits to my office, which pleased Ross greatly," White wrote me. "They would sit around on my couch and just study me, occasionally asking a question when they could think of one. The question I loved was when one of them said: 'Say, how did you get into writing, anyway?' I replied that I had just drifted into it."

The walls of Andy's office interested the detectives a lot. They contained some cockeyed drawings of mine, and the back jacket of Max Eastman's book, *The Enjoyment of Laughter,* which had a photograph of the handsome author laughing. I had taken a pencil and blacked out two of his fine even white teeth, drawn a lock of hair over his forehead, and given his eyes and eyebrows a demented look, the whole thing lending a tone of loony abandon to the office. Also, on one wall, Andy had written down the day and hour of an appointment with his dentist, and above the date I had scrawled *"Der Tag"* and above the hour *"l'heure."* I don't know what the cops made of this piece of cryptic trilingualism, but they must have wondered and worried about it. Andy got his car back finally, and the detectives were smart enough in the end to realize that the man who had just drifted into writing had not drifted into bank robbery, too.

The first major legal crisis, I remember, developed in 1927 when the magazine's Skyline department said that a new Fifth Avenue office building had the grace of a freight elevator and rashly went on to say that architects who walked past the building became sick. The *New Yorker* was promptly sued for half a million dollars by the architect of the new building. Ross sent me down to talk to one of the magazine's lawyers—we then had a firm in Wall Street—and I came back with a report that made him gloomy. The lawyers thought that it would be advisable to settle for a retraction, out of court, on the ground that a jury might decide the plaintiff's reputation had been inexcusably injured by a young smart-aleck magazine. Ross had planned a veritable Roman holiday in court. He was going to call to the witness stand some well-known critics of the theater and of books, Heywood Broun, Bob Benchley, Laurence Stallings, Woollcott, and at least half a dozen others. They would all testify that public buildings should be just as subject to criticism as plays or novels. My report took the wind out of that sail and the light out of the Ross face. I told him the lawyer had said that such testimony would be barred as immaterial, irrelevant, and irr-everything else. There was another point, too. The lawyer felt that the *New Yorker*'s crack about other architects getting attacks of nausea when they gazed upon the building would be regarded as malicious and far outside the bounds of privileged criticism. The case never came to court.

Ross's approach to the law was that of the plunging fullback, hitting the line with his eyes closed. When the Sherry Netherland was opened and the *New Yorker* wrote about it, another crisis was in the making. The new hotel didn't get mad, because it had been praised to the skies in a rave notice that said the place was so elegant even the floor maids wore a certain famous and expensive perfume. The *parfumeur,* one of the most celebrated in the world, did get mad, though, about the implication that his aristocratic product was worn by menials, and another lawsuit was threatened. "I'll send every one of those dames a quart of the stuff!" Ross yelled. When somebody told him what this particular perfume cost, he cut down the boastful size of his containers. "Well, what's the smallest bottle there is? I'll send each one of them the smallest bottle." I think he would have, too, although his lawyers were scarcely enthusiastic about such a tactical move. In the end, the whole thing quietly died out like the fragrance of white clover at summer's end.

Ross disturbed his legal advisers by his rough and tumble approach to everything in the field of jurisprudence, and also by his old newspaperman's idea of "getting something on" the plaintiff. "I know damn well they're digging up all they can about me," he would say. "That always happens in lawsuits. So I'm going to send out a couple of guys to dig up facts on them." His favorite reporter for such work was Eugene Kinkead, whom he admiringly called "the best gumshoe in the business."

When Pearl White, the illustrious heroine of the silent movie serial, *The Perils of Pauline,* died in Paris in 1938, Wolcott Gibbs wrote a nostalgic Comment about her and quoted the chorus of a song, "Poor Pauline," which came out about 1912. The *New Yorker* was promptly sued for having reprinted copyrighted material without permission. The case was decided in favor of the *New Yorker,* and it established the rule that copyrighted song lyrics could be lawfully used without permission in fiction and nonfiction for the purpose of establishing mood and background, provided the use was reasonable and not excessive.

I had my own legal troubles, too. The late Charles Yale Harrison jumped or flew to the conclusion that "The Secret Life of Walter Mitty" had been inspired by a novel of his, *Meet Me on the Barricades,* and he wrote me a polite letter saying he felt I had been the victim of what he called "a psychological deep freeze"; that is, I had read his novel, stored it in my unconscious, and used it unbeknownst to myself. Nobody can be so implacable as an author who thinks he has been plagiarized, and it did no good for the *New Yorker* lawyers to tell Harrison that I had been in Europe when his novel appeared, had not read it or any reviews of it, and had written daydreamer stories for Ross long before *The Barricades* appeared, one of them, "Mr. Pendley and the Poindexter," having given me the idea for "Mitty." Mr. Harrison wrote a long comparison of his novel and my short story, in which he tried to establish similarity between a drumbeat in his book and my own "ta pocketa pocketa," which had been as close as I could come to the sound of the idling of a gas engine. Ross was jocund about all this and, after his fashion, both shared my indignation and was entertained by it. I refused to submit the case to an arbitration board made up of five writers, and Harrison did not bring a legal action against me and the *New Yorker*.

When I was in London in 1938, I had written a casual called "The Macbeth Murder Mystery," and the authors of a parody mystery novel based on Shakespeare's *Macbeth* figured I must have been inspired by their book. Ross was gleeful, as always in triumph, when it was established that my piece had been written and submitted to the *New Yorker* before their book had appeared on the stands. Then, in one of a series of pieces I wrote on soap opera, I inadvertently left out the conclusion of some litigation in Chicago, which had been settled out of court. Lawyers for the aggrieved soap opera writer wired Ross that he would be hearing from them further in apt season. This was all amicably smoothed out when, in a subsequent piece, I apologized for my oversight and explained what had taken place out of court. But Ross continued to have a lot of fun with me about these cases. Every now and then he would break in on me, grin, and say, "How's the defendant?" or "You haven't got a leg to stand on, Thurber."

Far and away the most important legal case in the history of the magazine, and the only one that ever reached the United States Supreme Court, resulted from an article in the *New Yorker* of August 14, 1937, entitled "April Fool." It was one of the "Where Are They Now?" series, for which I did the rewrite. The series naturally dealt with once famous front page figures who had been lost to public view for considerable lengths of time. One of these was William James Sidis, son of a psychotherapist named Boris Sidis. The article, which was to become forever celebrated in legal and publishing circles everywhere because of the important precedent established by the courts, affecting all so-called "right-of-privacy" cases, began like this:

> One snowy January evening in 1910 about a hundred professors and advanced students of mathematics from Harvard University

> gathered in a lecture hall in Cambridge, Massachusetts, to listen to a speaker by the name of William James Sidis. He had never addressed an audience before, and he was abashed and a little awkward at the start. His listeners had to attend closely, for he spoke in a small voice that did not carry well, and he punctuated his talk with nervous, shrill laughter. A thatch of fair hair fell far over his forehead, and keen blue eyes peered out from what one of those present later described as a 'pixielike' face. The speaker wore black velvet knickers. He was eleven years old . . .

The astonishingly brilliant boy could have passed the entrance examinations for Harvard when he was only nine, but he was not permitted to matriculate there until he was twelve. There was a precedent for that. It was the same age at which Cotton Mather had entered Harvard. In July, 1938, the lawyers for Sidis filed suit in the Federal Court on two counts of breach of the right of privacy and on one count for libel. (The libel charge, at first held in abeyance, was decided as late as 1944, in favor of Sidis. The judgment was small, for the libel, whatever it was, had been a minor slip and not intentional denigration.) Judge Goddard in the lower court and three judges of the Circuit Court of Appeals decided in favor of the *New Yorker,* sustaining the argument of Alexander Lindey that a decision in favor of Sidis would, to summarize it briefly, result in continual and multitudinous cases of public figures suing the authors and publishers of newspapers, magazines, books and encyclopedias. The opinion of the judges could be condensed into eight words: "Once a public figure, always a public figure." More than three years after the suit was instituted, it reached the United States Supreme Court, which refused to review it, and so the long legal saga ended in favor of the *New Yorker.*

The Circuit Court had agreed with the *New Yorker* counsel on the point of law, but the three judges sympathized with Sidis. In the course of the opinion, written by Judge Clark, it was not contended that "the manner of the author" was unfriendly, but the piece as a whole was described as a merciless and ruthless exposure of a once public character who had sought privacy, or, as one lawyer expressed it to me recently, "espoused obscurity." The general tenor of the article was called "amusing and instructive" but nowhere was there any indication whatever of what I thought had stood out all through my story, implicit though it was—my sincere feeling that the piece would help to curb the great American thrusting of talented children into the glare of fame or notoriety, a procedure in so many cases disastrous to the later career and happiness of the exploited youngsters.

The great importance of the Sidis case lies in its having become the principal authority in all similar cases in which the right of privacy is claimed by a person who is, or once was, a notable public figure. It was to save the *New Yorker* from a similar suit which came about following the publication, in August, 1953, of St. Clair McKelway's "The Perils of Pearl and Olga," one of the magazine's "Annals of Crime" series. This was McKelway's lead:

> On the morning of December 31, 1946, two young women, among many other people, got on a subway train separately at the Fifty-fifth Street B.M.T. station in Brooklyn, and sat down across from each other in a car as the train moved off toward Manhattan. They had never met, had never spoken, but their lives had been drawn together and the entwinement was a sinister one. They were both working girls and more than ordinarily attractive. One of them was tall, with pale, clear skin and large, dark eyes and shining black hair; she was twenty-eight years old, and her face, besides being beautiful, had an interesting, troubled look about it. She had noticed that the other girl was carrying a gift-wrapped package about the size of a large shoe box. It had an aperture at one end, from which protruded what looked like the lens of a camera. Without thinking much about it, she wondered idly what kind of gift was inside the package. The other girl was barely nineteen and was small and blond . . .

The young woman with the gift-wrapped box had been duped into believing that it contained an X-ray camera that might reveal stolen jewels under the clothing of the other woman. This situation had been carefully plotted by the dark lady's husband, who called himself Allen La Rue. What the box actually contained was not a camera but a sawed-off shotgun, and when it was set off on the subway platform, one of the most terrible scenes in New York police annals occurred. The dark woman lost most of one leg, later sued the city, charging negligence on the part of the police, but lost that suit. Then, when the *New Yorker* revived the story, she sued for violation of her right to privacy. The judge, personally sympathetic to the plaintiff, had to abide by the precedent established in the Sidis case.

Questions and Assignments

1. How do terms such as "dicks" and "state cops" affect the tone of "Up Popped the Devil"? Find other similar terms.

2. List as many of the metaphors and similes in this selection as you can. Which ones are clearly dead metaphors or overused clichés? Which seem particularly effective and why?

3. Thurber is a master of a lucid, entertaining style. Note, in addition to his diction and figurative language, his sentence structure. Study closely, for example, the first paragraph. What is the effect of the final phrase in the first sentence? How does he manage by punctuation to convey the progress of the detective's question in the third sentence? What is the effect of the brevity of the final sentence in the fifth paragraph? Comment on the effectiveness of other sentences.

4. Recount the legal troubles of the *New Yorker*. Is there anything in the style of the magazine which might account for some of its legal difficulties?

5. Perhaps you could write a theme in the Thurber manner recounting legal difficulties of your own or of someone you know.

6. Thurber describes two instances in which he was charged with plagiarism and explains that both charges were based on coincidence. Write a theme describing an instance in which you were charged with a wrong that you did not commit.

Inaugural Address

JOHN F. KENNEDY

We observe today not a victory of party but a celebration of freedom —symbolizing an end as well as a beginning—signifying renewal as well as change. For I have sworn before you and Almighty God the same solemn oath our forebears prescribed nearly a century and three quarters ago.

The world is very different now. For man holds in his mortal hands the power to abolish all forms of human poverty and to abolish all forms of human life. And yet the same revolutionary beliefs for which our forebears fought are still at issue around the globe—the belief that the rights of man come not from the generosity of the state but from the hand of God.

We dare not forget today that we are the heirs of that first revolution. Let the word go forth from this time and place, to friend and foe alike, that the torch has been passed to a new generation of Americans—born in this century, tempered by war, disciplined by a cold and bitter peace, proud of our ancient heritage—and unwilling to witness or permit the slow undoing of those human rights to which this nation has always been committed, and to which we are committed today.

Let every nation know, whether it wish us well or ill, that we shall pay any price, bear any burden, meet any hardship, support any friend or oppose any foe in order to assure the survival and success of liberty.

This much we pledge—and more.

To those old allies whose cultural and spiritual origins we share, we pledge the loyalty of faithful friends. United, there is little we cannot do in a host of new cooperative ventures. Divided, there is little we can do—for we dare not meet a powerful challenge at odds and split asunder.

To those new states whom we now welcome to the ranks of the free, we pledge our word that one form of colonial control shall not have passed merely to be replaced by a far more iron tyranny. We shall not always expect to find them supporting our every view. But we shall always hope to find them always strongly supporting their own freedom—and to remember that, in the past, those who foolishly sought to find power by riding on the tiger's back inevitably ended up inside.

To those peoples in the huts and villages of half the globe struggling to break the bonds of mass misery, we pledge our best efforts to help them help themselves, for whatever period is required—not because the Communists are doing it, not because we seek their votes, but because it is right. If the free society cannot help the many who are poor, it can never save the few who are rich.

To our sister republics south of our border, we offer a special pledge—to convert our good words into good deeds—in a new alliance for progress—to assist free men and free governments in casting off the chains of poverty. But this peaceful revolution of hope cannot become the prey of hostile powers. Let all our neighbors know that we shall join with them to oppose aggression or subversion anywhere in the Americas. And let every other power know that this hemisphere intends to remain the master of its own house.

To that world assembly of sovereign states, the United Nations, our last best hope in an age where the instruments of war have far out-paced the instruments of peace, we renew our pledge of support—to prevent its becoming merely a forum for invective—to strengthen its shield of the new and the weak—and to enlarge the area to which its writ may run.

Finally, to those nations who would make themselves our adversary, we offer not a pledge but a request: that both sides begin anew the quest for peace, before the dark powers of destruction unleashed by science engulf all humanity in planned or accidental self-destruction.

We dare not tempt them with weakness. For only when our arms are sufficient beyond doubt can we be certain beyond doubt that they will never be employed.

But neither can two great and powerful groups of nations take comfort from their present course—both sides overburdened by the cost of modern weapons, both rightly alarmed by the steady spread of the deadly atom, yet both racing to alter that uncertain balance of terror that stays the hand of mankind's final war.

So let us begin anew—remembering on both sides that civility is not a sign of weakness, and sincerity is always subject to proof. Let us never negotiate out of fear. But let us never fear to negotiate.

Let both sides explore what problems unite us instead of belaboring the problems that divide us.

Let both sides, for the first time, formulate serious and precise proposals for the inspection and control of arms—and bring the absolute power to destroy other nations under the absolute control of all nations.

Let both sides join to invoke the wonders of science instead of its terrors. Together let us explore the stars, conquer the deserts, eradicate disease, tap the ocean depths and encourage the arts and commerce.

Let both sides unite to heed in all corners of the earth the command of Isaiah—to "undo the heavy burdens . . . (and) let the oppressed go free."

And if a beach-head of cooperation can be made in the jungles of suspicion, let both sides join in the next task: creating, not a new balance of power, but a new world of law, where the strong are just and the weak secure and the peace preserved forever.

All this will not be finished in the first one hundred days. Nor will it be finished in the first one thousand days, nor in the life of this administration, nor even, perhaps, in our lifetime on this planet. But let us begin.

In your hands, my fellow citizens, more than in mine, will rest the final success or failure of our course. Since this country was founded, each generation has been summoned to give testimony to its national loyalty. The graves of young Americans who answered that call encircle the globe.

Now the trumpet summons us again—not as a call to bear arms, though arms we need—not as a call to battle, though embattled we are—but a call to bear the burden of a long twilight struggle, year in and year out, "rejoicing in hope, patient in tribulation"—a struggle against the common enemies of man: tyranny, poverty, disease and war itself.

Can we forge against these enemies a grand and global alliance, north and south, east and west, that can assure a more fruitful life for all mankind? Will you join in that historic effort?

In the long history of the world, only a few generations have been granted the role of defending freedom in its hour of maximum danger. I do not shrink from this responsibility—I welcome it. I do not believe that any of us would exchange places with any other people or any other generation. The energy, the faith and the devotion which we bring to this endeavor will light our country and all who serve it—and the glow from that fire can truly light the world.

And so, my fellow Americans: Ask not what your country will do for you—ask what you can do for your country.

My fellow citizens of the world: Ask not what America will do for you, but what together we can do for the freedom of man.

Finally, whether you are citizens of America or of the world, ask of us the same high standards of strength and sacrifice that we shall ask of you. With a good conscience our only sure reward, with history the final judge of our deeds, let us go forth to lead the land we love, asking His blessing and His help, but knowing that here on earth God's work must truly be our own.

Questions and Assignments

1. Make a list of the figurative language in President Kennedy's speech. Are all the metaphorical usages equally expressive? Which seem most effective, which least? Try translating figurative expressions into literal language and comment on the effectiveness of the latter.

2. In attempting to express the faiths and aspirations of a nation—or perhaps of many nations—Kennedy obviously had to solve a major problem in tone. To what extent did his use of figurative language help? What elements of heritage and general belief does Kennedy appeal to? Note, for example, the many implicit and explicit references to the days of the American Revolution in the first few paragraphs.

3. Perhaps the most obvious stylistic feature of this selection is the way Kennedy sought to make himself immediately understood. Note, for instance, the many devices of antithesis, parallelism, climax, and repetition. Find examples of these devices and comment on their effectiveness.

4. This speech set forth the major goals of our nation at a crucial period in history. What were those goals? How successful have we been in carrying out these

intentions? Write a theme discussing the successes or failures of the aspirations outlined in this speech.

5. Do you agree or disagree with the ideas and plans set forth in this speech? Write a theme expressing what you feel would be an improved, or more suitable, program.

A Visit to Grandpa's

DYLAN THOMAS

Dylan Thomas was an important modern British poet who died in 1953. He also wrote numerous short stories, notable especially for their imagination and figurative language.

In the middle of the night I woke from a dream full of whips and lariats as long as serpents, and runaway coaches on mountain passes, and wide, windy gallops over cactus fields, and I heard the old man in the next room crying, "Gee-up!" and "Whoa!" and trotting his tongue on the roof of his mouth.

It was the first time I had stayed in grandpa's house. The floorboards had squeaked like mice as I climbed into bed, and the mice between the walls had creaked like wood as though another visitor was walking on them. It was a mild summer night, but curtains had flapped and branches beaten against the window. I had pulled the sheets over my head, and soon was roaring and riding in a book.

"Whoa there, my beauties!" cried grandpa. His voice sounded very young and loud, and his tongue had powerful hooves, and he made his bedroom into a great meadow. I thought I would see if he was ill, or had set his bed-clothes on fire, for my mother had said that he lit his pipe under the blankets, and had warned me to run to his help if I smelt smoke in the night. I went on tiptoe through the darkness to his bedroom door, brushing against the furniture and upsetting a candlestick with a thump. When I saw there was a light in the room I felt frightened, and as I opened the door I heard grandpa shout, "Gee-up!" as loudly as a bull with a megaphone.

He was sitting straight up in bed and rocking from side to side as though the bed were on a rough road; the knotted edges of the counterpane were his reins; his invisible horses stood in a shadow beyond the bedside candle. Over a white flannel nightshirt he was wearing a red waistcoat with walnut-sized brass buttons. The over-filled bowl of his pipe smouldered among his whiskers like a little, burning hayrick on a stick. At the sight of me, his hands dropped from the reins and lay blue and quiet, the bed stopped still on a level road, he muffled his tongue into silence, and the horses drew softly up.

"Is there anything the matter, grandpa?" I asked, though the clothes were not on fire. His face in the candlelight looked like a ragged quilt pinned upright on the black air and patched all over with goat-beards.

He stared at me mildly. Then he blew down his pipe, scattering the sparks and making a high, wet dog-whistle of the stem, and shouted: "Ask no questions."

After a pause, he said slyly: "Do you ever have nightmares, boy?"

I said: "No."

"Oh, yes, you do," he said.

I said I was woken by a voice that was shouting to horses.

"What did I tell you?" he said. "You eat too much. Who ever heard of horses in a bedroom?"

He fumbled under his pillow, brought out a small, tinkling bag, and carefully untied its strings. He put a sovereign in my hand, and said "Buy a cake." I thanked him and wished him good night.

As I closed my bedroom door, I heard his voice crying loudly and gaily, "Gee-up! gee-up!" and the rocking of the travelling bed.

In the morning I woke from a dream of fiery horses on a plain that was littered with furniture, and of large, cloudy men who rode six horses at a time and whipped them with burning bed-clothes. Grandpa was at breakfast, dressed in deep black. After breakfast he said, "There was a terrible loud wind last night," and sat in his arm-chair by the hearth to make clay balls for the fire. Later in the morning he took me for a walk, through Johnstown village and into the fields on the Llanstephan road.

A man with a whippet said, "There's a nice morning, Mr Thomas," and when he had gone, leanly as his dog, into the short-treed green wood he should not have entered because of the notices, grandpa said: "There, do you hear what he called you? Mister!"

We passed by small cottages, and all the men who leant on the gates congratulated grandpa on the fine morning. We passed through the wood full of pigeons, and their wings broke the branches as they rushed to the tops of the trees. Among the soft, contented voices and the loud, timid flying, grandpa said, like a man calling across a field: "If you heard those old birds in the night, you'd wake me up and say there were horses in the trees."

We walked back slowly, for he was tired, and the lean man stalked out of the forbidden wood with a rabbit held as gently over his arm as a girl's arm in a warm sleeve.

On the last day but one of my visit I was taken to Llanstephan in a governess cart pulled by a short, weak pony. Grandpa might have been driving a bison, so tightly he held the reins, so ferociously cracked the long whip, so blasphemously shouted warning to boys who played in the road, so stoutly stood with his gaitered legs apart and cursed the demon strength and wilfulness of his tottering pony.

"Look out, boy!" he cried when we came to each corner, and pulled and tugged and jerked and sweated and waved his whip like a rubber sword. And when the pony had crept miserably round each corner, grandpa turned to me with a sighing smile: "We weathered that one, boy."

When we came to Llanstephan village at the top of the hill, he left the cart by the Edwinsford Arms and patted the pony's muzzle and gave it sugar, saying: "You're a weak little pony, Jim, to pull big men like us."

He had strong beer and I had lemonade, and he paid Mrs Edwinsford with a sovereign out of the tinkling bag; she inquired after his health, and he said that Llangadock was better for the tubes. We went to look at the churchyard and the sea, and sat in the wood called the Sticks, and stood on the concert platform in the middle of the wood where visitors sang on midsummer nights and, year by year, the innocent of the village was elected mayor. Grandpa paused at the churchyard and pointed over the iron gate at the angelic headstones and the poor wooden crosses. "There's no sense in lying there," he said.

We journeyed back furiously: Jim was a bison again.

I woke late on my last morning, out of dreams where the Llanstephan sea carried bright sailing-boats as long as liners; and heavenly choirs in the Sticks, dressed in bards' robes and brass-buttoned waistcoats, sang in a strange Welsh to the departing sailors. Grandpa was not at breakfast; he rose early. I walked in the fields with a new sling, and shot at the Towy gulls and the rooks in the parsonage trees. A warm wind blew from the summer points of the weather; a morning mist climbed from the ground and floated among the trees and hid the noisy birds; in the mist and the wind my pebbles flew lightly up like hailstones in a world on its head. The morning passed without a bird falling.

I broke my sling and returned for the midday meal through the parson's orchard. Once, grandpa told me, the parson had bought three ducks at Carmarthen Fair and made a pond for them in the centre of the garden; but they waddled to the gutter under the crumbling doorsteps of the house, and swam and quacked there. When I reached the end of the orchard path, I looked through a hole in the hedge and saw that the parson had made a tunnel through the rockery that was between the gutter and the pond and had set up a notice in plain writing: "This way to the pond."

The ducks were still swimming under the steps.

Grandpa was not in the cottage. I went into the garden, but grandpa was not staring at the fruit-trees. I called across to a man who leant on a spade in the field beyond the garden hedge: "Have you seen my grandpa this morning?"

He did not stop digging, and answered over his shoulder: "I seen him in his fancy waistcoat."

Griff, the barber, lived in the next cottage. I called to him through the open door: "Mr Griff, have you seen my grandpa?"

The barber came out in his shirtsleeves.

I said: "He's wearing his best waistcoat." I did not know if it was important, but grandpa wore his waistcoat only in the night.

"Has grandpa been to Llanstephan?" asked Mr Griff anxiously.

"We went there yesterday in a little trap," I said.

He hurried indoors and I heard him talking in Welsh, and he came out again with his white coat on, and he carried a striped and coloured walking-stick. He strode down the village street and I ran by his side.

When we stopped at the tailor's shop, he cried out, "Dan!" and Dan Tailor stepped from his window where he sat like an Indian priest but wearing a derby hat. "Dai Thomas has got his waistcoat on," said Mr Griff, "and he's been to Llanstephan."

As Dan Tailor searched for his overcoat, Mr Griff was striding on. "Will Evans," he called outside the carpenter's shop, "Dai Thomas has been to Llanstephan, and he's got his waistcoat on."

"I'll tell Morgan now," said the carpenter's wife out of the hammering, sawing darkness of the shop.

We called at the butcher's shop and Mr Price's house, and Mr Griff repeated his message like a town crier.

We gathered together in Johnstown square. Dan Tailor had his bicycle, Mr Price his pony-trap. Mr Griff, the butcher, Morgan Carpenter, and I climbed into the shaking trap, and we trotted off towards Carmarthen town. The tailor led the way, ringing his bell as though there were a fire or a robbery, and an old woman by the gate of a cottage at the end of the street ran inside like a pelted hen. Another woman waved a bright handkerchief.

"Where are we going?" I asked.

Grandpa's neighbours were as solemn as old men with black hats and jackets on the outskirts of a fair. Mr Griff shook his head and mourned: "I didn't expect this again from Dai Thomas."

"Not after last time," said Mr Price sadly.

We trotted on, we crept up Constitution Hill, we rattled down into Lammas Street, and the tailor still rang his bell and a dog ran, squealing, in front of his wheels. As we clip-clopped over the cobbles that led down to the Towy bridge, I remembered grandpa's nightly noisy journeys that rocked the bed and shook the walls, and I saw his gay waistcoat in a vision and his patchwork head tufted and smiling in the candlelight. The tailor before us turned round on his saddle, his bicycle wobbled and skidded. "I see Dai Thomas!" he cried.

The trap rattled on to the bridge, and I saw grandpa there; the buttons of his waistcoat shone in the sun, he wore his tight, black Sunday trousers and a tall, dusty hat I had seen in a cupboard in the attic, and he carried an ancient bag. He bowed to us. "Good morning, Mr Price," he said, "and Mr Griff and Mr Morgan and Mr Evans." To me, he said "Good morning, boy."

Mr Griff pointed his coloured stick at him.

"And what do you think you are doing on Carmarthen bridge in the middle of the afternoon," he said sternly, "with your best waistcoat and your old hat?"

Grandpa did not answer, but inclined his face to the river wind, so that his beard was set dancing and wagging as though he talked, and watched the coracle men move, like turtles, on the shore.

Mr Griff raised his stunted barber's pole. "And where do you think you are going," he said, "with your old black bag?"

Grandpa said: "I am going to Llangadock to be buried." And he watched the coracle shells slip into the water lightly, and the gulls complain over the fish-filled water as bitterly as Mr Price complained:

"But you aren't dead yet, Dai Thomas."

For a moment grandpa reflected, then: "There's no sense in lying dead in Llanstephan," he said. "The ground is comfy in Llangadock; you can twitch your legs without putting them in the sea."

His neighbours moved close to him. They said: "You aren't dead, Mr Thomas."

"How can you be buried, then?"

"Nobody's going to bury you in Llanstephan."

"Come on home, Mr Thomas."

"There's strong beer for tea."

"And cake."

But grandpa stood firmly on the bridge, and clutched his bag to his side, and stared at the flowing river and the sky, like a prophet who has no doubt.

Questions and Assignments

1. Give an account of the highly imaginative quality of this story. What is the grandfather's condition?

2. Thomas is famous for his similes, such as "the floorboards had squeaked like mice," and for his metaphors, such as "his tongue had powerful hooves, and he made his bedroom into a great meadow." Find at least half a dozen more of each of these figures of speech and discuss their significance for the style and plot of the story.

3. What sort of relationship exists between the grandfather and the boy? How do you know? How old do you think the boy is? What part do these things play in the story: horses, the sea, Llanstephan, the waistcoat?

An Exercise in Figurative Language. Re-examine the wording used in several of the selections given previously in this book, and be prepared to comment on its effects in those selections. Does it add to clarity, force, and vividness? Is it original? Does it fit in naturally and match with the tone of the selection, or is it farfetched, strained, and out of place? (A few suggestions: criticize the following: "the first surge of yelling had overshot the eastern ridge," "like a short flapping blanket," "to run the heart completely out of them" in "Adam Helmer's Run"; "half-closed her eyes like a movie star" in "Mick Kelly Dresses"; "the pen originates the thought," "the author wraps his meaning in mystery" in "Lucidity"; "occasionally rides," "zero at the bone" in "A

Narrow Fellow in the Grass"; "king of the snakes" from "The World's Most Dangerous Snake"; "a coal-black current," "wrapped . . . as in a mantle" in "Liaison with a Black Snake"; "lassitude flowed round her," "a writhing dimness," "like a hurt animal" in "The Death of Leora.")

There are obvious dangers in using figurative language. You may find yourself trying an inappropriate figure. You may write something like "we were burning with eagerness to try our skis on the newly fallen snow." You may try the figurative in a situation in which your reader will naturally expect the literal. Once a girl wrote the following in a theme: "later that month I did fall through the ice into four feet of water, but this did not dampen my enthusiasm." You may mix figures, that is, use two figures that do not fit together, like "the royal British lion will never shrink back into its shell." We like to remember this one: "Every student has a spark of genius which the kindly instructor will carefully water." But if you think about what you are writing, and if you follow the advice of this book and keep revising, you will probably eliminate most of these inept uses of figurative language.

Perhaps you will find it enjoyable to try some original similes and metaphors. Evaluate the effectiveness of some of these examples. What is the sound of an ambulance siren like, and what does it do? Is it in itself a quivering cry for help, a scissors whose thrusts rip the night silence, a banshee portending death, a shrill slap that pushes other vehicles aside, a hemorrhage of sound, the whine of a speeding missile, the tantrum of the spoiled child of traffic, a tarantella in the midst of an orderly waltz, a hyena mockery of hope, a shrapnel hail of sound, a mad violence in a symphony, a strident defiance of death and injury? What is the coming of dusk—the rising tide of night, a soft messenger of coming sleep and rest, an ascendancy of powers of darkness, the dropping of a soft veil, an art critic that bans the lurid and permits only the pastel, the fall of the theatre curtain on the day's act, a gray animal encircling the city, the first whiff of an anaesthetic? What is the sun? One can call it a ball of fire; one can liken it to great lamps and candles. Edna St. Vincent Millay said that it was a bucketful of gold. The ancients thought it might be a divinity's chariot wheeling through the heavens. Primitives have seen in it a great dragon encircling the world. It has been called the eye of day. What else is it? A blast furnace in continuous operation, a mammoth atomic laboratory, the anchor for the planets, an inexorable father that keeps potentially rebellious offspring in order, a kindly mother who gives us all our food and energy, an angry blister on the skin of heaven, a fat orange blimp, an envelope of flaming gas? What is suspicion within one's mind of friend or partner or wife? A cancer that eats at one's insides, an acid etching malevolence in the soul, an unlubricated bearing that grinds, a flaw in a mirror of security, a rank weed in a garden growth of thought, a venomous snake in a herbarium, a treacherous shoal calling for careful piloting, a strident note in a sonata, an ulcer? What is it like to have to extract the main thoughts from a wordy and poorly written book when there is to be a test on that book tomorrow? Swimming in crude oil, walking through hardening concrete, picking a few good coals from an endless run of slate and shale, trying to go through a cave without a light, trying to drive at sixty in low gear, having to stop continually to wipe spider webs of words away as one tries to go through the woods? Try this sort of thing for yourself with the first five things, persons, emotions, or situations that you can think of.

A Paragraph Rewritten. The following selection recounts one experience involving writing labeled as jargon. John Dewey was for many years Professor of Philosophy at Columbia University. He exerted a powerful influence on American thought, particularly on education. Joseph Warren Beach was a Professor of English Literature and wrote a number of critical studies of literature.

(Dewey's Original Paragraph)[1]

> But no matter how much men in authority have turned moral rules into an agency of class supremacy, any theory which attributes the origin of rule to deliberate design is false. To take advantage of conditions after they have come into existence is one thing: to create them for the sake of an advantage to accrue is quite another thing.

[1] From *Human Nature and Conduct* by John Dewey. Reprinted by permission of Holt, Rinehart and Winston, Inc.

We must go back to the bare fact of social division into superior and inferior. To say that accident produced social conditions is to perceive that they were not produced by intelligence. Lack of understanding of human nature is the primary cause of disregard of it. Lack of insight always ends in despising or else unreasoned admiration. When men had no scientific knowledge of physical nature they either passively submitted to it or sought to control it magically. What cannot be understood cannot be managed intelligently. It has to be forced into subjection from without. The opaqueness of human nature to reason is equivalent to a belief in its intrinsic irregularity. Hence a decline in the authority of social oligarchy was accompanied by a rise of scientific interest in human nature. This means that the make-up and working of human forces affords a basis for moral ideas and ideals. Our science of human nature in comparison with physical sciences is rudimentary, and morals which are concerned with the health, efficiency and happiness of a development of human nature are correspondingly elementary. These pages are a discussion of some phases of the ethical change involved in positive respect for human nature when the latter is associated with scientific knowledge.

(Dewey's Paragraph Rewritten by Beach)[1]

But no matter how much men in authority have turned moral rules into an agency of class supremacy, *it would be a mistake to suppose that these rules were created originally with the* deliberate design *of using them for this purpose.* It is one thing to take advantage of conditions after they have come into existence; it is quite another thing to create them for the sake of an advantage to accrue. *To understand a system of morals,* we must go back to the division into classes—into superior and inferior. *We shall find that social conditions grew up spontaneously, and that is as much as to say that they were not the product of deliberate thought. Just the contrary, they were the product of a want of intelligence in interpreting human nature. Human nature was disregarded in framing moral rules because it was not understood.* Lack of insight *into anything* leads to its being despised or else admired unreasonably. *It is so with* physical nature; when men had no knowledge of it, they either

[1] Reprinted from *The Outlook for American Prose* by Joseph Warren Beach by permission of the University of Chicago Press. Copyright 1926 by the University of Chicago.

passively submitted to it or sought to control it magically. What cannot be understood cannot be managed intelligently. It has to be forced into subjection from without. *In the case of* human nature, *the difficulty of understanding it leads to the assumption that it is essentially arbitrary in its action, only to be controlled from without. This is the assumption of all social oligarchy, and it is an assumption which social oligarchy finds it to its advantage to maintain. And this in turn prevents the growth of any scientific study of human nature. But* a decline in the authority of social oligarchy is *naturally* accompanied by the rise of *that* scientific interest in human nature *to which social oligarchy has been opposed. The scientific assumption is that the principles of morality should be sought in the very constitution of human nature, and based on a study of* the make-up and *actual* working of human forces. *It must be acknowledged that,* in comparison with the physical sciences, our science of human nature is rudimentary, and morals—*which are concerned with the development of human nature into something* healthful, efficient and happy—are correspondingly elementary. These pages *will be taken up with* a discussion of some phases of the ethical change involved in *that* respect for human nature *which results from its being studied in connection* with scientific knowledge *in general.*

(Beach's Critique)[1]

It would be too long an undertaking to explain the necessity of the several dozen changes made in order that the course of this thought may be clear to the reader, if indeed I have succeeded in making it clear. But it would be worth our while to analyze, through several sentences, the process of trial and error, of guess and reconstruction, in which the reader must at every point engage in order to make any connected sense. Let us begin with the sentence a little below the middle of the passage. "The opaqueness of human nature to reason is equivalent to a belief in its intrinsic irregularity." The first thing the reader does instinctively is to get rid of the words "equivalent to." No fact about human nature is equivalent to any belief about it. Facts are one thing, beliefs another. The general

[1] Reprinted from *The Outlook for American Prose* by Joseph Warren Beach by permission of the University of Chicago Press. Copyright 1926 by the University of Chicago.

connection makes the reader understand that the author means to say, "The opaqueness of human nature to reason leads to a belief in its intrinsic irregularity." The reader then approaches the phrase, "the opaqueness of human nature to reason." He first translates the figurative phrase into one more consistent with English idiom, and has, "the imperviousness of human nature to reason." He supposes it to mean the fact that human nature is dense and irrational, that reason cannot penetrate into it. And so he reads, for simplification: "The irrationality of human nature leads to a belief in its intrinsic irregularity." But that, in the particular connection, makes no sense, and the reader tries again. He takes his cue from the statement two sentences back that what cannot be understood cannot be managed intelligently. Perhaps the author means, not the imperviousness of human nature to reason in the abstract, the irrationality of human nature, but its imperviousness to the understanding of the observer—the difficulty of understanding it. So he tries that. "The difficulty of understanding human nature leads to a belief in its intrinsic irregularity." That does make sense in the connection, providing one develops a little the connotations of the word "irregularity." A thing that is irregular is arbitrary in its action, not to be controlled by reference to its own laws, but only to be forced into subjection from without. So the reader puts the sentence into a form that will suggest that connection, and he proceeds to the following sentence: "The difficulty of understanding human nature leads to an assumption that it is essentially irregular, or arbitrary, in its action. Hence a decline in the authority of social oligarchy was accompanied by a rise of scientific interest in human nature."

Here the reader is plunged into very great difficulties by the use of the logical connective "hence." He does not yet know that Mr. Dewey is particularly cavalier in the use of just this category of words which imply the strictest of logical bonds—that when he uses "in short" very likely he is not summing up the points already made but proceeding to add a new one; that when he says "therefore" he may be meaning "on the other hand." And so that reader takes the word "hence" in its strict sense, and tries to understand how it can be that "since the difficulty of understanding human nature leads to the assumption that it is arbitrary in its action, therefore the decline in the authority of social oligarchy was accompanied by a rise of scientific interest in human nature." He understands the contention that it is the social oligarchs who fail to understand human nature and who, assuming that it is arbitrary in its action, find that they can control it only by forcing it into subjection from without. He can also understand how a rise in scientific interest in human nature would result in a better understanding of it and would consequently undermine the authority of the social oligarchs. But he cannot see that the decline in the authority of the oligarchs would be accompanied by a spontaneous rise of scientific interest in human nature. It must be that some step in the chain of reasoning has been omitted. Perhaps Mr. Dewey means to say that the social oligarchs, finding it to their personal advantage to maintain the supposition that human nature is essentially arbitrary, instinctively discourage the rise of scientific interest in human nature for fear that it will undermine their prestige, and that consequently the rise of scientific interest in human nature is delayed until, through other causes, their authority begins to decline. In that case the missing link will have to be supplied by the reader.

The difficulty of understanding human nature leads to the assumption that it is essentially arbitrary in its action, only to be controlled by being forced into subjection from without. This is the assumption of all social oligarchy, and it is an assumption which social oligarchy finds it to its own advantage to maintain. And this in turn prevents the growth of any scientific study of human nature. But the decline in the authority of social oligarchy was naturally accompanied by the rise of that scientific interest in human nature to which the social oligarchy had been opposed.

A Student Theme Rewritten

The Anxious Generation

(Original Student Theme)

I am a member of the anxious generation; the kids for whom there is no room, the products of a moment of alleviation, the post war babies. Most of us are in our late teenage years, studying and waiting for society to find a place for us. We wonder if we will ever see a place other than a battlefield or a grave. While our time should be spent learning of the nature of things and thought, we spend our energies in the tensions of indecision. Our thoughts checked as for fear of insurrection. We are ready to begin control of our era but our parents hold tightly still. Previous generations mold the following ones. Our parents can't find the fairy-tale ending to theirs and have left with anxieties for success before we've begun.

Previous generation was assimilated into society in their early teens and assumed positions which were created especially for them. They had the glory, the spoils of war. There were many openings in business, science, and the arts. Many had died. There was no bitter competition. Many knew there was a place for them and worked only as much as necessary to get that position.

We of the anxious generation must create our own futures. We not only must fabricate an occupation but study for that life's work. We are presented with overwhelming problems of science and told to find answers. We are all told such. There is no room elsewhere but the exploration of the rest of the universe should keep us busy.

We of this generation are at the point where we don't need an explanation for the world. We want to have that "go of it" before we become the adult-children of a senile society. Our parents are delaying too long before relinquishing the opportunities to us. We are being held to teenage thoughts and living. We are physically ready and our maturity is only "unripe" from this check. We are the old children of the anxious generation.

Ideas in this theme are often obscured by faulty diction. Although there are numerous weaknesses in this theme, the writer should concentrate initially on word choices, jargon and improper development of root metaphors. Regarding this final point: notice the phrase (in the fifth sentence from the end) "go of it." The confusion caused by this phrase is traceable to the writer's failure to express clearly the metaphor implied in these words. Observe the student's attempt to improve his language in his rewritten version. How successful is he?

The Anxious Generation
(Rewritten Student Theme)

The generation of which I write and in which I include myself, has been more considered in back yard debates, daily scandal sheets, and state and national communication systems than any other. We have even reached that enviable extreme in literature where by a single phrase we are recognized among all others in history. We are the "post war babies"—products of a moment of alleviation, the first really free Americans, the anxious generation.

The anxiety associated with this generation is of the type bred by restraint. Paradoxical though it may seem, we are being restrained by understanding. Harold Taylor, in his essay "The Unillusioned Generation," says of the beat generation that they lacked "a strong line of parental authority." Most of us too receive approval for things our parents would never have thought of mentioning in their homes. Unlimited car privileges, unchaperoned parties, skiing weekends, etc. We even choose our own schools and companions. We may do as we desire as long as we don't wish to be adults.

Mr. Taylor also sketches the cause of anxiety in our too understood generation clearly stating that "in such an atmosphere of acceptance and freedom from restriction, young people feel a deep emotional fatigue from continually being forced to make their own decisions before they have had enough experience to feel able to do so." While Taylor here analyzes the beats, the same is applicable to us. Our parents have given us these freedoms but have not yet mentioned the roles we should now be assuming as young adults in society.

Our parents were assimilated into society early in life and assumed the many available positions in most fields—some created especially for them. Such are the spoils of war. To some extent in the aftermath of war there is a man shortage and competition is less bitter. They were a trustworthy lot, our national defenders, and they took their positions with a zeal derived from the confidence of others.

The "understanding" we get from our parents is a type of confidence, yet we don't have that zeal. Perhaps the difference lies in the fact that our parents were not forced to rule themselves until they were experienced. When they were ready, though at a young age, immediate success reinforced their aspirations. One may only read any daily newspaper today to learn of the poor decisions of immature, and inexperienced minds.

Those who appear in headlines, of course, are the small minority. Actually, all is not lost for us though to the psychologist we have passed the formative stage. Unlike many of our parents, we are receiving this experience in the form of extensive education. They have not given us the benefit of their experiences, so we search on our own impetus. Our anxiety increases as we grow older yet we are not accepted as adults. Our parents are desperately clinging to their world. If they wonder why we are not interested in following their work they might try to remember how many times they discussed it with us; how many times they showed other than financial care for it.

As some of us begin having babies under our parents' roofs, it should be evident that we have been held too long to the high school-bannered room at home. Dad looks for the slot in the curtain that he might leave the stage but finds more folds there now than when he came out. He didn't find the world this way and perhaps is ashamed to leave it so to the offspring he's been trying to save from the cruel world he grew up in. Of such "favors" we have had more than enough.

If our parents don't start retiring, in spirit at least, we shall be forced to mold our futures in a unique way. We shall have to think of a new type of occupation (the conventional ones are filled by our dads) and then try to prepare for it. Just how it will be possible for all of us to find so many now inexistent positions . . .

This generation is at the point where we don't need or want an explanation for the world. We need to have that "go of it" before we become the adult-children of a senile society. Our parents are delaying too long before relinquishing the opportunities to us. We are being held to teenage living though our thoughts and minds are adult. We have made too many short term decisions and have had our share of trials. We, the senescent youth of the anxious generation are ready. How long must we wait?

A Poem Rewritten by Robert Frost

In White (1912)

A dented spider like a snow drop white
On a white Heal-all, holding up a moth
Like a white piece of lifeless satin cloth—
Saw ever curious eye so strange a sight?—
Portent in little, assorted death and blight
Like the ingredients of a witches' broth?—
The beady spider, the flower like a froth,
And the moth carried like a paper kite.

What had that flower to do with being white,
The blue prunella every child's delight.
What brought the kindred spider to that height?
(Make me no thesis of the miller's plight.)
What but design of darkness and of night?
Design, design! Do I use the word aright?

Design (1936)

I found a dimpled spider, fat and white,
On a white heal-all, holding up a moth
Like a white piece of rigid satin cloth—
Assorted characters of death and blight
Mixed ready to begin the morning right,
Like the ingredients of a witches' broth—
A snow-drop spider, a flower like a froth,
And dead wings carried like a paper kite.

What had that flower to do with being white,
The wayside blue and innocent heal-all?
What brought the kindred spider to that height,

Then steered the white moth thither in the night?
What but design of darkness to appall?—
If design govern in a thing so small.

A CHECKLIST FOR REWRITING. The main principle to keep in mind about language as you rewrite is the principle underlying this entire section—language should be straightforward but not platitudinous. We achieve clarity by precision in diction and sentence pattern and by adding whatever explanatory details are necessary. We avoid the trite and platitudinous by making sure we are saying something of importance and by saying it in a forceful style. A forceful style is a blend of so many diverse factors that it cannot be prescribed or formulated by any combination of *do's* and *don'ts*. Without by any means trying to summarize everything we have already said about language, and indirectly about style, we would, however, have you keep in mind five points about language. Four of these points are rather simply stated, the fifth requires copious and, to some extent, involved illustration.

1. Try to find the most appropriate synonym, the exact one for your purposes.

2. Given a choice, try to be specific, try to proceed along an abstraction scale toward the more specific rather than toward the more general.

3. Try to determine, as closely as you can, the tone of a word when you are thinking of using it; try to determine whether it has an appropriate suggestion over and above its specific denotation.

4. Try to evolve appropriate similes and metaphors—and these appropriate figures will show a similarity between things not commonly compared or thought of as similar; they will show a concentration of your attention on one, two, or three specific characteristics of very unlike things.Throughout these four maxims, the specific is stressed.

5. Vary your sentence patterns. Nothing can be more obvious than that after picking appropriate words and figures you frame them in sentences. Most of the time your sentences should accord with the standard sentence patterns explained on pp. 97-99. About sentences and sentence patterns two main things need to be said:

First, aim at variety in length and in type. Generally you do not have to be concerned about how short or how long a sentence should be. A sentence may be composed of only one or two words; it may be composed of one or two hundred. But try to show variety in sentence length. If sentence one is seventeen words in length, sentence two is nineteen, and sentence three is sixteen, experiment with using only seven in sentence four or with using forty-two. Most student writing errs, when it does in this particular, through inability or unwillingness to try longer sentences. Literature will sometimes show very effective passages composed only of short sentences. But, far from being simple, this kind of writing represents a difficult art.

Unless you are entirely sure that repetition of pattern is effective and that your reader can tell that it is conscious and intentional, try to vary sentence patterns, to use various kinds of sentences. Any accidental repetition is likely to be monotonous and unpleasant:

> When we discussed the matter, we decided that somebody ought to visit the cabin. After we talked about it further, we thought that Joe and Bob should go. When we suggested this to Joe, he said that he couldn't make the trip. When we asked Carl, he consented to go in Joe's place. When Bob tried to start his car, he found that the battery was dead. When he told us that, we . . .

> There were many things to be repaired and renovated about the old house. The curbing would need repairs and the cement walk was cracked and uneven. The fence had several holes in it and the gates were sagging on their hinges. The lawn was overgrown with weeds and the trees badly needed trimming. The front porch steps were old and unsafe and several boards on the porch needed to be replaced. The plaster was badly cracked in the front hall and the woodwork needed repainting.

At all costs try to avoid the monotonous repetition of sentence patterns illustrated by the sentences in these paragraphs.

Second, you can effectively vary from the word order illustrated in the explanation of the main sentence patterns on pp. 97-99. It is most important to say that you can do so only very, very occasionally. Variations in the order of sentence parts are, generally speaking, effective only if they occur in not more than one sentence out of fifty or a hundred or five hundred. Otherwise they are likely to become unpleasant and ineffective stylistic mannerisms. A physician may on occasion prescribe strychnine or digitalis or even trinitroglycerine, but you will realize at once that he will do so only in very slight quantities. Variations in order away from established patterns are similar; very bad results follow if they are overused.

What are some variations possible for occasional use? The following discussion is incomplete; it is designed merely to be suggestive rather than comprehensive:

A. Subject—verb (S—V) *The men hooted.* Without modifiers accompanying the verb it is hard to vary this pattern. When the verb form is composed of more than one word, one can do so:

He swore that he would escape from the prison camp. And escape he did.

He could becloud the facts, he could suggest an incorrect interpretation, he could equivocate. But lie he could not.

As is indicated, this sort of arrangement is unlikely in an introductory sentence; it is likely only in a sentence that serves as a sequal to one preceding.

B. Subject—verb—object (S—V—O) *Casey swung his bat.* One way to vary this pattern is to put the object first—to adopt an O—S—V order:

His rifle Adam Helmer threw into the stream.

A fine picture he painted of the gathering storm.

This man we picked as our leader.

This variation is more likely to occur in a sequel sentence than in an introductory one. If you ever use it, you must notice that you must be sure that your reader interprets it as a full sentence and that he cannot interpret it as a sentence fragment, a noun modified by a dependent clause without a relative pronoun. Notice that the words "the woman I had met before" can be interpreted both as "I had met the woman before" and "the woman whom (or *that*) I had met before . . ."

C. Subject—verb—predicate nominative (S—V—PN) *He became*

president. Sentences of this kind can show two variations in order, although not every single sentence can be varied in both ways. We can say: *He said that he would become president. And president he became.* This last sentence of course shows PN—S—V order. We can often, if we wish to, adopt a PN—V—S order, with the actual predicate nominative first:

A brave man was Captain Wilkins.

A silly fool was she.

Like others previously mentioned, this variation is likely to be found only in following sentences, sequel sentences, echo sentences. We have, then, three possible arrangements.

This was a startling discovery.

A startling discovery this was.

A startling discovery was this.

D. Subject—verb—predicate adjective (S—V—PA) *She grew faint.* Foregoing discussions have probably suggested variations in this pattern:

He was wise to save his money.

Wise was he to save his money.

Wise he was to save his money.

The defenders were brave.

Brave the defenders were.

Brave were the defenders.

E. Subject—verb—adverbial modifier (S—V—AM) *The foremen work Saturdays.* In English there is often a considerable amount of freedom in the placing of adverbial units. We can write either "the flood waters rapidly rose" or "the flood waters rose rapidly." If we transpose the adverbial modifier to the beginning of the sentence we can have two other arrangements:

Rapidly the flood waters rose.

Rapidly rose the flood waters.

We can then have the following:

The lions roared savagely.

The lions savagely roared.

Savagely the lions roared.

Savagely roared the lions.

F. Subject—verb—indirect object—object (S—V—IO—O) *My father gave me the news.* This pattern is usually varied by changing the indirect object to being the object of a preposition, usually *to,* sometimes *for,* and putting the resulting prepositional phrase at the end of the sentence:

They awarded him the medal.

They awarded the medal to him.

My sister baked me a birthday cake.

My sister baked a birthday cake for me.

Other variations from the pattern are noticeably uncommon. One *could* say "him they awarded the medal," but this is rare.

G. Subject—verb—object—objective complement (S—V—O—OC) *They made Jennings chairman.* Occasionaly this pattern is varied by putting the direct object first: Jennings they made chairman. Other arrangements—like "chairman they made Jennings" or "Jennings made they chairman"—are so uncommon that they are implausible or impossible.

H. Expletive—verb—subject (Ex—V—S) *There was a bus.* This kind of sentence needs a little explanation. There is a strong tendency on the part of many students to feel that *there* is the subject. Most grammarians maintain very resolutely that *bus* is the subject (although very occasionally a grammarian may permit one to call *there* an "anticipatory subject"). There is a strong tendency on the part of many other students to call *there* an adverb. It is if one expands the class of adverbs until it is virtually meaningless. *There* in the sentence given has neither the meaning nor the use of *there* as a location adverb. Notice the difference between the *there*'s in "we walked down to Elkins Square; there there was a bus to Exeter." *There* in our first illustration—"there was a bus"—is a meaningless filler word. Somehow in English we show a reluctance simply to say or write: "A bus was." We prefer to start such statements with *there*. This *there* is often called an expletive.

One can vary this pattern a bit by putting the noun that is really the subject first and then following with *there was* or *there is*:

There was a tree near the lake shore.

A tree there was near the lake shore.

(Notice that "a tree was there near the lake shore" means something else.)

There is a reason for his silence.

A reason there is for his silence.

We can vary the order of things after *there is* and *there was*:

There was an antique silver set on the buffet.

There was on the buffet an antique silver set.

But very often it is effective to break away from the use of the expletive completely and reframe the sentence according to another pattern:

There was a ladder leaning against the barn.

A ladder was leaning against the barn.

In general, main parts of English sentences—subjects, sentence or clause verbs or main verbs or finite verbs, and objects and complements—are likely to appear in set positions. Notice, however, that many sentences lend themselves to the placement of modifiers—adjectives and adverbs (interpreting both of these terms loosely)—to different positions. There is a considerable amount of freedom in the placing of paired and coordinated adjectives, and in that of adjectives accompanied by phrases, in English sentences. Suppose we start with the following:

The brave and resolute boy stood on the burning deck.

We can also use these arrangements:

Brave and resolute, the boy stood on the burning deck.

The boy, brave and resolute, stood on the burning deck.

The boy stood on the burning deck brave and resolute.

When we have an adjective accompanied by a prepositional phrase we find that we can place the whole unit anywhere but in the position in which an adjective is most commonly placed. We can't say:

The hot with anger old man clenched his fist.

We can say either of the following:

Hot with anger, the old man clenched his fist.

The old man, hot with anger, clenched his fist.

We have similar leeway in the placement of a variety of elements called adverbial:

However, the plane did not leave on schedule.

The plane, however, did not leave on schedule.

The plane did not leave on schedule, however.

The nurse skilfully bandaged the cut.

The nurse bandaged the cut skilfully.

Skilfully the nurse bandaged the cut.

Ruth will fly with us if her father consents.

If her father consents, Ruth will fly with us.

Ruth, if her father consents, will fly with us.

Sometimes insertion of the adverbial element between subject and verb is awkward—as you may feel it to be in the last illustration. But it is impossible here to analyze the effect of each of the variations that we have listed—variations in modifier position immediately above and variations away from dominant sentence patterns before that. The important thing is that you realize the possibility of these variations. Try them. One characteristic (as C. C. Fries has pointed out) that marks writing by the unlettered is a lack of variation in sentence arrangements.

PART THREE

Beginnings

The Straightforward Beginning
The Blanket Beginning
The Feint Beginning

Endings

Middle: Developing the Ideas

Readings: Chronology

The Legends of Shakespeare's Life by Marchette Chute
The Sinking of the Bismarck by George Whalley

Readings: Classification

The Three Ages of Man by Aristotle
The Four Idols by Francis Bacon
What to Listen for in Music by Aaron Copland

Readings: Comparison and Contrast

The Middle Ages by Johan Huizinga
On Translating Homer Once More by Kenneth G. Wilson
The Working Methods of Pope and Dryden by Samuel Johnson

Readings: Analogy

The Hedgehog and the Fox by Isaiah Berlin
The Morals of Chess by Benjamin Franklin

THIS section is primarily concerned with developing ideas—with what we shall call the "middle" of the essay. But an essay must have an appropriate beginning and ending. For this reason we shall discuss beginnings and endings before turning to the more involved problems of developing the middle.

Beginnings

That first impressions are lasting is, unfortunately, all too often true. For this reason the importance of a good beginning cannot be overemphasized, for it may make the difference between success or failure in the rest of the essay. A good beginning does more than open an essay; it brings the mind of the reader into focus with the mind of the writer. Just as a good personal introduction always supplies more than the names of those being introduced, a good beginning tries to say something important, relevant, and interesting about the subject to be discussed.

There are as many different ways of beginning as there are different subjects and it is dangerous to generalize. But examples of some of the more common types may prove useful. There are three general types of openings: the straightforward, the blanket, and the feint. The straightforward approach is the statement of some important fact, or of the writer's first point, or of the main idea of the essay. The blanket approach seeks to cover, or outline, the main points the essay will deal with. The feint beginning is an attempt to arrest the reader's attention with some startling but relevant thought.

THE STRAIGHTFORWARD BEGINNING. One of the simplest ways to begin an essay is to express simply and clearly the most important idea to be discussed. Emerson, in an essay on farming, begins with the clear idea that underlies his attitude toward the subject, "The glory of the farmer is that, in the division of labors, it is his part to create."

Adlai Stevenson's essay on patriotism (p. 301) presents the main idea both in the title and in the two opening sentences: "It is not easy to be a patriot these days—not because it is difficult to love one's country. The difficulty lies with loving one's country in the right way."

In presenting his main idea a writer may also indicate how his idea differs from the ideas of others on the same subject. Thus Schopenhauer begins his essay "On Noise," "Kant wrote a treatise on the Vital Powers. I should prefer to write a dirge for them. The superabundant display of vitality, which takes the form of knocking, hammering, and tumbling things about, has proved a daily torment to me all my life long."

Marya Mannes, in a satirical essay on the lack of appreciation for female intelligence (p. 287), indicates the contradiction in attitudes which she will discuss by opening this way: "Every now and then there is a resounding call for a national resource—largely untapped and unmustered—referred to as the intelligence of women, or the female brain."

The comparison-contrast opening is so frequent in scholarly writing that it is almost a trademark of literary criticism. Examples of this can be found in several selections in this book. William Y. Tindall, for instance, begins his critical analysis of the short story "Clay" by noting how that story compares and contrasts with the typical naturalistic story.

Another type of opening consists of stating one's purpose: "In this essay I shall propose the question: May the principal structure of a poem be of a logical rather than of an alogical sort?" ("Logic and Lyric," p. 482.) Or one may indicate the importance of one's subject, as does Shaw (p. 467) when he says that he is going to talk "about Democracy objectively: that is, as it exists and as we must all reckon with it."

One of the most straightforward approaches is to begin with the first step. Almost all narrative writing follows a chronological order, as do many descriptions of processes. Saint-Exupéry (p. 560) starts out "On the Guadalajara front I sat at night in a dugout with a Republican squad. . . ." And Edmund Wilson's descriptive reflections on "The Old Stone House" (p. 114) also proceed chronologically, "As I go north for the first time in years. . . ."

THE BLANKET BEGINNING. A "blanket" beginning is one that "covers" the subject. Anyone who has read or heard traditional religious sermons will readily recognize such openings. A sermon often begins, "Our text for today is . . ." and goes on to quote a few lines from scripture. The remainder of the talk will be an expansion of the opening quotation. The use of quotations in this way is applicable to many subjects. If one can find a particularly appropriate quotation, from a source worth quoting, it may not only provide an excellent "blanket" beginning, but also catch the interest and inspire the curiosity of the reader. In our selection called "The Hedgehog and the Fox" (p. 281) the author uses such a quotation as the "blanket" beginning for a whole book: "There is a line among the fragments of the Greek poet Archilochus which says: 'The fox knows many things, but the hedgehog knows one big thing.' "

A question which indicates the problem to be answered in the rest of an essay may also be a good opening. Bertrand Russell began his discussion of the table (parts of which you read in the Introduction), "Is there any knowledge in the world which is so certain that no reasonable man could doubt it?" This question covers all his subsequent material. Students, however, should be cautioned against resorting to the question beginning too frequently. They often begin with a question which actually reveals an insufficient consideration of the subject. An opening like "How can we define liberty?" is so general that it cannot be considered to say anything important, relevant, or interesting about the subject.

Another type of "blanket" beginning is the statement of a principle related to the purpose of your essay. After finding a subject, outlining an approach and formulating an organizing concept, we should be able to fashion a statement with general validity and specific relevance. Thus Orwell begins his essay on Gandhi (p. 308) with an intentionally controversial statement of principle: "Saints should always be judged guilty until they are proved innocent, but the tests that have to be applied to them are not, of course, the same in all cases."

A variation of the statement of principle is the inclusion of a division or classification in the opening words. This kind of beginning is quite common, perhaps because it is so useful and effective for both writer and reader. It "covers" not only the thought of the essay, but the form as well, so that one knows precisely where the essay is going and how it will get there. For example, Bacon begins his classic "Of Studies" (p. 79), "Studies serve for delight, for ornament, and for ability." G. K. Chesterton, in an essay called "A Defense of Nonsense," opens: "There are two equal and eternal ways of looking at this twilight world of ours: we may see it as the twilight of evening or the twilight of morning; we may think of anything down to the acorn, as a descendant or as an ancestor." Division of some sort may be found in the opening sentences of many essays in this book, such as Aaron Copland's "What to Listen for in Music" (p. 252) or the Birks' "Persuasion by Logical Argument" (p. 390).

THE FEINT BEGINNING. In contrast to the blanket or straightforward beginning, the "feint" beginning may be described as an attempt not only to attract or startle the reader but at the same time to excite his curiosity by leaving him somewhat in the dark as to what the author is going to say. A quotation may be used for this purpose very successfully. Or an anecdote, like the one in the opening paragraph of Hutchins' "Why Think?" (p. 44), or an example, like the one in the beginning of Kirk's "May Professors Profess Principles?" (p. 459), or in Menninger's "Verdict Guilty—Now What?" (p. 443).

The feint beginning may be a simple understatement such as opens Csezlaw Milosz' book *The Captive Mind,* "Like many of my generation, I could have wished that my life had been a more simple affair." Jacques Barzun's gently conciliatory opening to his discussion of capital punishment (p. 433) masks the highly charged polemicism of the rest of the essay. Shaw's extended sea analogy in his first paragraph (p. 467) is designed to win the reader's approval *before* he reveals some of the controversial things he has to say. The detailed and personal opening sentence of "A Discussion of Botulism" (p. 140) is a masterful example of how to arouse interest in what might otherwise be thought a boring and unreadable subject: "Toward dusk on Friday, November 25, 1949, the day after Thanksgiving, a forty-year-old resident of Craryville, Columbia County, New York, whom I will call Charles Pappone, was helped by his wife and their teen-age daughter into the receiving room of the Albany Hospital."

Obviously, the "feint" is one of the more difficult approaches, especially for the beginning writer. Just as an after-dinner speaker may win, or lose, his audience by the quality of the joke he tells to start with, the writer may enrich, or ruin, the rest of his essay by the relevance and interest which is present or lacking in his "feint" beginning. A quotation or anecdote which has no intrinsic relationship to the writer's purpose will do more harm than good. A shocking or exciting beginning to a dully written essay will only enhance its dullness. But, in general, one of the indisputable marks of good writing is the ability to compose good beginnings.

Endings

Before we discuss the "middle" of the essay, the various methods of development, it might be well to say a few words about endings. If a theme has a good beginning and a well-organized development, its conclusion should follow quite naturally. Now and then, however, a writer finds himself at a loss for words when it comes to closing his discussion. The student-writer is often tempted to do no more than stop—leaving the reader wondering vaguely what happened. Every essay should have some sort of conclusion, even if it is only a few sentences or a brief paragraph.

There are three basic types of conclusions. One obvious type is summarization. Using such phrases as "in brief," "finally," "thus," "therefore," "in conclusion," the author sums up his ideas or his argument and leaves the reader with some specific statement which is to be considered the main point of the essay. Related to this type of conclusion is a second kind which repeats or clearly refers to the opening words or thoughts. This conclusion closes the circle, as it were, and, like the drawstring of a bag, pulls the whole essay together.

The third type of conclusion, and one of the most difficult to handle properly, is similar to the others but purposefully climactic—sometimes dramatic. This is the favorite device of public speakers and a classic example is Patrick Henry's "Give me liberty or give me death!" Any such "either-or" conclusion tends to the same effect. Possibly a more suitable technique for students is the one used by Stevenson (p. 301) in climaxing his definition of patriotism with a pertinent quotation. But students should be cautioned to avoid dramatic conclusions unless they are *convinced* of their appropriateness.

Middle: Developing the Ideas

The principal techniques of developing ideas may, for the sake of illustration, be reduced to seven methods. It should be emphasized from the outset that these techniques of developing a subject are not mutually exclusive, nor are they always neat and clearly defined. Just the opposite—every good essay will most likely contain examples of several different techniques. Specific techniques are further complicated by the fact that once the author "divides" his subject he has to expand it, and once he begins expanding a subject he may have to make divisions as he goes along. Nevertheless, it is valuable for the student to be able to recognize and to use various methods of development.

Since the techniques of developing ideas are so closely related, it follows that some of the writings used to illustrate one technique might also be used to illustrate some other type. Isaiah Berlin's selection, for example, utilizes three methods: classification, comparison and contrast, and analogy. But we cite it only as an example of analogy because his use of the other two methods seems to us grounded in analogy.

The seven methods that we will illustrate in this section are: chronology, classification, comparison and contrast, analogy, cause and effect, definition, and explication. We have no separate category for the most obvious ways of expanding an idea—by enumerating details or by giving examples. The reason for this has already been implied—details and examples are used extensively in all of the other categories and thus do not need special emphasis. Explication, the final method of development considered in this section, is, generally speaking, a method of expanding. In the most common kind of explication the writer simply follows the order of the text by providing enlightening comments on successive words, phrases, sentences, allusions, and ideas.

Readings: Chronology

The simplest form of division is chronological. Such a division may be based on time—past, present, and future—or on the steps of a process. Any subject which lends itself to a discussion about background, present circumstances, future possibilities, or about origins, maturity, decline, is especially suited to development by means of chronology. Most biographical or historical essays are obvious examples of this. Chronology is also a means of dividing the subject into simple sequential events: "To drive a car, first turn on the ignition key. . . ."

Marchette Chute, contemporary biographer of several major British writers, traces the reliability of many legends that were once accepted about Shakespeare's life by discussing the biographies in historical order. This selection is an appendix to her well-known *Shakespeare of London.* George Whalley, Professor of English at Queen's University, Kingston, describes the World War II battle in which the *Bismarck* finally went down. At that time he was a young sublieutenant with the Royal Navy, and calls this report his "private record of the sensation of actual warfare."

The Legends of Shakespeare's Life

MARCHETTE CHUTE

There was no attempt to record the facts of Shakespeare's life until the Restoration, and by then it was found that almost no information was available.

Thomas Fuller published a book in 1662 which he called *The History of the Worthies of England.* He divided the book into counties, and under the heading of Warwickshire he included a short account of William Shakespeare. Fuller had exact information on some of his "worthies," like Ben Jonson. He had no exact information on Shakespeare, and short as the account was, he was obliged to pad it with references to Martial, Ovid, Plautus, Heraclitus and Democritus. His chief information about Shakespeare was that "his learning was very little" and that he used to have "wit combats" with Jonson. He was not even certain of the date of Shakespeare's death and left a space for the information to be filled in later. But at least it could be said of Thomas Fuller that he did not invent anything, and it could be wished that other writers of the period had followed his example.

At about this same time a Stratford vicar named John Ward was filling a series of fifteen manuscript volumes with notes on sermons, anecdotes, medical recipes and any other stray pieces of information that interested him. It occurred to Ward that he should have read the works of his great fellow townsman and he wrote a reminder to himself in one of the volumes: "Remember to peruse Shakespeare's plays, to be much versed in them, that I may not be ignorant in that matter." He also jotted down some random notes on Shakespeare's life, and thus made the first attempt at what might be called a biography.

Since Ward was a Stratford man, most of his exact information centered around Shakespeare's daughters. He knew there were two of them, and that one had married Dr. Hall and was the mother of the present Lady Bernard. He does not mention the other daughter, Judith, by name, but she was still living when he wrote his notes and he speaks of her in another connection. Judith Quiney was in her late seventies and died in 1662, so that there was probably no opportunity to ask her about her father; and this is the whole of Ward's knowledge about William Shakespeare:

> I have heard that Mr. Shakespeare was a natural wit, without any art at all; he frequented the plays all his younger time, but in his elder days lived at Stratford, and supplied the stage with two plays every year, and for it had an allowance so large, that he spent at the rate of £1,000 a year, as I have heard. Shakespeare, Drayton and Ben Jonson had a merry meeting, and it seems drank too hard, for Shakespeare died of a fever there contracted.

Although Ward was writing nearly half a century after Shakespeare's death, it might be hoped that he had acquired a piece of authentic information about the drinking party. It was true that Ben Jonson was a friend of Shakespeare's and that he was a heavy drinker. It is also true that Michael Drayton, although he was not a heavy drinker and was in fact famous for his sobriety, was a Warwickshire man and later a patient of Dr. Hall's, and he may very well have been a friend of Shakespeare's and a frequent visitor at New Place. But Ward's trustworthiness as a biographer collapses when he states that Shakespeare spent at the rate of a thousand pounds a year. This preposterous sum destroys any possible respect for Ward as a biographer, and if the story of the drinking party rests on no better basis than this it remains both unproven and unprovable.

The next attempt to write a biography of Shakespeare was made about twenty years later. Anthony Wood, the noted antiquarian, was doing research for a book, and a friend of his named John Aubrey undertook to help him by compiling manuscript notes on some of the people involved. The more Aubrey worked on his own series of biographies the more excited he became, until he finally announced with enthusiasm, "I believe never any in England were delivered so faithfully and with so good authority."

Aubrey was reliable enough when it came to describing his own family, and it is on good authority that the reader learns that the eyes of the author's mother are at present a little sore and that the author himself once had the measles. But Aubrey is not so reliable when it comes to describing events of the past, although his intentions are obviously excellent. He gives an account, for instance, of a castle near Newbury that was once the home of an individual he calls "Sir" Geoffrey Chaucer. The fact that Chaucer used to sit under a special oak outside this castle is proved by the fact that the oak was eventually cut down, and Aubrey heard the whole story from an attorney who attended the Star Chamber trial of the wretch who had thus offended against literature. It is not stated where Aubrey's "able attorney" got all this information in the first place, since Chaucer was not a knight and did not own Dunnington Castle or any other.

In his account of Shakespeare, Aubrey showed the same good intentions and the same trusting willingness to believe any story that came his way. He filled a whole page with information on Shakespeare that he had gathered together, recording it slightly uphill in his slanting hand, and as a further mark of respect he drew a small laurel wreath in the left margin.

It was not lack of good intentions on Aubrey's part that made his account so poor; it was lack of information.

Aubrey started off briskly and inaccurately by stating that Shakespeare's father was a butcher. He brought up his son in the same trade, and there was another butcher's son in town who was just as clever as William. "This William, being naturally inclined to poetry and acting, came to London I guess about eighteen," not a very good guess since the twins were born in Stratford when Shakespeare was twenty-one.

Aubrey makes some vague remarks about the virtues of Shakespeare as an actor and playwright, and then continues with some stories he has picked up. He says that a constable lived on the road from London to Stratford, and that Shakespeare used him as the model of the constable in *A Midsummer Night's Dream*. Aubrey is quite undeterred by the fact there is no constable in this play, for a friend of his, a Mr. Howe, knew the original of the character well. Another story that Aubrey found was that an "old rich usurer" of Stratford named Combe was to be buried and Shakespeare wrote a mocking rhymed epitaph for his grave. It is true there was once a rhyme about usury on John Combe's grave but it is unlikely it was put there by that landed country gentleman, William Shakespeare, whom John Combe remembered in his will. Aubrey also states that Shakespeare left a yearly income of two or three hundred pounds "to a sister." The sister is presumably Joan Hart; but Shakespeare left her twenty pounds, and his total cash estate was not more than £350.

For a brief period during the making of his notes, Aubrey had access to a man who could have given him some information about the old days in the theatre before the Civil War. He had the good fortune to meet old William Beeston, whose father, Christopher Beeston, had been an apprentice of Augustine Phillips and had acted briefly with Shakespeare's company before he joined a rival organization. Aubrey was tremendously excited at meeting old Mr. Beeston, although he did not quite catch the name, and he made a note in his book on the first of September, 1681: "I have met with old Mr. —— who knew all the old English poets, whose lives I am taking from him; his father was master of the —— playhouse." In time Aubrey discovered the man's name and wrote a memorandum to himself that Mr. Beeston lived at Hog Lane and Shoreditch and must be consulted for particulars on the lives of both Shakespeare and Jonson. The next note of Aubrey's on the subject is a sad one: "Old Mr. Beeston . . . died at his house in Bishopsgate Street Without, about Bartholomew-tide, 1682."

The man whom Dryden had called "the chronicle of the stage" was no more, and Aubrey was left to get his theatrical information from men as unreliable as Sir Edward Shirburn, who gave him the astonishing information that Ben Jonson had killed "Marlowe, the poet, on Bunhill, coming from the Green-Curtain playhouse." A statement of this kind is unfortunately typical of the state of Restoration information on the Elizabethans, and it results from a telescoping of the fact that Marlowe died a violent death, that five years later Jonson killed an actor named Gabriel Spencer in a duel, and that there was a playhouse named the Curtain which had been erected on the Curtain estate long before the days when green curtains were used in the theatres.

Aubrey managed to get one piece of information about Shakespeare from old William Beeston before he died: the statement that Shakespeare "had been in his younger years schoolmaster in the country." This statement would have more value if it had come from a more direct source than the son of one of the Queen's Men, or if it could have been transmitted by someone less careless than Aubrey. It is not likely that Shakespeare could have been a "master" of a school in his early twenties, since this was an office that was handled under a rigid system of licenses from the Worcester diocese, whether the applicant wished to teach in a public school or in a private family, and almost invariably required university training. Shakespeare may have assisted a schoolmaster or done some informal teaching before he went to London, but since no documentary evidence survives there is no way of knowing.

Elsewhere in his huge collection of biographies, Aubrey wrote down the life of the late Poet Laureate of England, Sir William D'Avenant. Before Sir William changed the spelling, the name had been Davenant, and his father owned a tavern on High Street in Oxford which had often been honored with the presence of William Shakespeare. The eldest son, Robert, who later became a parson, remembered that when he was a child Shakespeare had "given him a hundred kisses," and Shakespeare was such a close friend of the family that the second son, William, was probably named for him. The Davenants had seven children, whom they brought up with great care, and they were evidently a devoted couple; when John Davenant died during his term as mayor of Oxford, a contemporary elegy attributes his death to the loss of his wife a fortnight earlier.

Sir William D'Avenant was only ten years old when Shakespeare died, but he liked to feel that he had received Shakespeare's mantle as a dramatist. He liked to be called the swan of Isis as Shakespeare was called the swan of Avon, and announced that he wrote with the "very spirit" of Shakespeare. When he was slightly drunk and with sympathetic companions, D'Avenant was not above reinforcing his claims as a writer by hinting rather broadly that he was actually Shakespeare's son. D'Avenant lived in a casual age and was careless enough in his own affairs, for "he got a terrible clap of a black handsome wench that lay in Axeyard, Westminster"; but it was quite another thing to call his mother a whore, even though at the time he was being "pleasant over a glass of wine." Although Aubrey was a born gossip he disliked this particular story and crossed it out in his manuscript so that it would not get into print; but his precaution was not sufficient and in the next century the respectable Mrs. Davenant was firmly established in the popular mind as an adulteress.

The next writer to attempt a biography of Shakespeare was Nicholas Rowe, who brought out a six-volume edition of Shakespeare's plays in 1709 and prefaced it with a life of the poet. Rowe's biography was the first to get into print, since the work of both Ward and Aubrey had remained in manuscript; and Rowe did his best to make the account reliable. He even consulted the famous actor, Thomas Betterton, for information about Stratford, and Betterton admired Shakespeare so deeply that he had made a special trip into Warwickshire to collect biographical data. Unfortunately, Betterton was not familiar with the uses of old documents, and although he inspected the Stratford register he thought Shakespeare was one of ten children, since he did not know there were two Joans instead of one and accidentally added three children from a different Shakespeare family in Stratford. Betterton was even more careless when he came to Shakespeare's own children, since he thought that Judith was the oldest and that Hamnet was a girl. As for John Shakespeare's occupation, the "butcher" had now become a dealer in wool and trained his son in the same business.

Rowe had heard the popular story of Shakespeare and the thousand pounds, but according to Rowe's information the money had been given to him by the Earl of Southampton. Even to Rowe this seemed an exceedingly improbable sum, and he said that he would not have ventured to mention it, "if I had not been assured that the story was handed down by Sir William D'Avenant." It would be difficult to find a more unreliable witness than Sir William D'Avenant, and the story is chiefly interesting because it marks the beginning of the long association between Shakespeare and Southampton in the minds of all subsequent biographies.

Shakespeare must have received a handsome sum from Southampton in return for dedicating two successful books to the earl just before he turned back to writing for the stage, but any other "marks of favor and friendship from the Earl of Southampton" belong in the realm of conjecture. The instinct to connect Shakespeare with an earl was evidently the same one that made the seventeenth century persist in calling Chaucer a "knight," and as Shakespeare's reputation grew the impulse to link him with lords grew with it. Each writer amplified the statements of his predecessors, and by the end of the nineteenth century it was almost an article of faith that Shakespeare had been a close personal friend of Southampton's and intimately concerned with all his doings.[1]

Nicholas Rowe did his best with the various stories that had come his way, although he had no way of judging whether or not any of them were true. He repeated the story of the doggerel verses on John Combe's tomb and added that "the sharpness of the satire is said to have stung the man so severely, that he never forgave it"—an embellishment to the story he would have omitted if he could have seen John Combe's bequest to Shakespeare in his will. He told the story of Queen Elizabeth commissioning *The Merry Wives of Windsor,* which he got from a contemporary of his, and added another story to the effect that Ben Jonson was "altogether unknown" until Shakespeare persuaded his fellow actors to produce one of Jonson's plays. It is a pretty story, but Jonson's first production with the Chamberlain's Men was in 1598, and by that time his work for Henslowe

[1] A poem was published in 1594, written in praise of a constant wife. It was published just after *The Rape of Lucrece,* and a verse preceding the poem announces that the heroine of the poem, a lady named Avisa, is more chaste even than Lucrece. The introduction of the poem is interesting because it is the first mention of Shakespeare's name as a narrative writer. He is one of the "brave poets" who have written of chaste women.

The poem, which was called *Willobie His Avisa,* continues with an account of various assaults made on the lady's impregnable virtue. Various suitors try to tempt her, among whom is a Frenchman named D.B. and an Englishman named H.W. According to the poem itself, H.W. stands for Henry Willoby; but since he had a friend named W.S. it was suggested in the twentieth century that W.S. was William Shakespeare and H.W. was Henry Wriothesley, Earl of Southampton. It seems safe to say that such a suggestion could never have been made, since it had no support in the poem itself, if it had not been for the many generations of scholars who had worked to connect Shakespeare with the Earl of Southampton. By the twentieth century, Shakespeare towered so far above all his contemporaries that it seemed natural to assume that no other W.S. had ever existed, although the initials were actually so common that, in the single year of 1597, Richard Burbage was intimately associated in his profession with three men who had those initials: William Sly, William Shakespeare, and William Smith.

was so well known that Francis Meres listed him as one of "the best for tragedy."

But the most popular story that Rowe brought before the public was the deer-stealing story. This had first been written down by the Rev. Richard Davies of Gloucestershire, who inherited a collection of manuscript biographies from a friend of his and made several additions to them before he himself died in 1708. The orginal manuscript biography on Shakespeare was of no interest but the Rev. Davies improved it by two startling additions. One was that Shakespeare had died a Papist. The other one, delivered in a single breathless sentence, was that Shakespeare was "much given to all unluckiness in stealing venison and rabbits, particularly from Sir —— Lucy, who had him oft whipped and sometimes imprisoned, and at last made him fly his native country to his great advancement, but his revenge was so great that he is his Justice Clodpate, and calls him a great man, and that in allusion to his name bore three louses rampant for his arms."

Rowe was able to improve on the story, for he knew that "Sir —— Lucy" must be Sir Thomas Lucy of Charlecote, and that "Justice Clodpate" would be Justice Shallow of *The Merry Wives of Windsor*. He did not know that the Lucy family did not have a deer park in the sixteenth century, a piece of information that destroys the whole story, and he was in fact so pleased with the deer that he abandoned the Rev. Davies' "rabbits" entirely.

Rowe made quite a vivid little story out of the deer-stealing in which Shakespeare indulged after his marriage. "He had, by a misfortune common enough to young fellows, fallen into ill company, and amongst them, some that made a frequent practice of deer-stealing engaged him with them more than once in robbing a park that belonged to Sir Thomas Lucy, of Charlecote, near Stratford. For this he was prosecuted by that gentleman . . . to that degree that he was obliged to leave his business and family in Warwickshire for some time and shelter himself in London." Later on in his biography, Rowe added that Shakespeare had made Falstaff "a deer-stealer, that he might at the same time remember his Warwickshire prosecutor under the name of Justice Shallow; he has given him very near the same coat of arms."

The subsequent vitality of the story has been extraordinary. Some of this may be attributed to eighteenth-century love of gossip, but most of it comes from the little circumstantial touch about Justice Shallow and the twelve luces on his coat of arms. Sir Thomas Lucy bore three luces on his coat of arms, and therefore he must have been the model for Justice Shallow, and therefore the deer-stealing story must be true. No one was deterred by the fact that the comic characterization of Shallow has nothing in common with Sir Thomas Lucy, soldier and gentleman, or that Shakespeare gave respectful prominence to an ancestor of his, Sir William Lucy, in *Henry VI*. Nor was anyone deterred by the fact that the luce, a fresh water pike, appears on many of the arms of the period, from the Gascoigne family to the company of London fishmongers, and from Justice Gardiner to the Earl of Northampton, who actually had the "twelve luces" that are given to Shallow. Sir Charles Percy quartered three luces on his coat of arms because one of his ancestors had married into the Lucy family, and Sir Charles once actually compared himself to Shakespeare's Justice Shallow. But Sir Charles was not thinking of coats of arms, but of characterization. Justice Shallow and his colleague, Justice Silence, had been so popular on the London stage that they had become a kind of byword for rustic justices of the peace; and Sir Charles had been so busy with country matters that he wrote ruefully to London: "If I stay here so long in this fashion, at my return I think you will find me so dull that I shall be taken for Justice Silence or Justice Shallow."

A few other legends about Shakespeare grew up in the course of the eighteenth century. The story that had the longest life was supposed to have originated with D'Avenant and consisted of the theory that when Shakespeare first came up to London he held horses for the customers outside the theatres. This story was then expanded into a tale that he organized a collection of other young horse-holders who were known as "Shakespeare's boys."

At the end of the eighteenth century, Edmund Malone made the first determined effort to disentangle fact from legend in Shakespeare biographies. Malone was the first, and one of the greatest, of the real Shakespearian scholars, and Malone said frankly that he did not believe the horse-holding story. Nor did he believe the deer-stealing story, since, as he pointed out, Sir Thomas Lucy had no deer. Nor did he believe a great many other stories that were currently circulating about Shakespeare. In fact, said Malone bitterly, Nicholas Rowe had made eleven statements about Shakespeare's life and eight of them could be proven to be false.

Malone had very great influence as an editor, but he had almost none from the biographical point of view. Although he tried to remove the legends about Shakespeare he had nothing to offer in their place, and the legends took root again at once and flourished as though they had never been disturbed. There is nothing like a colorful story for surviving, no matter how unsupported its basis may be; and if a story is both colorful and disreputable, its immortality is practically assured.

Questions and Assignments

1. How many steps are there in this chronology? How does the author introduce each step? Notice the variations in the opening sentences of each paragraph. Why are they there?

2. How would you describe the author's main purpose in tracing these records of Shakespeare's life? Why is the beginning so abrupt? Is the conclusion satisfactory?

3. How important to the essay is the slim factual basis for the legends? How important is Fuller's negative virtue: "at least . . . he did not invent anything"? How does the author's tone here affect your responses to later biographers?

4. How do Aubrey's "good intentions" affect his reliability?

5. How reliable is the testimony of D'Avenant? Which was the first biography to get in print? Does this help account for the vitality of the deer-stealing story?

6. Does Miss Chute prove that any of these legends are false? Does she attempt to? Does she convince you? What do your answers show about evidence of this order?

7. How do Malone's "good intentions" differ from those of the earlier biographers? Why was he less influential?

8. Write a chronological essay on one of the following subjects:
   - Ideas about the shape of the earth and the solar system
   - Events which led up to the Revolutionary War, the Civil War, the First or Second World War
   - The steps involved in building a house or making an engine
   - A description of how you learned to cook, to sew, to take care of children, to drive a car
   - The steps involved in growing a garden, raising an animal
   - The various steps and events in your decision to come to this college

The Sinking of the Bismarck

GEORGE WHALLEY

It wasn't much like farm boys hunting rats in a barn with pitchforks. The German battleship *Bismarck,* at about 42,500 tons, with a main armament of eight fifteen-inch guns, was the most powerful battleship in the world when she completed working up in the Baltic in March, 1941. On 18 May she sailed from Gdynia with the new eight-inch gun crusier *Prinz*

From *The Atlantic Monthly.* Reprinted by permission of Professor Whalley.

Eugen in company and refueled in Korsfjord just south of Bergen: it was clear then that she intended to break through the British blockade into the Atlantic. The commander in chief, home fleet, Sir John Tovey, had already made cruiser dispositions to cover the variants on that probability; he now sailed the battle cruiser *Hood* and battleship *Prince of Wales* and waited for final developments. On the evening of 21 May, air reconnaissance found the anchorage at Korsfjord empty, and at 10:45 that night the main British fleet sailed from Scapa Flow—*King George V,* five cruisers, and five destroyers.

This prompt action was soon rewarded. At 7:22 on the evening of 23 May, the patrolling cruisers *Norfolk* and *Suffolk* sighted the *Bismarck* and *Prinz Eugen* passing through the Denmark Straits. The cruisers, shadowing with great skill in extremely difficult conditions, delivered *Bismarck* for destruction into the hands of *Hood* and *Prince of Wales* in the early morning of 24 May. But *Hood* did not survive the accurate savagery of *Bismarck's* shooting, and *Prince of Wales,* damaged, was obliged to break off the engagement. *Bismarck* continued to the south, and the shadowing continued with the object of delivering her to C.I.C.'s fleet. And so, steaming farther to the south on other matters, the battleship *Rodney* was drawn into the pursuit and finally into the kill.

The *Rodney* was long overdue for a refit; she had sailed from the Clyde for Boston at one P.M. on 22 May, escorting the liner *Britannic* and escorted by four tribal destroyers of the 6th Flotilla—*Somali, Tartar, Mashona,* and *Eskimo.* According to more than one printed account of the *Bismarck* action, *Tartar* was not in at the end and could not have seen what happened. But we were and did. In evidence: this letter written on 11 June, 1941, by myself as a twenty-five-year-old sublieutenant of the Royal Canadian Volunteer Reserve, appointed ten weeks earlier to *Tartar* additional and for training as a watchkeeping officer.

In wartime, Prime Ministers and Presidents can perhaps allow themselves the luxury of large public indiscretions; junior people, though less likely to possess crucial information, were enjoined to a strict secrecy, were forbidden to keep diaries or to write in letters any factual detail of places, times, events, units, ships, targets. No doubt the enemy thereby were kept in ignorance of much that would neither have profited them nor amused them; surely it has deprived us altogether of many vivid and strange records that otherwise would have been set down.

In 1941, when all things were desperate, most of us, impressed by the importunity if not the example of our seniors, were for the most part silent, not sure that a piece of writing would be worth another man's life. But every now and then an event would occur so notorious that even the enemy said he knew about it or politically so praiseworthy that reticence would have been superhuman, and some more or less accurate information was made public. Then journalists would come on board and drink our gin with an engaging enough grace. I hope we weren't discourteous, but I don't think we ever welcomed them in the manner customary to wardrooms. We would answer their questions, but with a clumsy and suspicious evasiveness, perhaps not because they were journalists but because they were outsiders and because they had not taken part in the experience and so could not be expected to understand it. As a result, their accounts, with the best will in the world, were often unfocused and awry; the central facts were often right enough, but not the color and tone.

Yet, as long as the papers published some information—names of some ships, losses, positions, times—these could harmlessly be repeated to provide a not entirely ghostly matrix within which a personal account could take shape. The impulse was neither to record nor to express but to release into the hard crystals of words the mordant and impacted sense of horror and awe and beauty, to make the human token of a few gale-tormented sea-weary days and nights and the terrible spectacle of a major naval gun action.

ABOARD *H.M.S. TARTAR,* JUNE 11, 1941

When the first word of the sighting of *Bismarck* [by *Suffolk*] came through, we were already at sea with *Rodney*. Already it had been a disgusting trip as regards weather. We were rolling through a great angle and pitching as well. After the second day we did not bother to stand up the wardroom chairs unless we wanted to sit in them.

The news of the sighting of *Bismarck* came not long before we were due to turn back. [At noon, 24 May, *Eskimo* was detached with *Britannic* and our speed was at once increased to *Rodney's* maximum, which, although not a great increase, made the discomfort even greater.] At that time, with the fleet dispositions as they were, it seemed most unlikely that we should be any more than an also-ran. We plugged on.

It seemed to me always to be night. I was only standing night watches [on the bridge]; for the rest of the time on cypher watch in the W/T office.

There it was like watching a gigantic chess game with the whole North Atlantic as board and each unit with the freedom of movement of a queen but without her devastating disregard for distance. The problem resolved itself into the question whether the shadowing cruisers could keep contact until dawn on Sunday morning [25 May]. Already the Fleet Air Arm [actually Coastal Command], *Prince of Wales,* and *Hood* had had a crack at *Bismarck.* The enemy was damaged and her speed slightly reduced. *Hood* had suddenly disappeared. [The signal sent out at six A.M. on the twenty-fourth simply said, "Hood has blown up."] It still does not seem possible that such a big ship, with beauty and speed in her lines, should suddenly have gone, that our ship's company taking their ease on deck will no more eye her with satisfaction and delight. A new grimness and determination entered the pursuit. If before it had been important to engage *Bismarck,* it was now a necessity. It was up to the cruisers, who so far had survived great danger in shadowing her through the diabolical visibility of the Greenland Sea.

I had the first watch on the Saturday night in the W/T office, also the middle. We thought we were going into action the next day. The seas were mountainous, so that we rolled down with a slow wounded motion, once or twice to fifty degrees in the morning watch, and on the bridge it felt as if she would never come back. Unpleasant weather for high-speed maneuvering for torpedo attack.

The sighting signals [from the cruisers *Suffolk* and *Norfolk*] came through rapidly, checked, improved again. Our spirits rose and fell according to the contents of those signals. The dawn would be early; only two or three more hours of successful shadowing by the cruisers, and *Bismarck* would be trapped and brought to action. At 3:06 A.M., 25 May, the cruisers lost contact and failed to regain it. We hoped to find her in the first light, but as the day wore on and no report came, a lethargy of disappointment spread through the ship. The storm had been easing. Now we turned and ran back into it again. There was little to cheer the men on mess decks flooded with water and rearing like a horse with an unpredictable motion. There was time for sleep for some, and sleep brought fresh hope.

I have lost track of the days. It seems, in looking back, like one long twilit day punctuated by meals that would scarcely stay on the table long enough to be eaten. There was an added anxiety, in that we had already steamed a good distance: if the action did not materialize soon, we should have to turn for home, ignominiously. The chase was now eastward, the right direction for us. It was at this time that one of the petty officers remarked how lucky we were to get the port anchor secured the first night out. It had walked back on its slip and was banging badly. There had been a period of five minutes while altering course [as soon as we left harbor] when the forecastle was fairly dry. A party rushed forward and secured the anchor. It was very wet; at any other time up till the time of battle no man could have even attempted to reach the anchor.

Then the sighting reports came in again [at 10:30 A.M., 26 May]. The correct estimation had been made of the enemy's movements; he was actually on the suggested track our captain had drawn the night contact was lost. We started again to think in terms of hours of darkness. All disappointment was forgotten now. The net was closing rapidly. The Fleet Air Arm [aircraft for the carrier *Ark Royal*] were attacking; their torpedoes slowed her down. There was no escape for *Bismarck*. But it was an anxious afternoon while we waited for the air reports.

[Since early afternoon, *King George V* had been approaching us on a converging course; we joined her at six P.M. *Somali,* late in the afternoon, had to return to harbor to fuel. *Tartar* and *Mashona,* though very short of fuel, were given permission to remain as the only escort to the two battleships, *King George V* and *Rodney*.]

The dusk came, and the darkness. We went to action stations in a ship moving wildly through a heavy sea. The mess decks were wet and slippery. The various crews and supply parties stood to their stations, deriving what comfort they could from wet duffle coats. It was in the early dark of that night that the other tribals [of the 4th Flotilla, from Gibraltar under Captain Viaw] delivered their torpedo attacks under heavy fire. *Bismarck* was hit, slowed down, stopped once. [From nine P.M. on she was steering erratic and illogical courses—north northeast, northeast, north—away from her harbor at Brest.] We were closing her rapidly, and the dawn would see the action.

In the first light we maneuvered for position. The course took us to the westward. Our fuel problem was acute. [Shortly before sunrise and] before *Bismarck* was sighted, we left the battleships and shaped away, our hearts in our boots. [The commander in chief, since midnight, had been steering north northeast to north and working around to the westward to get *Bismarck* against the eastern sky at dawn. The destroyers could not possibly any longer steam away from harbor.] To have come so far, the only destroyers to engage in the hunt from start to finish, and then to have to turn back within an hour or less of the battle . . . The battleships were only six or seven miles astern when we saw them turn toward us again. We met and spoke to a cruiser [*Norfolk*] who gave us a sighting report: In a rain squall to the southward was *Bismarck,* about ten miles away.

All this I saw from the bridge. The others were below in the wardroom (all who were not on watch), most of them asleep in the chairs, although it was not ten minutes since they had come below. I ran below to give them the news, came on deck at once just as *Rodney* opened fire. The rain squall had cleared. When I reached the bridge, *Bismarck's* upper works could be seen against the sky; also the flash of her guns and the white columns of water growing near her.

With insignificant gun range we lay off near the cruiser [*Norfolk*], maneuvering with her to keep the battle in sight [and serve as flank markers]. If we could do nothing at the moment, we might be able to torpedo her when her heavy guns were out of action or pick up survivors. It is impossible to imagine our sense of detachment, watching a battle between capital ships as one watches a tennis match or a film. There was now a bright sun in a sky only partly filled with white cumulus. The wind, still fresh, made a great play of blue and green on the water, stippling it, marbling it, whipping the tops from the short high seas, sending a lacelike drive of spray fingering its way over forecastle, guns, and bridge.

Against this dazzle of color and light the whole pageant, itself brightly colored, moved. For it seemed a pageant, majestic, wild, but surely not involving thousands of lives—it looked too clean for such a grim purpose, the daylight too clear. Against the sky we saw the enemy, now in full view, her almost-white, massive upper works, her long forecastle plunging, water lipping and creaming each time she lifted her head. By contrast, our ships, a darker blue-gray, their funnels white with salt from the heavy weather, the battle ensigns startlingly conspicuous. [*Bismarck* was sighted at 8:43; *Rodney* opened fire at 8:47; *King George V* immediately after; and *Bismarck* at 8:50.]

We watched the vivid orange-red flame shoot from the guns, saw the clouds of yellow smoke disperse in the wind, heard the silky sounds of the shells occasionally down the wind. The shell splashes mounted up, white, monstrously high, hung, and slowly drifted away like a clinging mist. *Bismarck's* gunnery was at first good, but although she already straddled *Rodney, Rodney* was closing her rapidly, and the enemy could not hold the range. *King George V* (being farther from us) we could not see clearly, but the flash of her guns was always on or near the horizon. *Rodney* soon had the range and was hitting hard. A dull red glow showed for an instant where a shell had hit. Soon *Bismarck* could no longer manage controlled firing and, judging from the spasmodic shooting, went into local control. She was engaging both *Rodney* and *K.G.V.* and using her secondary armament for smaller fry.

How long the firing had been going on, one could not say. After she had gone into local control she fought on, but not with persistent fierceness or accuracy. The silences between her salvos became longer. There was a heavy hit aft. A light smoke trailed out astern. She was hit again aft. There was a great sheet of flame, after which the whole ship abaft the bridge was hidden in a cloud of black smoke. At times she turned directly toward us, and when she brought her beam to us again the smoke cleared for a moment, so that we could see that her afterpart now had a far different silhouette than earlier.

Fire had apparently broken out forward. A line of flame ran along her fo'c'sle and disappeared, but shortly afterwards, two forward magazines went up with a burst of flame that seemed to move quite slowly as high as the bridge. First one magazine went, then the other immediately afterwards. By then her guns had almost ceased. Only her secondary armament was firing, and now that stopped. She appeared no longer to be making way through the water. Her long fo'c'sle rose and fell heavily in the seas, but little white water was breaking over her. If she was moving at all, it was only very slowly. Her foremost turrets were awry and derelict. No detailed damage could be seen—except that she looked different. Her upper works looked unusually massive when first we sighted her; now she looked a very large ship, although she was half enveloped in the smoke of her own burning. All the time more ships were opening fire. The splashes of the sixteen-inch guns were about twice *Bismarck's* height.

With that sort of detachment, we watched through our glasses, calling the fall of shot as an announcer calls the strokes of a cricket match. But all the time there was running through my mind a vivid picture of the people in that ship. It made the sunlight and color unearthly and nightmarish. I could see men, dazed with lack of sleep, rolling out of their hammocks, running along the decks to action stations; or had the gray dawn and the early rain found them, as it had us, sleepless and cold at their guns and ammunition hoists? For days they had been driven and harried by ships and aircraft. The respite of thirty hours would give them little peace of mind or confidence. An afternoon of aerial torpedoing, and then, when the darkness came, it brought with it, throughout the night, the wolfish attacks by destroyers that brought her speed down, smashed her rudder, and for a time made her unmanageable.

After what her men had come through, these intermittent attacks must have left them with raw nerves. But they did their best to beat off each attack. If they were lucky, they did not know how close we were to her that night, that we were only waiting for the light, that there was no possible escape. When they saw *Rodney* and *King George V* that morning, they must have known; that was soon enough. I don't know what men think or do or look like when they know what those men knew. But I fancy they opened fire as one sees our chaps in action. They look the same men, they do their jobs automatically, they curse fluently and joke and laugh in the lulls, and two of a supply party will be talking quietly to each other. But these men would be tired, and shortly they would be dazed and numb with the concussion. What that ship was like inside after an hour and a half of shelling does not bear thinking of: her guns smashed, the ship full of fire, her people hurt; and surely all men are much the same when they are hurt. It was a great relief that we were not sent in to torpedo, a dirty job.

We stood by for half an hour or so after our ships had ceased firing. The cruisers and destroyers were closing her when we turned away and shaped for home. The black cloud of smoke grew indistinct and disappeared beyond the horizon. The sea had moderated, but it was bad weather for picking up survivors. We did not see the end. It was 10:30 when we turned away [and started for home independently, at economical speed of 15 knots: it seemed unlikely that our fuel would last to get us around the north of Ireland]. Shortly after 11:00 we heard that it was all over. [*Bismarck* sank at 10:36, after being torpedoed by a cruiser.] Those who could, slept—anywhere; for myself, under a table in the wardroom beside the radio, and was not wakened until three P.M. for the first Dog.

Looking back over those twenty-four hours, I remember coming down to the wardroom flat, at about 3:00 on the morning of the battle, to fetch something from my cabin. The supply party were asleep there, waiting for a call. It was almost impossible to walk through them without treading on someone. They were all in duffle coats, sleeping, as only a sailor can, in any attitude, wherever he happens to be. There was a complete silence, a sense of no soul about; only the sound of the ship in a seaway, the creaking sounds, the wash, the drumming of the screws. There was no light except that coming through the slats of the pantry door. It fell across the still shapes in bars and moved across the duffle coats and outflung arms as the light swung to the ship's motion. It was strangely still and beautiful and ominous.

When I turned in at one A.M. the night after the action, it was said that the weather was moderating. I am no authority, being busy at the time with sleep. But scarcely, it seemed, had I rolled into my bunk than I found myself pulling on my sea boots and reaching for my cap. There was a sound of urgent ringing. It slowly dawned on me that it was [the alarm gongs for an] aircraft attack. As I dodged forward against the gun crews who were running aft, I noticed that the sea was still considerable, that the wind still gave us a list to starboard, and that there were four aircraft in sight.

We were soon no strangers to the rising whistle of bombs and the crunching gurgle of their entry into the water. The close ones made a pronounced *ping* against the ship's side. You will have heard how *Mashona* was lost and how a providential lull in the bombing made it possible to pick up most of her people. It was sad that it should be the ship with whom we were especially friendly, from the mess decks up; yet we also felt that, if it had to happen, we should prefer that we were there rather than any other ship.

In an air raid on land, one feels that the attack is objective and of diffused purpose. Air attack on a ship is very different. There is an unpleasant strain of personal malice in it. You know that the enemy is trying to get you and nobody else. They attacked methodically and with determination. Our fire kept them high, but even so, there must have been someone looking after us. The captain's avoiding action saved us on several occasions. The nearest stick, about fifteen to twenty yards off our stern, failed to explode.

So the day went on. When the planes were overhead, we were busy; and when there was a lull, I wandered aft to yarn with the gunner on the torpedo tubes. We had aboard then nearly 150 survivors crowded onto the mess decks, dressed in the most extraordinary clothes imaginable, or blankets only [and the wardroom and sick bay full of wounded]. It seemed that if there were any justice, the bombs would not get us with our precious cargo. But each cry of "Aircraft port quarter" became more like cold air on an exposed nerve and made the survivors thoughtful. At about ten in the evening we managed to get some food—since dinner the night before, two cups of tea. We were still drowsing over the finished meal when the last alarm sounded at 11:30 P.M. The enemy's bombs fell wide, and one of our aircraft drove him away.

I stayed up for what was left of the night and from the bridge saw the dawn come cold and gray over the land. How solid and comfortable the land looked—and how unconcerned. Everybody asleep ashore; and if they had been awake, they could never have guessed what incoherent prayers of thanksgiving had risen that day from a salt-weathered little ship with proud lines. Nor could they have guessed how others were waking to find no comfort in the dawn, hoping that they would wake again from a dream within a dream. There were many who never came aboard *Tartar,* and there were others who did who never reached the land. Late in the afternoon, after a rain squall had been hiding the ship for half an hour, tired men shambled aft in blankets and borrowed clothes. They passed me at the torpedo tubes; a long line of men who walked in silence and did not look up.

I think the horrors that normally confront an infantryman in action must be very terrible and take perhaps a long time to live down. A ship heavily hit in action is not pretty, certainly; neither are her people, particularly if you see them in the sea, where shock and the cold quickly reduce them to infantile helplessness. But, for the most part, naval fighting is relatively clean; killing—if one must—at a distance. But the bodies of drowned men, whether killed outright and with intent by an enemy, or by some futile error of judgment like breaking one's neck with a life jacket, or at length after a very long struggle with cold and the darkness, or caught in a squall in a mishandled sailing boat, whether crusted with burnt oil scum in the bitter Atlantic water or lolling idle as seaweed under a Mediterranean sun; the bodies of the drowned men eventually lie face down in the sea, humped up in a posture of uniform and poignant ungainliness, suggesting no image of life. Of *Hood's* ninety officers and more than twelve hundred men, there were three men only who survived; over a hundred of *Bismarck's* people lived, but her complement was near two thousand, and many men had to be left in the water when the U-boat warnings came.

The engineer officer of *Tartar* got his brass hat soon after the *Bismarck* action, and his ship was torpedoed on the Murmansk run soon after: he would have lasted only a few minutes in that water. The first lieutenant of *Tartar* in 1944 was given command of *Icarus,* one of the destroyers that hunted for *Hood's* survivors. I am told that on one of those restless, still summer nights off the Normandy coast, flank guarding and patrolling to the northward of the assault anchorage, *Icarus* was lost without a trace. It was at night, so nobody saw the breaking of the ship or the breaking of the bodies; and no man turned from his plow furrow to remark with placid wonder so meteoric and mundane a disaster.

Questions and Assignments

1. This essay uses a straightforward temporal sequence. Does this method of development increase your interest? To what extent does it rely upon exciting subject-matter?

2. Why does Whalley state that the loss of the *Hood* made battle with the *Bismarck* a necessity?

3. Explain why Whalley and others on his ship felt such extreme detachment at a crucial stage in the battle. What does such detail add to the psychological credibility?

4. What is added by the final contrasts between an air raid on land and on a ship? Of infantry against naval action?

5. What does Whalley add to his account by his many intrusions concerning his own experience and reactions? Attempt to discriminate material which is general knowledge from material which is that of an eye-witness.

6. To what extent does Whalley use his own knowledge to change the general tone and intensity of his description?

7. Write an essay using a chronological method of development on one of the following:

An automobile accident
A quarrel with your sister or your roommate or your parents
The death of someone you know
Some significant event which took place on a hike, at a party, on a vacation trip, during your summer job

Readings: Classification

Classification is a fundamental function of the mind when faced with complicated or disorganized material. Isaiah Berlin describes it as "a point of view from which to look and compare, a starting-point for genuine investigation." All scientific study is based upon classifications, such as organic and inorganic, animate and inanimate, air-breathing and water-breathing, vertebrate and invertebrate. Whenever we formulate a principle of difference or similarity, we usually formulate a class. For example, Russell Lynes a few years ago classified people as "Highbrow," "Lowbrow," and "Middlebrow" according to their intellectual pretensions. An author may also use classification to make an arbitrary division in his subject for the purpose of discussion.

The divisions, or categories, of a classification must be logically consistent. If, for example, one maintained that a top-priority college must be within commuting distance, have a first-rate football team, a good library, and a favorable boy-girl ratio, the principle governing the class "top-priority college" would be confusing. One can hardly commute to college and enjoy the football team, the boy-girl ratio, *and* the library.

The first reading in this unit, "The Three Ages of Man," employs one obvious principle of classification—age. This principle yields the categories youth, prime of life, and old age. Hidden beneath the emotional-moral and fortune distinction, moreover, is another principle of classification—the determinants of character. Aristotle views emotional and moral sensibilities as inner causes of character, and fortune (birth, power, money) as an outer influence on character.

The other selections in this unit, "The Four Idols" and "What to Listen for in Music," are also divided according to logical principles of classification.

The author of our first classification is one of the greatest Greek philosophers, Aristotle. Francis Bacon was probably the most important philosopher of Elizabethan England. Aaron Copland is one of the major contemporary American composers.

The Three Ages of Man

ARISTOTLE

Let us now consider the various types of human character, in relation to the emotions and moral qualities, showing how they correspond to our various ages and fortunes. By emotions I mean anger, desire, and the like; these we have discussed already. By moral qualities I mean virtues and vices; these also have been discussed already, as well as the various things that various types of men tend to will and to do. By ages I mean youth,

From *Aristotle,* ed. W. D. Ross, "Rhetorica," trans. W. Rhys Roberts, Book II, Chapters 12-14, by permission of the Clarendon Press, Oxford.

the prime of life, and old age. By fortune I mean birth, wealth, power, and their opposites—in fact, good fortune and ill fortune.

To begin with the Youthful type of character. Young men have strong passions, and tend to gratify them indiscriminately. Of the bodily desires, it is the sexual by which they are most swayed and in which they show absence of self-control. They are changeable and fickle in their desires, which are violent while they last, but quickly over: their impulses are keen but not deep-rooted, and are like sick people's attacks of hunger and thirst. They are hot-tempered and quick-tempered, and apt to give way to their anger; bad temper often gets the better of them, for owing to their love of honour they cannot bear being slighted, and are indignant if they imagine themselves unfairly treated. While they love honour, they love victory still more; for youth is eager for superiority over others, and victory is one form of this. They love both more than they love money, which indeed they love very little, not having yet learnt what it means to be without it—this is the point of Pittacus' remark about Amphiaraus. They look at the good side rather than the bad, not having yet witnessed many instances of wickedness. They trust others readily, because they have not yet often been cheated. They are sanguine; nature warms their blood as though with excess of wine; and besides that, they have as yet met with few disappointments. Their lives are mainly spent not in memory but in expectation; for expectation refers to the future, memory to the past, and youth has a long future before it and a short past behind it: on the first day of one's life one has nothing at all to remember, and can only look forward. They are easily cheated, owing to the sanguine disposition just mentioned. Their hot tempers and hopeful dispositions make them more courageous than older men are; the hot temper prevents fear, and the hopeful disposition creates confidence; we cannot feel fear so long as we are feeling angry, and any expectation of good makes us confident. They are shy, accepting the rules of society in which they have been trained, and not yet believing in any other standard of honour. They have exalted notions, because they have not yet been humbled by life or learnt its necessary limitations; moreover, their hopeful disposition makes them think themselves equal to great things—and that means having exalted notions. They would always rather do noble deeds than useful ones: their lives are regulated more by moral feeling than by reasoning; and whereas reasoning leads us to choose what is useful, moral goodness leads us to choose what is noble. They are fonder of their friends, intimates, and companions than older men are, because they like spending their days in the company of others, and have not yet come to value either their friends or anything else by their usefulness to themselves. All their mistakes are in the direction of doing things excessively and vehemently. They disobey Chilon's precept by overdoing everything; they love too much and hate too much, and the same with everything else. They think they know everything, and are always quite sure about it; this, in fact, is why they overdo everything. If they do wrong to others, it is because they mean to insult them, not to do them actual harm. They are ready to pity others, because they think every one an honest man, or anyhow better than he is: they judge their neighbour by their own harmless natures, and so cannot think he deserves to be treated in that way. They are fond of fun and therefore witty, wit being well-bred insolence.

Such, then, is the character of the Young. The character of Elderly Men—men who are past their prime—may be said to be formed for the most part of elements that are the contrary of all these. They have lived many years; they have often been taken in, and often made mistakes; and life on the whole is a bad business. The result is that they are sure about nothing and *under-do* everything. They "think," but they never "know"; and because of their hesitation they always add a "possibly" or a "perhaps," putting everything this way and nothing positively. They are cynical; that is, they tend to put the worse construction on everything. Further, their experience makes them distrustful and therefore suspicious of evil. Consequently they neither love warmly nor hate bitterly, but following the hint of Bias they love as though they will some day hate and hate as though they will some day love. They are small-minded, because they have been humbled by life: their desires are set upon nothing more exalted or unusual than what will help them to keep alive. They are not generous, because money is one of the things they must have, and at the same time their experience has taught them how hard it is to get and how easy to lose. They are cowardly, and are always anticipating danger, unlike that of the young, who are warm-blooded, their temperament is chilly; old age has paved the way for cowardice; fear is, in fact, a form of chill. They love life; and all the more when their last day has come, because the object of all desire is something we have not got, and also because we desire most strongly that which we need most urgently. They are too fond of themselves; this is one form that small-mindedness takes. Because of this, they guide their lives too much by considerations of what is useful and too little by what is noble—

for the useful is what is good for oneself, and the noble what is good absolutely. They are not shy, but shameless rather; caring less for what is noble than for what is useful, they feel contempt for what people may think of them. They lack confidence in the future; partly through experience—for most things go wrong, or anyhow turn out worse than one expects; and partly because of their cowardice. They live by memory rather than by hope; for what is left to them of life is but little as compared with the long past; and hope is of the future, memory of the past. This, again, is the cause of their loquacity; they are continually talking of the past, because they enjoy remembering it. Their fits of anger are sudden but feeble. Their sensual passions have either altogether gone or have lost their vigour: consequently they do not feel their passions much, and their actions are inspired less by what they do feel than by the love of gain. Hence men at this time of life are often supposed to have a self-controlled character; the fact is that their passions have slackened, and they are slaves to the love of gain. They guide their lives by reasoning more than by moral feeling; reasoning being directed to utility and moral feeling to moral goodness. If they wrong others, they mean to injure them, not to insult them. Old men may feel pity, as well as young men, but not for the same reason. Young men feel it out of kindness; old men out of weakness, imagining that anything that befalls any one else might easily happen to them, which, as we saw, is a thought that excites pity. Hence they are querulous, and not disposed to jesting or laughter—the love of laughter being the very opposite of querulousness.

Such are the characters of Young Men and Elderly Men. People always think well of speeches adapted to, and reflecting, their own character: and we can now see how to compose our speeches so as to adapt both them and ourselves to our audiences.

As for Men in their Prime, clearly we shall find that they have a character between that of the young and that of the old, free from the extremes of either. They have neither that excess of confidence which amounts to rashness, nor to much timidity, but the right amount of each. They neither trust everybody nor distrust everybody, but judge people correctly. Their lives will be guided not by the sole consideration either of what is noble or of what is useful, but by both; neither by parsimony nor by prodigality, but by what is fit and proper. So, too, in regard to anger and desire; they will be brave as well as temperate, and temperate as well as brave; these virtues are divided between the young and the old; the young are brave but intemperate, the old temperate but cowardly. To put it generally, all the valuable qualities that youth and age divide between them are united in the prime of life, while all their excesses or defects are replaced by moderation and fitness. The body is in its prime from thirty to five-and-thirty; the mind about forty-nine.

Questions and Assignments

1. What is the procedure Aristotle uses to divide his subject? Does the opening sentence seem casual or carefully planned?

2. Aristotle is actually using two different classifications at once—the emotions and moral qualities, and the different ages and fortunes of men. Make a detailed outline of this selection showing how he works out this classification as he writes. Why does he discuss middle age last and how does this contribute to his thought and his conclusion?

3. To what extent does Aristotle use contrast to establish his concept of each of his three ages? To what extent is contrast the essential rhetorical device of his individual sentences? Does this establish a rhythm in your thinking?

4. Write a paper in which you agree or disagree with Aristotle's conception of the young man. Be sure to give explicit reasons to support your generalizations.

5. Write a paper agreeing with Aristotle's basic ethical principle, that virtue is "free from the extremes?" Or write a paper disagreeing.

6. Write a theme based on a careful classification which involves one of the following subjects:

The various aspects of human character
Different types of girls, or boys
Different types of students, or professors
Different types of love
Different types of goals for living

The Four Idols

FRANCIS BACON

There are four classes of Idols which beset men's minds. To these for distinction's sake I have assigned names, calling the first class *Idols of the Tribe;* the second, *Idols of the Cave;* the third, *Idols of the Market-place;* the fourth, *Idols of the Theatre.*

The formation of ideas and axioms by true induction is no doubt the proper remedy to be applied for the keeping off and clearing away of idols. To point them out, however, is of great use, for the doctrine of Idols is to the Interpretation of Nature what the doctrine of the refutation of Sophisms is to common Logic.

The Idols of the Tribe have their foundation in human nature itself and in the tribe or race of men. For it is a false assertion that the sense of man is the measure of things. On the contrary, all perceptions as well of the sense as of the mind are according to the measure of the individual and not according to the measure of the universe. And the human understanding is like a false mirror, which, receiving rays irregularly, distorts and discolours the nature of things by mingling its own nature with it.

The Idols of the Cave are the idols of the individual man. For every one (besides the errors common to human nature in general) has a cave or den of his own, which refracts and discolours the light of nature, owing either to his own proper and peculiar nature, or to his education and conversation with others, or to the reading of books, and the authority of those whom he esteems and admires, or to the differences of impressions, accordingly as they take place in a mind preoccupied and predisposed or in a mind indifferent and settled, or the like. So that the spirit of man (according as it is meted out to different individuals) is in fact a thing variable and full of perturbation, and governed as it were by chance. Whence it was well observed by Heraclitus that men look for sciences in their own lesser worlds and not in the greater or common world.

There are also Idols formed by the intercourse and association of men with each other, which I call Idols of the Market-place on account of the commerce and consort of men there. For it is by discourse that men associate, and words are imposed according to the apprehension of the vulgar. And therefore the ill and unfit choice of words wonderfully obstructs the understanding. Nor do the definitions or explanations, wherewith in some things learned men are wont to guard and defend themselves, by any means set the matter right. But words plainly force and overrule the understanding, and throw all into confusion, and lead men away into numberless empty controversies and idle fancies.

Lastly, there are Idols which have immigrated into men's minds from the various dogmas of philosophies and also from wrong laws of demonstration. These I call Idols of the Theatre, because in my judgement all the received systems are but so many stage-plays, representing worlds of their own creation after an unreal and scenic fashion. Nor is it only of the systems now in vogue or only of the ancient sects and philosophies that I speak, for many more plays of the same kind may yet be composed and in like artificial manner set forth, seeing that errors the most widely different have nevertheless causes for the most part alike. Neither again do I mean this only of entire systems, but also of many principles and axioms in science, which by tradition, credulity, and negligence have come to be received.

But of these several kinds of Idols I must speak more largely and exactly, that the understanding may be duly cautioned.

Questions and Assignments

1. Bacon's divisions are straightforward. He is troubled by those things that mislead or confuse the understanding, and he divides these confusions into four Idols: the weakness of the mind itself, individual shortcomings, the confusions arising from language, and dogmatic systems of thought. What means does he use to develop these classifications? What does he claim is the proper remedy for them?

2. Explain the relation of the Idols of the Tribe to the individual. Explain more fully why human understanding is like a false mirror.

3. Discuss from your own experience distortions caused by Idols of the Cave. How thorough is Bacon's list of examples?

4. Expand Bacon's insistent statement that "words are imposed according to the apprehension of the vulgar." Why are learned men thrown into confusion by the Idols of the Market Place?

5. Paraphrase Bacon's distinction that explains the two types of Idols of the Theatre. Does he find this idol inherent in the nature of systems themselves?

6. Bacon writes that "for distinction's sake I have assigned names" to the idols. He implies that the classes exist as classes before they are names. Find and discuss the reasoning he uses to put the idols into his particular categories.

7. Write a theme using classification as a method of development on one of the following:

   "human understanding is like a false mirror"
   "everyone . . . has a cave or den of his own"
   "words . . . throw all into confusion"
   "all the received systems are but so many stage-plays"

What to Listen for in Music

AARON COPLAND

We all listen to music according to our separate capacities. But, for the sake of analysis, the whole listening process may become clearer if we break it up into its component parts, so to speak. In a certain sense we all listen to music on three separate planes. For lack of a better terminology, one might name these: (1) the sensuous plane, (2) the expressive plane, (3) the sheerly musical plane. The only advantage to be gained from mechanically splitting up the listening process into these hypothetical planes is the clearer view to be had of the way in which we listen.

The simplest way of listening to music is to listen for the sheer pleasure of the musical sound itself. That is the sensuous plane. It is the plane on which we hear music without thinking, without considering it in any way. One turns on the radio while doing something else and absent-mindedly bathes in the sound. A kind of brainless but attractive state of mind is engendered by the mere sound appeal of the music.

You may be sitting in a room reading this book. Imagine one note struck on the piano. Immediately that one note is enough to change the atmosphere of the room—proving that the sound element in music is a powerful and mysterious agent, which it would be foolish to deride or belittle.

The surprising thing is that many people who consider themselves qualified music lovers abuse that plane in listening. They go to concerts in order to lose themselves. They use music as a consolation or an escape. They enter an ideal world where one doesn't have to think of the realities of everyday life. Of course they aren't thinking about the music either. Music allows them to leave it, and they go off to a place to dream, dreaming because of and apropos of the music yet never quite listening to it.

Yes, the sound appeal of music is a potent and primitive force, but you must not allow it to usurp a disproportionate share of your interest. The sensuous plane is an important one in music, a very important one, but it does not constitute the whole story.

There is no need to digress further on the sensuous plane. Its appeal to every normal human being is self-evident. There is, however, such a thing as becoming more sensitive to the different kinds of sound stuff as used by various composers. For all composers do not use that sound stuff in the same way. Don't get the idea that the value of music is commensurate with its sensuous appeal or that the loveliest sounding music is made by the greatest composer. If that were so, Ravel would be a greater creator than Beethoven. The point is that the sound element varies with each composer, that his usage of sound forms an integral part of his style and must be taken into account when listening. The reader can see, therefore, that a more conscious approach is valuable even on this primary plane of music listening.

The second plane on which music exists is what I have called the expressive one. Here, immediately, we tread on controversial ground. Composers have a way of shying away from any discussion of music's expressive side. Did not Stravinsky himself proclaim that his music was an "object," a "thing," with a life of its own, and with no other meaning than its own purely musical existence? This intransigent attitude of Stravinsky's may be due to the fact that so many people have tried to read different meanings into so many pieces. Heaven knows it is difficult enough to say precisely what it is that a piece of music means, to say it definitely, to say it finally so that everyone is satisfied with your explanation. But that should not lead one to the other extreme of denying to music the right to be "expressive."

My own belief is that all music has an expressive power, some more and some less, but that all music has a certain meaning behind the notes and that that meaning behind the notes constitutes, after all, what the piece is saying, what the piece is about. This whole problem can be stated quite simply by asking, "Is there a meaning to music?" My answer to that would be, "Yes." And "Can you state in so many words what the meaning is?" My answer to that would be, "No." Therein lies the difficulty.

Simple-minded souls will never be satisfied with the answer to the second of these questions. They always want to have a meaning, and the more concrete it is the better they like it. The more the music reminds them of a train, a storm, a funeral, or any other familiar conception the more expressive it appears to be to them. This popular idea of music's meaning—stimulated and abetted by the usual run of musical commentator—should be discouraged wherever and whenever it is met. One timid lady once confessed to me that she suspected something seriously lacking in her appreciation of music because of her inability to connect it with anything definite. That is getting the whole thing backward, of course.

Still, the question remains, How close should the intelligent music lover wish to come to pinning a definite meaning to any particular work? No closer than a general concept, I should say. Music expresses, at different moments, serenity or exuberance, regret or triumph, fury or delight. It expresses each of these moods, and many others, in a numberless variety of subtle shadings and differences. It may even express a state of meaning for which there exists no adequate word in any language. In that case, musicians often like to say that it has only a purely musical meaning. They sometimes go farther and say that *all* music has only a purely musical meaning. What they really mean is that no appropriate word can be found to express the music's meaning and that, even if it could they do not feel the need of finding it.

But whatever the professional musician may hold, most musical novices still search for specific words with which to pin down their musical reactions. That is why they always find Tschaikovsky easier to "understand" than Beethoven. In the first place, it is easier to pin a meaning-word on a Tschaikovsky piece than on a Beethoven one. Much easier. Moreover, with the Russian composer, every time you come back to a piece of his it almost always says the same thing to you, whereas with Beethoven it is often quite difficult to put your finger right on what he is saying. And any musician will tell you that that is why Beethoven is the greater composer. Because music which always says the same thing to you will necessarily soon become dull music, but music whose meaning is slightly different with each hearing has a greater chance of remaining alive.

Listen, if you can, to the forty-eight fugue themes of Bach's *Well-Tempered Clavichord*. Listen to each theme, one after another. You will soon realize that each theme mirrors a different world of feeling. You will also soon realize that the more beautiful a theme seems to you the harder it is to find any word that will describe it to your complete satisfaction. Yes, you will certainly know whether it is a gay theme or a sad one. You will be able, in other words, in your own mind, to draw a frame of emotional feeling around your theme. Now study the sad one a little closer. Try to pin down the exact quality of its sadness. Is it pessimistically sad or resignedly sad; is it fatefully sad or smilingly sad?

Let us suppose that you are fortunate and can describe to your own satisfaction in so many words the exact meaning of your chosen theme. There is still no guarantee that anyone else will be satisfied. Nor need they be. The important thing is that each one feel for himself the specific expressive quality of a theme or, similarly, an entire piece of music. And if it is a great work of art, don't expect it to mean exactly the same thing to you each time you return to it.

Themes or pieces need not express only one emotion, of course. Take such a theme as the first main one of the *Ninth Symphony,* for example. It is clearly made up of different elements. It does not say only one thing. Yet anyone hearing it immediately gets a feeling of strength, a feeling of power. It isn't a power that comes simply because the theme is played loudly. It is a power inherent in the theme itself. The extraordinary strength and vigor of the theme results in the listener's receiving an impression that a forceful statement has been made. But one should never try to boil it down to "the fateful hammer of life," etc. That is where the trouble begins. The musician, in his exasperation, says it means nothing but the notes themselves, whereas the nonprofessional is only too anxious to hang on to any explanation that gives him the illusion of getting closer to the music's meaning.

Now, perhaps, the reader will know better what I mean when I say that music does have an expressive meaning but that we cannot say in so many words what that meaning is.

The third plane on which music exists is the sheerly musical plane. Besides the pleasurable sound of music and the expressive feeling that it gives off, music does exist in terms of the notes themselves and of their manipulation. Most listeners are not sufficiently conscious of this third plane. . . .

Professional musicians, on the other hand, are, if anything, too conscious of the mere notes themselves. They often fall into the error of becoming so engrossed with their arpeggios and staccatos that they forget the deeper aspects of the music they are performing. But from the layman's standpoint, it is not so much a matter of getting over bad habits on the sheerly musical plane as of increasing one's awareness of what is going on, in so far as the notes are concerned.

When the man in the street listens to the "notes themselves" with any degree of concentration, he is most likely to make some mention of the melody. Either he hears a pretty melody or he does not, and he generally lets it go at that. Rhythm is likely to gain his attention next, particularly if it seems exciting. But harmony and tone color are generally taken for granted, if they are thought of consciously at all. As for music's having a definite form of some kind, that idea seems never to have occurred to him.

It is very important for all of us to become more alive to music on its sheerly musical plane. After all, an actual musical material is being used. The intelligent listener must be prepared to increase his awareness of the musical material and what happens to it. He must hear the melodies, the rhythms, the harmonies, the tone colors in a more conscious fashion. But above all he must, in order to follow the line of the composer's thought, know something of the principles of musical form. Listening to all of these elements is listening on the sheerly musical plane.

Let me repeat that I have split up mechanically the three separate planes on which we listen merely for the sake of greater clarity. Actually, we never listen on one or the other of these planes. What we do is to correlate them—listening in all three ways at the same time. It takes no mental effort, for we do it instinctively.

Perhaps an analogy with what happens to us when we visit the theater will make this instinctive correlation clearer. In the theater, you are aware of the actors and actresses, costumes and sets, sounds and movements. All these give one the sense that the theater is a pleasant place to be in. They constitute the sensuous plane in our theatrical reactions.

The expressive plane in the theater would be derived from the feeling that you get from what is happening on the stage. You are moved to pity, excitement, or gaiety. It is this general feeling, generated aside from the particular words being spoken, a certain emotional something which exists on the stage, that is analogous to the expressive quality in music.

The plot and plot development is equivalent to our sheerly musical plane. The playwright creates and develops a character in just the same way that a composer creates and develops a theme. According to the degree of your awareness of the way in which the artist in either field handles his material will you become a more intelligent listener.

It is easy enough to see that the theatergoer never is conscious of any of these elements separately. He is aware of them all at the same time. The same is true of music listening. We simultaneously and without thinking listen on all three planes.

In a sense, the ideal listener is both inside and outside the music at the same moment, judging it and enjoying it, wishing it would go one way and watching it go another—almost like the composer at the moment he composes it; because in order to write his music, the composer must also be inside and outside his music, carried away by it and yet coldly critical of it. A subjective and objective attitude is implied in both creating and listening to music.

What the reader should strive for, then, is a more *active* kind of listening. Whether you listen to Mozart or Duke Ellington, you can deepen your understanding of music only by being a more conscious and aware listener —not someone who is just listening, but someone who is listening *for* something.

Questions and Assignments

1. Why does Copland feel that any attempt to express the "meaning" of music in "so many words" can only be futile?

2. Do you normally expect "a great work of art . . . to mean exactly the same thing to you each time you return to it?" Is Copland's objection to such uniformity applicable to a story, a painting, or a movie? How would the length of the work affect his general rule?

3. Why does Copland repeat at the end of his essay that each plane of his discussion exists only in combination with the other two?

4. Is Copland's analysis of the theatre as effective as that of music? Does the relative superficiality seem to you indicative of his own interests or of the position of this analogy in his argument?

5. Using this essay as a model, discuss one of the following subjects by dividing it into what you consider its component parts:

Poetry
The process of studying, reading, thinking
Love, friendship
Goodness
Beauty
Football, baseball, basketball, tennis, skiing, etc.
Science, history, mathematics

Readings: Comparison and Contrast

Comparison and contrast involve a discussion of the subject in relation to some other subject. Just as we may appreciate our homes even more after we have been away, or we may realize the unpleasantness of last week's blind date when we compare him or her to the one we met this week, so by comparison and contrast in writing we may reveal the subject at hand. Similarities and differences may be described by discussing one whole subject at a time or by discussing one aspect at a time as it appears in each subject. Or the contrast may remain implicit as in our first essay, "The Middle Ages," (p. 259) which contrasts the Middle Ages with modern times in regard to ritual and emotion, calamities and indigence, publicity, silence and sound. Our second essay compares two translations of Homer, showing both similarities and differences as it goes along, and then concludes with a value judgment based on this comparison. The third essay concentrates on one person involved in the comparison, then on the second.

Johan Huizinga is an influential Dutch historian. This selection is from the opening of his book on *The Waning of the Middle Ages,* a study of the characteristics of a particular historical period. His first step in writing this type of book is to contrast the period about which he is writing with the modern period which his readers presumably are well acquainted with. For this reason he does not need to be explicit about the characteristics of modern times, although his phraseology requires us to take them into consideration. Where there is any doubt about the contrast, he does become explicit, as in the reference to the suburbs of a modern city or the light and noise which we are accustomed to.

Kenneth Wilson, Professor of English at the University of Connecticut and a specialist in linguistics, contrasts the poetic principles, the syntax, and the diction of two contemporary translations of Homer. This essay is interesting not only as a fine example of comparison and contrast, but also for the insight it should give you into the use of different words and syntax to express the same thoughts.

Samuel Johnson, an important eighteenth-century British critic and man-of-letters, provides similar insights into the different methods of writing and rewriting as practiced by two great poets.

The Middle Ages

JOHAN HUIZINGA

To the world when it was half a thousand years younger, the outlines of all things seemed more clearly marked than to us. The contrast between suffering and joy, between adversity and happiness, appeared more striking. All experience had yet to the minds of men the directness and absoluteness of the pleasure and pain of child-life. Every event, every action, was still embodied in expressive and solemn forms, which raised them to the dignity of a ritual. For it was not merely the great facts of birth, marriage and death which, by the sacredness of the sacrament, were raised to the rank of mysteries; incidents of less importance, like a journey, a task, a visit, were equally attended by a thousand formalities: benedictions, ceremonies, formulae.

Calamities and indigence were more afflicting than at present; it was more difficult to guard against them, and to find solace. Illness and health presented a more striking contrast; the cold and darkness of winter were more real evils. Honours and riches were relished with greater avidity and contrasted more vividly with surrounding misery. We, at the present day, can hardly understand the keenness with which a fur coat, a good fire on the hearth, a soft bed, a glass of wine, were formerly enjoyed.

Then, again, all things in life were of a proud or cruel publicity. Lepers sounded their rattles and went about in processions, beggars exhibited their deformity and their misery in churches. Every order and estate, every rank and profession, was distinguished by its costume. The great lords never moved about without a glorious display of arms and liveries, exciting fear and envy. Executions and other public acts of justice, hawking, marriages and funerals, were all announced by cries and processions, songs and music. The lover wore the colours of his lady; companions the emblem of their confraternity; parties and servants the badges or blazon of their lords. Between town and country, too, the contrast was very marked. A medieval town did not lose itself in extensive suburbs of factories and villas; girded by its walls, it stood forth as a compact whole, bristling with innumerable turrets. However tall and threatening the houses of noblemen or merchants might be, in the aspect of the town the lofty mass of the churches always remained dominant.

The contrast between silence and sound, darkness and light, like that between summer and winter, was more strongly marked than it is in our lives. The modern town hardly knows silence or darkness in their purity, nor the effect of a solitary light or a single distant cry.

All things presenting themselves to the mind in violent contrasts and impressive forms, lent a tone of excitement and of passion to everyday life and tended to produce that perpetual oscillation between despair and distracted joy, between cruelty and pious tenderness which characterize life in the Middle Ages.

Questions and Assignments

1. Examine the words and sentences of this selection to see how the author has maintained the comparative method throughout. Look especially for the use of semicolons with parallel main clauses, and the repetition of parallel ideas and phrases.

2. What particular words are necessary to this implicit comparison—for example, the word *still* in the fourth sentence? What would happen if you took out all such words?

3. How does the author use examples to illustrate his comparison? Check the whole selection to see how many abstract and how many concrete statements are presented in support of his comparison.

4. Pick one of the following subjects and compare it with something that your reader should know well, using the methods of implicit comparison which were used by Huizinga:

The older generation
Colonial or victorian architecture
College life
The psychology of girls (if you are a boy)
The psychology of boys (if you are a girl)
Another part of the country
A season of the year
The days of the pioneers
Methods of communication a hundred years ago
City or country life

On Translating Homer Once More

KENNETH G. WILSON

Homer is rapid, plain, direct, and noble, Matthew Arnold says. Arnold makes clear the nature of rapidity, plainness, and directness in illustrating his points with what still remain the most accurate and useful descriptions of Homeric qualities. But what of nobility? To Arnold, nobility was the ultimate, the most important quality of all. The translator might imitate Homer perfectly in the first three qualities, but if his translation lacked nobility, it could not succeed. Arnold's descriptions of nobility are maddeningly vague, and his examples of it are often far from explicit. Speaking of the translator's choice of diction, he remarks, "No doubt a true poetic feeling is the Homeric translator's best guide in the use of words. . . ." Other means of attaining nobility appear to be equally a matter of intuition or luck. If all goes well, nobility, according to Arnold's description, will inhere in the translation which achieves the other three qualities—the rapidity, the plainness, and the directness which the translator *can* attempt consciously to achieve.

Among recent translators of Homer into English, Richmond Lattimore achieves nobility, while W. H. D. Rouse assumes that nobility is no longer to be hoped for, and refuses even indirectly to seek it. Forgetting for the moment the distinctions between poetry and prose, let us consider this difference of assumption in order to discover how it happens that, although in rapidity and directness Rouse's *Iliad* has never been exceeded, and in plainness—the lack of ornament—it has good success, yet in nobility his translation is so completely lacking. Lattimore's translation, on the other hand, achieves rapidity, directness, and plainness—and nobility too. That is, although both translators strive for three of the qualities Arnold describes, one comes naturally to achieve the fourth, while the other omits it completely.

To be sure, neither translator attempts nobility. Richmond Lattimore only hopes for it. W. H. D. Rouse assumes instead that nobility does not concern the modern reader and offers him nothing which he can understand or will want to experience. Rouse believes, it seems to me, that nobility is a

From *The University of Kansas City Review,* 1959. Reprinted by permission.

quality which the modern reader cannot grasp, and that even if he could grasp it, he would not admire it. Surely, if these assumptions are to be granted, Rouse's rapid, direct, *modern* prose translation deserves our praise (and it has received a good deal of it). The character of the translation is strikingly different from the tradition of Lang, Leaf, and Myers. Rouse stresses the comic, the farcical, the colloquial, the slangy. His gods speak a good deal of cheerful chatter, and "What ho!" Hera says to Zeus, "You dreadful creature! What a thing to say!" They are rather like musical comedy deities. They converse in a half-whimsical style most of the time, so that Rouse's gods might well walk into a Shavian comedy without appearing out of place. They are fully aware of their own amusing behavior, sensitive to others' judgments of seriousness, anticipating and warding off any suggestion of their being "sincere." Above all they are gods who disarm our criticism of their actions by means of a full, modern self-consciousness which through its own sense of irony protects them from the irony of others. There is none of this in Lattimore's gods, and I conclude that by avoiding it he has caught the flavor of nobility. I believe also that in the translators' differences of opinion there are important implications for contemporary moral values.

First of all, however, let us consider the nature of nobility itself as it appears in heroic poetry. In *The Song of Roland* this quality is surprisingly simple to discover. It is often inexactly described as a child-like quality which makes the hero stand erect and deliver himself of long, proud speeches full of confidence in himself and his values, and without a trace of doubt of the worth of his efforts. Roland announces his virtues again and again, and he insists on his ability to perform. He states directly his earnest desire to do well, nor does he ever doubt that he will. As the late Erich Auerbach has pointed out, Roland's world is without real problems. Roland believes in his God and in the right as he sees it, and he has no moments of doubt about possibly virtuous pagans on the one hand or possibly fallible courage or ability in himself on the other. Above all, he never asks whether he is fighting for the right, or whether in his simple values there may be some flaw. In the following, the battle at Roncevals is about to begin, and the pagans approach with trumpets blaring.

> Then saith Oliver: "Sir comrade, methinks we shall have ado with the Saracens." "Now God grant it be as thou sayest," Roland answers him, "for to make stand here for our King is to do as good men ought to do. Verily, for his liege a man well ought to suffer

> pain and woe, and endure both great heat and great cold, and should hold him ready to lose both hide and hair in his lord's service. Now let each have a care that he strikes good blows and great, that no man may mis-say us in his songs. These misbelieving men are in the wrong, and right is with the Christians, and for my part I will give ye no ill example."

Nowhere in the poem is there any change from the position stated in this simple credo; none of these values ever comes under question. Most contemporary heroes could not make such a speech, or, if one did, either *his* sense of it or ours would be ironic. He might be a Felix Krull or some other *picaro* whose view of such sentiments would be completely calculated, or else he would be filled with conflicting doubts, either then or later. A modern hero—Raskolnikov or Julien Sorel, for example—does not live in such a simple world. A modern heroic narrative (if we may ignore the implicit contradictions in the term *heroic* used here) would almost inevitably concern itself with the examination and the revaluation of the ideas so calmly accepted in *The Song of Roland.* Auerbach concludes his splendid essay on *The Song of Roland* by remarking on the nature of the "elevated style" of the poem, and by pointing out its grip on reality:

> Confronting the reality of life, this style is neither able nor willing to deal with its breadths or depths. It is limited in time, place, and social milieu. It simplifies the events of the past by stylizing and idealizing them. The feeling it seeks to arouse in its auditor is admiration and amazement for a distant world, whose instincts and ideals, though they certainly remain his own, yet evolve in such uncompromising purity and freedom, in comparison with the friction and resistance of real life, as his practical existence could not possibly attain. Human movements and great, towering exemplary figures appear with striking effect; his own life is not there at all.

The "uncompromising purity and freedom" of the world of the narrative make the difference. Within that frame, the narrator and his heroes may stand unafraid of laughter and judgment. They may be absolutely unselfconscious.

It is this lack of self-consciousness (it may be childlike in some respects, but children fear laughter aimed at themselves; perhaps the best use of the word is in the distinction between *childlike* and *childish*) which makes poems like *The Song of Roland* seem almost to be parodies if they are read in the rigorously self-conscious frame of mind and protectively ironic tone of voice peculiar to the modern intellectual. One need argue only that Roland has mistaken his value or that the things in which he believes are foolish, and at once *The Song of Roland* becomes a parody. There is always only a narrow circle of protection for the man who takes himself seriously; we can accept him only by willingly suspending our disbelief in the "uncompromising purity and freedom" of his world. If we will not make that suspension, if we cannot accept a world without compromise—and Rouse cannot—then *The Song of Roland* certainly becomes a parody, and *The Iliad* may too.

The Iliad and *The Song of Roland* are of course very different in other important ways, but in this respect it seems to me that their difference is one of degree rather than of kind. I would argue that the quality of unselfconsciousness is, in fact, peculiar to all the great heroic narratives of Western literature, and that it is the major force in that quality in Homer which Arnold calls nobility. The heroic posture is that of a man standing erect, fearing no laughter, human or cosmic. The great heroic poems have the peculiar quality of making that posture appear glorious, never ludicrous.

The problem for the translator is therefore how to make acceptable to the reader the necessity for this world of no compromise, this world where the ironic sense of human futility and triviality is ultimately put away in favor of a glorious, reverent belief in human courage. The problems raised in translating such a poem can perhaps be illustrated simply enough if we describe *The Iliad* as a poem dealing with either "the wrath of Achilles" or "the squabble between Achilles and Agamemnon"; the choice of the latter phrasing implies the triviality, the fallibility of the motivations. The choice of "the wrath of Achilles," or Lattimore's "the anger of Peleus' son Achilleus and its devastation," simply ignores the possibility that anything might be questioned. Such diction argues rather that this wrath and these actions are of the highest dignity and importance. That there could be any question never enters the narrator's mind.

Nobleness, the most important of Arnold's list of Homeric characteristics, can be illustrated in the heroes and their actions and in the style, the *manner* in which the poet tells their story. Arnold called it "the grand manner." A comparison of the translations by Lattimore and Rouse will illustrate the point. Consider first this simple little discussion of Euchenor, a very minor Achaian, as Lattimore translates it. Paris, seeking to avenge the death of a friend,

let fly a bronze-shod arrow.
There was a man, Euchenor, son of the seer Polyidos,
a rich man and good, who lived in his house at Korinth,
who knew well that it was his death when he went on shipboard,
that he must die in his own house of a painful sickness
or go with the ships of the Achaians and be killed by the Trojans.
He therefore chose to avoid the troublesome price the Achaians
would ask, and the hateful sickness so his heart might not be afflicted.
Paris struck him by jaw and ear, and at once the life spirit
fled from his limbs, and the hateful darkness closed in about him.

The statement of Euchenor's troubled choice is clear; there are two possibilities, with a minor economic advantage accompanying the choice of the heroic death. Irony is not stressed in the modern way; the man's choice is dignified and brave; he is noble. Rouse tells the story thus:

> [Paris] took a shot in revenge. There was a man there, the son of Polyidos the diviner, one Euchenor of Corinth, a man both wealthy and brave. He knew well what his fate would be before he embarked; for the good old man Polyidos had told him often enough, that he was either to die of a cruel disease in his own house, or to fall by a Trojan hand in the great war. *So he avoided two evils at the same time, the fatal disease and a heavy fine, and saved himself a great deal of discomfort.* Paris hit this man near the jawbone under the ear: a quick death for him when the darkness took him.

The understatement of the italicized sentence avoids nobility and adds a touch of the modern's vaunted irony; it is almost flippant. What the sentence does is to make Euchenor's choice acceptable to a modern realist. In the brevity of the statement and the stress on the logic, any idealistic quality in Euchenor's character which might have been suggested in the Lattimore translation is removed. Euchenor here is a sensible, courageous businessman, not a hero exemplifying Arnold's *nobleness.* He may also be the butt of ironic laughter.

Diction and syntax both accomplish these different ends, but the whole distinction involves a grasp of what seems "properly explained and adequately motivated" for the modern reader. Rouse's assumption is that no one now can accept men who act with the naïveté of Boy Scouts or with such sturdy Harry Watsonesque belief in the virtue of virtue and the absolute acceptability of ideal behavior. Lattimore assumes that we can.

The word which often suggests itself to me in these connections is *quixotic*: I have caught myself about to say that Homer's heroes, as Lattimore sees them, are quixotic. They are not. At least they are not if we insist that the quixotic hero carries on his idealistic activities in a world which is clearly real and not at all suited to such actions, so that there is explicit a conscious judgment of his error. Everyone in Lattimore's *Iliad,* from the narrator and Achilles and Hector to the Euchenors, accepts the ideal forms and values. There is no one *in* the narrative to stress an ironic awareness of the folly of human beings who cannot see themselves as trivial and silly in their heroic posturings. If we are to see any such quality—and lose nobility—we must bring it from outside; we must deny, as Rouse does, the acceptability to the modern reader of a world of "uncompromising purity and freedom."

Another word Arnold employed for this air so peculiar to Homer's great poem is *elevation;* he argued that the tone of the narrative, its subject, and its very diction were elevated, and that it was in the imitation of this elevation that so many had gone astray—he stressed some translations particularly, whose diction, while elevated, was not elevated in the Homeric manner. Efforts to achieve this kind of separateness from the affairs and representations of the world of men have been of many sorts; Arnold described most of the kinds in *On Translating Homer, I.* All the main problems seemed to turn on the kind of meter, the kind of syntax, the kind of rhetoric, and the kind of diction employed by the translator. In his famous dictum, Arnold phrased it this way:

> The translator of Homer should above all be penetrated by a sense of four qualities of his author: that he is eminently rapid; that he is eminently plain and direct both in the evolution of his thought and in the expression of it, that is, both in his syntax and in his words; that he is eminently plain and direct in the substance of his thought, that is, in his matter and ideas; and, finally that he is eminently noble . . .

He then continued to illustrate how Chapman, Pope, Cowper, Newman, and other English translators of *The Iliad* had failed in one or another of these qualities. Pope's translation was "highly intellectualized" and "oratorical," and while it did all these rhetorical things well, it was not Homer; Arnold characterized Pope's *Iliad* as having an "artificial evolution of thought and a literary cast of style"; these were virtues in Pope's own verse, but they were flaws in the translation of Homer. Cowper was too Miltonic; his blank verse, like Pope's and Chapman's rime, was out of place. The "inversion and pregnant conciseness of Milton" were "the very opposites of the directness and flowingness of Homer . . ." Cowper's blank verse and its compact syntax, like Pope's antitheses and rime, broke the flow of direct, simple thought. Chapman failed because he was given to the fantastic elaboration, the conceits, of the Elizabethans; "he cannot forbear to interpose a play of thought between his object and its expression."

If we set aside the purely prosodic considerations here, except as they influence syntax and the order of words where these reflect the order of the idea, we can see that Arnold argues essentially for a natural word order of some sort, a syntax with no consciously rhetorical rearrangement, no stress on antitheses or epigrammatic statement. The modern linguist may therefore be able to supply us with the proper term. But first observe in what respects the Lattimore and Rouse translations are syntactically similar. Here, from the Lattimore version, is the oft-repeated description of a sacrificial offering:

And when all had made prayer and flung down the scattering barley
first they drew back the victims' heads and slaughtered them and skinned them,
and cut away the meat from the thighs and wrapped them in fat,
making a double fold, and laid shreds of flesh upon them.
The old man burned these on a cleft stick and poured the gleaming
wine over, while the young men with forks in their hands stood about him.
But when they had burned the thigh pieces and tasted the vitals,
they cut all the remainder into pieces and spitted them
and roasted all carefully and took off the pieces.
Then after they had finished the work and got the feast ready
they feasted, nor was any man's hunger denied a fair portion.

And the same passage in Rouse's prose:

> And when they all had prayed and cast the barley-grains, they first drew back the heads, and killed, and flayed, carved out the thigh-slices and rolled them between pieces of fat, and laid more raw flesh upon them: then the old priest burnt them upon sticks of wood, and poured sparkling wine over, while the young men held

> their five-pronged forks ready by his side. After the thigh-pieces were burnt and the inner parts were divided, they chopped up the rest and ran spits through the meat, roasted all properly and drew it off. This work done, they prepared their meal and enjoyed it, and no one lacked a fair share.

The order of the words is almost identical. Two points of difference appear besides those of diction: (1) occasionally, as in the last sentence in the passage, Rouse compresses the longer, full introductory clause into a phrase; (2) Lattimore has a way of spelling out in full who did what and to what and how. He never omits pronouns, and he seems always to state grammatical objects in full, no matter how clearly they might be understood. Rouse, on the other hand, attempts to combine and to let series constructions permit him to omit repetition of some pronouns: compare the stated details in Lattimore's "first they drew back the *victims'* heads and slaughtered *them* and skinned *them,*" etc., with Rouse's "they first drew back the heads, and killed, and flayed," etc.

From the same passage we can illustrate this syntactic difference even further. Lattimore is not at all afraid of the long string of *and*-connected verbs and clauses, but Rouse prefers to vary the pace by interrupting with a series construction. Lattimore seems always to seek the steady addition of detail, the unselfconscious repetition of a comfortable pattern, while Rouse seems to seek variety. Having established a series, he will then simplify it, omit obvious words, and generally economize. Lattimore moves methodically and calmly through the entire pattern without shortening or saving anything. I believe the differences in syntax just described are typical of these two translations.

In direct narrative, when the voice of the poem simply tells how this man struck that man with a spear—describing the course of the spear and the place of the wound and such matters—Rouse and Lattimore translate very much alike, except for the differences just mentioned. In Book VII, during the fight with Aias, Hector is hit by a spear:

> *All the way through the glittering shield went the heavy spearhead,*
> *and crashed its way through the intricately worked corselet;*
> *straight ahead by the flank the spearhead shore through his*
> *tunic, yet he bent away to one side and avoided the dark death.*

> Right through it went, and through corselet also. The blade cut the tunic on Hector's side, but he swerved, and saved his life.

There are the same number of clauses here, and their order is essentially identical. The difference is in the detail; wherever he can, Rouse makes a single verb do the work of verb, object, and modifiers.

If the syntactic differences are least in direct narrative, they are greatest in dialogue. Here, the difference between Lattimore's syntax and Rouse's syntax is often of kind as well as degree. Consider these two speeches from Book X, where Menelaos encounters Agamemnon at night. Lattimore has the following:

> *It was Menelaos of the great war cry who spoke first:*
> *"Why this arming, my brother? Is it some one of your companions*
> *you are stirring to go and spy on the Trojans? Yet I fear sadly*
> *there will not be any man to undertake this endeavour,*
> *going against enemy fighters to spy on them, alone, through*
> *the immortal night. Such a man will have to be very bold-hearted."*
> *Then in turn powerful Agamemnon answered him:*
> *"You and I, illustrious, O Menelaos, have need now*
> *of crafty counsel, if any man is to defend and rescue*
> *the Argives and their ships, since the heart of Zeus is turned from us.*
> *For the sacrifices of Hektor have stirred his heart more than ours have.*
> *No, for I never saw nor heard from the lips of another*
> *of a single man in a day imagining so much evil*
> *as Hektor, beloved of Zeus, has wrought on the sons of the Achaians,*
> *alone, being called true son neither of a god nor a goddess.*
> *He has done things I think the Argives will remember with sorrow*
> *long into the future, such harm has he devised the Achaians.*
> *But go now, running lightly beside the ships, and call to us*
> *Idomeneus and Aias, while I shall go after Nestor*
> *the brilliant, and waken him to rise, if he might be willing*
> *to approach the sacred duty of the guards, or give orders to them.*
> *Above all, these would listen to him, seeing that his own son*
> *commands the pickets, and with him the follower of Idomeneus,*
> *Meriones. To these above all we entrusted the duty."*

The same passage in Rouse reads:

> Menelaos said: "Why are you arming, my dear fellow? Do you think of sending out a spy? I'm dreadfully afraid you will not find a

> man ready for that job—to go out all alone in the depth of night and spy in the enemy camp! He will be a plucky man!"
>
> Agamemnon answered: "We must find some plan, you and I, my dear Menelaos, something useful, to save our people and our ships, now Zeus has changed his mind. Hector's offerings, as it seems, are more to his mind than ours. For I never saw or heard in my life that one man in one day did so much mischief as Hector has done against us, just by himself! He's no son of a god or goddess. But he has done things that our nation will lament for ever and ever. What a mess he has made! Come along, run as fast as you can and call Aias and Idomeneus; I will look up Nestor, and see if he will come with us to the young fellows on outpost duty, and tell them what to do. They will listen to him more than any one, for his son is in command of the outposts, he and Meriones, the friend of Idomeneus. We put them in general charge."

The differences in diction leap out, but let us put them aside for the moment and concentrate on syntax, on the order of words and its relationship to patterns with which we are familiar. The "natural order" of the syntax which was similar in the passages of direct narrative above has changed a good deal. Both versions may still be natural, but they are no longer alike. Terms like *formal* and *informal, platform speech* and *informal colloquial speech* come to mind as we seek to describe the difference. Rouse's syntax is sometimes elliptical; it employs contractions; it is full of the parenthesis of conversational English; along with the diction of the colloquial idiom comes colloquial syntax: "What a mess he has made!" Again in the Rouse version there is economy of syntax, but here in the dialogue there is a good deal more of it, and it is more than simply a shortening of otherwise similar syntactic patterns while retaining the outlines of the patterns themselves. Here the attempt is to imitate the flow of speech itself, the varied pace of utterance, the ellipsis, and the broken or delayed syntax of informal colloquial English.

Lattimore's translation has none of these characteristics. There is no attempt to imitate real speech, with its syntactic false starts and its other structural uniqueness. Lattimore's language is much like that which he employed for the direct narrative discussed above. It is full, steady, and unhurried. There is none of the syntax peculiar only to informal colloquial utterance. This dialogue is unlike formal or platform speech, moreover, in that its rhetoric is not consciously studied; it does not turn periods or antitheses or do anything in the nature of formal rhetoric. Above all, it has a quality of calm. That there are no exclamation points is indicative; the same passage in the Rouse version has several. Syntax contributes to this calmness—or perhaps is dictated by it—in that patterns are meticulously filled out, without any omission, without any hurried parenthesis. If parenthesis is necessary, it receives full clausal status. It is perhaps in this respect, in the firm control of the subordination of one idea to another—such as human argument and discussion require—that Lattimore's dialogue achieves its noblest air.

Auerbach makes the distinction between *parataxis,* wherein there is little subordination and the narrative consists simply of a series of assertive statements following one another (as in *The Song of Roland*), and *hypotaxis,* wherein there is subordination in syntax as in thought. Auerbach's extremely interesting comments on this matter are surely apposite here. Perhaps nobility, if it *is* related to this quality of unselfconsciousness of which I have spoken, relies a good deal on a relatively paratactic narrative. A man certain of the soundness of his beliefs and the rightness of his actions does not feel it necessary to hedge and qualify his statements. But a man unsure—a man in a real world where "uncompromising purity and freedom" do not hold sway, or where he fears that they do not—this man must protect himself with carefully subordinated arguments and meticulously qualified statements. Hence there is a good deal of difference between the "childlike" simplicity of Roland's utterance quoted earlier, and the tormented prose of J. D. Salinger's *The Catcher in the Rye.* It is my contention, further, that the Homeric narrator, like his heroes, has this same wonderful confidence in the rightness of his values and the absolute dignity of the actions he is describing. Hence Lattimore's Homer's voice is calm; he can run rapidly, but not without dignity; his language is dressed for that occasion. When his heroes speak, they too never lose their dignity; their syntax is natural but never colloquial. It is here that Rouse's translation seems to suffer a division in itself, since, as we have said, his narrator's voice, though more economical, more brisk and efficient, is usually not widely different from that of the Lattimore narrator. But when the Rouse *heroes* talk, there is a marked change, a shift in the "world of the narrative," and what before has been pure and free is now compromised; these men are, at least in their speech, just like everybody else; they live in our impure, unfree world. Their speech reflects "the friction and resistance of real life."

I am inclined to agree with Arnold in this one point, at any rate: it is bootless to attempt to write a translation of Homer which will be to us exactly as was Homer's original to the ears either of his own audience (of whom we know little) or of an audience in Pericles' Athens (of whom we know a good deal, but still not enough). My main interest is conditioned by the assumptions that each of these translators makes: Lattimore assumes that a "noble" *Iliad* is what the modern reader needs; it seems to him to be *true,* an accurate translation. Rouse, on the other hand, argues that a "colloquial" *Iliad* is what the modern reader wants, where colloquial stands for the language of men as our ears hear it *spoken* daily, with its slang and its changing meanings and its economy and its pace. Why should there be this disagreement? If we cannot solve the historical question, can we at least attack the question of the modern reader's taste? Why will he accept, if Rouse is right, only a narrative which makes him everywhere conscious of "the friction and resistance of real life"? It seems to me that the whole problem, linguistic and interpretative, centers about the problem of self-consciousness and unselfconsciousness, and the possibilities in the reader for the willing suspension of disbelief.

Nobility, I believe, consists largely in the forgetting of self, in unselfconsciousness, even before enormously grand values of courage and greatness, values which men can accept without fear, or cavil, or doubt, or qualification. In Lattimore's *Iliad,* it consists in the narrator's sense of security: these were great men, greater than ours; these men were indeed godlike and glorious. Homer assumes it, and he does not ask pardon for digression or detail in describing their smallest actions. Nothing they do can be trivial. Achilles assumes it; so do Agamemnon and Nestor. Nestor's long reminiscences are not, in Lattimore's *Iliad,* the boring chatter of a garrulous old man, and this to me makes sense in the face of the obvious admiration he receives from so impatient a man as Agamemnon; Rouse makes him another sort of man, an amusing old soldier whose words are sympathetically heard, but who cannot be taken seriously except as a relic of his former self. It is incongruous in the Rouse version, then, to see the other Achaians give him more reverence than that due to the shell of a former hero.

Hector comes the closest of any of Lattimore's heroes to losing this nobleness, this unselfconscious quality. Achilles sulks, we say, but we never really consider his action childish, when Lattimore describes it. But Hector, in the scene where he bids good-bye to wife and son, seems close to doubt; this is the scene which more than any other in the translation makes the modern first-time reader a Trojan-sympathizer. Here, as Hector listens to

Andromache's plea, it seems he is about to falter, and new readers feel, "Yes, yes! *Our* wars have told us she is right; therefore stay home! Let glory go, and save yourself!" They seldom even see that he rejects her request without really entertaining it at all; it is only Andromache's weakness, not his. Yet that passage is one the first-time reader remembers above all, regardless of the translation, because, I think, he cannot even see what Hector sees: that there really is no other fate possible—for a *hero.* No man here—from Euchenor to Achilles—who has had the offer of alternative fates (Achilles' offer was a long life at home, devoid of fame, or a short but glorious life as the Achaians' greatest warrior), has any hesitation in his choosing, and none ever chooses safety over glory.

When we recover Homer, as I believe Lattimore has done, however, we do not fail to see that glorious courage reigns supreme. Hector does not falter. There is, in his world, no room for self-conscious doubt. Achilles' very withdrawal illustrates the point: when Agamemnon takes Briseis, Achilles doubts the gods and struggles against himself. But in the end the hero turns away from bitter introspection; he was wrong to doubt. Heroic action, and magnanimity—these are the qualities of the greatest man. Nobility. That is what the *Iliad* is all about.

Rouse retells "the story of Achilles" for the modern reader, and the effect is very different from that of Lattimore's *Iliad.* His heroes are self-conscious. Their language is symptomatic of their inner conflicts. Few of them can talk without irony, without a comic sense. And if they do not perceive their folly, we the readers do. In his preface, Rouse remarks:

> . . . Homer is full of merriment, full of open fun and delicate comedy, even farce—as when Ares, wounded, bursts up to Olympus like a bomb. And the divine family! What a delightful natural party—human beings raised a degree or two, but all the funnier for that.

I claim that much of the humor—certainly the bulk of the sardonic comment on the gods, is Rouse's doing, and his reader's. Rouse sees in the *Odyssey,* and in the *Iliad* too, a great deal of irony, until the word *godlike* in itself must become a nasty word, full of an opposite meaning. I submit that this cannot be, if Achilles is to be a great man; if we read and translate Homer in this way then the only thing we can see anywhere in the tale is comedy, the piddling little tempests which men create in teapots—poor, silly, little men! And then Homer's remark on the size of these heroes as compared with men nowadays becomes a crushing sarcasm.

Christopher Morley once wrote a comic narrative he called the *Trojan Horse,* "the *Iliad* in Modern Dress." It is most amusing, with its football atmosphere and locker room chatter, its roadhouse, Sarpedoni's, for the post-game celebration, and so on. But surely it is no surprise to discover that a heroic poem can be parodied? What could be easier? A heroic poem, with its troop of solemn heroes and their earnest, noble speeches is essentially its own parody. One needs only to read its speeches in a certain mirthful or effeminate or Algeresque or other special tone of voice and the thing can be done without the change of a word. We laugh, because we see what these heroes never can, that their world isn't real and true at all; it is all a giant misconception, and they are fools. Roland is the easiest one to destroy in this way, because his world—that part of reality which the poet has selected and stylized and simplified because in his view it is the *significant* part—is so obviously "uncompromisingly pure and free." Only a little exaggeration is needed to bring it down, and *The Pilgrimage of Charlemagne to Jerusalem* points out one easy way; the French themselves knew how to parody it. Since the hero—and the narrator—do not protect themselves by a sense of irony, or a perception of folly, or a hedging-in with realistic matter, the parody is always there for us to take; all we need do is (as with *The Sorrows of Young Werther*) refuse to believe. Laughter is then inevitable.

The *Iliad* is not quite so easy, because the tripods, shields, chariots, and other material objects are there to supply what seems to be realism. But, as in Don Quixote's discourse on the height and weight of giants, these details are not enough to protect it from our laughter if we will not believe. The world of the *Iliad*—that selection of the significant things, of what according to the poem is the only true reality—is easy to refute. One need say only that courage is not virtue, and that men are poor, weak, sniveling things, more sheep than lions, and the job is done. Or, as Rouse sometimes does, one need merely suggest that these values may be doubtful. But it is easier still to refute it if in the middle of that special world are men who talk like us, instead of like themselves. Rouse, without I think desiring to make a parody at all, has succeeded fairly well in establishing some aspects of the world; much of his description is rapid, plain, direct—and potentially noble. But Rouse's dialogue, his heroes' speeches, the *drama*—the very things which dominate and distinguish the great heroic narratives

—are from *our* world, not Homer's. Noble his heroes are not; and there's the rub.

Now let us turn once more to Arnold:

> To suppose that it is *fidelity* to an original to give its matter, unless at the same time you give its manner; or rather, to suppose that you can really give its matter at all, unless you can give its manner, is just the mistake of our Pre-Raphaelite school of painters, who do not understand that the peculiar effect of nature resides in the whole and not in the parts.

Each of our translators has tried to give us matter and manner as he sees it. Rouse points out however that he has had a good bit to omit in his version:

> This book . . . is a translation into plain English of the plain story of Homer, omitting the embellishments which were meant only to please the ear—stock epithets and recurring phrases where the meaning is of no account.

The case he makes (in "Homer's Words") for these omissions has its merits. But its first assumption interests me most: for the modern reader, apparently, not all of Homer is germane. We must adapt and modify the values of the poem exactly as we must translate its language. Tastes in values change like language, and there is no going back. The next step is to argue that there is no willing suspension of disbelief, to this extent at least; and there I cannot follow him.

The Rouse *Iliad* is, it seems to me, a bitter and frightening document, despite all its good humor, all the gaiety of gods and men. Perhaps the position it represents is existential; in any case it seems to claim that there can be no real nobility, and that no man dare be unselfconscious, even in his artistic experiences. This I cannot accept. Therefore I am cheered immeasurably by Lattimore's translation of *The Iliad,* for it seems to me not only noble in a way which Arnold would have liked, but also capable of what any great work of art must be capable—of permitting us to leave our world and ourselves to the extent of willingly suspending disbelief in great values—here, in the gods and the fates, in courage and nobility. It lets us accept the unselfconscious hero, however lost to our world we may now think he is, and be lifted by him. At least in art, if *only* there, we can have nobility in our time. If Rouse's *Iliad* is an accurate reflection of our world, then surely we need Lattimore's *Iliad* the more.

Questions and Assignments

1. Formulate the distinction that Wilson makes in his first paragraphs between the two translations. How can nobility be the basic subject if in Arnold its "descriptions . . . are maddeningly vague"?

2. How does your answer to the last question suggest to you the movement of Wilson's essay? How does his statement that "neither translator attempts nobility" fit in with this direction of the essay?

3. Explain how "unselfconsciousness," that Wilson declares the peculiar quality of all great heroic narratives in Western literature, is lost in the comic diction of Rouse. Have you ever responded to the heroic as if it were ludicrous? Do you think that the heroic quality can survive this response?

4. Analyze the first four paragraphs and provide an outline of their organization. What is the purpose in this essay of the extended reference to the *Song of Roland*? Are there, then, two comparisons being made in this essay? What are they and what is their relationship to one another?

5. What does Wilson consider to be the problem of the translator of an epic poem like the *Iliad*? How well does his conclusion accord with the organization and purpose of his essay? In what way and where has he anticipated and prepared his reader for the final sentence of this essay?

6. Does Wilson merely compare two whole translations in general, or does he utilize some sort of division in the course of his comparison? What aspects of the different translations does he discuss? Perhaps you will need to outline this part of the essay in order to perceive the careful organization.

7. After reading this essay, are you inclined to agree or disagree with Wilson about the quality of the two translations of Homer? If you disagree, write a paper based on the information in his essay, showing why you think Rouse is better.

8. Write an essay discussing the idea that "nobility is a quality which the modern reader cannot grasp, and . . . even if he could grasp it, he would not admire it." Choose two plays, movies, or books which can be compared in order to prove your point. If your two examples differ in subject matter, they should at least both be attempting nobility. Or else you may choose two examples written or produced about similar subjects, but not equally noble. For example, you might compare two different productions of a Shakespearean play, or two different movies on a Biblical theme, or two different books with obviously contrasting views on morality and the meaning of life.

The Working Methods of Pope and Dryden

SAMUEL JOHNSON

Pope was one of those few whose labour is their pleasure: he was never elevated to negligence, nor wearied to impatience; he never passed a fault unamended by indifference, nor quitted it by despair. He laboured his works first to gain reputation and afterwards to keep it.

Of composition there are different methods. Some employ at once memory and invention, and, with little intermediate use of the pen, form and polish large masses by continued meditation, and write their productions only when, in their own opinion, they have completed them. It is related of Virgil, that his custom was to pour out a great number of verses in the morning, and pass the day in retrenching exuberances and correcting inaccuracies. The method of Pope, as may be collected from his translation, was to write his first thoughts in his first words, and gradually to amplify, decorate, rectify, and refine them.

With such faculties, and such dispositions, he excelled every other writer in poetical prudence; he wrote in such a manner as might expose him to few hazards. He used almost always the same fabric of verse; and, indeed, by those few essays which he made of any other, he did not enlarge his reputation. Of this uniformity the certain consequence was readiness and dexterity. By perpetual practice, language had, in his mind, a systematical arrangement; having always the same use for words, he had words so selected and combined as to be ready at his call. This increase of facility he confessed himself to have perceived in the progress of his translation.

But what was yet of more importance, his effusions were always voluntary, and his subjects chosen by himself. His independence secured him from drudging at a task, and labouring upon a barren topic: he never exchanged praise for money, nor opened a shop of condolence or congratulation. His poems, therefore, were scarce ever temporary. He suffered coronations and royal marriages to pass without a song, and derived no opportunities from recent events, nor any popularity from the accidental disposition of his readers. He was never reduced to the necessity of soliciting the sun to shine upon a birthday, of calling the Graces and Virtues to a wedding, or of saying what multitudes have said before him. When he could produce nothing new, he was at liberty to be silent.

His publications were for the same reason never hasty. He is said to have sent nothing to the press till it had lain two years under his inspection: it is at least certain that he ventured nothing without nice examination. He suffered the tumult of imagination to subside, and the novelties of invention to grow familiar. He knew that the mind is always enamoured of its own productions, and did not trust his first fondness. He consulted his friends, and listened with great willingness to criticism; and, what was of more importance, he consulted himself, and let nothing pass against his own judgment.

He professed to have learned his poetry from Dryden, whom, whenever an opportunity was presented, he praised through his whole life with unvaried liberality; and perhaps his character may receive some illustration, if he be compared with his master.

Integrity of understanding and nicety of discernment were not allotted in a less proportion to Dryden than to Pope. The rectitude of Dryden's mind was sufficiently shown by the dismission of his poetical prejudices, and the rejection of unnatural thoughts and rugged numbers. But Dryden never desired to apply all the judgment that he had. He wrote, and professed to write, merely for the people; and when he pleased others, he contented himself. He spent no time in struggles to rouse latent powers; he never attempted to make that better which was already good, nor often to mend what he must have known to be faulty. He wrote, as tells us, with very little consideration; when occasion or necessity called upon him, he poured out what the present moment happened to supply, and, when once it had passed the press, ejected it from his mind; for when he had no pecuniary interest, he had no further solicitude.

Pope was not content to satisfy; he desired to excel, and therefore always endeavoured to do his best: he did not court the candour, but dared the judgment of his reader, and, expecting no indulgence from others, he showed none to himself. He examined lines and words with minute and punctilious observation, and retouched every part with indefatigable diligence, till he had left nothing to be forgiven.

For this reason he kept his pieces very long in his hands, while he considered and reconsidered them. The only poems which can be supposed to have been written with such regard to the times as might hasten their publication were the two satires of *Thirty-eight;* of which Dodsley told me that they were brought to him by the author, that they might be fairly copied. "Almost every line," he said, "was then written twice over; I gave him a clean transcript, which he sent some time afterwards to me for the press, with almost every line written twice over a second time."

His declaration that his care for his works ceased at their publication was not strictly true. His parental attention never abandoned them; what he found amiss in the first edition, he silently corrected in those that followed. He appears to have revised the *Iliad,* and freed it from some of its imperfections; and the *Essay on Criticism* received many improvements after its first appearance. It will seldom be found that he altered without adding clearness, elegance, or vigour. Pope had perhaps the judgment of Dryden; but Dryden certainly wanted the diligence of Pope.

In acquired knowledge, the superiority must be allowed to Dryden, whose education was more scholastic, and who before he became an author had been allowed more time for study, with better means of information. His mind has a larger range, and he collects his images and illustrations from a more extensive circumference of science. Dryden knew more of man in his general nature, and Pope in his local manners. The notions of Dryden were formed by comprehensive speculation, and those of Pope by minute attention. There is more dignity in the knowledge of Dryden, and more certainly in that of Pope.

Poetry was not the sole praise of either; for both excelled likewise in prose; but Pope did not borrow his prose from his predecessor. The style of Dryden is capricious and varied; that of Pope is cautious and uniform. Dryden observes the motions of his own mind; Pope constrains his mind to his own rules of composition. Dryden is sometimes vehement and rapid; Pope is always smooth, uniform, and gentle. Dryden's page is a natural field, rising into inequalities, and diversified by the varied exuberance of abundant vegetation; Pope's is a velvet lawn, shaven by the scythe, and levelled by the roller.

Of genius, that power which constitutes a poet; that quality without which judgment is cold, and knowledge is inert; that energy which collects, combines, amplifies, and animates; the superiority must, with some hesitation, be allowed to Dryden. It is not to be inferred that of this poetical vigour Pope had only a little, because Dryden had more; for every other writer since Milton must give place to Pope; and even of Dryden it must be said, that, if he has brighter paragraphs, he has not better poems. Dryden's performances were always hasty, either excited by some external occasion, or extorted by domestic necessity; he composed without consideration, and published without correction. What his mind could supply at call, or gather in one excursion, was all that he sought, and all that he gave. The dilatory caution of Pope enabled him to condense his sentiments, to multiply his images, and to accumulate all that study might produce or chance might supply. If the flights of Dryden therefore are higher, Pope continues longer on the wing. If of Dryden's fire the blaze is brighter, of Pope's the heat is more regular and constant. Dryden often surpasses expectation, and Pope never falls below it. Dryden is read with frequent astonishment, and Pope with perpetual delight.

This parallel will, I hope, when it is well considered, be found just; and if the reader should suspect me, as I suspect myself, of some partial fondness for the memory of Dryden, let him not too hastily condemn me; for meditation and inquiry may, perhaps, show him the reasonableness of my determination.

Questions and Assignments

1. This contrast comes from Johnson's long essay on the life and work of Pope. What are Johnson's six points of comparison between Dryden and Pope? Where and how are they developed? Does the order of their development have any special value? Are the first six paragraphs related to the comparison?

2. Why does Johnson feel Pope's own criticism "of more importance" to his work than that of others? Can you substantiate this from your personal experience?

3. Contrast Pope's care in revision with Dryden's. Why does Johnson insist upon the importance of Pope's refusal to write for particular occasions?

4. Distinguish between the range of Dryden and that of Pope. Would you expect either to excel both in range and in careful revision?

5. Show how much Johnson condenses in his opening paragraph about the nature of work. How rare are the virtues he praises? What especially is unusual in his praise "he never passed a fault unamended by indifference"?

6. Analyze the style and organization of the next-to-the-last paragraph. Aside from the careful comparison, can you find in this paragraph a definition? An analogy?

7. Write an essay comparing the working methods or the characters of two of the following:

Yourself and your roommate
Two of your friends
Your mother and father
Two teachers
Two literary characters
Two writers that you know well

Readings: Analogy

An analogy is a particular kind of comparison by which one subject is discussed according to terms which apply to the other. Simple analogies are often used in good writing, and extended analogies provide a very useful method of development for certain types of subjects. In the case of Franklin's discussion of "The Morals of Chess," the analogy between chess and life serves to illuminate both subjects by indicating the significance of chess as a means of understanding the "game" of life. Berlin's essay called "The Hedgehog and the Fox" is, as he says, a form of classification, but the principle of classification is an analogy without which the subject would be almost too complicated for coherent discussion.

Isaiah Berlin is a University Lecturer in Philosophy at Oxford. This selection is from the first chapter of a book about Tolstoy, the great Russian novelist.

Benjamin Franklin needs no introduction. A philosopher, scientist, writer, and statesman, apparently he was also an accomplished chess-player.

The Hedgehog and the Fox

ISAIAH BERLIN

There is a line among the fragments of the Greek poet Archilochus which says: "The fox knows many things, but the hedgehog knows one big thing." Scholars have differed about the correct interpretation of these dark words, which may mean no more than that the fox, for all his cunning, is defeated by the hedgehog's one defence. But, taken figuratively, the words can be made to yield a sense in which they mark one of the deepest differences which divide writers and thinkers, and, it may be, human beings in general. For there exists a great chasm between those, on one side, who relate everything to a single central vision, one system less or more coherent or articulate, in terms of which they understand, think and feel—a single, universal, organizing principle in terms of which alone all that they are and say has significance—and, on the other side, those who pursue many ends, often unrelated and even contradictory, connected, if at all, only in some *de facto* way, for some psychological or physiological cause, related by no moral or aesthetic principle; these last lead lives, perform acts, and entertain ideas that are centrifugal rather than centripetal, their thought is scattered or diffused, moving on many levels, seizing upon the essence of a vast variety of experiences and objects for what they are in themselves, without, consciously or unconsciously, seeking to fit them into, or exclude them from, any one unchanging, all-embracing, sometimes self-contradictory and incomplete, at times fanatical, unitary inner vision. The first kind of intellectual and artistic personality belongs to the hedgehogs, the second to the foxes; and without insisting on a rigid classification, we may, without too much fear of contradiction, say that, in this sense, Dante belongs to the first category, Shakespeare to the second; Plato, Lucretius, Pascal, Hegel, Dostoevsky, Nietzsche, Ibsen, Proust are, in varying degrees, hedgehogs; Herodotus, Aristotle, Montaigne, Erasmus, Molière, Goethe, Pushkin, Balzac, Joyce are foxes.

Of course, like all over-simple classifications of this type, the dichotomy becomes, if pressed, artificial, scholastic, and ultimately absurd. But if it is not an aid to serious criticism, neither should it be rejected as being merely superficial or frivolous; like all distinctions which embody any degree of truth, it offers a point of view from which to look and compare, a starting-point for genuine investigation. Thus we have no doubt about the violence of the contrast between Pushkin and Dostoevsky; and Dostoevsky's celebrated speech about Pushkin has, for all its eloquence and depth of feeling, seldom been considered by any perceptive reader to cast light on the genius of Pushkin, but rather on that of Dostoevsky himself, precisely because it perversely represents Pushkin—an arch-fox, the greatest in the nineteenth century—as a being similar to Dostoevsky who is nothing if not a hedgehog; and thereby transforms, indeed distorts, Pushkin into a dedicated prophet, a bearer of a single, universal message which was indeed the centre of Dostoevsky's own universe, but exceedingly remote from the many varied provinces of Pushkin's protean genius. Indeed, it would not be absurd to say that Russian literature is spanned by these gigantic figures—at one pole Pushkin, at the other Dostoevsky; and that the characteristics of other Russian writers can, by those who find it useful or enjoyable to ask that kind of question, to some degree be determined in relation to these great opposites. To ask of Gogol, Turgenev, Chekhov, Blok how they stand in relation to Pushkin and to Dostoevsky leads—or, at any rate, has led—to fruitful and illuminating criticism. But when we come to Count Lev Nikolaevich Tolstoy, and ask this of him—ask whether he belongs to the first category or the second, whether he is a monist or a pluralist, whether his vision is of one or of many, whether he is of a single substance or compounded of heterogeneous elements, there is no clear or immediate answer. The question does not, somehow, seem wholly appropriate; it seems to breed more darkness than it dispels. Yet it is not lack of information that makes us pause: Tolstoy has told us more about himself and his views and attitudes than any other Russian, more, almost, than any other European writer; nor can his art be called obscure in any normal sense: his universe has no dark corners, his stories are luminous with the light of day; he has explained them and himself, and argued about them and the methods by which they are constructed, more articulately and with greater force and sanity and lucidity than any other writer. Is he a fox or a hedgehog? What are we to say? Why is the answer so curiously difficult to find? Does he resemble Shakespeare or Pushkin more than Dante or Dostoevsky? Or is he wholly unlike either, and is the question therefore unanswerable because it is absurd? What is the mysterious obstacle with which our inquiry seems faced?

I do not propose in this essay to formulate a reply to this question, since this would involve nothing less than a critical examination of the art and thought of Tolstoy as a whole. I shall confine myself to suggesting that the difficulty may be, at least in part, due to the fact that Tolstoy was himself not unaware of the problem, and did his best to falsify the answer. The hypothesis I wish to offer is that Tolstoy was by nature a fox, but believed in being a hedgehog; that his gifts and achievement are one thing, and his beliefs, and consequently his interpretation of his own achievement, another; and that consequently his ideals have led him, and those whom his genius for persuasion has taken in, into a systematic misinterpretation of what he and others were doing or should be doing. No one can complain that he has left his readers in any doubt as to what he thought about this topic: his views on this subject permeate all his discursive writings—diaries, recorded *obiter dicta,* autobiographical essays and stories, social and religious tracts, literary criticism, letters to private and public correspondents. But the conflict between what he was and what he believed emerges nowhere so clearly as in his view of history to which some of his most brilliant and most paradoxical pages are devoted. This essay is an attempt to deal with his historical doctrines, and to consider both his motives for holding the views he holds and some of their probable sources. In short, it is an attempt to take Tolstoy's attitude to history as seriously as he himself meant his readers to take it, although for a somewhat different reason—for the light it casts on a single man of genius rather than on the fate of all mankind.

Questions and Assignments

1. How important is the analogy to this discussion? If no analogy had been made, how could the author have made his classification? Would it have been as successful? As interesting?

2. Berlin uses many examples which are perhaps not familiar to the average reader. Why are these examples acceptable and understandable nevertheless?

3. Where and how does Berlin define the terms of his analogy? Was this necessary to his essay?

4. Why does Berlin start his second paragraph with a topic sentence that describes his own classification as "over-simple" and "if pressed, artificial, scholastic, and ultimately absurd"? Does this undermine his argument or reinforce it?

5. Notice that Berlin uses his basic distinctions as an introduction to his analysis of Tolstoy and Tolstoy's theory of history. How well does his general theory prepare us for the conflict between belief and accomplishment that is Berlin's major thesis?

6. In effect, Berlin has set up an analogy and a classification which applies to his chief subject, Tolstoy, in a different way than to other writers. Why then did he make such a division?

7. Write an essay based on the same analogy concerning hedgehogs and foxes and apply it to several specific people that you know, being careful to provide plenty of details and examples. You may use the analogy to classify a number of people, or to compare two people. Or you may write an essay proving that most people are both foxes and hedgehogs.

8. Find an analogy of your own and write an essay based upon it. For example, you could write on "all the world's a stage," or "all water flows into the ocean," or "where there's smoke there's fire." Be sure to define your analogy before you apply it to the subject you discuss.

The Morals of Chess

BENJAMIN FRANKLIN

The game of chess is not merely an idle amusement. Several very valuable qualities of the mind useful in the course of human life are to be acquired or strengthened by it, so as to become habits, ready on all occasions. For life is a kind of chess, in which we have points to gain, and competitors or adversaries to contend with, and in which there is a vast variety of good and ill events that are in some degree the effects of prudence or the want of it. By playing chess, then, we learn:

First, Foresight, which looks a little into futurity, and considers the consequences that may attend an action; for it is continually occurring to the player, If I move this piece what will be the advantage to my new situation? What use can my adversary make of it to annoy me? What other moves can I make to support it and to defend myself from his attacks?

Second, Circumspection, which surveys the whole chessboard or scene of action—the relations of the several pieces and situations, the dangers they are respectively opposed to, the several possibilities of their aiding each other, the probabilities that the adversary may make this or that move and attack this or that piece, what different means can be used to avoid this stroke or turn its consequences against him.

Third, Caution, not to make our moves too hastily. This habit is best acquired by observing strictly the laws of the game, such as, If you touch a piece you must move it somewhere; if you set it down you must let it stand. It is best that these rules should be observed, as the game thereby becomes more the image of human life, and particularly of war, in which if you incautiously put yourself into a bad and dangerous position, you cannot obtain your enemy's leave to withdraw your troops and place them more securely, but you must abide all the consequences of your rashness.

And lastly, we learn by chess the habit of not being discouraged by present bad appearance in the state of our affairs, the habit of hoping for a favorable change, and that of persevering in the search of resources. The game is so full of events, there is such a variety of turns in it, the fortunes of it are so subject to sudden vicissitudes, and one so frequently after long contemplation discovers the means of extricating oneself from a supposed insurmountable difficulty, that one is encouraged to continue the contest to the last in the hope of a victory by our own skill or at least of getting a stalemate by the negligence of our adversary. And whoever considers, what in chess he often sees instances of, that particular pieces of success are apt to produce presumption and its consequent inattention, will learn not to be too much discouraged by the present success of his adversary, nor to despair of final good fortune upon every little check he receives in the pursuit of it.

Questions and Assignments

1. What is the analogy in this selection? Is the author discussing life or chess or both?

2. How would you characterize the opening sentence? How effective is the conclusion?

3. How is this essay divided for the sake of development? What part does the analogy play in this development?

4. Write an essay based on a similar analogy as it applies to football, baseball, basketball, skiing, tennis, checkers, skating, swimming, bridge.

5. Use an analogy to describe the importance of music, poetry, good food, happy homes, mountain climbing, friendship.

Readings: Cause and Effect

An essay organized according to cause and effect relationships examines reasons why something is true or the result of some particular event or state of mind. Here again, authors will probably make use of other methods of development too, but the overall structure of the particular essay will be based on the relationship of causes and effects. For example, our first essay examines the "effects" it is concerned with—namely, that women do not and will not use their intelligence, and then it examines the causes of this attitude and what needs to be done to bring about a change.

Marya Mannes is a contemporary journalist and a member of the staff of *The Reporter*. Arnold Bennett, the author of the other excerpt in this section, was a twentieth-century British critic and novelist.

Female Intelligence: Who Wants It?

MARYA MANNES

Every now and then there is a resounding call for a national resource—largely untapped and unmustered—referred to as the intelligence of women, or the female brain. Editorial writers, tired of outer space, say that if we are to win the race of survival and keep up with the Russians we must not squander this precious resource but rather press it into service.

Commenting on the number of women doctors, engineers, physicists and laboratory technicians in the Soviet Union compared to our paltry own, citing the desperate shortages in fields where the productive intellect is essential, they cry: "To the drawing-board, to the laboratories, to the computers!" And presidents of women's colleges beseech their students: "Use this brain you've got and we're training: society needs it!"

Gratifying though it may be to have the female intelligence not only publicly acknowledged but officially sought, these calls are met by a massive wave of indifference emanating from women even more than from men. We do not really believe either the acknowledgment or the demand for the kind of intelligence they speak of and claim they want, nor do we see any signs of a public attitude which would make its application either welcome or practical on a national scale.

The college presidents, the editorialists, the recruiters of resources are talking not of the intelligence which every woman needs to be a successful wife and mother or even a competent worker in office or factory or civic affairs. They are talking of the kind of free and independent intelligence which can analyze, innovate and create: the mind of the scientist and the artist, at liberty to roam in the world of abstractions and intangibles until, by will and effort, a concrete and tangible pattern is made clear.

Are women capable of this kind of intelligence? If they are not to the degree of genius—and the long history of man has produced no female Bachs or Shakespeares or Leonardos or Galileos—and although a Madame Curie is in lonely company, women have in every time given to the mainstream of the arts, letters and sciences. And when even a Jesuit priest-sociologist, Father Lucius F. Cervantes—whose recent book "And God Made

Man and Woman" is a long and satisfied reiteration of the sacred differences between the two sexes—writes, "As far as has been ascertained there is no inherent intellectual capacity differential between men and women," then surely women are not by nature denied the ability to think creatively and abstractly.

It is rather that this ability is unpopular with men. Our prior need, in short, is to be loved. And if the possession of this kind of intelligence is a deterrent to love, then it is voluntarily restricted or denied by women themselves.

I have seen enough of this deterrence and this denial, since my youth, to believe it the common experience. And although it has not always been mine (I am fortunate in a happy marriage), I recognize only too well the signal of alarm in the eyes of men when a woman of intellect challenges their own.

It flashed even before I recognized it: boys at dances would forsake me soon for others, not—in Marty's language—because I was a "dog," but because I talked to them of sonnets or senses instead of about themselves. Used to a family where ideas were as much a part of the dinner table as food, I knew of no special kind of talk geared to men rather than to women. Worse, I thought that to be interesting one had to say interesting things. This was possibly the greatest miscalculation since the Charge of the Light Brigade.

For most men, I duly discovered, prefer the woman whose interest lies not in her thoughts nor her speech nor her talents, but in her interest in them. Mind, they believe, interferes with this attention, and to some extent they are right. Right or wrong, the average American male is uneasy in the presence of markedly intelligent women; and the woman who wishes to change this unease into love must spend a good part of her life reining in her wits in the reluctant admission that they do her more harm than good.

Now there is a great paradox in all this. On the one hand, more girls go to college than ever before, and more colleges are equipped to develop their minds toward whatever intellectual goals they might aspire to. On the other hand, as President Thomas C. Mendenhall of Smith College recently—and sharply—declared, there is a 60 per cent dropout of women students before graduation and most of this is due to their early marriage and almost immediate proliferation of the species.

In an open forum recently, I asked Millicent C. McIntosh, president of Barnard, and Dr. George N. Shuster of Hunter what they considered the purpose of higher education for women if they left the campus in droves for a career of total domesticity. Their answer, roughly, was this: "Our main aim is to turn out women who can apply a trained intelligence to the problems of daily living, and whose intellectual resources can enrich their lives and those of their children."

They agreed that only a small proportion of girls manifested a genuine drive toward intellectual excellence, or a sustained dedication necessary to the mastery of any art or science, and they deplored this. But the shared opinion seemed to be that a girl who went to college would not only be a more intelligent wife and mother than the girl who did not, but that in later life and increased freedom she could draw on greater reserves of mind and spirit.

And yet an English teacher at one of the Eastern universities said: "There is a terrible waste here. I've taught girls with as much, if not more, talent than many of the boys I've had in my classes: first-class writers and thinkers. And what do they do when they leave here? Work? Not on your life. They marry and have four children, and that's that."

The argument, widely used, that a woman so trained can always return to her field when her children are grown and her time is her own, is specious, to say the least. In the sciences, if not in the arts, advances in theory and techniques are so rapid that a fifteen-year gap becomes unbreachable. Quite apart from that, the muscle of intellect degenerates with lack of use. The servantless young mother with small children has not the time, the place or the isolation necessary for any orderly process of thought or any sustained practice of the imagination.

Yet society—including most of the young women involved in this early and long domesticity—does not consider this condition even remotely tragic. On the contrary, there appears to be widespread approval of the return of women from the spurious and aggressive "independence" of their mothers to their prime function as the creators and guardians of the family.

Young girls themselves in countless numbers have chosen the security and closeness of a full household rather than the lonely road of individual fulfillment as creative identities. And although many young women work out of the home before and even after marriage, it is less for love of work than for love of a home in which a standard of living is more important than a standard of thinking.

Only a few seem to work because of an urgent need to be for once—if only part of every day—out of context and into their own skin, applying their intelligence singly toward matters not concerned with their personal lives.

Even this need, usually condoned for economic reasons ("She has to work to make ends meet") is criticized by those professionally concerned with allocating roles to the sexes, as an evasion of woman's prime responsibility and an indication either of maladjustment or of a false sense of values. And, although the country is full of educators charged with the development of the female intelligence, every social pressure is exerted on women from their childhood on toward one goal: marriage—the earlier the better—and babies, the more the better. And the girl who feels that she has something to give beyond her natural functions as a wife and mother is lonely, indeed—pitied even when she succeeds.

If television drama serials and mass magazine fiction are any indication of the national temper, there is only one "right" fulfillment for all women. The "career woman" may be admired for her success, but her absorption in her work—whether it be medicine, law, letters or art—is a tacit admission of her lack of fulfillment as a woman. And even if she marries and bears children, the assumption prevails that both her husband and her offspring will suffer from her preoccupation with the world outside.

Many housewives may secretly long for their independence, but they are secure in the knowledge that their own absorption in the home and the community is a guarantee against a continual conflict of loyalties and, indeed, against the natural hostility of men; a resentment, however covert, against the competition of the kind of female intelligence which, precisely because of its independence, is still called "masculine."

If it is true that this kind of intelligence is undesirable to the majority of men, accustomed as they are to the "liberated" woman of today, what are the reasons?

I suspect that in the stormy sea of "equality," men are uncertain of the extent and nature of their dominance—if, indeed, they believe in it—and that they need a constant reassurance of their superiority in one field at least, that of the creative intellect.

They need not look far to see that it is they who formulate national policies, send rockets into space and govern the world of business, art and science. The challenge from women in these fields is still negligible, but it exists; a source of discomfort rather than satisfaction. And although many men are generous in their admiration of the few women who have achieved distinction in the laboratory or in letters or in scholarship, most men have no desire to be married to them. They take too much trouble.

And here we come, I think, to the root of the matter: a masculine laziness in the ways of love which inclines them to avoid rather than surmount this particular kind of challenge. It is far easier to choose the relaxed and compliant woman than one who makes demands on the intelligence. They may be intrigued by the brilliant woman, but they rarely want her for themselves.

For the qualities that form a creative intellect are hard to live with. The woman cursed with them can retain the love of men and the approval of society only if she is willing to modify and mute them as much as she can without reducing them to impotence. As one so cursed, however modestly, I herewith submit some hard-won suggestions:

I would counsel the woman of intellect to watch her wit. Though it need not be tinged with malice, it has of necessity an astringency which many people find disconcerting. In a bland society, the unsheathed dart can draw blood, if only from vanity. And after the tide of laughter at a woman's wit has ebbed, the wrack left in the public mind is a sort of malaise: "She has a sharp tongue" or "I wouldn't like to tangle with her."

Candor is a second danger. The woman who is honest with men is so at her own risk if this honesty requires either criticism or skepticism of their position. And if she has convictions opposed to those of the man she speaks with she will be wise to withhold them or speak them so softly that they sound like concurrence.

She must, above all, have no conviction that what she has to say is of importance, but train herself instead to listen quietly to men no more knowledgeable in a given subject than herself and, what is more, to defer to their judgment. This is not always easy, but a woman cannot afford the luxury of declarations, however pertinent, if she seeks—and what woman does not?—to attract.

A man who is intense or excited about his work can be highly attractive, but woe to the woman who is either. Most people cannot distinguish between the tiresome garrulity of a woman preoccupied with her affairs and the purely abstract passion of a woman concerned with the process of thought. A state of tension is inseparable from active intelligence but it is socially unpermissible in women.

If such women are artists—and I use this to cover all forms of creative expression—and particularly if they have achieved any stature as such, they may have the attraction of rarity. There are even men who are mature enough and secure enough to cherish in them the capacity to create abstractly as well as biologically.

But they are rarer still, for the care and cultivation of an artist is a job that wives are trained for and few husbands want. The woman artist who has a husband and children must then, to quote Phyllis McGinley, have "three hands"—a mutation still infrequent but which the irradiation of women's minds may yet produce.

Is this irradiation really desirable? Are the full resources of the feminine intelligence really needed? And if they are to be mobilized for the national good, what is to be done about a climate of opinion satisfied with the overwhelming emphasis, on the part of the younger generation, on domesticity and large families? Do we need more babies or do we need more doctors and scientists and thinkers and innovators? Is it enough that we have a great pool of college graduates applying their intelligence to the problems of their homes and towns, or do we really need more women able to come to grips with the major issues of our time?

If we do, changes will have to be made, many of which may well be unattainable at this time. But if the nation's leaders really want and need this kind of woman, the opinion molders of the mass media will have to start right now giving her an honorable place in society, and men will have to start giving her an honorable place in their hearts as well as in their professions.

For one thing, parents with daughters who show a genuine intellectual talent and aspiration in any field should not feel compelled to enter her in the infantile mating-marathon that pushes a girl toward marriage from the age of 12 on. It should be possible for such a girl to prefer an exciting book to a dull date without the censure of her family or her peers, and to continue her training through her twenties without courting celibacy.

Much has been said about the new sense of responsibility shown by the young in their early acceptance of marriage and parenthood. But time may show that the cocoon of a large-familied home is—like that of a large corporation—the best protection from the loneliness of thought and a voluntary abdication of the burdens of personal freedom.

If a woman wishes to resume her chosen work after marriage and the bearing of children, there should be no stigma attached if she can afford to hire outside help for either home tasks or the care of the young. And we might begin to consider a pattern of community-supported nurseries which would permit the woman who cannot afford to pursue her profession to be at least partially free from the continuous demands of child care.

A few months ago a delegation of Russian professional women visited this country, and one of them remarked in amazement at the lack of any such service. Our profusion of labor-saving gadgets did not, it seems, blind her eyes to the domestic entrapment of the young American woman.

As for college education, there should, I believe, be a division made between students merely marking time before marriage and girls seriously bent on a career or profession, confining the domestic-minded to a two-year course of liberal arts and reserving the four-year, degree-granting course for the latter. After these have graduated, their entrance into the laboratories and offices of the country should be made on the same basis as that for equally qualified men—not, that is, as an interim occupation but as a chosen, sustained career.

And here, of course, is where the woman herself must be prepared to pay a fairly high price. If work is important to her she cannot allow herself the luxury of a large family or the kind of man who insists on one. Nor can she afford the close, and often cozy, community huddle in which women share their domestic preoccupations daily with one another. She must be prepared to fight for the freedom she wants at the risk of loneliness and the denial of a number of things dear to any woman.

As for men, they will have to stop thinking in terms of competition and think in terms of alliance instead: the alliance of companion intellects toward similar goals. If they can bring themselves to consider women primarily as human beings, they will be able to treat them intellectually as men and emotionally as women. If they do that, they will find the brilliant woman surprisingly docile and far from unfeminine.

If, however, men continue to subscribe to the prevailing belief that the American heroine must never be too intelligent for her own good and their own comfort, the cry for female brains will go largely unheeded—unless a national emergency makes it clear that we have for years been wasting one of the resources on which our strength depends and which other civilizations are using to their advantage.

Questions and Assignments

1. What does Miss Mannes consider the main cause that more women do not think creatively and abstractly? What is your initial reaction to her point? Does it

seem an adequate or a partial explanation? Does she succeed in convincing you in the course of the essay?

2. Distinguish the different reasons why, according to the author, men object to the "liberated woman."

3. To what extent do the author's justifications of herself interfere with the objectivity of her argument?

4. What tone does Miss Mannes adopt for her first counsels to the woman of intelligence? How do her final constructive proposals differ?

5. Write a paper agreeing or disagreeing with Miss Mannes about the reasons why women do not make use of their intelligence. In order to write this you will have to read the essay closely first and perhaps make a list of the reasons Miss Mannes gives.

6. Write a paper showing that Miss Mannes' analysis of the effects is wrong and that women really are using their intelligence. Be sure to include specific details and examples, and, if possible, show some of the effects of their intelligence in order to prove that it is used.

7. Write a cause and effect essay on one of the following:

"The average American male is uneasy in the presence of markedly intelligent women."
"The muscle of intellect degenerates with lack of use."
"A standard of living is more important than a standard of thinking."
"There is only one 'right' fulfillment for all women."
"Men are uncertain of the extent and nature of their dominance."
"Men may be intrigued by the brilliant woman, but they rarely want her for themselves."
"The unsheathed dart can draw blood, if only from vanity."
"A state of tension is inseparable from active intelligence."
"the infantile mating-marathon"
"the domestic entrapment of the young American woman"

Why a Classic Is a Classic

ARNOLD BENNETT

The large majority of our fellow citizens care as much about literature as they care about airplanes or the program of the legislature. They do not ignore it; they are not quite indifferent to it. But their interest in it is faint and perfunctory; or, if their interest happens to be violent, it is spasmodic. Ask the two hundred thousand persons whose enthusiasm made the vogue of a popular novel ten years ago what they think of that novel now, and you will gather that they have utterly forgotten it, and that they would no more dream of reading it again than of reading Bishop Stubbs's *Select Charters*. Probably if they did read it again they would not enjoy it—not because the said novel is a whit worse now than it was ten years ago; not because their taste has improved—but because they have not had sufficient practice to be able to rely on their taste as a means of permanent pleasure. They simply don't know from one day to the next what will please them.

In the face of this one may ask: Why does the great and universal fame of classical authors continue? The answer is that the fame of classical authors is entirely independent of the majority. Do you suppose that if the fame of Shakespeare depended on the man in the street it would survive a fortnight? The fame of classical authors is originally made, and it is maintained, by a passionate few. Even when a first-class author has enjoyed immense success during his lifetime, the majority have never appreciated him so sincerely as they have appreciated second-rate men. He has always been reënforced by the ardor of the passionate few. And in the case of an author who has emerged into glory after his death, the happy sequel has been due solely to the obstinate perseverance of the few. They could not leave him alone; they would not. They kept on savoring him, and talking about him, and buying him, and they generally behaved with such eager zeal, and they were so authoritative and sure of themselves, that at last the majority grew accustomed to the sound of his name and placidly agreed to the proposition that he was a genius; the majority did not care very much either way.

And it is by the passionate few that the renown of genius is kept alive from one generation to another. These few are always at work. They are always rediscovering genius. Their curiosity and enthusiasm are exhaustless, so that there is little chance of genius being ignored. And, moreover, they are always working either for or against the verdicts of the majority. The majority can make a reputation, but it is too careless to maintain it. If, by accident, the passionate few agree with the majority in a particular instance, they will frequently remind the majority that such and such a reputation has been made, and the majority will idly concur: "Ah, yes. By the way, we must not forget that such and such a reputation exists." Without that persistent memory-jogging the reputation would quickly fall into the oblivion which is death. The passionate few only have their way by reason of the fact that they are genuinely interested in literature, that literature matters to them. They conquer by their obstinacy alone, by their eternal repetition of the same statements. Do you suppose they could prove to the man in the street that Shakespeare was a great artist? The said man would not even understand the terms they employed. But when he is told ten thousand times, and generation after generation, that Shakespeare was a great artist, the said man believes—not by reason, but by faith. And he, too, repeats that Shakespeare was a great artist, and he buys the complete works of Shakespeare and puts them on his shelves, and he goes to see the marvelous stage affects which accompany *King Lear* or *Hamlet,* and comes back religiously convinced that Shakespeare was a great artist. All because the passionate few could not keep their admiration of Shakespeare to themselves. This is not cynicism; but truth. And it is important that those who wish to form their literary taste should grasp it.

What causes the passionate few to make such a fuss about literature? There can be only one reply. They find a keen and lasting pleasure in literature. They enjoy literature as some men enjoy beer. The recurrence of this pleasure naturally keeps their interest in literature very much alive. They are forever making new researches, forever practicing on themselves. They learn to understand themselves. They learn to know what they want. Their taste becomes surer and surer as their experience lengthens. They do not enjoy today what will seem tedious to them tomorrow. When they find a book tedious, no amount of popular clatter will persuade them that it is pleasurable; and when they find it pleasurable no chill silence of the street crowds will affect their conviction that the book is good and permanent. They have faith in themselves. What are the qualities in a book which give keen and lasting pleasure to the passionate few? This is a question so difficult that it has never yet been completely answered. You may talk lightly about truth, insight, knowledge, wisdom, humor, and beauty. But these comfortable words do not really carry you very far, for each of them has to be defined, especially the first and last. It is all very well for Keats in his airy manner to assert that beauty is truth, truth beauty, and that that is all he knows or needs to know. I, for one, need to know a lot more. And I never shall know. Nobody, not even Hazlitt or Sainte-Beuve, has ever finally explained why he thought a book beautiful. I take the first fine lines that come to hand—

The woods of Arcady are dead,
And over is their antique joy—

and I say that those lines are beautiful because they give me pleasure. But why? No answer! I only know that the passionate few will broadly agree with me in deriving this mysterious pleasure from these lines. I am only convinced that the liveliness of our pleasure in those and many other lines by the same author will ultimately cause the majority to believe, by faith, that W. B. Yeats is a genius. The one reassuring aspect of the literary affair is that the passionate few are passionate about the same things. A continuance of interest does, in actual practice, lead ultimately to the same judgments. There is only the difference in width of interest. Some of the passionate few lack catholicity, or, rather, the whole of their interest is confined to one narrow channel; they have none left over. These men help specially to vitalize the reputations of the narrower geniuses such as Crashaw. But their active predilections never contradict the general verdict of the passionate few; rather they reënforce it.

A classic is a work which gives pleasure to the minority which is intensely and permanently interested in literature. It lives on because the minority, eager to renew the sensation of pleasure, is eternally curious and is therefore engaged in an eternal process of rediscovery. A classic does not survive for any ethical reason. It does not survive because it conforms to certain canons, or because neglect would not kill it. It survives because it is a source of pleasure, and because the passionate few can no more neglect it than a bee can neglect a flower. The passionate few do not read "the right things" because they are right. That is to put the cart before the horse. "The right things" are the right things solely because the passionate few *like* reading them. Hence—and I now arrive at my point—the one primary essential to literary taste is a hot interest in literature. If you have that, all the rest will come. It matters nothing that at present you fail to find pleasure in certain classics. The driving impulse of your interest will force you to acquire experience, and experience will teach you the use of the means of pleasure. You do not know the secret ways of yourself; that is all. A continuance of interest must inevitably bring you to the keenest joys. But, of course, experience may be acquired judiciously or injudiciously, just as Putney may be reached *via* Walham Green or *via* St. Petersburg.

Questions and Assignments

1. What does Bennett cite as the principal cause for a classic being considered a classic? What reasons does he cite in support of this?

2. How does this cause bring about the effect? How does Bennett handle the problem of variety of taste?

3. Is it possible that someone with a passionate interest in literature may *not*

like some particular classic? In such a case where does Bennett consider the fault to lie—in the classic involved or in the particular reader? Is there any reversal of his cause and effect development here? How does this affect the validity of his discussion?

4. What is the meaning of the last sentence of this selection?

5. Write a cause and effect essay on one of the following:

Why students go to college
Why children love their parents
Why parents love their children
Why rain is important to the earth
Why some particular novel is considered great
Why trees and wild life should be saved
Why the sunset or the ocean or autumn foliage is beautiful
Why a happy person is happy

Readings: Definition

Definition draws upon all the methods of developing we have already discussed. It frequently uses chronology, comparison-contrast, causality, and analogy. It is most closely associated with classification in that the initial step in defining is to place a term or an idea in a class of related terms or ideas. Definition differs from classification, however, in a second step which emphasizes how the term or idea being defined differs from the other terms or ideas in the class.

The clearest instances of these two essential steps in definition are found in logic and science. A dolphin, for example, is defined as a cetacean (class) having a snout formed into a beak (thus distinguishing it from other members of its class).

Writers usually define by more informal methods of classifying and differentiating. The three most common methods are: synonymous statement, naming of parts, and negation. Stevenson in his definition of patriotism (pp. 301-307) uses all three of these methods. He begins by associating patriotism with its near synonyms—sentimental attachment, love of country, nationalism. Patriotism, he says, is "loving one's country." Love of country, however, is a broad class and thus Stevenson goes on immediately to suggest how true patriotism differs from other kinds of love for country by the criterion—"in the right way." In order to make this vague phrase clear Stevenson divides patriotism into some of its parts: sentimental and historical associations, political and moral commitments, and the ideal of liberty. Stevenson employs negation when he points out that patriotism is *not* mere sentimental attachment, *not* adherence to a business mentality, *not* enforced conformity. The other selections in this unit also employ synonymous expression, divide their subject into appropriate divisions, and use negation in order to define.

The author of our first definition, on the meaning of "plot," is E. M. Forster, a well-known modern British novelist and critic. Adlai Stevenson, formerly Democratic candidate for President, is now U. S. Ambassador to the United Nations. George Orwell, popular British novelist and satirist until his death in 1950, is also the author of *1984*, a novel about the possibility of an absolute totalitarian state.

Plot

E. M. FORSTER

Let us define a plot. We have defined a story as a narrative of events arranged in their time-sequence. A plot is also a narrative of events, the emphasis falling on causality. "The king died and then the queen died" is a story. "The king died, and then the queen died of grief" is a plot. The time-sequence is preserved, but the sense of causality overshadows it. Or again: "The queen died, no one knew why, until it was discovered that it was through grief at the death of the king." This is a plot with a mystery in it, a form capable of high development. It suspends the time-sequence, it moves as far away from the story as its limitations will allow. Consider the death of the queen. If it is in a story we say "and then?" If it is in a plot we ask "why?" That is the fundamental difference between these two aspects of the novel. A plot cannot be told to a gaping audience of cave-men or to a tyrannical sultan or to their modern descendant the movie-public. They can only be kept awake by "and then—and then——." They can only supply curiosity. But a plot demands intelligence and memory also.

Curiosity is one of the lowest of the human faculties. You will have noticed in daily life that when people are inquisitive they nearly always have bad memories and are usually stupid at bottom. The man who begins by asking you how many brothers and sisters you have is never a sympathetic character, and if you meet him in a year's time he will probably ask you how many brothers and sisters you have, his mouth again sagging open, his eyes still bulging from his head. It is difficult to be friends with such a man, and for two inquisitive people to be friends must be impossible. Curiosity by itself takes us a very little way, nor does it take us far into the novel—only as far as the story. If we would grasp the plot we must add intelligence and memory.

Intelligence first. The intelligent novel-reader, unlike the inquisitive one who just runs his eye over a new fact, mentally picks it up. He sees it from two points of view: isolated, and related to the other facts that he has read on previous pages. Probably he does not understand it, but he does not expect to do so yet awhile. The facts in a highly organized novel (like *The Egoist*) are often of the nature of cross-correspondences and the ideal spectator cannot expect to view them properly until he is sitting up on a hill at the end. This element of surprise or mystery—the detective element as it is sometimes rather emptily called—is of great importance in a plot. It occurs through a suspension of the time-sequence; a mystery is a pocket in time, and it occurs crudely, as in "Why did the queen die?" and more subtly in half-explained gestures and words, the true meaning of which only dawns pages ahead. Mystery is essential to a plot, and cannot be appreciated without intelligence. To the curious it is just another "and then——." To appreciate a mystery, part of the mind must be left behind, brooding, while the other part goes marching on.

That brings us to our second qualification: memory.

Memory and intelligence are closely connected, for unless we remember we cannot understand. If by the time the queen dies we have forgotten the existence of the king we shall never make out what killed her. The plot-maker expects us to remember, we expect him to leave no loose ends. Every action or word ought to count; it ought to be economical and spare; even when complicated it should be organic and free from dead-matter. It may be difficult or easy, it may and should contain mysteries, but it ought not to mislead. And over it, as it unfolds, will hover the memory of the reader (that dull glow of the mind of which intelligence is the bright advancing edge) and will constantly rearrange and reconsider, seeing new clues, new chains of cause and effect, and the final sense (if the plot has been a fine one) will not be of clues or chains, but of something aesthetically compact, something which might have been shown by the novelist straight away, only if he had shown it straight away it would never have become beautiful. We come up against beauty here—for the first time in our inquiry: beauty at which a novelist should never aim, though he fails if he does not achieve it. I will conduct beauty to her proper place later on. Meanwhile please accept her as part of a completed plot. She looks a little surprised at being there, but beauty ought to look a little surprised: it is the emotion that best suits her face, as Botticelli knew when he painted her risen from the waves, between the winds and the flowers. The beauty who does not look surprised, who accepts her position as her due—she reminds us too much of a prima donna.

Questions and Assignments

1. How does Forster distinguish story from plot? Is this distinction valid? Are the examples he gives sufficient to indicate his meaning?

2. What does Forster's discussion of curiosity do in terms of the structure of his definition? What about his treatment of memory and intelligence? And how does beauty enter in? Is his treatment of this satisfactory to you? Why does he introduce beauty so tangentially?

3. Find the specific definition Forster gives of the meaning of *memory* and *intelligence*. Why are these definitions interesting and good?

4. Apply Forster's distinction between story and plot to one or more novels or stories you have read.

5. Write a definition based on one of the following quotations from Forster:

"Curiosity is one of the lowest of the human faculties"
"for two inquisitive people to be friends must be impossible"
"a mystery is a pocket in time"
"unless we remember we cannot understand"
"beauty ought to look a little surprised"

The Hard Kind of Patriotism

ADLAI E. STEVENSON

It is not easy to be a patriot these days—not because it is difficult to love one's country. The difficulty lies with loving one's country in the right way.

The love itself is profound and instinctive, rooted in our childhood discovery of all the infinite delights of being alive—for me, the vast skies, the spring green of the corn, the fall colors and winter snow of the Illinois prairie; for all of us, the shining Christmas trees, the colored mesas and bright flowers of the desert, the rocky shores and pounding seas "way down East," the aspens showering autumn gold on the slopes of the Rockies.

It doesn't matter what your picture is. For all of us, it is "home," the place where we spent the endless, dream-filled days of childhood, the place that still nourishes our secret, life-giving imagination, the place we love as we love bread, as we love the earliest image of maternal care, as we love life itself. In doing so, we love what has largely made us what we are. The difficulty is, as I have said, to love it in the right way.

I think the complexity of modern technological society makes the loving difficult for everybody, but here in America we have some quite special problems, which come not from our complex present but from our historical inheritance.

Some states emerge from some pre-existing tribal unity, some grow up within an already established culture, and some are forged by conquest, with victor and vanquished settling down to a new synthesis.

None of these routes was followed by America. Our people have come from every "tribal" group; they have largely had to create their own civilization as they went along to absorb a continent. They have never been conquered or had any sort of synthesis imposed upon them. Their community had, in fact, a unique beginning—it was from the moment of its birth a land "dedicated to a proposition"—that men are born equal, that government is a government of laws, not men, and exists to serve them, that "life, liberty, and the pursuit of happiness" are man's inalienable right.

But consider the consequences of this astonishing start. We are Americans because we belong to a certain ideal, visionary type of political and social order. We can't point back to a long, shared civilization. It is true, most of us have Europe and the West behind us. But not all—and, anyway, it is a concept of the West that we create rather than inherit. And no one is standing on our necks keeping us down and together.

The result is a community, surely, whose instinctive, rooted, taken-for-granted unity has to be all the more dynamic. If we are not dedicated to our fundamental propositions, then the natural cement in our society may not be enough to take the strain.

I would agree that there are substitutes. When a President said that "the business of America is business," he told us something about the degree to which a standard of living can do stand-in duty for a way of life. But the question, "What manner of people are we?" cannot be everlastingly answered in terms of two-car families or split-level homes.

America is much more than an economic or geographical fact. It is a political and moral fact—the first community in which men set out in principle to institutionalize freedom, responsible government, and human equality. And we love it for this audacity! How easy it is, contemplating this vision, to see in it—as Jefferson or Lincoln saw in it—"The last, best hope of man." To be a nation founded on an ideal in one sense makes our love of country a more vital force than any instinctive pieties of blood and soil.

But it also demands a more complex and discriminating love. Will the fabric hold if the ideal fades? If the effort to realize our citizens' birthright of freedom and equality is not constantly renewed, on what can we fall back? As a going concern, we can no doubt survive many shocks and shames. It was Adam Smith who remarked that "There is a great deal of ruin in every state." But can we survive, as a confident and growing community, if the essentially liberal thrust of our origins is forgotten, if we equate liberty with passive noninterference, if we exclude large minorities from our standards of equality, if income becomes a substitute for idealism, consumption for dedication, privilege for neighborly good will?

Well, you may say, "Why be so concerned; after all, one of the most forceful elements of our free society is precisely our discontent with our own shortcomings. Because we are free, because we are not the victims of censorship and manipulated news, because no dictatorial government imposes on us its version of the truth, we are at liberty to speak up against our shortcomings. We don't confuse silence with success. We know that 'between the idea and the reality . . . falls the shadow,' and we are determined to chase away that shadow in the uncompromising light of truth."

But *are we*? It is at this point that our patriotism, our love of country, has to be a discriminating, not a blind force. All too often, voices are raised, in the name of some superpatriotism, to still all criticism and to denounce honest divergencies as the next thing to treason. We have risen up from the pit of McCarthy's time, when honest men could lose their jobs for questioning whether there were 381 known Communists in the State Department. But the intolerant spirit which equates responsible criticism with "selling the country short" or "being soft on communism" or "undermining the American way of life" is still abroad.

I can give you no comfort in suggesting there is an easy way around this type of criticism. Our position today *is* equivocal. We *are* in one sense a very conservative people—for no nation in history has had so much to conserve. Suggestions that everything is not perfect and that things must be changed *do* arouse the suspicion that something *I* cherish and *I* value may be modified. Even Aristotle complained that "every one thinks chiefly of his own, hardly ever of the public interest." And our instinct is to preserve what we have, and then to give the instinct a colored wrapping of patriotism.

This is in part what the great Dr. Johnson meant when he said: "Patriotism is the last refuge of a scoundrel." To defend every abuse, every self-interest, every encrusted position of privilege in the name of love of country—when in fact it is only love of the status quo—that indeed is the lie in the soul to which any conservative society is prone.

We do not escape it—but with us, an extra edge of hypocrisy attaches to the confusion. For our basic reason for being a state is our attempt to build a dynamic and equal society of free men. Societies based on blood ties can perhaps safely confuse conservatism and patriotism. People with long backward-looking traditions can perhaps do so. Countries under the heel of dictators must do so. But if the world's first experiment in the open society uses patriotism as a cloak for inaction or reaction, then it will cease to be open—and then, as a social organism, it will lose its fundamental reason for existence.

Do not, therefore, regard the critics as questionable patriots. What were Washington and Jefferson and Adams but profound critics of the colonial status quo? Our society can stand a large dose of constructive criticism just because it is so solid and has so much to conserve. It is only if keen and lively minds constantly compare the ideal and the reality and see the shadow—the shadow of self-righteousness, of suburban sprawl, of racial discrimination, of interminable strikes—it is only then that the shadow can be dispelled and the unique brightness of our national experiment can be seen and loved.

The patriots are those who love America enough to wish to see her as a model to mankind. This is not treachery. This—as every parent, every teacher, every friend must know—is the truest and noblest affection. No patriots so defaced America as those who, in the name of Americanism, launched a witch-hunt which became a byword around the world. We have survived it. We shall survive John Birchism and all the rest of the super-patriots—but only at the price of perpetual and truly patriotic vigilance.

This discriminating and vigilant patriotism is all the more necessary because the world at large is one in which a simple, direct, inward-looking nationalism is not enough.

We face in Communist hostility and expansionism a formidable force, whether Mr. Khrushchev and Mr. Mao Tse-tung pull together or apart. They disagree so far only on whether capitalism should be peacefully or violently buried. They are both for the funeral. So long as this fundamental objective remains, we must regard the Communist Bloc as a whole with extreme wariness.

Even if the Communists are divided and confused everywhere—even if they have scored of late none of the victories in Africa, East Asia, and the Middle East our doomsayers predicted—still the Communist Bloc is aggressive and powerful and determined to grow more so. Taken individually, the European states are all outnumbered. Even America has only a margin of superiority over the tough, austere Soviet Union. Even if the Russian forces in Cuba are not going to conquer the Americas, still their presence in this hemisphere endangers the peace.

So we have sensibly concluded in the NATO Alliance that our separate sovereignties and nationalisms must be transcended in a common, overwhelming union of deterrent strength. Together our weight keeps the balance of power firmly down on our side, and it removes from each state the temptation of playing off one state against another and weakening the overall power in order to strengthen its own. This is the first reason for transcending narrow nationalism.

The second follows from our economic interdependence. The Atlantic world has taken 70 per cent of world trade and absorbed 70 per cent of its own investments for the last seventy years. We are an interwoven international economy. Bank rates in Britain affect investments in New York. Restrictions here affect carpet makers in Belgium. French farmers affect everybody. We can only avoid the mismanagement of this community if we pursue joint policies. My friend Jean Monnet has outlined the essential list: expansion of demand, currency stability, investment overseas, trade with the developing nations, reserves for world trade. Without joint policies here, we could easily slip back to the debacle of the period between the great civil wars of Europe of 1914 and 1939.

In this context, separate, divisive nationalism is not patriotism. It cannot be patriotism to enlarge a country's illusory sense of potency and influence, and reduce its security and economic viability. True patriotism demands that, in some essential categories, purely national solutions be left behind in the interest of the nation itself. It is this effort to transcend narrow nationalism that marked the supremely successful Marshall Plan. It marks the great enterprise of European unification—after so many tribal wars. It could mark the building of an Atlantic partnership as a secure nucleus of world order.

So our vision must be of the open society fulfilling itself in an open world. This we can love. This gives our country its universal validity. This is a patriotism which sets no limits to the capacity of our country to act as the organizing principle of wider and wider associations, until in some way not yet foreseen we can embrace the family of man.

And here our patriotism encounters its last ambiguity. There are misguided patriots who feel we pay too much attention to other nations, that we are somehow enfeebled by respecting world opinion. Well, "a decent respect for the opinions of mankind" was the very first order of business when the Republic was created; the Declaration of Independence was written, not to proclaim our separation, but to explain it and win other nations to our cause. The founding fathers did not think it was "soft" or "un-American" to respect the opinions of others, and today for a man to love his country truly, he must also know how to love mankind. The change springs from many causes. The two appalling wars of this century, culminating in the atom bomb, have taught all men the impossibility of war. Horace may have said: "It is sweet and fitting to die for one's country." But to be snuffed out in the one brief blast of an atomic explosion bears no relation to the courage and clarity of the old limited ideal.

Nor is this a simple shrinking from annihilation. It is something much deeper—a growing sense of our solidarity as a human species on a planet made one and vulnerable by our science and technology.

For, on this shrunken globe, men can no longer live as strangers. Men can war against each other as hostile neighbors, as we are determined not to do; or they can coexist in frigid isolation, as we are doing. But our prayer is that men everywhere will learn, finally, to live as brothers, to respect each other's differences, to heal each other's wounds, to promote each other's progress, and to benefit from each other's knowledge. If the evangelical virtue of charity can be translated into political terms, aren't these our goals?

Aristotle said that the end of politics must be the good of man. Man's greatest good and greatest present need is, then, to establish world peace. Without it, the democratic enterprise—one might even say the human enterprise—will be utterly, fatally doomed. War under modern conditions is bereft of even that dubious logic it may have had in the past. With the development of modern technology, "victory" in war has become a mockery. What victory—victory for what or for whom?

Perhaps younger people are especially sensitive to this growing conviction that nowadays all wars are civil wars and all killing is fratricide. The movement takes many forms—multilateral diplomacy through the United Nations, the search for world peace through world law, the universal desire for nuclear disarmament, the sense of sacrifice and service of the Peace Corps, the growing revulsion against Jim Crowism, the belief that dignity rests in man as such and that all must be treated as ends, not means.

But whatever its form, I believe that, far from being in any sense an enemy to patriotism, it is a new expression of the respect for life from which all true love springs. We can truly begin to perceive the meaning of our great propositions—of liberty and equality—if we see them as part of the patrimony of all men. We shall not love our corner of the planet less for loving the planet too, and resisting with all our skill and passion the dangers that would reduce it to smoldering ashes.

I can, therefore, wish no more for the profound patriotism of Americans than that they add to it a new dedication to the world-wide brotherhood of which they are a part and that, together with their love of America, there will grow a wider love which seeks to transform our earthly city, with all its races and peoples, all its creeds and aspirations, into Saint Augustine's "Heavenly city where truth reigns, love is the law, and whose extent is eternity."

Questions and Assignments

1. What is Stevenson's first step in defining his subject? Did you expect this method from reading his title?

2. How precise is the distinction Stevenson makes in his first two sentences? What effect does he gain by initially expanding the first kind of patriotism—the kind which is not his subject?

3. How does the author make his transition from America as "an economic or geographical fact" to America as "a political and moral fact"?

4. What does Stevenson mean by the danger of patriotism as a blind force? For him can one be both intolerant and patriotic?

5. Why is patriotism not satisfied by the "instinct . . . to preserve and cherish what we have?" How does Stevenson link contemporary America with Washington, Jefferson, and Adams on this point?

6. Show how the statement that we cannot "survive as a confident and growing community . . . if we equate liberty with passive noninterference" is central to Stevenson's argument. To what extent does this formulation go beyond partisan considerations?

7. Expand in an essay Stevenson's statements "In this context, separate, divisive nationalism is not patriotism" or "Our instinct is to preserve what we have, and then to give the instinct a colored wrapping of patriotism."

8. Write a definition of one of the following:

Home
Freedom
Equality
Responsible government
Responsible criticism
The dignity of man
Love
Friendship
Success
Optimism
Fear

Reflections on Gandhi

GEORGE ORWELL

Saints should always be judged guilty until they are proved innocent, but the tests that have to be applied to them are not, of course, the same in all cases. In Gandhi's case the questions one feels inclined to ask are: to what extent was Gandhi moved by vanity—by the consciousness of himself as a humble, naked old man, sitting on a praying mat and shaking empires by sheer spiritual power—and to what extent did he compromise his own principles by entering politics, which of their nature are inseparable from coercion and fraud? To give a definite answer one would have to study Gandhi's acts and writings in immense detail, for his whole life was a sort of pilgrimage in which every act was significant. But this partial autobiography,[1] which ends in the nineteen-twenties, is strong evidence in his favor,

[1] *The Story of My Experiments with Truth.* By M. K. Gandhi. Translated from the Gujarati by Mahadex Desai. Public Affairs Press.

all the more because it covers what he would have called the unregenerate part of his life and reminds one that inside the saint, or near-saint, there was a very shrewd, able person who could, if he had chosen, have been a brilliant success as a lawyer, an administrator or perhaps even a business-man.

At about the time when the autobiography first appeared I remember reading its opening chapters in the ill-printed pages of some Indian news-paper. They made a good impression on me, which Gandhi himself at that time did not. The things that one associated with him—home-spun cloth, "soul forces" and vegetarianism—were unappealing, and his medievalist program was obviously not viable in a backward, starving, over-populated country. It was also apparent that the British were making use of him, or thought they were making use of him. Strictly speaking, as a Nationalist, he was an enemy, but since in every crisis he would exert himself to prevent violence—which, from the British point of view, meant preventing any ef-fective action whatever—he could be regarded as "our man." In private this was sometimes cynically admitted. The attitude of the Indian millionaires was similar. Gandhi called upon them to repent, and naturally they pre-ferred him to the Socialists and Communists who, given the chance, would actually have taken their money away. How reliable such calculations are in the long run is doubtful; as Gandhi himself says, "in the end deceivers deceive only themselves"; but at any rate the gentleness with which he was nearly always handled was due partly to the feeling that he was useful. The British Conservatives only became really angry with him when, as in 1942, he was in effect turning his non-violence against a different conqueror.

But I could see even then that the British officials who spoke of him with a mixture of amusement and disapproval also genuinely liked and admired him, after a fashion. Nobody ever suggested that he was corrupt, or ambitious in any vulgar way, or that anything he did was actuated by fear or malice. In judging a man like Gandhi one seems instinctively to apply high standards, so that some of his virtues have passed almost un-noticed. For instance, it is clear even from the autobiography that his natural physical courage was quite outstanding: the manner of his death was a later illustration of this, for a public man who attached any value to his own skin would have been more adequately guarded. Again, he seems to have been quite free from that maniacal suspiciousness which, as E. M. Forster rightly says in *A Passage to India,* is the besetting Indian vice, as hypocrisy is the British vice. Although no doubt he was shrewd enough in detecting dishonesty, he seems wherever possible to have believed that other people were acting in good faith and had a better nature through which they could be approached. And though he came of a poor middle-class family, started life rather unfavorably, and was probably of unimpressive physical appearance, he was not afflicted by envy or by the feeling of inferiority. Color feeling when he first met it in its worst form in South Africa, seems rather to have astonished him. Even when he was fighting what was in effect a color war, he did not think of people in terms of race or status. The governor of a province, a cotton millionaire, a half-starved Dravidian coolie, a British private soldier were all equally human beings, to be approached in much the same way. It is noticeable that even in the worst possible circumstances, as in South Africa when he was making himself unpopular as the champion of the Indian community, he did not lack European friends.

Written in short lengths for newspaper serialization, the autobiography is not a literary masterpiece, but it is the more impressive because of the commonplaceness of much of its material. It is well to be reminded that Gandhi started out with the normal ambitions of a young Indian student and only adopted his extremist opinions by degrees and, in some cases, rather unwillingly. There was a time, it is interesting to learn, when he wore a top hat, took dancing lessons, studied French and Latin, went up the Eiffel Tower and even tried to learn the violin—all this was the idea of assimilating European civilization as thoroughly as possible. He was not one of those saints who are marked out by their phenomenal piety from childhood onwards, nor one of the other kind who forsake the world after sensational debaucheries. He makes full confession of the misdeeds of his youth, but in fact there is not much to confess. As a frontispiece to the book there is a photograph of Gandhi's possessions at the time of his death. The whole outfit could be purchased for about £5, and Gandhi's sins, at least his fleshly sins, would make the same sort of appearance if placed all in one heap. A few cigarettes, a few mouthfuls of meat, a few annas pilfered in childhood from the maidservant, two visits to a brothel (on each occasion he got away without "doing anything"), one narrowly escaped lapse with his landlady in Plymouth, one outburst of temper—that is about the whole collection. Almost from childhood onwards he had a deep earnestness, an attitude ethical rather than religious, but, until he was about thirty, no very definite sense of direction. His first entry into anything describable as public life was made by way of vegetarianism. Underneath his less ordinary qualities one feels all the time the solid middle-class businessmen who were his ancestors. One feels that even after he had abandoned personal ambition he must have been a resourceful, energetic lawyer and a hard-headed political organizer, careful in keeping down expenses, an adroit handler of committees and an indefatigable chaser of subscriptions. His character was an extraordinarily mixed one, but there was almost nothing in it that you can put your finger on and call bad, and I believe that even Gandhi's worst enemies would admit that he was an interesting and unusual man who enriched the world simply by being alive. Whether he was also a lovable man, and whether his teachings can have much value for those who do not accept the religious beliefs on which they are founded, I have never felt fully certain.

Of late years it has been the fashion to talk about Gandhi as though he were not only sympathetic to the Western Left-wing movement, but were integrally part of it. Anarchists and pacifists, in particular, have claimed him for their own, noticing only that he was opposed to centralism and State violence and ignoring the other-worldly, anti-humanist tendency of his doctrines. But one should, I think, realize that Gandhi's teachings cannot be squared with the belief that Man is the measure of all things and that our job is to make life worth living on this earth, which is the only earth we have. They make sense only on the assumption that God exists and that the world of solid objects is an illusion to be escaped from. It is worth considering the disciplines which Gandhi imposed on himself and which—though he might not insist on every one of his followers observing every detail—he considered indispensable if one wanted to serve either God or humanity. First of all, no meat-eating, and if possible no animal food in any form. (Gandhi himself, for the sake of his health, had to compromise on milk, but seems to have felt this to be a backsliding.) No alcohol or tobacco, and no spices or condiments even of a vegetable kind, since food should be taken not for its own sake but solely in order to preserve one's strength. Secondly, if possible, no sexual intercourse. If sexual intercourse must happen, then it should be for the sole purpose of begetting children and presumably at long intervals. Gandhi himself, in his middle thirties, took the vow of *brahmacharya,* which means not only complete chastity but the elimination of sexual desire. This condition, it seems, is difficult to attain without a special diet and frequent fasting. One of the dangers of milk-drinking is that it is apt to arouse sexual desire. And finally—this is the cardinal point—for the seeker after goodness there must be no close friendships and no exclusive loves whatever.

Close friendships, Gandhi says, are dangerous, because "friends react on one another" and through loyalty to a friend one can be led into wrongdoing. This is unquestionably true. Moreover, if one is to love God, or to love humanity as a whole, one cannot give one's preference to any individual person. This again is true, and it marks the point at which the humanistic and the religious attitude cease to be reconcilable. To an ordinary human being, love means nothing if it does not mean loving some people more than others. The autobiography leaves it uncertain whether Gandhi behaved in an inconsiderate way to his wife and children, but at any rate it makes clear that on three occasions he was willing to let his wife or a child die rather than administer the animal food prescribed by the doctor. It is true that the threatened death never actually occurred, and also that Gandhi—with, one gathers, a good deal of moral pressure in the opposite direction—always gave the patient the choice of staying alive at the price of committing a sin: still, if the decision had been solely his own, he would have forbidden the animal food, whatever the risks might be. There must, he says, be some limit to what we will do in order to remain alive, and the limit is well on this side of chicken broth. This attitude is perhaps a noble one, but, in the sense which—I think—most people would give to the word, it is inhuman. The essence of being human is that one does not seek perfection, that one *is* sometimes willing to commit sins for the sake of loyalty, that one does not push asceticism to the point where it makes friendly intercourse impossible, and that one is prepared in the end to be defeated and broken up by life, which is the inevitable price of fastening one's love upon other human individuals. No doubt alcohol, tobacco, and so forth, are things that a saint must avoid, but sainthood is also a thing that human beings must avoid. There is an obvious retort to this, but one should be wary about making it. In this yogi-ridden age, it is too readily assumed that "non-attachment" is not only better than a full acceptance of earthly life, but that the ordinary man only rejects it because it is too difficult: in other words, that the average human being is a failed saint. It is doubtful whether this is true. Many people genuinely do not wish to be saints, and it is probable that some who achieve or aspire to sainthood have never felt much temptation to be human beings. If one could follow it to its psychological roots, one would, I believe, find that the main motive for "non-attachment" is a desire to escape from the pain of living, and above all from love, which, sexual or non-sexual, is hard work. But it is not necessary here to argue whether the other-worldly or the humanistic ideal is "higher." The point is that they are incompatible. One must choose between God and Man, and all "radicals" and "progressives," from the mildest Liberal to the most extreme Anarchist, have in effect chosen Man.

However, Gandhi's pacifism can be separated to some extent from his other teachings. Its motive was religious, but he claimed also for it that it was a definite technique, a method, capable of producing desired political results. Gandhi's attitude was not that of most Western pacifists. *Satyagraha,* first evolved in South Africa, was a sort of non-violent warfare, a way of defeating the enemy without hurting him and without feeling or arousing hatred. It entailed such things as civil disobedience, strikes, lying down in front of railway trains, enduring police charges without running away and without hitting back, and the like. Gandhi objected to "passive resistance" as a translation of *Satyagraha:* in Gujarati, it seems, the word means "firmness in the truth." In his early days Gandhi served as a stretcher-bearer on the British side in the Boer War, and he was prepared to do the same again in the war of 1914-18. Even after he had completely abjured violence he was honest enough to see that in war it is usually necessary to take sides. He did not—indeed, since his whole political life centred round a struggle for national independence, he could not—take the sterile and dishonest line of pretending that in every war both sides are exactly the same and it makes no difference who wins. Nor did he, like most Western pacifists, specialize in avoiding awkward questions. In relation to the late war, one question that every pacifist had a clear obligation to answer was: "What about the Jews? Are you prepared to see them exterminated? If not, how do you propose to save them without resorting to war?" I must say that I have never heard, from any Western pacifist, an honest answer to this question, though I have heard plenty of evasions, usually of the "you're another" type. But it so happens that Gandhi was asked a somewhat similar question in 1938 and that his answer is on record in Mr. Louis Fischer's *Gandhi and Stalin.* According to Mr. Fischer, Gandhi's view was that the German Jews ought to commit collective suicide, which "would have aroused the world and the people of Germany to Hitler's violence." After the war he justified himself: the Jews had been killed anyway, and might as well have died significantly. One has the impression that this attitude staggered even so warm an admirer as Mr. Fischer, but Gandhi was merely being honest. If you are not prepared to take life, you must often be prepared for lives to be lost in some other way. When, in 1942, he urged non-violent resistance against a Japanese invasion, he was ready to admit that it might cost several million deaths.

At the same time there is reason to think that Gandhi, who after all was born in 1869, did not understand the nature of totalitarianism and saw everything in terms of his own struggle against the British government. The important point here is not so much that the British treated him forbearingly as that he was always able to command publicity. As can be seen from the phrase quoted above, he believed in "arousing the world," which is only possible if the world gets a chance to hear what you are doing. It is difficult to see how Gandhi's methods could be applied in a country where opponents of the régime disappear in the middle of the night and are never heard of again. Without a free press and the right of assembly, it is impossible not merely to appeal to outside opinion, but to bring a mass movement into being, or even to make your intentions known to your adversary. Is there a Gandhi in Russia at this moment? And if there is, what is he accomplishing? The Russian masses could only practice civil disobedience if the same idea happened to occur to all of them simultaneously, and even then, to judge by the history of the Ukraine famine, it would make no difference. But let it be granted that non-violent resistance can be effective against one's own government, or against an occupying power: even so, how does one put it into practice internationally? Gandhi's various conflicting statements on the late war seem to show that he felt the difficulty of this. Applied to foreign politics, pacifism either stops being pacifist or becomes appeasement. Moreover the assumption, which served Gandhi so well in dealing with individuals, that all human beings are more or less approachable and will respond to a generous gesture, needs to be seriously questioned. It is not necessarily true, for example, when you are dealing with lunatics. Then the question becomes: Who is sane? Was Hitler sane? And is it not possible for one whole culture to be insane by the standards of another? And, so far as one can gauge the feelings of whole nations, is there any apparent connection between a generous deed and a friendly response? Is gratitude a factor in international politics?

These and kindred questions need discussion, and need it urgently, in the few years left to us before somebody presses the button and the rockets begin to fly. It seems doubtful whether civilization can stand another major war, and it is at least thinkable that the way out lies through non-violence. It is Gandhi's virtue that he would have been ready to give honest consideration to the kind of question that I have raised above; and, indeed, he probably did discuss most of these questions somewhere or other in his innumerable newspaper articles. One feels of him that there was much that he did not understand, but not that there was anything that he was frightened of saying or thinking. I have never been able to feel much liking for Grandhi, but I do not feel sure that as a political thinker he was wrong in the main, nor do I believe that his life was a failure. It is curious that when he was assassinated, many of his warmest admirers exclaimed sorrowfully that he had lived just long enough to see his life work in ruins, because India was engaged in a civil war which had always been foreseen as one of the by-products of the transfer of power. But it was not in trying to smooth down Hindu-Moslem rivalry that Gandhi had spent his life. His main political objective, the peaceful ending of British rule, had after all been attained. As usual the relevant facts cut across one another. On the other hand, the British did get out of India without fighting, an event which very few observers indeed would have predicted until about a year before it happened. On the other hand, this was done by a Labour government, and it is certain that Conservative government, especially a government headed by Churchill, would have acted differently. But if, by 1945, there had grown up in Britain a large body of opinion sympathetic to Indian independence, how far was this due to Gandhi's personal influence? And if, as may happen, India and Britain finally settle down into a decent and friendly relationship, will this be partly because Gandhi, by keeping up his struggle obstinately and without hatred, disinfected the political air? That one even thinks of asking such questions indicates his stature. One may feel, as I do, a sort of aesthetic distaste for Gandhi, one may reject the claims of sainthood made on his behalf (he never made any such claim himself, by the way), one may also reject sainthood as an ideal and therefore feel that Gandhi's basic aims were anti-human and reactionary: but regarded simply as a politician, and compared with the other leading political figures of our time, how clean a smell he has managed to leave behind!

Questions and Assignments

1. Orwell "defines" Gandhi by showing first some of the things he is not. What are these and where does Orwell discuss them? In what particular group does Orwell finally locate Gandhi as a worthwhile figure?

2. Analyze the elements which Orwell considers to be essential to the concept

of sainthood. Is it possible that Orwell is confused about what sanctity implies? If Orwell's definition of saintliness is wrong, does this have any significant effect on the validity of his argument?

3. How would you characterize Orwell's beginning? Why does Orwell say that "saints should always be judged guilty"? What does this reveal to you about his attitude toward sanctity as well as toward Gandhi?

4. How substantial are such statements as "politics . . . of their nature are inseparable from coercion and fraud" and "maniacal suspiciousness . . . is the besetting Indian vice, as hypocrisy is the British vice"? Does the use of such assertions weaken to any extent the reliability of the author?

5. How does Orwell's insistence that he has "never been able to feel much liking for Gandhi" strengthen his praise? How clear-eyed and sensible does his evaluation seem in retrospect? How has your opinion changed since his opening sentence?

6. Write a paper in which you, like Orwell, attempt to capture the qualities of a man or woman you admire. If you can, use his method of expressing also those qualities the person possesses which you do not value.

7. Write a definition based on one of the following quotations:

"the essence of being human"
"the inevitable price of . . . love"
"our job is to make life worth living on this earth"
"in the end deceivers deceive only themselves"
"in war it is usually necessary to take sides"

Readings: Explication and Paraphrase

Explication and paraphrase is a form of analysis which is applied to a work of literature. Its purpose is to restate, to clarify, to expand upon, the words and the meaning of the work in question. An early, and still important, form of explication is Biblical exegesis—the examination of and commentary on specific passages in the Bible. Explication of this sort is also carried out on many other forms of writing—everything from the *Bhagavad Gita* of Hinduism to the works of Marx and Lenin. The legal decision which appears in Part Two, "Brown v. Board of Education" (p. 173), is also a kind of explication. As you will see in the humorous selection by James Thurber, an explicator who writes from too many of his own preconceived preferences and opinions may produce rather extraordinary results.

Our first selection, by Heinz Politzer, Professor of German at the University of California, shows the complex and varied implications of a ten-line parable by Franz Kafka. Kafka himself was a Czech writer whose symbolic stories and fantasies were published after his death. The other parable reprinted here is an excerpt from his well-known novel *The Trial.* It is not intended to be taken literally, or to put it differently, it may have several different literal meanings. Using the internal explications as examples, as well as Politzer's explication of the first story, the student can use this selection as an opportunity for practising his own explicative skill.

The selection by Wayne Booth, Professor of English at Earlham College and a well-known literary critic, is from the opening chapter of his book *The Rhetoric of Fiction.* By brief explications and discussions of excerpts from the Book of Job and the work of Homer, Boccaccio, and Ring Lardner, Booth shows some of the different methods used by authors of fiction and the different responses which readers must make to those methods. The story by Nathaniel Hawthorne provides a subject for student explication. Hawthorne was an important nineteenth-century American novelist, author of such well-known books as *The Scarlet Letter* and *The House of Seven Gables.*

James Thurber's "explication" of *Macbeth* has been included here just for fun. Thurber, who died recently after many years on the staff of *The New Yorker,* was one of America's greatest humorists.

"Give It Up!": A Kafka Parable

HEINZ POLITZER

"It was very early in the morning, the streets clean and deserted, I was on my way to the railroad station. As I compared the tower clock with my watch I realized it was already much later than I had thought, I had to hurry, the shock of this discovery made me feel uncertain of the way, I was not very well acquainted with the town as yet, fortunately there was a policeman nearby, I ran to him and breathlessly asked him the way. He smiled and said: 'From me you want to learn the way?' 'Yes,' I said, 'since I cannot find it myself.' 'Give it up, give it up,' said he, and turned away with a great sweep, like someone who wants to be alone with his laughter" (*DS*, 201).

This paragraph was discovered among the papers which Franz Kafka left at his death. On its upper left corner the manuscript page shows in faded ink, but unmistakably in Kafka's handwriting, the title "A Commentary." Max Brod published the piece in 1936 calling it: "Give It Up!" Presumably it was written during Kafka's last years.

At first sight it is simple enough. It does not make any extravagant demands on the reader's sensitivity or imagination, nor does it lead to any staggering conclusions. It seems to be self-contained and to say neither more nor less than what it actually says. For this reason it may serve us as an example of Kafka's narrative style. We shall try to determine its form and meaning, then apply some current methods of interpretation to test their validity for this particular text, and finally draw a few conclusions of our own. In the chapters to come there will be ample opportunity to check these conclusions against the evidence offered by Kafka's work at large.

At the outset one must admit that the form of our literary document is somewhat puzzling. It is both a narrative and a statement of truth, although a negative one. Its few lines contain lyrical impressions as well as a dramatic dialogue which is resolved at the end into one decisive silent gesture. For the moment one might call the piece an aphorism extended into an anecdote.

The hybrid form of the story is appropriately reflected by the variety of stylistic devices Kafka has brought into play. The first sentence is composed of three short and almost disconnected phrases; its character is determined by monosyllabic words, which occur much less frequently in German than they do in English. The statement it makes is realistic. The early hour of the day explains the clean and empty streets. Undoubtedly the city will be full of noise and dirt once dawn has turned into day, and people have appeared to fill the streets. Nor is there anything conspicuous about the man who is introduced in the first person as "I." One is tempted to feel that he represents the narrator. At the same time he seems to be shy, for it strikes us as a personal trait that he mentions himself only after having described the time and place of the sketch. The early hour provides a good setting for him; we imagine him to be as fresh and lonely as the streets through which he makes his way to the railroad station.

There is no one to accompany him, nor does he mention anyone whom he may leave behind. He does not say why he turns his back on the place, nor does he indicate where he wants to go. We see him before us, but his figure is determined by what we are not told about him rather than by a description dwelling upon his distinctive features. We are able to make a few assumptions about his person; yet they are not based on what he actually is or does but on what he fails to disclose about himself.

The basic structure of the second sentence resembles that of the first except that the number of individual phrases is now greater, which makes the tempo of the whole sequence seem faster. Here the many commas no longer separate the short statements: instead they have the effect of clamping the parts together. The musical cadence of this sentence has a staccato quality. The word "breathlessly" which falls toward its end expresses the character of the whole. Thus the story moves to its climax; we are astonished, however, to notice that even though this sentence marks a turning point in the narrative, it does not abandon reality anywhere. It reports nothing a realist could not have expressed in exactly the same terms. On the other hand, if we probe the sentence for its actual content, we shall see that the words have been chosen in such a way that the reader is forced to focus his attention on what remains hidden behind and below the realistic narrative.

Let us examine this second sentence more carefully. The man compares his watch with a clock in a tower and discovers that he is late. This is an everyday occurrence; yet we feel strangely compelled to ask for the motivation of the wanderer's trivial action. His watch was slow; he must have sensed that he was behind time, or he would have had no reason to check up on it. Here two time systems seem to diverge: the man's personal time which had determined his way, the time which he carries as a watch on his own body and which has become almost as much a part of himself as his own heart, dissociates itself from the impersonal time, which runs its way up on the tower, completely unconcerned with the wanderer and the watch that had been setting his pace. He "had" believed in it. Kafka deliberately chooses the pluperfect tense to indicate a past now left behind by the man. He starts to run. Now he no longer believes in his personal time; without even the slightest hesitation he accepts the impersonal time as correct. And yet—is it not possible that his personal time was right and that the clock in the tower was too fast?

The fact that the wanderer's watch disagrees with the clock in the tower has led him to what he calls a "discovery": he realizes that it is later than he thought. Because of the urgency of this insight he fails to consult a third watch or to check the time on the clock before he completely surrenders to panicky haste. The reader will sympathize with the man in the anecdote, for he may remember having done the same thing himself. Thus an identification with the man is established which will prevail until the end of the story. It may have been that the wanderer was overcome by the height, the nearness to heaven, of the clock in the tower. More likely than not, however, he was swayed by the mere fact that this clock showed a time outside and beyond himself. Not only is he willing to give precedence to whatever is outside of himself—as the first sentence of the anecdote has already demonstrated—he feels compelled to trust the extrapersonal power of the clock without any further ado. Hence the word "shock," which breaks through the hitherto smooth surface of the narration with primitive force. The panic causes a second awakening, but this time the man is intellectually awakened. He realizes that his walk is no longer in step with a higher order of things. This realization tempts him to run; yet by running, he loses his way. Or to say it in other words, the attempt to regain the right time by running deprives him of the right direction in space.

At this point of the story we meet the phrase, "I was not very well acquainted with the town." First and foremost it seems to suggest that the narrator is neither a native nor a casual visitor, for in neither case would the problem of familiarity with the town have arisen. The fact that the man was not quite familiar with the city could explain his insecurity. Then his fear of being late would be associated with his fear of being a stranger, and both fears could have been allayed if he had only stayed in the neighborhood long enough to become acquainted with it. "Why don't you know your way?" he seems to be asking himself. "You could have known it better if only you had stayed a little longer."

Again, and this time more urgently, we are asking for the reasons behind the man's departure. The haste to which he has succumbed suggests a possible solution to the puzzle: it was impatience which caused him to leave the city before he had become sufficiently familiar with it. Because of impatience the wanderer was likewise incapable of stopping to check the time again or to contemplate his condition. Instead he surrendered to a panic incommensurate with the simple discovery that his watch was slow. Here is another, deeper motivation for the man's following the clock in the tower instead of his own watch: the fact that the impersonal time of the clock was later than his own time met his innate impatience halfway.

Impatience brings a sigh of relief from the wanderer when he catches sight of the policeman. German uses the words *Polizist* and *Schutzmann* interchangeably; yet here Kafka introduces the policeman deliberately as *Schutzmann.* It is *Schutz* which the man now craves most—protection from the strange city, from the elapsed time, from his own insecurity. Moreover, the policeman has not appeared suddenly, nor did he catch the eye of the running man by mere chance. He was nearby, standing there as if he had been on that very spot since time immemorial and intended to remain there forever. Towering there, the policeman seems to be associated with the tower that holds the clock; like the clock tower he represents a system of order ruling the world outside. And just as the man previously had accepted the "outer" time of the tower, so now he surrenders to the extrapersonal authority of the policeman. He does not stop to think or ask himself what business the officer had in this place at so early an hour. Because the street itself is deserted and free from traffic, a policeman is not needed. Destiny itself has clearly ordered the *Schutzmann* to take up his position at this spot and to protect the man for whom he seems to have been waiting.

The word "fortunately" is intended to express the fact that the man believes he has found again a complete agreement between the reality outside and the sense of direction inside himself; he again sees the relationship between the time shown by the clock in the tower and the way he was afraid he had lost, between a well-ordered world and his position in it. His haste now proves to have been utterly unnecessary. The policeman is to show him the way to the railroad station, the lost time will be regained, and all will end well. Our wanderer now relaxes to the extent that, for the first and only time in the story, he is able to describe himself directly. By calling himself "breathless," he reflects the impression which he is bound to give the policeman. For one split second he sees himself as he must appear to the outside world. Yet in this moment of extraversion he accepts, ironically, the policeman's point of view; from now on he will doubt the information given him by the official as little as the time revealed to him by the clock.

During this second, fate appears to be favorably inclined toward the hapless wanderer. The policeman smiles. However, the smile immediately assumes a second, ominous meaning by the words which the policeman adds to it. Kafka has formulated the sentence in which this change occurs in a peculiarly skillful way. Its meaning is at first hidden under the policeman's smile, which only later turns out to have been false or at least ambiguous. The discomfort that the change intends to convey arises in the reader only gradually. Some time is needed to realize the strangeness of this information giver who answers a question with a counterquestion: "From me you want to learn the way?" Signposts are meant to point the way, not to raise questions about themselves. Nor can we miss the undertone of arrogance and indignation in the words of the policeman, who puts himself first in his question (in contrast to the man who had hidden himself at the end of the introductory sentence). The "I" of the official towers so forcefully above the "Thou" of the man that we do not realize right away the presumption underlying his words. He actually addresses the man with a "Thou" (*du*), instead of the formal "you" (*Sie*). In German one says *du* to inferiors, to children, or to animals, not to a solid citizen, with whom one conducts an official exchange of words. Putting his Ego before the humiliating "Thou," the policeman downgrades the information seeker.

And yet, are we not falling prey to a deception when we accept the impression the policeman is giving the man? His counterquestion, which is bound to sound like the epitome of unreasonable pride to the ears of the disappointed questioner, may just as well have been prompted by diffidence or uncertainty. The policeman may have resorted to parrying question with question because the answer was not known to him either. He may not have been familiar with this part of the city, may himself have been ignorant of the right way. The ambiguity of his return question may have been a sign of his incompetence, the *du* of his address an attempt to ingratiate himself with the man, for the German *du* also implies human proximity and brotherliness. Again the wanderer is offered an opportunity to deliberate and evaluate the situation confronting him. Again he misses it. Meekly, like a horrified child, he admits his helplessness.

The exchange between man and policeman is restricted to the barest minimum of words. While it is taking place, however, a general change occurs, unnoticeably but undeniably. In the beginning an ordinary man was asking for an ordinary way, but by now it has become clear to us that it could not have been the everyday way to an everyday railroad station which was on the policeman's mind. Although his counterquestion is phrased in the simplest of words, it points to another, more complex meaning of the word "way." It hints at an infinite variety of ways, without pointing them out or making a binding statement about them. After all, what answer could be more noncommittal than a question? Although man and policeman are conversing in the same language, they do not agree on the exact meaning of this one syllable "way." They talk past one another. Nevertheless, it is not impossible that the man, out of submissiveness and self-denial, eventually will make the policeman's deeper and darker idea of the way his own—whatever this idea may be.

Simultaneously the background of the story has changed without, to be sure, resulting in a change of the external scene. Since the way with which the policeman is concerned, cannot possibly be identical with the one sought by the man in reality, the very reality of the street on which the encounter is taking place has begun to dissolve. The setting which we assumed at first to have the three-dimensional quality of a real town has become unreal and intangible. Even the clock tower has disappeared from the story. Thus the man is deprived of his last pointer, and nothing is left to give him direction.

We are now prepared for the words, "Give it up!" with which the information giver finally dismisses the man. The finality of these words is stressed by their being repeated. On the other hand, it could also be that this repetition is due to the policeman's realization of the man's limited understanding: he talks to him as one talks to an infant or a person who is hard of hearing. We remain in the dark about the precise meaning of these syllables, which descend upon the man like a sixfold thunderbolt. What is he being asked to give up? As little as Kafka allows himself to be pinned down with regard to the meaning of the word "way," so little does he enlighten the reader about the intention of the truly impersonal pronoun "it" in "Give it up!"[1] This "it" is so elastic that it can easily be extended to mean the man's unreasonable haste. If this were the case, the policeman would seem to intimate that the man should abandon his breathlessness and impatience, that is, that he should quiet down. Similarly, the "it" may be understood as a reference to the man's travels and wanderings, or his departure in particular. Then the grim warning would have changed its tone completely and have become a friendly invitation encouraging the man to stay in the city, to look around and linger a while until he would know his way better than before. And yet we are already so intensely identified with the man and his way of thinking that we, too, hasten to substitute an "everything" for this "it." "Give everything up!" the policeman seems to be saying, "let all hope go, abandon the way and the desire ever to find it, give up your quest, your drive and your yearning, your very

[1] In the German original this "it" is even more obscure: there the pronoun *"es"* has been reduced to the letter *s*, which is fused with the imperative *gib* to *"Gibs auf!"* where "it" becomes almost inaudible.

existence—yourself!" He has pronounced this verdict without giving his reasons, without specifying how it should be carried out, without even pronouncing it. He has simply repeated a few syllables, which can mean anything from benevolent advice to the most sinister urge to self-destruction.

The man listens to the verdict in complete silence. He neither questions nor contradicts it and seems to accept it fully. He still notices the "great sweep," with which the official turns away: yet this baroque gesture of the policeman seems even to precipitate the man's disappearance from the scene. The information giver remains silent with a flourish, as it were; thus he avoids giving an answer and shuns, ultimately, his duty. He "turned away . . . , as people do who want to be left alone with their laughter." Kafka uses the present tense here: the policeman's preoccupation with himself is meant to continue as a *praesens infinitum* while the narrator narrates and the reader reads this story.

The policeman returns to his duty, which, whatever it may be, has nothing to do with the claims the man has made upon him. The man has disappeared like the town around him. This statement is, however, only a surmise, unsupported by any textual evidence. By interrupting his narrative at this point, Kafka saves himself the trouble of informing us about the eventual outcome of his story. We are never told whether the man really found his way in the end.

Nor do we find any indication of the outcome in the tone of the story. We cannot decide whether we have been reading a tragic or a grotesquely comic tale. Its scene is plunged in a twilight in which the horrible freely blends with the absurd, and if we are in the right mood, even with the funny. The policeman smiles when his eyes catch the man; the man sees in the information giver a figure of monumental seriousness. The wanderer appears ludicrous to the reader, the official petty, pompous, and awe-inspiring. Yet Kafka does not decide for any one of these conflicting points of view. Instead he forces the reader to change continuously from one to another. Moreover, these shifts of perspective occur so quickly that the contrasts are blurred, the opposites merge, and the contradictions are shrouded by an all-encompassing ambiguity.

Whoever intends to extract an unequivocal meaning from this story will, like the man who is its central figure, hear a question instead of an answer. The policeman's "Give it up!" is also spoken to all those interpreters of Kafka who seem to assume that he believed in the existence of only one way leading in one direction to one aim.

Questions and Assignments

1. In the opening pages of his book *Franz Kafka: Parable and Paradox,* Politzer uses the method of close and exhaustive interpretation of a brief text. This method has been central in French literary study for students in the high schools. Why does Politzer distinguish his initial impression of the whole paragraph from the far deeper insight given by his explication? How superficial does his initial impression seem when you have read the whole selection? Is this superficiality intended? Why?

2. How does this initial general impression serve as a foundation for the details that follow?

3. What was your initial reaction to the word "fortunately" in Kafka's parable? From what point of view is the word used? Is it used to show a change in time during the parable? How?

4. How many of Politzer's conclusions about the narrator have you assumed? Do you in other words, seem to make some of them unconsciously? Do they at first seem familiar or incredible?

5. Do you agree with the adjectives Politzer uses to describe the policeman? Can you think of others that may be more precise—or which provide helpful additional qualification?

6. Consider the structure and movement of Politzer's long paragraph that analyzes the brief phrase, "Give it up!" Why does he first consider the "finality" of the words? Why do the following paragraphs shift from a discussion of finality to one of "changes," of shades of meaning, and of ambiguity?

7. Do you identify with the narrator as Politzer argues that we do? To what extent do you think the author intends you to?

Before the Law

FRANZ KAFKA

Both were now silent for a long time. In the prevailing darkness the priest certainly could not make out K.'s features, while K. saw him distinctly by the light of the small lamp. Why did he not come down from the pulpit? He had not preached a sermon, he had only given K. some information which would be likely to harm him rather than help him when he came to consider it. Yet the priest's good intentions seemed to K. beyond question, it was not impossible that they could come to some agreement if the man would only quit his pulpit, it was not impossible that K. could obtain decisive and acceptable counsel from him which might, for instance, point the way, not toward some influential manipulation of the case, but toward a circumvention of it, a breaking away from it altogether, a mode of living completely outside the jurisdiction of the Court. This possibility must exist, K. had of late given much thought to it. And should the priest know of such a possibility, he might perhaps impart his knowledge if he were appealed to, although he himself belonged to the Court and as soon as he heard the Court impugned had forgotten his own gentle nature so far as to shout K. down.

"Won't you come down here?" said K. "You haven't got to preach a sermon. Come down beside me." "I can come down now," said the priest, perhaps repenting of his outburst. While he detached the lamp from its hook he said: "I had to speak to you first from a distance. Otherwise I am too easily influenced and tend to forget my duty."

K. waited for him at the foot of the steps. The priest stretched out his hand to K. while he was still on the way down from a higher level. "Have you a little time for me?" asked K. "As much time as you need," said the priest, giving K. the small lamp to carry. Even close at hand he still wore a certain air of solemnity. "You are very good to me," said K. They paced side by side up and down the dusky aisle. "But you are an exception among those who belong to the Court. I have more trust in you than in any of the others, though I know many of them. With you I can speak openly." "Don't be deluded," said the priest. "How am I being deluded?" asked K. "You are deluding yourself about the Court," said the priest. "In the writings which preface the Law that particular delusion is described thus: before the Law stands a doorkeeper. To this doorkeeper there comes a man from the country who begs for admittance to the Law. But the doorkeeper says that he cannot admit the man at the moment. The man, on reflection, asks if he will be allowed, then, to enter later. 'It is possible,' answers the doorkeeper, 'but not at this moment.' Since the door leading into the Law stands open as usual and the doorkeeper steps to one side, the man bends down to peer through the entrance. When the doorkeeper sees that, he laughs and says: 'If you are so strongly tempted, try to get in without my permission. But note that I am powerful. And I am only the lowest doorkeeper. From hall to hall, keepers stand at every door, one more powerful than the other. And the sight of the third man is already more than even I can stand.' These are difficulties which the man from the country has not expected to meet, the Law, he thinks, should be accessible to every man and at all times, but when he looks more closely at the doorkeeper in his furred robe, with his huge pointed nose and long thin Tartar beard, he decides that he had better wait until he gets permission to enter. The doorkeeper gives him a stool and lets him sit down at the side of the door. There he sits waiting for days and years. He makes many attempts to be allowed in and wearies the doorkeeper with his importunity. The doorkeeper often engages him in brief conversation, asking him about his home and about other matters, but the questions are put quite impersonally, as great men put questions, and always conclude with the statement that the man cannot be allowed to enter yet. The man, who has equipped himself with many things for his journey, parts with all he has, however valuable, in the hope of bribing the doorkeeper. The doorkeeper accepts it all, saying, however, as he takes each gift: 'I take this only to keep you from feeling that you have left something undone.' During all these long years the man watches the doorkeeper almost incessantly. He forgets about the other doorkeepers, and this one seems to him the only barrier between himself and the Law. In the first years he curses his evil fate aloud; later, as he grows old, he only mutters to himself. He grows childish, and since in his prolonged study of the doorkeeper he has learned to know even the fleas in his fur collar, he begs the very fleas to help him and to persuade the doorkeeper to change his mind. Finally his eyes grow dim and he does not know whether the world is really darkening around him or whether his eyes are only deceiving him. But in the darkness he can now perceive a radiance that streams inextinguishably from the door of the Law. Now his life is drawing to a close. Before he dies, all that he has experienced during the whole time of his sojourn condenses in his mind into one question, which he has never yet put to the doorkeeper. He beckons the doorkeeper, since he can no longer raise his stiffening body. The doorkeeper has to bend far down to hear him, for the difference in size between them has increased very much to the man's disadvantage. 'What do you want to know now?' asks the doorkeeper, 'you are insatiable.' 'Everyone strives to attain the Law, answers the man, 'how does it come about, then, that in all these years no one has come seeking admittance but me?' The doorkeeper perceives that the man is nearing his end and his hearing is failing, so he bellows in his ear: 'No one but you could gain admittance through this door, since this door was intended for you. I am now going to shut it.' "

"So the doorkeeper deceived the man," said K. immediately, strongly attracted by the story. "Don't be too hasty," said the priest, "don't take over someone else's opinion without testing it. I have told you the story in the very words of the scriptures. There's no mention of deception in it." "But it's clear enough," said K., "and your first interpretation of it was quite right. The doorkeeper gave the message of salvation to the man only when it could no longer help him." "He was not asked the question any earlier," said the priest, "and you must consider, too, that he was only a doorkeeper, and as such fulfilled his duty." "What makes you think he fulfilled his duty?" asked K. "He didn't fulfill it. His duty might have been to keep all strangers away, but this man, for whom the door was intended, should have been let in." "You have not enough respect for the written word and you are altering the story," said the priest. "The story contains two important statements made by the doorkeeper about admission to the Law, one at the beginning, the other at the end. The first statement is: that he cannot admit the man at the moment, and the other is: that this door was intended only for the man. If there were a contradiction between the two, you would be right and the doorkeeper would have deceived the man. But there is no contradiction. The first statement, on the contrary, even implies the second. One could almost say that in suggesting to the man the possibility of future admittance the doorkeeper is exceeding his duty. At that time his apparent duty is only to refuse admittance and indeed many commentators are surprised that the suggestion should be made at all, since the doorkeeper appears to be a precisian with a stern regard for duty. He does not once leave his post during these many years, and he does not shut the door until the very last minute; he is conscious of the importance of his office, for he says: 'I am powerful'; he is respectful to his superiors, for he says: 'I am only the lowest doorkeeper'; he is not garrulous, for during all these years he puts only what are called 'impersonal questions'; he is not to be bribed, for he says in accepting a gift: 'I take this only to keep you from feeling that you have left something undone'; where his duty is concerned he is to be moved neither by pity nor rage, for we are told that the man 'wearied the doorkeeper with his importunity'; and finally even his external appearance hints at a pedantic character, the large, pointed nose and the long, thin, black, Tartar beard. Could one imagine a more faithful doorkeeper? Yet the doorkeeper has other elements in his character which are likely to advantage anyone seeking admittance and which make it comprehensible enough that he should somewhat exceed his duty in suggesting the possibility of future admittance. For it cannot be denied that he is a little simple-minded and consequently a little conceited. Take the statements he makes about his power and the power of the other doorkeepers and their dreadful aspect which even he cannot bear to see—I hold that these statements may be true enough, but that the way in which he brings them out shows that his perceptions are confused by simpleness of mind and conceit. The commentators note in this connection: 'The right perception of any matter and a misunderstanding of the same matter do not wholly exclude each other.' One must at any rate assume that such simpleness and conceit, however sparingly manifest, are likely to weaken his defense of the door; they are breaches in the character of the doorkeeper. To this must be added the fact that the doorkeeper seems to be a friendly creature by nature, he is by no means always on his official dignity. In the very first moments he allows himself the jest of inviting the man to enter in spite of the strictly maintained veto against entry; then he does not, for instance, send the man away, but gives him, as we are told, a stool and lets him sit down beside the door. The patience with which he endures the man's appeals during so many years, the brief conversations, the acceptance of the gifts, the politeness with which he allows the man to curse loudly in his presence the fate for which he himself is responsible—all this lets us deduce certain feelings of pity. Not every doorkeeper would have acted thus. And finally, in answer to a gesture of the man's he bends down to give him the chance of putting a last question. Nothing but mild impatience—the doorkeeper knows that this is the end of it all—is discernible in the words: 'You are insatiable.' Some push this mode of interpretation even further and hold that these words express a kind of friendly admiration, though not without a hint of condescension. At any rate the figure of the doorkeeper can be said to come out very differently from what you fancied." "You have studied the story more exactly and for a longer time than I have," said K. They were both silent for a little while. Then K. said: "So you think the man was not deceived?" "Don't misunderstand me," said the priest, "I am only showing you the various opinions concerning that point. You must not pay too much attention to them. The scriptures are unalterable and the comments often enough merely express the commentators' despair. In this case there even exists an interpretation which claims that the deluded person is really the doorkeeper." "That's a far-fetched interpretation," said K. "On what is it based?" "It is based," answered the priest, "on the simple-mindedness of the doorkeeper. The argument is that he does not know the Law from inside, he knows only the way that leads to it, where he patrols up and down. His ideas of the interior are assumed to be childish, and it is supposed that he himself is afraid of the other guardians whom he holds up as bogies before the man. Indeed, he fears them more than the man does, since the man is determined to enter after hearing about the dreadful guardians of the interior, while the doorkeeper has no desire to enter, at least not so far as we are told. Others again say that he must have been in the interior already, since he is after all engaged in the service of the Law and can only have been appointed from inside. This is countered by arguing that he may have been appointed by a voice calling from the interior, and that anyhow he cannot have been far inside, since the aspect of the third doorkeeper is more than he can endure. Moreover, no indication is given that during all these years he ever made any remarks showing a knowledge of the interior, except for the one remark about the doorkeepers. He may have been forbidden to do so, but there is no mention of that either. On these grounds the conclusion is reached that he knows nothing about the aspect and significance of the interior, so that he is in a state of delusion. But he is deceived also about his relation to the man from the country, for he is inferior to the man and does not know it. He treats the man instead as his own subordinate, as can be recognized from many details that must be still fresh in your mind. But, according to this view of the story, it is just as clearly indicated that he is really subordinated to the man. In the first place, a bondman is always subject to a free man. Now the man from the country is really free, he can go where he likes, it is only the Law that is closed to him, and access to the Law is forbidden him only by one individual, the doorkeeper. When he sits down on the stool by the side of the door and stays there for the rest of his life, he does it of his own free will; in the story there is no mention of any compulsion. But the doorkeeper is bound to his post by his very office, he does not dare go out into the country, nor apparently may he go into the interior of the Law, even should he wish to. Besides, although he is in the service of the Law, his service is confined to this one entrance; that is to say, he serves only this man for whom alone the entrance is intended. On that ground too he is inferior to the man. One must assume that for many years, for as long as it takes a man to grow up to the prime of life, his service was in a sense an empty formality, since he had to wait for a man to come, that is to say someone in the prime of life, and so he had to wait a long time before the purpose of his service could be fulfilled, and, moreover, had to wait on the man's pleasure, for the man came of his own free will. But the termination of his service also depends on the man's term of life, so that to the very end he is subject to the man. And it is emphasized throughout that the doorkeeper apparently realizes nothing of all this. That is not in itself remarkable, since according to this interpretation the doorkeeper is deceived in a much more important issue, affecting his very office. At the end, for example, he says regarding the entrance to the Law: 'I am now going to shut it,' but at the beginning of the story we are told that the door leading into the Law always stands open, and if it always stands open, that is to say at all times, without reference to the life or death of the man, then the doorkeeper cannot close it. There is some difference of opinion about the motive behind the doorkeeper's statement, whether he said he was going to close the door merely for the sake of giving an answer, or to emphasize his devotion to duty, or to bring the man into a state of grief and regret in his last moments. But there is no lack of agreement that the doorkeeper will not be able to shut the door. Many indeed profess to find that he is subordinate to the man even in knowledge, toward the end, at least, for the man sees the radiance that issues from the door of the Law while the doorkeeper in his official position must stand with his back to the door, nor does he say anything to show that he has perceived the change." "That is well argued," said K., after repeating to himself in a low voice several passages from the priest's exposition. "It is well argued, and I am inclined to agree that the doorkeeper is deceived. But that has not made me abandon my former opinion, since both conclusions are to some extent compatible. Whether the doorkeeper is clear-sighted or deceived does not dispose of the matter. I said the man is deceived. If the doorkeeper is clear-sighted, one might have doubts about that, but if the doorkeeper himself is deceived, then his deception must of necessity be communicated to the man. That makes the doorkeeper not, indeed, a deceiver, but a creature so simple-minded that he ought to be dismissed at once from his office. You mustn't forget that the doorkeeper's deceptions do himself no harm but do infinite harm to the man." "There are objections to that," said the priest. "Many aver that the story confers no right on anyone to pass judgment on the doorkeeper. Whatever he may seem to us, he is yet a servant of the Law; that is, he belongs to the Law and as such is beyond human judgment. In that case one must not believe that the doorkeeper is subordinate to the man. Bound as he is by his service, even only at the door of the Law, he is incomparably greater than anyone at large in the world. The man is only seeking the Law, the doorkeeper is already attached to it. It is the Law that has placed him at his post; to doubt his dignity is to doubt the Law itself." "I don't agree with that point of view," said K., shaking his head, "for if one accepts it, one must accept as true everything the doorkeeper says. But you yourself have sufficiently proved how impossible it is to do that." "No," said the priest, "it is not necessary to accept everything as true, one must only accept it as necessary." "A melancholy conclusion," said K. "It turns lying into a universal principle."

K. said that with finality, but it was not his final judgment. He was too tired to survey all the conclusions arising from the story, and the trains of thought into which it was leading him were unfamiliar, dealing with impalpabilities better suited to a theme for discussion among Court officials than for him. The simple story had lost its clear outline, he wanted to put it out of his mind, and the priest, who now showed great delicacy of feeling, suffered him to do so and accepted his comment in silence, although undoubtedly he did not agree with it.

They paced up and down for a while in silence, K. walking close beside the priest, ignorant of his whereabouts. The lamp in his hand had long since gone out. The silver image of some saint once glimmered into sight immediately before him, by the sheen of its own silver, and was instantaneously lost in the darkness again. To keep himself from being utterly dependent on the priest, K. asked: "Aren't we near the main doorway now?" "No," said the priest, "we're a long way from it. Do you want to leave already?" Although at that moment K. had not been thinking of leaving, he answered at once: "Of course, I must go. I'm the Chief Clerk of a Bank, they're waiting for me, I only came here to show a business friend from abroad round the Cathedral." "Well," said the priest, reaching out his hand to K., "then go." "But I can't find my way alone in this darkness," said K. "Turn left to the wall," said the priest, "then follow the wall without leaving it and you'll come to a door." The priest had already taken a step or two away from him, but K. cried out in a loud voice, "Please wait a moment." "I am waiting," said the priest. "Don't you want anything more from me?" asked K. "No," said the priest. "You were so friendly to me for a time," said K., "and explained so much to me, and now you let me go as if you cared nothing about me." "But you have to leave now," said the priest. "Well, yes," said K., "you must see that I can't help it." "You must first see who I am," said the priest. "You are the prison chaplain," said K., groping his way nearer to the priest again; his immediate return to the Bank was not so necessary as he had made out, he could quite well stay longer. "That means I belong to the Court," said the priest. "So why should I want anything from you? The Court wants nothing from you. It receives you when you come and it dismisses you when you go."

Questions and Assignments

1. How do the introductory phrases, "You are deluding yourself. . . . In the writings which preface the Law that particular delusion is described, thus . . . ," color your interpretation of the priest's story? How much individuality is left to the case of K.?

2. Try to state precisely your reactions and sympathies at the end of the priest's parable. How are these altered by K.'s response? By the priest's rebuke?

3. Why does the priest describe the various commentaries to K.? Do they enlighten K., confuse him more—or both?

4. Explain in your own words the meaning and effect of the priest's words, "No, it is not necessary to accept everything as true, one must only accept it as necessary." How does K.'s answer, "It turns lying into a universal principle," alter your response?

5. What relationship do the last two paragraphs have to the rest of the story?

6. Trace the way your reactions to the parable change. Attempt to be precise and to discover how unstated implications and general allusions influence you. How does the simplicity of the surface of Kafka's writing contribute to the various possible interpretations of his story?

7. From the comments of the priest, attempt to work out the manner in which the Law operates. How do K.'s coments change your opinions?

8. Attempt to assess the reliability of the priest's statements. Of K.'s responses. To what extent do your sympathies coincide with their reliability?

9. Write your own explication of the doorkeeper parable.

Telling and Showing

WAYNE C. BOOTH

One of the most obviously artificial devices of the storyteller is the trick of going beneath the surface of the action to obtain a reliable view of a character's mind and heart. Whatever our ideas may be about the natural way to tell a story, artifice is unmistakably present whenever the author tells us what no one in so-called real life could possibly know. In life we never know anyone but ourselves by thoroughly reliable internal signs, and most of us achieve an all too partial view even of ourselves. It is in a way strange, then, that in literature from the very beginning we have been told motives directly and authoritatively without being forced to rely on those shaky inferences about other men which we cannot avoid in our own lives.

"There was a man in the land of Uz, whose name was Job; and that man was perfect and upright, one that feared God, and eschewed evil." With one stroke the unknown author has given us a kind of information never obtained about real people, even about our most intimate friends. Yet it is information that we must accept without question if we are to grasp the story that is to follow. In life if a friend confided his view that *his* friend was "perfect and upright," we would accept the information with qualifications imposed by our knowledge of the speaker's character or of the general fallibility of mankind. We could never trust even the most reliable of witnesses as completely as we trust the author of the opening statement about Job.

We move immediately in Job to two scenes presented with no privileged information whatever: Satan's temptation of God and Job's first losses and lamentations. But we conclude the first section with another judgment which no real event could provide for any observer: "In all this Job sinned not, nor charged God foolishly." How do we know that Job sinned not? Who is to pronounce on such a question? Only God himself could know with certainty whether Job charged God foolishly. Yet the author pronounces judgment, and we accept his judgment without question.

It might at first appear that the author does not require us to rely on his unsupported word, since he gives us the testimonial of God himself, conversing with Satan, to confirm his view of Job's moral perfection. And after Job has been pestered by his three friends and has given his own opinion about his experience, God is brought on stage again to confirm the truth of Job's view. But clearly the reliability of God's statements ultimately depends on the author himself; it is he who names God and assures us that this voice is truly His.

This form of artificial authority has been present in most narrative until recent times. Though Aristotle praises Homer for speaking in his own voice less than other poets, even Homer writes scarcely a page without some kind of direct clarification of motives, of expectations, and of the relative importance of events. And though the gods themselves are often unreliable, Homer—the Homer we know—is not. What he tells us usually goes deeper and is more accurate than anything we are likely to learn about real people and events. In the opening lines of the *Iliad,* for example, we are told, under the half-pretense of an invocation, precisely what the tale is to be about: "the anger of Peleus' son Achilles and its devastation." We are told directly that we are to care more about the Greeks than the Trojans. We are told that they were "heroes" with "strong souls." We are told that it was the will of Zeus that they should be "the delicate feasting of dogs." And we learn that the particular conflict between Agamemnon, "the lord of men," and "brilliant" Achilles was set on by Apollo. We could never be sure of any of this information in real life, yet we *are* sure as we move through the *Iliad* with Homer constantly at our elbow, controlling rigorously our beliefs, our interests, and our sympathies. Though his commentary is generally brief and often disguised as simile, we learn from it the precise quality of every heart; we know who dies innocent and who guilty, who foolish and who wise. And we know, whenever there is any reason for us to know, what the characters are thinking: "the son of Tydeus pondered doubtfully / . . . Three times in his heart and spirit he pondered turning . . . (Book VIII, ll. 167-69).

In the *Odyssey* Homer works in the same explicit and systematic way to keep our judgments straight. Though E. V. Rieu is no doubt correct in calling Homer an "impersonal" and "objective" author, in the sense that the life of the real Homer cannot be discovered in his work, Homer "intrudes" deliberately and obviously to insure that our judgment of the "heroic," "resourceful," "admirable," "wise" Odysseus will be sufficiently favorable. "Yet all the gods were sorry for him, except Poseidon, who pursued the heroic Odysseus with relentless malice till the day when he reached his own country."

Indeed, the major justification of the opening scene in the palace of Zeus is not as mere exposition of the facts of Odysseus' plight. What Homer requires of us is sympathetic involvement in that plight, and Athene's opening reply to Zeus provides authoritative judgment on what is to follow. "It is for Odysseus that my heart is wrung—the wise but unlucky Odysseus, who has been parted so long from all his friends and is pining on a lonely island far away in the middle of the seas." To her accusation of neglect, Zeus replies, "How could I ever forget the admirable Odysseus? He is not only the wisest man alive but has been the most generous in his offerings. . . . It is Poseidon . . . who is so implacable towards him. . . ."

When we come to Odysseus' enemies, the poet again does not hesitate either to speak in his own person or to give divine testimony. Penelope's suitors must look bad to us; Telemachus must be admired. Not only does Homer dwell on Athene's approval of Telemachus, he lays on his own direct judgments with bright colors. The "insolent," "swaggering," and "ruffianly" suitors are contrasted to the "wise" (though almost helplessly young) Telemachus and the "good" Mentor. "Telemachus now showed his good judgment." Mentor "showed his good will now by rising to admonish his compatriots." We seldom encounter the suitors without some explicit attack by the poet: "This was their boastful way, though it was they who little guessed how matters really stood." And whenever there might be some doubt about where a character stands, Homer sets us straight: " 'My Queen,' replied Medon, who was by no means a villain. . . ." Hundreds of pages later, when Medon is spared from Odysseus' slaughter, we can hardly be surprised.

The result of all this direct guidance, when it is joined with Athene's divine attestation that the gods "have no quarrel" with Telemachus and have settled that he "shall come home safe," is to leave us, as we enter upon Odysseus' first adventure in Book Five, perfectly clear about what we should hope for and what fear; we are unambiguously sympathetic toward the heroes and contemptuous of the suitors. It need hardly be said that another poet, working with the same episodes but treating them from the suitors' point of view, could easily have led us into the same adventures with radically different hopes and fears.

Direct and authoritative rhetoric of the kind we have seen in Job and in Homer's works has never completely disappeared from fiction. But as we all know, it is not what we are likely to find if we turn to a typical modern novel or short story.

> Jim had a great trick that he used to play w'ile he was travelin'. For instance, he'd be ridin' on a train and they'd come to some little town like, well, like, we'll say, like Benton. Jim would look out of the train window and read the signs on the stores.
>
> For instance, they'd be a sign, "Henry Smith, Dry Goods." Well, Jim would write down the name and the name of the town and when he got to wherever he was goin' he'd mail back a postal card to Henry Smith at Benton and not sign no name to it, but he'd write on the card, well, somethin' like "Ask your wife about that book agent that spent the afternoon last week," or "Ask your Missus who kept her from gettin' lonesome the last time you was in Carterville." And he'd sign the card, "A Friend."
>
> Of course, he never knew what really come of none of these jokes, but he could picture what probably happened and that was enough. . . . Jim was a card.

Most readers of Lardner's "Haircut" (1926) have recognized that Lardner's opinion of Jim is radically different here from the speaker's. But no one in the story has said so. Lardner is not present to say so, not, at least, in the sense that Homer is present in his epics. Like many other modern authors, he has effaced himself, renounced the privilege of direct intervention, retreated to the wings and left his characters to work out their own fates upon the stage.

> In sleep she knew she was in her bed, but not the bed she had lain down in a few hours since, and the room was not the same but it was a room she had known somewhere. Her heart was a stone lying upon her breast outside of her; her pulses lagged and paused, and she knew that something strange was going to happen, even as the early morning winds were cool through the lattice. . . .
>
> Now I must get up and go while they are all quiet. Where are my things? Things have a will of their own in this place and hide where they like. . . . Now what horse shall I borrow for this journey I do not mean to take? . . . Come now, Graylie, she said, taking the bridle, we must outrun Death and the Devil. . . .

The relation between author and spokesman is more complex here. Katherine Anne Porter's Miranda ("Pale Horse, Pale Rider" [1936]) cannot be simply classified, like Lardner's barber, as morally and intellectually deficient; the ironies at work among character, author, and reader are considerably more difficult to describe. Yet the problem for the reader is essentially the same as in "Haircut." The story is presented without comment, leaving the reader without the guidance of explicit evaluation.

Since Flaubert, many authors and critics have been convinced that "objective" or "impersonal" or "dramatic" modes of narration are naturally superior to any mode that allows for direct appearances by the author or his reliable spokesman. Sometimes, as we shall see in the next three chapters, the complex issues involved in this shift have been reduced to a convenient distinction between "showing," which is artistic, and "telling," which is inartistic. "I shall not *tell* you anything," says a fine young novelist in defense of his art. "I shall allow you to eavesdrop on my people, and sometimes they will tell the truth and sometimes they will lie, and you must determine for yourself when they are doing which. You do this every day. Your butcher says, 'This is the best,' and you reply, 'That's *you* saying it.' Shall my people be less the captive of their desires than your butcher? I can *show* much, but show only. . . . You will no more expect the novelist to tell you precisely *how* something is said than you will expect him to stand by your chair and hold your book."

But the changed attitudes toward the author's voice in fiction raise problems that go far deeper than this simplified version of point of view would suggest. Percy Lubbock taught us forty years ago to believe that "the art of fiction does not begin until the novelist thinks of his story as a matter to be *shown,* to be so exhibited that it will tell itself." He may have been in some sense right—but to say so raises more questions than it answers.

Why is it that an episode "told" by Fielding can strike us as more fully realized than many of the scenes scrupulously "shown" by imitators of James or Hemingway? Why does some authorial commentary ruin the work in which it occurs, while the prolonged commentary of *Tristram Shandy* can still enthral us? What, after all, does an author do when he "intrudes" to "tell" us something about his story? Such questions force us to consider closely what happens when an author engages a reader fully with a work of fiction; they lead us to a view of fictional technique which necessarily goes far beyond the reductions that we have sometimes accepted under the concept of "point of view."

Our task will be simpler if we begin with some stories written long before anyone worried very much about cleaning out the rhetorical impurities from the house of fiction. The stories in Boccaccio's *Decameron,* for example, seem extremely simple—perhaps even simple-minded and inept —if we ask of them the questions which many modern stories invite us to ask. It is bad enough that the characters are what we call two-dimensional, with no revealed depths of any kind; what is much worse, the "point of view" of the narrator shifts among them with a total disregard for the kind of technical focus or consistency generally admired today. But if we read these stories in their own terms, we soon discover a splendid and complex skill underlying the simplicity of the effect.

The material of the ninth story of the fifth day is in itself conventional and shallow indeed. There was once a young lover, Federigo, who impoverished himself courting a chaste married woman, Monna Giovanna. Rejected, he withdrew to a life of poverty, with only a beloved falcon remaining of all his former possessions. The woman's husband died. Her son, who had grown fond of Federigo's falcon, became seriously ill and asked Monna to obtain the falcon for his comfort. She reluctantly went to Federigo to request the falcon. Federigo was overwhelmed with excitement by her visit, and he was determined, in spite of his poverty, to entertain her properly. But his cupboard was bare, so he killed the falcon and served it to her. They discovered their misunderstanding, and the mother returned empty-handed to her boy, who soon died. But the childless widow, impressed by Federigo's generous gesture in offering his falcon, chose him for her second husband.

Such a story, reduced in this way to a bare outline, could have been made into any number of fully realized plots with radically different effects. It could have been a farce, stressing Federigo's foolish extravagance, his ridiculous antics in trying to think of something to serve his beloved for breakfast, and the absurdity of the surprise ending. It could have been a meditative or a comic piece on the ironical twists of fate, emphasizing the transformation in Monna from proud resistance to quick surrender—something on the order of Christopher Fry's *A Phoenix Too Frequent* as derived from Petronius. It could have been a sardonic tale written from the point of view of the husband and son who, like the falcon, must be killed off, as it were, to make the survivors happy. And so on.

As it is, every stroke is in a direction different from these. The finished tale is designed to give the reader the greatest possible pleasure in the sympathetic comedy of Monna's and Federigo's deserved good fortune, to make the reader delight in this instance of the announced theme for all the tales told on the fifth day: "good fortune befalling lovers after divers direful or disastrous adventures." Though one never views these characters or their "direful or disastrous adventures" in anything like a tragic light, and though, in fact, one laughs at the excesses of Federigo's passion and at his willingness to pursue it even to poverty, our laughter must always be sympathetic. Much as Federigo deserves his disasters, in the finished tale he also deserves the supreme good fortune of winning Monna.

To insure our pleasure in such an outcome—a pleasure which might have been mild indeed considering that there are nine other tales attempting something like the same effect—the two main characters must be established with great precison. First the heroine, Monna Giovanna, must be felt to be thoroughly worthy of Federigo's "extravagant" love. In a longer, different kind of story, this might have been done by showing her in virtuous action; one could take whatever space was required for episodes dramatizing her as worthy of Federigo's fantastic devotion. But here economy is at least as important as precision. And the economical method of imposing her virtues on the reader is for the narrator to *tell* us about them, supporting his telling with some judiciously chosen, and by modern standards very brief and unrealistic, episodes. These can be of two kinds, either in the form of what James was later to call "going behind" to reveal the true workings of the heroine's mind and heart or in the form of overt action. Thus, the narrator begins by describing her as the "fairest" and "most elegant," and as "no less virtuous than fair." In a simple story of this kind, her beauty and elegance require for validation no more than Federigo's dramatized passion. Our belief in her virtue, however—certainly in Boccaccio a more unlikely gift than beauty and elegance—is supported both by her sustained chastity in the face of his courtship and, far more important, by the quality of what is revealed whenever we enter her thoughts.

> Whereupon the lady was silent a while, bethinking her what she should do. She knew that Federigo had long loved her, and had never had so much as a single kind look from her: wherefore she said to herself:—How can I send or go to beg of him this falcon, which by what I hear is the best that ever flew, and moreover is his sole comfort? And how could I be so unfeeling as to seek to deprive a gentleman of the one solace that is now left him? And so, albeit she very well knew that she might have the falcon for the asking, she was perplexed, and knew not what to say, and gave her son no answer. At length, however, the love she bore the boy carried the day, and she made up her mind, for his contentment . . . to go herself and fetch him the falcon.

The interest in this passage lies of course in the moral choice that it presents and in the effect upon our sentiments that is implicit in that choice. Though the choice is in one respect a relatively trivial one, it is far more important than most choices faced by the characters who people Boccaccio's world. Dramatized at greater length, it could in fact have been made into the central episode for the story—though the story that resulted would be a far different one from what we now have. As it is treated here, the choice is given precisely the degree of importance it should have in the whole. Because we experience Monna's thoughts and feelings at first hand, we are forced to agree with the narrator's assessment of her great worth. She is not simply virtuous in conventional matters like chastity, but she is also capable of moral delicacy in more fundamental matters: unlike the majority of Boccaccio's women, she is above any casual manipulation of her lover for her own purposes. Even this delicacy, admirable in itself, can be overridden by a more important value, "the love she bore the boy." Yet all this is kept strictly serviceable to our greater interest in

Federigo and the falcon; there is never any question of our becoming side-tracked into deep psychological or sentimental involvement with her as a person.

Because the narrator has *told* us what to think of her, and then *shown* her briefly in support of his claims, all the while keeping our sympathy and admiration carefully subordinated to the comic effect of the whole, we can move to the most important episode with our expectations clear and—in their own kind—intense. We can move to Monna's relatively long and wonderfully delicate speech to Federigo requesting the falcon, with our hopes centered clearly on the "good fortune" of their ultimate union.

If all this skilful presentation of the admirable Monna is to succeed, we must see Federigo himself as an equally admirable, though not really heroic, figure. Too much moral stature will spoil the comedy; too little will destroy our desire for his success. It is not enough to show his virtues through his actions; his only admirable act is the gift of the falcon and that might be easily interpreted in itself as a further bit of foolish extravagance. Unless the story is to be lengthened unduly with episodes showing that he is worthy, in spite of his extravagance, the narrator must give us briefly and directly the necessary information about his true character. He is therefore described, unobtrusively but in terms that only an omniscient narrator could use with success, as "gallant," "full of courtesy," "patient," and most important of all, as "more in love than ever before"; the world of *his* desires is thus set off distinctly from the world of many of the other tales, where love is reduced for comic purposes to lust.

These completely straightforward statements of the narrator's opinions are supported by what we see of Federigo's own mind. His comic distress over not having anything to feed his beloved visitor, and his unflinching sacrifice of the bird, are rendered in intimate detail, with frequent—though by modern standards certainly shallow—inside views; his poverty "was brought home to him," he was "distressed beyond measure," he "inwardly" cursed "his evil fortune." "Sorely he longed that the lady might not leave his house altogether unhonoured, and yet to crave help of his own husbandman was more than his pride could brook." All this insures that the wonderful comedy of the breakfast will be the comedy of sympathetic laughter: we are throughout completely in favor of Federigo's suit. And our favor is heightened by the method of presenting the scene of discovery. "No sooner had Federigo apprehended what the lady wanted, than, *for grief that 'twas not in his power to serve her* . . . he fell a-weeping. . . ." At first

Monna supposed that " 'twas only because he was loath to part with the brave falcon that he wept." We might have made the same mistake but for the author's help provided in the clause I have italicized.

Once we have become assured of his character in this way, Federigo's speeches, like Monna Giovanna's, become the equivalent of inside views, because we know that everything he says is a trustworthy reflection of his true state of mind. His long speech of explanation about the falcon serves, as a result, to confirm all we have learned of him; when he concludes, "I doubt I shall ever know peace of mind more," we believe in his sincerity, though of course we know with complete certainty, and have known from the beginning, that the story is to end with "good fortune."

Having seen this much, we need little more. To make Monna the heiress as provided in the will, her son must die in a passage only one or two lines longer than the one or two lines earlier given to the death of the husband. Her "inward commendation" of Federigo's "magnanimity" leads her to the decision to marry him rather than a wealthy suitor: "I had rather have a man without wealth than wealth without a man." Federigo *is* a man, as we know by now. Though his portrait is conventional, "flat," "two-dimensional," it includes everything we need. We can thus accept without irony the narrator's concluding judgment that married to such a wife he lived happily to the end of his days. Fiammetta's auditors all "praised God that He had worthily rewarded Federigo."

If we share in the pleasure of seeing the comic but worthy hero worthily rewarded, the reason is thus not to be found in any inherent quality of the materials but rather in the skilful construction of a living plot out of materials that might have been used in many different ways. The deaths of the husband and son, which in the finished version are merely conveniences for Federigo's exaltation, would in any truly impartial account occupy considerably more space than Federigo's anxiety over not having anything to serve his mistress. Treated impartially, the boy's death would certainly be dramatized as fully as the mother's hesitation about troubling Federigo for his falcon. But the demands of this plot are for a technique that wins us to Federigo's side.

Quite obviously this technique cannot be judged by modern standards of consistency; the story could not have been written from a consistent point of view without stretching it to three times its present length and thereby losing its taut comic force. To tell it entirely through Federigo's eyes would require a much longer introductory section, and the comedy of the visit to fetch the falcon would be partially lost if we did not see more of the preparation for it than Federigo can possibly be aware of. Yet since it is primarily Federigo's story, to see it through Monna's eyes would require a great deal of manipulation and extension. Such conjectural emendations are in a way absurd, since they almost certainly would never have occurred to Boccaccio. But they help to make emphatic the great gap that separates Boccaccio's technique from the more obviously rigorous methods we have come to look for. In this story there is no important revelation of truth, no intensity of illusion, no ironic complexity, no prophetic vision, no rich portrayal of moral ambiguities. There is some incidental irony, it is true, but the greatness of the whole resides in unequivocal intensity not of illusion but of comic delight produced in extraordinarily brief compass.

Any temptation we might have to attribute its success to unconscious or accidental primitivism can be dispelled by looking at the radically different experience offered by other tales. Since his different effects are based on different moral codes, Boccaccio can never assume that his readers will hold precisely the correct attitudes as they approach any one story. He certainly does not assume that his readers will approve of the license of his most licentious tales. Even Dioneo, the most lewd of all the ten narrators, must spend a good deal of energy manipulating us into the camp of those who can laugh with a clear conscience at his bawdy and often cruel stories. In the potentially distressing tale of how the holy man, Rustico, debauches the young and innocent Alibech by teaching her how to put the devil in hell (third day, tenth tale), great care is taken with the character and ultimate fate of the simple-minded girl in order to lead us to laugh at conduct that in most worlds, including the world in which Boccaccio lived, would be considered cruel and sacrilegious rather than comic.

If Dioneo, the lusty young courtier, must use care with his rhetoric in a bawdy tale, Fiammetta, the lovely lady, must use even more when she comes to praise infidelity. On the seventh day the subject is "the tricks which, either for love or for their deliverance from peril, ladies have heretofore played on their husbands, and whether they were by the said husbands detected, or no." In "The Falcon" Fiammetta worked to build admiration for the virtue of Federigo and Monna Giovanna; she now (fifth tale) employs a different rhetoric. Since her task is to insure our delight in the punishment of a justifiably jealous husband, her commentary tells us directly what is borne out by our views of the husband's mind: he is "a poor creature, and of little sense" who deserves what he gets. More important, she prefaces the story with a little oration, about one-seventh of the length of the whole story, setting our values straight: "For which reason, to sum up, I say that a wife is rather to be commended than censured, if she take her revenge upon a husband that is jealous without cause."

In support of this general argument, the whole tale is manipulated in such a way as to make the reader desire the comic punishment of the husband. Most of it is seen through the eyes of the woman, with great stress on her comic suffering at the hands of the great bullying fool. The climax is his full punishment, in the form of a clever, lashing speech from his wife. Few readers can feel that he has received anything but what he deserves when Fiammetta concludes that the cuckold's wife has now earned her "charter of indulgence."

Questions and Assignments

1. What is the essential contrast Booth makes between our responses in "real life" and as readers? Why does he stress the distinction between the "natural" and artificial? Do you make this distinction when you read? Should you?

2. When you read—or when you think back about what you have read—do you recognize that the author, like Homer, has been "controlling rigorously our beliefs, our interests, and our sympathies"? How important for such control is the reader's conscious recognition?

3. What is the main difference Booth describes between the narration in Homer or the Bible and that of such recent writers as Lardner and Porter? To what extent does Lardner "control" your interests and sympathies as did Homer in his example? How vital do you find this distinction in your own responses as a reader of fiction?

4. Notice Booth's technique of beginning his analyses of complex problems with "simple" early examples. Why does he choose as the two types of simplicity the "two-dimensional" characters and the disregard for "focus or consistency"? Do these characteristics disturb you in Boccaccio? Can you think of examples in recent fiction or in movies you have seen? Do they disturb you there? How can you start to explain the difference?

5. Develop some of the possibilities of the different effects that Booth says could have been gained from Boccaccio's basic plot. How do these comparisons help you understand better the story as it is told?

6. Why are "precision and economy" the qualities necessary for effectively gaining the reader's sympathy? Why are these particular qualities appropriate for this tale?

7. How important is Booth's distinction that the author "all the while keeps our sympathy and admiration carefully subordinated to the comic effect of the whole"? Notice that this sort of distinction depends upon a critical interpretation

of what is of primary importance for the whole. Why would "too much moral stature . . . spoil the comedy"?

The Minister's Black Veil

NATHANIEL HAWTHORNE

The sexton stood in the porch of Milford meeting-house, pulling busily at the bell-rope. The old people of the village came stooping along the street. Children, with bright faces, tripped merrily beside their parents, or mimicked a graver gait, in the conscious dignity of their Sunday clothes. Spruce bachelors looked sidelong at the pretty maidens, and fancied that the Sabbath sunshine made them prettier than on week days. When the throng had mostly streamed into the porch, the sexton began to toll the bell, keeping his eye on the Reverend Mr. Hooper's door. The first glimpse of the clergyman's figure was the signal for the bell to cease its summons.

"But what has good Parson Hooper got upon his face?" cried the sexton in astonishment.

All within hearing immediately turned about, and beheld the semblance of Mr. Hooper, pacing slowly his meditative way towards the meeting-house. With one accord they started, expressing more wonder than if some strange minister were coming to dust the cushions of Mr. Hooper's pulpit.

"Are you sure it is our parson?" inquired Goodman Gray of the sexton.

"Of a certainty it is good Mr. Hooper," replied the sexton. "He was to have exchanged pulpits with Parson Shute, of Westbury; but Parson Shute sent to excuse himself yesterday, being to preach a funeral sermon."

The cause of so much amazement may appear sufficiently slight. Mr. Hooper, a gentlemanly person, of about thirty, though still a bachelor, was dressed with due clerical neatness, as if a careful wife had starched his band, and brushed the weekly dust from his Sunday's garb. There was but one thing remarkable in his appearance. Swathed about his forehead, and hanging down over his face, so low as to be shaken by his breath, Mr. Hooper had on a black veil. On a nearer view it seemed to consist of two folds of crape, which entirely concealed his features, except the mouth and chin, but probably did not intercept his sight, further than to give a darkened aspect to all living and inanimate things. With this gloomy shade before him, good Mr. Hooper walked onward, at a slow and quiet pace, stooping somewhat, and looking on the ground, as is customary with abstracted men, yet nodding kindly to those of his parishioners who still waited on the meeting-house steps. But so wonder-struck were they that his greeting hardly met with a return.

"I can't really feel as if good Mr. Hooper's face was behind that piece of crape," said the sexton.

"I don't like it," muttered an old woman, as she hobbled into the meeting-house. "He has changed himself into something awful, only by hiding his face."

"Our parson has gone mad!" cried Goodman Gray, following him across the threshold.

A rumor of some unaccountable phenomenon had preceded Mr. Hooper into the meeting-house, and set all the congregation astir. Few could refrain from twisting their heads towards the door; many stood upright, and turned directly about; while several little boys clambered upon the seats, and came down again with a terrible racket. There was a general bustle, a rustling of the women's gowns and shuffling of the men's feet, greatly at variance with that hushed repose which should attend the entrance of the minister. But Mr. Hooper appeared not to notice the perturbation of his people. He entered with an almost noiseless step, bent his head mildly to the pews on each side, and bowed as he passed his oldest parishioner, a white-haired great grandsire, who occupied an arm-chair in the centre of the aisle. It was strange to observe how slowly this venerable man became conscious of something singular in the appearance of his pastor. He seemed not fully to partake of the prevailing wonder, till Mr. Hooper had ascended the stairs, and showed himself in the pulpit, face to face with his congregation, except for the black veil. That mysterious emblem was never once withdrawn. It shook with his measured breath, as he gave out the psalm; it threw its obscurity between him and the holy page, as he read the Scriptures; and while he prayed, the veil lay heavily on his uplifted countenance. Did he seek to hide it from the dread Being whom he was addressing?

Such was the effect of this simple piece of crape, that more than one woman of delicate nerves was forced to leave the meeting-house. Yet perhaps the pale-faced congregation was almost as fearful a sight to the minister, as his black veil to them.

Mr. Hooper had the reputation of a good preacher, but not an energetic one: he strove to win his people heavenward by mild, persuasive influences, rather than to drive them thither by the thunders of the Word. The sermon which he now delivered was marked by the same characteristics of style and manner as the general series of his pulpit oratory. But there was something, either in the sentiment of the discourse itself, or in the imagination of the auditors, which made it greatly the most powerful effort that they had ever heard from their pastor's lips. It was tinged, rather more darkly than usual, with the gentle gloom of Mr. Hooper's temperament. The subject had reference to secret sin, and those sad mysteries which we hide from our nearest and dearest, and would fain conceal from our own consciousness, even forgetting that the Omniscient can detect them. A subtle power was breathed into his words. Each member of the congregation, the most innocent girl, and the man of hardened breast, felt as if the preacher had crept upon them, behind his awful veil, and discovered their hoarded iniquity of deed or thought. Many spread their clasped hands on their bosoms. There was nothing terrible in what Mr. Hooper said, at least, no violence; and yet, with every tremor of his melancholy voice, the hearers quaked. An unsought pathos came hand in hand with awe. So sensible were the audience of some unwonted attribute in their minister, that they longed for a breath of wind to blow aside the veil, almost believing that a stranger's visage would be discovered, though the form, gesture, and voice were those of Mr. Hooper.

At the close of the services, the people hurried out with indecorous confusion, eager to communicate their pent-up amazement, and conscious of lighter spirits the moment they lost sight of the black veil. Some gathered in little circles, huddled closely together, with their mouths all whispering in the centre; some went homeward alone, wrapt in silent meditation; some talked loudly, and profaned the Sabbath day with ostentatious laughter. A few shook their sagacious heads, intimating that they could penetrate the mystery; while one or two affirmed that there was no mystery at all, but only that Mr. Hooper's eyes were so weakened by the midnight lamp, as to require a shade. After a brief interval, forth came good Mr. Hooper also, in the rear of his flock. Turning his veiled face from one group to another, he paid due reverence to the hoary heads, saluted the middle aged with kind dignity as their friend and spiritual guide, greeted the young with mingled authority and love, and laid his hands on the little children's heads to bless them. Such was always his custom on the Sabbath day. Strange and bewildered looks repaid him for his courtesy. None, as on former occasions, aspired to the honor of walking by their pastor's side. Old Squire

Saunders, doubtless by an accidental lapse of memory, neglected to invite Mr. Hooper to his table, where the good clergyman had been wont to bless the food, almost every Sunday since his settlement. He returned, therefore, to the parsonage, and, at the moment of closing the door, was observed to look back upon the people, all of whom had their eyes fixed upon the minister. A sad smile gleamed faintly from beneath the black veil, and flickered about his mouth, glimmering as he disappeared.

"How strange," said a lady, "that a simple black veil, such as any woman might wear on her bonnet, should become such a terrible thing on Mr. Hooper's face!"

"Something must surely be amiss with Mr. Hooper's intellects," observed her husband, the physician of the village. "But the strangest part of the affair is the effect of this vagary, even on a sober-minded man like myself. The black veil, though it covers only our pastor's face, throws its influence over his whole person, and makes him ghostlike from head to foot. Do you feel it so?"

"Truly do I," replied the lady; "and I would not be alone with him for the world. I wonder he is not afraid to be alone with himself!"

"Men sometimes are so," said her husband.

The afternoon service was attended with similar circumstances. At its conclusion, the bell tolled for the funeral of a young lady. The relatives and friends were assembled in the house, and the more distant acquaintances stood about the door, speaking of the good qualities of the deceased, when their talk was interrupted by the appearance of Mr. Hooper, still covered with his black veil. It was now an appropriate emblem. The clergyman stepped into the room where the corpse was laid, and bent over the coffin, to take a last farewell of his deceased parishioner. As he stooped, the veil hung straight down from his forehead, so that, if her eyelids had not been closed forever, the dead maiden might have seen his face. Could Mr. Hooper be fearful of her glance, that he so hastily caught back the black veil? A person who watched the interview between the dead and living, scrupled not to affirm, that, at the instant when the clergyman's features were disclosed, the corpse had slightly shuddered, rustling the shroud and muslin cap, though the countenance retained the composure of death. A superstitious old woman was the only witness of this prodigy. From the coffin Mr. Hooper passed into the chamber of the mourners, and thence to the head of the staircase, to make the funeral prayer. It was a tender and heart-dissolving prayer, full of sorrow, yet so imbued with celestial hopes, that the music of a heavenly harp, swept by the fingers of the dead, seemed faintly to be heard among the saddest accents of the minister. The people trembled, though they but darkly understood him when he prayed that they, and himself, and all of mortal race, might be ready, as he trusted this young maiden had been, for the dreadful hour that should snatch the veil from their faces. The bearers went heavily forth, and the mourners followed, saddening all the street, with the dead before them, and Mr. Hooper in his black veil behind.

"Why do you look back?" said one in the procession to his partner.

"I had a fancy," replied she, "that the minister and the maiden's spirit were walking hand in hand."

"And so had I, at the same moment," said the other.

That night, the handsomest couple in Milford village were to be joined in wedlock. Though reckoned a melancholy man, Mr. Hooper had a placid cheerfulness for such occasions, which often excited a sympathetic smile where livelier merriment would have been thrown away. There was no quality of his disposition which made him more beloved than this. The company at the wedding awaited his arrival with impatience, trusting that the strange awe, which had gathered over him throughout the day, would now be dispelled. But such was not the result. When Mr. Hooper came, the first thing that their eyes rested on was the same horrible black veil, which had added deeper gloom to the funeral, and could portend nothing but evil to the wedding. Such was its immediate effect on the guests that a cloud seemed to have rolled duskily from beneath the black crape, and dimmed the light of the candles. The bridal pair stood up before the minister. But the bride's cold fingers quivered in the tremulous hand of the bridegroom, and her deathlike paleness caused a whisper that the maiden who had been buried a few hours before was come from her grave to be married. If ever another wedding were so dismal, it was that famous one where they tolled the wedding knell. After performing the ceremony, Mr. Hooper raised a glass of wine to his lips, wishing happiness to the new-married couple in a strain of mild pleasantry that ought to have brightened the features of the guests, like a cheerful gleam from the hearth. At that instant, catching a glimpse of his figure in the looking-glass, the black veil involved his own spirit in the horror with which it overwhelmed all others. His frame shuddered, his lips grew white, he spilt the untasted wine upon the carpet, and rushed forth into the darkness. For the Earth, too, had on her Black Veil.

The next day, the whole village of Milford talked of little else than Parson Hooper's black veil. That, and the mystery concealed behind it, supplied a topic for discussion between acquaintances meeting in the street, and good women gossiping at their open windows. It was the first item of news that the tavern-keeper told to his guests. The children babbled of it on their way to school. One imitative little imp covered his face with an old black handkerchief, thereby so affrighting his playmates that the panic seized himself, and he well-nigh lost his wits by his own waggery.

It was remarkable that all of the busybodies and impertinent people in the parish, not one ventured to put the plain question to Mr. Hooper, wherefore he did this thing. Hitherto, whenever there appeared the slightest call for such interference, he had never lacked advisers, nor shown himself averse to be guided by their judgment. If he erred at all, it was by so painful a degree of self-distrust, that even the mildest censure would lead him to consider an indifferent action as a crime. Yet, though so well acquainted with this amiable weakness, no individual among his parishioners chose to make the black veil a subject of friendly remonstrance. There was a feeling of dread, neither plainly confessed nor carefully concealed, which caused each to shift the responsibility upon another, till at length it was found expedient to send a deputation of the church, in order to deal with Mr. Hooper about the mystery, before it should grow into a scandal. Never did an embassy so ill discharge its duties. The minister received them with friendly courtesy, but became silent, after they were seated, leaving to his visitors the whole burden of introducing their important business. The topic, it might be supposed, was obvious enough. There was the black veil swathed round Mr. Hooper's forehead, and concealing every feature above his placid mouth, on which, at times, they could perceive the glimmering of a melancholy smile. But that piece of crape, to their imagination, seemed to hang down before his heart, the symbol of a fearful secret between him and them. Were the veil but cast aside, they might speak freely of it, but not till then. Thus they sat a considerable time, speechless, confused, and shrinking uneasily from Mr. Hooper's eye, which they felt to be fixed upon them with an invisible glance. Finally, the deputies returned abashed to their constituents, pronouncing the matter too weighty to be handled, except by a council of the churches, if, indeed, it might not require a general synod.

But there was one person in the village unappalled by the awe with which the black veil had impressed all beside herself. When the deputies returned without an explanation, or even venturing to demand one, she, with the calm energy of her character, determined to chase away the strange cloud that appeared to be settling round Mr. Hooper, every moment more darkly than before. As his plighted wife, it should be her privilege to know what the black veil concealed. At the minister's first visit, therefore, she entered upon the subject with a direct simplicity, which made the task easier both for him and her. After he had seated himself, she fixed her eyes steadfastly upon the veil, but could discern nothing of the dreadful gloom that had so overawed the multitude: it was but a double fold of crape, hanging down from his forehead to his mouth, and slightly stirring with his breath.

"No," said she aloud, and smiling, "there is nothing terrible in this piece of crape, except that it hides a face which I am always glad to look upon. Come, good sir, let the sun shine from behind the cloud. First lay aside your black veil: then tell me why you put it on."

Mr. Hooper's smile glimmered faintly.

"There is an hour to come," said he, "when all of us shall cast aside our veils. Take it not amiss, beloved friend, if I wear this piece of crape till then."

"Your words are a mystery, too," returned the young lady. "Take away the veil from them, at least."

"Elizabeth, I will," said he, "so far as my vow may suffer me. Know, then, this veil is a type and a symbol, and I am bound to wear it ever, both in light and darkness, in solitude and before the gaze of multitudes, and as with strangers, so with my familiar friends. No mortal eye will see it withdrawn. This dismal shade must separate me from the world: even you, Elizabeth, can never come behind it!"

"What grievous affliction hath befallen you," she earnestly inquired, "that you should thus darken your eyes forever?"

"If it be a sign of mourning," replied Mr. Hooper, "I, perhaps, like most other mortals, have sorrows dark enough to be typified by a black veil."

"But what if the world will not believe that it is the type of an innocent sorrow?" urged Elizabeth. "Beloved and respected as you are, there may be whispers that you hide your face under the consciousness of secret sin. For the sake of your holy office, do away this scandal!"

The color rose into her cheeks as she intimated the nature of the rumors that were already abroad in the village. But Mr. Hooper's mildness did not forsake him. He even smiled again—that same sad smile, which always appeared like a faint glimmering of light, proceeding from the obscurity beneath the veil.

"If I hide my face for sorrow, there is cause enough," he merely replied; "and if I cover it for secret sin, what mortal might not do the same?"

And with this gentle, but unconquerable obstinacy did he resist all her entreaties. At length Elizabeth sat silent. For a few moments she appeared lost in thought, considering, probably, what new methods might be tried to withdraw her lover from so dark a fantasy, which, if it had no other meaning, was perhaps a symptom of mental disease. Though of a firmer character than his own, the tears rolled down her cheeks. But, in an instant, as it were, a new feeling took the place of sorrow: her eyes were fixed insensibly on the black veil, when, like a sudden twilight in the air, its terrors fell around her. She arose, and stood trembling before him.

"And do you feel it then, at last?" said he mournfully.

She made no reply, but covered her eyes with her hand, and turned to leave the room. He rushed forward and caught her arm.

"Have patience with me, Elizabeth!" cried he, passionately. "Do not desert me, though this veil must be between us here on earth. Be mine, and hereafter there shall be no veil over my face, no darkness between our souls! It is but a mortal veil—it is not for eternity! O! you know not how lonely I am, and how frightened, to be alone behind my black veil. Do not leave me in this miserable obscurity forever!"

"Lift the veil but once, and look me in the face," said she.

"Never! It cannot be!" replied Mr. Hooper.

"Then farewell!" said Elizabeth.

She withdrew her arm from his grasp, and slowly departed, pausing at the door, to give one long shuddering gaze, that seemed almost to penetrate the mystery of the black veil. But, even amid his grief, Mr. Hooper smiled to think that only a material emblem had separated him from happiness, though the horrors, which it shadowed forth, must be drawn darkly between the fondest of lovers.

From that time no attempts were made to remove Mr. Hooper's black veil, or, by a direct appeal, to discover the secret which it was supposed to hide. By persons who claimed a superiority to popular prejudice, it was reckoned merely an eccentric whim, such as often mingles with the sober actions of men otherwise rational, and tinges them all with its own semblance of insanity. But with the multitude, good Mr. Hooper was irreparably a bugbear. He could not walk the street with any peace of mind, so conscious was he that the gentle and timid would turn aside to avoid him, and that others would make it a point of hardihood to throw themselves in his way. The impertinence of the latter class compelled him to give up his customary walk at sunset to the burial ground; for when he leaned pensively over the gate, there would always be faces behind the gravestones, peeping at his black veil. A fable went the rounds that the stare of the dead people drove him thence. It grieved him, to the very depth of his kind heart, to observe how the children fled from his approach, breaking up their merriest sports, while his melancholy figure was yet afar off. Their instinctive dread caused him to feel more strongly than aught else, that a preternatural horror was interwoven with the threads of the black crape. In truth, his own antipathy to the veil was known to be so great, that he never willingly passed before a mirror, nor stooped to drink at a still fountain, lest, in its peaceful bosom, he should be affrighted by himself. This was what gave plausibility to the whispers, that Mr. Hooper's conscience tortured him for some great crime too horrible to be entirely concealed, or otherwise than so obscurely intimated. Thus, from beneath the black veil, there rolled a cloud into the sunshine, an ambiguity of sin or sorrow, which enveloped the poor minister, so that love or sympathy could never reach him. It was said that ghost and fiend consorted with him there. With self-shudderings and outward terrors, he walked continually in its shadow, groping darkly within his own soul, or gazing through a medium that saddened the whole world. Even the lawless wind, it was believed, respected his dreadful secret, and never blew aside the veil. But still good Mr. Hooper sadly smiled at the pale visages of the worldly throng as he passed by.

Among all its bad influences, the black veil had the one desirable effect, of making its wearer a very efficient clergyman. By the aid of his mysterious emblem—for there was no other apparent cause—he became a man of awful power over souls that were in agony for sin. His converts always regarded him with a dread peculiar to themselves, affirming, though but figuratively, that, before he brought them to celestial light, they had been with him behind the black veil. Its gloom, indeed, enabled him to sympathize with all dark affections. Dying sinners cried aloud for Mr. Hooper, and would not yield their breath till he appeared; though ever, as he stooped to whisper consolation, they shuddered at the veiled face so near their own. Such were the terrors of the black veil, even when Death had bared his visage! Strangers came long distances to attend service at his church, with the mere idle purpose of gazing at his figure, because it was forbidden them to behold his face. But many were made to quake ere they departed! Once, during Governor Belcher's administration, Mr. Hooper was appointed to preach the election sermon. Covered with his black veil, he stood before the chief magistrate, the council, and the representatives, and wrought so deep an impression, that the legislative measures of that year were characterized by all the gloom and piety of our earliest ancestral sway.

In this manner Mr. Hooper spent a long life, irreproachable in outward act, yet shrouded in dismal suspicions; kind and loving, though unloved, and dimly feared; a man apart from men, shunned in their health and joy, but ever summoned to their aid in mortal anguish. As years wore on, shedding their snows above his sable veil, he acquired a name throughout the New England churches, and they called him Father Hooper. Nearly all his parishioners, who were of mature age when he was settled, had been borne away by many a funeral: he had one congregation in the church, and a more crowded one in the churchyard; and having wrought so late into the evening, and done his work so well, it was now good Father Hooper's turn to rest.

Several persons were visible by the shaded candlelight, in the death chamber of the old clergyman. Natural connections he had none. But there was the decorously grave, though unmoved physician, seeking only to mitigate the last pangs of the patient whom he could not save. There were the deacons, and other eminently pious members of his church. There, also, was the Reverend Mr. Clark, of Westbury, a young and zealous divine, who had ridden in haste to pray by the bedside of the expiring minister. There was the nurse, no hired handmaiden of death, but one whose calm affection had endured thus long in secrecy, in solitude, amid the chill of age, and would not perish, even at the dying hour. Who, but Elizabeth! And there lay the hoary head of good Father Hooper upon the death pillow, with the black veil still swathed about his brow, and reaching down over his face, so that each more difficult gasp of his faint breath caused it to stir. All through life that piece of crape had hung between him and the world: it had separated him from cheerful brotherhood and woman's love, and kept him in that saddest of all prisons, his own heart; and still it lay upon his face, as if to deepen the gloom of his darksome chamber, and shade him from the sunshine of eternity.

For some time previous, his mind had been confused, wavering doubtfully between the past and the present, and hovering forward, as it were, at intervals, into the indistinctness of the world to come. There had been feverish turns, which tossed him from side to side, and wore away what little strength he had. But in his most convulsive struggles, and in the wildest vagaries of his intellect, when no other thought retained its sober influence, he still showed an awful solicitude lest the black veil should slip aside. Even if his bewildered soul could have forgotten, there was a faithful woman at this pillow, who, with averted eyes, would have covered that aged face, which she had last beheld in the comeliness of manhood. At length the death-stricken old man lay quietly in the torpor of mental and bodily exhaustion, with an imperceptible pulse, and breath that grew fainter and fainter, except when a long, deep, and irregular inspiration seemed to prelude the flight of his spirit.

The minister of Westbury approached the bedside.

"Venerable Father Hooper," said he, "the moment of your release is at hand. Are you ready for the lifting of the veil that shuts in time from eternity?"

Father Hooper at first replied merely by a feeble motion of his head; then, apprehensive, perhaps, that his meaning might be doubted, he exerted himself to speak.

"Yea," said he, in faint accents, "my soul hath a patient weariness until that veil be lifted."

"And is it fitting," resumed the Reverend Mr. Clark, "that a man so given to prayer, of such a blameless example, holy in deed and thought, so far as mortal judgment may pronounce; is it fitting that a father in the church should leave a shadow on his memory, that may seem to blacken a life so pure? I pray you, my venerable brother, let not this thing be! Suffer us to be gladdened by your triumphant aspect as you go to your reward. Before the veil of eternity be lifted, let me cast aside this black veil from your face!"

And thus speaking, the Reverend Mr. Clark bent forward to reveal the mystery of so many years. But, exerting a sudden energy, that made all the beholders stand aghast, Father Hooper snatched both his hands from beneath the bedclothes, and pressed them strongly on the black veil, resolute to struggle, if the minister of Westbury would contend with a dying man.

"Never!" cried the veiled clergyman. "On earth, never!"

"Dark old man!" exclaimed the affrighted minister, "with what horrible crime upon your soul are you now passing to the judgment?"

Father Hooper's breath heaved; it rattled in his throat; but, with a mighty effort, grasping forward with his hands, he caught hold of life, and held it back till he should speak. He even raised himself in bed; and there he sat, shivering with the arms of death around him, while the black veil hung down, awful, at that last moment, in the gathered terrors of a lifetime. And yet the faint, sad smile, so often there, now seemed to glimmer from its obscurity, and linger on Father Hooper's lips.

"Why do you tremble at me alone?" cried he, turning his veiled face round the circle of pale spectators. "Tremble also at each other! Have men avoided me, and women shown no pity, and children screamed and fled, only for my black veil? What, but the mystery which it obscurely typifies, has made this piece of crape so awful? When the friend shows his inmost heart to his friend; the lover to his best beloved; when man does not vainly shrink from the eye of his Creator, loathsomely treasuring up the secret of his sin; then deem me a monster, for the symbol beneath which I have lived, and die! I look around me, and, lo! on every visage a Black Veil!"

While his auditors shrank from one another, in mutual affright, Father Hooper fell back upon his pillow, a veiled corpse, with a faint smile lingering on the lips. Still veiled, they laid him in his coffin, and a veiled corpse they bore him to the grave. The grass of many years has sprung up and withered on that grave, the burial stone is moss-grown, and good Mr. Hooper's face is dust; but awful is still the thought that it mouldered beneath the Black Veil!

The Macbeth Murder Mystery

JAMES THURBER

"It was a stupid mistake to make," said the American woman I had met at my hotel in the English lake country, "but it was on the counter with the other Penguin books—the little sixpenny ones, you know, with the paper covers—and I supposed of course it was a detective story. All the others were detective stories. I'd read all the others, so I bought this one without really looking at it carefully. You can imagine how mad I was when I found it was Shakespeare." I murmured something sympathetically. "I don't see why the Penguin-books people had to get out Shakespeare plays in the same size and everything as the detective stories," went on my companion. "I think they have different-colored jackets," I said. "Well, I didn't notice that," she said. "Anyway, I got real comfy in bed that night and all ready to read a good mystery story and here I had 'The Tragedy of Macbeth'—a book for high-school students." "Like 'Ivanhoe,' or 'Lorna Doone,' " I said. "Exactly," said the American lady. "And I was just crazy for a good Agatha Christie, or something. Hercule Poirot is my favorite detective." "Is he the rabbity one?" I asked. "Oh, no," said my crime-fiction expert. "He's the Belgian one. You're thinking of Mr. Pinkerton, the one that helps Inspector Bull. He's good, too."

Over her second cup of tea my companion began to tell the plot of a detective story that had fooled her completely—it seems it was the old family doctor all the time. But I cut in on her. "Tell me," I said. "Did you read 'Macbeth'?" "I *had* to read it," she said. "There wasn't a scrap of anything else to read in the whole room." "Did you like it?" I asked. "No, I did not," she said, decisively. "In the first place, I don't think for a moment that Macbeth did it." I looked at her blankly. "Did what?" I asked. "I don't think for a moment that he killed the king," she said. "I don't think the Macbeth woman was mixed up in it, either. You suspect them the most, of course, but those are the ones that are never guilty—or shouldn't be, anyway." "I'm afraid," I began, "that I—" "But don't you see?" said the American lady. "It would spoil everything if you could figure out right away who did it. Shakespeare was too smart for that. I've read that people never have figured out 'Hamlet,' so it isn't likely Shakespeare would have made 'Macbeth' as simple as it seems." I thought this over while I filled my pipe. "Who do you suspect?" I asked, suddenly. "Macduff," she said, promptly. "Good God!" I whispered, softly.

"Oh Macduff did it, all right," said the murder specialist. "Hercule Poirot would have got him easily." "How did you figure it out?" I demanded. "Well," she said, "I didn't right away. At first I suspected Banquo. And then, of course, he was the second person killed. That was good right there, that part. The person you suspect of the first murder should always be the second victim." "Is that so?" I murmured. "Oh, yes," said my informant. "They have to keep surprising you. Well, after the second murder I didn't know who the killer was for a while." "How about Malcolm and Donalbain, the King's sons?" I asked. "As I remember it, they fled right after the first murder. That looks suspicious." "Too suspicious," said the American lady. "Much too suspicious. When they flee, they're never guilty. You can count on that." "I believe," I said, "I'll have a brandy," and I summoned the waiter. My companion leaned toward me, her eyes bright, her teacup quivering. "Do you know who discovered Duncan's body?" she demanded. I said I was sorry, but I had forgotten. "Macduff discovers it," she said, slipping into historical present. "Then he comes running downstairs and shouts, 'Confusion has broke open the Lord's anointed temple' and 'Sacrilegious murder has made his masterpiece' and on and on like that." The good lady tapped me on the knee. "All that stuff was rehearsed," she said. "You wouldn't say a lot of stuff like that, offhand, would you—if you had found a body?" She fixed me with a glittering eye. "I—" I began. "You're right!" she said. "You wouldn't! Unless you had practiced it in advance. 'My God, there's a body in here!' is what an innocent man would say." She sat back with a confident glare.

I thought for a while. "But what do you make of the Third Murderer?" I asked. "You know, the Third Murderer has puzzled 'Macbeth' scholars for three hundred years." "That's because they never thought of Macduff," said the American lady. "It was Macduff, I'm certain. You couldn't have one of the victims murdered by two ordinary thugs—the murderer always has to be somebody important." "But what about the banquet scene?" I asked, after a moment. "How do you account for Macbeth's guilty actions there, when Banquo's ghost came in and sat in his chair?" The lady leaned forward and tapped me on the knee again. "There wasn't any ghost," she said. "A big, strong man like that doesn't go around seeing ghosts—especially in a brightly lighted banquet hall with dozens of people around. Macbeth was *shielding somebody*!" "Who was he shielding?" I asked. "Mrs. Macbeth, of course," she said. "He thought she did it and he was going to take the rap himself. The husband always does that when the wife is suspected." "But what," I demanded, "about the sleepwalking scene, then?" "The same thing, only the other way around," said my companion. "That time *she* was shielding *him*. She wasn't asleep at all. Do you remember where it says, 'Enter Lady Macbeth with a taper'?" "Yes," I said. "Well, people who walk in their sleep *never carry lights*!" said my fellow-traveler. "They have a second sight. Did you ever hear of a sleepwalker carrying a light?" "No," I said, "I never did." "Well, then, she wasn't asleep. She was acting guilty to shield Macbeth." "I think," I said, "I'll have another brandy," and I called the waiter. When he brought it, I drank it rapidly and rose to go. "I believe," I said, "that you have got hold of something. Would you lend me that 'Macbeth'? I'd like to look it over tonight. I don't feel, somehow, as if I'd ever really read it." "I'll get it for you," she said. "But you'll find that I am right."

I read the play over carefully that night, and the next morning, after breakfast, I sought out the American woman. She was on the putting green, and I came up behind her silently and took her arm. She gave an exclamation. "Could I see you alone?" I asked, in a low voice. She nodded cautiously and followed me to a secluded spot. "You've found out something?" she breathed. "I've found out," I said, triumphantly, "the name of the murderer!" "You mean it wasn't Macduff?" she said. "Macduff is as innocent of those murders," I said, "as Macbeth and the Macbeth woman." I opened the copy of the play, which I had with me, and turned to Act II, Scene 2. "Here," I said, "you will see where Lady Macbeth says, 'I laid their daggers ready. He could not miss 'em. Had he not resembled my father as he slept, I had done it.' Do you see?" "No," said the American woman, bluntly, "I don't." "But it's simple!" I exclaimed. "I wonder I didn't see it years ago. The reason Duncan resembled Lady Macbeth's father as he slept is that *it actually was her father*!" "Good God!" breathed my companion, softly. "Lady Macbeth's father killed the King," I said, "and, hearing someone coming, thrust the body under the bed and crawled into the bed himself." "But," said the lady, "you can't have a murderer who only appears in the story once. You can't have that." "I know that," I said, and I turned to Act II, Scene 4. "It says here, 'Enter Ross with an old Man.' Now, that old man is never identified and it is my contention he was old Mr. Macbeth, whose ambition it was to make his daughter Queen. There you have your motive." "But even then," cried the American lady, "he's still a minor character!" "Not," I said, gleefully, "when you realize that he was also *one of the weird sisters in disguise*!" "You mean one of the three witches?" "Precisely," I said. "Listen to this speech of the old man's. 'On Tuesday last, a falcon towering in her pride of place, was by a mousing owl hawk'd at and kill'd.' Who does that sound like?" "It sounds like the way the three witches talk," said my companion, reluctantly. "Precisely!" I said again. "Well," said the American woman, "maybe you're right, but—" "I'm sure I am," I said. "And do you know what I'm going to do now?" "No," she said. "What?" "Buy a copy of 'Hamlet,' " I said, "and solve *that*!" My companion's eye brightened. "Then," she said, "you don't think Hamlet did it?" "I am,"

I said, "absolutely positive he didn't." "But who," she demanded, "do you suspect?" I looked at her cryptically. "Everybody," I said, and disappeared into a small grove of trees as silently as I had come.

Questions and Assignments

1. What is the butt of Thurber's spoofing? Shakespeare? Detective story writers? Detective story readers? Shakespearean scholars? American tourists?

2. What is the "cream of the jests"? How does Thurber, himself an American of course, use the American lady's reading habits?

3. How would you characterize the dominant tone Thurber uses? He clearly makes his character seem foolish, but is there appreciable bitterness in his satire?

4. How does Thurber insure that the reader can grasp the general flow of his narrative even if he doesn't recognize every reference? Explain then why he uses so many particular literary comments?

5. What, for example, is the point of *Ivanhoe* and *Lorna Doone* in relation to *Macbeth* and to detective stories?

6. Trace the peaks and the lows of this story. What is the point of the narrator's conclusion? How is it appropriate to both the story and the tone? Could Thurber leave us with the lady's solution we learned on the first page?

Rewriting

Rewriting an essay, as we have pointed out before, is not just a matter of correcting spelling and punctuation, finding different words and rearranging sentences. Writers, both student and professional, must often reorganize an entire essay or a significant part of it. The organization may be unclear or it may be inadequate so that the addition of a specific definition or division, for example, is necessary. Or there may be a need for expansion and the addition of comparisons, analogies, causes, and so forth.

John A. Kouwenhoven's extended definition of jazz is a fine example of revision. It is an excerpt from a long essay called "What's American about America?" We have included the first and second published versions here. Professor Kouwenhoven says that there were two other versions in between these two and that he made further changes when he included the definition in his book *The Beer Can by the Highway,* published in 1961. The student should be able to learn a great deal about the art of revision from a careful examination of this definition of jazz. Professor Kouwenhoven is a well-known educator and writer who teaches English at Barnard College, Columbia University.

Immediately following Professor Kouwenhoven's rewritten definition of jazz is a student theme in its original and rewritten versions. A Checklist for Rewriting closes this section.

A Definition of Jazz

JOHN A. KOUWENHOVEN

(Original Version)

It was Le Corbusier who first noted the relation between New York skyscrapers and American jazz. The city, he said, is "hot jazz in stone and steel"—which at first may sound as if it were merely a slick up-dating of "Architecture is frozen music." But it is more than that, if you think in terms of the structural principles we have been discussing and the structural principles of jazz.

What is distinctive about jazz? This is a complicated and technical subject, and I will have to oversimplify. Roughly speaking, however, the essence of jazz, the thing which differentiates it from music of the Western European classical tradition, is its rhythm. That rhythm, as Winthrop Sargeant has pointed out, is a product of two devices: syncopation and polyrhythm, both of which have the effect of constantly upsetting rhythmical expectation. Both displace the normal accents, so that the accent falls, in highly irregular patterns, upon the off-beats.

As you can easily hear—if you will listen to any good jazz performance (whether of the Louis Armstrong or Benny Goodman or Lennie Tristano variety)—the delight (or agony, if you're of that ilk) created by the upsetting of rhythmic expectation depends upon there being a clearly defined basic rhythmic pattern which enforces the expectations which are to be upset. That basic pattern is the four-four or two-four beat which underlies jazz. Hence the importance of the percussive instruments in a jazz band—the drums, the guitar and banjo, the bull fiddle, and the piano. Hence also that insistent thump, thump, thump, thump which is so boring when

From "What's American about America?" Reprinted by permission of *The Colorado Quarterly* and John Kouwenhoven.

you only half-hear jazz—either because you are too far away, across the lake or in the next room, or simply because you won't listen attentively.

The structure of a jazz performance is, like that of the New York skyline, a tension of cross-purposes. In what is called a jam session—which, if the musicians are good and in top form, is jazz at its best—each player seems to be and has the illusion of being on his own. Each goes his own way, inventing rhythmic and melodic patterns which seem to have as little relevance to one another as the U.N. building does to the Empire State. In classical Western European music, themes are developed; in jazz they are toyed with, and irreverently dismantled.

And yet, while all this is going on, every man apparently for himself, the outcome is—at its best—a dazzlingly precise creative unity. And the thing which holds the performance together is the very thing which each of the players is flouting: namely, the basic four-four beat, that simple rhythmic gridiron of identical and infinitely extendable units. As I have said elsewhere, jazz thereby becomes the first art form to meet the Emersonian ideal of a union in which "all the uniters are isolated."

As you would by now expect, the esthetics of jazz, like those of the skyscrapers, have little to do with proportion and symmetry. Like the skyscrapers, the jazz performance does not reach a climax or conclusion; it simply stops. There is no inherent structural reason why it should not continue for another twelve or twenty-four or thirty-two measures (for those are the cages which in jazz correspond to the floors in a building). Its limits, as a matter of fact, are chiefly determined by custom, derived from the arbitrary time limit of the conventional ten-inch phonograph record.

Here again, as in the skyscraper, the esthetic effect is one of motion. The off-beat rhythms create what can only be called momentum. When the rhythm of one voice (say the trumpeter, off on a rhythmic excursion) lags behind the underlying beat, it carries over into a succeeding measure, which has begun before the lagging voice has finished the preceding one. When it anticipates the beat, it starts a new measure before the other has ended. And the result is a momentum, a forward motion, which is crucial to the particular effects of jazz. Hence the importance, in jazz, of timing; and hence the delight and amusement of the so-called "break," in which the underlying four-four beat ceases, and a soloist goes off on a flight of rhythmic and melodic fancy which nevertheless comes back surprisingly to meet the basic beat precisely where it would have been if it had kept going.

A Definition of Jazz

JOHN A. KOUWENHOVEN

(Rewritten Version)

It was the French architect, LeCorbusier, who described New York's architecture as "hot jazz in stone and steel." At first glance this may sound as if it were merely a slick updating of Schelling's "Architecture . . . is frozen music," but it is more than that if one thinks in terms of the structural principles we have been discussing and the structural principles of jazz.

Let me begin by making clear that I am using the term jazz in its broadest significant application. There are circumstances in which it is important to define the term with considerable precision, as when you are involved in discussion with a disciple of one of the many cults, orthodox or progressive, which devote themselves to some particular subspecies of jazz. But in our present context we need to focus upon what all the subspecies (Dixieland, Be-bop, Swing, or Cool Jazz) have in common; in other words, we must neglect the by no means uninteresting qualities which differentiate one from another, since it is what they have in common which can tell us most about the civilization which produced them.

There is no definition of jazz, academic or otherwise, which does not acknowledge that its essential ingredient is a particular kind of rhythm. Improvisation is also frequently mentioned as an essential; but even if it were true that jazz always involves improvisation, that would not distinguish it from a good deal of Western European music of the past. It is the distinctive rhythm which differentiates all types of jazz from all other music and which gives to all of its types a basic family resemblance.

It is not easy to define that distinctive rhythm. Winthrop Sargeant has described it as the product of two superimposed devices; syncopation and polyrhythm, both of which have the effect of constantly upsetting rhythmical expectations. André Hodeir, in his recent analysis, *Jazz: Its Evolution and Essence,* speaks of "an unending alternation" of syncopations and

From "What's American about America?" Reprinted from *Harper's Magazine,* 1956, with permission of John Kouwenhoven.

of notes played *on* the beat, which "gives rise to a kind of expectation that is one of jazz's subtlest effects."

As you can readily hear, if you listen to any jazz performance (whether of the Louis Armstrong, Benny Goodman, or Charlie Parker variety), the rhythmical effect depends upon there being a clearly defined basic rhythmic pattern which enforces the expectations which are to be upset. That basic pattern is the 4/4 or 2/4 beat which underlies all jazz. Hence the importance of the percussive instruments in jazz: the drums, the guitar or banjo, the bull fiddle, the piano. Hence too the insistent thump, thump, thump, thump which is so boring when you only half-hear jazz—either because you are too far away, across the lake or in the next room, or simply because you will not listen attentively. But hence also the delight, the subtle effects, which good jazz provides as the melodic phrases evade, anticipate, and return to, and then again evade the steady basic four-beat pulse which persists, implicitly or explicitly, throughout the performance.

In other words, the structure of a jazz performance is, like that of the New York skyline, a tension of cross-purposes. In jazz at its characteristic best, each player seems to be—and has the sense of being—on his own. Each goes his own way, inventing rhythmic and melodic patterns which, superficially, seem to have as little relevance to one another as the United Nations building does to the Empire State. And yet the outcome is a dazzling precise creative unity.

In jazz that unity of effect is, of course, the result of the very thing which each of the players is flouting: namely, the basic 4/4 beat—that simple rhythmic gridiron of identical and infinitely extendible units which holds the performance together. As Louis Armstrong once wrote, you would expect that if every man in a band "had his own way and could play as he wanted, all you would get would be a lot of jumbled up, crazy noise." But, as he goes on to say, that does not happen, because the players know "by ear and sheer musical instinct" just when to leave the underlying pattern and when to get back on it.

What it adds up to, as I have argued elsewhere, is that jazz is the first art form to give full expression to Emerson's ideal of a union which is perfect only "when all the uniters are isolated." That Emerson's ideal is deeply rooted in our national experience need not be argued. Frederick Jackson Turner quotes a letter written by a frontier settler to friends back East, which in simple, unself-conscious words expresses the same reconciling of opposites. "It is a universal rule here," the frontiersman wrote, "to help one another, each one keeping an eye single to his own business."

One need only remember that the Constitution itself, by providing for a federation of separate units, became the infinitely extendible framework for the process of reconciling liberty and unity over vast areas and conflicting interests. Its seven brief articles, providing for checks and balances between interests, classes, and branches of the government, establish, in effect, the underlying beat which gives momentum and direction to a political process which Richard Hofstadter has called "a harmonious system of mutual frustration"—a description which fits a jazz performance as well as it fits our politics.

The aesthetic effects of jazz, as Winthrop Sargeant long ago suggested, have as little to do with symmetry and proportion as have those of a skyscraper. Like the skyscraper, a jazz performance does not build to an organically required climax; it can simply cease. The "piece" which the musicians are playing may, and often does, have a rudimentary Aristotelian pattern of beginning, middle, and end; but the jazz performance need not. In traditional Western European music, themes are developed. In jazz they are toyed with and dismantled. There is no inherent reason why the jazz performance should not continue for another 12 or 16 or 24 or 32 measures (for these are the rhythmic cages which in jazz correspond to the cages of a steel skeleton in architecture). As in the skyscraper, the aesthetic effect is one of motion, in this case horizontal rather than vertical.

Jazz rhythms create what can only be called momentum. When the rhythm of one voice (say the trumpet, off on a rhythmic and melodic excursion) lags behind the underlying beat, its four-beat measure carries over beyond the end of the underlying beat's measure into the succeeding one, which has already begun. Conversely, when the trumpet anticipates the beat, it starts a new measure before the steady underlying beat has ended one. And the result is an exhilarating forward motion which the jazz trumpeter Wingy Malone once described as "feeling an increase in tempo though you're still playing at the same tempo." Hence the importance in jazz of timing, and hence the delight and amusement of the so-called "break," in which the basic 4/4 beat ceases and a soloist goes off on a flight of rhythmic and melodic fancy which nevertheless comes back surprisingly and unerringly to encounter the beat precisely where it would have been if it had kept going.

Once the momentum is established, it can continue until—after an interval dictated by some such external factor as the conventional length of phonograph records or the endurance of dancers—it stops. And as if to guard against any Aristotelian misconceptions about an end, it is likely to stop on an unresolved chord, so that harmonically as well as rhythmically everything is left up in the air. Even the various coda-like devices employed by jazz performers at dances, such as the corny old "without a shirt" phrase of blessed memory, are harmonically unresolved. They are merely conventional ways of saying "we quit," not, like Beethoven's insistent codas, ways of saying, "There now; that ties off all the loose ends; I'm going to stop now; done; finished; concluded; signed, sealed, delivered."

Thoughts on Optimism

(Original Student Theme)

I am an optimist. I'm told that the world hates an optimist, but it doesn't matter because I love the world. I believe that everything that happens can, must, and will turn out for the best—with a little push. The world to me is an essentially beautiful place, a place where the wind and the rain and the fog, as well as the sun, are beautiful. Everything that exists is a message of God, every star a blessing, every sunset a benediction. Music is His voice, poetry His revelation. As Browning put it, "God's in His heaven—all's right with the world."

To many people the word optimist conveys the image of a foolish idealist who, sitting happily remote from life, proclaims, nevertheless, that the world is the best possible world and everything as happy as it can be. Even the dictionary would support this definition. But the dictionary also gives other meanings which to me seem far more valid. It says that optimism is "the doctrine that reality is essentially good," and that it is "the doctrine that the good of life overbalances the pain and evil of it." Finally it defines the word as "an inclination to put the most favorable construction upon actions and happenings, or anticipate the best possible outcome." (A small parable may serve to illustrate the truth of the latter.) Two men, observing half a glass of water sitting on a table, each see exactly the same image. One man describes the glass as half-empty; the other says it is half-full.

Optimism is the essence of life. We may wake up and go to sleep, eat and move about, laugh and cry, but not until we have sensed that there is a purpose to existence do we begin to live. Nevertheless, optimism is often considered a youthful virtue. In a sense that is true. Many of us in youth are caught into the urgent belief that there is a solution to every problem of life and of the world—but we want the solution now. We think that in another week, another month, another year it will be found and, perhaps unconsciously, that each of us is the potential discoverer. Few, very few, have the courage to wait, knowing that it may be years, generations, centuries before the answers can be reached. Optimism must extend into eternity, and eternity is a concept which no human mind can ever grasp. Those who have most nearly grasped it are the ones who are able to maintain their optimism as a force no matter how adverse the circumstances.

Perhaps one of the best examples of this type of optimism today is Winston Churchill. He became Prime Minister of Great Britain in 1940 when his country faced the greatest crisis in its history, yet he was able to say, "What is our aim? I can answer in one word: Victory—victory at all costs, victory in spite of all terror; victory, however long and hard the road may be; for without victory, there is no survival. . . . But I take up my task with buoyancy and hope. I feel sure that our cause will not be suffered to fail among men." Then, as the war drew to a successful close, due in large part to his efforts, he was voted out of office in favor of the socialist Labor Party. For a man of his age to receive such a defeat after having given his whole life to the service of his country—although much of that service was unappreciated, his warnings against Hitler and the Japanese during the Thirties, for example—it would have been much easier to retire to a well-deserved rest. Winston Churchill did nothing of the sort. He continued in vigorous opposition until his party was finally re-elected in the fall of 1951. At that time, with almost 77 years of experience in life as well as in world politics, he said, "There lies before us a difficult time. I have seen worse and had to face worse. I do not doubt we shall come through. . . ."

Another man, Christ, was undoubtedly the greatest of all optimists. He believed in the brotherhood of man and in the possibility of perfection on earth. He taught that men's souls are eternal and that each is equally valuable, that the basic law of Nature is love, and that there is a Will behind all things. He was an optimist with his feet on the ground, for he put into practice every article of his belief. At last he died willingly, putting his faith in every future generation of man to accept the truth of his doctrines from the handful of followers he had left.

Optimism is a giant Atlas holding up the sky and making visible the unreachable stars above it. Therefore, like Atlas, we must put our heads above the clouds to find "the substance of things hoped for, the evidence of things not seen" (Hebrews XI:1), while our feet, rooted to the ground, translate those things into reality. The greatest men have been those who have had faith in the future: Plato, who believed that a man could discover the absolute truth; the American pioneers, who conquered and settled a wilderness; Thomas Jefferson, who believed in the ability of the "common man" to successfully rule a nation; Winston Churchill, who is known for his profound faith in Great Britain; and, of course, Jesus Christ, who died to prove his faith in all men.

It is my belief also that even in suffering we may be optimists. This should be true not only for individuals but for nations and and for the world. First of all, it is a purgative. It turns the soul inside out and forces old values to be re-examined and new values to be added. Suffering builds character as nothing else can, for by a man's reaction to suffering he becomes stronger—or weaker. Perhaps most important of all, however, is suffering's contribution to the fullness of personality. Kahlil Gibran in *The Prophet* expresses this idea beautifully: "And the selfsame well from which your laughter rises was oftentimes filled with your tears. And how else can it be? The deeper that sorrow carves into your being, the more joy you can contain."

Optimism is in part the ability to compromise with the facts of life. Thackeray wrote: "The world is a looking-glass, and gives back to every man the reflection of his own face. Frown at it and it will in turn look sourly upon you; laugh at it and with it, and it is a jolly kind companion." Life should seldom be taken too seriously. We must be able to laugh at our troubles and to withstand our griefs. We must be able to see the whole picture and, while recognizing the faults, be encouraged by the good qualities. And most of all, we must be willing to give and give and give in a self-forgetfulness which will make every gift back to us doubly appreciated.

In Nature we may find the final manifestation of optimism in practice. Each year dies and is reborn, despite wars and plagues, depressions and oppressions, democracies or dictatorships. As Longfellow put it, " 'Tis always morning somewhere, and above/The awakening continents, from shore to shore,/Somewhere the birds are singing evermore." Even if man cannot see God's perfection he can be sure that it exists and that it is good. If skies are grey, there is no need to look for the proverbial silver lining; inevitably they will turn blue again. A gale cannot blow forever, the rain must cease to fall. Nothing man can do can halt the endless pattern. Perhaps it is best expressed in the Old Testament Ecclesiastes: "For everything there is a season, and a time for every purpose under heaven: a time to be born, and a time to die; a time to plant, and a time to pluck up that which is planted; . . . a time to love, and a time to hate; a time for war, and a time for peace. . . . He hath made everything beautiful in its time: also he hath set eternity in their heart, yet so that man cannot find out the work that God hath done from the beginning even to the end. I know that there is nothing better for them, than to rejoice, and to do good so long as they live." What could be better advice to the people of today than this from the unknown optimist of twenty-five centuries ago!

This essay tends toward oversentimentality and is in need of some reorganization. There are several mixed metaphors, the one about Atlas, for example, and in the discussion of Christ as an optimist there is an inevitable oversimplification which would be better avoided altogether. Whatever the author's beliefs, it would take a much longer essay to expand such oversimplification sufficiently. In several places the essay goes off the point altogether, as in the second sentence of the third paragraph, and transitions throughout need to be improved. The conclusion is also rather poor. The author needs to recognize that he is writing a definition, not just a discussion of his thoughts about optimism.

He will then be able to organize the whole essay more tightly and more appropriately.

The Meaning of Optimism

(Rewritten Student Theme)

I've been told that the world hates an optimist—but I'm an optimist just the same. I believe that everything that happens can, must, and will turn out for the best—with a little push. And so, if the world hates me, I'm sure its opinion will change sooner or later!

Many people think of an optimist as a foolish idealist who, sitting happily remote from life, proclaims nevertheless that the world is the best possible world and everything as happy as can be. Even the dictionary would support this definition. But the dictionary also gives other meanings which to me seem far more valid. It says that optimism is "the doctrine that reality is essentially good," and that it is "the doctrine that the good of life overbalances the pain and evil of it." Finally, it defines the word as "an inclination to put the most favorable construction upon actions and happenings, or anticipate the best possible outcome."

Perhaps the best definition of all is the one about two men observing a glass of water on a table. The pessimist describes the glass as half-empty; the optimist says it is half-full.

Optimism is often considered a youthful virtue. In a limited sense that is true. Many of us in youth are caught into the urgent belief that there is a solution to every problem of life and of the world—but we want the solution now. We think that in another week, another month, another year, it will be found and, perhaps unconsciously, that each of us is the potential discoverer. Few, very few, have the courage to wait, knowing that it may be years, generations, centuries before the answers can be reached. True optimism must extend into eternity, and eternity is a concept no human mind can grasp. Those who have most nearly grasped it are the ones who are able to maintain their optimism even into old age and no matter how adverse the circumstances.

For the truth is that even in suffering we may be optimists.

This is true not only for individuals but for nations and for the whole world. First of all, suffering is a purgative. It turns the soul inside out and forces the re-examination of old values and the addition of new ones. Suffering also builds character, for by a man's reaction to suffering he becomes stronger—or weaker. But the pessimist will never reap the benefits of difficulty. Only the optimist will be able to recognize and accept the value of pain and upheaval to the fullness of personality and the development of civilization. He alone will understand the words of Kahlil Gibran from *The Prophet,* "The deeper that sorrow carves into your being, the more joy you can contain."

Optimism is, in part, the ability to compromise with the facts of life. Thackeray wrote: "The world is a looking-glass, and gives back to every man the reflection of his own face. Frown at it and it will in turn look sourly upon you; laugh at it and with it, and it is a jolly kind companion." Life should never be taken too seriously. We must be able to laugh at our troubles and to withstand our griefs. We must be able to see the whole picture and, while recognizing the faults, be encouraged by the good qualities. And most of all, we must be willing to give and give and give in a self-forgetfulness which will make every gift back to us doubly appreciated.

In fact, optimism has no value at all if it is not translated into practice. The self-forgetfulness of happiness must be turned into the self-forgetfulness of joyful action, so that we may share our enthusiasm with others. Enthusiasm which is not shared is quickly lost. Hope in the future which takes no part in the present is a contradiction in terms. The greatest men have been those who have put their heads above the clouds to find "the substance of things hoped for, the evidence of things not seen," while their feet, rooted to the ground, have enabled them to translate those things into reality. Among them are: Plato, who believed that a man could discover the absolute truth; the American pioneers, who conquered and settled a wilderness; Thomas Jefferson, who believed in the ability of the "common man" to rule a nation; and Winston Churchill, who is known for his profound faith in Great Britain.

Winston Churchill is, in fact, one of the best of modern examples. He became Prime Minister of Great Britain in 1940 when his country faced the greatest crisis in its history, yet his optimism, at least in public, never failed. He said as he took office: "What is our aim? I can answer in one word: Victory—victory at all costs, victory in spite of all terror; victory, however long and hard the road may be; for without victory, there is no survival. . . . But I take up my task with buoyancy and hope. I feel sure that our cause will not be suffered to fail among men." Then, as the war drew to a successful close, due in large part to his efforts, he was voted out of office in favor of the socialist Labor Party. For a man of his age to receive such a defeat after having given his whole life to the service of his country, it would have been much easier to retire to a well-deserved rest. Winston Churchill did nothing of the sort. He continued in vigorous opposition until his party was finally re-elected in the fall of 1951. At that time, with almost seventy-seven years of experience in life as well as in world politics, he said, "There lies before us a difficult time. I have seen worse and had to face worse. I do not doubt we shall come through. . . ."

Nature itself provides the final unquestionable manifestation of optimism in practice. Each year dies and is reborn, despite wars and plagues, depressions and oppressions, democracies or dictatorships. As Longfellow put it,

> *'Tis always morning somewhere, and above*
> *The awakening continents, from shore to shore,*
> *Somewhere the birds are singing evermore.*

If skies are grey, there is no need to look for the proverbial silver lining; inevitably they will turn blue again. A gale cannot blow forever, the rain must cease to fall. Nothing man can do can halt the endless pattern. An unknown optimist of twenty-five centuries ago perceived this and wrote it down in the book of Ecclesiastes: "For everything there is a season, and a time for every purpose under heaven: a time to be born, and a time to die; a time to plant, and a time to pluck up that which is planted; . . . a time to love, and a time to hate; a time for war, and a time for peace. . . . He hath made everything beautiful in its time: also He hath set eternity in their heart, yet so that man cannot find out the work that God hath done from the beginning even to the end. I know that there is nothing better for them, than to rejoice, and to do good so long as they live."

A Checklist for Rewriting

1. Make sure your beginning is interesting, important, and relevant. Consider other types of beginnings (see pp. 219-223) to see if your opening is as effective as it could be.

2. Is your conclusion satisfactory? Make sure that a summary really summarizes, that a restatement of your main point does not change the point, that a dramatic ending is not melodramatic.

3. You should be able to see the general outline of your paper clearly as you reread it. If you cannot, there are several things which might need revising. Are your transitions, especially between paragraphs, satisfactory? Have you included irrelevant thoughts and details? Did you lose track of your organization somewhere along the line?

4. Check the methods of development you have used. If you have used a chronological method, is your sequential relationship clear and yet sufficiently varied to maintain interest? If every new thought begins with something like "and then," you need to improve your sentence structure and perhaps add some analogies or comparisons to clarify and brighten what you are saying.

5. If you have used classification, you should check for any irrelevant categories. Your groupings should include closely related ideas and the less important ones should be eliminated. Apparent contradictions should be clarified by further divisions or distinctions or else eliminated altogether. If you have divided your subject into several arbitrary parts, as Copland does the process of listening to music, make sure that you have not added an extra part in your discussion and that you have given sufficient attention to each of your categories. In either case, it may be that your categories were faulty to begin with and the correction should be made in your division.

6. If your purpose was to write a definition, check to see that everything you have written contributes to that purpose. Have you shown what the subject is not, either by discussing its antonym or by locating

it in relation to some larger group? Have you used a dictionary meaning? If so, is it a real contribution to your discussion, or would it be just as well left out? Have you explained any other definitions which may have been given for your subject, and is it clear to your reader how your definition differs?

7. Check to see if your comparisons and contrasts are natural or forced. If it requires a real stretch of the imagination to see any relationship, your comparison will be a failure. For example, if you wanted to describe the acting ability of Marlon Brando, it would be a mistake to choose Danny Kaye as a basis for comparison. In order to show similarities or differences between two subjects, there must be some basic likeness of purpose to begin with. Is your comparison or contrast valid, or will it strike your reader as an arbitrary and unjustifiable distinction? Does your comparison serve to illuminate your subject and to support the main point of your essay? If not, you need to reword it or to rethink it altogether.

8. Do your analogies really fit wherever you use them? As with comparison and contrast, if your analogy is forced it cannot be convincing. Have you developed your analogy as fully as possible? Have you worked out all its valuable ramifications? And have you forestalled disbelief or criticism by clearly limiting the ways in which you intend the analogy to be understood?

9. Make sure that your explication really reveals the thought of the material to be explicated and not just your own ideas. Go over each point that you have made and check it with the original to be sure you were not carried away by your own eloquence. Then check to see if you have explained everything that can be explained. Make sure there are no details of the original which would tend to disprove your explanation. If so, you must either incorporate them into your discussion or you must revise your interpretation.

PART FOUR

Argument

ARGUMENT is the valid use of evidence and the accurate exercise of reasoning. The ability to follow an argument or to argue convincingly is one of the marks of a mature and intelligent mind. This ability is, in one sense, the climax or the goal of a college education, and all this section on argument can hope to do is to acquaint the student with a few of the kinds and forms of argument that one is likely to encounter.

Understanding Argument

Introducing "Argument" are two very different approaches. The first essay by philosopher Warner A. Wick defines various kinds of rational thought, from science to philosophy, as arguments. For him there are as many kinds of logic as there are reasonable minds and the logic typified by the syllogism is only one form of argument. The second selection, by two professors of English, Newman and Genevieve Birk, is specifically concerned with logical argument and emphasizes the knowledge and use of syllogisms.

We have included these two essays not only to provide different views, but also to provide alternate methods. In the questions following the readings, however, students will not be expected to use formal syllogisms, which require specialized study. Generally the selections you will read in this part of the book are discussed "according to rules or principles which every reasonable person can recognize" (Wick). We do, nevertheless, ask students to utilize some of the more common terms described by the Birks, such as *hasty generalization, post hoc, ad hominem, arguing in a circle.* Regardless of whether syllogisms seem restrictive or liberating, the terms of informal logic should be a part of the vocabulary of "every reasonable person."

Argument

WARNER A. WICK

If "Plot is the soul of tragedy," then argument is the life and soul of philosophy. Just as in drama "the play's the thing," and it is the subordination of many elements to the unifying plot that makes the play, so in philosophy "the argument's the thing." I do not mean to say that arguments are found only in philosophy; they are found in many other contexts, as I shall explain. But it is in philosophy that they appear in their clearest form and where everything depends on the argument itself.

If this is true, the ways of reading that are especially appropriate to philosophy will concern the analysis of an argument. To show that it is true is to resort to an argument whose subject is the nature of argument itself. My argument, then, will be a live illustration of what it talks about. First I must spend some time in outlining, in a general way, what is meant by an argument and how arguments function in the sciences and arts which make us civilized. After explaining the sort of thing an argument is, I shall go on to discuss in more detail how one is to be read and studied. Finally, I shall try to show why the significance of a philosophy is to be understood only by understanding its argument.

An argument can be defined very generally as a systematic structure of reasoning. Reasoning is discourse—thought expressible in speech or writing—in which, when something is laid down or assumed, something else follows, either necessarily or probably, according to rules or principles which every reasonable person can recognize. An argument, then, is something that claims objective validity, regardless of the feelings, prejudices, or convictions of the people to whom it is addressed. It is rather a kind of thought in which opinions and convictions are tested. The validity of an argument can be ignored or forgotten; it cannot be denied by a reasonable man unless, after a counterargument, he has shown in some detail that its claim of validity was falsely made.

It follows from this that, contrary to the way we often talk, a dispute or wrangle need not be an argument in our sense of the word—in fact, usually it is not. A dispute is often a tiresome series of counterassertions—

From "The Argument in Philosophy," by Warner A. Wick, *The Journal of General Education,* 1953. Reprinted by permission of The Pennsylvania State University Press.

of 'Tis's and 'Tain'ts—in which there is no argument because there is no common appeal to evidence or rational principles which would settle the matter by relating evidence to the problem being discussed. And people do not wrangle unless genuine communication between them has broken down—that is, until they are no longer able or willing to recognize common principles on which an orderly argument could be constructed.

We could say that an argument is a sort of logical construction; but, when we say that, we are in danger of limiting ourselves too much, since "logic" may suggest some rather special form of thought like the syllogism or one of the formal patterns of modern mathematical logic. But there are as many ways of building arguments as there are of being reasonable, and each can be said to have its own "logic." Newton's famous *Principia* is built on a mathematical framework of great elegance. And among the authors represented here you will—if you are skilful—find many syllogisms in Aristotle but few in Plato or Dewey. Yet all give us arguments with their own characteristic structures, based upon rules and principles which you ought to be able to discover.

The ability to follow an argument, or to construct one for ourselves, is what people are usually talking about when they say that the purpose of a liberal education is to teach you to think. In a way, "to teach you to think" has a silly sound, because, of course, everybody thinks without being taught. We all put two and two together and, by some sort of mental chemistry, come out with something new and different, though we may be helpless when we try to give an account of the process to ourselves or to explain to someone else the reasons why we should be justified in drawing the conclusions that we believe are sound. Still, we cannot think in the full sense of the word until we can think self-consciously and explicitly—that is, until we can, through argument, lay out the bases, as well as the results, of our thinking and communicate them to other people for their judgment, criticism, and perhaps acceptance.

To think in this complete sense is difficult; the ability to do it is not only so valuable that it is largely what makes civilized life possible, but also it is rare—so rare that perhaps most people do not really believe in its possibility. They do not, however, stand up and deny that it is possible, giving their reasons. To do that, they would have to understand what that sort of thinking would be; and that is just what they do not succeed in doing. Moreover, to give reasons for their denial would be to present an argument, so that their action would be—like the baby whose mother claimed she never knew any men—the living contradiction of their plea. The possibility of argument is denied in other ways: by the look of puzzled suspicion in the eyes, by the shrug that puts off attempts to discuss a question as "a lot of propaganda," or by the direct action of Socrates' accusers, who found that he talked too much.

We can learn some of the basic facts about an argument from a story in a very wise book that should be better known. In *Life among the Lowbrows* Eleanor Wembridge reports her experiences as a social worker with the not very bright. She says:

> Neither Flora nor any of her moron friends could master the problem [If two pencils cost five cents, how many can you get for fifty cents?]. We knew because we had asked them. Flora's answer was twenty-five, because two into fifty is twenty-five. Her friend Lucille's, on the other hand, was a hundred, because two times fifty is a hundred. Another friend, Annie, ventured a still more generous estimate. She said, "Five times fifty, because five cents times fifty cents is five times fifty—whatever that is."

Chuck answered ten, because "You get two for five, and two times five is ten." Mrs. Wembridge's comment indicates the important distinction. "It will be observed that all of them knew that *something* must be done in the way of arithmetic, and that their arithmetic was generally correct—except for the fact that they could not select the right process to employ." In a sense, they all knew their arithmetic—except for the girl who did not know what five times fifty was. That is, they knew the elements and operations that arithmetic is built out of—its materials; but they had no conception of arithmetic as a rational structure. Now arithmetic as a rational structure is a system of thought of the kind that we call an "argument."

There are other whole ranges of life that depend on similar rational structures. We become acquainted with some of the elements that function in them— i.e., with numbers and rules of manipulating them—and we may operate with them more or less successfully without understanding them very well. And because we do not understand them, there are occasions when we are likely to look upon them as cobwebs of fictions, or, at best, of talk. The distinctions of the law, for example, which give such powers and significance to bits of paper bearing the proper signs and seals, are constantly mistrusted by ordinary citizens; and even its successful technicians sometimes think of the law as a bag of ready-made tricks for them to exploit. In the same way science, as an activity of rational inquiry and explanation, is not very widely understood among the people who are casually acquainted with its agents and materials (men in white surrounded by complicated wiring and glassware) or with its by-products, from nylons to pronouncements on what "Science says." Its specialized technicians may understand it little better. So it is not surprising that impatient people sometimes push aside the lawyers' red tape to take direct action or that they fail to understand why scientists should be allowed to cut up live dogs or to entertain outrageous ideas.

The essential point here is that the life of science and the law is the life of thought, and the kind of thought that we call "argument." It is this which gives meaning to the symbols and instruments which the technicians use and which directs their routines. And to speak of thought as the "life" —or, as Aristotle might have said, the "soul" or life-giving principle—of science and law is, though a metaphor, not an idle one; for, like all living organisms, they must grow in order to function at all. They grow by constantly being reconstructed and reorganized to deal with new problems and materials; and most important, for our present purposes, is the fact that this reinterpretation proceeds by discussion and argument—a discussion in which members of the scientific and legal communities test alternative constructions. While it is often convenient, therefore, to follow the fashion for semantics and treat these systems of thought as systems of symbols or "languages," it is necessary to remember that a symbol symbolizes. It is used to stand for something. What makes a word a word is neither its sound nor its look on a printed page but the activity of thought which gives it its meaning and reference. In the same way the symbolic materials of law and the sciences do their work only because of the thought that sustains them.

There is one more everyday embodiment of argument that ought to be mentioned in this preliminary survey. Without science and the law, kept alive by discussion among their special experts, no complex society could exist. A free society requires something more—that the purposes to be served by these and other specialized activities and the general regulations that govern them should be determined by a discussion in which people who are not experts can take part. Now government by discussion (we call it "democracy") depends upon an appeal to standards of reasonableness which can mediate the clash of interests, opinions, and prejudices which is the material of politics. Where there is no community which recognizes common principles of argument—at least, the principle that decisions are to be sought through discussion—then discussion breaks down. When discussion breaks down, force in one form or another decides the question. Sometimes the force is mild, and the breakdown of communication is limited; and, indeed, the decisions of no actual government can be always, or even usually, unanimous. There comes a point, sometimes in the faculty staff meetings of your courses as well as in Congress, at which, in the words of Jack Garner, "There's no use talking any more, Cap'n. You just don't have the votes." But this limited force of the majority vote is kept harmless because it occurs within a wider framework of communication and agreement on the principle of majority rule. When no communication is possible or when it is believed to be impossible, then the less lovely forms of force take over. Talk may still go on, but according to the principle that "ideas are weapons" rather than means of argument and communication. Socrates is told he may stay in Athens if he follows the party line and promises to quit asking questions. I might add that the tendency, in some "advanced" circles, to think as if ideas in politics were *nothing but* weapons is one of the danger signals of our century. It is, incidentally, an indirect way of denying the possibility of argument.

To sum up, then, the comunicable form of thinking that we call "argument" is the priceless ingredient in science, the law, and the discussions by which we try to manage our affairs. In each of these contexts the argument is to some extent subordinated to other materials—to the data which it makes intelligible in science, to the institutions and practices maintained by the rules of law, and to the opinions and interests which we are advocating or defending in the rhetoric of politics. In philosophy, however, argument is not just the condition of health and life, but the life itself. This is because the arguments in philosophy are used less to demonstrate truths, settle cases, or convince doubters than to test the principles and assumptions that make proofs and judgments cogent and connect theories with their data. This kind of argument may be called "dialectic," although there are some special "dialectics" with which it should not be confused. It is the highest form of thinking, so it is not surprising that it should be impossible to practice it without intelligence and discipline or that to people who lack either one it should seem like a lot of idle talk—of which we already have too much.

To detect talk which is really idle, really mystification and sophistry, or really self-delusion is a task which is never finished and never easy. There is no simple test for detecting it, since its outward and visible signs are the same as those of honest argument. Sophists, fools, and able thinkers are alike in making distinctions, laying down propositions, and drawing conclusions. Since the differences between them are in the coherence of their arguments and the communicability of their principles, it is only by the analysis of arguments that they can be distinguished, although a dishonest rather than a simply deluded reasoner often gives himself away by refusing to test his argument in discussion.

Now we should plant our feet on the ground again, as Socrates did when he began the serious part of his argument in the *Phaedo,* and deal with some specific problems of analyzing an argument. Many of them, we should find, are well on the way to being solved if we have succeeded in understanding these general remarks about what an argument is.

The most important thing about the study of argument follows from the fact that an argument does not consist of the words or symbols that it informs but in the thought which unites these materials into a whole. This means that an argument is never understood until it has been brought to life again in your own thought. Arguments are learned, or grasped, or communicated by being re-enacted or reconstructed. It follows that not much can be learned "about" one. You can memorize all the words in all propositions that occur in it, and you can remember that a certain conclusion was said to follow from it all. You can learn about the circumstances under which it took place, who the participants were, their case histories, interests, and expectations. You can also discover what the participants said the problem was which gave rise to the discussion. But you will not have the argument. What you can learn *about* is always something else, the elements or parts, the occasion and other circumstances, and its historical effects. All these things, taken broadly, are its materials.

The argument itself is the activity of thinking which brings all these materials together into a unity and, according to our ruling metaphor, gives them life. The moral of this is that, since philosophy is thinking, you will never learn philosophy except by thinking—hard—yourself.

The various factors that I have called the "materials" of argument may be of many kinds and of more or less relevance, according to the nature of the argument. In a Platonic dialogue, as you will learn, all these background materials usually make a contribution to the progress and significance of the discussion. This does not contradict my remark that a knowledge of all the materials will not of itself bring the argument to life. It is rather that, when once the glow of thought begins in your minds, you should find that these elements reflect its light and so make their own contribution to the general illuminiation. In Aristotle's work, contrariwise, you will have a much more limited range of materials to interpret, since you can rely almost entirely on his explicit statements. There will be no participants except you and Aristotle; the occasion will not be datable, either B.C. or A.D., and the problem will be stated in timeless terms. The data of the problem will be those he gives you in his statements or propositions, plus your own experience and judgment as a reasonable person who is able and willing to follow what he says. In the case of Dewey, the kinds of materials will widen out again, with the unique situation which presented the problem being given a great deal of attention. Besides, Dewey will tell you, his experimental thinking relies heavily on things that are done and made, as well as on what is said. It would follow from this that, if his *Essays in Experimental Logic* contain samples of experimental reasonings, you would have to *do* a great deal before you could reconstruct his arguments. But it may be—and this you will have to look out for—that he will give you nonexperimental arguments *about* the nature and principles of experimental reasoning, in which case the situation might be different. But in every case and for every author, to possess the materials is no more to possess the argument than to own a dictionary is to own the literature of one's culture.

All this may no doubt seem obvious enough, but it is surprising how many people behave as if the study of philosophy were quite a different matter. An extreme case is a proud announcement that came from a certain university a couple of years ago. It said that audiovisual techniques had at last been used successfully in teaching philosophy, and, since the ability to read is alleged to be disappearing, this would be a great gain. The conclusive experiment consisted in helping students associate the name of an ancient Greek philosopher with that particular one of the so-called four "elements" (earth, air, fire, or water) which he thought was the basic one, from which the others were generated. And so the connection of the name of Thales with water was made forever memorable by turning on the water tap and having the sound-effects man play "Old Man River" when his name was mentioned. Now if to engrave associations with philosophers' names on one's memory is to learn philosophy, then, of course, philosophy can be taught in this way; and it can be taught to dogs as well as to people. (That *would* be something for the public relations department!) What is missing, of course, is the argument. To have shown how water or fire could function as a principle of explanation in the investigation of nature would have been to make some progress. But this, the construction of an argument, could not begin until the audiovisual aids had been put back into the cupboard.

It is not quite so silly—though it is still beside the point—to try to teach philosophy by means of lectures. The point will be clear if you remember the old joke that the lecture is a way of transferring the materials of argument from the lecturer's notes to the hearer's notes without their having passed through the mind of either. But a lecture or an essay can do other useful things. Let me illustrate. Suppose our subject were swimming. It is obvious that you cannot learn to swim by going to lectures. But before you started swimming you might profit by having someone tell you what to try to do when you get into the water, warn you about the difficulties you might expect to encounter, give you useful pointers, describe the operation in a general way, and try to stir up some enthusiasm to carry you over the first humps—this by describing the importance of swimming, its place in civilization, and the pleasures and renown that are to be enjoyed in it. Then, after you had swum a little, you would be able to benefit from more lectures on the different styles of swimming and their peculiar uses and advantages, stories of the great swimmers, their exploits, and their contributions to the sport which you had been learning. So you can be helped to philosophize by lectures and essays, but you should appreciate their limits.

The same is true of books *about* philosophizing. Remember what you could reasonably expect from a book about swimming.

A more usual and more philosophical way to study an argument is to misread it by imposing one's own pattern of thinking on the materials, so as to give an alien account of the significance of what has been said. Instead of reconstructing the argument, that is, you put a different one in its place, using some or all of the original materials but in such a way that, though the words may be the same, their meanings will all be different because the organizing thought will not be the same.

Let me illustrate how this happens. If we assume, for example, that the quaint and touching things that Socrates says about the soul in the *Phaedo* are utterly absurd, in view of the progress of the sciences and the decline of superstition, we may want to account for the fact that Socrates—a well-intentioned character, no doubt—happened to say what he did. So we construct a theory or argument to explain his opinions. Accordingly, we study Greek society to unearth the current opinions of men about town, we look up Socrates' biography, and we may even study what he said very carefully indeed. But we consider what he said not in the context of his argument, for we have ignored it as an argument, but as a sign of something else, the underlying causes which led him to utter such opinions. In other words, we look for "reasons" in the sense of causes of his opinions rather than for reasons in the sense of the grounds which he presented to justify them.

This way of reading an argument—though it is not really a way of reading an argument at all but of inventing one—is very popular. In Chancellor Hutchins' farewell speech to the students when he left the University of Chicago, he said that, so far as he could tell, most students were either imitation Freudians or counterfeit Marxists. What makes these philosophies attractive is their usefulness, for bull-session purposes, in sterilizing arguments which are embarrassing to one's cherished beliefs. Pseudo-Marx and pseudo-Freud sterilize arguments by treating them as symptoms. The other fellow's view arises from his sick soul or his place in a sick society. According to popular psychoanalysis, for example, it is easy to surmise that Socrates may be suffering from a castration complex. If so, he would naturally try to rationalize his suppressed resentment of his bodily functions. It might even lead him to compulsive behavior, amounting in this case to forcing himself (subconsciously) into a situation in which he would apparently have to destroy his libido by drinking hemlock. And this under the delusion—expressed by his assertion that philosophy is a prelude to the death of the body and the life of the soul—that in doing so he would become an immortal, disembodied intellect! Now this account of his devious ways of expressing the death instinct is all very fine. It certainly takes care of Socrates' argument, but it does so by condemning it without a hearing.

It would be easy, in a similar way, to give a crypto-Marxist account of Socrates' talk of eternal ideas in terms of the ideology of an outworn class system, all tied up in contradictions with the realities of an emerging popular culture. Books have been written which do this, but you easily can fill in the details for yourself. Try it some time.

The obvious fact about both these stratagems is that they ignore the argument. They do not help you to understand Socrates or to establish communication with him. They rather destroy the significance of Socrates —or anyone—as a thinker. But let us ask the amateur Freudian some questions: "You have developed a theory which puts the materials of Socrates' life and thought in an intelligible order. Are you sure that this behavior is not just a symptom of yours? So you don't want to be upset in the firm faith of your unbelief in immortality by paying attention to the argument of the *Phaedo*? Aha! So you develop a nice theoretical structure which rationalizes your subconscious rejection of immortality. So why should we listen to you? What you say makes sense when we treat it as a symptom of your own compulsions, and we can understand you very well without taking seriously what you say. Now, one can do the same with this argument. So where do we end? The trend of this line of argument is that arguments can be ignored. But this trend itself can be justified only by means of argument!"

The point here is that we eventually come to a point where somebody's argument has to be examined on its own merits. We might as well begin with your original principle that what a man says is to be understood as the outward and visible sign of an inward and compulsive subconscious. If it is taken as a principle for testing ideas, what follows in regard to both Socrates' argument and your own? If it is denied, what follows? What other alternatives are there? In other words, we shall be engaged in dialectic, the type of argument in which principles for constructing and testing arguments are identified, analyzed, tested, and made to show what they can do and what one is committed to by accepting them. By questioning our assumptions, we will have been imitating Socrates, acting according to his precept that the unexamined life is not worthy of a man, that our business as reasonable beings is to know ourselves, and that the greatest evil that can befall a man is misology, the distrust of reason in argument.

I have now said nearly all that I intend to say. The materials of any argument can be organized in a number of ways, each of which will turn out to be a distinct rational structure, or argument. In each one the words, sentences, and other elements will take on a different meaning and significance; and this should make it clear that the true elements of arguments are not so much the words and sentences as what the logicians call "terms" and "propositions"—that is, words and sentences whose natural ambiguities have been removed by being given determinate meanings through the organizing activity of thought. It should also be clear that there is a great difference between an original argument, found in one of the landmarks of philosophical literature and reconstructed in its own terms, and other rational orders that we can impose on the same material. But, though it is easy to see the difference in general terms, it is not so easy to be assured that the argument we may construct is, in fact, the original argument reconstructed. Communication, which occurs when we understand each other in the same terms, is difficult, especially so when we try to communicate with someone whose thought lives only through his written words and who cannot answer our questions.

We should, no doubt, as students, be pious in the attempt to reconstruct the arguments of the great philosophers. But, as I have said before, in philosophy it is the argument that counts—not who said it. When we have got one going, the really important thing is the argument itself, its significance, its consequences, its validity. We may not have revived Socrates, but we shall be philosophizing, and he will have helped us to do so.

Who judges the soundness and validity of arguments? The answer has already been suggested in what I have been saying. It is the community of reasonable men in comunication with one another. There are no other judges. You will remember that Socrates refers to his colleagues in the discussion as his judges; and if you think about it you will see the sense in which Socrates is on trial in the *Phaedo* more fundamentally than he was before the assembly which condemned him. Here he is tested by the argument before a jury of his peers. Not only that, he is fighting for his life. His life is his philosophy. It is impious, as he says, to take one's own life. Had he submitted to the conditions of the trial by ceasing to philosophize or if he had fallen into misology—that hatred of ideas which is the worst thing that can happen to a man—he would indeed have committed suicide, for Socrates' character would have been obliterated. But, instead of seeing this, the world persisted in thinking that he was committing suicide by defying the decree that he stop philosophizing, though the penalty was to drink the hemlock. But when the appeal to reason is rejected and decisions are made by standards which are not submitted to the test of argument, misology is always at work.

Piety before the principles of communication by discussion has never been more dramatically illustrated than in the arguments and deeds of Socrates. But he has had no monopoly of such piety. It is the common possession of civilized men, though we have to be reminded of it generation by generation and each new generation has to be introduced to the meaning of its demands and of being loyal to them. Here is another reminder that came twenty-two hundred years after Socrates:

> Reason must in all its undertakings subject itself to criticism; should it limit freedom of criticism by any prohibitions, it must harm itself, drawing upon itself a damaging suspicion. Nothing is so important through its usefulness, nothing so sacred, that it may be exempted from this searching examination, which knows no

> respect for persons. Reason depends on this freedom for its very existence. For reason has no dictatorial authority; its verdict is always simply the agreement of free citizens, of whom each one must be permitted to express, without let or hindrance, his objections or even his veto.[1]

The recurring danger is that we have to know what an argument is before we know the meaning of being loyal to the principles by which one is regulated and judged. And we never know what an argument is until we have constructed one for ourselves.

[1] Immanuel Kant, *Critique of Pure Reason,* Part II, chap. i, sec. 2.

Questions and Assignments

1. Early in this essay, Wick sets forth his main divisions. What are they? Discuss these divisions as they are developed in the essay.

2. How does Wick define argument? Trace some of the details in his definition. Would it be accurate to say that Wick finally defines argument as intelligent thought or as precise understanding?

3. Explain the following phrases and ideas in your own words: "Reasoning is discourse" (paragraph three), "to teach you to think" (paragraph six), "the life of science and the law is the life of thought" (paragraph eleven).

4. Wick uses many of the techniques for development discussed in Part III. For example, the first nine paragraphs make use of definition, comparison and contrast, analogy. Find these and other techniques as they are used throughout the essay.

5. In paragraph 15 Wick signals a shift from general remarks to "specific problems" of analysis. Cite some of the specific problems he turns to.

6. Explain what Wick means by "imposing one's own pattern of thinking" on an argument. Have you ever seen this happen in your own experience?

7. What is the difference between the "words and sentences" of an argument and the "terms" of an argument?

8. What, according to Wick, is the final determinant of "the soundness and validity of arguments"?

Persuasion by Logical Argument

NEWMAN AND GENEVIEVE BIRK

The closely organized logical argument usually follows a basic plan of this kind: (1) The writer or speaker states the question clearly and fairly, defining any terms that might be ambiguous, and limiting the argument to the specific isues which he regards as important; he may in this preliminary step of his argument consider the history of the question and its present significance. (2) He states his position and supports that position by citing facts and authorities, and by reasoning from the evidence he presents. (3) He recognizes and refutes any outstanding arguments against his ideas. (4) He summarizes his argument and emphasizes the merits of his position or his proposal. Less formal arguments are likely to include these four steps too, but to follow a more personal, less orderly plan.

The writer of convincing argument must have studied his subject thoroughly. He must know exactly what the major issues are, so that he will not waste words in arguing trivial side issues or points on which there is general agreement. He must have not merely facts and authorities to support his position, but trustworthy, representative, up-to-date facts and reputable authorities. He must know his subject well enough to know more than one side of it. Argument, unlike some other kinds of persuasion, assumes opposition; understanding that opposition, being able to concede its strength on some points, but also to demonstrate its weakness on vital points, may be a large part of successful argumentation. In order to see weaknesses in the opposition, and in order to evaluate his own evidence and to arrive at sound conclusions, the writer needs, in addition to knowledge, skill in logical reasoning.

The reader of argument also needs this skill. If he is a critical reader, he will ask two questions about a piece of argumentative prose: Is the evidence good? Is the reasoning sound? In answering the first question he will be helped immeasurably, of course, if he has read and thought about the subject, if he himself has some command of the facts and some acquaintance with the recognized authorities in the field. But without this knowledge he still can make valid judgments about the evidence on which the writer's

From *Understanding and Using English* (Third Edition, 1958), by Newman and Genevieve Birk.

conclusions are based. He can see how well the writer's statements are substantiated. Some of them may be unsubstantiated, or practically so: "leading scientists agree," or "as psychologists tell us," or "the facts are well known," or "experiments have proved" is not equivalent to quoting scientists, psychologists, facts, or results of specific experiments. Some statements may have unreliable substantiation because the sources are unauthoritative or prejudiced: "the Podunk *Post-Examiner* of April 10, 1958, says . . ."; "the last issue of *Popular Reading* contains an article which settles this issue for all time"; "John Smith's authoritative study [written in 1935] says the last word on college football"; "the *Democratic Digest* gives an impartial account of the political situation." The reader can also recognize the citing of irrelevant authority—Thomas Jefferson, for example, quoted to support an argument against national health insurance; or a famous chemist quoted on old age pensions, or a prominent businessman on modern art. Persons competent in one field are not necessarily authorities in another. Finally, a reader can make some judgment of the evidence by asking himself how much of it there is, and whether the writer seems to have minimized or ignored evidence on the other side.

In answering the second question—Is the reasoning sound?—the reader is aided by a knowledge of logic. Frequently, while reading or listening to argument, one has an elusive sense of illogic in the thinking, a feeling of something's-wrong-but-I-can't-put-my-finger-on-it. A knowledge of the two kinds of logical thinking called *induction* and *deduction,* and of the common errors in logic, called *fallacies,* makes it easier to detect weaknesses in reasoning and also to recognize and to practice sound reasoning.

A. Induction

Induction is the kind of reasoning by which we examine a number of particulars or specific instances and on the basis of them arrive at a conclusion. The scientific method is inductive when the scientist observes a recurrent phenomenon and arrives at the conclusion or hypothesis that under certain conditions this phenomenon will always take place; if in the course of time further observation supports his hypothesis and if no exceptions are observed, his conclusion is generally accepted as truth and is sometimes called a law. In everyday living, too, we arrive at conclusions by induction. Every cat we encounter has claws; we conclude that all cats have claws. Every rose we smell is fragrant; we conclude that all roses are fragrant. An acquaintance has, on various occasions, paid back money he has borrowed; we conclude that he is frequently out of funds but that he pays his debts. Every Saturday morning for six weeks the new paper boy is late in delivering the paper; we conclude that he sleeps on Saturday mornings and we no longer look for the paper before nine o'clock. In each case we have reasoned inductively from a number of instances; we have moved from an observation of some things to a generalization about all things in the same category.

Occasionally, in restricted situations, it is possible to examine every instance. For example, a teacher may note that student A is present in class today, student B is present, C is present, and so on through the whole class list; by simple counting, the teacher can conclude that all members of the class are present today. Ordinarily, though, it is impossible to examine every instance—the claws of every cat, for example, or the nervous system of every cockroach, or every case of diphtheria, or every ruptured appendix, or the opinion of every voter. One must make an inductive jump from the instances he can know to a conclusion embracing things of the same sort that he cannot know. Inductive reasoning arrives, therefore, not at "truth" or "law," but at probability. The probability grows stronger and the induction becomes sounder when a substantial number of instances are examined, when the instances examined are typical, and when the exceptions, if any, are infrequent and explainable.

A conclusion based on too few instances or on untypical instances is called a *hasty generalization.* It is the most common fallacy in inductive reasoning, and is responsible for much misinformation and prejudice: "Negroes are lazy" "Why do you say that?" "Well, we had a Negro cook who was the laziest mortal I ever saw, and look at Bob Jones—he doesn't even try to get a job." The speaker is, of course, generalizing on the basis of only two examples, assuming that these examples are typical, and ignoring the countless exceptions. The hasty generalization may also occur in scientific research; further research may reveal exceptions which modify or invalidate the earlier conclusion.

Cause-effect induction is reasoning about why things happened and about the relationship between them. We observe effects and arrive at a conclusion about their cause; or we observe a set of circumstances (causes) and draw a conclusion about their effects; or we observe some effects and reason from them that there will be other effects. A doctor examines a patient, learns his symptoms, and from the data makes a diagnosis; he has started with the effects of the illness and reasoned to the cause of them. In cause-to-effect thinking the process is reversed because we can see the causes and, usually with the help of past inductions, can predict the effects. A student visits football practice two days before the opening game; he observes that two players are fighting on the field, that the captain and the coach are on bad terms, that the team's best passer is on the bench with a broken arm, and that the backfield is slow; seeing these causes, he predicts that this will not be a successful team. Effect-to-effect thinking is chain reasoning which also usually relies on past inductions: "That little accident [cause] smashed the right front fender [observed effect]; Father will be angry and will make me pay for a new fender [further effect reasoned on the basis of past instances]; I won't be able to take Jane to the prom [ultimate effect]."

A great deal of scientific investigation deals with causal relationships; that is, with observing and describing those orderly connections between elements and events in the universe, on the basis of which causes can be assigned and effects predicted with accuracy. In our daily thinking, too, we make numerous cause-effect inductions, many of which, however, lack scientific exactitude; they need to be verified before they can be held as logical conclusions. The following effect-to-cause inductions are fairly typical of the kind of reasoning we hear and perhaps do every day. During a storm, the back door slams with such force that the glass breaks; we assume that the wind blew the door. A friend is obviously depressed on the day grades come out; we say that he is badly disappointed in his grades. An engagement is broken a month after the engaged girl's family loses its money; we conclude that the engagement was broken for that reason. All these inductions need further verification, for the cause in each case may well be different from the one assigned; the door may have been slammed by a member of the family who is happy to have the storm blamed for it; the friend may be depressed and the engagement may have been broken for any number of reasons.

These examples illustrate two common fallacies in cause-effect induction. The first fallacy is oversimplifying, and attributing to a single cause effects which actually have complex causes. "I failed the course because the teacher was unreasonably hard" is sometimes an example of this oversimplification. Other familiar examples are: "The atomic bomb won World War II"; "The Hoover administration was responsible for the depression of the nineteen thirties"; "The reason for the high cost of living is the high wages paid to labor."

Often closely related to oversimplification of the cause is the logical fallacy of seeing a cause-effect relationship between events which have only an accidental time relationship. This fallacy is called *post hoc ergo propter hoc,* Latin for "after that therefore because of that." A common instance of this reasoning is a statement like "I won't vote for the Democrats again. Six months after they got into office the city taxes went up two dollars." It is possible, of course, that the Democrats were responsible for the tax increase; but it is also possible that any administration would have found higher taxes necessary. Asserting without proof a cause-effect relationship simply because one event follows another is as illogical as asserting that breakfast causes lunch. Many superstitions are maintained by this *post hoc ergo propter hoc* thinking. A superstitious person walks under a ladder, and an hour later, for reasons entirely unrelated to that incident, has a quarrel with a good friend; he forgets or ignores the real causes of the quarrel, falls into the logical confusion of after-I-walked-under-the-ladder-therefore-because-I-walked-under-the-ladder, and is confirmed in his original faulty induction that walking under ladders brings bad luck.

Induction by analogy occurs when one observes that two things are similar in some ways, and then reasons, from the observed likenesses, that they are also similar in other ways. For example, Sir Isaac Newton observed that certain combustible substances—oils, turpentine, camphor, etc.—had refractive power two or three times greater than might be expected from their densities. He reasoned by analogy that the diamond, with its very high refractive powers, was also combustible. This inference was correct.

Reasoning from analogy is dangerous, however, and argument by analogy alone is seldom convincing, because analogous situations or objects have differences as well as similarities and the differences may outweigh the similarities. Sir David Brewster, a nineteenth-century physicist and biographer of Sir Isaac Newton, pointed out that if Newton had reasoned from analogy the combustibility of greenockite and octahedrite, which also have high refractive powers, he would have been wrong. His reasoning about the diamond simply happened to be right. Long observation of Mars has given astronomers a body of data from which they have arrived inductively at a number of conclusions about that planet. Some people have reasoned by analogy that since Mars has atmosphere, temperatures, and seasonal changes comparable to earth's, it must also have life like ours. This conclusion is questionable; it disregards the observed differences between the two planets.

Analogy is not logical proof. In informative writing it is, as we have said earlier, a useful method of clarifying a difficult subject. Skillful analogy also has great persuasive power. But it should be used in conjunction with, not as a substitute for, more strictly logical reasoning; and it is effective only when the similarities are striking and the differences slight between the things being compared. The following induction by analogy is weak because the comparison is far-fetched and the differences are glaring:

> Even the most durable machines break down if they are worked constantly for long periods of time. Their parts wear out; they become inefficient. Are students supposed to be stronger than machines? Do they deserve less attention and care? We should have shorter assignments and longer vacations.

The following famous passage illustrates effective analogy. The comparison is used not to prove, but to describe and to persuade:

> In the field of world policy I would dedicate this Nation to the policy of the good neighbor—the neighbor who resolutely respects himself and because he does so, respects the rights of others—the neighbor who respects his obligations and respects the sanctity of his agreements in and with a world of neighbors.—Franklin D. Roosevelt, *First Inaugural Address.*

B. Deduction

Inductive reasoning, as we have seen, moves from individual circumstances or instances to a conclusion; this conclusion, unless every possible instance has been examined, expresses probability; the probability is as strong as the weight of evidence which supports it. Deduction is reasoning from stated propositions or premises to a conclusion. If the conclusion follows logically from the premises and if the premises are true, deduction arrives at proof or certainty.

> All men are mortal.
> John is a man.
> Therefore John is mortal.

The statement above is a syllogism, the pattern in which, in formal logic, a deductive argument is expressed. The syllogism consists of three statements—two premises and a conclusion. It contains three and only three main terms, each of which appears twice, but not twice in the same statement. The terms are given these names: the *major term* is the predicate of the conclusion; the *minor term* is the subject of the conclusion; and the *middle term* appears in both premises. The major term in the syllogism above is "mortal," and the premise in which it appears is called the *major premise.* The minor term is "John," and the premise in which it appears is called the *minor premise.* The middle term, "man/men," appears in both premises.

Diagraming the syllogism sometimes makes the relationship of statements clearer:

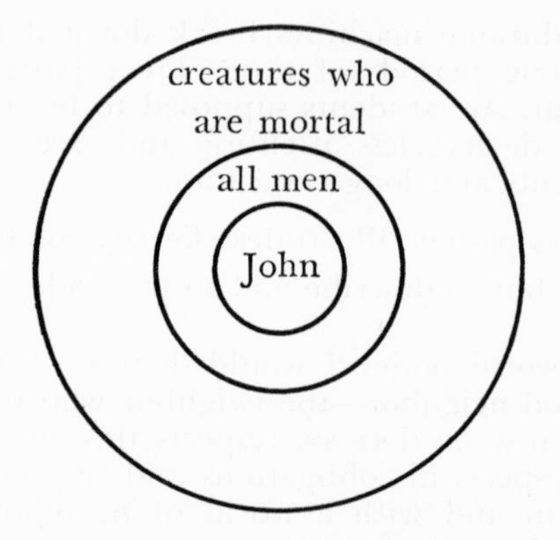

If all men are included in the larger group of mortal things (major premise), and if John is included in the group of all men (minor premise), then John is inevitably included in the group of those who are mortal (conclusion).

There are four patterns of the syllogism, in which the terms have different positions. In the following examples, the middle term (the term which appears in both premises) is printed in capital letters to show its position in the four patterns or "figures" of the syllogism:

Figure 1: All DOGS are carnivorous.
My cocker is a DOG.
Therefore my cocker is carnivorous.

Figure 2: No thief CAN BE TRUSTED.
All good men CAN BE TRUSTED.
Therefore no good men are thieves.

Figure 3: Every COLLEGE STUDENT has great opportunities.
Some COLLEGE STUDENTS are poor.
Therefore some poor people have great opportunities.

Figure 4: Most people devote themselves to MATERIAL GAIN.
MATERIAL GAIN is not a worthy goal in life.
Therefore most people do not devote themselves to a worthy goal in life.

When a syllogism has any of these four relationships between terms and between premises and conclusion, its argument is said to be *valid.* It is worth noting here that a "valid" argument is not necessarily *factually true.* For example, for some readers, the conclusions in the second and fourth syllogism above will seem untrue because one or both of the two premises seem untrue. Perhaps the point will be clearer if we look at more obvious examples:

Major premise: All Irishmen have hot tempers.
Minor premise: He is Irish.
Conclusion: Therefore he is hot-tempered.

Major premise: Poisonous snakes should be killed.
Minor premise: Garter snakes are poisonous.
Conclusion: Therefore garter snakes should be killed.

These two arguments are "valid" because they have the logical form of Figure 1 of the syllogism. However, the conclusions are unreliable because the major premise of the first syllogism is a hasty generalization, and the minor premise of the second syllogism is a misstatement of fact. In judging the truth or reliability of a deductive argument, one must ask two questions: Are the premises true? Is the argument valid? If the answer to both questions is "yes," the deduction can be accepted as true.[1]

C. Fallacies

We have mentioned earlier the common fallacies in inductive reasoning: hasty generalization, oversimplification of complex causes, *post hoc ergo propter hoc* argument, and faulty analogy. The most common fallacies in deductive argument come from the faulty relationship of parts of the syllogism. Such fallacies sometimes produce a slippery illogic in the reasoning, difficult to detect. For example, in the first figure of the syllogism illustrated on page 396, the subject of the major premise is the predicate of the minor premise; the form of the syllogism is *All X is Y; Z is X; therefore Z is Y.* In the following syllogism of the same pattern, the terms are shifted:

All tigers are felines. (X is Y)
My cat is a feline (Z is Y)
Therefore my cat is a tiger. (∴ Z is X)

[1] True premises and a valid argument can produce only a true conclusion. Untrue premises, as we have seen, can produce questionable or untrue conclusions. But it may be worth noting that a conclusion may happen to be true even though it is drawn from false premises: All cats are birds; all pigeons are cats; therefore all pigeons are birds. The conclusion here is true for reasons other than those stated in the premises.

The illogic here is made apparent by the absurdity of the conclusion; but it may not be so apparent in a similarly constructed syllogism:

All communists say Russia doesn't want war.
He says Russia doesn't want war.
Therefore he is a communist.

Diagraming such arguments is a good way of seeing why they are invalid:

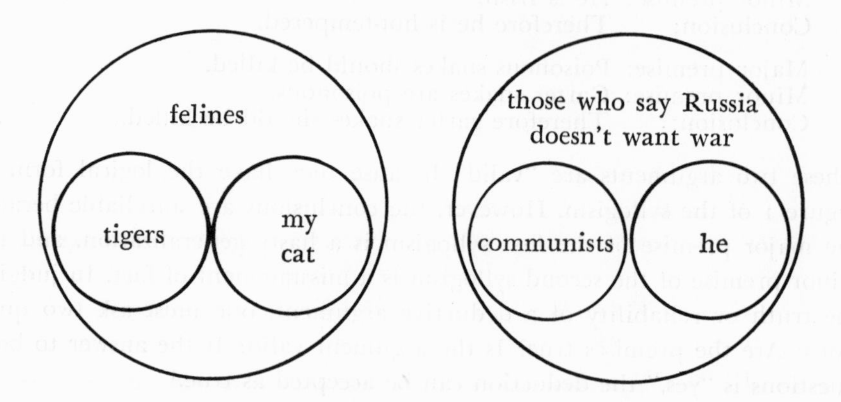

My cat and *he* are in the large circles of *felines* and *those who say Russia doesn't want war,* but not necessarily in the smaller circles of *tigers* and *communists.* There is no established relationship between the terms (tigers and my cat; communists and he) except the fact that they are both members of a larger group.

Another fallacy is in conclusions drawn from negative premises. If one premise is negative, the conclusion must be negative in a valid argument; if both premises are negative, no conclusion can be drawn.

Valid: All those attending the meeting are freshmen.
John is not a freshman.
Therefore John is not attending the meeting.

Invalid: No freshmen are attending the meeting.
John is not a freshman.
Therefore John is attending the meeting.

No conclusion can be drawn from the last two negative premises; John may or may not be attending the meeting.

In a valid argument, the conclusion follows inevitably from the premises. *Non-sequitur* (Latin for "it does not follow") is the fallacy of leaping to a conclusion not warranted by the premises. Drawing a conclusion from negative premises is one form of *non-sequitur*. Other examples are:

> Anyone who works hard deserves a vacation now and then.
> I work hard.
> Therefore my parents should give me a trip to Bermuda.
>
> Men who have made sacrifices for their country should be honored.
> I have made sacrifices for my country.
> Therefore I should be President.

The faults in the two preceding syllogisms are closely related to another fallacy of logical relationship—*the shifting of the meaning of terms between the major and the minor premise.* The shifted meaning is equivalent to a fourth term in the syllogism. For example:

> Man is the only creature capable of reason.
> Mary is not a man.
> Therefore Mary is incapable of reason.

The meaning of man has been shifted from *mankind* in the major premise to *male* in the minor premise. Other examples of shifted meanings are:

> Men who have devoted themselves to the service of the community should hold public office.
> I have devoted myself to the service of the community by running a bakery for fifteen years.
> Therefore I should hold public office.
>
> Government employees who are sympathetic with Russian policy should be discharged.
> This government employee belonged in 1943 to an organization which was friendly toward Russia.
> Therefore he should be discharged.

We seldom encounter the complete syllogism except in discussions of logic and in very formal argument. More usual is a reduced form of the syllogism in which one or two of the three parts, though implied, are not stated. The reduced syllogism is called an *enthymeme*. Sometimes in the enthymeme the conclusion of the syllogism is omitted because it is obvious: *Students who are found cheating on examinations fail the course; Clarence has been found cheating on an examination;* [the obvious omitted conclusion: therefore Clarence will fail the course]. Sometimes the minor premise is omitted for the same reason: *I like candidates who speak their minds; I'm going to vote for you* [omitted premise: you speak your mind]. Sometimes both the minor premise and the conclusion are omitted because the major premise adequately communicates them: *I date only men who have cars;* [omitted: you don't have a car; therefore I won't have a date with you]. Most frequently the major premise is omitted because the communicator assumes (often wrongly) that it is universally accepted and so does not require proof or even statement. One of the most useful skills of the hearer or reader of argument, therefore, is the ability to supply the omitted major premise. By recognizing that premise and examining it critically, he can better judge the reliability of the argument. The enthymemes below are familiar informal arguments; the major premise on which each one is based is put in brackets.

Jim must have been in a fight; he has a black eye. [Major premise. All black eyes are the result of fights.]

So he forgot he made the appointment. What can you expect? He's a college professor. [Major premise: College professors usually forget appointments. *Or,* College professors are absent-minded.]

He must be a grind! He got all A's last semester. [Students who get A records are grinds.]

He can't be a good doctor. He's in favor of socialized medicine. [No good doctor is in favor of socialized medicine.]

You're crazy, saying the meat tastes spoiled. I got it at the store just an hour ago. [Meat is always fresh when it is bought at stores.]

What a coward. He's a conscientious objector, you know. [All conscientious objectors are cowards.]

Naturally he's a delinquent. He reads ten comic books a week. [Reading comics always produces delinquency.]

Of course it's true. I read it in the paper. [Everything printed in the newspapers is true.]

They won't be happy together; he's two years younger than she. [Marriages are always unhappy if the man is younger than the woman.]

I think they'll be very nice neighbors. They have a new Cadillac. [People are nice neighbors if they have a new Cadillac.]

We're not talking about the same girl. The one I knew last summer had blond hair. [Once a blonde always a blonde.]

His mother has trained him to be neat around the house; he'll make a wonderful husband. [Any man who is neat around the house is a wonderful husband; also, a man trained by his mother to be neat around the house will continue to be neat when he is married.]

Two other logical fallacies, not peculiar to induction or to deduction, but involving the quality of the whole argument, are *begging the question* and *ignoring the question.*

Begging the question is assuming, without proof, the truth of a proposition which actually needs proof. If an arguer says, "This senseless language requirement should be abolished," he is, with the word *senseless,* begging the question; the question is whether or not the language requirement is senseless; if it is, it should of course be abolished; simply calling it senseless is not a logical argument in its disfavor. "This corrupt political machine should be replaced by good government" is another example of begging the question. No proof is offered that the government under attack is a "corrupt political machine," or that the government supported by the speaker will be "good." Both propositions are simply assumed. *Arguing in a circle* is one form of begging the question:

> People who are poor lack ambition because if they didn't lack ambition they wouldn't be poor.
>
> The study of literature is worthwhile because literature is a worthwhile subject.

Such argument in a circle is sometimes baffling, particularly when the argument is long and the circular motion is therefore difficult to detect. What the arguer in a circle does, technically, is offer as proof of his first proposition a second proposition which can be proved only by proving the first.

Ignoring the question is diverting attention from the real issues, or shifting the argument to some other ground. It has many forms. Name-calling, introducing irrelevant facts, and using other devices of charged language may be means of ignoring the real question. Sometimes a new argument is introduced in an effort to obscure the original issue: "I don't see why not. Susan Jones has a new coat. I should think you'd want me to be well dressed. It's a good thing someone in this family takes some pride in appearance. You haven't even shaved today." Arguing that an accused murderess should be acquitted because she is the mother of three children, and that a candidate should be mayor because he is a veteran of two wars are examples of ignoring the question by shifting from the central issues; the questions here are "Did she commit the murder?" and "Will he make a good mayor?" What is called argument *ad hominem* (to the man) is a way of ignoring the question by a shift from reasonable consideration of a measure to an attack on the character of the opponent; his ancestry, his religion, the fact that his first wife divorced him, that his son was arrested for speeding, etc. may be introduced to appeal to prejudice while the real question—the merits and defects of the measure itself—is ignored.

D. The Texture of Logical Thought

Although we have separated induction and deduction for purposes of discussion, the two processes work together in most acts of reasoning. A simple illustration of the interplay between them is this: A friend asks you one afternoon to go with him to a movie at the neighborhood theatre. You say, "No; it's Saturday." Behind your refusal lies an induction, based on instances in your own experience, that on Saturday afternoons many school children attend this theatre and are very noisy. You make a quick deduction: Every Saturday afternoon this theatre is full of noisy school children; this is Saturday; therefore the theatre will be full of noisy school children. Another inductive-deductive process also takes place. You have arrived at the generalization that you do not enjoy a movie if you cannot hear all of it. You reason: I do not want to go to a movie if I cannot hear all of it; I will not be able to hear all of it today (because of the noise of the children); therefore I do not want to go to this movie on this day. Still another reasoning process about your relationship with the friend who has asked you to go to the movie may occur. From your past experience with him you may have induced: Jack is not offended if for some good reason I refuse his invitations. Now you may deduce: I am refusing this invitation for a good reason; therefore Jack will not be offended. In this kind of thinking, the inductions and deductions are almost automatic. In more complex reasoning they are formulated only after conscious and disciplined thought.

We have said earlier that induction is important in scientific thinking; it enables human beings to arrive at generalizations and hypotheses about the world they live in, to see cause-effect relationships, and, on the basis of established probabilities, to make predictions and produce effects by controlling causes. As a science advances and its inductive hypotheses are further substantiated, the substantiated hypotheses supply premises from which deductive conclusions are drawn. One kind of reasoning leads to, supports, and leads back to the other. In the same way, in a logical argument, observed instances have perhaps led the speaker or writer inductively to the position he takes in the argument. From his inductions he may reason deductively about what should be done in a particular situation.

Closely interwoven though the two kinds of reasoning are, it is useful to have some knowledge of their differences, of the different kinds of reliability they can arrive at, and of the common fallacies in each kind of thinking. Being able to reduce a confusing argument to syllogistic form will enable one to see more clearly its premises and its validity. Being alert to hasty generalization, to faulty cause-effect reasoning, to conclusions which do not follow the premises, to question-begging and to ignoring of the question will help one judge the soundness of an argument. A knowledge of the processes of reasoning, in short, provides instruments of analysis with which one can better examine the texture of his own argument and the arguments of others.

E. Tone

In persuasion by logical argument, the writer may be formal or informal in his attitude toward his audience; but he is usually less concerned with getting their liking than with winning their respect. For this respect, he depends largely on the quality of the argument itself. If he presents the issues fairly; if he is reasonable in considering opposing points of view; if his evidence is good and his thinking clear and sound; if he respects the intelligence of his audience and assumes that they will not be convinced by slippery illogic and devices like arguments *ad hominem,* he will almost certainly gain a respectful hearing for what he has to say.

As a rule, the most skillful argument is reasonable in tone as well as in thought; it gives the impression of trying to arrive at truth, not merely to win a case; it is good tempered, and free from dogmatism and conceit. Fighting-mad arguments and dogmatic statements do sometimes affect already-sympathetic or prejudiced audiences; but they are likely to alienate and offend an impartial audience. Benjamin Franklin, wise in argument and diplomacy, wrote in his autobiography:

> I made it a rule to forbear all direct contradiction to the sentiments of others, and all positive assertion of my own. I even forbade myself . . . the use of every word or expression in the language that imported a fix'd opinion, such as *certainly, undoubtedly,* etc., and I adopted, instead of them, *I conceive, I apprehend,* or *I imagine* a thing to be so or so; or it *so appears to me at present.* When another asserted something that I thought an error, I deny'd myself the pleasure of contradicting him abruptly, and of showing immediately some absurdity in his proposition; and in answering I began by observing that in certain cases of circumstances

his opinion would be right but in the present case there *appear'd* or *seem'd* to me some difference, etc. I soon found the advantage of this change in my manner; the conversations I engag'd in went on more pleasantly. The modest way in which I propos'd my opinions procur'd them a readier reception and less contradiction; I had less mortification when I was found to be in the wrong, and I more easily prevail'd with others to give up their mistakes and join with me when I happened to be in the right.

And this mode, which I at first put on with some violence to natural inclination, became at length so easy, and so habitual to me, that perhaps for these fifty years past no one has ever heard a dogmatical expression escape me. And to this habit (after my character of integrity) I think it principally owing that I had early so much weight with my fellow-citizens when I proposed new institutions, or alterations in the old, and so much influence in public councils when I became a member; for I was but a bad speaker, never eloquent, subject to much hesitation in my choice of words, hardly correct in language, and yet I generally carried my points.

Questions and Assignments

1. This essay begins by pointing out that logical argument falls into four parts. What are the parts? In our Introduction we said that analysis tends toward argumentation. Look back at some analytical essays such as "The Hard Kind of Patriotism" and determine whether or not they fall into four parts.

2. Why do the authors emphasize particular skills for the reader and for the writer? What is the relationship between the skills they emphasize?

3. Explain the difference between evidence and reasoning.

4. "Inductive reasoning arrives, therefore, not at 'truth' or 'law,' but at probability." What does this statement mean?

5. Find original instances of these fallacies: hasty generalization, oversimplification, faulty analogy, faulty causality. Are any of these related to errors in deductive reasoning? Which of the errors in deductive reasoning do you think are the most common?

6. Why do the writers draw a distinction between what is *valid* and what is *factually true*? In other words, what is the relationship between a false premise and a valid deduction?

7. Toward the end of this essay, three additional errors in reasoning are cited. What are they?

8. The essay by Wick and this one by the Birks are both concerned with argument, but the two essays differ a great deal. What accounts for this difference? Is there any difference in language and tone? Do both essays use the same terms in the same way? For example, do both essays mean the same thing by *reasoning*?

Premises and Fallacies

Every argument has a premise. Whether he implies it or whether he states it, an author argues from a particular point of view, a particular belief, or a particular set of facts which he holds to be true. Whether or not it *is* true the reader or hearer has to decide for himself on the basis of his own experience or knowledge as well as the opinions of other "reasonable" men.

For example, we may believe that frogs cause warts and argue against handling frogs, or we may hold that bushy eyebrows are a sign of malicious character and argue against trusting people with bushy eyebrows. But all such reasoning, valid as it may be, will carry no conviction because the premises are obviously untrue, and these premises, in turn, fail to convince because evidence suggests that they are not valid.

It is not always so easy, however, to decide whether a premise is true or false, as the readings in this section will show. And sometimes it is not even easy to find the premise, for it is often merely implied rather than specifically stated. If someone were to say, "I believe in the superiority of the Nordic race and am opposed to changing or liberalizing our immigration laws," his premise would be perfectly clear. But if someone said, "I am opposed to any further increase in our immigration quotas," the premise is completely concealed. The speaker may be arguing from the same racist principle as the first, but he may be arguing from a fear of overpopulation or for purely economic reasons.

In the second example, we do not have sufficient evidence to spot the premise. But if the speaker were to continue, we would probably very shortly be able to determine his implied premise. In many of the readings which follow premises are implied rather than stated, but close attention to the details of the selections should quickly reveal them.

Whatever the reader's judgment about the truth of the premise, he must also be able to judge the validity of the argument. For this purpose he must be alert for the various types of fallacies which were pointed out in the essay by the Birks. Spotting the fallacies, where they appear, may help the reader to make an accurate judgment of the premise as well as of the conclusion. And if there are no fallacies, if the argument is valid, then we must either accept the conclusion or reject the premise. Therefore, it should be obvious how important it is to be able to recognize fallacious reasoning. The five selections which follow should provide interesting material for study with this in mind.

The first selection is taken from the novel *Crime and Punishment* by the great nineteenth-century Russian novelist, Fyodor Dostoyevsky. Bertrand Russell, the author of the second selection, is a twentieth-century philsopher and mathematician. Shakespeare is the author of the third selection, and Robert Browning, a nineteenth-century English poet, is the author of "My Last Duchess." Luigi Pirandello is a well-known twentieth-century writer.

Great Men as Criminals

FYODOR DOSTOYEVSKY

Readers should know that the main speaker, Raskolnikov, has recently committed a murder for no other motive than to prove that he was capable of such a deed. Razumihin, his friend, does not know this, and Porfiry, the police inspector, apparently *does not know it either.*

"How did you find out that the article was mine? It's only signed with an initial."

"I only learnt it by chance, the other day. Through the editor; I know him. . . . I was very much interested."

"It analysed, if I remember, the psychology of a criminal before and after the crime."

"Yes, and you maintained that the perpetration of a crime is always accompanied by illness. Very, very original, but . . . it was not that part of your article that interested me so much, but an idea at the end of the article which I regret to say you merely suggested without working it out clearly. There is, if you recollect, a suggestion that there are certain persons

From *Crime and Punishment* by Fyodor Dostoyevsky (Constance Garnett translation), Random House, Inc.

who can . . . that is, not precisely are able to, but have a perfect right to commit breaches of morality and crimes, and that the law is not for them."

Raskolnikov smiled at the exaggerated and intentional distortion of his idea.

"What? What do you mean? A right to crime? But not because of the influence of environment?" Razumihin inquired with some alarm even.

"No, not exactly because of it," answered Porfiry. "In his article all men are divided into 'ordinary' and 'extraordinary.' Ordinary men have to live in submission, have no right to transgress the law, because, don't you see, they are ordinary. But extraordinary men have a right to commit any crime and to transgress the law in any way, just because they are extraordinary. That was your idea, if I am not mistaken?"

"What do you mean? That can't be right?" Razumihin muttered in bewilderment.

Raskolnikov smiled again. He saw the point at once, and knew where they wanted to drive him. He decided to take up the challenge.

"That wasn't quite my contention," he began simply and modestly. "Yet I admit that you have stated it almost correctly; perhaps, if you like, perfectly so." (It almost gave him pleasure to admit this.) "The only difference is that I don't contend that extraordinary people are always bound to commit breaches of morals, as you call it. In fact, I doubt whether such an argument could be published. I simply hinted that an 'extraordinary' man has the right . . . that is not an official right, but an inner right to decide in his own conscience to overstep . . . certain obstacles, and only in case it is essential for the practical fulfilment of his idea (sometimes, perhaps, of benefit to the whole of humanity). You say that my article isn't definite; I am ready to make it as clear as I can. Perhaps I am right in thinking you want me to; very well. I maintain that if the discoveries of Kepler and Newton could not have been made known except by sacrificing the lives of one, a dozen, a hundred, or more men, Newton would have had the right, would indeed have been in duty bound . . . to *eliminate* the dozen or the hundred men for the sake of making his discoveries known to the whole of humanity. But it does not follow from that that Newton had a right to murder people right and left and to steal every day in the market. Then, I remember, I maintain in my article that all . . . well, legislators and leaders of men, such as Lycurgus, Solon, Mahomet, Napoleon, and so on, were all without exception criminals, from the very fact that, making a new law, they transgressed the ancient one, handed down from their ancestors and held sacred by the people, and they did not stop short at bloodshed either, if that bloodshed—often of innocent persons fighting bravely in defence of ancient law—were of use to their cause. It's remarkable, in fact, that the majority, indeed, of these benefactors and leaders of humanity were guilty of terrible carnage. In short, I maintain that all great men or even men a little out of the common, that is to say capable of giving some new word, must from their very nature be criminals—more or less, of course. Otherwise it's hard for them to get out of the common rut; and to remain in the common rut is what they can't submit to, from their very nature again, and to my mind they ought not, indeed, to submit to it. You see that there is nothing particularly new in all that. The same thing has been printed and read a thousand times before. As for my division of people into ordinary and extraordinary, I acknowledge that it's somewhat arbitrary, but I don't insist upon exact numbers. I only believe in my leading idea that men are *in general* divided by a law of nature into two categories, inferior (ordinary), that is, so to say, material that serves only to reproduce its kind, and men who have the gift or the talent to utter *a new word.* There are, of course, innumerable sub-divisions, but the distinguishing features of both categories are fairly well marked. The first category, generally speaking, are men conservative in temperament and law-abiding; they live under control and love to be controlled. To my thinking it is their duty to be controlled, because that's their vocation, and there is nothing humiliating in it for them. The second category all transgress the law; they are destroyers or disposed to destruction according to their capacities. The crimes of these men are of course relative and varied; for the most part they seek in very varied ways the destruction of the present for the sake of the better. But if such a one is forced for the sake of his idea to step over a corpse or wade through blood, he can, I maintain, find within himself, in his conscience, a sanction for wading through blood—that depends on the idea and its dimensions, note that. It's only in that sense I speak of their right to crime in my article (you remember it began with the legal question). There's no need for such anxiety, however; the masses will scarcely ever admit this right, they punish them or hang them (more or less), and in doing so fulfil quite justly their conservative vocation. But the same masses set these criminals on a pedestal in the next generation and worship them (more or less). The first category is always the man of the present, the second the man of the future. The first preserve the world and people it, the second move the world and lead it to its goal. Each class has an equal right to exist. In fact, all have equal rights with me—and *vive la guerre éternelle*—till the New Jerusalem, of course!"

"Then you believe in the New Jerusalem, do you?"

"I do," Raskolnikov answered firmly; as he said these words and during the whole preceding tirade he kept his eyes on one spot on the carpet.

. . . .

"You don't say so. . . . I asked from curiosity. Excuse me. But let us go back to the question; they are not always executed. Some, on the contrary . . ."

"Triumph in their lifetime? Oh, yes, some attain their ends in this life, and then . . ."

"They begin executing other people?"

"If it's necessary; indeed, for the most part they do. Your remark is very witty."

"Thank you. But tell me this: how do you distinguish those extraordinary people from the ordinary ones? Are there signs at their birth? I feel there ought to be more exactitude, more external definition. Excuse the natural anxiety of a practical law-abiding citizen, but couldn't they adopt a special uniform, for instance, couldn't they wear something, be branded in some way? For you know if confusion arises and a member of one category imagines that he belongs to the other, begins to 'eliminate obstacles,' as you so happily expressed it, then . . ."

"Oh, that very often happens! That remark is wittier than the other."

"Thank you."

"No reason to; but take note that the mistake can only arise in the first category, that is among the ordinary people (as I perhaps unfortunately called them). In spite of their predisposition to obedience very many of them, through a playfulness of nature, sometimes vouchsafed even to the cow, like to imagine themselves advanced people, 'destroyers,' and to push themselves into the 'new movement,' and this quite sincerely. Meanwhile the really *new* people are very often unobserved by them, or even despised as reactionaries of grovelling tendencies. But I don't think there is any considerable danger here, and you really need not be uneasy for they never go very far. Of course, they might have a thrashing sometimes for letting their fancy run away with them and to teach them their place, but no more; in fact, even this isn't necessary as they castigate themselves, for they are very conscientious: some perform this service for one another and others chastise themselves with their own hands. . . . They will impose various public acts of penitence upon themselves with a beautiful and edifying effect; in fact you've nothing to be uneasy about. . . . It's a law of nature."

"Well, you have certainly set my mind more at rest on that score; but there's another thing worries me. Tell me, please, are there many people who have the right to kill others, these extraordinary people? I am ready to bow down to them, of course, but you must admit it's alarming if there are a great many of them, eh?"

"Oh, you needn't worry about that either," Raskolnikov went on in the same tone. "People with new ideas, people with the faintest capacity for saying something *new,* are extremely few in number, extraordinarily so in fact. One thing only is clear, that the appearance of all these grades and sub-divisions of men must follow with unfailing regularity some law of nature. That law, of course, is unknown at present, but I am convinced that it exists, and one day may become known. The vast mass of mankind is mere material, and only exists in order by some great effort, by some mysterious process, by means of some crossing of races and stocks, to bring into the world at last perhaps one man out of a thousand with a spark of independence. One in ten thousand perhaps—I speak roughly, approximately—is born with some independence, and with still greater independence one in a hundred thousand. The man of genius is one of millions, and the great geniuses, the crown of humanity, appear on earth perhaps one in many thousand millions. In fact I have not peeped into the retort in which all this takes place. But there certainly is and must be a definite law, it cannot be a matter of chance."

"Why, are you both joking?" Razumihin cried at last. "There you sit, making fun of one another. Are you serious, Rodya?"

Raskolnikov raised his pale and almost mournful face and made no reply. And the unconcealed, persistent, nervous, and *discourteous* sarcasm of Porfiry seemed strange to Razumihin beside that quiet and mournful face.

"Well, brother, if you are really serious . . . You are right, of course, in saying that it's not new, that it's like what we've read and heard a thousand times already; but what is really *original* in all this, and is exclusively your own, to my horror, is that you sanction bloodshed *in the name of conscience,* and, excuse my saying so, with such fanaticism. . . . That, I take it, is the point of your article. But that sanction of bloodshed *by conscience* is to my mind . . . more terrible than the official, legal sanction of bloodshed. . . ."

"You are quite right, it is more terrible," Porfiry agreed.

"Yes, you must have exaggerated! There is some mistake, I shall read it. You can't think that! I shall read it."

"All that is not in the article, there's only a hint of it," said Raskolnikov.

"Yes, yes." Porfiry couldn't sit still. "Your attitude to crime is pretty clear to me now, but . . . excuse me for my impertinence (I am really ashamed to be worrying you like this), you see, you've removed my anxiety as to the two grades' getting mixed, but . . . there are various practical possibilities that make me uneasy! What if some man or youth imagines that he is a Lycurgus or Mahomet—a future one of course—and suppose he begins to remove all obstacles. . . . He has some great enterprise before him and needs money for it . . . and tries to get it . . . do you see?"

Zametov gave a sudden guffaw in his corner. Raskolnikov did not even raise his eyes to him.

"I must admit," he went on calmly, "that such cases certainly must arise. The vain and foolish are particularly apt to fall into that snare; young people especially."

"Yes, you see. Well then?"

"What then?" Raskolnikov smiled in reply; "that's not my fault. So it is and so it always will be. He said just now (he nodded at Razumihin) that I sanction bloodshed. Society is too well protected by prisons, banishment, criminal investigators, penal servitude. There's no need to be uneasy. You have but to catch the thief."

"And what if we do catch him?"

"Then he gets what he deserves."

"You are certainly logical. But what of his conscience?"

"Why do you care about that?"

"Simply from humanity."

"If he has a conscience he will suffer for his mistake. That will be his punishment—as well as the prison."

"But the real geniuses," asked Razumihin frowning, "those who have the right to murder? Oughtn't they to suffer at all even for the blood they've shed?"

"Why the word *ought?* It's not a matter of permission or prohibition. He will suffer if he is sorry for his victim. Pain and suffering are always inevitable for a large intelligence and a deep heart. The really great men must, I think, have great sadness on earth," he added dreamily, not in the tone of the conversation.

He raised his eyes, looked earnestly at them all, smiled, and took his cap. He was too quiet by comparison with his manner at his entrance, and he felt this. Every one got up.

Questions and Assignments

1. Compare the diction and tone of Raskolnikov's argument with the comments of his friend Razumihin and the questions of Inspector Porfiry. Raskolnikov sounds the most confident and rational. Is he therefore more logical than the others?

2. The point of this argument is stated by three different speakers in different ways. Raskolnikov says that Porfiry's statement is not quite correct. Is the difference he points out a logical one or does he go off on a tangent?

3. Raskolnikov acknowledges that his division of men may be "somewhat arbitrary." How logically does he justify the division? Can you see where he contradicts himself in regard to those who transgress the law?

4. According to Raskolnikov, which comes first, criminal behavior or greatness? How much depends upon one's definition of "greatness" and "criminal behavior"?

5. The premise of this argument is that the end justifies the means. Even if you grant that the ends Raskolnikov cites are good, do you think he gives sufficient proof that there is no danger that the wrong people will use illegal means?

6. Choose a particular law or a moral principle—anything from stopping at stop signs to thou shalt not kill—and write an essay proving that the rule does or does not apply to everyone. Be sure to give an adequate definition of the principle, an accurate statement of opposing arguments, and a logical description of how it applies and to whom.

7. Write an essay proving that Raskolnikov is wrong or right, using examples especially from twentieth-century history.

Respect for Law

BERTRAND RUSSELL

Under the influence of the romantic movement, a process began about a hundred and fifty years ago, which has continued ever since—a process of revaluing the traditional virtues, placing some higher on the scale than before, and others lower. The tendency has been to exalt impulse at the expense of deliberation. The virtues that spring from the heart have come to be thought superior to those that are based upon reflection: a generous man is preferred to a man who is punctual in paying his debts. *Per contra,* deliberate sins are thought worse than impulsive sins: a hypocrite is more harshly condemned than a murderer.

The upshot is that we tend to estimate virtues, not by their capacity for providing human happiness, but by their power of inspiring a personal liking for the possessors, and we are apt to include among the qualities for which we like people, a habit of reflecting before making an important decision.

The men who started this movement were, in the main, gentle sentimentalists who imagined that, when the fetters of custom and law were removed, the heart would be free to display its natural goodness. Human nature, they thought, is good, but institutions have corrupted it; remove the institutions and we shall all become angels. Unfortunately, the matter is not so simple as they thought. Men who follow their impulses establish governments based on pogroms, clamour for war with foreign countries, and murder pacifists and Negroes. Human nature unrestrained by law is violent and cruel. In the London Zoo, the male baboons fought over the females until all the females were torn to pieces; human beings, left to the ungoverned impulse, would be no better. In ages that have had recent experience of anarchy, this has been obvious. All the great writers of the middle ages were passionate in their admiration of the law; it was the Thirty Years' War that led Grotius to become the first advocate of international law. Law, respected and enforced, is in the long run the only alternative to violent and predatory anarchy; and it is just as necessary to realize this now as it was in the time of Dante and Grotius.

What is the essence of law? On the one hand, it takes away from private citizens the right of revenge, which it confers upon the government. If a man steals your money, you must not steal it back, or thrash him, or shoot him; you must establish the facts before a neutral tribunal, which inflicts upon him such punishment as has seemed just to the disinterested legislators. On the other hand, when two men have a dispute, the law provides a machinery for settling it, again on principles laid down in advance by neutrals. The advantages of law are many. It diminishes the amount of private violence, and settles disagreements in a manner more nearly just than that which would result if the disputants fought it out by private war. It makes it possible for men to work without being perpetually on the watch against bandits. When a crime has been committed it provides a skilled machine for discovering the criminal.

Without law, the existence of civilized communities is impossible. In international law, there is as yet no effective law, for lack of an international police force capable of overpowering national armies, and it is daily becoming more evident that this defect must be remedied if civilization is to survive. Within single nations there is a dangerous tendency to think that moral indignation excuses the extra-legal punishment of criminals. In Germany an era of private murder (on the loftiest grounds) preceded and followed the victory of the Nazis. In fact, nine-tenths of what appeared as just indignation was sheer lust for cruelty; and this is equally true in other countries where mobs rob the law of its functions. In any civilized community, toleration of mob rule is the first step towards barbarism.

Questions and Assignments

1. Try expressing the opening thought of paragraph four in an ordinary sentence. Why is the question more effective?

2. Is the syntax of the second paragraph sufficiently clear? How would you rewrite it in order to clarify the two main thoughts and the transition between them?

3. Does Russell state his premise before or after his exposition of the opposing point of view? What examples does he cite? What assumption underlies the analogy of the baboons in the third paragraph?

4. Does Russell's definition of law follow logically from his premise? Examine the reasoning in the last paragraph to see how it is based on the preceding argument and how it leads up to the final conclusion.

5. Compare this selection with the Dostoyevsky piece. Is there any similarity in their premises? In their conclusions? How would Russell refute the arguments of Raskolnikov?

6. In light of Russell's essay, rewrite the essay you wrote after reading the Dostoyevsky essay.

7. Or take one of the topics suggested after that selection and write a short essay modeled on the form of Russell's. You may need to provide yourself with an outline of Russell's essay in order to copy it coherently.

8. Would Russell advocate respect for an unjust law? Write a theme discussing some possible circumstances in which respect for the law might not be a good thing.

Measure for Measure

WILLIAM SHAKESPEARE

In the second scene of Act II in MEASURE FOR MEASURE, *the heroine Isabella pleads with the deputy Angelo that he pardon her brother, Claudio. Angelo is acting ruler during the Duke's absence. One of Angelo's first acts as ruler was to reinstate an ancient statute which demanded the death penalty for all found guilty of fornication. Isabella's brother has been found guilty of fornicating with his betrothed, Juliet. This scene consists principally of Isabella's argument for justice tempered by mercy and of Angelo's arguments for an impartial and inflexible enforcement of the law, but by the end of the scene reasons are being overwhelmed by emotions.*

SCENE II

Enter PROVOST *and a* SERVANT.

Serv. He's hearing of a cause; he will come straight.
I'll tell him of you.
Prov. Pray you, do.
[*Exit Servant.*]
I'll know
His pleasure; may be he will relent. Alas,
He hath but as offended in a dream!
All sects, all ages smack of this vice; and he 5
To die for't!

Enter ANGELO.

Ang. Now, what's the matter, Provost?
Prov. Is it your will Claudio shall die to-morrow?
Ang. Did not I tell thee yea? Hadst thou not order?
Why dost thou ask again?
Prov. Lest I might be too rash.
Under your good correction, I have seen 10

When, after execution, judgement hath
Repented o'er his doom.

Ang. Go to; let that be mine.
Do you your office, or give up your place,
And you shall well be spar'd.

Prov. I crave your honour's pardon.
What shall be done, sir, with the groaning Juliet?
She's very near her hour.

Ang. Dispose of her 16
To some more fitter place, and that with speed.

[*Re-enter* SERVANT.]

Serv. Here is the sister of the man condemn'd
Desires access to you.

Ang. Hath he a sister?

Prov. Ay, my good lord; a very virtuous maid,
And to be shortly of a sisterhood, 21
If not already.

Ang. Well, let her be admitted.

[*Exit Servant.*]

See you the fornicatress be remov'd.
Let her have needful but not lavish means;
There shall be order for't.

Enter ISABELLA *and* LUCIO.

Prov. [God] save your honour!

Ang. Stay a little while. [*To Isab.*] You're welcome; what's your will? 26

Isab. I am a woeful suitor to your honour,
Please but your honour hear me.

Ang. Well; what's your suit?

Isab. There is a vice that most I do abhor,
And most desire should meet the blow of justice;
For which I would not plead, but that I must; 31
For which I must not plead, but that I am
At war 'twixt will and will not.

Ang. Well; the matter?

Isab. I have a brother is condemn'd to die.
I do beseech you, let it be his fault, 35
And not my brother.

Prov. [*Aside.*] Heaven give thee moving graces!
Ang. Condemn the fault, and not the actor of it?
Why, every fault's condemn'd ere it be done.
Mine were the very cipher of a function,
To fine the faults whose fine stands in record, 40
And let go by the actor.
Isab. O just but severe law!
I had a brother, then. Heaven keep your honour!
Lucio. [*Aside to Isab.*] Give't not o'er so. To him again, entreat him,
Kneel down before him, hang upon his gown.
You are too cold. If you should need a pin, 45
You could not with more tame a tongue desire it.
To him, I say!
Isab. Must he needs die?
Ang. Maiden, no remedy.
Isab. Yes; I do think that you might pardon him,
And neither heaven nor man grieve at the mercy.
Ang. I will not do't.
Isab. But can you, if you would? 51
Ang. Look, what I will not, that I cannot do.
Isab. But might you do't, and do the world no wrong,
If so your heart were touch'd with that remorse
As mine is to him?
Ang. He's sentenc'd; 'tis too late.
Lucio. [*Aside to Isab.*] You are too cold. 56
Isab. Too late? Why, no, I, that do speak a word,
May call it [back] again. Well, believe this,
No ceremony that to great ones longs, 59
Not the king's crown, nor the deputed sword,
The marshal's truncheon, nor the judge's robe,
Become them with one half so good a grace
As mercy does.
If he had been as you and you as he,
You would have slipt like him; but he, like you, 65
Would not have been so stern.

Ang. Pray you, be gone.
Isab. I would to heaven I had your potency,
And you were Isabel! Should it then be thus?
No; I would tell what 'twere to be a judge,
And what a prisoner.
Lucio. [*Aside to Isab.*] Ay, touch him; there's the vein. 70
Ang. Your brother is a forfeit of the law,
And you but waste your words.
Isab. Alas, alas!
Why, all the souls that were were forfeit once;
And He that might the vantage best have took
Found out the remedy. How would you be 75
If He, which is the top of judgement, should
But judge you as you are? O, think on that;
And mercy then will breathe within your lips,
Like man new made.
Ang. Be you content, fair maid.
It is the law, not I condemn your brother. 80
Were he my kinsman, brother, or my son,
It should be thus with him. He must die to-morrow.
Isab. To-morrow! O, that's sudden! Spare him, spare him!
He's not prepar'd for death. Even for our kitchens
We kill the fowl of season. Shall we serve Heaven
With less respect than we do minister 86
To our gross selves? Good, good my lord, bethink you:
Who is it that hath died for this offence?
There's many have committed it.
Lucio. [*Aside to Isab.*] Ay, well said.
Ang. The law hath not been dead, though it hath slept. 90
Those many had not dar'd to do that evil,
If [but] the first that did th' edict infringe
Had answer'd for his deed. Now 'tis awake,
Takes note of what is done, and, like a prophet,

Looks in a glass that shows what future evils,
Either [new], or by remissness new-conceiv'd, 96
And so in progress to be hatch'd and born,
Are now to have no successive degrees,
But, [ere] they live, to end.

Isab. Yet show some pity.

Ang. I show it most of all when I show justice,
For then I pity those I do not know, 101
Which a dismiss'd offence would after gall;
And do him right that, answering one foul wrong,
Lives not to act another. Be satisfied.
Your brother dies to-morrow. Be content. 105

Isab. So you must be the first that gives this sentence,
And he, that suffers. O, it is excellent
To have a giant's strength; but it is tyrannous
To use it like a giant.

Lucio. [*Aside to Isab.*] That's well said.

Isab. Could great men thunder 110
As Jove himself does, Jove would ne'er be quiet;
For every pelting, petty officer
Would use his heaven for thunder,
Nothing but thunder! Merciful Heaven, 114
Thou rather with thy sharp and sulphurous bolt
Splits the unwedgeable and gnarled oak
Than the soft myrtle; but man, proud man,
Dress'd in a little brief authority,
Most ignorant of what he's most assur'd,
His glassy essence, like an angry ape, 120
Plays such fantastic tricks before high heaven
As makes the angels weep; who, with our spleens,
Would all themselves laugh mortal.

Lucio. [*Aside to Isab.*] O, to him, to him, wench! he will relent.
He's coming; I perceive't.

Prov. [*Aside.*] Pray Heaven she win him! 125

Isab. We cannot weigh our brother with ourself.
Great men may jest with saints; 'tis wit in them,

But in the less foul profanation.

Lucio. [*Aside.*] Thou'rt i' th' right, girl. More o' that.

Isab. That in the captain's but a choleric word,
Which in the soldier is flat blasphemy. 131

Lucio. [*Aside to Isab.*] Art avis'd o' that? More on't.

Ang. Why do you put these sayings upon me?

Isab. Because authority, though it err like others,
Hath yet a kind of medicine in itself, 135
That skins the vice o' th' top. Go to your bosom;
Knock there, and ask your heart what it doth know
That's like my brother's fault. If it confess
A natural guiltiness such as is his,
Let it not sound a thought upon your tongue 140
Against my brother's life.

Ang. [*Aside.*] She speaks and 'tis
Such sense, that my sense breeds with it. Fare you well.

Isab. Gentle my lord, turn back.

Ang. I will bethink me. Come again to-morrow.

Isab. Hark how I'll bribe you. Good my lord, turn back. 145

Ang. How! bribe me?

Isab. Ay, with such gifts that Heaven shall share with you.

Lucio. [*Aside to Isab.*] You had marr'd all else.

Isab. Not with fond shekels of the tested gold,
Or stones whose [rates] are either rich or poor 150
As fancy values them; but with true prayers
That shall be up at heaven and enter there
Ere sun-rise, prayers from preserved souls,
From fasting maids whose minds are dedicate
To nothing temporal.

Ang. Well, come to me to-morrow.

Lucio. [*Aside to Isab.*] Go to; 'tis well. Away!

Isab. Heaven keep your honour safe!

Ang. [*Aside.*] Amen! 157

For I am that way going to temptation,
Where prayers cross.
Isab. At what hour to-morrow
Shall I attend your lordship?
Ang. At any time 'fore noon. 160
Isab. 'Save your honour!
[*Exeunt Isabella, Lucio, and Provost.*]
Ang. From thee, even from thy virtue.
What's this, what's this? Is this her fault or mine?
The tempter or the tempted, who sins most?
Ha!
Not she, nor doth she tempt; but it is I 165
That, lying by the violet in the sun,
Do, as the carrion does, not as the flower,
Corrupt with virtuous season. Can it be
That modesty may more betray our sense
Than woman's lightness? Having waste ground
enough, 170
Shall we desire to raze the sanctuary
And pitch our evils there? O, fie, fie, fie!
What dost thou, or what art thou, Angelo?
Dost thou desire her foully for those things
That make her good? O, let her brother live!
Thieves for their robbery have authority 176
When judges steal themselves. What, do I love
her,
That I desire to hear her speak again
And feast upon her eyes? What is't I dream on?
O cunning enemy, that, to catch a saint, 180
With saints dost bait thy hook! Most dangerous
Is that temptation that doth goad us on
To sin in loving virtue. Never could the strumpet,
With all her double vigour, art and nature,
Once stir my temper; but this virtuous maid
Subdues me quite. Ever till now, 186
When men were fond, I smil'd and wond'red how.
[*Exit.*]

Questions and Assignments

1. In line 16, Angelo, the judge, gives orders regarding the pregnant Juliet, Claudio's "partner in crime." What do you learn of his character from these and other words that he uses?

2. What analogy does Isabella draw in lines 73-79? How does it effect Angelo's premises and how does it forward Isabella's argument?

3. What, in your own words, is Isabella saying in lines 126-141?

4. Compare Angelo's words in lines 38-41 with his last speech in lines 162-187. What change has taken place and how does it effect Angelo's attitude toward justice and mercy?

5. How does Angelo's original premise differ from Isabella's and why is he finally convinced? Which one of them is more logical and why?

6. Compare this selection with those by Dostoyevsky and Russell. Are there any similarities?

7. Imagine yourself in Isabella's position and your brother or sister in jail. Write an argument to show why he or she should not be punished for the crime committed. Your argument will, of course, depend upon the particular law which has been broken, such as robbery, speeding, assault and battery, murder, forgery.

8. Reread Russell's essay and then write a theme defending Angelo's original point of view—that by enforcing this law others will be deterred from similar behavior. Or write a theme explaining why Angelo is wrong. Or write a theme showing how both justice and mercy could be obtained by some other solution than either Angelo's or Isabella's.

My Last Duchess

ROBERT BROWNING

That's my last Duchess painted on the wall,
Looking as if she were alive. I call
That piece a wonder, now: Frà Pandolf's hands
Worked busily a day, and there she stands.
Will't please you sit and look at her? I said
"Frà Pandolf" by design, for never read
Strangers like you that pictured countenance,
The depth and passion of its earnest glance,
But to myself they turned (since none puts by
The curtain I have drawn for you, but I)

And seemed as they would ask me, if they durst,
How such a glance came there; so, not the first
Are you to turn and ask thus. Sir, 'twas not
Her husband's presence only, called that spot
Of joy into the Duchess' cheek: perhaps
Frà Pandolf chanced to say "Her mantle laps
Over my lady's wrist too much," or "Paint
Must never hope to reproduce the faint
Half-flush that dies along her throat:" such stuff
Was courtesy, she thought, and cause enough
For calling up that spot of joy. She had
A heart—how shall I say?—too soon made glad,
Too easily impressed; she liked whate'er
She looked on, and her looks went everywhere.
Sir, twas all one! My favor at her breast,
The dropping of the daylight in the West,
The bough of cherries some officious fool
Broke in the orchard for her, the white mule
She rode with round the terrace—all and each
Would draw from her alike the approving speech,
Or blush, at least. She thanked me,—good! but thanked
Somehow—I know not how—as if she ranked
My gift of a nine-hundred-years-old name
With anybody's gift. Who'd stoop to blame
This sort of trifling? Even had you skill
In speech—(which I have not)—to make your will
Quite clear to such an one, and say, "Just this
Or that in you disgusts me; here you miss,
Or there exceed the mark"—and if she let
Herself be lessoned so, nor plainly set
Her wits to yours, forsooth, and made excuse,
—E'en then would be some stooping; and I choose
Never to stoop. Oh sir, she smiled, no doubt,
Whene'er I passed her; but who passed without
Much the same smile? This grew; I gave commands;
Then all smiles stopped together. There she stands
As if alive. Will't please you rise? We'll meet
The company below, then. I repeat,

The Count your master's known munificence
Is ample warrant that no just pretence
Of mine for dowry will be disallowed;
Though his fair daughter's self, as I avowed
At starting, is my object. Nay, we'll go
Together down, sir. Notice Neptune, though,
Taming a sea-horse, thought a rarity,
Which Claus of Innsbruck cast in bronze for me!

Questions and Assignments

1. This poem is a dramatic monologue with only one speaker, who obviously assumes the complete agreement and submission of his listener. How then can you perceive the author's point of view? And the listener's?

2. What ironic devices appear in the last eight lines of the poem and why are they so effective? Find other examples of irony in the poem.

3. What is the significance within the poem of the words, "Nay, we'll go/ Together down, sir."?

4. In what way does the irony of the whole poem depend upon the basic premises of the speaker, the listener, and the reader? If you accept the Duke's premise, is his argument logical?

5. Compare the theme of this poem with the selections by Dostoyevsky, Russell, and Shakespeare.

6. Write a brief essay explaining the behavior (real or imaginary) of yourself or someone you know. Choose a subject like "Running away from home," "Breaking my sister's doll," "Cheating on exams," "Speeding on highways," "Torturing cats," "Avoiding work," "Getting rid of roommates." Decide on your basic premise and argue accordingly. Consider whether you want to sound serious (as in "My Last Duchess") or humorous, and then be careful to choose your examples and maintain your tone.

War

LUIGI PIRANDELLO

The passengers who had left Rome by the night express had had to stop until dawn at the small station of Fabriano in order to continue their journey by the small old-fashioned local joining the main line with Sulmona.

At dawn, in a stuffy and smoky second-class carriage in which five people had already spent the night, a bulky woman in deep mourning was hoisted in—almost like a shapeless bundle. Behind her—puffing and moaning, followed her husband—a tiny man, thin and weakly, his face death-white, his eyes small and bright and looking shy and uneasy.

Having at last taken a seat he politely thanked the passengers who had helped his wife and who had made room for her; then he turned round to the woman trying to pull down the collar of her coat, and politely inquired:

"Are you all right, dear?"

The wife, instead of answering, pulled up her collar again to her eyes, so as to hide her face.

"Nasty world," muttered the husband with a sad smile.

And he felt it his duty to explain to his traveling companions that the poor woman was to be pitied for the war was taking away from her her only son, a boy of twenty to whom both had devoted their entire life, even breaking up their home at Sulmona to follow him to Rome, where he had to go as a student, then allowing him to volunteer for war with an assurance, however, that at least for six months he would not be sent to the front and now, all of a sudden, receiving a wire saying that he was due to leave in three days' time and asking them to go and see him off.

The woman under the big coat was twisting and wriggling, at times growling like a wild animal, feeling certain that all those explanations would not have aroused even a shadow of sympathy from those people who —most likely—were in the same plight as herself. One of them, who had been listening with particular attention, said:

"You should thank God that your son is only leaving now for the front. Mine has been there since the first day of the war. He has already come back twice wounded and been sent back again to the front."

"What about me? I have two sons and three nephews at the front," said another passenger.

"Maybe, but in our case it is our *only* son," ventured the husband.

"What difference can it make? You may spoil your only son with excessive attentions, but you cannot love him more than you would all your other children if you had any. Paternal love is not like bread that can be broken into pieces and split amongst the children in equal shares. A father gives *all* his love to each one of his children without discrimination, whether it be one or ten, and if I am suffering now for my two sons, I am not suffering half for each of them but double . . ."

"True . . . true . . ." sighed the embarrassed husband, "but suppose (of course we all hope it will never be your case) a father has two sons at the front and he loses one of them, there is still one left to console him . . . while . . ."

"Yes," answered the other, getting cross, "a son left to console him but also a son left for whom he must survive, while in the case of the father of an only son if the son dies the father can die too and put an end to his distress. Which of the two positions is the worse? Don't you see how my case would be worse than yours?

"Nonsense," interrupted another traveler, a fat, red-faced man with bloodshot eyes of the palest gray.

He was panting. From his bulging eyes seemed to spurt inner violence of an uncontrolled vitality which his weakened body could hardly contain.

"Nonsense," he repeated, trying to cover his mouth with his hand so as to hide the two missing front teeth. "Nonsense. Do we give life to our children for our own benefit?"

The other travelers stared at him in distress. The one who had had his son at the front since the first day of the war sighed: "You are right. Our children do not belong to us, they belong to the Country. . . ."

"Bosh," retorted the fat traveler. "Do we think of the Country when we give life to our children? Our sons are born because . . . well, because they must be born and when they come to life they take our own life with them. This is the truth. We belong to them but they never belong to us. And when they reach twenty they are exactly what we were at their age. We too had a father and mother, but there were so many other things as well . . . girls, cigarettes, illusions, new ties . . . and the Country, of course, whose call we would have answered—when we were twenty—even if father and mother had said no. Now at our age, the love of our Country is still great, of course, but stronger than it is the love for our children. Is there any one of us here who wouldn't gladly take his son's place at the front if he could?"

There was a silence all round, everybody nodding as to approve.

"Why then," continued the fat man, "shouldn't we consider the feelings of our children when they are twenty? Isn't it natural that at their age they should consider the love for their Country (I am speaking of decent boys, of course) even greater than the love for us? Isn't it natural that it should be so, as after all they must look upon us as upon old boys who cannot move any more and must stay at home? If Country exists, if Country is a natural necessity, like bread, of which each of us must eat in order not to die of hunger, somebody must go to defend it. And our sons go, when they are twenty, and they don't want tears, because if they die, they die inflamed and happy (I am speaking, of course, of decent boys). Now, if one dies young and happy, without having the ugly sides of life, the boredom of it, the pettiness, the bitterness of disillusion . . . what more can we ask for him? Everyone should stop crying; everyone should laugh, as I do . . . or at least thank God—as I do—because my son, before dying, sent me a message saying that he was dying satisfied at having ended his life in the best way he could have wished. That is why, as you see, I do not even wear mourning. . . ."

He shook his light fawn coat as to show it; his livid lip over his missing teeth was trembling, his eyes were watery and motionless, and soon after he ended with a shrill laugh which might well have been a sob.

"Quite so . . . quite so . . ." agreed the others.

The woman who, bundled in a corner under her coat, had been sitting and listening had—for the last three months—tried to find in the words of her husband and her friends something to console her in her deep sorrow, something that might show her how a mother should resign herself to send her son not even to death but to a probably dangerous life. Yet not a word had she found amongst the many which had been said . . . and her grief had been greater in seeing that nobody—as she thought—could share her feelings.

But now the words of the traveler amazed and almost stunned her. She suddenly realized that it wasn't the others who were wrong and could not understand her but herself who could not rise up to the same height of those fathers and mothers willing to resign themselves, without crying, not only to the departure of their sons but even to their death.

She lifted her head, she bent over from her corner trying to listen with great attention to the details which the fat man was giving to his companions about the way his son had fallen as a hero, for his King and his Country, happy and without regrets. It seemed to her that she had stumbled into a world she had never dreamt of, a world so far unknown to her and she was so pleased to hear everyone joining in congratulating that brave father who could so stoically speak of his child's death.

Then suddenly, just as if she had heard nothing of what had been said and almost as if waking up from a dream, she turned to the old man, asking him:

"Then . . . is your son really dead?"

Everybody stared at her. The old man, too, turned to look at her, fixing his great, bulging, horribly watery light gray eyes, deep in her face. For some little time he tried to answer, but words failed him. He looked and looked at her, almost as if only then—at that silly, incongruous question—he had suddenly realized at last that his son was really dead—gone for ever—for ever. His face contracted, became horribly distorted, then he snatched in haste a handkerchief from his pocket and, to the amazement of everyone, broke into harrowing, heart-rending, uncontrollable sobs.

Questions and Assignments

1. Despite its brevity, this story's theme may be said to be the meaning of love and grief. The author's premises and conclusion are only implied. Can you state the theme of this story in your own words?

2. Each of the three men—the husband and the two other travelers—has certain premises from which he tries to reason logically. What are they?

3. In what way does the fat traveler's argument differ from the other two? Why is the woman so impressed? What effect does her question and his reaction have on his argument?

4. Why is it significant that the woman in this story is merely described to begin with and only speaks at the very end? After studying the behavior and thoughts of this woman, do you see any sort of logic in her position?

5. Choose one of the following as a premise and write an essay in its support:
   It's an unjust world (or a just world).
   An only child is more (or less) loved than several children.
   No one understands another's grief (or happiness).
   Children exist for the benefit of their parents.
   Parents exist for the benefit of their children.
   Family relationships are more (or less) important than patriotism.
   It is better (or worse) to die young.

Inferences and Conclusions

To infer means to reason or to come to a conclusion. By inferring we endeavor to move from unknowing to knowing, from confusion to understanding. Inference involves the drawing together of miscellaneous facts into a unity and also involves carrying out ideas to their logical ends. The simplest example to begin with—if a person were to return from a vacation and find his neighbor's house a charred ruin, he would infer that the house had been destroyed by fire. His mind would have instinctively sought to understand what he did not know by applying what he had learned from experience—that charred ruins indicate fire.

Our ability to make complicated inferences depends directly upon the knowledge we bring to new situations. Most of us would not be content to know that our neighbor's house had burned down. We would want to know the circumstances: Was anyone injured? Was the house insured? For how much? Where is the owner now? Does he plan to rebuild?

In order to answer these and related questions we could observe the condition of the house, we could gather information by talking to witnesses and experts (of whom the owner would probably be the foremost), and we could find what general procedure has been followed in similar cases. As a neighbor, of course, our gathering of information and our inferences would be relatively uncomplicated. An identical process of acquiring knowledge and drawing inferences, but on a much more complicated basis, might be followed by a fire marshal or an insurance investigator.

For the sake of clarity, logicians have divided inferences into two general classes: inductive inferences and deductive inferences. A close rereading of "Persuasion by Logical Argument" (pages 390-404) should clarify the specific uses and pitfalls involved in logical inferences. A brief summary may be of assistance. Inductive reasoning is of three kinds—inferences based on a number of particular instances, inferences based on an analogy, and inferences based on cause and effect. In the first type we must be aware of hasty generalizations, in the second of false analogies, and in the third of the *post hoc ergo propter hoc* fallacy. Deductive reasoning relates what we know about general principles to particular instances, or what we know about a class to members of that class. Here again there are two frequent errors. The general principle may not be accurate (we may be uninformed or misinformed about material in one of the premises), or we may be making unjustifiable inferences based on our first principle. This last error is particularly common. Take a statement such as this: "Because every Communist is pro-labor, no good American is pro-labor." Put into syllogistic form the statement would run: "Every Communist is pro-labor/ No good

American is a Communist/ Therefore no good American is pro-labor." If we think about the premise carefully, we should realize that being pro-labor is not a total definition of being a Communist. Communism has many other characteristics and there are many people who are pro-labor but who do not share those other characteristics. Therefore the inference made in the original statement is unjustifiable.

It is not necessary to put statements into syllogistic form in order to spot fallacies in reasoning. It is necessary only to determine precisely what is being said. This is what the reader should do in the following six essays. That is to say, as we have said several times before, the reader must determine the organizing principle of the selection. Once he knows exactly what the writer is saying, he must trace out the means used to support the ideas, that is, what is the premise, what conclusions are drawn from that premise, what arguments, what evidence, causes, examples, precedents, are cited to bolster the contentions.

The first three essays in this unit are concerned with capital punishment. We begin with a brief, straightforward statement on the subject by a law enforcement official, J. Edgar Hoover. Next, Jacques Barzun, Dean of Faculties and Provost of Columbia University, expresses an opinion similar to Hoover's. Barzun's is an essay, not a memorandum, and it therefore presents the case in favor of capital punishment in much greater detail. The third essay, opposing capital punishment, was written by a noted psychiatrist, Dr. Karl Menninger.

These three essays are followed by two selections which deal with the pressure for conformity in modern society. The first one, by Professor Morris, co-ordinator of Teacher Education at Douglass College, Rutgers University, discusses the current emphasis on adjustment and respectability in the education and guidance of students. The second, by Professor Kirk, a philosopher and essayist, describes the pressures on professors to "adjust" their principles regarding intellectual standards.

The unit concludes with a provocative essay on democracy by George Bernard Shaw.

A Memorandum on Capital Punishment

J. EDGAR HOOVER

The following is not an argument in the formal sense of the term. It is a special directive, or memorandum, issued to all law enforcement officials by the director of the Federal Bureau of Investigation.

The question of capital punishment has sent a storm of controversy thundering across our Nation—millions of spoken and written words seek to examine the question so that decisions may be reached which befit our civilization.

The struggle for answers concerning the taking of men's lives is one to which every American should lend his voice, for the problem in a democracy such as ours is not one for a handful of men to solve alone.

As a representative of law enforcement, it is my belief that a great many of the most vociferous cries for abolition of capital punishment emanate from those areas of our society which have been insulated against the horrors man can and does perpetrate against his fellow beings. Certainly, penetrative and searching thought must be given before considering any blanket cessation of capital punishment in a time when unspeakable crimes are being committed. The savagely mutilated bodies and mentally ravaged victims of murderers, rapists and other criminal beasts beg consideration when the evidence is weighed on both sides of the scales of Justice.

At the same time, nothing is so precious in our country as the life of a human being, whether he is a criminal or not, and on the other side of the scales must be placed all of the legal safeguards which our society demands.

Experience has clearly demonstrated, however, that the time-proven deterrents to crime are sure detection, swift apprehension, and proper punishment. Each is a necessary ingredient. Law-abiding citizens have a right to expect that the efforts of law enforcement officers in detecting and apprehending criminals will be followed by realistic punishment.

It is my opinion that when no shadow of a doubt remains relative to

From the *FBI Law Enforcement Bulletin,* June 1960. Reprinted by permission.

the guilt of a defendant, the public interest demands capital punishment be invoked where the law so provides.

Who, in all good conscience, can say that Julius and Ethel Rosenberg, the spies who delivered the secret of the atomic bomb into the hands of the Soviets, should have been spared when their treachery caused the shadow of annihilation to fall upon all of the world's peoples? What place would there have been in civilization for these two who went to their deaths unrepentant, unwilling to the last to help their own country and their own fellow men? What would have been the chances of rehabilitating Jack Gilbert Graham, who placed a bomb in his own mother's luggage and blasted her and 43 other innocent victims into oblivion as they rode an airliner across a peaceful sky?

A judge once said, "The death penalty is a warning, just like a lighthouse throwing its beams out to sea. We hear about shipwrecks, but we do not hear about the ships the lighthouse guides safely on their way. We do not have proof of the number of ships it saves, but we do not tear the lighthouse down."

Despicable crimes must be dealt with realistically. To abolish the death penalty would absolve other Rosenbergs and Grahams from fear of the consequences for committing atrocious crimes. Where the death penalty is provided, a criminal's punishment may be meted out commensurate with his deeds. While a Power transcending man is the final Judge, this same Power gave man reason so that he might protect himself. Capital punishment is an instrument with which he may guard the righteous against the predators among men.

We must never allow misguided compassion to erase our concern for the hundreds of unfortunate, innocent victims of bestial criminals.

Questions and Assignments

1. In what way do the adjectives used whenever Hoover refers to crime and criminals help to reveal the premise of his argument? Is the tone of this argument emotional or rational or both?

2. Consider the diction of the fourth paragraph, especially the phrase "at the same time" and the conjunction "and."

3. Where and how well does this selection handle the arguments of the opposition?

4. Hoover uses the analogy of the scale to make a distinction and to provide a proof. Does he weight the scales in any way?

5. What is Hoover's assumption about the reliability of our investigative and judicial processes? What connection does Hoover assume between the guilt of a defendant and the fact that he has been arrested or indicted or convicted? How valid is the analogy between the death penalty and the lighthouse? What substantiation does Hoover provide for his evidence?

6. Write your own argument for or against capital punishment on the basis of this selection and your own knowledge. Do not read the next two essays yet.

In Favor of Capital Punishment

JACQUES BARZUN

A passing remark of mine in the *Mid-Century* magazine has brought me a number of letters and a sheaf of pamphlets against capital punishment. The letters, sad and reproachful, offer me the choice of pleading ignorance or being proved insensitive. I am asked whether I know that there exists a worldwide movement for the abolition of capital punishment which has everywhere enlisted able men of every profession, including the law. I am told that the death penalty is not only inhuman but also unscientific, for rapists and murderers are really sick people who should be cured, not killed. I am invited to use my imagination and acknowledge the unbearable horror of every form of execution.

I am indeed aware that the movement for abolition is widespread and articulate, especially in England. It is headed there by my old friend and publisher, Mr. Victor Gollancz, and it numbers such well-known writers as Arthur Koestler, C. H. Rolph, James Avery Joyce and Sir John Barry. Abroad as at home the profession of psychiatry tends to support the cure principle, and many liberal newspapers, such as the *Observer,* are committed to abolition. In the United States there are at least twenty-five state leagues working to the same end, plus a national league and several church councils, notably the Quaker and the Episcopal.

The assemblage of so much talent and enlightened goodwill behind a single proposal must give pause to anyone who supports the other side, and in the attempt to make clear my views, which are now close to unpopular, I start out by granting that my conclusion is arguable; that is, I am still open to conviction, *provided* some fallacies and frivolities in the abolitionist argument are first disposed of and the difficulties not ignored but overcome. I should be glad to see this happen, not only because there is pleasure in the spectacle of an airtight case, but also because I am not more sanguinary than my neighbor and I should welcome the discovery of safeguards—for society *and* the criminal—other than killing. But I say it again, these safeguards must really meet, not evade or postpone, the difficulties I am about to describe. Let me add before I begin that I shall probably not answer any more letters on this arousing subject. If this printed exposition does not do justice to my cause, it is not likely that I can do better in the hurry of private correspondence.

I readily concede at the outset that present ways of dealing out capital punishment are as revolting as Mr. Koestler says in his harrowing volume, *Hanged by the Neck.* Like many of our prisons, our modes of execution should change. But this objection to barbarity does not mean that capital punishment—or rather, judicial homicide—should not go on. The illicit jump we find here, on the threshold of the inquiry, is characteristic of the abolitionist and must be disallowed at every point. Let us bear in mind the possibility of devising a painless, sudden and dignified death, and see whether its administration is justifiable.

The four main arguments advanced against the death penalty are: *1.* punishment for crime is a primitive idea rooted in revenge; *2.* capital punishment does not deter; *3.* judicial error being possible, taking life is an appalling risk; *4.* a civilized state, to deserve its name, must uphold, not violate, the sanctity of human life.

I entirely agree with the first pair of propositions, which is why, a moment ago, I replaced the term capital punishment with "judicial homicide." The uncontrollable brute whom I want put out of the way is not to be punished for his misdeeds, nor used as an example or a warning; he is to be killed for the protection of others, like the wolf that escaped not long ago in a Connecticut suburb. No anger, vindictiveness or moral conceit need preside over the removal of such dangers. But a man's inability to control his violent impulses or to imagine the fatal consequences of his acts should be a presumptive reason for his elimination from society. This generality covers drunken driving and teen-age racing on public highways, as well as incurable obsessive violence; it might be extended (as I shall suggest later) to other acts that destroy, precisely, the moral basis of civilization.

But why kill? I am ready to believe the statistics tending to show that the prospect of his own death does not stop the murderer. For one thing he is often a blind egotist, who cannot conceive the possibility of his own death. For another, detection would have to be infallible to deter the more imaginative who, although afraid, think they can escape discovery. Lastly, as Shaw long ago pointed out, hanging the wrong man will deter as effectively as hanging the right one. So, once again, why kill? If I agree that moral progress means an increasing respect for human life, how can I oppose abolition?

I do so because on this subject of human life, which is to me the heart of the controversy, I find the abolitionist inconsistent, narrow or blind. The propaganda for abolition speaks in hushed tones of the sanctity of human life, as if the mere statement of it as an absolute should silence all opponents who have any moral sense. But most of the abolitionists belong to nations that spend half their annual income on weapons of war and that honor research to perfect means of killing. These good people vote without a qualm for the political parties that quite sensibly arm their country to the teeth. The West today does not seem to be the time or place to invoke the absolute sanctity of human life. As for the clergymen in the movement, we may be sure from the experience of two previous world wars that they will bless our arms and pray for victory when called upon, the sixth commandment notwithstanding.

"Oh, but we mean the sanctity of life *within* the nation!" Very well: is the movement then campaigning also against the principle of self-defense? Absolute sanctity means letting the cutthroat have his sweet will of you, even if you have a poker handy to bash him with, for you might kill. And again, do we hear any protest against the police firing at criminals on the street—mere bank robbers usually—and doing this, often enough, with an excited marksmanship that misses the artist and hits the bystander? The absolute sanctity of human life is, for the abolitionist, a slogan rather than a considered proposition.

Yet it deserves examination, for upon our acceptance or rejection of it depend such other highly civilized possibilities as euthanasia and seemly suicide. The inquiring mind also wants to know, why the sanctity of *human* life alone? My tastes do not run to household pets, but I find something less than admirable in the uses to which we put animals—in zoos, laboratories and space machines—without the excuse of the ancient law, "Eat or be eaten."

It should moreover be borne in mind that this argument about sanctity applies—or would apply—to about ten persons a year in Great Britain and to between fifty and seventy-five in the United States. These are the average numbers of those executed in recent years. The count by itself should not, of course, affect our judgment of the principle: one life spared or forfeited is as important, morally, as a hundred thousand. But it should inspire a comparative judgment: there are hundreds and indeed thousands whom, in our concern with the horrors of execution, we forget: on the one hand, the victims of violence; on the other, the prisoners in our jails.

The victims are easy to forget. Social science tends steadily to mark a preference for the troubled, the abnormal, the problem case. Whether it is poverty, mental disorder, delinquency or crime, the "patient material" monopolizes the interest of increasing groups of people among the most generous and learned. Psychiatry and moral liberalism go together; the application of law as we have known it is thus coming to be regarded as an historic prelude to social work, which may replace it entirely. Modern literature makes the most of this same outlook, caring only for the disturbed spirit, scorning as bourgeois those who pay their way and do *not* stab their friends. All the while the determinism of natural science reinforces the assumption that society causes its own evils. A French jurist, for example, says that in order to understand crime we must first brush aside all ideas of Responsibility. He means the criminal's and takes for granted that of society. The murderer kills because reared in a broken home or, conversely, because at an early age he witnessed his parents making love. Out of such cases, which make pathetic reading in the literature of modern criminology, is born the abolitionist's state of mind: we dare not kill those we are beginning to understand so well.

If, moreover, we turn to the accounts of the crimes committed by these unfortunates, who are the victims? Only dull ordinary people going about their business. We are sorry, of course, but they do not interest science on its march. Balancing, for example, the sixty to seventy criminals executed annually in the United States, there were the seventy to eighty housewives whom George Cvek robbed, raped and usually killed during the months of a career devoted to proving his virility. "It is too bad." Cvek alone seems instructive, even though one of the law officers who helped track him down quietly remarks: "As to the extent that his villainies disturbed family relationships, or how many women are still haunted by the specter of an experience they have never disclosed to another living soul, these questions can only lend themselves to sterile conjecture."

The remote results are beyond our ken, but it is not idle to speculate about those whose death by violence fills the daily two inches at the back of respectable newspapers—the old man sunning himself on a park bench and beaten to death by four hoodlums, the small children abused and strangled, the middle-aged ladies on a hike assaulted and killed, the family terrorized by a released or escaped lunatic, the half-dozen working people massacred by the sudden maniac, the boatload of persons dispatched by the skipper, the mindless assaults upon schoolteachers and shopkeepers by the increasing horde of dedicated killers in our great cities. Where does the sanctity of life begin?

It is all very well to say that many of these killers are themselves "children," that is, minors. Doubtless a nine-year-old mind is housed in that 150 pounds of unguided muscle. Grant, for argument's sake, that the misdeed is "the fault of society," trot out the broken home and the slum environment. The question then is, What shall we do, not in the Utopian city of tomorrow, but here and now? The "scientific" means of cure are more than uncertain. The apparatus of detention only increases the killer's antisocial animus. Reformatories and mental hospitals are full and have an understandable bias toward discharging their inmates. Some of these are indeed "cured"—so long as they stay under a rule. The stress of the social free-for-all throws them back on their violent modes of self-expression. At that point I agree that society has failed—twice: it has twice failed the victims, whatever may be its guilt toward the killer.

As in all great questions, the moralist must choose, and choosing has a price. I happen to think that if a person of adult body has not been endowed with adequate controls against irrationally taking the life of another, that person must be judicially, painlessly, regretfully killed before that mindless body's horrible automation repeats.

I say "irrationally" taking life, because it is often possible to feel great sympathy with a murderer. Certain *crimes passionnels* can be forgiven without being condoned. Blackmailers invite direct retribution. Long provocation can be an excuse, as in that engaging case of some years ago, in which a respectable carpenter of seventy found he could no longer stand the incessant nagging of his wife. While she excoriated him from her throne in the kitchen—a daily exercise for fifty years—the husband went to his bench and came back with a hammer in each hand to settle the score. The testimony to his character, coupled with the sincerity implied by the two hammers, was enough to have him sent into quiet and brief seclusion.

But what are we to say of the type of motive disclosed in a journal published by the inmates of one of our Federal penitentiaries? The author is a bank robber who confesses that money is not his object:

> My mania for power, socially, sexually, and otherwise can feel no degree of satisfaction until I feel sure I have struck the ultimate of submission and terror in the minds and bodies of my victims. . . . It's very difficult to explain all the queer fascinating sensations pounding and surging through me while I'm holding a gun on a victim, watching his body tremble and sweat. . . . This is the moment when all the rationalized hypocrisies of civilization are suddenly swept away and two men stand there facing each other morally and ethically naked, and right and wrong are the absolute commands of the man behind the gun.

This confused echo of modern literature and modern science defines the choice before us. Anything deserving the name of cure for such a man presupposes not only a laborious individual psychoanalysis, with the means to conduct and to sustain it, socially and economically, but also a re-education of the mind, so as to throw into correct perspective the garbled ideas of Freud and Nietzsche, Gide and Dostoevski, which this power-seeker and his fellows have derived from the culture and temper of our times. Ideas are tenacious and give continuity to emotion. Failing a second birth of heart and mind, we must ask: How soon will this sufferer sacrifice a bank clerk in the interests of making civilization less hypocritical? And we must certainly question the wisdom of affording him more than one chance. The abolitionists' advocacy of an unconditional "let live" is in truth part of the same cultural tendency that animates the killer. The Western peoples' revulsion from power in domestic and foreign policy has made of the state a sort of counterpart of the bank robber: both having power and neither knowing how to use it. Both waste lives because hypnotized by irrelevant ideas and crippled by contradictory emotions. If psychiatry were sure of its ground in diagnosing the individual case, a philosopher might consider whether such dangerous obsessions should not be guarded against by judicial homicide *before* the shooting starts.

I raise the question not indeed to recommend the prophylactic execution of potential murderers, but to introduce the last two perplexities that the abolitionists dwarf or obscure by their concentration on changing an isolated penalty. One of these is the scale by which to judge the offenses society wants to repress. I can for example imagine a truly democratic state in which it would be deemed a form of treason punishable by death to create a disturbance in any court or deliberative assembly. The aim would be to recognize the sanctity of orderly discourse in arriving at justice, assessing criticism and defining policy. Under such a law, a natural selection would operate to remove permanently from the scene persons who, let us say, neglect argument in favor of banging on the desk with their shoe. Similarly, a bullying minority in a diet, parliament or skupshtina would be prosecuted for treason to the most sacred institutions when fists or flying inkwells replace rhetoric. That the mere suggestion of such a law sounds ludicrous shows how remote we are from civilized institutions, and hence how gradual should be our departure from the severity of judicial homicide.

I say gradual and I do not mean standing still. For there is one form of barbarity in our law that I want to see mitigated before any other. I mean imprisonment. The enemies of capital punishment—and liberals generally—seem to be satisfied with any legal outcome so long as they themselves avoid the vicarious guilt of shedding blood. They speak of the sanctity of life, but have no concern with its quality. They give no impression of ever having read what it is certain they have read, from Wilde's *De Profundis* to the latest account of prison life by a convicted homosexual. Despite the infamy of concentration camps, despite Mr. Charles Burney's remarkable work, *Solitary Confinement,* despite riots in prisons, despite the round of escape, recapture and return in chains, the abolitionists' imagination tells them nothing about the reality of being caged. They read without a qualm, indeed they read with rejoicing, the hideous irony of "Killer Gets Life"; they sigh with relief instead of horror. They do not see and suffer the cell, the drill, the clothes, the stench, the food; they do not feel the sexual racking of young and old bodies, the hateful promiscuity, the insane monotony, the mass degradation, the impotent hatred. They do not remember from Silvio Pellico that only a strong political faith, with a hope of final victory, can steel a man to endure long detention. They forget that Joan of Arc, when offered "life," preferred burning at the stake. Quite of another mind, the abolitionists point with pride to the "model prisoners" that murderers often turn out to be. As if a model prisoner were not, first, a contradiction in terms, and second, an exemplar of what a free society should not want.

I said a moment ago that the happy advocates of the life sentence appear not to have understood what we know they have read. No more do they appear to read what they themselves write. In the preface to his useful volume of cases, *Hanged in Error,* Mr. Leslie Hale, M.P., refers to the tardy recognition of a minor miscarriage of justice—one year in jail: "The prisoner emerged to find that his wife had died and that his children and his aged parents had been removed to the workhouse. By the time a small payment had been assessed as 'compensation' the victim was incurably insane." So far we are as indignant with the law as Mr. Hale. But what comes next? He cites the famous Evans case, in which it is very probable that the wrong man was hanged, and he exclaims: "While such mistakes are possible, should society impose an irrevocable sentence?" Does Mr. Hale really ask us to believe that the sentence passed on the first man, whose wife died and who went insane, was in any sense *revocable?* Would not any man rather be Evans dead than that other wretch "emerging" with his small compensation and his reasons for living gone?

Nothing is revocable here below, imprisonment least of all. The agony of a trial itself is punishment, and acquittal wipes out nothing. Read the heart-rending diary of William Wallace, accused quite implausibly of having murdered his wife and "saved" by the Court of Criminal Appeals—but saved for what? British ostracism by everyone and a few years of solitary despair. The cases of Adolf Beck, of Oscar Slater, of the unhappy Brooklyn bank teller who vaguely resembled a forger and spent eight years in Sing Sing only to "emerge" a broken, friendless, useless, "compensated" man—all these, if the dignity of the individual has any meaning, had better have been dead before the prison door ever opened for them. This is what counsel always says to the jury in the course of a murder trial and counsel is right: far better hang this man than "give him life." For my part, I would choose death without hesitation. If that option is abolished, a demand will one day be heard to claim it as a privilege in the name of human dignity. I shall believe in the abolitionist's present views only after he has emerged from twelve months in a convict cell.

The detached observer may want to interrupt here and say that the argument has now passed from reasoning to emotional preference. Whereas the objector to capital punishment *feels* that death is the greatest of evils, I *feel* that imprisonment is worse than death. A moment's thought will show that feeling is the appropriate arbiter. All reasoning about what is right, civilized and moral rests upon sentiment, like mathematics. Only, in trying to persuade others, it is important to single out the fundamental feeling, the prime intuition, and from it to reason justly. In my view, to profess respect for human life and be willing to see it spent in a penitentiary is to entertain liberal feelings frivolously. To oppose the death penalty because, unlike a prison term, it is irrevocable is to argue fallaciously.

In the propaganda for abolishing the death sentence the recital of numerous miscarriages of justice commits the same error and implies the same callousness: what is at fault in our present system is not the sentence but the fallible procedure. Capital cases being one in a thousand or more, who can be cheerful at the thought of all the "revocable" errors? What the miscarriages point to is the need for reforming the jury system, the rules of evidence, the customs of prosecution, the machinery of appeal. The failure to see that this is the great task reflects the sentimentality I spoke of earlier, that which responds chiefly to the excitement of the unusual. A writer on Death and the Supreme Court is at pains to point out that when that tribunal reviews a capital case, the judges are particularly anxious and careful. What a left-handed compliment to the highest judicial conscience of the country! Fortunately, some of the champions of the misjudged see the issue more clearly. Many of those who are thought wrongly convicted now languish in jail because the jury was uncertain or because a doubting governor commuted the death sentence. Thus Dr. Samuel H. Sheppard, Jr., convicted of his wife's murder in the second degree is serving a sentence that is supposed to run for the term of his natural life. The story of his numerous trials, as told by Mr. Paul Holmes, suggests that police incompetence, newspaper demagogy, public envy of affluence and the mischances of legal procedure fashioned the result. But Dr. Sheppard's vindicator is under no illusion as to the conditions that this "lucky" evader of the electric chair will face if he is granted parole after ten years: "It will carry with it no right to resume his life as a physician. His privilege to practice medicine was blotted out with his conviction. He must all his life bear the stigma of a parolee, subject to unceremonious return to confinement for life for the slightest misstep. More than this, he must live out his life as a convicted murderer."

What does the moral conscience of today think it is doing? If such a man is a dangerous repeater of violent acts, what right has the state to let him loose after ten years? What is, in fact, the meaning of a "life sentence" that peters out long before life? Paroling looks suspiciously like an expression of social remorse for the pain of incarceration, coupled with a wish to avoid "unfavorable publicity" by freeing a suspect. The man is let out when the fuss has died down; which would mean that he was not under lock and key for our protection at all. He *was* being punished, just a little—for so prison seems in the abolitionist's distorted view, and in the jury's and the prosecutor's, whose "second-degree" murder suggests killing someone "just a little."[1]

If, on the other hand, execution and life imprisonment are judged too severe and the accused is expected to be harmless hereafter—punishment being ruled out as illiberal—what has society gained by wrecking his life and damaging that of his family?

What we accept, and what the abolitionist will clamp upon us all the more firmly if he succeeds, is an incoherence which is not remedied by the belief that second-degree murder merits a kind of second-degree death; that a doubt as to the identity of a killer is resolved by commuting real death into intolerable life; and that our ignorance whether a maniac will strike again can be hedged against by measuring "good behavior" within the gates and then releasing the subject upon the public in the true spirit of experimentation.

These are some of the thoughts I find I cannot escape when I read and reflect upon this grave subject. If, as I think, they are relevant to any discussion of change and reform, resting as they do on the direct and concrete perception of what happens, then the simple meliorists who expect to breathe a purer air by abolishing the death penalty are deceiving themselves and us. The issue is for the public to judge; but I for one shall not sleep easier for knowing that in England and America and the West generally a hundred more human beings are kept alive in degrading conditions to face a hopeles future; while others—possibly less conscious, certainly less controlled—benefit from a premature freedom dangerous alike to themselves and society. In short, I derive no comfort from the illusion that in giving up one manifest protection of the law-abiding, we who might well be in any of these three roles—victim, prisoner, licensed killer—have struck a blow for the sanctity of human life.

[1] The British Homicide Act of 1957, Section 2, implies the same reasoning in its definition of "diminished responsibility" for certain forms of mental abnormality. The whole question of irrationality and crime is in utter confusion, on both sides of the Atlantic.

Questions and Assignments

1. Why is this essay written in the familiar style of the first person? How does this relate to the author's conclusion that capital punishment is better than imprisonment?

2. Where and with what effect does Barzun use loaded words and phrases? Find his rhetorical questions and consider their effect on both the tone and the course of the argument.

3. Analyze the form and the function of the introduction.

4. Where and how does Barzun present the opposition argument? How does this presentation serve to limit and define what he has to say? Outline briefly the rest of his essay. Is this generally an argument by deduction? Explain why.

5. Is there any fallacy involved in discussing the sanctity of human life in terms of "absolute sanctity"? Barzun also uses an analogy involving the "sanctity of orderly discourse." Is this valid?

6. How well does Barzun substantiate his point of view regarding psychiatry and modern criminology? Compare with Menninger's essay to see where these two agree and disagree.

7. Barzun agrees and disagrees with Hoover on several points. Find where and how. How does Barzun deal with the possibility of judicial error?

8. Suggestions for writing follow the next essay by Menninger.

Verdict Guilty—Now What?

KARL MENNINGER, M.D.

Since ancient times criminal law and penology have been based upon what is called in psychology the pain-pleasure principle. There are many reasons for inflicting pain—to urge an animal to greater efforts, to retaliate for pain received, to frighten, or to indulge in idle amusement. Human beings, like all animals, tend to move away from pain and toward pleasure. Hence the way to control behavior is to reward what is "good" and punish what is "bad." This formula pervades our programs of child-rearing, education, and the social control of behavior.

With this concept three out of four readers will no doubt concur.

"Why, of course," they will say. "Only common sense. Take me for example. I know the speed limit and the penalty. Usually I drive moderately because I don't want to get a ticket. One afternoon I was in a hurry; I had an appointment, I didn't heed the signs. I did what I knew was forbidden and I got caught and received the punishment I deserved. Fair enough. It taught me a lesson. Since then I drive more slowly in that area. And surely people are deterred from cheating on their income taxes, robbing banks, and committing rape by the fear of punishment. Why, if we didn't have these crime road blocks we'd have chaos!"

This sounds reasonable enough and describes what most people think —*part of the time*. But upon reflection we all know that punishments and the threat of punishments do *not* deter *some* people from doing forbidden things. Some of them take a chance on not being caught, and this chance is a very good one, too, better than five to one for most crimes. Not even the fear of possible death, self-inflicted, deters some speedsters. Exceeding the speed limit is not really regarded as criminal behavior by most people, no matter how dangerous and self-destructive. It is the kind of a "crime" which respectable members of society commit and condone. This is not the case with rape, bank-robbing, check-forging, vandalism, and the multitude of offenses for which the prison penalty system primarily exists. And from these offenses the average citizen, including the reader, is deterred by quite different restraints. For most of us it is our conscience, our self-respect, and our wish for the good opinion of our neighbors which are the determining factors in controlling our impulses toward misbehavior.

Today it is no secret that our official, prison-threat theory of crime control is an utter failure. Criminologists have known this for years. When pocket-picking was punishable by hanging, in England, the crowds that gathered about the gallows to enjoy the spectacle of an execution were particularly likely to have their pockets picked by skillful operators who, to say the least, were not deterred by the exhibition of "justice." We have long known that the perpetrators of most offenses are never detected; of those detected, only a fraction are found guilty and still fewer serve a "sentence." Furthermore, we are quite certain now that of those who do receive the official punishment of the law, many become firmly committed thereby to a continuing life of crime and a continuing feud with law enforcement officers. Finding themselves ostracized from society and blacklisted by industry they stick with the crowd they have been introduced to in jail and try to play the game of life according to this set of rules. In this way society skillfully converts individuals of borderline self-control into loyal members of the underground fraternity.

The science of human behavior has gone far beyond the common sense rubrics which dictated the early legal statutes. We know now that one cannot describe rape or bank-robbing or income-tax fraud simply as pleasure. Nor, on the other hand, can we describe imprisonment merely as pain. Slapping the hand of a beloved child as he reaches to do a forbidden act is utterly different from the institutionalized process of official punishment. The offenders who are chucked into our county and state and federal prisons are not anyone's beloved children; they are usually unloved children, grown-up physically but still hungry for human concern which they never got or never get in normal ways. So they pursue it in abnormal ways—abnormal, that is, from *our* standpoint.

What might deter the reader from conduct which his neighbors would not like does not necessarily deter the grown-up child of vastly different background. The latter's experiences may have conditioned him to believe that the chances of winning by undetected cheating are vastly greater than the probabilities of fair treatment and opportunity. He knows about the official threats and the social disapproval of such acts. He knows about the hazards and the risks. But despite all this "knowledge," he becomes involved in waves of discouragement or cupidity or excitement or resentment leading to episodes of social offensiveness.

These episodes may prove vastly expensive both to him and to society. But sometimes they will have an aura of success. Our periodicals have only recently described the wealth and prominence for a time of a man described as a murderer. Konrad Lorenz, the great psychiatrist and animal psychologist, has beautifully described in geese what he calls a "triumph reaction." It is a sticking out of the chest and flapping of the wings after an encounter with a challenge. All of us have seen this primitive biological triumph reaction—in some roosters, for example, in some businessmen and athletes and others—*and* in some criminals.

In general, though, the gains and goals of the social offender are not those which most men seek. Most offenders whom we belabor are not very wise, not very smart, not even very "lucky." It is not the successful criminal upon whom we inflict our antiquated penal system. It is the unsuccessful criminal, the criminal who really doesn't know how to commit crimes, and who gets caught. Indeed, until he is caught and convicted a man is technically not even called a criminal. The clumsy, the desperate, the obscure, the friendless, the defective, the diseased—these men who commit crimes that do not come off—are bad actors, indeed. But they are not the professional criminals, many of whom occupy high places. In some instances the crime is the merest accident or incident or impulse, expressed under unbearable stress. More often the offender is a persistently perverse, lonely, and resentful individual who joins the only group to which he is eligible—the outcasts and the anti-social.

And what do we do with such offenders? After a solemn public ceremony we pronounce them enemies of the people, and consign them for arbitrary periods to institutional confinement on the basis of laws written many years ago. Here they languish until time has ground out so many weary months and years. Then with a planlessness and stupidity only surpassed by that of their original incarceration they are dumped back upon society, regardless of whether any change has taken place in them for the better and with every assurance that changes have taken place in them for the worse. Once more they enter the unequal tussle with society. Proscribed for employment by most concerns, they are expected to invent a new way to make a living and to survive without any further help from society.

Intelligent members of society are well aware that the present system is antiquated, expensive, and disappointing, and that we are wasting vast quantities of manpower through primitive methods of dealing with those who transgress the law. In 1917 the famous Wickersham report of the New York State Prison Survey Committee recommended the abolition of jails, the institution of diagnostic clearing houses or classification centers, the development of a diversified institutional system and treatment program, and the use of indeterminate sentences. *Forty-two years have passed.* How little progress we have made! In 1933 the American Psychiatric Association, the American Bar Association, and the American Medical Association officially and jointly recommended psychiatric service for every criminal and juvenile court to assist the court and prison and parole officers with all offenders.

That was twenty-six years ago! Have these recommendations been carried out anywhere in the United States? With few exceptions offenders continue to be dealt with according to old-time instructions, written by men now dead who knew nothing about the present offender, his past life, the misunderstandings accumulated by him, or the provocation given to him.

The sensible, scientific question is: What kind of treatment could be instituted that would deter him or be most likely to deter him? Some of these methods are well known. For some offenders who have the money or the skillful legal counsel or the good luck to face a wise judge go a different route from the prescribed routine. Instead of jail and deterioration, they get the sort of re-education and re-direction associated with psychiatric institutions and the psychiatric profession. Relatively few wealthy offenders get their "treatment" in jail. This does not mean that justice is to be bought, or bought off. But it does mean that some offenders have relatives and friends who *care* and who try to find the best possible solution to the problem of persistent misbehavior, which is NOT the good old jail-and-penitentiary and make-'em-sorry treatment. It is a reflection on the democratic ideals of our country that these better ways are so often—indeed, *usually*—denied to the poor, the friendless, and the ignorant.

If we were to follow scientific methods, the convicted offender would be detained indefinitely pending a decision as to whether and how and when to reintroduce him successfully into society. All the skill and knowledge of modern behavioral science would be used to examine his personality assets, his liabilities and potentialities, the environment from which he came, its effect upon him, and his effects upon it.

Having arrived at some diagnostic grasp of the offender's personality, those in charge can decide whether there is a chance that he can be redirected into a mutually satisfactory adaptation to the world. If so, the most suitable techniques in education, industrial training, group administration, and psychotherapy should be selectively applied. All this may be best done extramurally or intramurally. It may require maximum "security" or only minimum "security." If, in due time, perceptible change occurs, the process should be expedited by finding a suitable spot in society and industry for him, and getting him out of prison control and into civil status (with parole control) as quickly as possible.

The desirability of moving patients out of institutional control swiftly is something which we psychiatrists learned the hard way, and recently. Ten years ago, in the state hospital I know best, the average length of stay was five years; today it is three months. Ten years ago few patients were discharged under two years; today 90 per cent are discharged within the first year. Ten years ago the hospital was overcrowded; today it has eight times the turnover it used to have; there are empty beds and there is no waiting list.

But some patients do not respond to our efforts, and they have to remain in the hospital, or return to it promptly after a trial home visit. And if the *prisoner,* like some of the psychiatric patients, cannot be changed by genuine efforts to rehabilitate him, we must look *our* failure in the face, and provide for his indefinitely continued confinement, regardless of the technical reasons for it. This we owe society for its protection.

There will be some offenders about whom the most experienced are mistaken, both ways. And there will be some concerning whom no one knows what is best. There are many problems for research. But what I have outlined is, I believe, the program of modern penology, the program now being carried out in some degree in California and a few other states, and in some of the federal prisons.

This civilized program, which would save so much now wasted money, so much unused manpower, and so much injustice and suffering, is slow to spread. It is held back by many things—by the continued use of fixed sentences in many places; by unenlightened community attitudes toward the offender whom some want tortured; by the prevalent popular assumption that burying a frustrated individual in a hole for a short time will change his warped mind, and that when he is certainly worse, he should be released because his "time" has been served; by the persistent failure of the law to distinguish between crime as an accidental, incidental, explosive event, crime as a behavior pattern expressive of chronic unutterable rage and frustration, and crime as a business or elected way of life. Progress is further handicapped by the lack of interest in the subject on the part of lawyers, most of whom are proud to say that they are not concerned with criminal law. It is handicapped by the lack of interest on the part of members of my own profession. It is handicapped by the mutual distrust of lawyers and psychiatrists.

The infestation or devil-possession theory of mental disease is an outmoded, pre-medieval concept. Although largely abandoned by psychiatry, it steadfastly persists in the minds of many laymen, including, unfortunately, many lawyers.

On the other hand, most lawyers have no really clear idea of the way in which a psychiatrist functions or of the basic concepts to which he adheres. They cannot understand, for example, why there is no such thing (for psychiatrists) as "insanity." Most lawyers have no conception of the meaning or methods of psychiatric case study and diagnosis. They seem to think that psychiatrists can take a quick look at a suspect, listen to a few anecdotes about him, and thereupon be able to say, definitely, that the awful "it"—the dreadful miasma of madness, the loathsome affliction of "insanity"—is present or absent. Because we all like to please, some timid psychiatrists fall in with this fallacy of the lawyers and go through these preposterous antics.

It is true that almost any offender—like anyone else—when questioned for a short time, even by the most skillful psychiatrist, can make responses and display behavior patterns which will indicate that he is enough like the rest of us to be called "sane." But a barrage of questions is not a psychiatric examination. Modern scientific personality study depends upon various specialists—physical, clinical, and socioligical as well as psychological. It takes into consideration not only static and presently observable factors, but dynamic and historical factors, and factors of environmental interaction and change. It also looks into the future for correction, re-education, and prevention.

Hence, the same individuals who appear so normal to superficial observation are frequently discovered in the course of prolonged, intensive scientific study to have tendencies regarded as "deviant," "peculiar," "unhealthy," "sick," "crazy," "senseless," "irrational," "insane."

But now you may ask, "Is it not possible to find such tendencies in any individual if one looks hard enough? And if this is so, if we are all a little crazy or potentially so, what is the essence of your psychiatric distinctions? Who is it that you want excused?"

And here is the crux of it all. We psychiatrists don't want *anyone* excused. In fact, psychiatrists are much more concerned about the protection of the public than are the lawyers. I repeat: psychiatrists don't want anyone excused, certainly not anyone who shows antisocial tendencies. We consider them all responsible, which lawyers do not. And we want the prisoner to take on that responsibility, or else deliver it to someone who will be concerned about the protection of society and about the prisoner too. We don't want anyone excused, but neither do we want anyone stupidly disposed of, futilely detained, or prematurely released. We don't want them tortured, either sensationally with hot irons or quietly by long-continued and forced idleness. In the psychiatrist's mind nothing should be done in the name of punishment, though he is well aware that the offender may regard either the diagnostic procedure or the treatment or the detention incident to the treatment as punitive. But this is in *his* mind, not in the psychiatrist's mind. And in our opinion it should not be in the public's mind, because it is an illusion.

It is true that we psychiatrists consider that all people have potentialities for antisocial behavior. The law assumes this, too. Most of the time most people control their criminal impulses. But for various reasons and under all kinds of circumstances some individuals become increasingly disorganized or demoralized, and then they begin to be socially offensive. The man who does criminal things is less convincingly disorganized than the patient who "looks" sick, because the former more nearly resembles the rest of us, and seems to be indulging in acts that we have struggled with and controlled. So we get hot under the collar about the one and we call him "criminal" whereas we pityingly forgive the other and call him "lunatic." But a surgeon uses the same principles of surgery whether he is dealing with a "clean" case, say some cosmetic surgery on a face, or a "dirty" case which is foul-smelling and offensive. What we are after is results and the emotions of the operator must be under control. Words like "criminal" and "insane" have no place in the scientific vocabulary any more than pejorative adjectives like "vicious," "psychopathic," "bloodthirsty," etc. The need is to find all the *descriptive* adjectives that apply to the case, and this is a scientific job—not a popular exercise in name-calling. Nobody's insides are very beautiful; and in the cases that require social control there has been a great wound and some of the insides are showing.

Intelligent judges all over the country are increasingly surrendering the onerous responsibility of deciding in advance what a man's conduct will be in a prison and how rapidly his wicked impulses will evaporate there. With more use of the indeterminate sentence and the establishment of scientific diagnostic centers, we shall be in a position to make progress in the science of *treating* antisocial trends. Furthermore, we shall get away from the present legal smog that hangs over the prisons, which lets us detain with heartbreaking futility some prisoners fully rehabilitated while others, whom the prison officials know full well to be dangerous and unemployable, must be released, *against our judgment,* because a judge far away (who has by this time forgotten all about it) said that five years was enough. In my frequent visits to prisons I am always astonished at how rarely the judges who have prescribed the "treatment"come to see whether or not it is effective. What if doctors who sent their seriously ill patients to hospitals never called to see them!

As more states adopt diagnostic centers directed toward getting the prisoners *out* of jail and back to work, under modern, well-structured parole systems, the taboo on jail and prison, like that on state hospitals, will begin to diminish. Once it was a lifelong disgrace to have been in either. Lunatics, as they were cruelly called, were feared and avoided. Today only the ignorant retain this phobia. Cancer was then considered a *shameful* thing to have, and victims of it were afraid to mention it, or have it correctly treated, because they did not want to be disgraced. The time will come when offenders, much as we disapprove of their offenses, will no longer be unemployable untouchables.

To a physician discussing the wiser treatment of our fellow men it seems hardly necessary to add that under no circumstances should we kill them. It was never considered right for doctors to kill their patients, no matter how hopeless their condition. True, some patients in state institutions have undoubtedly been executed without benefit of sentence. They were a nuisance, expensive to keep and dangerous to release. Various people took it upon themselves to put an end to the matter, and I have even heard them boast of it. The Hitler regime had the same philosophy.

But in most civilized countries today we have a higher opinion of the rights of the individual and of the limits to the state's power. We know, too, that for the most part the death penalty is inflicted upon obscure, impoverished, defective, and friendless individuals. We know that it intimidates juries in their efforts to determine guilt without prejudice. We know that is is being eliminated in one state after another, most recently Delaware. We know that in practice it has almost disappeared—for over seven thousand capital crimes last year there were less than one hundred executions. But vast sums of money are still being spent—let us say wasted—in legal contests to determine whether or not an individual, even one known to have been mentally ill, is now healthy enough for the state to hang him. (I am informed that such a case has recently cost the State of California $400,000!)

Most of all, we know that no state employees—except perhaps some that ought to be patients themselves—want a job on the killing squad, and few wardens can stomach this piece of medievalism in their own prisons. For example, two officials I know recently quarreled because each wished to have the hanging of a prisoner carried out on the other's premises.

Capital punishment is, in my opinion, morally wrong. It has a bad effect on everyone, especially those involved in it. It gives a false sense of security to the public. It is vastly expensive. Worst of all it beclouds the entire issue of motivation in crime, which is so importantly relevant to the question of what to do for and with the criminal that will be most constructive to society as a whole. Punishing—and even killing—criminals may yield a kind of grim gratification; let us all admit that there are times when we are so shocked at the depredations of an offender that we persuade ourselves that this is a man the Creator didn't intend to create, and that we had better help correct the mistake. But playing God in this way has no conceivable moral or scientific justification.

Let us return in conclusion to the initial question: "Verdict guilty—now what?" My answer is that now we, the designated representatives of the society which has failed to integrate this man, which has failed him in some way, hurt him and been hurt by him, should take over. It is *our* move. And our move must be a constructive one, an intelligent one, a purposeful one—not a primitive, retaliatory, offensive move. We, the agents of society, must move to end the game of tit-for-tat and blow-for-blow in which the offender has foolishly and futilely engaged himself and us. We are not driven, as he is, to wild and impulsive actions. With knowledge comes power, and with power there is no need for the frightened vengeance of the old penology. In its place should go a quiet, dignified, therapeutic program for the rehabilitation of the disorganized one, if possible, the protection of society during his treatment period, and his guided return to useful citizenship, as soon as this can be effected.

Questions and Assignments

1. Can you find any emotionalism, sentimentality, loaded terminology, oversimplification in this essay? Examine Menninger's rhetorical questions and compare their use and purpose with those of Barzun and Hoover.

2. How appropriate is the analogy of a surgeon which appears near the end of this essay?

3. Menninger begins with the statement and the refutation of one important opposing argument. Where and how does this essay handle the other elements of the opposing argument? Is this an argument by induction? Explain why.

4. What distinction does Menninger make in the fourth paragraph? Why does he consider the "pain-pleasure" principle fallacious?

5. Compare Menninger's assumption about police detection and the judicial system with Hoover's point of view. Barzun and Menninger seem to agree on this point, yet they arrive at opposite conclusions. What particular points does Menninger make which could be used to refute Barzun?

6. Now that you have read two more essays on the subject of capital punishmen and its ramifications, rewrite your first theme, making use of what you have learned from these essays. You may still take either side, or you may argue against all these essays—provided you can supply a satisfactory conclusion of your own. Be sure to substantiate your evidence and avoid fallacies. Make use of the four-part outline described in the first paragraph of the essay by Newman and Genevieve Birk (p. 390), although you need not follow this outline in the same order.

Conformity, Rebellion and the Authentic Life

VAN CLEVE MORRIS

America suffers from a new and baffling social disease: acute isomorphy. Whether we like it or not, we are growing more and more alike, not simply in terms of the superficial features of living—our clothing, our automobiles, our houses, our tastes—but, more troublingly, in the bedrock conceptions we have of life: what it is all about, what we are in the world for, and what we are supposed to be doing with our precious three-score and ten.

It is now, of course, a common public sport to comment upon and, if possible, document this strange social disease. The customary theme—from the pulpit or on the editorial page, from the commencement platform or in the Sunday supplement—is a kind of worrisome wringing of the hands over the way this paralysis seems to be gripping personality development in our land. But no one has ever stopped to ask whether we are actually *producing* this disease, year after year, in one of our primary social institutions—the school!

Social commentators like Riesman and Whyte and Packard and a host of others have finally given us a terminology to deal with this new malady. It is time now to apply this terminology to the school and to see how this strange pathology first appears in the individual in connection with the work of those who have built an industry out of guiding the young. I propose here to describe one of the theoretical premises on which all guidance specialists operate, examine and offer criticism of this premise, and suggest possible new avenues of action in dealing with growing young people.

To come immediately to the point: in an age of conformity, when we might reasonably expect to find guidance on the side of "individual differences" (which it claims to be), on the side of developing the unique personality, indeed, on the side of idiosyncrasy, we find it instead on the side of an educational doctrine which perhaps unwittingly but nevertheless very effectively serves to aggravate the very problem it seeks to solve—the growing uniformity of youth. I refer, in general terminology, to the doctrine in education of the "social man," by which we view the maturation process principally as a career in coming into adjustment with the complex and

From *Teachers College Record*, 1959. Reprinted by permission of the publisher and Van Cleve Morris.

multifaceted form of corporate social life we have come to know in the Western world.

This doctrine holds that education generally, and guidance particularly as an ancillary function in the total educational enterprise, must proceed on the assumption that boys and girls grow up by viewing themselves as members of a social system which requires them to be cooperative, team-minded, well-adjusted individuals. This mentality—the so-called "organization man" mentality—reaches all the way from big business to the neighborhood play group.

This principle stipulates that the genuinely mature individual in our social system is the one who responds in flexible and harmonious ways to his peers; indeed, the very definition of social maturity is held to be a continually adjustable and empathetic relationship with other human beings. In this frame, the individual submits generally to an unwritten constitution of behavioral expectations set by others, and, since he is part of the "legislative process," he levies these same expectations upon others. Whatever claim he has to maturity is founded on his ability to relate to other people.

To say that the individual does all this within the scope of a benign form of voluntarism does not gainsay the fact that this interlace of rather standardized behavioral requirements represents the very texture of social conduct in American life. At the more primitive levels this entire outlook values "good human relations" and "getting along with others." In more sophisticated circles it subscribes to "effective team effort," "good public relations," and "a good press."

Any study of the American educational industry will reveal that this ideology has taken hold of school teachers and guidance counselors as well. Indeed, we in education have invented a whole basketful of educational devices—social promotion, group methods in teaching, even group guidance—by which we institutionalize this ideology, give it force and meaning in the minds of young people, so that they will come to resemble the prototype "social" creature we have pedagogically in mind, the creature who aspires to a maturity of harmonious, socialized union with his fellow man.

By this I do not mean that we turn out boys and girls who are identical. But we *do* turn them out all equipped with the *same method* of making life choices—the method of choosing mate, college, extracurricular activity, lodge, union, church, indeed an entire career—on the basis of its total *social* impact on the individual's life. That is to say, we have them ask, "What will be the effect of this choice on the life I must lead *with* and *among other people*?"

Guidance, at root, is the institutionalization of the process of choice-making. What people do with their lives is the strategic result of the one-by-one tactical choices they make in their formative years. Since these tactical choices are so important, we have come to feel that some charge must be taken of the process by which they are made, and so we have "invented" guidance counselors, interview methods, material-gathering procedures, aptitude test batteries, and a host of other paraphernalia which we place at the disposal of young people to enable them, as we say, to make more intelligent choices.

Now this great undertaking is the result of considerable effort, and generally we can say that it deserves our applause. But what we forget is that with the institutionalization of choice-making, we inadvertently institutionalize the choices, that is, we help to shape the choices of young people for college or career along lines which are considered acceptable, orthodox, in short, *socially* legitimate in our day and time.

Suppose, for instance, that a high school boy, reasonably intelligent and sensitive to life, decides to quit school in the spring of his junior year, buy a motorcycle, and start out on a trip around the world. Suppose also that his father, without seeming to dictate his future, nevertheless wishes the boy to finish school and perhaps spend a couple of years in college before going into the business world. At this point, or perhaps even earlier, the whole apparatus of the guidance division of his school begins surrounding this youth with materials, information, impressions of teachers and counselors, and direct advice from adults, all of which is designed to illustrate to him the long-run social consequences of this motorcycle trip vis-à-vis the long-run social consequences of completing high school and taking college work.

Through it all, there slowly descends a kind of miasma of orthodoxy which, by design or inadvertence, has the effect of placing the guidance division and the school as a whole normatively on the side of the latter choice —certainly not in every case, but usually. Most guidance counselors have never been around the world on a motorcycle; and for this reason what they think of the social consequences of this adventure will have to be rather uninformed and inarticulate. On the other hand, all of them have gone to college, and for better or worse, most of them would be likely to think that a high school diploma and a college career, however foreshortened by lack of ability, would lead to a higher kind of life than a motorcycle trip around the world.

They may be right, of course, and educators and counselors of my acquaintance never tire of citing instances in which a youngster returns to them years later to express gratitude that they made him hew to an orthodox line in his school years when so-called immature impulse dictated otherwise. But how many others are there who at this very moment represent what Thoreau was talking about when he said "the mass of men lead lives of quiet desperation," and who, with neither rancor nor unforgiveness, nevertheless look back upon their teachers and counselors as unwitting accomplices to the creation of their present humdrum and witless existence?

In preparing this paper, I got to thinking about one Garry Davis, son of band-leader Meyer Davis. Shortly after World War II, young Davis renounced his American citizenship and proclaimed himself a "citizen of the world." For the past dozen years he has been waging a one-man, One-World campaign and has, from time to time, attracted the attention of the press. The editorial reaction has usually been one of condescending amusement and not a little scorn. But I have been musing to myself, What opportunities exist today in American high schools—in classrooms and in guidance offices—for a student to find encouragement from his teachers and counselors to emulate this adventurer in international understanding?

This young man, after more than a decade of lonesome espousal of a splendid cause, has finally given in, altogether frustrated by the glacial indifference of the world's governments. But while he held out, he was a symbol, a nagging, annoying symbol, of what we all know is right—a unitarian conception of membership in the human race.

On a more prosaic level, I have also found myself thinking of Lew Hoad, amateur tennis player recently turned pro, who, according to a story in *Life* Magazine, did not at the time exhibit the orthodox and standard attitude toward playing the game of tennis that all professional players possess, namely, the aggressive, fanatic, do-or-die will to win. As a result, his promoter, fearing this would detract from Mr. Hoad's box-office appeal, launched upon an ingenious educational program to recondition the athlete along more desirable and more conformist lines. Hoad, like Davis, has finally succumbed to the treatment; he is now refashioned into a splendid, commercial, athletic commodity. But here we must ask, Is there a tennis coach or a guidance counselor who would not attempt the same program of reform on a potential champion in some American high school today?

The amusing irony of our predicament is that those who wring their hands the most over our conformist tendencies (*Life* Magazine itself, as a matter of fact, which a few months earlier had run a series of editorials on the subject) are full of scorn for even the mild eccentricities represented by the behavior of these two individuals. And, let's be frank, school teachers and guidance counselors are in the same camp: *adventuresomeness in the ideals of private conscience is not employed today as an educational instrument for motivating young people.*

And I am saying that it should be. We lose a great measure of human development by quietly assenting to the public pressures for orthodox and respectable choices by our young people. Rebellion for its own sake is of no particular merit. Rebelliousness and unorthodoxy as general traits are no more attractive than quiet submission. They are the marks of the social delinquent, the self-styled odd-ball, or the practicing, "card-carrying" Bohemian. But veering away from standard public expectations is but a small beginning of what a youngster can potentially do with his own life. Without the encouragement to make these tentative probes into the unexpected or unorthodox, these young people, like adults themselves, will shortly find themselves locked in place in the regularized patterns of adult social conduct. And I say this is a tragic loss, not only for them but for society as a whole.

What *does* matter, in guiding young people, is the degree to which we can awaken them to the possibilities for making an authentic life. In reality we have fallen asleep in the business of making life choices, adults even more than youngsters. We have grown numb to the possibilities that this life holds—for effort, for service, for intelligence, for love. We choose instead the life of the coffee-break culture, we scorn the do-gooder, we have come only lately to a reluctant regard for the egghead, and we are skeptical of love and warmth, whether God's or man's. We default because we have been *socialized* to within an inch of our human integrity. And we have compounded this default in the rearing of the young.

In school life, as in the wider society, there should be no moral imperative either to be different or to blend into the social landscape, but only the ultimate imperative to know who one is, to know what one is choosing out of life, and to take final responsibility for those choices.

The task of the educational counselor is not to provide choices ready-made for young people; we have certainly outgrown this point of view. Nor is it merely to provide the experiences and circumstances in which choices can be made, a theory which is currently in the ascendancy. At root the function of the educator and counselor is to show young people that they must *take charge of their own lives.* Test results, depth interviews, sophisticated psychometry, or unsophisticated advice from adults may provide valuable background for maturing young people, but these data must never be used to justify or rationalize a human choice except on the superficial level of social necessity. No one *has* to abide by the findings of the psychometric counselor's apparatus.

The only thing one *has* to do is to make his life choices express what he thinks his human life is for. And what an individual thinks his life is for can be discovered only in the active functioning of a human self trying to assess its own meaning in a complicated and troubled world. Every individual must be made to realize that if he means to build a life that is worth living, rather than one that is merely socially successful, if he wishes to make his life count in the total scheme of things, he must recognize and understand the very private and personal quality of his choice-making. It is in this tiny, quiet chamber of decision that a human being makes himself truly human.

Questions and Assignments

1. Look up the word "isomorphy" in the dictionary. Why did the author apply a biological term to a "social disease" and why in the opening sentence?

2. Check the dictionary to see how the author's use of the word "aggravate," which is correct, differs from the meaning you may be accustomed to.

3. What is the value and effect of such phrases as "whole basketful of educational devices," "miasma of orthodoxy," "the practicing, 'card-carrying' Bohemian," "coffee-break culture"?

4. After a brief introduction establishing the relevance of his subject, the author of this essay provides a clear outline of his whole argument. How well does he follow this outline?

5. What, precisely, is the premise which Morris is arguing against? Do you think his examples are valid and appropriate?

6. The author says he is not advocating rebellion for its own sake. How does his opinion differ? What does he mean by distinguishing between the life that is socially successful and the life that is worth living?

7. Choose a particular decision in your own life, perhaps the one you wrote on in Part II of this book, and write an argument concerning the advice you were given (or that you gave to yourself) and whether or not the advice and your decision were right. You would be wise to imitate the form of this essay closely, that is, set up the premise upon which the decision was made, examine the alternatives and the opposition, and draw your conclusion.

8. Write the same sort of essay based on someone you know or some historical

figure like Lincoln, Columbus, Martin Luther King, the Pilgrims, Einstein, one of the astronauts.

9. Write an essay explaining what you think are the most important things to be considered in choosing a career and why. You might make use of some of the examples in Morris' essay and argue for or against his conclusions.

May Professors Profess Principles?

RUSSELL KIRK

On March 7, 1959, the *Saturday Evening Post* published an article with the title, "Are We Making a Playground out of College?" Jerome Ellison, an associate professor of journalism at Indiana University, wrote it. On last January 9, a second article by Mr. Ellison appeared in the *Post*—"American Disgrace: College Cheating." Shortly before the second article came out, Professor Ellison was given notice by the university, and will teach no more at Bloomington.

While in itself an interesting case, this dismissal of a well-known writer and teacher has a larger significance. It is one engagement in a struggle fought for the past several years on hundreds of college campuses—particularly, as Mr. Ellison suggests, at the "Big Ten" universities and other middle western institutions. On one side are certain college administrators interested primarily in larger enrollments; on the other, college professors interested primarily in the works of the mind.

During the next decade, the controversy about academic freedom may shift from the debate concerning Communist and fellow-traveling teachers to a fierce argument over whether professors have the right to uphold intellectual standards.

That Mr. Ellison was dismissed because he had presumed to criticize the "Second Curriculum" at American universities seems to be established beyond reasonable doubt. His observations had included some passing comments on life at Indiana University—though only as one among many campuses. Five years earlier, the university had engaged Mr. Ellison as a teacher of journalism. His qualifications were remarkably good: he had been managing editor of *Collier's* and editor of *Liberty*. His performance as a teacher at Indiana seems to have been superior: his student editorial team won the national college yearbook championship, many of his stu-

From the *Southwest Review,* Autumn 1960. Reprinted by permission of the publisher and Russell Kirk.

dents placed their writings in national magazines, he was commended for proficiency in teaching journalism by a national accreditation committee, and he published more articles of his own than did his eight departmental colleagues combined. With his wife, he founded a successful national magazine, *Best Articles and Stories,* which reprints selections from the scholarly and critical quarterlies. He was promoted from assistant to associate professor. In two more years, he would have acquired tenure at the university. But then he trod upon the perilous ground of educational criticism.

To suggest that anything might conceivably be unsatisfactory at one of our great state universities now requires some boldness in a professor at such an institution. Not many take the risk—especially if they have two years to go before they obtain tenure. Mr. Ellison wrote in his first *Post* article:

> Entering the academic life from the "outside world," one is disappointed by the banality of conversation at social gatherings, and by attitudes of old-fashioned trade-unionism centering on "tenure," a word which means that after they've kept you on for seven years it's almost impossible for them to fire you. This concern for tenure bends many teachers toward cautious utterance, often blunting the kind of searching, outspoken discourse that might explode into exciting teaching and learning.

Once his article on College Playgrounds was published, the administrators of the university made it clear to Professor Ellison that his brand of outspoken discourse was not desired at Bloomington. The university's public-relations bureau burst into activity, sending out news releases hostile to Mr. Ellison and angry letters against him, including a demand to the *Post* that the editors apologize for publishing such stuff—on pain, it was hinted, of retaliation against the magazine. The president of Indiana University, Dr. Herman Wells, personally directed the preparation of a dossier questioning Mr. Ellison's personal integrity and professional competence.

Ellison choose, according to the dean of the graduate school, "to pander to an insatiable appetite for the comic strip and Hollywood version of college life." The acting dean of students cried out that Ellison's work was "a lot of bosh," and that Ellison was "searching for sensationalism." The university's public-relations chief diligently publicized these temperate comments. An Indianapolis newspaper columnist wrote, shortly after Mr. Ellison's first article was published, that he had "official word" Ellison would be dropped from the Indiana faculty in punishment. Soon other university administrators joined in the chorus against Mr. Ellison, though a number of their complaints seem curiously irrelevant to what he had written in the *Post*.

Some students hanged Professor Ellison in effigy before the journalism building. "Apparently I have arrived," Mr. Ellison observed. "I stand on my thirty years' work and my record for integrity. I said what I had to say in that article."

By the middle of December, the Department of Journalism decided that Professor Ellison's contract would not be renewed, because the tenure members of the department had concluded that "the teaching, counseling, and sharing of duties [by Mr. Ellison] did not meet the requirements we wanted in a person retained on a permanent basis." They added that of course Mr. Ellison's *Post* article had nothing to do with their action.

President Wells was even more emphatic on this point. "I'm absolutely confident," he said in a statement for the student newspaper, "the article did not have anything to do with his not being reappointed. This office simply takes the recommendations of the department in all such matters." It was Dr. Wells who had ordered the preparation of documents against Mr. Ellison. In the Indiana faculty handbook is this passage concerning academic freedom: "No restraint shall be placed upon the teacher's freedom in investigation. . . . In speaking and writing outside of the institution upon subjects beyond the scope of his own field of study [the teacher] is entitled to precisely the same freedom, but is subject to the same responsibility as attaches to all other citizens." But the administrators at Bloomington gave Professor Ellison the freedom to do his writing somewhere else—if he could find a post. The widely-circulated press releases against him might injure his oportunities elsewhere; and there have been attempts, sometimes successful, to blacklist stubborn professors who resign or are dismissed.

Mr. Ellison is one of the best-known professors of journalism in America. Until he published his *Post* article, he was given no notice that his work at Indiana seemed unsatisfactory to the administrative hierarchy. Having looked carefully into this case, I am convinced that Professor Ellison was discharged simply because he had the effrontery to criticize many American colleges and universities, including his own, in a popular magazine.

Now what outrageous charges did Mr. Ellison make against the higher learning in America? If one takes the trouble to read his article on College Playgrounds, one finds a temperate, sincere, well-documented account of the "Second Curriculum" at the great majority of our colleges and universities. My own observations—and I have visited more than a hundred campuses—coincide with Mr. Ellison's. And I doubt that any competent professor of arts or science can deny, in his heart, the truth of what Mr. Ellison writes.

The Second Curriculum is the fun-fair which overshadows book-learning. It is the marriage-market, the athletics craze, the passion for snap courses. In Mr. Ellison's words, it

> is that odd mixture of status hunger, voodoo, tradition, lust, sterotyped dissipation, love, solid achievement, and plain good fun sometimes called "college life." It drives a high proportion of our students through college chronically short of sleep, behind in their work, and uncertain of the exact score in any department of life.

With examples from many campuses—chiefly from state universities—Mr. Ellison combines information from various reliable surveys of the state of our colleges, notably the Hazen Foundation report, *Changing Values in College*. His purpose is not mere denunciation, but rather the restoration of first principles in higher education. He puts this very well toward the end of his second *Post* article:

> The first step in a school concerned about its cheating, I would think, should be to ask itself what it stands for. Does it rest its reputation on having the biggest enrollment in its state? As fielding the best football team? As offering the greatest variety of courses? As having the handsomest fraternity houses and the most luxurious student-union building? None of these things, I suggest, offers the kind of challenge required. The school must assign itself some inspired goal, some lofty set of aims which has won the passionate loyalty of a dedicated faculty. These aims, whatever may be their specific nature, should have their roots in an undeviating allegiance to the truth.
>
> The practical, national importance of truth is, I think, too little recognized. I am speaking now, not of ideals that tend to become fuzzily poetic, but of the hardheaded business of getting along in the job of being a nation.

Mr. Ellison's prudence and good nature impress me; there is in his articles nothing of the "sensationalism" which the deans at Indiana professed to find. But I do not propose here to open the general question of the effects of the Second Curriculum. My immediate point is that many able American professors, of whom Mr. Ellison is a representative specimen, are convinced that intellectual and moral standards have suffered a marked decline in our colleges since World War II. And that many American college and university administrators shut their eyes to this decline, being intent on bigger enrollments. And—this last being my main theme—that some of the administrators have made up their minds to close the mouths of the protesting professors.

This struggle between administrators and teachers obtains public attention only rarely. For the majority of professorial objectors to the lowering of standards and the disregard of traditional disciplines do nothing but grumble with their colleagues. "This is a city of brave children and timid men," a nonacademic friend once said to me as we walked the streets of a college town. The permissively-reared professors' children swaggered past us; but the professors themselves looked excessively meek—not with the meekness of Moses, or of the sort that shall inherit the earth. To protest, even in a faculty meeting, against the Second Curriculum, the prevalence of cheating, or the proliferation of trifling courses may provoke the frowns of president and deans; and that can mean a teacher might be passed over for advancement, or—like Mr. Ellison—suddenly be found wanting in pedagogical techniques and counseling skills. Once I was present, and vocal, at a faculty meeting in which a half-dozen professors, indeed, ventured to speak against a proposed lowering of grade-standards. As each of the objectors rose, a cynical colleague at my elbow murmured, "He's a full professor, with tenure," or, "He's a single man."

When a scholar does have sufficient resolution to object, within or without a college, to the decay of the higher learning, few people hear about it—or about what warnings to him or positive measures of retaliation may have come from the college administration. I described several such instances in my book *Academic Freedom* (1955). The administrators of the state universities and colleges have at their service an elaborate and well-paid public-relations bureau; the average professor is obscure enough, without friends among the newspaper editors or the members of the state legislature. As Tocqueville says of the dissenter under democratic despotism, he may find himself deserted by his former friends, crushed by the weight of a vague disapproval rather than by positive punishments, and so regret that he ever spoke out.

Yet occasionally some single combat in this contest between empire-building administrators and intellect-respecting professors comes to public attention. Before the Ellison case, the most startling episode of this sort in recent years occurred at the University of Nevada, in 1953. There Dr. Frank Richardson, a professor of biology, was summarily dismissed by the university's president, Dr. (of education) Minard Stout, because Dr. Richardson had ventured to distribute among the faculty copies of a pamphlet by Professor Arthur Bestor, *Aimlessness in Education*—and because Dr. Richardson was known to believe in reasonably high academic standards. After prolonged controversy and litigation, the Supreme Court of Nevada ordered Dr. Richardson's reinstatement, because he had possessed tenure; a committee appointed by the Nevada legislature reported against President Stout; the people of Nevada elected new university regents, who removed Stout from the presidency. Even though Dr. Richardson meanwhile had left Reno for less troubled waters, this was a real victory for academic freedom. But it occurred because of Dr. Richardson's courage and persistence.

Generally it is less injurious to a professor for him to be accused of Communist sympathies than for him to be found wanting in enthusiasm for indiscriminate expansion of college enrollments. If he is in danger of dismissal for his radicalism, often a crowd rushes to his defense: a considerable segment of the press, eminent liberal politicians and publicists, the American Association of University Professors, the Civil Liberties Union. But if he has clashed with president and dean over academic standards, he may find no one interested except his nervous family. Much of the public does not understand the issue at all, and can be easily won to the administrators' side by facile slogans about how "our wonderful boys and girls deserve college educations, as many of them as we can find room for." Even the AAUP has been markedly reluctant to intervene in such controversies.

And the public assumes, usually, that the administrators know best; so, too, most of the alumni assume; so, perhaps, the college trustees or the educational committees of the state legislature. A college president is Constituted Authority—with a public-relations bureau next door; a professor is only an impractical intellectual, probably full of crotchets.

What the public and the alumni and the trustees and the legislators often forget is that university administrators, like the rest of us, are afflicted by the *libido dominandi*. Swelling college enrollments mean more divisions and departments for an administrator to control; more faculty appointments at his disposal; handsome new buildings on his campus; a larger body of alumni, eventually, through whom he can exert influence; perhaps a larger salary for himself; certainly more attention in the newspapers. It is not easy for an administrator to resist these temptations; and it is so unpleasant to be thinking all the time about high standards and old disciplines, and so convenient not to know exactly what goes on in crowded classrooms. So the interest of an administrator need not always coincide with the interest of his faculty, or of the students (at least the more serious students among them), or of the university's intellectual reputation, or—in the long run—of the public. And this divergence of interest comes about the more easily if the administrator is not himself educated in any genuinely humane or scientific discipline, but has been trained only in administrative methods, technical skills, or Education (Teachers' College variety).

I am not saying that the crotchety professor always is right, or that the harried administrator always is wrong. There are teachers whose chief delight it is to vex presidents and deans, simply by way of passing the time; while some of my better friends are college administrators—and are as devoted to decent standards as is the most tradition-directed professor. The flood of students into our colleges and universities since World War II has created problems that demand fresh approaches.

But I am saying that professors ought to be allowed to discuss these real problems, and ought to be protected in their right to criticize reasonably the ends and means of college administrators. If scholars and teachers have no freedom to discuss educational standards, whatever is academic freedom meant for? It is important, I know, that professors enjoy a high degree of freedom of expression upon political questions. But it is still more important that they be free to affirm their educational first principles. If political expression is curbed, only those teachers interested in politics are directly affected; but if educational opinions are repressed, every conscientious teacher is at once injured. Politics, after all, is a secondary concern for the professor: he does not rule the state. Educational ends and means, however, are the primary concern of the professor: they constitute the essence of his vocation. If he is not free to criticize the standards of the university, he enjoys no real liberty—nor will he be competent to impart intellectual disciplines meant for free men.

Professor Ellison's very readable articles, founded upon personal observation, are precisely the sort of discussion our university administrators ought to encourage. The president or dean who flies into a rage at such criticism must suffer from a bad conscience, I suspect. Mr. Ellison makes a number of practical proposals for reform. These his administrative adversaries do not deign to examine. Bigotry is nowhere more destructive than at the top of a foundation for higher learning.

In the *Georgias,* Socrates remarks that most men do not take kindly to the preacher of moral reform, the pursuer of the good. "There is no telling," Socrates says, "what may happen to such a man." What the possessors of administrative power have done to Professor Ellison is quite clear: they have deprived him of his post and have tried to injure his reputation. Similar things will happen, these next few years, to other preachers of educational reform. For there are among us certain titular guardians of the Academy who conceal the decay of learning, condone cheating, and consign to outer darkness the conscientious teacher.

Questions and Assignments

1. What is implied by phrases like "presumed to criticize" or "his brand of outspoken discourse"? Compare the nouns and verbs in paragraph seven with those in the latter half of the essay.

2. What purpose is served by the phrase *libido dominandi* and what does it mean?

3. Is there any comparison and contrast involved in the author's use of quotations in this essay?

4. Of what value is the reference to Socrates aside from the quotation itself?

5. Does the title contribute to the understanding of the essay in any way? How?

6. What is the premise of this argument? Is it basically inductive or deductive in form?

7. What is the function of the case of Mr. Ellison in Kirk's essay? What other examples does Kirk provide? Is the evidence sufficient to prove everything Kirk says?

8. Does the author say that college administrators are always opposed to high educational standards? Does he say that professors should be free to say anything they please? What are the "principles" this article is concerned with?

9. If some professor at your college were to do as Mr. Ellison did, how would you react? What about your parents? Write a theme, using at least one real or hypothetical example, defending or opposing Kirk's point of view.

10. Using the thought attributed to Tocqueville—that "the dissenter under democratic despotism . . . may find himself deserted by his former friends, crushed by the weight of a vague disapproval . . . and so regret that he ever spoke out," argue the case of yourself or someone you know who has been in a similar situation.

Democracy

GEORGE BERNARD SHAW

Shaw was the greatest British playwright of his era. "Democracy" is an address delivered over the British Broadcasting System in October, 1929. At the time he gave his talk Shaw says he "was determined that this time 'Votes for Everybody' and 'Every Authority Elected by Vote' should not escape by wearing its imposing mask." Democracy did not escape the satiric and provocative force of Shaw's intelligence, as the following selection shows.

Your Majesties, your Royal Highnesses, your Excellencies, your Graces and Reverences, my Lords, Ladies and Gentlemen, fellow-citizens of all degrees: I am going to talk to you about Democracy objectively: that is, as it exists and as we must all reckon with it equally, no matter what our points of view may be. Suppose I were to talk to you not about Democracy, but about the sea, which is in some respects rather like Democracy! We all have our own views of the sea. Some of us hate it and are never well when we are at it or on it. Others love it, and are never so happy as when they are in it or on it or looking at it. Some of us regard it as Britain's natural realm and surest bulwark: others want a Channel Tunnel. But certain facts about the sea are quite independent of our feelings towards it. If I take it for granted that the sea exists, none of you will contradict me. If I say that the sea is sometimes furiously violent and always uncertain, and that those who are most familiar with it trust it least, you will not immediately shriek out that I do not believe in the sea; that I am an enemy of the sea; that I want to abolish the sea; that I am going to make bathing illegal; that I am out to ruin our carrying trade and lay waste all our seaside resorts and scrap the British Navy. If I tell you that you cannot breathe in the sea, you will not take that as a personal insult and ask me indignantly if I consider you inferior to a fish. Well, you must please be equally sensible when I tell you some hard facts about Democracy. When I tell you that it is sometimes furiously violent and always dangerous and treacherous, and that those who are familiar with it as practical statesmen trust it least, you must not once denounce me as a paid agent of Benito Mussolini, or declare that I have become a Tory Die-hard in my old age, and accuse me of wanting to take away your votes and make an end of parliament, and the franchise, and free speech, and public meeting, and trial by jury. Still less must you rise in your places and give me three rousing cheers as a champion of medieval monarchy and feudalism. I am quite innocent of any such extravagances. All I mean is that whether we are Democrats or Tories, Catholics or Protestants, Communists or Fascists, we are all face to face with a certain force in the world called Democracy; and we must understand the nature of that force whether we want to fight it or to forward it. Our business is not to deny the perils of Democracy, but to provide against them as far as we can, and then consider whether the risks we cannot provide against are worth taking.

Democracy, as you know it, is seldom more than a long word beginning with a capital letter, which we accept reverently or disparage contemptuously without asking any questions. Now we should never accept anything reverently until we have asked it a great many very searching questions, the first two being What are you? and Where do you live? When I put these questions to Democracy the answer I get is 'My name is Demos; and I live in the British Empire, the United States of America, and wherever the love of liberty burns in the heart of man. You, my friend Shaw, are a unit of Democracy: your name is also Demos: you are a citizen of a great democratic community: you are a potential constituent of the Parliament of Man, the Federation of the World.' At this I usually burst into loud cheers, which do credit to my enthusiastic nature. Tonight, however, I shall do nothing of the sort: I shall say 'Dont talk nonsense. My name is not Demos: it is Bernard Shaw. My address is not the British Empire, nor the United States of America, nor wherever the love of liberty burns in the heart of man: it is at such and such a number in such and such a street in London; and it will be time enough to discuss my seat in the Parliament of Man when that celebrated institution comes into existence. I dont believe your name is Demos: nobody's name is Demos; and all I can make of your address is that you have no address, and are just a tramp—if indeed you exist at all.'

You will notice that I am too polite to call Demos a windbag or a hot air merchant; but I am going to ask you to begin our study of Democracy by considering it first as a big balloon, filled with gas or hot air, and sent up so that you shall be kept looking up at the sky whilst other people are picking your pockets. When the balloon comes down to earth every five years or so you are invited to get into the basket if you can throw out one of the people who are sitting tightly in it; but as you can afford neither the time nor the money, and there are forty millions of you and hardly room for six hundred in the basket, the balloon goes up again with much the same lot in it and leaves you where you were before. I think you will admit that the balloon as an image of Democracy corresponds to the parliamentary facts.

Now let us examine a more poetic conception of Democracy. Abraham Lincoln is represented as standing amid the carnage of the battlefield of Gettysburg, and declaring that all that slaughter of Americans by Americans occurred in order that Democracy, defined as government *of* the people *for* the people *by* the people, should not perish from the earth. Let us pick this famous peroration to pieces and see what there really is inside it. (By the way, Lincoln did not really declaim it on the field of Gettysburg; and the American Civil War was not fought in defence of any such principle, but, on the contrary, to enable one half of the United States to force the other half to be governed as they did not wish to be governed. But never mind that. I mentioned it only to remind you that it seems impossible for statesmen to make speeches about Democracy, or journalists to report them, without obscuring it in a cloud of humbug.)

Now for the three articles of the definition. Number One: Government *of* the people: that, evidently, is necessary: a human community can no more exist without a government than a human being can exist without a co-ordinated control of its breathing and blood circulation. Number Two: Government *for* the people, is most important. Dean Inge put it perfectly for us when he called Democracy a form of society which means equal consideration for all. He added that it is a Christian principle, and that, as a Christian, he believes in it. So do I. That is why I insist on equality of income. Equal consideration for a person with a hundred a year and one with a hundred thousand is impossible. But Number Three: Government *by* the people, is quite a different matter. All the monarchs, all the tyrants, all the dictators, all the Die-hard Tories are agreed that we must be governed. Democrats like the Dean and myself are agreed that we must be governed with equal consideration for everybody. But we repudiate Number Three on the ground that the people cannot govern. The thing is a physical impossibility. Every citizen cannot be a ruler any more than every boy can be an engine driver or a pirate king. A nation of prime ministers or dictators is as absurd as an army of field marshals. Government by the people is not and never can be a reality: it is only a cry by which demagogues humbug us into voting for them. If you doubt this—if you ask me 'Why should not the people make their own laws?' I need only ask you 'Why should not the people write their own plays?' They cannot. It is much easier to write a good play than to make a good law. And there are not a hundred men in the world who can write a play good enough to stand daily wear and tear as long as a law must.

Now comes the question, If we cannot govern ourselves, what can we do to save ourselves from being at the mercy of those who *can* govern, and who may quite possibly be thoroughpaced grafters and scoundrels? The primitive answer is that as we are always in a huge majority we can, if rulers oppress us intolerably, burn their houses and tear them to pieces. This is not satisfactory. Decent people never do it until they have quite lost their heads; and when they have lost their heads they are as likely as not to burn the wrong house and tear the wrong man to pieces. When we have what is called a popular movement very few people who take part in it know what it is all about. I once saw a real popular movement in London. People were running excitedly through the streets. Everyone who saw them doing it immediately joined in the rush. They ran simply because everyone else was doing it. It was most impressive to see thousands of people sweeping along at full speed like that. There could be no doubt that it was literally a popular movement. I ascertained afterwards that it was started by a runaway cow. That cow had an important share in my education as a political philosopher; and I can assure you that if you will study crowds, and lost and terrified animals, and things like that, instead of reading books and newspaper articles, you will learn a great deal about politics from them. Most general elections, for instance, are nothing but stampedes. Our last but one was a conspicuous example of this. The cow was a Russian one.

I think we may take it that neither mob violence nor popular movements can be depended on as checks upon the abuse of power by governments. One might suppose that at least they would act as a last resort when an autocrat goes mad and commits outrageous excesses of tyranny and cruelty. But it is a curious fact that they never do. Take two famous cases: those of Nero and Tsar Paul the First of Russia. If Nero had been an ordinary professional fiddler he would probably have been no worse a man than any member of the wireless orchestra. If Paul had been a lieutenant in a line regiment we should never have heard of him. But when these two poor fellows were invested with absolute powers over their fellow-creatures they went mad, and did such appalling things that they had to be killed like mad dogs. Only, it was not the people that rose up and killed them. They were dispatched quite privately by a very select circle of their own bodyguards. For a genuinely democratic execution of unpopular statesmen we must turn to the brothers De Witt, who were torn to pieces by a Dutch mob in the seventeenth century. They were neither tyrants nor autocrats. On the contrary, one of them had been imprisoned and tortured for his resistance to the despotism of William of Orange; and the other had come to meet him as he came out of prison. The mob was on the side of the autocrat. We may take it that the shortest way for a tyrant to get rid of a troublesome champion of liberty is to raise a hue and cry against him as an unpatriotic person, and leave the mob to do the rest after supplying them with a well tipped ringleader. Nowadays this is called direct action by the revolutionary proletariat. Those who put their faith in it soon find that proletariats are never revolutionary, and that their direct action, when it is controlled at all, is usually controlled by police agents.

Democracy, then, cannot be government by the people: it can only be government by consent of the governed. Unfortunately, when democratic statesmen propose to govern us by our own consent, they find that we dont want to be governed at all, and that we regard rates and taxes and rents and death duties as intolerable burdens. What we want to know is how little government we can get along with without being murdered in our beds. That question cannot be answered until we have explained what we mean by getting along. Savages manage to get along. Unruly Arabs and Tartars get along. The only rule in the matter is that the civilized way of getting along is the way of corporate action, not individual action; and corporate action involves more government than individual action.

Thus government, which used to be a comparatively simple affair, today has to manage an enormous development of Socialism and Communism. Our industrial and social life is set in a huge communistic framework of public roadways, streets, bridges, water supplies, power supplies, lighting, tramways, schools, dockyards, and public aids and conveniences, employing a prodigious army of police, inspectors, teachers, and officials of all grades in hundreds of departments. We have found by bitter experience that it is impossible to trust factories, workshops, and mines to private management. Only by stern laws enforced by constant inspection have we stopped the monstrous waste of human life and welfare it cost when it was left uncontrolled by the Government. During the war our attempt to leave the munitioning of the army to private enterprise led us to the verge of defeat and caused an appalling slaughter of our soldiers. When the Government took the work out of private hands and had it done in national factories it was at once successful. The private firms were still allowed to do what little they could; but they had to be taught to do it economically, and to keep their accounts properly, by Government officials. Our big capitalist enterprises now run to the Government for help as a lamb runs to its mother. They cannot even make an extension of the Tube railway in London without Government aid. Unassisted private capitalism is breaking down or getting left behind in all directions. If all our Socialism and Communism and the drastic taxation of unearned incomes which finances it were to stop, our private enterprises would drop like shot stags, and we should all be dead in a month. When Mr Baldwin tried to win the last election by declaring that Socialism had been a failure whenever and wherever it had been tried, Socialism went over him like a steam roller and handed his office to a Socialist Prime Minister. Nothing could save us in the war but a great extension of Socialism; and now it is clear enough that only still greater extensions of it can repair the ravages of the war and keep pace with the growing requirements of civilization.

What we have to ask ourselves, then, is not whether we will have Socialism and Communism or not, but whether Democracy can keep pace with the developments of both that are being forced on us by the growth of national and international corporate action.

Now corporate action is impossible without a governing body. It may be the central Government: it may be a municipal corporation, a county council, a district council, or a parish council. It may be the board of directors of a joint stock company, or of a trust made by combining several joint stock companies. Such boards, elected by the votes of the shareholders, are little States within the State, and very powerful ones, too, some of them. If they have not laws and kings, they have by-laws and chairmen. And you and I, the consumers of their services, are more at the mercy of the boards that organize them than we are at the mercy of parliament. Several active politicians who began as Liberals and are now Socialists have said to me that they were converted by seeing that the nation had to choose, not between governmental control or industry and control by separate private individuals kept in order by their competition for our custom, but between governmental control and control by gigantic trusts wielding great power without responsibility, and having no object but to make as much money out of us as possible. Our Government is at this moment having much more trouble with the private corporations on whom we are dependent for our coals and cotton goods than with France or the United States of America. We are in the hands of our corporate bodies, public or private, for the satisfaction of our everyday needs. Their powers are life and death powers. I need not labor this point: we all know it.

But what we do not all realize is that we are equally dependent on corporate action for the satisfaction of our religious needs. Dean Inge tells us that our general elections have become public auctions at which the contending parties bid against one another for our votes by each promising us a larger share than the other of the plunder of the minority. Now that is perfectly true. The contending parties do not as yet venture to put it exactly in those words; but that is what it comes to. And the Dean's profession obliges him to urge his congregation, which is much wider than that of St Paul's (it extends across the Atlantic), always to vote for the party which pledges itself to go farthest in enabling those of us who have great possessions to sell them and give the price to the poor. But we cannot do this as private persons. It must be done by the Government or not at all. Take my own case. I am not a young man with great possessions; but I am an old man paying enough in income tax and surtax to provide doles for some hundreds of unemployed and old age pensioners. I have not the smallest objection to this: on the contrary, I advocated it strongly for years before I had any income worth taxing. But I could not do it if the Government did not arrange it for me. If the Government ceased taxing my superfluous money and redistributing it among people who have no incomes at all, I could do nothing by myself. What could I do? Can you suggest anything? I could send my war bonds to the Chancellor of the Exchequer and invite him to cancel the part of the National Debt that they represent; and he would undoubtedly thank me in the most courteous official terms for my patriotism. But the poor would not get any of it. The other payers of surtax and income tax and death duties would save the interest they now have to pay on it: that is all. I should only have made the rich richer and myself poorer. I could burn all my share certificates and inform the secretaries of the companies that they might write off that much of their capital indebtedness. The result would be a bigger dividend for the rest of the shareholders, with the poor out in the cold as before. I might sell my war bonds and share certificates for cash, and throw the money into the street to be scrambled for; but it would be snatched up, not by the poorest, but by the best fed and most able-bodied of the scramblers. Besides, if we all tried to sell our bonds and shares—and this is what you have to consider; for Christ's advice was not addressed to me alone but to all who have great possessions—the result would be that their value would fall to nothing, as the Stock Exchange would immediately become a market in which there were all sellers and no buyers. Accordingly, any spare money that the Government leaves me is invested where I can get the highest interest and the best security, as thereby I can make sure that it goes where it is most wanted and gives immediate employment. This is the best I can do without Government interference: indeed any other way of dealing with my spare money would be foolish and demoralizing; but the result is that I become richer and richer, and the poor become relatively poorer and poorer. So you see I cannot even be a Christian except through Government action; and neither can the Dean.

Now let us get down to our problem. We cannot govern ourselves; yet if we entrust the immense powers and revenues which are necessary in an effective modern Government to an absolute monarch or dictator, he goes more or less mad unless he is a quite extraordinary and therefore very seldom obtainable person. Besides, modern government is not a one-man job: it is too big for that. If we resort to a committee or parliament of superior persons, they will set up an oligarchy and abuse their power for their own benefit. Our dilemma is that men in the lump cannot govern themselves; and yet, as William Morris put it, no man is good enough to be another man's master. We need to be governed, and yet to control our governors. But the best governors will not accept any control except that of their own consciences; and, as we who are governed are also apt to abuse any power of control we have, our ignorance, our passions, our private and immediate interests are constantly in conflict with the knowledge, the wisdom, and the public spirit and regard for the future of our best qualified governors.

Still, if we cannot control our governors, can we not at least choose them and change them if they do not suit?

Let me invent a primitive example of democratic choice. It is always best to take imaginary examples: they offend nobody. Imagine then that we are the inhabitants of a village. We have to elect somebody for the office of postman. There are several candidates; but one stands out conspicuously, because he has frequently treated us at the public-house, has subscribed a shilling to our little flower show, has a kind word for the children when he passes, and is a victim of oppression by the squire because his late father was one of our most successful poachers. We elect him triumphantly; and he is duly installed, uniformed, provided with a red bicycle, and given a batch of letters to deliver. As his motive in seeking the post has been pure ambition, he has not thought much beforehand about his duties; and it now occurs to him for the first time that he cannot read. So he hires a boy to come round with him and read the addresses. The boy conceals himself in the lane whilst the postman delivers the letters at the house, takes the Christmas boxes, and gets the whole credit of the transaction. In course of time he dies with a high reputation for efficiency in the discharge of his duties; and we elect another equally illiterate successor on similar grounds. But by this time the boy has grown up and become an institution. He presents himself to the new postman as an established and indispensable feature of the postal system, and finally becomes recognized and paid by the village as such.

Here you have the perfect image of a popularly elected Cabinet Minister and the Civil Service department over which he presides. It may work very well; for our postman, though illiterate, may be a very capable fellow; and the boy who reads the addresses for him may be quite incapable of doing anything more. But this does not always happen. Whether it happens or not, the system is not a democratic reality: it is a democratic illusion. The boy, when he has ability enough to take advantage of the situation, is the master of the man. The person elected to do the work is not really doing it: he is a popular humbug who is merely doing what a permanent official tells him to do. That is how it comes about that we are now governed by a Civil Service which has such enormous power that its regulations are taking the place of the laws of England, though some of them are made for the convenience of the officials without the slightest regard to the convenience or even the rights of the public. And how are our Civil Servants selected? Mostly by an educational test which nobody but an expensively schooled youth can pass, thus making the most powerful and effective part of our government an irresponsible class government.

Now, what control have you or I over the Services? We have votes. I have used mine a few times to see what it is like. Well, it is like this. When the election approaches, two or three persons of whom I know nothing write to me soliciting my vote and enclosing a list of meetings, an election address, and a polling card. One of the addresses reads like an article in *The Morning Post,* and has a Union Jack on it. Another is like *The Daily News* or *Man-*

chester Guardian. Both might have been compiled from the editorial waste paper baskets of a hundred years ago. A third address, more up-to-date and much better phrased, convinces me that the sender has had it written for him at the headquarters of the Labor Party. A fourth, the most hopelessly out of date of them all, contains scraps of the early English translations of the Communist Manifesto of 1848. I have no guarantee that any of these documents were written by the candidates. They convey nothing whatever to me as to their character or political capacity. The half-tone photographic portraits which adorn the front pages do not even tell me their ages, having been taken twenty years ago. If I go to one of the meetings I find a schoolroom packed with people who find an election meeting cheaper and funnier than a theatre. On the platform sit one or two poor men who have worked hard to keep party politics alive in the constituency. They ought to be the candidates; but they have no more chance of such eminence than they have of possessing a Rolls-Royce car. They move votes of confidence in the candidates, though as the candidate is a stranger to them and to everybody else present nobody can possibly feel any such confidence. They lead the applause for him; they prompt him when questions are asked; and when he is completely floored they jump up and cry 'Let me answer that, Mr Chairman!' and then pretend that he has answered it. The old shibboleths are droned over; and nothing has any sense or reality in it except the vituperation of the opposition party, which is received with shouts of relief by the audience. Yet it is nothing but an exhibition of bad manners. If I vote for one of these candidates, and he or she is elected, I am supposed to be enjoying a democratic control of the government—to be exercising government *of* myself, *for* myself, *by* myself. Do you wonder that the Dean cannot believe such nonsense? If I believed it I should not be fit to vote at all. If this is Democracy, who can blame Signor Mussolini for describing it as a putrefying corpse?

The candidates may ask me what more they can do for me but present themselves and answer any questions I may put to them. I quite admit that they can do nothing; but that does not mend matters. What I should like is a real test of their capacity. Shortly before the war a doctor in San Francisco discovered that if a drop of a candidate's blood can be obtained on a piece of blotting paper it is possible to discover within half an hour what is wrong with him physically. What I am waiting for is the discovery of a process by which on delivery of a drop of his blood or a lock of his hair we can ascertain what is right with him mentally. We could then have a graded series of panels of capable persons for all employments, public or private, and not allow any person, however popular, to undertake the employment of governing us unless he or she were on the appropriate panel. At the lower end of the scale there would be a panel of persons qualified to take part in a parish meeting; at the higher end a panel of persons qualified to act as Secretaries of State for Foreign Affairs or Finance Ministers. At present not more than two per thousand of the population would be available for the highest panel. I should then be in no danger of electing a postman and finding that he could neither read nor write. My choice of candidates would be perhaps more restricted than at present; but I do not desire liberty to choose windbags and nincompoops to represent me in parliament; and my power to choose between one qualified candidate and another would give me as much control as is either possible or desirable. The voting and counting would be done by machinery: I should connect my telephone with the proper office; touch a button; and the machinery would do the rest.

Pending such a completion of the American doctor's discovery, how are we to go on? Well, as best we can, with the sort of government that our present system produces. Several reforms are possible without any new discovery. Our present parliament is obsolete: it can no more do the work of a modern State than Julius Caesar's galley could do the work of an Atlantic liner. We need in these islands two or three additional federal legislatures, working on our municipal committee system instead of our parliamentary party system. We need a central authority to co-ordinate the federal work. Our obsolete little internal frontiers must be obliterated, and our units of local government enlarged to dimensions compatible with the recent prodigious advances in facility of communication and co-operation. Commonwealth affairs and supernational activities through the League of Nations or otherwise will have to be provided for, and Cabinet function to be transformed. All the pseudo-democratic obstructive functions of our political machinery must be ruthlessly scrapped, and the general problem of government approached from a positive viewpoint at which mere anarchic national sovereignty as distinguished from self-government will have no meaning.

I must conclude by warning you that when everything has been done that can be done, civilization will still be dependent on the consciences of the governors and the governed. Our natural dispositions may be good; but we have been badly brought up, and are full of anti-social personal ambitions and prejudices and snobberies. Had we not better teach our children to be better citizens than ourselves? We are not doing that at present. The Russians *are*. That is my last word. Think over it.

Questions and Assignments

1. How would you characterize Shaw's tone and style as evidenced by the examples he uses and words and phrases like "windbag," "humbug," "men in the lump," "fellow," "completely floored"? Is the intent of this essay serious or humorous? How do you know?

2. Shaw begins by stating his subject clearly and by providing an analogy to indicate what he is going to say. What other analogies does he use and what purpose do they serve?

3. Of what value to the structure of this essay is Lincoln's definition of democracy?

4. Outline the rest of Shaw's argument with particular attention to his topic sentences. Notice that his conclusion brings the argument full circle by affirming and redefining the principle which he had at first denied. Explain why and how this is done.

5. Evaluate to the best of your ability Shaw's examples of government administration and election campaigns in a democracy.

6. What is Shaw's opinion of democracy?

7. Write an argument in favor of democracy modeled on the basic form of this essay, but with your own analogies and examples. See if you can find another quotation or definition which could serve your purpose as Lincoln's did for Shaw.

8. Write a similar essay on student government, the honor system, world government, family living, fraternities, sororities.

Evidence and Reasoning in Poetry

Most writing on literary works seeks to convince the reader of the correctness of a particular interpretation. In writing on literature, as in every kind of writing, conviction depends upon the clarity and completeness of the critical analysis; and clarity and completeness, in turn, depend on the use of evidence and logical reasoning. What you have learned from your discussions of premises and inferences can readily be applied to the poems which follow, and to the short stories which are contained in the final part of the text.

Evidence in literary works may be divided into six categories or "contexts." Words are the primary level of evidence. And, naturally, words achieve their intended meanings within a grammatical context.

Thus the first two things a critic must do is to familiarize himself with the meaning of the words and to determine exact grammatical relationships. The third context of meaning, or level of evidence, is the complete literary work. We cannot understand the total meaning of a poem or a story until we have finished reading it and have comprehended how the beginning is related to the end and how the various lines, stanzas or paragraphs, images and symbols, extend the thought or prolong a mood.

These three levels of meaning are usually sufficient for beginning writers; there are, however, three additional levels that critics often use in their analyses: the body of work, the life of the writer, and the literary period. If a poem occurs in a particular book of poetry, or if it uses symbols which occur repeatedly in a poet's work, a critic may find corroboration or support for his reading of the poem in these aspects of the poet's work. Secondly, the meaning of a literary work is quite often clarified or altered by a knowledge of the author's life. Finally, no piece of literature is written in complete isolation. Other literature of the same period or other works of literature in the same genre may have influenced the writing. Therefore, a critic is assisted in his understanding of a satiric work, for example, when he knows something about other satiric works with which the author was most likely familiar.

Critics drawing upon these six levels of evidence reason for the most part inductively. The poet's language, his syntax, and his images are the prime facts from which a critic infers a general principle of meaning, or unifying thesis. Further "facts" or evidence are provided by the poet's life, his body of work, and the literary tradition in which he works. Occasionally, however, a critic cites a commonly accepted principle and reasons deductively. For example, in the essay on "Logic and Lyric" which you are about to read, the critic begins with the principle that sixteenth- and seventeenth-century poets were highly trained in logic and that they used logical forms in their poetry. From this principle he proceeds to demonstrate the logic in particular poems. Often the deductive principle will be somewhat more concealed and the reader will have to ask himself what assumptions lead a particular critic to emphasize some facts more than others. For example, why does one critic stress something which another critic passes over as an inconsequential piece of evidence?

As you read the poems in this section, and the short stories in Part Five, you may want to distinguish between the levels of evidence in critical argument. Although students will most likely need to confine their arguments to the first three levels—language, syntax, and complete work, the critics will be seen to use references to the other levels as well. The principle guiding the use of these various levels of evidence is simple: whenever the first three levels provide us with a completely satisfactory understanding, it may not be necessary to draw upon other evidence. However, when confusion or incompleteness results from a reading of the literary work as a self-sufficient entity, it may be necessary to argue from other levels.

The selections that follow include a famous poem by the seventeenth-century English poet Andrew Marvell, a discussion of the logic in this poem, and in another poem, by poet-teacher J. V. Cunningham, and three poems containing varying degrees of "logic." The student might well begin by reading the Marvell poem and preparing his own interpretation. Then he could read Cunningham's essay and interpretation. Finally, he will find it useful to apply the methods described in the essay, along with whatever modifications he may find necessary, to interpret the three poems that follow.

Sir Walter Raleigh's poem was written as a reply to Christopher Marlowe's, and Archibald MacLeish's poem is based on a thought contained in Marvell's "To His Coy Mistress."

To His Coy Mistress

ANDREW MARVELL

Had we but world enough, and time,
This coyness, lady, were no crime.
We would sit down, and think which way
To walk, and pass our long love's day.
Thou by the Indian Ganges' side

Should'st rubies find: I by the tide
Of Humber would complain. I would
Love you ten years before the Flood,
And you should, if you please, refuse
Till the conversion of the Jews.
My vegetable love should grow
Vaster than empires, and more slow.
An hundred years should go to praise
Thine eyes, and on thy forehead gaze:
Two hundred to adore each breast:
But thirty thousand to the rest;
An age at least to every part,
And the last age should show your heart.
For, lady, you deserve this state,
Nor would I love at lower rate.
But at my back I always hear
Time's wingèd chariot hurrying near:
And yonder all before us lie
Deserts of vast eternity.
Thy beauty shall no more be found;
Nor, in thy marble vault, shall sound
My echoing song: then worms shall try
That long-preserved virginity,
And your quaint honour turn to dust,
And into ashes all my lust.
The grave's a fine and private place,
But none, I think, do there embrace.
Now, therefore, while the youthful hue
Sits on thy skin like morning dew,
And while thy willing soul transpires
At every pore with instant fires,
Now let us sport us while we may;
And now, like amorous birds of prey,
Rather at once our Time devour,
Than languish in his slow-chapt power.
Let us roll all our strength and all
Our sweetness up into one ball,

And tear our pleasures with rough strife
Thorough the iron gates of life.
Thus, though we cannot make our sun
Stand still, yet we will make him run.

Logic and Lyric

J. V. CUNNINGHAM

In this essay I shall propose the question: May the principle structure of a poem be of a logical rather than of an alogical sort? For example, to confine ourselves to the Old Logic: May a lyric be solely or predominantly the exposition of a syllogism? and may the propositions of the lyric, one by one, be of the sort to be found in a logical syllogism?

The incautious romantic will deny the possibility, and with a repugnance of feeling that would preclude any further discussion. For logic and lyric are generally regarded as opposites, if not as contradictory terms. "It is a commonplace," says a recent writer on logic, "that poetry and logic have nothing to do with each other, that they are even opposed to one another."[1] You will find this explicitly stated, sometimes with the substitution of "science" for "logic," in most of the school handbooks on the study of literature, in most of the introductions to poetry. "The peculiar quality of poetry," we read in one of these, "can be distinguished from that of prose if one thinks of the creative mind as normally expressing itself in a variety of literary forms ranged along a graduated scale between the two contrasted extremes of scientific exposition and lyrical verse." And, a little later, "[Poetry] strives for a conviction begotten of the emotions rather than of the reason." Consequently, we are told, "The approach of poetry is indirect. It proceeds by means of suggestion, implication, reflection. Its method is largely symbolical. It is more interested in connotations than in denotations."[2] This is common doctrine. Poetry is in some way concerned with emotion rather than with reason, and its method is imaginative, indirect, implicit rather than explicit, symbolical rather than discursive, concerned with what its terms suggest rather than with what they state. The kind of

[1] Richard von Mises, *Positivism* (Cambridge, Mass., 1951), p. 289.

[2] Harold R. Walley and J. Harold Wilson, *The Anatomy of Literature* (New York, 1934), pp. 143, 144.

poetry which most fully possesses and exhibits these concerns, methods, and qualities is generally thought to be the lyric, and hence the lyric, of all poetry, is regarded as the most antithetical to reason, logic, and science.

This was not always the case. In the eighth century, for example, a scholiast of the school of Alcuin regarded not only grammar and rhetoric but dialectic or logic also as the disciplines that nourish and form a poet. In the medieval and Renaissance traditions of commentary on Aristotle's logic, poetic is sometimes regarded as a part, a subdivision, of logic—as, indeed, I consider it myself. So late as the eighteenth century, David Hume writes in an essay *Of the Standard of Taste:* "Besides, every kind of composition, even the most poetical, is nothing but a chain of propositions and reasonings; not always indeed the justest and most exact, but still plausible and specious, however disguised by the coloring of the imagination." And even today the writer on logic whom I quoted earlier asserts, in denial of the commonplace: "Every poem, except in rare extreme cases, contains judgements and implicit propositions, and thus becomes subject to logical analysis."[3]

But may the chain of propositions and reasonings be not merely plausible and specious but even sufficiently just and exact? May the poem be not merely subject to logical analysis but logical in form? May, to return to our point, the subject and structure of a poem be conceived and expressed syllogistically? Anyone at all acquainted with modern criticism and the poems that are currently in fashion will think in this connection of Marvell's "To His Coy Mistress." The apparent structure of that poem is an argumentative syllogism, explicitly stated. "Had we but world enough and time," the poet says,

> *This coyness, Lady, were no crime . . .*
> *But at my back I always hear*
> *Time's wingèd chariot hurry near . . .*
> *Now, therefore . . .*
> *. . . let us sport us while we may.*

If we had all the space and time in the world, we could delay consummation. But we do not. Therefore. The structure is formal. The poet offers to the lady a practical syllogism, and if she assents to it, the appropriate consequence, he hopes, will follow.

[3] Scholiast cited in Otto Bird, "The Seven Liberal Arts," in Joseph T. Shipley (ed.), *Dictionary of World Literature* (New York, 1943), p. 55; J. E. Spingarn, *A History of Literary Criticism in the Renaissance* (2d ed.; New York, 1908), pp. 24–27; David Hume, *Philosophical Works* (Boston and Edinburgh, 1854), III, 264; von Mises, *loc. cit.*

The logical nature of the argument here has been generally recognized, though often with a certain timidity. Mr. Eliot hazards: "the three strophes of Marvell's poem have something like a syllogistic relation to each other." And in a recent scholarly work we read: "The dialectic of the poem lies not only or chiefly in the formal demonstration explicit in its three stanzas, but in all the contrasts evoked by its images and in the play between the immediately sensed and the intellectually apprehended."[4] That is, the logic is recognized, but minimized, and our attention is quickly distracted to something more reputable in a poem, the images or the characteristic tension of metaphysical poetry. For Mr. Eliot the more important element in this case is a principle of order common in modern poetry and often employed in his own poems. He points out that the theme of Marvell's poem is "one of the great traditional commonplaces of European literature . . . the theme of . . . *Gather ye rosebuds,* of *Go, lovely rose.*" "Where the wit of Marvell," he continues, "renews the theme is in the variety and order of the images." The dominant principle of order in the poem, then, is an implicit one rather than the explicit principle of the syllogism, and implicit in the succession of images.

Mr. Eliot explains the implicit principle of order in this fashion:

> In the first of the three paragraphs Marvell plays with a fancy that begins by pleasing and leads to astonishment. . . . We notice the high speed, the succession of concentrated images, each magnifying the original fancy. When this process has been carried to the end and summed up, the poem turns suddenly with that surprise which has been one of the most important means of poetic effect since Homer:
>
> *But at my back I always hear*
> *Time's wingèd chariot hurrying near,*
> *And yonder all before us lie*
> *Deserts of vast eternity.*
>
> A whole civilization resides in these lines:
>
> *Pallida Mors aequo pulsat pede pauperum tabernas*
> *Regumque turres . . .**

[4] T. S. Eliot, *Selected Essays* (new ed.; New York, 1950), p. 254; Helen C. White, Ruth C. Wallerstein, and Ricardo Quintana (eds.), *Seventeenth Century Verse and Prose* (New York, 1951), I, p. 454.

* These lines are translated on page 488 as follows: "Pallid death with indifferent foot strikes the poor man's hut and the palaces of kings."

> A modern poet, had he reached the height, would very likely have closed on this moral reflection.

What is meant by this last observation becomes clear a little later where it is said that the wit of the poem "forms the crescendo and diminuendo of a scale of great imaginative power." The structure of the poem, then, is this: It consists of a succession of images increasing in imaginative power to the sudden turn and surprise of the image of time, and then decreasing to the conclusion. But is there any sudden turn and surprise in the image of time? and does the poem consist of a succession of images?

This talk of images is a little odd, since there seem to be relatively few in the poem if one means by "image" what people usually do—a descriptive phrase that invites the reader to project a sensory construction. The looming imminence of Time's wingèd chariot is, no doubt, an image, though not a full-blown one, since there is nothing in the phrasing that properly invites any elaboration of sensory detail. But when Mr. Eliot refers to "successive images" and cites "my *vegetable* love," with *vegetable* italicized, and "Till the conversion of the Jews," one suspects that he is provoking images where they do not textually exist. There is about as much of an image in "Till the conversion of the Jews" as there would be in "till the cows come home," and it would be a psychiatrically sensitive reader who would immediately visualize the lowing herd winding slowly o'er the lea. But "my *vegetable* love" will make the point. I have no doubt that Mr. Eliot and subsequent readers do find an image here. They envisage some monstrous and expanding cabbage, but they do so in ignorance. *Vegetable* is no vegetable but an abstract and philosophical term, known as such to the educated man of Marvell's day. Its context is the doctrine of the three souls: the rational, which in man subsumes the other two; the sensitive, which men and animals have in common and which is the principle of motion and perception; and, finally, the lowest of the three, the vegetable soul, which is the only one that plants possess and which is the principle of generation and corruption, of augmentation and decay. Marvell says, then, my love, denied the exercise of sense but possessing the power of augmentation, will increase "Vaster than empires." It is an intellectual image, and hence no image at all but a conceit. For if one calls any sort of particularity or detail in a poem an "image," the use of the wrong word will invite the reader to misconstrue his experience in terms of images, to invent sensory constructions and to project them on the poem.

A conceit is not an image. It is a piece of wit. It is, in the tradition in which Marvell was writing, among other possibilities, the discovery of a proposition referring to one field of experience in terms of an intellectual structure derived from another field, and often enough a field of learning, as is the case in "my vegetable love." This tradition, though it goes back to the poetry of John Donne, and years before that, was current in Marvell's day. The fashionable poetry at the time he was writing this poem, the poetry comparable to that of Eliot or of Auden in the last two decades, was the poetry of John Cleveland, and the fashionable manner was generally known as "Clevelandizing." It consisted in the invention of a series of witty hyperbolical conceits, sometimes interspersed with images, and containing a certain amount of roughage in the form of conventional erotic statements:

Thy beauty shall no more be found,
Nor in thy marble vault shall sound
My echoing song. . . .

It was commonly expressed in the octosyllabic couplet. Cleveland, for example, writes "Upon Phillis Walking in a Morning before Sun-rising":

The trees, (like yeomen of the guard,
Serving more for pomp than ward). . . .

The comparison here does not invite visualization. It would be inappropriate to summon up the colors and serried ranks of the guard. The comparison is made solely with respect to the idea: the trees, like the guard, serve more for pomp than ward. Again:

The flowers, called out of their beds,
Start and raise up their drowsy heads,
And he that for their color seeks
May find it vaulting to her cheeks,
Where roses mix,—no civil war
Between her York and Lancaster.[5]

One does not here picture in panorama the Wars of the Roses. One sees rather the aptness and the wit of York and Lancaster, the white rose and the red, reconciled in her cheeks, or one rejects it as forced and far-fetched. This is a matter of taste.

But if the poem is not a succession of images, does it exhibit that other

[5] John M. Berdan (ed.), *The Poems* (New Haven, 1911), pp. 80–81.

principle which Mr. Eliot ascribes to it—the turn and surprise which he finds in the abrupt introduction of Time's chariot and which forms a sort of fulcrum on which the poem turns? Subsequent critics have certainly felt that it has. In a current textbook we read:

> The poem begins as a conventional love poem in which the lover tries to persuade his mistress to give in to his entreaties. But with the introduction of the image of the chariot in l. 21, the poet becomes obsessed by the terrible onrush of time, and the love theme becomes scarcely more than an illustration of the effect which time has upon human life.[6]

. . . .

Let us question the fact. Does the idea of time and death come as any surprise in this context? The poem began, "Had we but world enough and time." That is, it began with an explicit condition contrary to fact, which, by all grammatical rules, amounts to the assertion that we do not have world enough and time. There is no surprise whatever when the proposition is explicitly made in line 21. It would rather have been surprising if it had not been made. Indeed, the only question we have in this respect, after we have read the first line, is: How many couplets will the poet expend on the ornamental reiteration of the initial proposition before he comes to the expected *but?* The only turn in the poem is the turn which the structure of the syllogism had led us to await.

Mr. Eliot compares the turn and surprise which he finds in this poem to a similar turn in an ode of Horace's, and the scholars seem to corroborate the comparison. This is the fourth ode of the first book:

> *Solvitur acris hiems grata vice veris et Favoni,*
> *trahuntque siccas machinae carinas . . .*

The poem begins with a picture of spring and proceeds by a succession of images, images of the external world and mythological images:

> Sharp winter relaxes with the welcome change to Spring and the west wind, and the cables haul the dry keels of ships. The herd no longer takes pleasure in its stalls or the farmer in his fire, and the pastures no longer whiten with hoar frost. Cytherean Venus leads her dancers beneath the overhanging moon, and the beautiful graces and nymphs strike the ground with alternate foot, while

[6] Wright Thomas and Stuart Gerry Brown (eds.), *Reading Poems* (New York, 1941), p. 702.

> blazing Vulcan visits the grim forges of the Cyclops. Now is the time to wind your bright hair with green myrtle or with the flowers that the thawed earth yields. Now is the time to sacrifice to Faunus in the shadowed woods, whether it be a lamb he asks or a kid:
>
> *Pallida mors aequo pulsat pede pauperum tabernas*
> *regumque turres.*
>
> Pallid death with indifferent foot strikes the poor man's hut and the palaces of kings. Now, fortunate Sestius, the brief sum of life forbids our opening a long account with hope. Night will soon hem you in, and the fabled ghosts, and Pluto's meagre house.

Death occurs in this poem with that suddenness and lack of preparation with which it sometimes occurs in life. The structure of the poem is an imitation of the structure of such experiences in life. And as we draw from such experiences often a generalization, so Horace from the sudden realization of the abruptness and impartiality of death, reflects

> *vitae summa brevis spem nos vetat incohare longam.*
>
> The brief sum of life forbids our opening a long account with hope.

But the proposition is subsequent to the experience; it does not rule and direct the poem from the outset. And the experience in Horace *is* surprising and furnishes the fulcrum on which the poem turns. It has, in fact, the characteristics which are ascribed to Marvell's poem but which Marvell's poem does not have. The two are two distinct kinds of poetry, located in distinct and almost antithetical traditions; both are valuable and valid methods, but one is not to be construed in terms of the other.

In brief, the general structure of Marvell's poem is syllogistic, and it is located in the Renaissance tradition of formal logic and of rhetoric. The structure exists in its own right and as a kind of expandable filing system. It is a way of disposing of, of making a place for, elements of a different order: in this case, Clevelandizing conceits and erotic propositions in the tradition of Jonson and Herrick. These reiterate the propositions of the syllogism. They do not develop the syllogism, and they are not required by the syllogism; they are free and extra. There could be more or less of them, since there is nothing in the structure that determines the number of interpolated couplets. It is a matter of tact and a matter of the appetite of the writer and the reader.

The notion of a structure as a kind of expandable filing system may deserve a few sentences. The narrative structure of a Shakespearean play can be regarded as a structure of this order. It exists in its own right, of course, but it is also a method for disposing various kinds of material of other orders, a set speech or passion here, an interpolated comic routine in another place. The structure offers a series of hooks upon which different things can be hung. Whether the totality will then form a whole, a unity, is a question of interpretation and a question of value. It is a question, for example, of what sort of unity is demanded and whether there are various sorts.

In Marvell's poem, only the general structure is syllogistic; the detail and development are of another order, and critics have been diligent in assigning the poetic quality of the whole to the nonsyllogistic elements. Is it possible, then, to write a lyric that will be wholly or almost wholly syllogistic? It is.

. . . .

I shall conclude with . . . a lyric of . . . renown in modern criticism. This is the song from *Summer's Last Will and Testament* by Thomas Nashe, "Adieu, farewell, earth's bliss." It, . . . has a refrain, though in English, a response from the Litany of Saints which was customarily recited through the streets of London in time of plague. The poem, . . . consists of a series of discrete, self-inclosed stanzas, in which each line is end-stopped. The structure of the poem is, like . . . Marvell's, a practical syllogism explicitly propounded, though not quite so formally as in the preceding poem. It opens with the rejection of earthly happiness. The argument is, to begin with the surpressed premise: true happiness is certain, but the world is uncertain; therefore worldly happiness is not true happiness. The world is uncertain since it is subject to the certainty of death and change. Nor can the goods of this world buy continued life, or the art of medicine procure it: the plague increases. What is best in this life—and here we have the structure of the next three stanzas—beauty, prowess, and wit, all fade:

Haste therefore each degree
To welcome destiny . . .

For the world after death is certain, and its happiness true happiness:

Adieu, farewell, earth's bliss!
This world uncertain is:
Fond are life's lustful joys,
Death proves them all but toys.

None from his darts can fly;
I am sick, I must die—
Lord, have mercy on us.

Rich men, trust not in wealth,
Gold cannot buy you health;
Physic himself must fade;
All things to end are made;
The plague full swift goes by;
I am sick, I must die—
Lord, have mercy on us.

Beauty is but a flower;
Which wrinkles will devour,
Brightness falls from the air;
Queens have died young and fair;
Dust hath closed Helen's eye;
I am sick, I must die—
Lord, have mercy on us.

Strength stoops unto the grave,
Worms feed on Hector brave;
Swords may not fight with fate;
Earth still holds ope her gate;
Come, come! the bells do cry—
I am sick, I must die—
Lord, have mercy on us.

Wit with his wantonness
Tasteth death's bitterness;
Hell's executioner
Hath no ears for to hear
What vain art can reply;
I am sick, I must die—
Lord, have mercy on us.

Haste therefore each degree
To welcome destiny;
Heaven is our heritage
Earth but a player's stage;

Mount we unto the sky;
I am sick, I must die—
Lord, have mercy on us.[7]

The poem is a series of fairly literal propositions, some exactly in logical form: *This world uncertain is, All things to end are made, Queens have died young and fair, Haste therefore each degree.* They are such propositions as might have been translated from the *Summa contra Gentiles* of Thomas Aquinas, and they are located in that general tradition. Thomas, for instance, discusses the following questions: That human happiness does not consist in carnal pleasures; that man's happiness does not consist in glory; that man's happiness does not consist in wealth; that happiness does not consist in wordly power; that happiness does not consist in the practice of art; that man's ultimate happiness is not in this life, "for if there is ulitmate happiness in this life, it will certainly be lost, at least by death."[8] But these are the propositions of Nashe's lyric, some literally, some more figuratively put.

Of the propositions in the poem, perhaps the most figurative is *Strength stoops unto the grave,* which yet is fairly literal as we see the suggestion of an aged figure bent over more and more until he is almost prone. And there are, of course, affective elements in the poem, as in *death's bitterness* and *Hell's executioner.* But the special distinction of the poem and the source of an unusual quality of feeling perhaps lies in the meter as much as in anything else. The six-syllable line glides from a regular iambic pattern into a triple movement—accented, unaccented, accented—and back again as if both were its mode of being and neither had precedence over the other:

Beauty is but a flower
Which wrinkles will devour;
Brightness falls from the air;
Queens have died young and fair...

The poem in this respect belongs to a curious episode in the history of English meter; for this phenomenon appears only, to my knowledge, in the songs written within a fairly short period, of perhaps ten or twenty years, in the 1590's and early 1600's. Of a similar sort is Shakespeare's:

[7] Modernized from Ronald B. McKerrow (ed.), *Works* (London, 1904–10), III, 283.

[8] *Contra Gentiles* iii. pp. 27, 29–31, 36, 48, in *Opera omnia* (Rome, 1882–1948), Vol. XIV; Anton C. Pegis (ed.), *Basic Writings of Saint Thomas Aquinas* (New York, 1945), Vol. II.

Come away, come away, death,
And in sad cypress let me be laid;
Fly away, fly away, breath;
I am slain by a fair cruel maid.

But the special distinction of the poem has usually been found in the line, *Brightness falls from the air.* This is certainly a proposition of a different order from those we have discussed, and one that has excited the sensibilities of innumerable modern readers. It is a line in the symbolist tradition. One remembers how Stephen Dedalus in the *Portrait of the Artist as a Young Man* recalls the line, though at first in an altered form:

> She had passed through the dusk. And therefore the air was silent save for one soft hiss that fell. And therefore the tongues about him had ceased their babble. Darkness was falling.
>
> *Darkness falls from the air.*
>
> A trembling joy, lambent as a faint light, played like a fairy host around him. But why? Her passage through the darkening air or the verse with its black vowels and its opening sound, rich and lutelike?
>
> He walked away slowly towards the deeper shadows at the end of the colonnade, beating the stone softly with his stick to hide his revery from the students whom he had left: and allowed his mind to summon back to itself the age of Dowland and Byrd and Nashe.
>
> Eyes, opening from the darkness of desire, eyes that dimmed the breaking east. What was their languid grace but the softness of chambering? And what was their shimmer but the shimmer of the scum that mantled the cesspool of the court of a slobbering Stuart. And he tasted in the language of memory ambered vines, dying fallings of sweet airs, the proud pavan. . . .
>
> The images he had summoned gave him no pleasure. They were secret and enflaming but her image was not entangled by them. . . .
>
> Yes; and it was not darkness that fell from the air. It was brightness.
>
> *Brightness falls from the air.*
>
> He had not even remembered right Nashe's line. All the images it had awakened were false.[9]

[9] James Joyce, *A Portrait of the Artist as a Young Man* ("Modern Library" ed.; New York, 1928), pp. 273–75.

But all the images it had awakened were false for still another reason. The line as Joyce quotes it is certainly an evocative line, a line in the symbolist tradition, and hence apt and fitted to entangle itself in reverie. But it seems out of place in the poem. It is so much a line in the symbolist tradition that the historical scholar grows wary and suspicious. He turns to the text. He looks in the great modern edition of Nashe, the edition of McKerrow, and he finds that the editor records with a sigh: "It is to be hoped that Nashe meant 'ayre,' but I cannot help strongly suspecting that the true reading is 'hayre,' which gives a more obvious, but far inferior, sense."[10] So we have the alternatives: *Brightness falls from the air* or *Brightness falls from the hair*. But the latter is a literal account of the effect of age and death. The proposition so read is of the same order as all the other propositions in the poem, of the same order as *Queens have died young and fair*. There is no doubt, then, as to the correct reading. In fact, the symbolistic line, however good, is a bad line in context, since it is out of keeping. And so the poem loses its last claim to modernity. It becomes a Renaissance poem. It returns to the park of logic from the forest of reverie. The experience of the poem is the experience of syllogistic thinking with its consequences for feeling, attitude, and action. It is a mode of experience that the Renaissance practiced and cherished, and expressed with power, dignity, and precision. It is a poetical experience and a logical, and it is both at once.

[10] McKerrow, IV, p. 440.

Questions and Assignments

1. Notice the clear, straightforward opening paragraph. What purpose does such an orderly and precise beginning serve? How does it affect the tone of the essay?

2. The author spends two paragraphs stating the problem of "Logic and Lyric." What is the effect of the phrase "incautious romantics" as a label for those who see a contradiction between logic and lyric? Is this a legitimate procedure?

3. How convincing (in paragraph three) is it to say "a scholiast of the school of Alcuin"? What is a *scholiast,* what is *the school of Alcuin*? Is Cunningham's case weakened by the "sometimes" in the third sentence of the third paragraph?

4. Is it possible that several of the terms used in the early paragraphs, for example, *logic, science, lyric, reason,* are equivocal terms? How would this affect the problem Cunningham is discussing? What would be the difference between quoting Hume on poetical composition and quoting a contemporary critic?

5. Summarize the difference between the way Cunningham reads "To His Coy Mistress" and the way others have apparently read the poem. Which do you

prefer? Why? Could you add anything to these readings? Is the argument in the poem valid or invalid? Must it necessarily follow that it is a crime to be "coy" because "time's wingèd chariot" is at the back? What does Cunningham mean by saying that in this poem "only the general structure is syllogistic; the detail and development are of another order"?

6. Do you find the poems by Marvel and Nashe equally persuasive? Which do you consider the better poem? Why?

7. What is the purpose of the illustration drawn from Joyce's novel? On the basis of the information given in the last paragraph, can you explain the terms "symbolist" and "Renaissance tradition"?

8. Does the final paragraph suggest to you that logic is particularly pertinent in a Renaissance poem? Does this fit with what Cunningham said in his opening paragraph?

9. Write a theme contradicting or further supporting Cunningham's contentions regarding logic and lyric poetry. Draw upon analyses of both poems that he discussed and also of the poems which follow this essay. You will be trying to prove that they are or are not logical, or perhaps that they are a little of both.

10. Write a theme based on question five.

The Passionate Shepherd to His Love

CHRISTOPHER MARLOWE

Come live with me and be my love,
And we will all the pleasures prove,
That valleys, groves, hills and fields,
Woods or steepy mountains yields.

And we will sit upon the rocks,
Seeing the shepherds feed their flocks
By shallow rivers, to whose falls
Melodious birds sing madrigals.

And I will make thee beds of roses,
And a thousand fragrant posies,
A cap of flowers and a kirtle
Embroidered all with leaves of myrtle;

A gown made of the finest wool,
Which from our pretty lambs we pull;
Fair-linèd slippers for the cold,
With buckles of the purest gold;

A belt of straw and ivy buds,
With coral clasps and amber studs;
And if these pleasures may thee move,
Come live with me and be my love.

The shepherd swains shall dance and sing
For thy delight each May morning;
If these delights thy mind may move.
Then live with me and be my love.

The Nymph's Reply to the Shepherd

SIR WALTER RALEIGH

If all the world and love were young
And truth in every shepherd's tongue,
These pretty pleasures might me move
To live with thee and be thy love.

Time drives the flocks from field to fold
When rivers rage and rocks grow cold,
And Philomel becometh dumb;
The rest complain of cares to come.

The flowers do fade, and wanton fields
To wayward winter reckoning yields;
A honey tongue, a heart of gall,
Is fancy's spring, but sorrow's fall.

Thy gowns, thy shoes, thy beds of roses
Thy cap, thy kirtle, and thy posies
Soon break, soon wither, soon forgotten,
In folly ripe, in reason rotten.

Thy belt of straw and ivy buds,
Thy coral clasps and amber studs,
All these in me no means can move
To come to thee and be thy love.

But could youth last and love still breed,
Had joys no date nor age no need,
Then these delights my mind might move
To live with thee and be thy love.

You, Andrew Marvell

ARCHIBALD MacLEISH

And here face down beneath the sun
And here upon earth's noonward height
To feel the always coming on
The always rising of the night:

To feel creep up the curving east
The earthy chill of dusk and slow
Upon those under lands the vast
And ever climbing shadow grow

And strange at Ecbatan the trees
Take leaf by leaf the evening strange
The flooding dark about their knees
The mountains over Persia change

And now at Kermanshah the gate
Dark empty and the withered grass
And through the twilight now the late
Few travelers in the westward pass

And Baghdad darken and the bridge
Across the silent river gone
And through Arabia the edge
Of evening widen and steal on

And deepen on Palmyra's street
The wheel rut in the ruined stone
The wheel rut in the ruined Crete
High through the clouds and overblown

And over Sicily the air
Still flashing with the landward gulls
And loom and slowly disappear
The sails above the shadowy hulls

And Spain go under and the shore
Of Africa the gilded sand
And evening vanish and no more
The low pale light across that land

Nor now the long light on the sea

And here face downward in the sun
To feel how swift how secretly
The shadow of the night comes on . . .

Questions and Assignments

1. On what premise does the "passionate shepherd's" argument depend? What is the offering—in modern terms? Hyperbole plays an important part in his argument. Does this help or hinder his argument, or both?

2. Why does the nymph reject the shepherd's argument? Express the idea of this poem in your own words. How logical is her reply?

3. You will notice that MacLeish's poem is not actually a completed sentence. The implications then are just as important as what is actually said. What are those implications? What is the relationship between this poem and "To His Coy Mistress" and what is the explanation for the title? How logical is this poem in Cunningham's terms?

4. If possible, follow the method outlined in "Logic and Lyric" and write a critical interpretation of one or all of these three poems. Remember that not all lyrics have a clear rational organization, much less a syllogistic structure. In fact, as Cunningham suggests at the beginning of his essay, many lyrics are expressions of emotion rather than examples of logical thought. You may want to examine each of these poems in terms of rational thought versus imagistic progression. Which seems more significant—the ideas (which are paraphrasable and definable) or the images (which may be to a large extent unparaphrasable and indefinable)? What is the relationship between logic and emotion in each of the poems?

Perspectives on a Poem

In this section we bring together three differing views on a single poem by the modern American poet, Wallace Stevens. In order to understand the interpretations of Stevens' poem we must read them as we would any argumentative essay. We must determine precisely what the writer is saying and what evidence he uses to support his views. The commentaries each take and support a slightly different reading of "A Glass of Water." The reader's first step should be to summarize the main ideas of each and then determine whether different assumptions or different understandings of language and image, or a combination of both, have caused the variation in interpretation.

As the selections themselves show, these essays are published in the same order as they were written. Each succeeding essay includes direct comments on the preceding selection. The student, however, should not simply accept the summary of previous commentaries given by the critics. Eric Sellin teaches at the University of Pennsylvania, Warren French at Kansas State University, and Sister Therese at Trinity College, Washington, D.C.

The Glass of Water

WALLACE STEVENS

That the glass would melt in heat,
That the water would freeze in cold,
Shows that this object is merely a state,
One of many, between two poles. So,
In the metaphysical, there are these poles.

Here in the centre stands the glass. Light
Is the lion that comes down to drink. There
And in that state the glass is a pool.
Ruddy are his eyes and ruddy are his claws
When light comes down to wet his frothy jaws

And in the water winding weeds move round.
And there and in another state—the refractions,
The metaphysica, *the plastic parts of poems*

Crash in the mind—But fat Jocundus, worrying
About what stands here in the centre, not the glass,

But in the centre of our lives, this time, this day,
It is a state, this spring among the politicians
Playing cards. In a village of the indigenes,
One would have still to discover. Among the dogs and dung,
One would continue to contend with one's ideas.

Stevens' "The Glass of Water"

ERIC SELLIN

In this poem of deceivingly simple subject matter and equally confusing contrast and paradoxes we have the crux of the Stevens cosmos. Whereas T. S. Eliot tells us of his ideas on relativity in *Burnt Norton* with the sweeping generalities

Time present and time past
Are both perhaps present in time future,
And time future contained in time past . . .

which are not particularly revolutionary or revelatory, Stevens takes a mundane object to illustrate to us his conception of relativity. This concept is, fittingly enough, handled differently in various poems. In "Thirteen Ways of Looking at a Blackbird" the same subject appears different and therefore *is* different according to light, movement, and setting, much like the subject of a series of Claude Monet impressionist studies. In the "Anecdote of the Jar" Stevens is concerned with a formal relativity such that the sculptured or geometric jar makes the forest take on new direction, organization, and personality, with the vessel as the hub or focal point. "The Glass of Water" is more complex than either of these poems, and it contains concepts found in both of them.

We are confronted with a simple glass of water. But in the first line we are reminded that the glass will melt in heat and is hence a liquid with very high freezing point. We are then told that the water could freeze and is hence a solid with a low melting point. The glass of water as we see it is not something we can be secure about, for its functional thirst-quenching state as we know it is merely one of many states between two poles. The relativity is not merely one of heat and time, then, but also one in which our conceptions of the real object are relative—by necessity "existential."

Thus if the observer's conception of the object cannot be securely established, if that object can vary in state, the actual nature of its meaning may not be established, i.e., is relative. Thus the light does not resemble a lion, but "is" a lion coming to drink. It is childish to say, "But a lion couldn't possibly be mistaken for a light on a glass of water." Stevens, in his theory of "correspondances"—not to be confused with Baudelaire's quite different theory—is not concerned with the physical lion or the physical glass of water once the relativity has been inferred. Once both are in that realm of physical and, what's more important, conceptual relativity, the objects themselves cease to have qualities that make them incompatible and are intermingled "metaphysica" on an unreal level, crashing the mind, giving birth to insight and art.

But even in this revelation of relativity the writer is confronted with the further relative fact that, if the object may change with heat or time or light along a continuum of "states" between two poles, so is his insight merely a "state" of metaphysical momentariness along with the indifference of the jovial drinker for whom the essence lies in the contents of the functional glass and the ignorance of those who have yet to set thought to such problems.

It is in the ebb and flood of this last relativity that even he who has discovered the conceptual relativity of "things" and functions must continue to contend with his own ideas which become relative themselves when compared to the "state" of mind of others ("the politicians" if you will) on a certain day at a certain time, not to mention his own ideas which may vary with the time and the day—for as Stevens tells us in line 5, the metaphysical has poles, too.

Stevens' "The Glass of Water"

WARREN G. FRENCH

Eric Sellin's explication of Wallace Stevens' "The Glass of Water" (EXP., Jan., 1959, XVII, 28) leaves the impression that the poem is a versified essay presenting through a homely metaphor only a concept of relativity. This presentation ends dramatically in the third stanza; the whole poem is more aptly described as a dramatic monologue recording an internal debate that culminates in the formulation of a credo for creators of speculative verse.

It is helpful to approach this astringent but idealistic poem through W. H. Auden's comments about the poet in modern society that conclude his contribution to *Poets at Work* (New York, 1948, pp. 180-81). The point of these is that the poet should not be distracted from pursuing his vision by the meretricious demands of a sick culture, but should reject its bribes to go on "humming quietly to himself." Stevens, too, speaks of subjects beyond the comprehension of those preoccupied with the transient, immediate, and obvious.

In the first two and a half stanzas of "The Glass of Water," the speaker is (as in many of Stevens' poems) lecturing—possibly only himself—demonstrating by analogy the concept of relativity Sellin explains—that a symbol of refreshment and fertility may in another potential state be the center of a fiery drama and in yet another a stagnant body. The explanation is unfinished, because the lecturer breaks off suddenly—as if exasperated by an indifferent audience (perhaps only his own mocking misgivings) —with the observation that the efforts to communicate concretely the poet's apprehensions cause intense mental activity, "crash in the mind."

These efforts are unappreciated by "fat Jocundus," Stevens' symbol for self-seeking mankind (including, ironically, the poet's unilluminated self), impatient with impractical abstractions irrelevant to his immediate situation. Why fritter away time on a glass of water when the world needs saving from political gamesmen?

The theorist's reply resembles Auden's. "This time, this day . . . this spring among the politicians" is unworthy of concern, since the state of a culture is no more permanent or essentially "real" than a state of the glass of water. The "real" thing, the organizing force in man (as Stevens argues elsewhere, especially in "The Idea of Order at Key West"), is not a transient state but the underlying process of which the state is but one manifestation. The man who "contends" with his ideas transcends "world affairs." In even the most primitive or degraded society he continues to lead an autonomous intellectual life, goes on "humming," as Auden said more lightly. What our "Jocundian" selves suppose the center of our lives is illusion, not worth the efforts of the mind, which should be a battleground where man's plastic concepts of the relativity of metaphysical as well as physical states struggle for communicable formulation.

A comparison with Auden's observation helps us see that Stevens makes here more than an objective comment about the relativity of states of mind; he expresses a conviction of the transcendence of the life of the mind over material squalor. The poem is not versified philosophy, but a brief drama of a significant clash between intellectualism and materialism that defines a concept of the role of the intellectual in a materialistic society.

Stevens' "The Glass of Water"

SISTER THERESE, S.N.D.

I believe that the explanations of this poem in Exp., Jan., 1959, XVII, 28, and Exp., Jan., 1961, XIX, 23, would be more satisfactory if they took into account the theory of poetry expressed by Stevens in *The Necessary Angel* (New York, 1951). Ignoring the poet's stated views, these explications distract from the appreciation of the poem as a well-integrated piece of art, though here the poet is making use of art to explain art.

The Necessary Angel carries as subtitle: *Essays on Reality and the Imagination.* From its scrutiny of the relation between poetry and reality, we are not surprised to find one after another of Stevens' poems expressing some aspect of this theme. Stevens considered the imagination as "one of the great human powers" (p. 138), as "the liberty of the mind" (p. 138), "the only genius" (p. 139). He asserts that poetry is a part of the structure of reality (p. 81) and concludes "that the structure of poetry and the structure of reality are one or, in effect, that poetry and reality are one, or should be." The definition of poetry as "an unofficial view of being" places poetry "in contrast with philosophy and at the same time establishes the relationship between the two" (p. 41). In approaching truth, philosophy uses reason; poetry, imagination: the two have, therefore, a kind of equality, though, as Stevens looks upon the fulfillment reached by the poet in contrast to the philosopher's too frequent despair, he concludes that "poetry, which we have been thinking of as at least the equal of philosophy, may be its superior" (p. 43). At the opposite pole of reality, politics offers itself for comparison with poetry. In the *Partisan Review* of August, 1948 (xv, 886), Stevens suggests the ironical impasse: "In the conflict between the poet and the politician the chief honor the poet can hope for is that of remaining himself. Life and reality, on the one hand, and politics, on the other, not withstanding the activity of politics, are not interchangeable terms."

Turning now to "The Glass of Water," we find set side by side philosophical reality, imaginative reality, and what I believe the poet would name political unreality. The diction and style of the first stanza is that of a scientific demonstration. The glass of water, it is concluded, is a state (a way, or form of being) within thermal polarity. The second stanza begins in the same tone. But at the end of the first line a metaphor is introduced: "Light / Is the lion that comes down to drink." With the mere turn of the verse we are in another world, accomplished, in part, by the leaping anapests and the alliteration of the two terms of comparison (light: lion); in large, by the stark image of the beast urged into action by elemental need. I would not call the figure "homely," but brilliant in its startling impact as it flashes before us the image of the sun as vital life-force. For the truth is, the reader here experiences some of the effects of "poetry at its source" (*The Necessary Angel,* p. 81): at once the lion-image, ruddy in eyes and claws, frothing as it sets boiling the weed-tangled waters, becomes a symbol of passion, the irrational, of brute violence. Already something of the "genius" of the imagination is grasped, something of poetry's power to relate, to order, to share insight.

Quietly the third stanza returns to the plain diction and style of the first. Here the poet does not hesitate to equate the technical term *metaphysica* with the imaginative "plastic parts of poems." To make clear that it is imagination which brings about this identification, with a kind of blasting force he uses the metaphor: "Crash in the mind." The last two lines of the third stanza and the entire concluding stanza are given to considering the relationship of poetry with politics. Entering the point of view of the self-indulgent pleasure-seeker, "fat Jocundus," the poet with intentional ambiguity explains that "this spring among the politicians playing cards" is likewise a state (a form of being, an actuality). Again, like a flash, in the irrationality of this state the reader finds an illustration of the lion-symbol just used. Scheming politicians, unscrupulous demagogues, can work such havoc of "winding weeds" that Jocundus may have reason to be troubled for his well-being (*fat Jocundus, worrying*). The style of the last two lines is too sophisticated, too ironic, to be tinged with the moralistic, as Warren French suggests: The poet says in brief that in any village off the jungle one still has the imagination (Stevens is again purposely ambiguous) to *uncover* the chicanery of barbaric scheming, and happily to *discover* the mind's own native poetic similitudes; one still has one's ideas to order.

I said that Stevens used art. In a word let me point to the poem's tension between the scientific in style and diction and the poetic which works out a patterning of tonality (assonance, consonance, alliteration) and parallelism that is at once simple and intricate. In the first stanza, consonance of final *t,* and assonance of the low-pitched *o,* especially in the position of rhyme, help to save the lines for poetry and prepare for the effective, if unobtrusive, alliteration in stanzas 3 and 4. Throughout the poem, the play of parallel thought and structure is worth noting: *That the glass . . . That the water* (st. 1); *Ruddy are his eyes . . . ruddy are his claws* (st. 2); *this object is merely a state* (st. 1) . . . *And there and in another state* (st. 3) . . . *It is a state* (st. 4); *Here in the centre stands* (st. 2) . . . *stands here in the centre* (st. 3) . . . *But in the centre* (st. 4); *This time, this day* (st. 4); *One would have still . . . One would continue* (st. 4). Form is thus made to accomplish a melding of prose style with poetic, an amalgamation of the intellective with the imaginative. As for the light-lion image of stanza 2, I would emphasize that this central climactic symbol is as effectively gaudy as it is—to use the epithet applied by the poet himself to an earlier poem—because of the structural ingenuity with which the imaginative is juxtaposed with the severely intellectual. As a result, in a short twenty lines, Stevens awakens the reader to the reality of the imaginative world side by side with the metaphysical and even the political. In other words, he demonstrates how "poetry and reality are one, or should be."

Questions and Assignments

1. Do these writers differ in their methods of interpreting a poem? Do their methods differ from that used by Cunningham?

2. Note the phrases or symbols which each critic emphasizes or ignores. Which phrases seem important to only one or two of the commentaries? Why?

3. Where do the commentaries agree most? Where do they disagree?

4. Which critic do you think gives the best reading of "A Glass of Water"? Why?

5. Distinguish any premises or "general truths" that the different critics appeal to. What levels of evidence are used by each commentator? Which level do they depend on most?

6. Professor French, author of the second interpretation (in a letter to the editors), asked that consideration be given to two questions relevant to Sr. Therese's interpretation: (1) "Are moralizing and sophistication mutually exclusive?" (2) "What does it prove to say that Stevens' poem illustrates his theories?" How would you answer these questions?

7. Write a comprehensive interpretation of "A Glass of Water" based upon all three critics. Be sure to acknowledge direct borrowings.

8. Write an argumentative analysis of the poem disagreeing with one or more of the critics.

9. If possible, write a fresh analysis of the poem.

Poems for Analysis

The nine poems which follow are divided into three groups, each group about a perennial theme not only of poetry but of all art—love, man, and mortality.

These poems should be both enjoyable and good material for writing and discussion. One of the easiest ways to decide if you understand, or if you are ready to write on one of these poems, is to ask yourself a few general questions. Begin your reading by conceiving of the poem as a voice or a group of voices, a meditation or a dialogue, and ask yourself who is speaking and what are the circumstances of his speaking? Does he characterize himself? Is he thinking out loud or is he addressing someone else? If addressing someone else, who are the other "voices" or silent actors in the poem? How are they characterized? Secondly, what is the dominant idea or mood of the poem? Is there any progression of idea or change of mood from stanza to stanza in the poem? How are the various images handled? Is one stressed or developed? Is there a relationship between the images? Naturally, you will want to look up proper names or allusions to mythical or Biblical personages. And if possible you will want to determine any obvious relationship between the form—the stanza pattern, the rhythm and rhyme, the sounds of the poem—and the meaning.

The first three poems are about various aspects of love. The seventeenth-century poet and clergyman John Donne describes the sorrows accompanying the separation of lovers in "A Valediction Forbidding Mourning." The next poem, "Adam's Curse," is by a man believed by many to be the finest poet of the twentieth century, W. B. Yeats. His is a dramatic poem reflecting on—among other things—the ravages inflicted on love by the passage of time. "Peter Quince at the Clavier," written by Wallace Stevens, blends individual emotions, a famous Biblical story, and a meditation on the eternality of love.

The next three poems have to do with the nature of man. George Herbert, a seventeenth-century Anglican priest and poet, uses in his famous poem an extended pun on the word "rest." He describes man as created by God with the blessings of strength, beauty, wisdom, honour, and pleasure—but not rest. Alexander Pope, writing in the eighteenth century, sees man's particular problem as doubt, the antagonism between mind and body which places him in a constant state of confusion. The selection by Pope is a short excerpt from his *Essay on Man,* a long philosophic poem. Dylan Thomas, an important modern poet, suggests that experience, knowledge, and the loss of innocence which comes with the passage of time are the source of man's discomfort.

The last three poems are concerned with mortality, the inevitability of death. John Keats, one of the great poets of the Romantic period, wrote this poem knowing that he was already dying of tuberculosis. Gerard Manley Hopkins' poem refers to the sorrow of autumn which prefigures the death "man was born for." The late Theodore Roethke, prize-winning poet and teacher at the University of Washington, describes the death of the spirit as well as the body in terms of the monotony and impersonality of bureaucracy.

A Valediction Forbidding Mourning

JOHN DONNE

As virtuous men pass mildly away,
And whisper to their souls to go,
Whilst some of their sad friends do say,
The breath goes now, and some say, No:

So let us melt, and make no noise,
No tear-floods, nor sigh-tempests move;
'Twere profanation of our joys
To tell the laity our love.

Moving of th' earth brings harms and fears,
Men reckon what it did, and meant;
But trepidation of the spheres,
Though greater far, is innocent.

Dull sublunary lovers' love
—Whose soul is sense—cannot admit
Absence, because it doth remove
Those things which elemented it.

But we by a love so much refined
That ourselves know not what it is,
Inter-assurèd of the mind,
Care less eyes, lips and hands to miss.

Our two souls therefore, which are one,
Though I must go, endure not yet
A breach, but an expansion,
Like gold to airy thinness beat.

If they be two, they are two so
As stiff twin compasses are two;
Thy soul, the fix'd foot, makes no show
To move, but doth, if th' other do.

And though it in the centre sit,
Yet, when the other far doth roam,
It leans, and hearkens after it,
And grows erect, as that comes home.

Such wilt thou be to me, who must,
Like th' other foot, obliquely run;
Thy firmness draws my circle just,
And makes me end where I begun.

Adam's Curse

W. B. YEATS

We sat together at one summer's end,
That beautiful mild woman, your close friend,
And you and I,[1] and talked of poetry.
I said: 'A line will take us hours maybe;
Yet if it does not seem a moment's thought,
Our stitching and unstitching has been naught.
Better go down upon your marrow-bones
And scrub a kitchen pavement, or break stones
Like an old pauper, in all kinds of weather;
For to articulate sweet sounds together
Is to work harder than all these, and yet
Be thought an idler by the noisy set
Of bankers, schoolmasters, and clergymen
The martyrs call the world.'

And thereupon
That beautiful mild woman for whose sake
There's many a one shall find out all heartache
On finding that her voice is sweet and low
Replied: 'To be born woman is to know—

From *Collected Poems of W. B. Yeats,* The Macmillan Company, publisher.

[1] The three people in this poem are Yeats himself, a woman with whom he was for a long time in love, Maud Gonne, and her sister, Mrs. Pilcher.

Although they do not talk of it at school—
That we must labour to be beautiful.'
I said: 'It's certain there is no fine thing
Since Adam's fall but needs much labouring.
There have been lovers who thought love should be
So much compounded of high courtesy
That they would sigh and quote with learned looks
Precedent out of beautiful old books;
Yet now it seems an idle trade enough.'

We sat grown quiet at the name of love;
We saw the last embers of daylight die,
And in the trembling blue-green of the sky
A moon, worn as if it had been a shell
Washed by time's waters as they rose and fell
About the stars and broke in days and years.

I had a thought for no one's but your ears:
That you were beautiful, and that I strove
To love you in the old high way of love;
That it had all seemed happy, and yet we'd grown
As weary-hearted as that hollow moon.

Peter Quince[1] *at the Clavier*

WALLACE STEVENS

I

Just as my fingers on these keys
Make music, so the self-same sounds
On my spirit make a music too.

[1] Peter Quince is a comic figure in Shakespeare's *A Midsummer Night's Dream.* The use of the name in the title is meant to associate the speaker in the poem with Shakespeare's character—apparently in the sense that the speaker too partakes of the human comedy in his feelings of love.

Music is feeling, then, not sound;
And thus it is that what I feel,
Here in this room, desiring you,

Thinking of your blue-shadowed silk,
Is music. It is like the strain
Waked in the elders by Susanna:[1]

Of a green evening, clear and warm,
She bathed in her still garden, while
The red-eyed elders, watching, felt

The basses of their being throb
In witching chords, and their thin blood
Pulse pizzicati of Hosanna.

II

In the green water, clear and warm,
Susanna lay.
She searched
The touch of springs,
And found
Concealed imaginings.
She sighed
For so much melody.

Upon the bank she stood
In the cool
Of spent emotions.
She felt, among the leaves,
The dew
Of old devotions.

She walked upon the grass,
Still quavering.
The winds were like her maids,
On timid feet,
Fetching her woven scarves,
Yet wavering.

[1] The story of Susanna and the Elders is found in the *Apocrypha* of the Old Testament, the Thirteenth Chapter of the Book of Daniel.

A breath upon her hand
Muted the night.
She turned—
A cymbal crashed,
And roaring horns.

III

Soon, with a noise like tambourines,
Came her attendant Byzantines.

They wondered why Susanna cried
Against the elders by her side:

And as they whispered, the refrain
Was like a willow swept by rain.

Anon their lamps' uplifted flame
Revealed Susanna and her shame.

And then the simpering Byzantines
Fled, with a noise like tambourines.

IV

Beauty is momentary in the mind—
The fitful tracing of a portal;
But in the flesh it is immortal.

The body dies; the body's beauty lives.
So evenings die, in their green going,
A wave, interminably flowing.

So gardens die, their meek breath scenting
The cowl of Winter, done repenting.
So maidens die to the auroral
Celebration of a maiden's choral.

Susanna's music touched the bawdy strings
Of those white elders; but, escaping,
Left only Death's ironic scraping.
Now, in its immortality, it plays
On the clear viol of her memory,
And makes a constant sacrament of praise.

The Pully

GEORGE HERBERT

When God at first made man,
Having a glass of blessings standing by—
"Let us," said He, "pour on him all we can;
Let the world's riches, which dispersed lie,
Contract into a span."

So strength first made a way,
Then beauty flow'd, then wisdom, honour, pleasure:
When almost all was out, God made a stay,
Perceiving that, alone of all His treasure,
Rest in the bottom lay.

"For if I should," said He,
"Bestow this jewel also on My creature,
He would adore My gifts instead of Me,
And rest in Nature, not the God of Nature:
So both should losers be.

"Yet let him keep the rest,
But keep them with repining restlessness;
Let him be rich and weary, that at least,
If goodness lead him not, yet weariness
May toss him to My breast."

Essay on Man

ALEXANDER POPE

Know then thyself, presume not God to scan,
The proper study of Mankind is Man.
Plac'd on this isthmus of a middle state,
A Being darkly wise, and rudely great:

With too much knowledge for the Sceptic side,
With too much weakness for the Stoic's pride,

He hangs between; in doubt to act, or rest;
In doubt to deem himself a God, or Beast;
In doubt his Mind or Body to prefer;
Born but to die, and reas'ning but to err;
Alike in ignorance, his reason such,
Whether he thinks too little, or too much:
Chaos of Thought and Passion, all confus'd;
Still by himself abus'd, or disabus'd;
Created half to rise, and half to fall;
Great lord of all things, yet a prey to all;
Sole judge of truth, in endless error hurl'd:
The glory, jest, and riddle of the world!

Self-love, the spring of motion, acts the soul;
Reason's comparing balance rules the whole.
Man, but for that, no action could attend,
And, but for this, were active to no end:
Fix'd like a plant on his peculiar spot,
To draw nutrition, propagate, and rot;
Or, meteor-like, flame lawless through the void,
Destroying others, by himself destroy'd.

Was There a Time

DYLAN THOMAS

Was there a time when dancers with their fiddles
In children's circuses could stay their troubles?
There was a time they could cry over books,
But time has set its maggot on their track.
Under the arc of sky they are unsafe.
What's never known is safest in this life.
Under the skysigns they who have no arms
Have cleanest hands, and, as the heartless ghost
Alone's unhurt, so the blind man sees best.

When I Have Fears That I May Cease to Be

JOHN KEATS

When I have fears that I may cease to be
Before my pen has gleaned my teeming brain,
Before high-pilèd books, in charact'ry,
Hold like rich garners the full-ripened grain;
When I behold, upon the night's starred face,
Huge cloudy symbols of a high romance,
And think that I may never live to trace
Their shadows, with the magic hand of chance;

And when I feel, fair creature of an hour!
That I shall never look upon thee more,
Never have relish in the faery power
Of unreflecting love;—then on the shore
Of the wide world I stand alone, and think,
Till Love and Fame to nothingness do sink.

Spring and Fall: To a Young Child

GERARD MANLEY HOPKINS

Margaret, are you grieving
Over Goldengrove unleaving?
Leaves, like the things of man, you
With your fresh thoughts care for, can you?
Ah! as the heart grows older
It will come to such sights colder
By and by, nor spare a sigh
Though worlds of wanwood leafmeal lie;
And yet you will weep and know why.
Now no matter, child, the name:
Sorrow's springs are the same.

Nor mouth had, no nor mind, expressed
What heart heard of, ghost guessed:
It is the blight man was born for,
It is Margaret you mourn for.

Dolor

THEODORE ROETHKE

I have known the inexorable sadness of pencils,
Neat in their boxes, dolor of pad and paper-weight,
All the misery of manila folders and mucilage,
Desolation in immaculate public places,
Lonely reception room, lavatory, switchboard,
The unalterable pathos of basin and pitcher,
Ritual of multigraph, paper-clip, comma,
Endless duplication of lives and objects.
And I have seen dust from the walls of institutions,
Finer than flour, alive, more dangerous than silica,
Sift, almost invisible, through long afternoons of tedium,
Dropping a fine film on nails and delicate eyebrows,
Glazing the pale hair, the duplicate gray standard faces.

Rewriting

Below are two examples of student rewriting. One theme is an argument on a topic of current interest, the other is a critical interpretation of one of the poems you have just read—"Adam's Curse."

As with the other student themes previously studied, these themes are not to be considered perfect—indeed with extremely proficient writing it is more difficult for students to be critical than with less proficient writing. Thus you should find it both profitable and enjoyable to analyze these particular themes. Rewriting an argument obviously draws upon all the principles mentioned in the three previous rewriting sections, plus the principles summarized in the immediately succeeding checklist. The principles of effective use of language and effective form are never in abeyance and you should keep these in mind as you concentrate on the use of evidence and on the reasoning demonstrated in the following papers.

Discrimination: North and South

(Original Student Theme)

Upon reading any daily newspaper in the United States one can always expect to find at least one article dealing with the problem of racial discrimination in this country. This problem is one of the most pressing problems of our day. It has weakened the whole nation both externally and internally.

The common action in both the North and the South is to point an accusing finger at one another. The South is accused of failing to grant equal Constitutional rights. The North in turn is accused of allowing unlawful and dangerous groups to roam in their cities. Both sides are somewhat accurate. Some southerners are ignorant and prejudiced; some Northern Negroes have participated in anti-social behavior.

Let us examine the cases further. In the South we find complete segregation, one school, one church, one store for each race. In the North the segregation is more subtle. Ghettos are fashioned and these in turn give rise to segregated schools, churches and stores.

In the North we find many minorities such as Catholics, Jews and Negroes, but instead of friendly smpathetic relations between these groups we usually find one group quietly working against the other. In the South highly traditional modes of behavior give the impression of public hospitality—"southern hospitality."

While the South has given the Negro no job opportunities, the North has given him very little. More northern companies will hire Negroes, but many times only if they cannot find qualified whites.

Socially the Negro is an outcast in a white society either North or South. Let a Negro apply to a Michigan country club and he will get nowhere—unless he applies as a caddy. Even the Washington

Redskins, a professional football team in the nation's capital, hesitated until just last year before hiring a Negro player.

Thus it can be seen that discrimination is not bounded on the North by the Mason-Dixon line. It is easy to live in the North, look down on the South, and criticize their way of life. There are some who say that outside of a few large cities racial discrimination is not a serious problem. This was a frequent reaction to Provost Wilson's recent appeal to attend to the problem of civil rights in our own backyard. This line of argument holds that all northerners can achieve economic status if they work hard, can vote if they go to the polls, can live where they want, and can attend whatever schools they wish. The reasoning behind this line of argument assumes that the Negro is not economically discriminated against and this is fallacious.

I do not want to appear too idealistic in this paper, but for me a little discrimination is just as bad as a lot. It's simply a matter of degree, but the same kind of injustice is present. It's like asking a person if he wants to lose 25 pay checks a year or 35. What difference does it make? After you've lost 25 pay days, you have to go on unemployment or relief, why not go on relief for an extra 10 weeks? The annual income northern negroes get to support a family is not usually sufficient to support a single person. College graduates with dark colored skin often have to find jobs as stock clerks or taxi drivers. Some Northerners say there are not more Negro executives because Negroes are not ambitious enough. But the truth of the matter is that the Negro has not been given the opportunity. Of course there may be a small handful of Negroes who have become business executives.

Provost Wilson's request that we concentrate on injustices in our own backyard expresses in one sentence what I have tried to demonstrate at some length. Our northern backyard is far from perfect and we are not going to improve it by marching through Georgia. I have neither the time nor the wisdom to provide a detailed solution to the problem of discrimination in the North, but I know that the first step in solving the problem is in recognizing that a serious degree of discrimination exists in the North. The final solution lies in education, and that is a job of many years.

This argument needs to be both rewritten and reconceived. Words, phrases, sentences must be reworked, and there are a number of hasty generalizations and unclear distinctions. Even the title is misleading since it does not reflect the real subject of the theme. But, most important, the overall argument of the theme is neither well organized nor convincing. The writer must begin his rewriting by determining which point he wishes to emphasize. It seems apparent that he wants to stress cleaning up his own backyard, but he seems not to have realized the importance of this idea until halfway through the essay. Once he formulates his central thesis more clearly, he will automatically be able to rearrange parts of his argument more cogently. To be more convincing, he must also find facts and details (evidence) to support his reasoning.

Discrimination in Our Own "Backyard"

(Rewritten Student Theme)

In an orientation talk earlier this fall Provost Wilson urged freshmen to "clean up your own backyards" before going off on crusades to other parts of the country. He gave two reasons for this view: He said our first job was to be students and we would lose less study time by staying close to campus. He further felt that the benefit of student social concern should be applied to communities closer to the university.

Student reaction to these remarks was sharply divided. Some felt the Provost was trying to soft pedal the civil rights controversy, others felt that his comments were unwarranted because there was no comparison between discrimination in the North and in the South.

Both of these reactions seem wrong to me. The best place for civil rights action for a northerner is in the North. I will admit that national leaders and celebrities help to focus public attention by traveling to other sections of the nation, but I do not feel this is true for the average student. What I am primarily concerned with attacking, however, is the contention that racial discrimination in the North is not comparable to that in the South. Not only did

Provost Wilson's remark express what was, to me, an obvious truth, it also seems a necessary first step in any effort to improve the lives of oppressed minorities.

There is a common practice in both the North and South of pointing the accusing finger at the other fellow. I do not intend to enter into this game of recrimination; there is often some measure of truth in even the most wild allegation. But it would be unjust to pretend that discrimination in the North is the same as that in the South. In the South there is complete segregation with some token exceptions. Each race has its own schools, churches, stores and entertainment places. In the North, however, much the same pattern is followed. In most cities Negroes are economically, if for no other reason, forced to live in a particular area—we would not be exaggerating to call it a ghetto. Surrounding this ghetto are Negro schools, churches, stores, and places for eating and entertainment.

What the South enforces by tradition, economics, law and sometimes brute force, the North enforces by economics. It should not be imagined that tradition, law and physical coercion are unimportant factors, nor should it be imagined that the Negro in the North is equally as poor as the Negro in the South. There are very important differences and the fact that hundreds of thousands of Negroes have migrated North in recent years says more than I can about the different degrees of discrimination that exist in the two sections of our country.

In court, in the polling booth, in job hunting, the Negro's position is more limited in the South than in the North. While a Negro finds it difficult to join a northern country club, it was impossible for a colored football player to play with the Washington Redskins until recently because Washington, D. C. has been considered a "southern" city. On the other hand, we must not be misled into believing that discrimination is bounded on the North by the Mason-Dixon line.

Those who hold that all northerners, regardless of race, can live where they wish, send their children to schools of their choice, or find the type of employment they are qualified for—those who hold these things are wrong. All of these freedoms are dependent on earning capacity and the Negro in the North is generally denied his rightful place in the economic picture. Let's look at some facts. In

1960 Negroes suffered 13.8% unemployment as compared to 7.7% in Northern industrial states. In these same states Negro workers earned only 58% as much as white workers. The President of Howard University said, "The image of the labor union held by the Negro is no longer one of inadequacy of performance in the struggle for civil rights, but is now that of the enemy." What the university official meant is obvious from the Congressional testimony of such workers as Francis Hardy. A young New York City electrician, Hardy said that his Local 3, International Brotherhood of Electrical Workers, had 80 Negro members out of a total membership of some 8,000, and out of 800 apprentices only two were Negro. The local's president pointed out at the same hearing that the electrical union was, "comparatively speaking," liberal.

Economic discrimination against Negroes extends to college graduates. Often college graduates with dark colored skin have to find jobs as stock clerks or taxi drivers. With such conditions only a small handful of Negroes ever rise to executive positions.

What begins in the employment office carries over to all areas of life. Writing in the *Nation* in October 1961, Jack Rothman said real estate and money lending institutions use "racism for profit." In Queens, New York, Mr. Rothman says, "Real estate brokers call up white residents in the community and offer to buy their homes, warning that Negroes will be moving into the neighborhood. Other brokers will show homes in the community to only Negro buyers to keep a section all Negro. Gradually both ends work toward the middle and a ghetto results." Mr. Rothman goes on, "Banks and lending institutions help out in the process. They make it difficult for non-white families to obtain a mortgage when they want to move into an all-white area."

Without opportunity or incentive many Negroes inevitably find themselves losing hope in bettering their lives. Some respond with lassitude, others with anti-social behavior. To cite indifference and criminality as reasons for the economic plight of the Negroes is to say "after this, therefore because of this." The only answer to such fallacious thought is the comment recently made by a Negro spokesman: "If you want us to act like staunch middle-class citizens, treat us that way."

Provost Wilson's request that we concentrate on injustices in our own backyard expresses in one sentence what I have tried to demonstrate in some detail. Our northern backyard is far from perfect and we are not going to improve it by marching through Georgia. We can help to tutor underprivileged children in nearby schools, we can support attempts for fair hiring, we can call attention to "racism for profit" and to trained and educated Negroes who are unable to find suitable employment. Whatever the practical steps we choose, the first step in solving the problem lies in recognizing the serious degree of discrimination which exists in the North. The final solution lies in education, and that is a job of many years.

Analysis of "Adam's Curse"

(Original Student Theme)

This poem is concerned with Maude Gonne, a woman with whom Yeats was in love but who never loved him. The poem tells of the labor of poet and woman and the weariness and hopelessness of a man's love for a woman. This is Yeats' curse, like Adam's —to love the wrong woman.

"Adam's Curse" is a dramatic poem containing parts of a conversation between a poet, his beloved and her sister. Its first three stanzas follow a rational progression while the last two stanzas emphasize an emotional state. The poet tells about the labor of writing poetry, his beloved's sister speaks of the labor of being beautiful, and, finally, the poem ends with the poet's inner feelings about the weariness even of loving. Now to demonstrate these observations in detail:

The first stanza gives the setting and tone. Yeats speaks of the time and effort that poets expend in the pursuit of their art in order to make it seem "a moment's thought." He then makes the point that the poet must work harder than a common laborer and ironically, he (the poet) is still regarded as an idler by the respectable pillars of society "the martyrs call the world."

The "beautiful, mild woman" extends the idea of worthwhile things being created only by labor, thus unifying the ideas of poetry and womanly beauty. "Women must labour to be beautiful"—just as the poet must spend hours "stitching and unstitching."

The poet speaks again in the third stanza and draws the natural inference from the preceding two stanzas. If poets must labor to create worthwhile poetry, if women must labor to be beautiful, it is logical to say, "there is no fine thing/ Since Adam's fall but needs much labouring." Then the stanza turns to love and the conversation stops as all present turn over the ideas of love and labor in their minds. The poet tells the reader that love and labor dominate the little group by the image of the moon. The moon is waning, only "a shell," and it (the timeless symbol of romance) too has been wearied by "time's waters."

A moon, worn as if it had been a shell
Washed by time's waters as they rose and fell
About the stars and broke in days and years.

In the final stanza, Yeats makes the point that everything seems futile. Poets must exert themselves to create poetry only to receive the criticism of society. Women must labor to be beautiful and learn all of the world's sadness. And Yeats has labored to love "in the old high ways of love" and has failed. Despite the fact that all had seemed happy, they had grown "weary-hearted as that hollow moon."

This is a remarkable poem because of the casualness of tone. It seems like a conversation. Thus Yeats has accomplished what he maintains is the prime purpose of good poetry—to make it seem "a moment's thought."

This paper contains several inaccuracies—many of them in the opening paragraph. It does not state its thesis clearly at the outset, and it is wordy and repetitive in places, notably in the opening and concluding paragraphs. It does not include a sufficient amount of verbal evidence to support its view. Since the student had a week to prepare this paper, he could also have consulted critics in order to draw upon other than purely verbal levels of evidence.

Analysis of "Adam's Curse"

(Rewritten Student Theme)

"Adam's Curse" is a dramatic poem based on three pieces of conversation and a reflection following the conversation. Three important statements are made in the poem: a poet's labor is difficult and unappreciated, a woman must labor to be beautiful, and even love is a labor which can make one weary. These things are clear. What is not clear, however, is the connection between these three points and consequently what the poem is saying. Is the poet equating his own labor, the beautiful woman's and the lover's? Does he finally criticize himself for having attempted to love in the wrong manner? Critics have found a great deal of meaning in this poem in connection with W. B. Yeats' life, and they have found this to be a very wonderful poem, but they have not, so far as I know, answered the important questions.

I know little about Yeats' life, nor do I know whether this is a great poem, but I would like to explain the meaning of the poem, based on the words and my meager knowledge of poetry.

The first three stanzas of "Adam's Curse" follow a logical progression, the last two follow an emotional line. A detailed analysis of these two considerations will show that the poem is about labor and the weariness which is part of human labor, especially the unsuccessful labor of love.

The title is ambiguous because one is first led to think that Maude Gonne, a woman with whom Yeats was in love but who never loved him, is being compared to Eve. It is easy to conclude from the title and the information given in the poem that Yeats' curse—like Adam's—was to love a woman. But this is not exactly right because Adam's curse was not Eve, but rather to "work by the sweat of his brow" all the days of his life. Thus even from the title one can gather the idea of labor and weariness.

The first stanza provides the setting and the tone. Yeats tells of the time and labor expended on a poem. But ironically the pillars of society, "the world," do not regard the poet's work as important. The poet has been "cursed" by work.

The "beautiful, mild woman" next introduces the idea that labor produces good, that even the beauty of woman, both physical and spiritual, is the result of labor. But the reader knows that Yeats finds this beauty sad and weary for he says: "There's many a one shall find out all heartache/ On finding that her voice is sweet and low."

The poet speaks again in the third stanza and draws the natural conclusion from the two preceding stanzas. If poets labor to create worthwhile poetry, if women must labor to be beautiful, it is logical to conclude: "there is no fine thing/ Since Adam's fall but needs much labouring." What is not so logical is Yeats' reference to lovers. We know that he is identifying the poet and the lover because he uses the word "idle" in both instances (lines 11 and 25). The kind of lover Yeats is talking about, however, is the important point. He is one "who would sigh and quote with learned looks/ Precedents out of beautiful old books." He, like the poet, is a labouring man.

When the stanza turns to the lover who has worked at love, like the poet at poetry, the conversation stops and all are overwhelmed by the lover who labors foolishly and in vain. The poet tells the reader that the thoughts of love and labor have brought weariness and sadness to the little group by using the image of the moon. The moon is waning, it is only a "shell," and, as the poetic symbol of romance, it too has been wearied by "time's waters."

In the final stanza Yeats summarizes the meaning of the preceding stanzas. Everything is silent and the unspoken thought of weariness—a lover's weariness—dominates the ending. The final stanza makes the point that "Adam's curse" makes everything seem futile. Women labor to be beautiful and then grow old, men labor to love "in the old high ways of love" and fail. Despite the fact that "all seemed happy," Yeats and his beloved had grown "weary-hearted as that hollow moon." Even the "fine thing" that needed "much labouring" and which had made them seem happy, now seems as hollow as the moon.

A Checklist for Rewriting. Part Four has been concerned with kinds of evidence and with the characteristics of logical argument, both in general topics and in literary works. We have stressed the need for careful examination of premises and of the inferences drawn from premises. Fallacious reasoning is common. Often it is difficult, sometimes impossible, for all save trained logicians to detect. As a method of summary we include below a checklist of steps to follow and pitfalls to avoid in writing and rewriting argument. This list is by no means exhaustive nor will it necessarily guarantee a logical and persuasive argument, but if you observe the following points your chances of writing sound arguments are measurably increased.

All suggestions made in the checklists at the end of Part I, Part II, and Part III are also pertinent to argument. The fundamental requirement of a sound argument is effective writing. In addition to the suggestions already made the following points should be kept in mind when rewriting.

1. Define the issues involved as clearly as possible at the outset. Discuss previous arguments on the same issue if you are aware of them.

2. State your own position as soon as possible and provide a clear outline of where your argument will lead and of some of the main points you intend to cover.

3. Marshal evidence to support your position. Gather details, facts, statistics; cite authority, draw upon your own experience.

4. Appeal to universally accepted truths ("all men are created equal," for example), and show how your position is in accord with such principles.

5. Compare and contrast, trace causes and effects to indicate the correctness of your position.

6. Examine and reject significant points of the opposite position.

7. Summarize your most effective points.

8. Know and avoid the following fallacies: hasty generalization, faulty causality (*post hoc ergo propter hoc*), shift in terms, *non sequitur*, begging the question (arguing in a circle), and ignoring the question (*ad hominem*).

9. Keep the tone of your essay persuasive rather than polemical. Grant as much as you can grant, agree on all nonessentials. Do not go to the other extreme, however. Don't be afraid to make positive assertions and don't qualify *all* your assertions with such phrases as "I believe," "it appears," or "perhaps," which tend to indicate weakness.

PART FIVE

Interpretation

Clay by James Joyce

"Clay": An Interpretation by William York Tindall
Concerning "Clay" by Marvin Magalaner and Richard M. Kain
The Witch Maria by Richard Carpenter and Daniel Leary
Joyce's "Clay": An Interpretation by William T. Noon, S.J.
Joyce's "Clay" by Florence L. Walzl

A Walled Garden by Peter Taylor

On the Guadalajara Front by Antoine de St. Exupéry

Two Lovely Beasts by Liam O'Flaherty

The Guest by Albert Camus

THE narratives, or short stories, presented in this section were chosen with specific attention to the possibility of student analysis. In varying degrees, all five stories lend themselves to different critical approaches. A discussion of useful approaches to writing on literary works has already been given in the unit on explication (pp. 316-360) and in "Evidence in Poetry" (pp. 478-505). Further models for writing are provided in this section following James Joyce's short story "Clay."

The five stories comprising this part of the book are all quite different from one another. But they all have important ingredients in common. Each of the stories explores the themes of man's relationship with man, of each man's essential isolation, and of each man's responsibilities to his fellow men.

The author of the first story, James Joyce, is regarded as one of the greatest prose writers, if not *the* greatest, of the twentieth century. Peter Taylor is a teacher of creative writing and a master of the short-story form. Antoine de St. Exupéry was not only a master stylist of twentieth-century French literature, but also a world-renowned flyer and a *Resistance* hero of World War II. The episode he is writing about in "On the Guadalajara Front" took place during the Spanish Civil War. Liam O'Flaherty, another modern writer, author of "Two Lovely Beasts," has written many works of fiction including the popular novel *The Informer*. Albert Camus, Algerian-born author of "The Guest," was Nobel Prize winner for Literature in 1957.

"Clay" and the critical commentaries following it should indicate some of the numerous possibilities for writing on characters and themes found in fiction. The commentaries following the first story illuminate the meaning of that story, illustrate critical analysis, and challenge the reader to select—and defend—the most persuasive interpretation.

Clay

JAMES JOYCE

The matron had given her leave to go out as soon as the women's tea was over and Maria looked forward to her evening out. The kitchen was spick and span: the cook said you could see yourself in the big copper boilers. The fire was nice and bright and on one of the side-tables were four very big barmbracks. These barmbracks seemed uncut; but if you went closer you would see that they had been cut into long thick even slices and were ready to be handed round at tea. Maria had cut them herself.

Maria was a very, very small person indeed but she had a very long nose and a very long chin. She talked a little through her nose, always soothingly: *"Yes, my dear,"* and *"No, my dear."* She was always sent for when the women quarrelled over their tubs and always succeeded in making peace. One day the matron had said to her:

"Maria, you are a veritable peace-maker!"

And the sub-matron and two of the Board ladies had heard the compliment. And Ginger Mooney was always saying what she wouldn't do to the dummy who had charge of the irons if it wasn't for Maria. Everyone was so fond of Maria.

The women would have their tea at six o'clock and she would be able to get away before seven. From Ballsbridge to the Pillar, twenty minutes; from the Pillar to Drumcondra, twenty minutes; and twenty minutes to buy the things. She would be there before eight. She took out her purse with the silver clasps and read again the words *A Present from Belfast.* She was very fond of the purse because Joe had brought it to her five years before when he and Alphy had gone to Belfast on a Whit-Monday trip. In the purse were two half-crowns and some coppers. She would have five shillings clear after paying tram fare. What a nice evening they would have, all the children singing! Only she hoped that Joe wouldn't come in drunk. He was so different when he took any drink.

Often he had wanted her to go and live with them; but she would have felt herself in the way (though Joe's wife was ever so nice with her), and she had become accustomed to the life of the laundry. Joe was a good fellow. She had nursed him and Alphy too; and Joe used often say:

"Mamma is mamma but Maria is my proper mother."

After the break-up at home the boys had got her that position in the *Dublin by Lamplight* laundry, and she liked it. She used to have such a bad opinion of Protestants but now she thought they were very nice people, a little quiet and serious, but still very nice people to live with. Then she had her plants in the conservatory and she liked looking after them. She had lovely ferns and wax-plants and, whenever anyone came to visit her, she always gave the visitor one or two slips from her conservatory. There was one thing she didn't like and that was the tracts on the walks; but the matron was such a nice person to deal with, so genteel.

When the cook told her everything was ready she went into the women's room and began to pull the big bell. In a few minutes the women began to come in by twos and threes, wiping their steaming hands in their petticoats and pulling down the sleeves of their blouses over their red steaming arms. They settled down before their huge mugs which the cook and the dummy filled up with hot tea, already mixed with milk and sugar in huge tin cans. Maria superintended the distribution of the barmbrack and saw that every woman got her four slices. There was a great deal of laughing and joking during the meal. Lizzie Fleming said Maria was sure to get the ring and, though Fleming had said that for so many Hallow Eves, Maria had to laugh and say she didn't want any ring or man either; and when she laughed her grey-green eyes sparkled with disappointed shyness and the tip of her nose nearly met the tip of her chin. Then Ginger Mooney lifted up her mug of tea and proposed Maria's health while all the other women clattered with their mugs on the table, and said she was sorry she hadn't a sup of porter to drink it in. And Maria laughed again till the tip of her nose nearly met the tip of her chin and till her minute body nearly shook itself asunder because she knew that Mooney meant well though, of course, she had the notions of a common woman.

But wasn't Maria glad when the women had finished their tea and the cook and the dummy had begun to clear away the tea-things! She went into her little bedroom and, remembering that the next morning was a mass morning, changed the hand of the alarm from seven to six. Then she took off her working skirt and her house-boots and laid her best skirt out on the bed and her tiny dress-boots beside the foot of the bed. She changed her blouse too and, as she stood before the mirror, she thought of how she used to dress for mass on Sunday morning when she was a young girl; and she looked with quaint affection at the diminutive body which she had so often adorned. In spite of its years she found it a nice tidy little body.

When she got outside the streets were shining with rain and she was glad of her old brown waterproof. The tram was full and she had to sit on the little stool at the end of the car, facing all the people, with her toes barely touching the floor. She arranged in her mind all she was going to do and thought how much better it was to be independent and to have your own money in your pocket. She hoped they would have a nice evening. She was sure they would but she could not help thinking what a pity it was Alphy and Joe were not speaking. They were always falling out now but when they were boys together they used to be the best of friends: but such was life.

She got out of her tram at the Pillar and ferreted her way quickly among the crowds. She went into Downes's cake-shop but the shop was so full of people that it was a long time before she could get herself attended to. She bought a dozen of mixed penny cakes, and at last came out of the shop laden with a big bag. Then she thought what else would she buy: she wanted to buy something really nice. They would be sure to have plenty of apples and nuts. It was hard to know what to buy and all she could think of was cake. She decided to buy some plumcake but Downes's plumcake had not enough almond icing on top of it so she went over to a shop in Henry Street. Here she was a long time in suiting herself and the stylish young lady behind the counter, who was evidently a little annoyed by her, asked her was it wedding-cake she wanted to buy. That made Maria blush and smile at the young lady; but the young lady took it all very seriously and finally cut a thick slice of plumcake, parcelled it up and said:

"Two-and-four, please."

She thought she would have to stand in the Drumcondra tram because none of the young men seemed to notice her but an elderly gentleman made room for her. He was a stout gentleman and he wore a brown hard hat; he had a square red face and a greyish moustache. Maria thought he was a colonel-looking gentleman and she reflected how much more polite he was than the young men who simply stared straight before them. The gentleman began to chat with her about Hallow Eve and the rainy weather. He supposed the bag was full of good things for the little ones and said it was only right that the youngsters should enjoy themselves while they were young. Maria agreed with him and favoured him with demure nods and hems. He was very nice with her, and when she was getting out at the Canal Bridge she thanked him and bowed, and he bowed to her and raised his hat and smiled agreeably; and while she was going up along the terrace, bending her tiny head under the rain, she thought how easy it was to know a gentleman even when he has a drop taken.

Everybody said: *"O, here's Maria!"* when she came to Joe's house. Joe was there, having come home from business, and all the children had their Sunday dresses on. There were two big girls in from next door and games were going on. Maria gave the bag of cakes to the eldest boy, Alphy, to divide and Mrs. Donnelly said it was too good of her to bring such a big bag of cakes and made all the children say:

"Thanks, Maria."

But Maria said she had brought something special for papa and mamma, something they would be sure to like, and she began to look for her plumcake. She tried in Downes's bag and then in the pockets of her waterproof and then on the hallstand but nowhere could she find it. Then she asked all the children had any of them eaten it—by mistake, of course—but the children all said no and looked as if they did not like to eat cakes if they were to be accused of stealing. Everybody had a solution for the mystery and Mrs. Donnelly said it was plain that Maria had left it behind her in the tram. Maria, remembering how confused the gentleman with the greyish moustache had made her, coloured with shame and vexation and disappointment. At the thought of the failure of her little surprise and of the two and fourpence she had thrown away for nothing she nearly cried outright.

But Joe said it didn't matter and made her sit down by the fire. He was very nice with her. He told her all that went on in his office, repeating for her a smart answer which he had made to the manager. Maria did not understand why Joe laughed so much over the answer he had made but she said that the manager must have been a very overbearing person to deal with. Joe said he wasn't so bad when you knew how to take him, that he was a decent sort so long as you didn't rub him the wrong way. Mrs. Donnelly played the piano for the children and they danced and sang. Then the two next-door girls handed round the nuts. Nobody could find the nutcrackers and Joe was nearly getting cross over it and asked how did they expect Maria to crack nuts without a nutcracker. But Maria said she didn't like nuts and that they weren't to bother about her. Then Joe asked would she take a bottle of stout and Mrs. Donnelly said there was port wine too in the house if she would prefer that. Maria said she would rather they didn't ask her to take anything: but Joe insisted.

So Maria let him have his way and they sat by the fire talking over old times and Maria thought she would put in a good word for Alphy. But Joe cried that God might strike him stone dead if ever he spoke a word to his brother again and Maria said she was sorry she had mentioned the matter. Mrs. Donnelly told her husband it was a great shame for him to speak that way of his own flesh and blood but Joe said that Alphy was no brother of his and there was nearly being a row on the head of it. But Joe said he would not lose his temper on account of the night it was and asked his wife to open some more stout. The two next-door girls had arranged some Hallow Eve games and soon everything was merry again. Maria was delighted to see the children so merry and Joe and his wife in such good spirits. The next-door girls put some saucers on the table and then led the children up to the table, blindfold. One got the prayer-book and the other three got the water; and when one of the next-door girls got the ring Mrs. Donnelly shook her finger at the blushing girl as much as to say: *O, I know all about it!* They insisted then on blindfolding Maria and leading her up to the table to see what she would get; and, while they were putting on the bandage, Maria laughed and laughed again till the tip of her nose nearly met the tip of her chin.

They led her up to the table amid laughing and joking and she put her hand out in the air as she was told to do. She moved her hand about here and there in the air and descended on one of the saucers. She felt a soft wet substance with her fingers and was surprised that nobody spoke or took off her bandage. There was a pause for a few seconds; and then a great deal of scuffling and whispering. Somebody said something about the garden, and at last Mrs. Donnelly said something very cross to one of the next-door girls and told her to throw it out at once: that was no play. Maria understood that it was wrong that time and so she had to do it over again: and this time she got the prayer-book.

After that Mrs. Donnelly played Miss McCloud's Reel for the children and Joe made Maria take a glass of wine. Soon they were all quite merry again and Mrs. Donnelly said Maria would enter a convent before the year was out because she had got the prayer-book. Maria had never seen

Joe so nice to her as he was that night, so full of pleasant talk and reminiscences. She said they were all very good to her.

At last the children grew tired and sleepy and Joe asked Maria would she not sing some little song before she went, one of the old songs. Mrs. Donnelly said *"Do, please, Maria!"* and so Maria had to get up and stand beside the piano. Mrs. Donnelly bade the children be quiet and listen to Maria's song. Then she played the prelude and said *"Now, Maria!"* and Maria, blushing very much, began to sing in a tiny quavering voice. She sang *I Dreamt that I Dwelt,* and when she came to the second verse she sang again:

I dreamt that I dwelt in marble halls
With vassals and serfs at my side,
And of all who assembled within those walls
That I was the hope and the pride.

I had riches too great to count; could boast
Of a high ancestral name,
But I also dreamt, which pleased me most,
That you loved me still the same.

But no one tried to show her her mistake; and when she had ended her song Joe was very much moved. He said that there was no time like the long ago and no music for him like poor old Balfe, whatever other people might say; and his eyes filled up so much with tears that he could not find what he was looking for and in the end he had to ask his wife to tell him where the corkscrew was.

"Clay": An Interpretation

WILLIAM YORK TINDALL

The story of virginal, old Maria, taken at face value, seems naturalistic; for she works in a laundry, and naturalists, delighting in whatever is ignoble, find laundry workers almost as congenial as drunken servant maids with illegitimate children. Maria's daily life and even her night out are tedious enough for naturalistic purposes. Her environment is indicated, if not displayed. If we take her story literally, it has little point beyond the exhibition of pointlessness. There seems more to it, however, than this. Symbolic devices indicate that Joyce intended something beyond a memorial to a frustrated, futile, and uninteresting life. There are allusions—such as Little Chandler esteems; and there are counterparts.

Maria's night out is on Halloween, a night when witches are out. The tip of her nose almost touches her chin, and this is the case with all the witches I have known. The copper boilers among which she works are a witch's equipment. But, far from proving Maria a witch, these circumstances only suggest that she is witch-like; for analogy or parallel does not establish identity. Maria remains Maria, witch, witch. That Maria is also like the Blessed Virgin Mary is suggested by her name and by the reactions of those around her. The matron hails her as a "peace-maker";[1] and, though she is not his actual mother, Joe hails her as his "proper mother." That she presides over a little garden in the wilderness and that she distributes tea and cakes add the possibility that she is also like the Church, often represented as a woman. No more than parallel to one another, these three parallels do not mean that the Virgin is a witch or that the Church is identical with the Virgin. The three parallels, agreeing as they can, make Maria seem more than a particular old woman.

These enlarging parallels seem subordinate to another, which, though less explicitly established, seems more important. Not only a poor old woman, Maria is like the Poor Old Woman or Ireland herself. That her particular figure serves as the traditional figure of Ireland is suggested by other circumstances. Like most in Ireland in her day, she works for the Protestants who control Ireland's purse. (Maria's purse is from Protestant Belfast.) Shopkeepers condescend to her; and when a British colonel is polite to her on the tram, she loses her cake. Distracted by colonels and condescended to by a nation of shopkeepers, Ireland had been losing her cake for several centuries. Moreover, Mother Ireland's sons, commonly drunk, were always quarreling among themselves. Alphy and Joe, Maria's "proper" sons, are always quarreling; and Joe, who is not altogether unlike Farrington, is certainly a drinker. As peace-maker, Maria seems ineffectual.

At Joe's Halloween party, they play the traditional game of saucers.

[1] "Peace-maker," which occurs in the Mass for All Saints' Day (the day after Halloween) is ultimately from the Beatitudes of the Sermon on the Mount (Matthew 5: 1-12). "Blessed" (the recurrent word of the Beatitudes) is the Virgin's adjective.

Failing to pick the ring (marriage), Maria picks clay (death), and then, given another chance, the prayer book. Her choice of death and prayer suits Joyce's idea of his moribund, pious country.

As we have been prepared for a meaning of "clay" by a reference in "A Little Cloud," so we have been prepared for Maria's song from *The Bohemian Girl* by a reference in "Eveline." Maria's conscious or unconscious omission of the second stanza, which concerns love and suitors, suits one who, lacking love and avoiding fertility, has chosen prayer and death.

Joe detects the meaning of her omission. "Very much moved" by it, he calls for the missing corkscrew (one of many lost or misplaced things in this story) and presumably for another bottle in which to drown his understanding. The epiphany, not Maria's but Joe's, is one of barrenness, lovelessness, disorder, and loss. Not even Balfe, thoughts of "the long ago," or drink itself can hide the bitterness.

Concerning "Clay"

MARVIN MAGALANER AND RICHARD M. KAIN

The story "Clay" shows most clearly the operation of symbolism on several levels simultaneously. Though a quick reading may deceive the reader into thinking that the sketch concerns nothing more than the frustrated longings of a timid old maid for the joys of life, a husband, children, and romance, careful examination leads to discovery of interesting patterns. All the social relationships in the story, for instance, are awry. Maria should be married but is not. Alphy and Joe, though brothers, fight continually. Mrs. Donnelly strives to keep peace in the family by calming her drunken husband. The laundresses quarrel often. The saleswoman in the cake shop is impudent to the most inoffensive of customers. The young men on the tram will not rise to give her a seat. And even the innocent children are half accused of stealing the missing cakes. Through this maze of human unpleasantness moves the old maid, Maria, a steadying and moderating influence on all those who have dealings with her.

Her role as peacemaker is stressed. In the Protestant laundry, she "was always sent for when the women quarrelled over their tubs and always

From *Joyce: The Man, the Work, the Reputation.* Reprinted by permission of New York University Press.

succeeded in making peace." Her employer compliments her on her ability as mediator: "Maria, you are a veritable peace-maker." Her calm moderation alone keeps Ginger Mooney from using violence against the "dummy who had charge of the irons." "Everyone," says Joyce, "was so fond of Maria." And rightly so. Her tact prevents a family quarrel over the loss of a nutcracker when she quickly says that "she didn't like nuts and that they weren't to bother about her." Though she does not wish a drink of wine offered by Joe, she "let him have his way." Maria's function as peacemaker, dovetailing as it does with a great many other details of the story, suggests the hypothesis that Joyce intended to build up a rough analogy between the laundry worker Maria and the Virgin Mary. Along certain lines, the relationship is fairly obvious.

Maria, of course, is a variant of the name Mary. Certainly there is nothing subtle about the associations that the name of the main character evokes. The Virgin is well known for her role as peacemaker, for the invocations to her, especially by women, to prevent conflict. Accordingly, she is invoked ("sent for") whenever the laundresses argue and she "always succeeded in making peace." Without her restraining and comforting influence, much more violence would occur. There is surely a suggestion of the church in Maria, for, like Mrs. Kearney and the two sisters, she offers a form of Communion to the women by distributing the barmbracks (raisin bread) and beverage.

Carrying the analogy further, Joyce makes much of the fact that Maria is a virgin. At the same time, and this is significant, she has children, though they are not born from her womb. "She had nursed . . . [Joe] and Alphy too; and Joe used often to say: 'Mamma is mamma but Maria is my proper mother.' " There would seem to be no reason, in a very short story, to quote Joe directly here unless more was intended by the author than the bare statement that Maria had aided his mother in bringing up her sons. There are additional Biblical parallels too. In the Gospel according to Luke, it is Elizabeth who announces to Mary that she is blessed and will have blessed offspring. Interestingly enough, in "Clay" it is Lizzie (Elizabeth) Fleming, Maria's co-worker in the laundry, who "said Maria was sure to get the ring and, though Fleming had said that for so many Hallow Eves, Maria had to laugh and say she didn't want any ring or man either. . . ."

Other similarities crowd in to lend support to the idea. Maria works in a laundry, where things are made clean; Mary is the instrument of cleansing on the spiritual plane. All the children sing for Maria, and two bear gifts to her on a Whitmonday trip. That one gift is a purse has ironic meaning in Joyce's mercenary Dublin. The laundress finds her appearance "nice" and "tidy" "in spite of its years," perhaps a circumspect way of saying that, after centuries, the freshness of Mary as a symbol is still untarnished. On the other hand, Maria finds on the tram that she is ignored by the young men and in the bakeshop treated insolently by the young girl. Only the elderly and the slightly drunk treat her with the respect which she enjoys but which she is too timid to demand. The meaning for Joyce of this situation needs no spelling out. The fact, finally, that Maria gets the prayer book, in the game of the three dishes, and is therefore slated to enter a convent and retire from the world is additional evidence of the author's symbolic intent.

Joyce is not content, however, with working on this single level. He has accomplished one purpose. Just as in *Ulysses* the juxtaposition of the heroic age and the human—of wily Odysseus and sly Leopold Bloom—serves to point up the contrast between the glory that was Greece and the mundane sphere that was Dublin for the artist of 1900, so the super-imposition of modern Maria upon the ancient and venerable symbol of Mary is aesthetically effective. Now he goes a step beyond.

The story, originally entitled "Hallow Eve," takes place on the spooky night of the thirty-first of October, "the night set apart for a universal walking abroad of spirits, both of the visible and invisible world; for . . . one of the special characteristics attributed to this mystic evening, is the faculty conferred on the immaterial principle in humanity to detach itself from its corporeal tenement and wander abroad through the realms of space. . . ." Putting this more bluntly than Joyce would have wished, Maria on the spirit level is a witch on this Halloween night, and as a traditional witch Joyce describes her. "Maria was a very, very small person indeed but she had a very long nose and a very long chin." To fix this almost caricature description in the minds of his readers, the author repeats that "when she laughed . . . the tip of her nose nearly met the tip of her chin." And two sentences further on, he reiterates the information for the third time, and for a fourth before the story is through. The intention is very plain. In addition to these frequent iterations, Joyce's first sentence in "Clay"—and his story openings are almost always fraught with special meaning—discloses that this was "her evening out." By right it should be, for witches walk abroad on Allhallow Eve. In itself, however, implying that the old woman is a witch is of minor significance. It derives fuller meaning from the illusion-reality motif.

This motif is central to the story, gives it, in fact, its point. Halloween is famous for its masquerades, its hiding of identities of celebrants, conjuring tricks, illusions of goblins and ghosts—in other words, famed for the illusions that are created in the name of celebrating the holiday. It is a night on which it is hard to tell the material from the spiritual, witch from woman, ghost from sheeted youngster. On this night, things are not what they seem.

In the first paragraph, Joyce touches gently upon the motif more than once. Maria's work in the kitchen is done. Barmbracks have been prepared. It is legitimate to wonder whether the baking was done in accordance with this Irish custom: unmarried girls would knead a cake "with their left thumbs. . . . in mute solemnity; a single word would have broken the charm and destroyed their ardent hopes of beholding their future husbands in their dreams after having partaken of the mystic 'dumb-cake.' " The finished barmbracks "seemed uncut; but if you went closer you would see that they had been cut into long thick even slices and were ready. . . . Maria had cut them herself." The contrast between the illusion of wholeness and the reality of the actual slices is given prominent mention only because it belongs within the larger framework of the motif. Also, in the same paragraph, the cook delights in the cleanliness of the big copper boilers in which "you could see yourself," another reference to illusion, possibly connected in Joyce's mind with the Allhallow Eve custom of looking into a mirror to see one's future husband.

In other respects, also, the spirits are at work in this story. Things, as things, lose their materiality and become invisible. At least they are missing and cannot be found. The plum cake disappears. "Nobody could find the nutcrackers." Finally, Joe trying to locate the corkscrew, "could not find what he was looking for." Maria herself is ambiguous, sometimes more a disembodied spirit than a person. Her body, though it exists, is "very, very small," and a hearty burst of laughter grips her "till her minute body nearly shook itself asunder." On this night she is able to get outside her body, almost, and look at it objectively: "she looked with quaint affection at the diminutive body which she had so often adorned . . . she found it a nice tidy little body."

It is in dreams, however, that Maria is able to put the greatest distance between illusion, namely, the love and adventure which have never entered her life, and reality, the drab, methodical existence of a servant in a laundry. Or if not in dreams, in the reverie induced by a dream song, "I dreamt that I dwelt in marble halls." The whole story builds up to this central split, at which point all the minor examples of the thin line between fantasy and actuality attain meaning and stature. In these rich and sensuous lines, sung in a "tiny quavering voice" by Maria, are packed the antitheses to the frustrating life of the average Dubliner. Mary in contemporary life has decayed in scope to Maria and is no more imposing a spiritual figure than a witch on a broomstick. The marble halls have been converted into laundry kitchens. Most tragic of all, there is no one in the world to whom the old maid can, with truth, sing "that you loved me just the same." In Maria's rendition of the song, she inadvertently omits the second and third stanzas and carelessly sings the first verse twice. Joyce emphasizes that "no one tried to show her her mistake." Little wonder that her audience remains tactfully silent about these missing verses:

I dreamt that suitors sought my hand
That knights on bended knee,
And with vows no maiden heart could withstand,
They pledged their faith to me.

And I dreamt that one of that noble band
Came forth my heart to claim,
But I also dreamt, which charmed me most,
That you loved me still the same.

Maria's error is probably attributable to an emotional block that prevents her from giving voice to remarks so obviously at variance with the reality of her dull life. Leopold Bloom suffers a similar lapse when of Boylan's affair with Molly he speaks of "the wife's admirers" and then in confusion adds, "The wife's advisers, I mean."

Joyce's decision to change the title of the story from "Hallow Eve" to "Clay" shifts the emphasis from the singing of the song to the ceremony of the three dishes. This familiar Irish fortunetelling game requires blindfolded players to select from a group of traditional objects the one which, so the story goes, will be symbolically revelatory of their future life. Poor Maria puts her fingers into a dish which the thoughtless children have jokingly filled with clay. She is to get neither the prayer book (life in a convent) or the ring (marriage). Death is her fate. There is a subdued shock when even the insensitive people present at the Halloween party realize the symbolic significance of selecting clay as an omen of things to come. Joyce, leaving nothing to chance, has earlier prepared the reader for the symbolic action by showing that Maria is half in love with easeful death: "She had her plants . . . and she liked looking after them. She had lovely ferns and wax-plants. . . ." The emblems of the Virgin Mary, it is interesting to note, are unlike the others, late-flowering plants and late-blossoming trees.

Joyce was a very young writer when he wrote "Clay." He seems uncertain where to place the emphasis, and perhaps he allows too many motifs, even though a tenuous connection among them does exist, to deflect from the central point of his narrative. Perhaps he has not sufficiently reinforced the relationship between the witch and the Virgin, though the history of the church holiday actually establishes all the parallel background he needs: the day set aside in honor of saints (like Mary) by Boniface IV has had its eve perverted by celebrants to the calling forth of witches. The two supernormal female figures, the saint and the witch, share this holiday. The writer who was soon to wrestle with the intricacies of interlocking symbolic levels in *Ulysses* was in "Clay" learning his trade. The result is a much more complicated story than commentators in the past have discovered.

In the B.B.C. magazine, *The Listener* (March 25, 1954), Stanislaus Joyce takes issue with such "scientific" explication of the early works of his brother as has been attempted in this chapter. He attacks particularly an "American critic," undoubtedly Magalaner, who "finds in the short story 'The Clay' [*sic*] three levels of significance on which Maria is successively herself, a witch, and the Virgin Mary." He continues:

> Though such critics are quite at sea, they can still have the immense satisfaction of knowing that they have dived into deeper depths than the author they are criticising ever sounded. I am in a position to state definitely that my brother had no such subtleties in mind when he wrote the story. In justice, though, I must say that exaggerations like those I have mentioned are not typical of American criticism. . . .

This type of personal-acquaintance criticism is understandably dangerous. What family of a deceased writer has not felt that blood relationship and lifelong closeness afforded deeper insight into the writer's work than detached criticism could? This is a natural and healthy family tendency; yet the results, as evidenced in authorized biographies and critical studies by sons and grandsons and nephews of nineteenth-century literary greats, are generally regarded with amusement or dismay by today's scholars. One should respect such prime sources of biographical information, but, at the same time, one may suspect critical judgments enunciated by such sources as the last word, on, say, literary symbolism.

Stanislaus Joyce admits that *Ulysses* was "intended by its author" to have "various levels of significance." One wonders whether, if Joyce had not "leaked" his intention to Stuart Gilbert and others, Stanislaus would not be insisting equally on the "pernicious" quality of explications of that novel. It is very difficult to be sure of Joyce's intentions in his poetry and short stories, as it is in *A Portrait.* Eugene Jolas records how "Joyce blanched" when Jolas guessed merely what the title of *Finnegans Wake* was to be. "Ah, Jolas, you've taken something out of me," was the author's sad reply. It is quite possible that the earlier Joyce might have been toying with the idea of multiple symbolic levels in the works before *Ulysses* without discussing his unformulated plans with his younger brother.

The Witch Maria

RICHARD CARPENTER AND DANIEL LEARY

Recent critical interpretations have cast much light on James Joyce's "Clay"—that slight but fascinating and much-anthologized story from *Dubliners.* Most particularly, Magalaner and Kain in their book on Joyce show us the symbolism inherent in this story, indicating that its central figure, Maria, can be considered simultaneously on two levels: as representing both the Virgin Mary and a witch, with her very long nose and very long chin, going abroad on Hallow Eve. In their Preface, however, Messrs. Magalaner and Kain "hope that the avenues opened by our exploratory analyses will lead easily to further, extended insights." And since their analysis of "Clay" dismisses Maria's being a witch as "of minor significance" we would like to extend that insight further. It seems to us that

From *The James Joyce Review,* Volume 3, Numbers 1-2, 1959. Reprinted by permission.

the insistence with which Joyce presents Maria-as-witch (for example, telling us four separate times that "when she laughed . . . the tip of her nose nearly met the tip of her chin," emphasizing her tiny size, and that her "night out" is Hallowe'en), indicates that this function is vital to the story and of major significance to its effect of pathos combined with irony. Also, seeing Maria as a witch serves, we believe, to explain more effectively some aspects of the story than does seeing her primarily as the Virgin.

Witches, as we all know, are of various gradations of evil from the relatively harmless to the positively fiendish. Some are content to sour milk and tangle horses' tails, while others eat little boys and girls. But they all have one thing in common: they are predisposed to bring unhappiness to mankind, and yet their success brings no happiness to themselves. Now Maria is obviously not a figure of evil—she is called a "veritable peacemaker" in the Protestant laundry where she works, and no one (at least in the beginning of the story) reacts to her in any way that would indicate she is disliked; she is too diminutive and too much a figure of pity to be feared. But it might be suspected in the light of later events that calling her a peacemaker is ironic and that she is predestined, in a witchlike fashion, to bring discord to those she most desires to share happiness with—and in turn does not find the happiness she anticipates in her visit to Joe and his family.

The first indication of this is in the reception given Maria by Joe's children who evidently join in the chorus of "Oh, here's Maria!" (which could be read as a less than ecstatic greeting) but are *made* to thank Maria for bringing a big bag of cakes. True it is that children do not always think to thank those bringing gifts; however, in a moment, when Maria cannot find the plumcake she has brought for Joe and his wife, she asks the children if any of them had "eaten it—by mistake, of course—but the children all said no and looked as if they did not like to eat cakes if they were to be accused of stealing." Maria has gone to considerable trouble and, to her, expense to get the plumcake; it is understandable she would be concerned, but she alienates herself from at least part of the company, taking some of the bloom from her visit when she thus accuses the children. Then comes the little incident of the nutcracker which has also unaccountably disappeared. Although Magalaner and Kain explain this as part of the pixie work of Hallowe'en, it is to be noted that Joe "was nearly getting cross over it and asked how did they expect Maria to crack nuts without a nutcracker." The displeasure of the children is conveyed to Joe as

Maria unconsciously goes about spreading dissension. In the next few lines she prefers not to take any stout or wine but Joe insists. She is not exactly a flexible guest.

Shortly she makes a worse blunder and, it would appear, nearly breaks up the party. We have already learned that Joe and his brother Alphy are deadly enemies, as deadly as only brothers can be, but Maria talks over old times and thinks she will "put in a good word for Alphy. But Joe cried that God might strike him stone dead if ever he spoke a word to his brother again and Maria said she was sorry she had mentioned the matter." For a veritable peacemaker Maria shows an outstanding lack of diplomacy; at this time we are led to wonder if her tact in the laundry might leave something to be desired.

The most positive indication comes in the next episode, however. After her blunder with Joe he resolves not to lose his temper, "on account of the night it was"—and asks his wife to open another bottle of stout. It should be noted parenthetically here that Maria has worried early in the story about Joe getting drunk but has through her faux pas caused him to drink more than he would have otherwise. Then all becomes merry again and they start the game which gives the story its title. It is a blindfold game in which a girl is supposed to touch a ring, a prayer-book, or water, indicating that she will be married, go into the convent, or go on a journey. Maria laughs and laughs until the tip of her nose nearly meets the tip of her chin when her turn comes, but the girls from next door have slipped in a dish of clay from the garden, which she touches. The inference seems obvious: clay is symbolic of death and it becomes an unfunny practical joke which makes Mrs. Donnelly very cross so that she tells one of the next-door girls to "throw it out at once." In effect, Maria is being told to drop dead; underneath the family gayety there is a hint of grimness. The very nature of the clay itself, cold, wet, and sticky, brings a shiver in the midst of the merriment, in the moment of holiday when everything should be harmony and happiness. We are reminded forcibly of the bitter quarrel over Christmas dinner which comes in the early part of *A Portrait of the Artist*. The ironic contrast between what should be and what is, between appearance and reality, is made explicit by this device.

The question arises, why is Maria to be looked on as a witch, bringing discord into the midst of a holiday party? What is she, or what has she done, to make her deserve this fate? Certainly she wants to bring happiness; she looks forward with eager anticipation to a good time, different from the drab routine of her work in the laundry. She is a tiny, shy, and pathetic old maid who deserves, one would ordinarily think, some small spark of joy in her life; but while this is not exactly denied her and she is happy after a fashion at the party, the results are far from delectable as she has anticipated. Of course, they never are. Simple realism of this sort hardly seems enough, however, to explain the chill that falls over the gathering every few moments.

It seems to us that there are two keys which may be used to answer this question: the reference to reflection found in the early part of the tale, and the final sentence in nearly every paragraph. In the opening of the story, everything in the kitchen is "spick and span: the cook said you could see yourself in the big copper boilers"; later, when Maria is getting ready to leave she stands before the mirror and looks "with quaint affection at the diminutive body which she had so often adorned. In spite of its years she found it a neat tidy little body." Although it is quite possible that these are simply details to give exposition and verisimilitude and should not be analyzed too extensively, with Joyce the chances are that they have another level of significance. Gazing at one's reflection implies some degree of Narcissism and self-regard; it is to be noted that Maria looks at herself with "quaint affection" and finds her body neat and tidy.

Combined with terminal sentences or phrases in nearly every paragraph these two references to reflection take on more depth. In one way or another the terminal sentences show, first, that Maria is a person so concerned with herself that she hardly discerns other people; and second, that her code of gentility prevents her understanding the rest of the world, warps and distorts her judgment because she is continually assessing people by her estimate of herself, as eminently genteel and respectable. For examples of the first aspect of Maria's character, here are some of the final sentences or phrases:

Paragraph No. 1. Maria had cut them herself.
Paragraph No. 2. "Maria, you are a veritable peacemaker!"
Paragraph No. 3. Everyone was so fond of Maria.
Paragraph No. 5. "Mamma is mamma but Maria is my proper mother."
Paragraph No. 8. . . . she found it a nice tidy little body.
Paragraph No. 17. She said they were all very good to her.

Recalling that we are seeing the story through Maria's eyes makes this constant reference to self and what people think of that self more than natural. Maria is undoubtedly a person who wants to be the center of attraction—perhaps this is one of the reasons she anticipates so eagerly going to Joe's because she knows she will be important there. This tendency is also evident in the insistent repetitions of gentility: she likes the matron in the Protestant laundry because she is "so genteel" (par. 6); the "colonel-looking gentleman" on the tram is easy to know as a gentleman "even when he has a drop taken" (par. 11)—quite different from her attitude toward Joe's drinking; Ginger Mooney, who has heartily toasted Maria's health "meant well enough, of course, she had the notions of a common woman." (par. 7) Maria is more than a bit of a snob, a snob of probably the worst sort, who, priding herself on respectability, condemns her inferiors because they are common yet is flattered by those who seem higher in the social scale despite their lack of respectability.

That these phrases all come at the end of paragraphs hardly seems an accident either, since Joyce as a stylist would be well aware of the impression such a position would create. It seems to us that he wants the reader to feel not only pathos toward Maria, whose position is certainly such as to warrant pity, but irony as well. Yearning for a proper place in the world she is perpetually an outsider; in the Protestant laundry among the big women with their "huge mugs" and earthy ways and the unbelievers with their tracts on the walls; buying plumcake from the superior young lady; at Joe's where the children wish she had not come and Joe is led from anger to drink and maudlin sentiment—all this is pathetic. Yet she brings on herself, through her self-regard, some of the pity of it all. She is not just a victim of a narrow drab life of the "scrupulous meanness" which Joyce said he wished to create in *Dubliners,* she is also *responsible* for that life, in part at least. And it is this combination of the pathetic and ironic which gives the story its unique flavor. We can neither merely feel sorry for Maria nor merely disdain her as an egoistic old maid. She is a witch because, seeking happiness and harmony, her own defect of character plus her inescapable situation perpetually deny these to her. In effect the witch sours the milk, tangles the horse's tail, and produces bad dreams when she wants to do exactly the opposite.

Emphasizing instead of minimizing the importance of seeing Maria as a witch going about her typical business on Hallow Eve does not clash either with the realistic dimension or the symbolic interpretations of this story. The plight of the spinster, without occupation yet too genteel to do menial labor, was and is acute even in sections of this country; it was much more so in Ireland fifty years ago: getting the ring would have been a kind of cruel irony since the prayer-book signified the only adequate recourse for such women as Maria. Moreover, the plight of the unwanted relative for whom one feels old affection and a sense of responsibility yet who manages through her difficult personality to make herself an agent of discord is not confined to any place or time. Symbolically, Maria as a Virgin Mary or Maria as Mother Ireland (William Tindall's interpretation) can be co-ordinated with Maria-as-witch. Maria's pathos lies in her situation, which Joyce may be implying is like that of Mary in latter-day Ireland—diminished, glory and fertility lost, forced into artificial circumstance where form takes the place of spirit. And Mother Ireland shows, from Joyce's point of view, the same vice which is the source of Maria's witchery—self-regard, provinciality and smug respectability.

Probably this is a sufficient extension of Magalaner and Kain's insight into "Clay." Joyce can be over-interpreted like any other symbolist. But it does seem that he intended for us to see Maria as an unintentional spirit of discord who pathetically and ironically does not even realize her own agency and stumbles through life feeling all eyes upon her while she gazes steadfastly, like the queen in Snow White, at the mirror on the wall.

Joyce's "Clay": An Interpretation

WILLIAM T. NOON, S.J.

Blessed are the peace-makers; they shall be counted the children of God.

In the James Joyce Collection at the University of Buffalo Library there is a large notebook containing in Joyce's own hand further notes to his already published works. The new notes to "Clay," one of the shortest of the *Dubliners* stories, are cryptic:

Gentleman horse (stallion):
sie studiert immer etwas:
murders child.

Such jottings are mysterious enough to afford several slants of the critical glass in an effort to catch the meaning of "Clay." Since these late marginal

From *College English,* November 1955. Reprinted with the permission of the National Council of Teachers of English and William T. Noon.

comments are outside of the story's own texture, the interpreter can hope at best to accommodate them to the meaning which emerges, which "epiphanizes," in the story itself. I should like to accommodate them to my own view of "Clay" as a spiritually revitalized version of a Hallowe'en tale. (I am grateful to the University Librarian for permission to quote the phrases.)

All Hallows Eve, or Hallowe'en, has a spiritual core of meaning in Catholic countries like Ireland which has been almost altogether forgotten in our own secular observance of the holiday. Hallow Eve, or "Holy Eve," began not just as a holiday of false faces and funny pranks, but as the vigil of holy day, the feast of All the Saints. Once a year at the end of the Church's liturgical cycle in the autumn, this holy day is observed in honor of all the little men and women, the G.I. Joes and Janes of the spiritual warfare, the unsung heroes, the "saints" (with a small *s*) who may not have done anything particularly memorable or striking by way of exploit, but who in the ordinary, everyday routine business of living showed holiness, saved their souls. This "feast" has always been a favorite with the vast rank and file of the faithful. It has been regarded in a very special way as their particular holy day. In a Catholic country like Ireland the evening before the holy day came to be celebrated with games and harmless pranks from which our Hallowe'en customs are derived.

Joyce's story "Clay" unfolds against this All Hallows background. Joyce takes advantage of the original meaning of All Hallows Eve to introduce us to a modern work-a-day saint, a saint with the small *s* indeed, somewhat vain and somewhat foolish, whose proudest moment of grace "epiphanizes" in the wordless, brave acceptance of herself as others see her—so much shapeless, loveless clay.

The plot-line of Joyce's story is simple. Maria, employee of a laundry (at Ballsbridge, the site of the annual Horse Show in Dublin), goes on Hallow Eve to the family of one of the Donnelly boys for whom she had been a childhood nurse. En route she purchases some cookies and a plumcake for the Hallowe'en party which Joe Donnelly and his wife have arranged for their own and a neighbor's children. On the tram a stout, elderly "gentleman," somewhat intoxicated, makes room for Maria, and they chat together. Arriving at the Donnelly home Maria is disconcerted when she cannot find her plumcake surprise. In the course of the evening's games the children trick Maria, who is blindfolded, into choosing, instead of the ring (prophetic of marriage) which she had hoped for, a wet lump of clay (prophetic of death). Joe scolds the children and he and his wife arrange that on the next try Maria will choose the prayer-book (prophetic, so they say, of Maria's entering a convent). The party closes with Maria's singing, at Joe's and his wife's insistence, two stanzas from one of "the old songs" of Balfe. Only, Maria omits the second stanza and sings the first stanza twice.

The plot-line of the story gives little idea, however, of how Joyce manages his "epiphany" of Maria as a kind of average saint, aware and unaware of the humility in self-knowledge which existence and sanctity require. Quietly, in a seemingly casual, unpremeditated way, Joyce prepares us for this understanding of Maria in the very opening of the story. The incident of Maria's settling the quarrels of the work-house laundry women has its point in the matron's words: "Maria, you are a veritable peace-maker." Though Joyce's overt allusion is to but one of the Beatitudes, covertly he manages to suggest, after a fashion, all the Beatitudes. "Blessed are you who are poor; the Kingdom of God is yours": in Maria's purse, we are told, there "were but two half-crowns and some coppers." Also, Maria is patient ("Blessed are the sad of heart") when she suspects that her cakes have been stolen by the children (as possibly they were), when the nut-cracker is misplaced by the children (most likely deliberately) so that she cannot eat any of the nuts. In a subtle way Maria "suffers persecutions" and yet tries to appear "glad and light-hearted."

The lyric-like ambiguity of the story, however, comes from Joyce's focus on Maria as a woman as well as a saint. For all her beautiful moral traits, on which she somewhat prided herself, Maria was not physically attractive. When she laughed, for instance, the tip of her very long nose nearly met the tip of her very long chin. The poor drudges of the laundry loved Maria anyway for her gentle character. Joe Donnelly and his wife were old enough, had lived long enough to take Maria for granted. But children were instinctively "put off" by her physical ugliness. And there had never been any "beaux" for Maria; no "suitors sought her hand, no knights upon bended knee."

This, Joyce implies, was a great sorrow. For Maria at heart thought of herself as a great lady. *Sie studiert immer etwas*: Maria was always "studying something." She had a knack of fitting whatever harsh thing might happen into her dream. "All that is lovely, all that is gracious in the telling"—all this truly was the argument of Maria's thought. Maria knew that she was a lady, not like Ginger Mooney, "a common woman." Since she was a lady, Maria thought she could tell a gentleman when she saw one.

After talking with the "colonel-looking gentleman" on the tram, she thought: "How easy it was to know a gentleman even when he has a drop taken." Maria was ever ready to make excuses. Maria was sometimes wrong. The gentleman of whom she had such a high opinion was in some respects, had she known them, hardly more than a stallion, a gentleman horse.

A lovely person like Maria should have been married, should have had a chance to know the love of a husband and children of her own, children who would have cared for her too much to have wanted to play tricks on her. It is only when we come to reflect on Maria's "mistake" at the end of the story that we realize how much the lack of love in her life had hurt Maria, how much it had cost her.

Joyce manages numerous details of the story in illumination of Maria's "mistake" at its close. The laundry-women laugh and jest about the ring in the barmbrack which they truly wish Maria to have. Maria seemingly regards the jest as lightheartedly as they do. Actually she has to try to convince herself "how much better it was to be independent and have your own money in your pocket." The stylish clerk's ironical question at the cake-shop, "was it wedding-cake she wanted to buy," made Maria blush. The cruelty of the children's jest in offering her a saucer filled with moist clay from the garden is seemingly not registered by Maria, only because the illumination is all within. The child who is "murdered" in the story is not any one of the children at the party. The child is inside Maria. In a flash the lady Maria sees herself as ridiculous and rather ugly. In that flash she loses hold on her dream.

The crucial test of Maria's gentle character comes to focus a little while later in her singing of Balfe's romantic love-song from *The Bohemian Girl,* "I Dreamt I Dwelt in Marble Halls." What an ironic contrast there is between Maria's actual situation and the words of the lyric as she sings them in her "tiny, quavering voice." There had been a time when Maria might have imagined that these words of the first stanza could conceivably come true in some sense for her. She was the hope and the pride of the laundry-folk, was she not? It was not altogether incongruous to *dream* that she could be rich, could have a high name. In spite of everything, she had once believed, or at least wanted to believe that people were good like herself—so that they would continue to love her *for what she was,* even if she were "to dwell in marble halls."

But Maria herself saw the incongruity of singing the second stanza of the lyric, hard as she had once tried to believe that people loved her just for what she was, and so she omitted:

I dreamt that suitors sought my hand,
That knights upon bended knee,
And with vows no maiden heart could
withstand
They pledged their faith to me.
And I dreamt that one of that noble band
Came forth my hand to claim.
But I also dreamt, which pleased me most,
That you loved me still the same.

Life had finally taught Maria the sheer impossibility of a dream like that ever coming true for her. Now after the games of the evening it would not be wise to expose herself to ridicule by singing this second verse. So, Joyce tells us, she sang the first verse twice. Joyce adds, "No one tried to show her her mistake!" Maria's goodness was not always able to restore peace: she had not succeeded that evening in making Joe any better disposed toward his estranged brother Alphy. But on this All Hallows Eve, she had succeeded in something. Her goodness was stronger than the children's hardness, their lack of understanding: "No one tried to show her her mistakes!" Her goodness was strong enough to trouble their parents' casual acceptance: Joe had to ask for the corkscrew. Life had been hard to Maria, but Maria had not become hard. Was Maria's singing the same stanza twice a mistake? Is living the life of the Beautitudes a mistake? Is it a mistake to be hallow on All Hallows Eve?

Joyce's "Clay"

FLORENCE L. WALZL

Conflicting elements in Maria, the heroine of James Joyce's "Clay" in *Dubliners,* have led to contradictory interpretations of the character: as saint (William T. Noon, "Joyce's 'Clay': An Interpretation," *College*

English, XVII, 1955, 93-95); as thematically disunified combination of laundress, witch, and Virgin Mary figure (Marvin Magalaner and Richard M. Kain, *Joyce: The Man, The Work, The Reputation,* New York, 1956, 84-91); and as unconsciously selfish troublemaker (Richard Carpenter and Daniel Leary, "The Witch Maria," *James Joyce Review,* III, 1959, 3-7). I believe "Clay" is a thematic whole based on a set of contrasts relating to the two church holidays which provide the setting and to the two fortunes the heroine receives in a fortune-telling game.

The setting is Halloween, the night in folk tradition when the dead walk, and (by the anticipation of the heroine) All Saints' Day, a feast honoring all the blessed, both those proclaimed publicly in canonization and those completely unknown to the world. The fact that it celebrates, especially, the unheralded saints of ordinary life has a thematic relationship to the story, as does the walking abroad of spirits on All Hallows' Eve.

The plot of "Clay" is simple. A middle-aged spinster named Maria, a humble kitchen worker in a laundry, spends Halloween with a family, perhaps relatives, for whom she has been nursemaid. While blindfolded in a game of fortunes, she chooses the clay portending death. Her friends quickly hide this choice from her and substitute a prayerbook prophetic of a future convent life. The pathos is deepened by the contrast between the emptiness and futility of her life as it is and as it might have been. For this little laundress has the potential qualities of ideal woman and mother, but their development has been stunted by the circumstances of her life.

In a sense, there are two Marias in this story: the Maria of the laundry and the Maria of the Halloween excursion. Within the confines of the laundry, several of Maria's qualities, her goodness, peaceableness, and loving motherliness, are greatly stressed. Both as a worker and a person her goodness is evident. She labors to make the scullery of the laundry a pleasant, happy place: the kitchen is "spic and span," the fire "nice and bright," the barmbracks perfectly cut, the plants well-kept. She sees that each laundress is well served at teatime. She spends her hard-earned money buying cakes for the children of the family and plumcake for their elders. Much also is made of her peaceableness. "She was always sent for when the women quarreled over their tubs and always succeeded in making peace." She always thinks the best of people. The matron of the laundry calls her "a veritable peace-maker." Finally, she is loving and motherly. She evokes the affection of the rough washerwomen who all are "so fond of Maria." She likes to recall the children she formerly nursed who called her their "proper mother." She looks forward happily to the family evening with "all the children singing." Even her name suggests the Church's prototype of the ideal maid and mother in the Virgin Mary. This Maria with her alarm clock set for the early morning mass of All Saints' Day suggests the very kind of saint this feast was inaugurated to honor.

But Maria on her Halloween visitation seems quite different. Though her goodness and generosity within the rounds of the laundry are effective, outside it they are not. In her timidity and lack of experience she loses the plumcake that was to have been her gift to the family and irritates the children over its loss. Moreover, her very presence upsets the adults because they feel the pathos of her life. At one point, Joe's eyes so fill with tears that he cannot find the corkscrew for the family toast. Her peaceableness, which is so marked within the laundry, is also ineffective without. She annoys the salesgirl in the bakeshop, is unable to heal the breach between the two brothers, and unwittingly provokes three near-quarrels: over Alphy, over some nuts, and over her choice of the clay. Also the emotional frustration of her life and its lack of human love are emphasized. Through a series of incidents suggesting romance, Joyce indicates that romantic and maternal love remain undeveloped in Maria. The laundresses' teasing about the ring, the shop girl's suggestion that the plumcake is for a wedding, the gallantry of the gentleman in the tram, and, above all, the verse from "I Dreamt That I Dwelt in Marble Halls" Maria forgets, a verse dealing with marriage proposals—all remind us of the sterility of her life. Finally, her appearance is that of "a very, very small person" with a "very long nose and a very long chin" which nearly meet. This Maria, ineffectual and trouble-making, suggests a Halloween witch.

What is Joyce's intent in this contrast which suggests saint and witch, life and death? I believe the answer is suggested in part by the two fortunes Maria receives at the party, the prayerbook and the clay—the first thematically associated with the saints' day, the second with the Halloween spirits. Both represent her future; both are death symbols.

The prayerbook, the fortune contrived by the family and forced upon her, is her immediate future, the life Irish society has molded for Maria. (In fact, her laundry job had been arranged for her by the family.) Her life in the laundry is a convent-like existence of narrow piety and goodness but without spiritual elevation, a life of small endeavors spent among women of a low class. Yet Maria had the potentialities for being the kind of heroic woman of full experience sainthood implies. Celibacy for a person ideally suited for marriage is a deprivation of life. The prayerbook for Maria is a sterility-death symbol.

Her hidden fortune, the clay, prophetic of death, suggests all that the ultimate future holds for her. In combination with Joyce's description of her as a Halloween wraith, it probably suggests also that she is not fully alive. Prevented by circumstances from full development of self, she represents virtue in an arrested state. Maria is one of the living dead of *Dubliners* who like Eliot's Hollow Men are "Shape without form, shade without colour,/ Paralyzed force, gesture without motion."

A Walled Garden

PETER TAYLOR

No, Memphis in autumn has not the moss-hung oaks of Natchez. Nor, my dear young man, have we the exotic, the really exotic orange and yellow and rust foliage of the maples at Rye or Saratoga. When our five-month summer season burns itself out, the foliage is left a cheerless brown. Observe that Catawba tree beyond the wall; and the leaves under your feet here on the terrace are mustard and khaki colored; and the air, the atmosphere (who would dare to breathe a deep breath!) is virtually a sea of dust. But we do what we can. We've walled ourselves in here with these evergreens and box and jasmine. You must know, yourself, young man, that no beauty is native to us but the verdure of early summer. And it's as though I've had to take my finger, just so, and point out to Frances the lack of sympathy that there is in the climate and in the eroded countryside of this region. I have had to build this garden and say, "See, my child, how nice and sympathetic everything can be." But now she does see it my way, you understand. You understand, my daughter has finally made her life with me in this little garden plot, and year by year she has come to realize how little else there is hereabouts to compare with it.

And you, you know nothing of flowers? A young man who doesn't know the zinnia from the aster! How curious that you and my daughter should have made friends. I don't know under what circumstances you two may have met. In her League work, no doubt. She *throws* herself so into whatever work she undertakes. Oh? Why, of course, I should have guessed. She simply *spent* herself on the Chest Drive this year. . . . But my daughter has most of her permanent friends among the flower-minded people. She makes so few friends nowadays outside of our little circle, sees so few people outside our own garden here, really, that I find it quite strange for there to be someone who doesn't know flowers.

No, nothing, we've come to feel, is ever very lovely, really lovely, I mean, in this part of the nation, nothing *but* this garden; and you can well imagine what even this little bandbox of a garden once was. I created it out of a virtual chaos of a backyard—Franny's playground, I might say. For three years I nursed that little magnolia there, for one whole summer did nothing but water the ivy on the east wall of the house; if only you could have seen the scrubby hedge and the unsightly servants' quarters of our neighbors that are beyond my serpentine wall (I suppose, at least, they're still there). In those days it was all very different, you understand, and Frances's father was about the house, and Frances was a child. But now in the spring we have what is truly a sweet garden here, modeled on my mother's at Rye; for three weeks in March our hyacinths are an inspiration to Frances and to me and to all those who come to us regularly; the larkspur and marigold are heavenly in May over there beside the roses.

But you do not know the zinnia from the aster, young man? How curious that you two should have become friends. And now you are impatient with her, and you mustn't be; I don't mean to be too indulgent, but she'll be along presently. Only recently she's become incredibly painstaking in her toilet again. Whereas in the last few years she's not cared so much for the popular fads of dress. Gardens and floral design have occupied her—with what guidance I could give—have been pretty much her life, really. Now in the old days, I confess, before her father was taken from us—I lost Mr. Harris in the dreadfully hot summer of '48 (People don't generally realize what a dreadful year that was—the worst year for perennials and annuals, alike, since Terrible '30. Things died that year that I didn't think would *ever* die. A dreadful summer)—why, she used then to run here and there with people of every sort, it seemed. I put no restraint upon her, understand. How many times I've said to my Franny, "You must make your own life, my child, as you would have it." Yes, in those days she used to run here and there with people of every sort and variety, it seemed to me. Where was it you say you met, for she goes so few places that are really *out* any more? But Mr. Harris would let me put no restraint upon her. I still remember the strongheadedness of her teens that had to be overcome and the testiness in her character when she was nearer to twenty than thirty. And you should have seen her as a tot of twelve when she would be somersaulting and rolling about on this very spot. Honestly, I see that child now, the mud on her middy-blouse and her straight yellow hair in her eyes.

When I used to come back from visiting my people at Rye, she would grit her teeth at me and give her confidence to the black cook. I would find my own child become a mad little animal. It was through this door here from the sun-room that I came one September afternoon—just such an afternoon as this, young man—still wearing my traveling suit, and called to my child across the yard for her to come and greet me. I had been away for the two miserable summer months, caring for my sick mother, but at the sight of me the little Indian turned and with a whoop she ran to hide in the scraggly privet hedge which was at the far end of the yard. I called her twice to come from out that filthiest of shrubs. "Frances Ann!" We used to call her by her full name when her father was alive. But she didn't stir. She crouched at the roots of the hedge and spied at her travel-worn mother between the leaves.

I pleaded with her at first quite indulgently and goodnaturedly and described the new ruffled dress and the paper cut-outs I had brought from her grandmother at Rye. (I wasn't to have Mother much longer, and I knew it, and it was hard to come home to this kind of scene.) At last I threatened to withhold my presents until Thanksgiving or Christmas. The cook in the kitchen may have heard some change in my tone, for she came to the kitchen door over beyond the lattice work which we've since put up, and looked out first at me and then at the child. While I was threatening, my daughter crouched in the dirt and began to mumble things to herself which I could not hear, and the noises she made were like those of an angry little cat. It seems that it was a warmer afternoon than this one—but my garden does deceive—and I had been moving about in my heavy traveling suit. In my exasperation I stepped out into the rays of the sweltering sun, and into the yard which I so detested; and I uttered in a scream the child's full name, "Frances Ann Harris!" Just then the black cook stepped out onto the back porch, but I ordered her to return to the kitchen. I began to cross the yard toward Frances Ann—that scowling little creature who was *incredibly* the same Frances you've met—and simultaneously she began to crawl along the hedgerow toward the wire fence that divided my property from the neighbor's.

I believe it was the extreme heat that made me speak so very harshly and with such swiftness as to make my words incomprehensible. When I saw that the child had reached the fence and intended climbing it, I pulled off my hat, tearing my veil to pieces as I hurried my pace. I don't actually know what I was saying—I probably couldn't have told you even a moment later—and I didn't even feel any pain from the turn which I gave my ankle in the gulley across the middle of the yard. But the child kept her nervous little eyes on me and her lips continued to move now and again. Each time her lips moved I believed I must have raised my voice in more intense rage and greater horror at her ugliness. And so, young man, striding straight through the hedge I reached her before she had climbed to the top of the wire fencing. I think I took her by the arm above the elbow, about here, and I said somethink like, "I shall have to punish you, Frances Ann." I did not jerk her. I didn't jerk her one bit, as she wished to make it appear, but rather, as soon as I touched her, she relaxed her hold on the wire and fell to the ground. But she lay there—in her canniness—only the briefest moment looking up and past me through the straight hair that hung over her face like an untrimmed mane. I had barely ordered her to rise when she sprang up and moved with such celerity that she soon was out of my reach again. I followed—running in those high heels—and this time I turned my other ankle in the gulley, and I fell there on the ground in that yard, this garden. You won't believe it—pardon, I must sit down. . . . I hope you don't think it too odd, my telling you all this. . . . You won't believe it: I lay there in the ditch and she didn't come to aid me with childish apologies and such, but instead she deliberately climbed into her swing that hung from the dirty old poplar that was here formerly (I have had it cut down and the roots dug up) and she began to swing, not high and low, but only gently, and stared straight down at her mother through her long hair—which, you may be sure, young man, I had cut the very next day at my own beautician's and curled into a hundred ringlets.

Questions and Assignments

1. This story takes the form of what is called a dramatic monologue, in which the words are always those of a single speaker whose listener remains silent. In most dramatic monologues (see "My Last Duchess," p. 422) what the speaker says and how he says it gradually reveal his own limitations until finally the reader

begins to question the reliability of the speaker's observations and judgments. Thus the words of a dramatic monologue reveal three things at the same time: (1) reality as the speaker sees it; (2) the character of the speaker; and (3) reality as the reader sees it in the light of his growing knowledge of the speaker. What are the limitations of this speaker and at what point do you first suspect them?

2. In this connection how revealing of the speaker's character is the formality of her diction in such expressions as "the verdure of early summer" and "painstaking in her toilet" (see "Tone: Levels of Usage," pp. 161-167)? And how revealing are recurrent turns of speech like "she *throws* herself into whatever work she undertakes," "she *spent* herself on the Chest Drive," "my daughter," "my own child," "my presents," "I wasn't to have Mother much longer," but "Frances's father," "her father"?

3. In view of the speaker's character, how reliable is her description of the surrounding countryside and of the beauties of her own garden and the beauties of Rye and Saratoga? Do you think that her account of the episode described in the last four paragraphs is accurate in every important detail? How valid is her judgment of the feelings and motives of the child in this episode? And how valid is her judgment of the present feelings and interests of her daughter? Consider the words: "Only recently she's become incredibly painstaking in her toilet again."

4. Try your skill at drawing inferences from available evidence (see "Inferences and Conclusions," pp. 428-430). Support or refute the following propositions: "The speaker, for all her shortcomings, is at least honestly devoted to natural beauty." "The speaker was not congenial with her husband, who was probably a man of unusually strong character." "The speaker has finally succeeded in recreating her daughter in her own image."

5. In the interpretations of "Clay" certain visible objects were said to represent invisible ones. Maria, for example, is said by one interpreter to represent the Church or the spirit of Ireland. Can you find similar examples of symbolism in "A Walled Garden"?

6. It is often said that the difference between appearance and reality is a major preoccupation of good prose fiction (see the preceding interpretations of "Clay"). Try to reconstruct in some detail the reality underlying appearances in "The Walled Garden." (See the definition of *irony*, p. 178.)

7. After considering these questions carefully, write an interpretation of "A Walled Garden," using as models, insofar as possible, the preceding interpretations of "Clay."

On the Guadalajara Front

ANTOINE DE ST. EXUPÉRY

On the Guadalajara front I sat at night in a dugout with a Republican squad made up of a lieutenant, a sergeant, and three men. They were about to go out on patrol duty. One of them—the night was cold—stood half in shadow with his head not quite through the neck of a sweater he was pulling on, his arms caught in the sleeves and waving slowly and awkwardly in the air like the short arms of a bear. Smothered curses, stubbles of beard, distant muffled explosions—the atmosphere was a strange compound of sleep, waking, and death. I thought of tramps on the road bestirring themselves, raising themselves up off the ground on heavy sticks. Caught in the earth, painted by the earth, their hands grubby with their gardenless gardening, these men were raising themselves painfully out of the mud in order to emerge under the stars. In these blocks of caked clay I could sense the awakening of consciousness, and as I looked at them I said to myself that across the way, at this very moment, the enemy was getting into his harness, was thickening his body with woolen sweaters; earth-crusted, he was breaking out of his mould of hardened mud. Across the way the same clay shaping the same beings was wakening in the same way into consciousness.

The patrol moved forward across fields through crackling stubble, knocking its toes against unseen rocks in the dark. We were making our way down into a narrow valley on the other side of which the enemy was entrenched. Caught in the cross-fire of artillery, the peasants had evacuated this valley, and their deserted village lay here drowned in the waters of war. Only their dogs remained, ghostly creatures that hunted their pitiful prey in the day and howled in the night. At four in the morning, when the moon rose white as a picked bone, a whole village bayed at the dead divinity.

"Go down and find out if the enemy is hiding in that village," the commanding officer had ordered. Very likely on the other side the same order had been given.

We were accompanied by a sort of political agent, a civilian, whose name I have forgotten, though not what he looked like. It seems to me he must have been rheumatic, and I remember that he leaned heavily on a knotted stick as we tramped forward in the night. His face was the face of a conscientious and elderly workman. I would have sworn that he was above politics and parties, above ideological rivalries. "Pity it is," he would say, "that as things are we cannot explain our point of view to the other fellow." He walked weighed down by his doctrine, like an evangelist. Across the way, meanwhile was the other evangelist, a believer just as enlightened as this one, his boots just as muddy, his duty taking him on exactly the same errand.

"You'll hear them pretty soon," my commissar said. "When we get close enough we'll call out to the enemy, ask him questions; and he may answer tonight."

Although we don't yet know it, we are in search of a gospel to embrace all gospels, we are on the march towards a stormy Sinai.

And we have arrived. Here is a dazed sentry, half asleep in the window of a stone wall.

"Yes," says my commissar, "sometimes they answer. Sometimes they call out first and ask questions. Of course they don't answer, too, sometimes. Depends on the mood they're in."

Just like the gods.

A hundred yards behind us lie our trenches. I strike a match, intending to light a cigarette, and two powerful hands duck my head. Everybody has ducked, and I hear the whistle of bullets in the air. Then silence. The shots were fired high and the volley was not repeated—a mere reminder from the enemy of what constitutes decorum here. One does not light a cigarette in the face of the enemy.

We are joined by three or four men, wrapped in blankets, who had been posted behind neighboring walls.

"Looks as if the lads across the way were awake," one of them remarks.

"Do you think they'll talk tonight? We'd like to talk to them."

"One of them, Antonio, he talks sometimes."

"Call him."

The man in the blanket straightens up, cups his hands round his mouth, takes a deep breath, and calls out slowly and loudly: "An . . . to . . . ni . . . o!"

The call swells, unfurls, floats across the valley and echoes back.

"Better duck," my neighbor advises. "Sometimes when you call them, they let fly."

Crouched behind the stone wall, we listen. No sound of a shot. Yet we cannot say we have heard nothing at all, for the whole night is singing like a sea-shell.

"Hi! Antonio . . . o! Are you . . ."

The man in the blanket draws another deep breath and goes on:

"Are you asleep?"

"Asleep?" says the echo. "Asleep?" the valley asks. "Asleep?" the whole night wants to know. The sound fills all space. We scramble to our feet and stand erect in perfect confidence. They have not touched their guns.

I stand imagining them on their side of the valley as they listen, hear, receive this human voice, this voice that obviously has not stirred them to anger since no finger has pressed a trigger. True, they do not answer, they are silent; but how attentive must be that silent audience from which, a moment ago, a match had sufficed to draw a volley. Borne on the breeze of a human voice, invisible seeds are fertilizing that black earth across the valley. Those men thirst for our words as we for theirs. But their fingers, meanwhile, are on their triggers. They put me in mind of those wild things we would try in the desert to tame and that would stare at us, eat the food and drink the water we set out for them, and would spring at our throats when we made a move to stroke them.

We squatted well down behind the wall and held up a lighted match above it. Three bullets passed overhead. To the match they said, "You are forgetting that we are at war." To us, "We are listening, nevertheless. We can still love, though we stick to our rules."

Another giant peasant rested his gun against the wall, stood up, drew a deep breath, and let go:

"Antonio . . . o! It's me! Leo!"

The sound moved across the valley like a ship new-launched. Eight hundred yards to the far shore, eight hundred back—sixteen hundred yards. If they answered, there would be five seconds of time between our questions and their replies. Five seconds of silence, in which all war would be suspended, would go by between each question and each answer. Like an embassy on a journey, each time. What this meant was that even if they answered, we should still feel ourselves separated from them. Between them and us the inertia of an invisible world would still be there to be stirred into action. For the considerable space of five seconds we should be like men shipwrecked and fearful lest the rescue party had not heard their cries.

". . . ooo!"

A distant voice like a feeble wave has curled up to die on our shore. The phrase, the word, was lost on the way and the result is an undecipherable message. Yet it strikes me like a blow. In this impenetrable darkness a sudden flash of light has gleamed. All of us are shaken by a ridiculous hope. Something has made known to us its existence. We can be sure now that there are men across the way. It is as if in invisibility a crack had opened, as if . . . Imagine a house at night, dark and its doors all locked. You, sitting in its darkness, suddenly feel a breath of cold air on your face. A single breath. What a presence!

There it comes again! ". . . time . . . sleep!"

Torn, mutilated as a truly urgent message must be, washed by the waves, and soaked in brine, here is our mesage. The men who fired at our cigarettes have blown up their chests with air in order to send us this mother bit of advice:

"Quiet! Go to bed! Time to sleep!"

It excites us. You who read this will perhaps think that these men were merely playing a game. In a sense they were. I am sure that, being simple men, if you had caught them at their sport they would have denied that it was serious. But games always cover something deep and intense, else there would be no excitement in them, no pleasure, no power to stir us. Here was a game that made our hearts beat too wildly not to satisfy a real though undefined need within us. It was as if we were marrying our enemy before dying of his blow.

But so slight, so fragile was the pontoon flung between our two shores that a question too awkward, a phrase too clumsy, would certainly upset it. Words lose themselves: only essential words, only the truth of truths would leave this frail bridge whole. And I can see him now, that peasant who stirred Antonio to speech and thus made himself our pilot, our ambassador; I can see him as he stood erect, as he rested his strong hands on the low stone wall and sent forth from his great chest that question of questions:

"Antonio! What are you fighting for?"

Let me say again that he and Antonio would be ashamed to think that you took them seriously. They would insist that it was all in fun. But I was there as he stood waiting, and I know that his whole soul gaped wide to receive the answer. Here is the truncated message, the secret mutilated by five seconds of travel across the valley as an inscription in stone is defaced by the passing of the centuries:

". . . Spain!"

And then I heard:

". . . You?"

He got his answer. I heard the great reply as it was flung forth into space:

"The bread of our brothers!"

And then the amazing:

"Good night, friend!"

And the response from the other side of the world:

"Good night, friend!"

And silence.

Their words were not the same, but their truths were identical. Why has this high communion never yet prevented men from dying in battle against each other?

Questions and Assignments

1. St. Exupéry's fine, lucid style comes through clearly even in translation. In Part Two of this book (pp. 85-216) we pointed to simple wording as an important aspect of clarity. Notice the relative length of St. Exupéry's sentences. Notice the positioning of verbs in successive sentences—an *is,* or a *was,* is usually surrounded by sentences of inverted word order, or by sentences with particularly strong verbs. Find instances of this. Study also the simplicity of diction—is there, in the whole episode, any word or phrase which is not immediately intelligible?

2. No small measure of St. Exupéry's stylistic strength is his use of metaphoric language. Find examples of his sustained sea imagery, such as, "Caught in the cross-fire of artillery, the peasants had evacuated this valley, and their deserted village lay here drowned in the waters of war." Why does he draw upon the sea as often as he does?

3. Explain the implications of the following: "these men were raising themselves painfully out of the mud in order to emerge under the stars." "He walked weighed down by his doctrine, like an evangelist." "It was as if we were marrying our enemy before dying of his blow." "At four in the morning, when the moon rose white as a picked bone, a whole village bayed at the dead divinity."

4. Is there a conflict between the references to "the enemy" and the constant emphasis on human brotherhood? How do you explain St. Exupéry, a Frenchman volunteering to fight in Spain, and then writing about the common humanity of "the enemy"? In your answer to that question explain this sentence: "Although we don't yet know it, we are in search of a gospel to embrace all gospels, we are on the march towards a stormy Sinai," and "The shots were fired high and

the volley was not repeated—a reminder from the enemy of what constitutes decorum here."

5. Examine the means by which St. Exupéry seeks to build interest and suspense during the exchange of comments between the opposing forces. Comment specifically on the waiting, on the details provided, on the echoes, and on the statement that "games always cover something deep and intense."

6. What is the difference between the two answers given to "What are you fighting for"?

7. Write an analysis of the theme of "On the Guadalajara Front."

8. Compare Joyce's treatment of Maria's isolation with St. Exupéry's treatment of the isolation of the soldiers.

9. Write an essay, using this story as a basic example, answering the final question of the author: "Why has this high communion never yet prevented men from dying in battle against each other?"

Two Lovely Beasts

LIAM O'FLAHERTY

The Derranes were having breakfast when a neighbour called Kate Higgins came running into their kitchen. She squatted on the floor by the wall to the right of the door, threw her apron over her face and began to wail at the top of her voice in most heartrending fashion.

"God between us and harm!" said Mrs. Derrane as she came over from the table. "What happened to you?"

She put an arm about the shoulders of the wailing neighbour and added tenderly:

"Tell us what happened, so that we can share your sorrow."

Colm Derrane came over with his mouth full of food. He had a mug of tea in his hand. The six children followed him. They all stood in a half-circle about Kate Higgins, who continued to wail incontinently.

"Speak up, in God's name," Colm said, after swallowing what he had been munching. "Speak to us so that we can help you, woman."

It was some time before Kate desisted from her lamentation. Then she suddenly removed her apron from before her face and looked fiercely at Colm through wild blue eyes that showed no sign of tears. She was a skinny little woman, with a pale face that was deeply lined with worry. Her husband had died a few months previously, leaving her with a large family that she was struggling to rear on next to nothing.

"Will you buy a calf?" she said to Colm in an angry tone.

"A calf?" said Colm in surprise. "I didn't know your cow had . . ."

"She dropped it a little while ago," the woman interrupted. "Then she died herself. Lord save us, she lay down and stretched herself out flat on the grass and shook her legs and that was all there was to it. She's as dead as a door-nail. There isn't a spark left in her. It must have been poison that she dragged up out of the ground with her teeth, while she was mad with the calf sickness."

The whole Derrane family received this news in open-mouthed silence. It was a calamity that affected every household in the village. Each family had but a single cow. By traditional law, those who had milk were bound to share with those who had none. So that the death of one cow, no matter to whom she belonged, was a calamity that affected all.

"Bloody woe!" Colm said at length. "Bloody mortal woe! That's a terrible blow, and you after losing your husband only the other day. There you are now with a house full of weak children and no cow. Ah! Bloody woe!"

"No use talking, Colm," Kate Higgins said fiercely. "Buy the calf from me. I'm asking you to do it for the love of God. He must get suck quickly or else he'll die of hunger. He'll stretch out there on the grass beside his mother and die, unless he gets suck. Buy him from me."

Colm and his wife looked at one another in perplexity. Their faces were racked with pity for their neighbour.

"Bloody woe!" Colm kept muttering under his breath.

There was no sign of pity in the faces of the children. They moved back to the table slowly after a few moments of open-mouthed consternation. They kept glancing over their shoulders at Kate Higgins with aversion. They hated her, now that they understood her calamity threatened to diminish their milk supply.

"I'm asking you for the love of God," Kate Higgins continued in a tone that had become quite savage. "The price will help me buy a new cow. I must have a cow for the children. The doctor said they must have plenty of milk, the two youngest of them especially. They are ailing, the poor creatures. Your cow has a fine udder, God bless her. She calved only a few days ago. She won't feel my fellow at her teats in addition to her own. She'll be well able for the two of them, God bless her. She will, 'faith and she'll leave plenty of milk for yourselves into the bargain. Praise be to God, I never saw such a fine big udder as she has."

Colm was on the point of speaking when his wife interrupted him.

"You know how it is with us," Mrs. Derrane said. "We are giving milk to three houses already. Their cows aren't due to calve for more than three weeks yet. We'll have to help you as well, now that your cow is gone. So how could we feed a second calf? It would be against the law of God and of the people. We couldn't leave neighbours without milk in order to fill a calf's belly."

Kate Higgins jumped to her feet and put her clenched fists against her lean hips.

"The calf will die unless you buy him," she cried ferociously. "There is nobody else to take him but you people. Nobody else has a cow after calving. The price would help me buy another cow. I must have a cow for the children. The doctor said . . ."

"That's enough, woman," Colm interrupted. "I'll put him on our cow for a couple of days. In the meantime, maybe you could get someone in another village to buy him."

Kate Higgins grew calm at once on hearing this offer. Tears came into her wild blue eyes.

"God spare your health, Colm," she said gently. "I was afraid he'd die of hunger before he could get suck. That would be the end of me altogether. I'd have nothing at all left if he died on me, stretched out on the grass beside his mother. When you have a few pounds, it's easier to borrow more than if you have none at all. God spare the two of you."

Colm went with her to the field, where they were already skinning the dead cow. He took the red bull calf in his arms to the paddock where his own cow was grazing. She consented to give the stranger suck after some persuasion.

"He's lovely, sure enough," Colm said as he looked with admiration at the wine-dark hide of the sucking calf. "I thought my own calf this year looked like a champion, but he's only in the halfpenny place compared to this one."

"He'll be a champion all right," Kate Higgins said. "He has the breed in him. Why wouldn't he? Nothing would do my husband, Lord have mercy on him, but to spend ten royal shillings for the use of the Government bull. Nothing less would satisfy him, 'faith. He wasn't much to look at, poor man, but he always liked to have the best of everything."

She suddenly rushed over to Colm and put her lips close in his ear. Now her wild blue eyes were full of cunning.

"You should buy him, Colm," she whispered. "Buy him and put him with your own calf. Then you'll have the makings of the two finest yearlings that were ever raised in this townland. You'll be the richest man in the village. You'll be talked about and envied from one end of the parish to the other."

Colm turned his back to her and took off his cap. He was quite young and yet his skull had already begun to go bald along the crown. He was a big awkward fellow with pigeon toes and arms that were exceptionally long, like those of an ape. He was noted in the district for his strength, his immense energy and his eagerness for work.

"Arrah! How could I buy him from you?" he said in a low voice. "How could I feed him and so many people depending on the milk?"

Then he turned towards her suddenly and raised his voice to a shout, as if he were arguing with some wild thought in his own mind.

"I have only twenty acres of land," he cried angrily. "The whole of it is practically barren. You wouldn't find more than a few inches of soil in the deepest part of it. You wouldn't find a foot of ground in all I possess where you could bury a spade to the haft. Bloody woe! Woman, I tell you that I haven't one good single half-acre. There is hardly enough grass for my cow, not to mention my unfortunate horse. You could count the bones right through my poor horse's hide. I'm hard put every year to find grass for my yearling. Woman alive, sure there isn't a man in this village that could feed two yearlings. It would be madness for me to try it."

"The English have started fighting the Germans a second time," Kate Higgins whispered. "They won't stop until they have dragged the whole world again into the war with them. The fight will last for years and years, same as it did before. There will be a big price for everything fit to eat. A man that would have two lovely beasts for sale . . ."

"Stop tempting me with your foolish talk, woman," Colm interrupted.

"Your cow could easily feed the two calves," Kate continued. "She could do it without any bother at all. She'd have plenty, besides, for yourselves and the neighbours. You needn't worry about grass, either. There's always plenty of grass for rent in the village of Pusach. You'll have plenty of money to spare for buying any extra grass you'll need, because there is going to be a great price for potatoes and fish. Man alive, there will be lashings of money, same as before. During the other big war, you remember, they were even buying rotten dog-fish. I declare to my God they were. They paid famine prices for the rotten dog-fish that the storms threw up on the beach beyond there."

Colm turned away from her again and lowered his voice to a whisper.

"It would be madness for me to try it," he said. "Nobody ever tried to raise two yearlings in this village. We all have the same amount of rocky land, twenty acres a head."

"You're different from everybody else, Colm," Kate said, raising her voice and speaking very rapidly. "The others only do what they have to do. They do barely enough to keep themselves and their families alive. You go out of your way looking for work. You never turn aside from an opportunity to earn an extra shilling. You are at it night and day, whenever you get the chance. The spunk is in you. There is no end to your strength. Oh! Indeed, it's well known that there is no holding you, when there is a job of work to be done. You spit on your hands and away you go like a wild stallion. God bless you, there is the strength of ten men in your body and you're not afraid to use it. You deserve to prosper on account of your willingness. You deserve to be rich and famous. All you need is courage."

"Nobody ever tried it," Colm whispered hoarsely. "Nobody ever did. It would be madness to try it."

Kate Higgins stepped back from him and threw out her arms in a dramatic gesture.

"Let you be the first, then," she shouted. "There's nothing stopping you but a want of courage. Let you be the first. Let you show them how to do it, Colm."

Colm also raised his voice to a shout as he answered her fiercely.

"Stop your foolish talk, woman," he said. "He can suck on my cow for a couple days, but I promise you no more."

Kate walked away from him hurriedly, gesticulating with both arms.

"Two lovely beasts!" she shouted back at him, when she was at a distance. "Think of that now. There's nothing standing in your way but a want of courage."

"Not another word out of you now," Colm shouted after her at the top of his voice. "What you're saying is against the law of God."

Even so, he could hardly sleep a wink that night through thinking of what the woman had said. In the morning he broached the idea of buying the calf during conversation with his wife.

"That's a lovely calf Kate Higgins has," he said. "It's a pity we can't buy it."

"Buy it?" said his wife. "Yerrah! How could we do that?"

"There is going to be a great price for beasts on account of the war," Colm continued. "With the English and the Germans at it again . . ."

"Have sense, man," his wife said. "Unless you've taken leave of your gumption, you know well it's impossible for us to buy that calf. Not even if we had grass for it, which we haven't."

"All the same," Colm said, "that young fellow makes my mouth water. I never saw such a young champion."

"Yerrah! How could we leave the neighbours without milk?" his wife said.

"I'm only talking, that's all," Colm said. "There is no harm in talk."

"Well! Say no more about it," his wife said. "People might hear you and be scandalised."

"You never saw such a colour as that calf has," Colm said as he went out of the house. "He's so red that he's almost black."

Kate Higgins came to him again that day, while he was smashing rocks with a sledge-hammer in the corner of a little field that he was trying to make arable. She began to pester him once more with the idea of having "two lovely beasts." He threw down the sledge-hammer and ran over to the fence against which she leant.

"Why don't you leave me alone?" he shouted at her. "Go to some other village and find a buyer for him."

"I've enquired everywhere," Kate Higgins said. "It's no use, Colm. Unless you buy him, I'll have to give him to the butcher at Kilmacalla. The few shillings that I'll get for his flesh and his hide won't be much. However, they'll be better than nothing."

"I promised to let him suck for a couple of days," Colm shouted. "I can promise you no more. I can't let the neighbours go without the milk that is due to them."

"It will be a mortal sin to slaughter such a lovely young fellow," Kate said as she walked away hurriedly. "What else can I do, though? I must get a pound or two, by hook or by crook. Then I can borrow more. I have to make up the price of a new cow one way or another. The doctor said that the young ones must have plenty of milk. Otherwise they'll die. So he said. He did, 'faith."

After the woman had gone, Colm went to the paddock for another look at the young bull calf that had a wine-dark hide.

"It would be a mortal sin surely to slaughter such a lovely creature," he said aloud. "He'll be every inch a champion if he lives."

Then his heart began to beat wildly as he watched the two calves cavort together with their tails in the air. He became intoxicated by the idea of possessing them both.

"Two lovely beasts!" he whispered.

He went for a walk to the cliff tops instead of returning to his sledgehammer. He stood on the brink of the highest cliff and looked down into the sea.

"Two lovely beasts!" he whispered again.

Then a frenzied look came into his pale blue eyes. He took off his cap and threw it on the ground behind him.

"Sure I have the courage," he muttered fiercely.

He spread his legs, leaned forward slightly and held out his hands in front of his hips, with the palms upturned and the fingers slightly crooked. He began to tremble.

"I have plenty of courage," he muttered.

The skin on the upper part of his forehead and on top of his baldish skull looked very pale above the brick-red colour of his bony cheeks. He had a long, narrow face, thick lips and buck teeth. His short nose had a very pointed ridge. His mouse-coloured hair stuck out in ugly little bunches above his ears and at the nape of his neck. His shoes were in tatters. His frieze trousers were covered with patches of varying colours. His grey shirt was visible through the numerous holes in his blue woollen sweater.

Yet he looked splendid and even awe-inspiring, in spite of his physical ugliness and his uncouth dress, as he stood poised that way on the brink of the tall cliff above the thundering sea, leaning forward on widespread legs, with his long arms stretched out and his fingers turned slightly inwards on his open palms, trembling with a frenzy of desire.

After a while he turned away from the sea and picked up his cap. He felt very tired as he walked homewards with downcast head. His arms swung limply by his sides. He kept glancing furtively from side to side, as if he were conscious of having committed a crime up there on the cliff top and feared pursuit as a consequence. There was a hard look in his pale blue eyes.

Again that night he could not sleep. He lay on his back thinking of the "two lovely beasts" and how he wanted to possess them. The thought gave him both pleasure and pain. The pleasure was like that derived from the anticipation of venery. The pain came from his conscience.

During the morning of the following day, Kate Higgins came to him again. She was wearing her best clothes.

"I'm on my way to the butcher at Kilmacalla," she said to him.

"All right," Colm said to her. "How much do you want for the calf?"

He was so excited by the decision at which he had arrived that he consented to the price she asked without bargaining.

"Come to the house with me," he said. "I'll hand over the money to you."

"God spare your health," Kate Higgins said. "With that money I can begin at once to look for another cow. When you have a few pounds you can always borrow more."

Mrs. Derrane got very angry when her husband came into the kitchen with Kate Higgins and asked her for the family purse.

"Is it to buy that calf?" she said.

"Hand me the purse," Colm repeated.

"Devil a bit of me," his wife said. "It would be against the law of God to put the people's milk into a calf's heathen belly. I won't give it to you."

Colm gripped the front of her bodice with his left hand and shook her.

"Hand it over, woman," he said in a low voice.

Her anger passed at once. She was a big, muscular woman, almost as strong as her husband and possessed of a stern will. Indeed, she had dominated Colm's simple nature ever since their marriage until now. Whenever he tried to rebel against her decisions, he had always been easily defeated. He had shouted, broken articles of furniture and even struck her cruel blows from time to time. She had always merely waited with folded arms and set jaws until his foolish anger had spent itself. Now it was different. He did not shout and she saw something in his pale blue eyes that frightened her.

So that she went quickly to the great chest and brought him the long cloth purse.

"What's come over you?" she said to him while he was undoing the string. "What are the neighbours going to say about this?"

Colm unrolled the purse and thrust his hand deep down into the long inner pocket. He again looked his wife straight in the eyes.

"Shut up, woman," he said quietly. "From now on don't meddle with things that don't concern you. I'm master in this house. Do you hear?"

Again she became frightened by what she saw in his eyes. She turned away from him.

"May God forgive you," she said. "I hope you have thought well about this before doing it."

"I've never in my life thought more about anything," Colm said.

Kate Higgins never uttered one word of thanks when she was given the money. She stuffed the notes into the front pocket of her skirt and rushed from the house.

"I'll go now," she cried as she hurried down the yard, "to try and get company for these few pounds. When you have money, it's always easier to borrow more. Those that have give only to those that have. To those that have not only crumbs are given, same as to a dog."

When Colm went that evening to the meeting place on the brow of the little hill that faced the village, silence fell among the men that were assembled there. He threw himself on the ground, put his back to a rock and lit his pipe. The others began to discuss the weather in subdued tones after a little while. Then again there was silence.

At length a man named Andy Gorum turned to Colm and said:

"We heard you bought the calf from Kate Higgins."

"I did," said Colm.

"Is it to slaughter him you bought him?" Gorum said.

"No," said Colm.

"Do you intend to rear him?" Gorum said.

"I do," said Colm.

Gorum got to his feet slowly and clasped his hands behind the small of his back. He came over and stood in front of Colm. He was an elderly man, very small and thin, with a wrinkled face that was the colour of old parchment. His eyes were weak and they had hardly any lashes, like those of a man blind from birth. He was the village leader because of his wisdom.

"I'm sorry you are doing this, Colm," he said. "You are a good man and everybody belonging to you was good, away back through the generations. This is a bad thing you intend to do, though."

"How could it be bad to help a widow?" Colm said.

"You know well it won't help a widow if you rear that calf on the people's milk," Gorum said.

"She begged me and begged me," Colm said, raising his voice. "She kept at me the whole time. How could I refuse her? She said that she had to have the money for another cow. She said her children would die unless . . ."

"You know you are breaking the law," Gorum interrupted. "It's no use trying to talk yourself out of it."

"How could it be against the law to help a widow?" Colm shouted.

"Indeed, it isn't," Gorum said. "We'll all help her, please God, as much as we can. That's how we live here in our village, by helping one another. Our land is poor and the sea is wild. It's hard to live. We only manage to live by sticking together. Otherwise we'd all die. It's too wild and barren here for any one man to stand alone. Whoever tries to stand alone and work only for his own profit becomes an enemy of all."

Colm jumped to his feet. He towered over Gorum.

"Are you calling me an enemy for helping a widow?" he shouted.

"If you put into a calf's belly," Gorum said, "the milk that you owe your neighbours, everybody will be against you."

"I'll do what I please," Colm shouted.

Thereupon he rushed from the meeting place.

"Come back, neighbour," Gorum called after him in a tone of entreaty.

"I have the courage to do what I think is right," Colm shouted.

"We are all fond of you," Gorum said. "We don't want to turn against you. Come back to us and be obedient to the law."

"I'll do what I think is right," Colm shouted as he crossed the stile into his yard. "I'll raise those two beasts if it's the last thing I'll do in this world. Let any man that dares try to stop me."

The Derranes became outcasts in the village from that day forward. Nobody spoke to them. Nobody gave them any help. Nobody entered their house. All other doors were closed against them.

Even Kate Higgins turned against her benefactors in most shameful fashion. Contrary to her expectations, the hapless woman was unable to borrow any more money, except for a solitary pound that she got from an aunt after lengthy importunities. Neither was she able to find any cow for sale, although she tramped the parish from end to end, over and over again. Her house went to rack and ruin during her continued absence. The ungoverned children burned the furniture to keep themselves warm. They grew so savage and filthy that the neighbour women removed their own children from all contact with them.

Unbalanced by her misfortunes, Kate forsook her peasant frugality and brought tidbits home to her starving brood after each fruitless day of wandering. The poor woman lacked courage to face them empty-handed. In that way she soon spent every penny of the money that she got from Colm and her aunt. There was none of it left after two months. When she had nothing more to give the little ones on her return, as they clutched at her apron with their filthy hands and whined pitifully for food, her mind began to get crazed.

She took to reviling Colm at the top of her voice in the roadway outside her house as she shuffled homeward with the fall of night.

"Colm Derrane is sold to the devil," she cried. "He put bad luck on me. I was grateful to him when he bought my calf, thinking he was doing me a favour and that I could borrow more, to put with what he gave me and make up the price of a new cow. Devil a bit of it. There was a curse on his money. People told me it was on account of the war they were unwilling to part with any of their share. They said they were bound to clutch all they had, for fear of disaster. The truth is that they would not lend to a woman that sold a calf to an enemy of the people. Here I am now without a red copper in my skirt, without a cow or a husband and my children ailing. They'll die on me, the poor little creatures, without the milk that the doctor ordered for them. I have no strength to care for them. I'm so tired every evening after my walking that I can't even pick the lice out of their hair. Ah! the poor little creatures! May God have pity on my orphans!"

Colm paid no more heed to this abuse than he did to the hostility of the people. After his outburst of anger on being told he was to be treated as an outcast, he maintained strict control over his temper. He became dour and silent and indifferent, except when he was in the presence of the two young beasts that he loved. It was only then that he smiled and uttered words of tenderness.

"Oh! You lovely creatures!" he said to them as he watched them suck at the cow's teats. "Drink up now and be strong. Don't leave a drop of that milk in the udder. I want the two of you to be champions."

He was as ruthless towards his family as he was tender towards the calves. He only brought enough milk to colour the tea into the house. He let the calves swallow all the rest. Lest there might be any cheating, he forbade his wife and children to go near the cow under threat of dire punishment.

His wife came to him shortly after the calves were weaned and protested.

"I can go without butter," she said, "although the children tear the heart in me with their whinging. They keep asking when there is going to be some. It is too much, though, when I can't get enough buttermilk to make our bread rise. All I ask is enough milk for one churning."

"You can't have it," Colm said coldly. "I can't let the calves go in want, just for the sake of making our bread rise. We can eat it flat just as well. Calves must get a good foundation during the first few months, by having every hole and corner of their bellies well stuffed the whole time. That's how they get bone and muscle and balance and plenty of room. Then it's easy, when the time comes, to pile on the good hard meat. The foundation will be there to carry the load."

His wife kept looking at him in amazement while he spoke. She could not understand how a man, who had formerly been so kind and considerate of his family's needs, could suddenly become ruthless. She burst into tears after he had finished.

"God will punish you for being cruel," she said.

"Silence," said Colm. "Don't take liberties, woman."

Midsummer came. That was the season of abundance for the poor people of that village. The new potatoes were being dug. The young onions were succulent in the house gardens. There was plenty of milk and butter in the houses. Great baskets of pollock and rock-fish and bream and mackerel were brought each day from the sea. The hens were laying and the spare cockerels from the spring hatchings made broth for the delicate. At supper-time, the people gorged themselves on their favourite dish of mashed new potatoes, with butter and scallions and boiled fish and fresh potatoes. Then a great lump of yellow butter was pressed down into the centre of the steaming dish. The table was laid before the open door, so that they could hear the birds singing in the drowsy twilight and see the red glory of the sunset on the sea while they ate. The men waddled out afterwards to the village meeting place, sending clouds of tobacco smoke into the air from their pipes. They laid down on their backs against the rocks and listened to the bird music in raptured content. Now and again, one of them joined his voice to those of the birds and gave thanks to God for His gracious bounty.

It was then that Mrs. Derrane rose up in rebellion against her husband. She took the tongs from the hearth one evening and stood in front of him.

"I'll stand no more of this, Colm," she said fiercely. "Here we are, living on potatoes and salt, while the neighbours are feasting. Everything is put aside for the calves. My curse on the pair of them. You won't even let us eat a bit of fresh fish. By your leave, you made me salt every single fish that you brought into the house this spring, to be sold later on, so that you can have money to buy grass for your beasts. We have to scavenge along the shore, the children and myself, looking for limpets and periwinkles, same as people did during the famine. Lord save us, the lining of our stomachs is torn into shreds from the purging that the limpets give us. We are put to shame, rummaging like sea-gulls for stinking food, while the people of our village are feasting. There has to be an end to this, or else I'll take the children and follow my face out of the house. You'll have to get rid of that calf you bought. Then we can live as we did before. We'll be outcasts no longer."

Colm got to his feet and looked at her coldly.

"I'm going to raise those two calves," he said solemnly, "even if you and the children and myself have to eat dung while I'm doing it. Let other people fill their bellies in midsummer and remain poor. I want to rise in the world. A man can do that only by saving."

His wife raised the tongs and threatened him with them.

"I'll have none of it," she cried. "I'm telling you straight to your face. You have to give in to me or I'll split your skull with these tongs."

"Put down those tongs," Colm said quietly.

"Are you going to get rid of that calf?" said his wife.

"Put them down," said Colm.

"I'll kill you with them," shouted his wife, becoming hysterical.

She struck at him with all her force, but he jumped aside nimbly and evaded the blow. Then he closed with her and quickly locked her arms behind her back.

"I'm going to give you a lesson now," he said quietly. "I'm going to chastise you in a way that you'll remember."

He dragged her down to the hearth.

"Call the neighbours," his wife cried to the children. "Run out into the yard and call the people to come and save me from this murderer."

The children ran out into the yard and began to call for help as Colm took down a dried sally rod that lay stretched on wooden pegs along the chimney place.

"You'll be obedient in future, my good woman," he said. "On my solemn oath you will."

He began to flog her. She tried to bite his legs. Then he put her flat on the ground and laid his foot to her back.

"I'll kill you when I get a chance," she cried. "I'll have your life while you are asleep."

Then she folded her arms beneath her face, gritted her teeth and received his blows in silence. He had to go on beating her for a long time before the sturdy creature surrendered and begged for mercy.

"All right, then," Colm said calmly when she had done so. "Do you promise to be obedient from now on and to make no more trouble about the calf?"

"I promise," his wife said.

"Get up, then, in God's name," Colm said gently, "and call in the children."

His wife looked up at him sideways in amazement. She did not rise. It puzzled her that he was so calm and spoke to her with tenderness, after beating her without mercy.

"Get up, woman," he continued. "Don't let us behave like this any more. It gives scandal to the children."

Then he took her tenderly in his arms and raised her to her feet. She ran out into the yard without looking at him.

"Get into the house," she said sternly to the children. "In with you."

She turned to some neighbours who had come in answer to the children's cries for help. They were standing out in the lane, in doubt as to whether they should enter the yard of a household that was outcast.

"What brought you here?" Mrs. Derrane shouted at them. "It's not for our good you came. Be off now and mind your own business."

That night in bed, she clasped Colm in her arms and put her cheek against his breast.

"I thought it was the devil got into you," she whispered as tears rolled down her cheeks. "Now I know different. You are trying to raise your family up in the world, while I'm only a hindrance to you and a dead weight around your neck. From now on, though, I'm going to help you. I will, 'faith!"

Colm took her head between his big rough hands and kissed her on the crown.

"God spare your health, darling," he said. "With your help there will be no stopping us."

Seeing their parents happily united again, the children also became imbued with enthusiasm. They willingly consented to make sacrifices for the common effort. Even the youngest boy, barely five years old, had a little job to do every day. The whole family worked like bees in a hive.

The village people soon became so impressed by this turn of events that they began to question the justice of their conduct towards the Derrane family.

"If what he is doing is bad, why does he prosper?" they said to one another. "Isn't it more likely that God is blessing his effort to rise in the world? Maybe it's us that are wicked on account of our laziness?"

At the village meeting place, Andy Gorum strove with all his skill to hold the men steadfast against Colm.

"You'll soon see him come back to us on his knees," Gorum said, "and he begging for mercy. He may seem to prosper now. His two calves are growing powerfully. His wife and children and himself are working night and day. He has a nimble hand in everything worth money. Wait till winter comes, though. Then he won't be able to find grass for his beasts. The butcher of Kilmacalla has bought a herd of black cattle, to fatten them for the fighting English. He has rented all the spare grass in the village of Pusach. Many more big people in the district have bought herds on account of the war. There won't be a single blade of grass left anywhere for a poor man to rent. The big people will have it all clutched. Colm will have to slaughter that dark-skinned calf. I declare to my God we'll be eating that dark fellow's meat when the Christmas candles are lit."

Gorum's prophecy proved false and Colm was able to find grass owing to the tragedy that again struck the Higgins family. As summer passed, the village people were no longer able to give more than the barest help to the widow and her orphans. Neither did the distraught woman put to the best use what little there was given. Indeed, she now turned on the whole village as she had formerly turned on Colm, denouncing the community at the top of her voice.

"Ah! Woe!" she cried as she marched back and forth before the houses in her bare feet. "Almighty God was cruel when he left me a widow among people that are worse than the heathen Turks. There I am, with my clutch of delicate creatures, without bite or sup from morning to night. You wouldn't see a good rush of smoke out of my chimney-top from Monday to Saturday. All I have to burn on my hearth is cow dung and a few miserable briars. There isn't a hot drop for the children's bellies. Ah! Woe! My curse on the hard hearts of my neighbours!"

There was a spell of cold weather towards the end of September and the two youngest children fell victims to it. They both died in the same week of pneumonia. The second death unhinged the mother's reason. Leaving the child unburied in the house, she wandered away at dead of night, with hardly a stitch of clothes on her starved body. They found her marching along the cliff tops on the evening of the following day and took her to the lunatic asylum. The remaining five children, finding no relatives willing to shelter them, were also lodged in a public institution. It then became apparent that the widow owed money right and left. Her creditors, who were chiefly shopkeepers of Kilmacalla, began to quarrel about disposal of the house and land. The case was brought into the district court.

"Here is my chance," Colm said to his wife. "Here is where I might be able to get grass this winter for my beasts."

On the day the case was to be tried, he put on his best clothes, took the family purse and went to the court-house at Kilmacalla. After listening to the arguments of the rival lawyers for some time, he got leave to address the magistrate.

"Your honour," he said, "it would be an injustice to the children if that farm is auctioned now, or divided up among these shopkeepers. It would be taking the bread out of the children's mouths. They have a right to do what they please later on with that land. When they grow up and come out into the world, it's for them to say if the land is to be sold, or given to one of themselves in order to raise a family on it. In the meantime, let me rent it from them, your honour. Year after year, I'll pay a good rent for it on the nail. Everybody knows me, sir. I'm a man of my word. I never went back on a pennyworth of promises in my natural life. Any man will tell you that, from the parish priest on down. The mother's debts can be paid out of the rent in no time at all. What more would these shopkeepers want, unless they are land-grabbers? In God's name, your honour, you'll be behaving like a Christian if you let me rent it, instead of letting these people slice it out among themselves. God bless you, sir!"

The magistrate finally agreed to Colm's suggestion for settling the dispute.

"Praised be God!" Colm cried on his return home. "I am secure now against the winter. Nothing can stop me from now on. In God's name, the two beasts are as good as raised."

Gorum was furious at this turn of events. He attacked Colm savagely that evening at the meeting place.

"There is a bloody heathen for you!" he cried. "The two little ones are barely dead in their graves when the bloodsucker that robbed them of their milk puts his two calves grazing on their mother's share. Ay! His two calves are lovely, sure enough. Why wouldn't they? Didn't they grow fat and strong on the milk that the little dead children should have drunk? Ah! The poor little dead creatures! It's a fine state of affairs truly, with two children dead and two beasts rolling in fat on their share of food. Mother of God! That's a cursed state of affairs for you! Beasts given rich food and children let die of hunger! Damnation has surely fallen on our village when such things are let happen here."

The men jeered at these remarks. They had lost faith in the old man.

"You are envious of Colm," they said to Gorum. "You are jealous of his success and his wisdom. You are no longer a wise man. Hatred has made a windbag of you."

One by one, they entered Colm's house, sat by his hearth and shared their pipes with him. Their wives brought presents to Mrs. Derrane and knitted with her on Sunday after Mass, at the women's hillock. The men came to Colm for advice, just as they had hitherto gone to Gorum. They put Colm in the place of honour at the meeting place. There was silence when he spoke.

"God is good to us," Colm said to his wife.

"He is, 'faith," Mrs. Derrane said. "Praised be His name."

Even so, it became more and more difficult for the family to make ends meet. The rent for the widow's farm put a heavy strain on their purse. The children's enthusiasm vanished during the winter in face of continual hunger. It became almost impossible to make them do a hand's turn.

Mrs. Derrane also forgot her solemn promise of co-operation and began to grumble out loud when Colm would not even allow an egg for the Christmas dinner.

"Great God!" she said. "There is a limit to everything. We haven't seen fish or meat since spring. You wouldn't let us buy a piece of holly or a coloured candle. We are a disgrace to the whole village, with nothing on our table but potatoes and salt for the feast of our Lord."

"Silence," Colm said. "This is no time of the year to become impudent."

To cap it all, he ordered that the cloth made from that year's wool be sold, instead of turning it into garments for the household.

"Our rags will do us well enough for another year," he said. "In any case, patched clothes are just as warm as new ones."

Everybody in the house got terribly thin and weak. Yet Colm's iron will buoyed them up to such an extent that there was no illness.

"We have only to hold on a little while," he kept saying, "and have courage. Then we'll rise in the world. We'll be rich and famous, from one end of the parish to the other."

He himself looked like a skeleton, for he practically went without food in order that the children might have as much as possible.

"You'll kill yourself," his wife said when he began to prepare the ground for the spring sowing. "You look like a sick man. For God's sake, let me take money out of the purse and buy a pig's cheek for you."

"Silence, woman," Colm said. "Not a penny must be touched. I have a plan. We'll need all we have and more to make my new plan work. It's not easy to become rich, I tell you."

The cow relieved the desperate plight of the family by having her calf a month earlier than usual, during the first week of March. The children became gay once more, for they were given plenty of the new milk to drink. There was buttermilk to make the bread rise. There was even beautiful, salty yellow butter, fresh from the churn and with pale drops of water glistening on its surface, to spread thickly on the long slices of crusty griddle cake.

The happy children began to whisper excitedly to one another in the evenings about the coming spring fair, when great riches were to come into the house from the sale of the pigs and the yearlings. Over and over again, they discussed the toys and trinkets that their mother would buy them in the town on fair day, as a reward for their help in raising the two beasts.

They were continually running to the field where the yearlings were gorging themselves on the luscious young grass.

"They are champions," they cried boastfully as they stared at the animals over the top of the stone fence. "Nobody ever before saw such lovely beasts."

Colm put an end to the children's dreams a few days before the fair.

"Listen to me, all of you," he told the family one evening after supper. "You have worked hard helping me with the two beasts. They are now fine yearlings, God bless them. We'll all have to work a little harder, though, so as to make them the two best bullocks that were ever seen."

Mrs. Derrane was dumbfounded on hearing this news. She dropped on to a stool and fanned her face with her apron.

"Are you out of your mind, Colm?" she said at length. "How could we keep those two beasts another year? How could we keep two bullocks? Won't we have this year's calf, too, growing up and eating on us?"

"I have a plan," Colm said. "We are going to open a shop."

His wife made the sign of the Cross on her forehead and looked at him in horror.

"Why not?" said Colm. "It's only shopkeepers that rise in the world."

"Are you crazy?" his wife said. "Where would we get the money to open a shop?"

"All we need is courage," Colm said. "The few pounds we have saved, together with the price of the pigs, will be enough to open it. I'm telling you, woman, that all we need is courage and willingness. If we all work hard together, night and day . . ."

"God Almighty!" his wife interrupted. "You've gone mad. Those two beasts have gone to your head."

"Now, then," said Colm. "That's not true at all. I was never wiser in my life. The war will last for years yet. It's only now the real fury is coming on the fighting nations. Very well, then. While the mad people are fighting and killing each other, let us make money out of them and rise in the world. There is going to be a demand for everything that can be eaten. There will be a price for everything fit to make your mouth water. Food is going to be more precious than gold. So will clothes. In God's name, then, let us open a shop and stock it with goods. Let us go around the parish with our horse and cart, buying up everything the people have to sell, eggs and butter and carigeen moss and fish and wool and hides and potatoes. We'll buy everything that can be parted away. We can pay them for what we buy with shop goods. Do you see? Then we'll sell what we buy from the people over in the town at a profit. Later on, we can buy sheep as well and . . ."

"Arrah! You're stark crazy," his wife interrupted angrily. "Stop talking like that, man alive, in front of the children."

At this moment all the children burst into tears, no longer able to contain their disappointment.

"Stop whinging," Colm shouted, as he leaped to his feet. "Is it crying you are because there will be nothing for you from the fair? Is it for sweets and crackers you are crying and dai-dais? All right, then. I'm telling you now there will be plenty of sweets and dai-dais for you when we have a shop. There will be sweets every day and dai-dais, too. Do you hear me? Every day in the year will be like a fair day for you."

His uncouth face, worn to the bone by privation and worry, now glowed with the light of ecstasy, as he struggled to wheedle his family into co-operation with his ambition to "rise in the world." Such was the power of the idea that possessed him that the children stopped crying almost at once. They listened with eagerness to his fantastic promises. Their little faces became as radiant as his own.

His wife also became affected as she saw her dour husband trying to win over the children by means of smiles and gaiety and honeyed words.

"I wouldn't believe it," she said, "only for I see it with my own two eyes."

Tears rolled down her cheeks and her upper lip trembled.

"In fifteen years," she muttered as she rubbed her eyes with a corner of her apron, "I never once saw him dance one of the children on his knee. No, 'faith, I never once saw him shake a rattle in front of a whinging baby. Yet there he is now, all of a sudden, trying to make a showman of himself. God Almighty! Only for I see it with my own two eyes . . ."

"There will be no end to the riches we'll have when we are shop-keepers," Colm continued. "We can have bacon for breakfast. Yes, indeed, we can eat great big rashers of it every morning in the year, except Fridays. The people of the village will be coming to smell the lovely food that's frying on our pan. Oh! I'm telling you that we can have bellies on us like tourists. We'll hardly be able to carry ourselves as we walk the road, on account of our fat. We'll have ribbons as well and velvet and a mirror in every room."

His wife and children were won over completely to his side once more. So they all went to work with enthusiasm and the shop was speedily installed. It was an immediate success. People came specially from a long distance in order to trade with the courageous man, who was trying to raise two bullocks on twenty acres of barren rocks.

"Blood in ounce!" the people said. "He'll never be able to do it, but you have to admire his courage all the same. He'll very likely end up in the asylum with Kate Higgins, but more power to him for trying. He's a credit to the parish."

When Colm went round with his horse and cart, accompanied by one or other of the children, everybody was eager to do business with him.

The people sold him whatever they had available and they forbore to drive a hard bargain. He soon had to take the house and barn that belonged to Kate Higgins, in order to store the great mass of his goods. Within a few months he was making trips to the town twice a week and getting high prices for all he had to sell.

Money kept coming into the house so quickly and in such large quantities that his wife became frightened.

"May God keep pride and arrogance out of our hearts," she used to say as she stuffed the notes into the long cloth purse. "It's dangerous to get rich so quickly."

"Have no fear, woman," Colm said to her. "We denied ourselves and we didn't lose heart when times were bad. So now God is giving us a big hansel as a reward. Be grateful, woman, and have no fear."

The promises that he had made to the children were fulfilled. There was full and plenty in the house. The little girls had ribbons to their hair and dai-dais to amuse their leisure. His wife got a velvet dress and a hat with feathers. There was bacon for breakfast.

"He must have touched the magic stone," said the astonished people of the village. "Everything he handles turns into lashings of money."

Andy Gorum alone continued to prophesy that misfortune would fall on Colm for attempting to "stand alone and rise above the people."

"You just wait," Gorum kept shouting on the hill before the village. "God will strike him down when he least expects it. Those two beasts, that are now so lovely, will never reach the fair green alive on their four legs."

This prophecy proved to be just as false as the previous one that Gorum had made. All through the winter and the following spring, Colm and his family lavished the greatest care on the two beasts that had brought them prosperity. So that they were really champions on fair day. The bullock with the wine-dark hide was acknowledged by all to be the finest animal of his age ever seen in the district. He fetched top price.

Tears poured down Colm's cheeks as he walked back from the railway station with his wife, after parting with his beasts.

"Those two lovely beasts brought me luck," he said. "I feel lonely for them now that they are gone. Only for them, I'd never think of rising in the world. Praised be God! He works in strange ways. He strikes one down and raises up another."

"True for you," his wife said. "Praised be His holy name! Who are we, miserable sinners that we are, to question His mysterious ways?"

"Only for that cow dying on Kate Higgins," Colm continued, "we'd always be land slaves, wrestling with starvation to the end of our days and never getting the better of any bout. Look at us now, woman. We're on our way towards riches. God alone knows where we'll stop."

"Enough of that talk now," his wife said. "Don't let arrogance get hold of us. Don't let us be boastful. The people are already becoming envious of us. I can see a begrudging look in the eyes of the neighbours."

"That's true," Colm said. "That's why I'm thinking of opening a shop in the town. It might be better to take ourselves out of the sight of people that knew us poor."

"A shop in the town?" his wife said. "Don't get too big for your boots, Colm."

"No fear," Colm said. "I know what I'm doing. I'm going to hire a few men and begin buying in earnest. There's money to be picked up by the bushel all over the place. All we need is courage, woman."

"In God's name!" his wife said.

When they were hitching the mare to their new jaunting car for the journey home, Andy Gorum came along with a group of intoxicated men.

"The mills of God grind slow," Gorum shouted, "but they grind sure. The bloodsuckers are taking the food out of our country. They are giving it to the fighting foreigners, while our children die of hunger. We are barefooted and in rags, but they give our wool and our hides to the war people. They are taking all our lovely beasts across the sea to fill the bellies of pagans. The time will soon come, though, when the bloodsuckers that are robbing us will be struck down by the hand of Almighty God. They will roast in Hell for the everlasting ages."

As Colm drove away in his new green jaunting car, quite a number of people whistled after him in hostility and derision. Now that he had risen so far, he had again become an enemy.

His gaunt face looked completely unaware of their jeers. His pale blue eyes stared fixedly straight ahead, cold and resolute and ruthless.

Questions and Assignments

1. Did Colm really help the widow Kate Higgins by buying her calf? Why then did she insist? Is there any similarity between the characters and attitudes of

these two people? What about the character of Kate's husband as revealed by the fact that he was so anxious to breed a champion calf?

2. Trace the various references to the war throughout the story. What is their significance, both to the unfolding of the action of the story and to the overall theme? Would Colm have achieved such success without the war?

3. What effect do the following phrases have on the reader's understanding of Colm's decision: "intoxicated by the idea of possessing them both," "he muttered fiercely," "frenzy of desire," "glancing furtively," "the anticipation of venery"? How does his decision affect his character?

4. Gorum serves as community spokesman in this story. What is his point of view and why? Who else is he a spokesman for? Compare Colm's remark near the end of the story, "God alone knows where we'll stop," with Gorum's final prophecy, "The bloodsuckers that are robbing us will be struck down by the hand of Almighty God. . . ." What is the significance of the story's end?

5. Is Colm really being altruistic in offering to rent the widow's land? Does his greater attention to the children in particular instances indicate greater love? Why is he so gentle to his wife after beating her? Is his family happier at the end of the story? Is the community better off? Is the world better for his action? Is he a better man?

6. Notice the references to God throughout the story. Kate Higgins refers to Him constantly. Is she a deeply religious person? How do the attitudes of Colm and his wife change in regard to God as the story progresses? Kate claims at one point that Colm has been possessed by the devil, but Colm and his wife claim that their success has come from God. What do you think about it? Are they more truly religious at the end or at the beginning of the story?

7. Write an essay showing that Colm's success is good, or evil, and why.

8. Explain the significance in the story of one of the characters, such as Kate Higgins, Gorum, Colm's children, the calves.

9. Explain the significance of some particular event in the story, such as the war, the death of Kate Higgins' children, the frugal Christmas dinner.

10. Write an essay based on one of the following quotations:

"We couldn't leave neighbours without milk in order to fill a calf's belly."

"You deserve to prosper on account of your intelligence."

"Those that have give only to those that have."

"Whoever tries to stand alone and work for his own profit becomes an enemy of all."

"It's dangerous to get rich so quickly."

The Guest

ALBERT CAMUS

The schoolmaster was watching the two men climb toward him. One was on horseback, the other on foot. They had not yet tackled the abrupt rise leading to the schoolhouse built on the hillside. They were toiling onward, making slow progress in the snow, among the stones, on the vast expanse of the high, deserted plateau. From time to time the horse stumbled. He could not be heard yet but the breath issuing from his nostrils could be seen. The schoolmaster calculated that it would take them a half hour to get onto the hill. It was cold; he went back into the school to get a sweater.

He crossed the empty, frigid classroom. On the blackboard the four rivers of France, drawn with four different colored chalks, had been flowing toward their estuaries for the past three days. Snow had suddenly fallen in mid-October after eight months of drought without the transition of rain, and the twenty pupils, more or less, who lived in the villages scattered over the plateau had stopped coming. With fair weather they would return. Daru now heated only the single room that was his lodging, adjoining the classroom. One of the windows faced, like the classroom windows, the south. On that side the school was a few kilometers from the point where the plateau began to slope toward the south. In clear weather the purple mass of the mountain range where the gap opened onto the desert could be seen.

Somewhat warmed, Daru returned to the window from which he had first noticed the two men. They were no longer visible. Hence they must have tackled the rise. The sky was not so dark, for the snow had stopped falling during the night. The morning had dawned with a dirty light which had scarcely become brighter as the ceiling of clouds lifted. At two in the afternoon it seemed as if the day were merely beginning. But still this was better than those three days when the thick snow was falling amidst unbroken darkness with little gusts of wind that rattled the double door of the classroom. Then Daru had spent long hours in his room, leaving it only to go to the shed and feed the chickens or get some coal. Fortunately the delivery truck from Tadjid, the nearest village to the north, had brought his supplies two days before the blizzard. It would return in forty-eight hours.

Besides, he had enough to resist a siege, for the little room was cluttered with bags of wheat that the administration had left as a supply to distribute to those of his pupils whose families had suffered from the drought. Actually they had all been victims because they were all poor. Every day Daru would distribute a ration to the children. They had missed it, he knew, during these bad days. Possibly one of the fathers or big brothers would come this afternoon and he could supply them with grain. It was just a matter of carrying them over to the next harvest. Now shiploads of wheat were arriving from France and the worst was over. But it would be hard to forget that poverty, that army of ragged ghosts wandering in the sunlight, the plateaus burned to a cinder month after month, the earth shriveled up little by little, literally scorched, every stone bursting into dust under one's foot. The sheep had died then by thousands, and even a few men, here and there, sometimes without anyone's knowing.

In contrast with such poverty, he who lived almost like a monk, in his remote schoolhouse, had felt like a lord with his whitewashed walls, his narrow couch, his unpainted shelves, his well, and his weekly provisioning with water and food. And suddenly this snow, without warning, without the foretaste of rain. This is the way the region was, cruel to live in, even without men, who didn't help matters either. But Daru had been born here. Everywhere else, he felt exiled.

He went out and stepped forward on the terrace in front of the schoolhouse. The two men were now halfway up the slope. He recognized the horseman to be Balducci, the old gendarme he had known for a long time. Balducci was holding at the end of a rope an Arab walking behind him with hands bound and head lowered. The gendarme waved a greeting to which Daru did not reply, lost as he was in contemplation of the Arab dressed in a faded blue *jellaba,* his feet in sandals but covered with socks of heavy raw wool, his head crowned with a narrow, short *chèche.* Balducci was holding back his horse in order not to hurt the Arab, and the group was advancing slowly.

Within earshot, Balducci shouted, "One hour to do the three kilometers from El Ameur!" Daru did not answer. Short and square in his thick sweater, he watched them climb. Not once had the Arab raised his head. "Hello," said Daru when they got up onto the terrace. "Come in and warm up." Balducci painfully got down from his horse without letting go of the rope. He smiled at the schoolmaster from under his bristling mustache. His little dark eyes, deep-set under a tanned forehead, and his mouth surrounded with wrinkles made him look attentive and studious. Daru took the bridle, led the horse to the shed, and came back to the two men who were now waiting for him in the school. He led them into his room. "I am going to heat up the classroom," he said. "We'll be more comfortable there."

When he entered the room again, Balducci was on the couch. He had undone the rope tying him to the Arab, who had squatted near the stove. His hands still bound, the *chèche* pushed back on his head, the Arab was looking toward the window. At first Daru noticed only his huge lips, fat, smooth, almost Negroid; yet his nose was straight, his eyes dark and full of fever. The *chèche* uncovered an obstinate forehead and, under the weathered skin now rather discolored by the cold, the whole face had a restless and rebellious look. "Go into the other room," said the schoolmaster, "and I'll make you some mint tea." "Thanks," Balducci said. "What a chore! How I long for retirement." And addressing his prisoner in Arabic, he said, "Come on, you." The Arab got up and, slowly, holding his bound wrists in front of him, went into the classroom.

With the tea, Daru brought a chair. But Balducci was already sitting in state at the nearest pupil's desk, and the Arab had squatted against the teacher's platform facing the stove, which stood between the desk and the window. When he held out the glass of tea to the prisoner, Daru hesitated at the sight of his bound hands. "He might perhaps be untied." "Sure," said Balducci. "That was for the trip." He started to get to his feet. But Daru, setting the glass on the floor, had knelt beside the Arab. Without saying anything, the Arab watched him with his feverish eyes. Once his hands were free, he rubbed his swollen wrists against each other, took the glass of tea and sucked up the burning liquid in swift little sips.

"Good," said Daru. "And where are you headed?"

Balducci withdrew his mustache from the tea. "Here, son."

"Odd pupils! And you're spending the night?"

"No. I'm going back to El Ameur. And you will deliver this fellow to Tinguit. He is expected at police headquarters."

Balducci was looking at Daru with a friendly little smile.

"What's this story?" asked the schoolmaster. "Are you pulling my leg?"

"No, son. Those are the orders."

"The orders? I'm not . . ." Daru hesitated, not wanting to hurt the old Corsican. "I mean, that's not my job."

"What! What's the meaning of that? In wartime people do all kinds of jobs."

"Then I'll wait for the declaration of war!"

Balducci nodded. "O.K. But the orders exist and they concern you too. Things are bubbling, it appears. There is talk of a forthcoming revolt. We are mobilized, in a way."

Daru still had his obstinate look.

"Listen, son," Balducci said. "I like you and you've got to understand. There's only a dozen of us at El Ameur to patrol the whole territory of a small department and I must be back in a hurry. He couldn't be kept there. His village was beginning to stir; they wanted to take him back. You must take him to Tinguit tomorrow before the day is over. Twenty kilometers shouldn't faze a husky fellow like you. After that, all will be over. You'll come back to your pupils and your comfortable life."

Behind the wall the horse could be heard snorting and pawing the earth. Daru was looking out the window. Decidedly the weather was clearing and the light was increasing over the snowy plateau. When all the snow was melted, the sun would take over again and once more would burn the fields of stone. For days still, the unchanging sky would shed its dry light on the solitary expanse where nothing had any connection with man.

"After all," he said, turning around toward Balducci, "what did he do?" And, before the gendarme had opened his mouth, he asked, "Does he speak French?"

"No, not a word. We had been looking for him for a month, but they were hiding him. He killed his cousin."

"Is he against us?"

"I don't think so. But you can never be sure."

"Why did he kill?"

"A family squabble, I think. One owed grain to the other, it seems. It's not at all clear. In short, he killed his cousin with a billhook. You know, like a sheep, *kreezk!*"

Balducci made the gesture of drawing a blade across his throat, and the Arab, his attention attracted, watched him with a sort of anxiety. Daru felt a sudden wrath against the man, against all men with their rotten spite, their tireless hates, their blood lust.

But the kettle was singing on the stove. He served Balducci more tea, hesitated, then served the Arab again, who drank avidly a second time. His raised arms made the *jellaba* fall open, and the schoolmaster saw his thin, muscular chest.

"Thanks, son," Balducci said. "And now I'm off."

He got up and went toward the Arab, taking a small rope from his pocket.

"What are you doing?" Daru asked dryly.

Balducci, disconcerted, showed him the rope.

"Don't bother."

The old gendarme hesitated. "It's up to you. Of course, you are armed?"

"I have my shotgun."

"Where?"

"In the trunk."

"You ought to have it near your bed."

"Why? I have nothing to fear."

"You're crazy, son. If there's an uprising, no one is safe; we're all in the same boat."

"I'll defend myself. I'll have time to see them coming."

Balducci began to laugh, then suddenly the mustache covered the white teeth. "You'll have time? O.K. That's just what I was saying. You always have been a little cracked. That's why I like you; my son was like that."

At the same time he took out his revolver and put it on the desk. "Keep it; I don't need two weapons from here to El Ameur."

The revolver shone against the black paint of the table. When the gendarme turned toward him, the schoolmaster caught his smell of leather and horseflesh.

"Listen, Balducci," Daru said suddenly, "all this disgusts me, beginning with your fellow here. But I won't hand him over. Fight, yes, if I have to. But not that."

The old gendarme stood in front of him and looked at him severely.

"You're being a fool," he said slowly. "I don't like it either. You don't get used to putting a rope on a man even after years of it, and you're even ashamed—yes, ashamed. But you can't let them have their way."

"I won't hand him over," Daru said again.

"It's an order, son, and I repeat it."

"That's right. Repeat to them what I've said to you: I won't hand him over."

Balducci made a visible effort to reflect. He looked at the Arab and at Daru. At last he decided.

"No, I won't tell them anything. If you want to drop us, go ahead; I'll not denounce you. I have an order to deliver the prisoner and I'm doing so. And now you'll just sign this paper for me."

"There's no need. I'll not deny that you left him with me."

"Don't be mean with me. I know you'll tell the truth. You're from around these parts and you are a man. But you must sign; that's the rule."

Daru opened his drawer, took out a little square bottle of purple ink, the red wooden penholder with the "sergeant-major" pen he used for models of handwriting, and signed. The gendarme carefully folded the paper and put it into his wallet. Then he moved toward the door.

"I'll see you off," Daru said.

"No," said Balducci. "There's no use being polite. You insulted me."

He looked at the Arab, motionless in the same spot, sniffed peevishly, and turned away toward the door. "Good-by, son," he said. The door slammed behind him. His footsteps were muffled by the snow. The horse stirred on the other side of the wall and several chickens fluttered in fright. A moment later Balducci reappeared outside the window leading the horse by the bridle. He walked toward the little rise without turning around and disappeared from sight with the horse following him.

Daru walked back toward the prisoner, who, without stirring, never took his eyes off him. "Wait," the schoolmaster said in Arabic and went toward the bedroom. As he was going through the door, he had a second thought, went to the desk, took the revolver, and stuck it in his pocket. Then, without looking back, he went into his room.

For some time he lay on his couch watching the sky gradually close over, listening to the silence. It was this silence that had seemed painful to him during the first days here, after the war. He had requested a post in the little town at the base of the foothills separating the upper plateaus from the desert. There rocky walls, green and black to the north, pink and lavender to the south, marked the frontier of eternal summer. He had been named to a post farther north, on the plateau itself. In the beginning, the solitude and the silence had been hard for him on these wastelands peopled only by stones. Occasionally, furrows suggested cultivation, but they had been dug to uncover a certain kind of stone good for building. The only plowing here was to harvest rocks. Elsewhere a thin layer of soil accumulated in the hollows would be scraped out to enrich paltry village gardens. This is the way it was: bare rock covered three quarters of the region. Towns sprang up, flourished, then disappeared; men came by, loved one another or fought bitterly, then died. No one in this desert, neither he nor his guest, mattered. And yet, outside this desert neither of them, Daru knew, could have really lived.

When he got up, no noise came from the classroom. He was amazed at the unmixed joy he derived from the mere thought that the Arab might have fled and that he would be alone with no decision to make. But the prisoner was there. He had merely stretched out between the stove and the desk and he was staring at the ceiling. In that position, his thick lips were particularly noticeable, giving him a pouting look. "Come," said Daru. The Arab got up and followed him. In the bedroom the schoolmaster pointed to a chair near the table under the window. The Arab sat down without ceasing to watch Daru.

"Are you hungry?"

"Yes," the prisoner said.

Daru set the table for two. He took flour and oil, shaped a cake in a frying pan, and lighted the little stove that functioned on bottled gas. While the cake was cooking, he went out to the shed to get cheese, eggs, dates, and condensed milk. When the cake was done he set it on the window sill to cool, heated some condensed milk diluted with water, and beat up the eggs into an omelette. In one of his motions he bumped into the revolver stuck in his right pocket. He set the bowl down, went into the classroom, and put the revolver in his desk drawer. When he came back to the room, night was falling. He put on the light and served the Arab. "Eat," he said. The Arab took a piece of the cake, lifted it eagerly to his mouth, and stopped short.

"And you?" he asked.

"After you. I'll eat too."

The thick lips opened slightly. The Arab hesitated, then bit into the cake determinedly.

The meal over, the Arab looked at the schoolmaster. "Are you the judge?"

"No, I'm simply keeping you until tomorrow."

"Why do you eat with me?"

"I'm hungry."

The Arab fell silent. Daru got up and went out. He brought back a camp cot from the shed and set it up between the table and the stove, at right angles to his own bed. From a large suitcase which, upright in a corner, served as a shelf for papers, he took two blankets and arranged them on the cot. Then he stopped, felt useless, and sat down on his bed. There was nothing more to do or to get ready. He had to look at this man. He looked at him therefore, trying to imagine his face bursting with rage. He couldn't do so. He could see nothing but the dark yet shining eyes and the animal mouth.

"Why did you kill him?" he asked in a voice whose hostile tone surprised him.

The Arab looked away. "He ran away. I ran after him."

He raised his eyes to Daru again and they were full of a sort of woeful interrogation. "Now what will they do to me?"

"Are you afraid?"

The Arab stiffened, turning his eyes away.

"Are you sorry?"

The Arab stared at him openmouthed. Obviously he did not understand. Daru's annoyance was growing. At the same time he felt awkward and self-conscious with his big body wedged between the two beds.

"Lie down there," he said impatiently. "That's your bed."

The Arab didn't move. He cried out, "Tell me!"

The schoolmaster looked at him.

"Is the gendarme coming back tomorrow?"

"I don't know."

"Are you coming with us?"

"I don't know. Why?"

The prisoner got up and stretched out on top of the blankets, his feet toward the window. The light from the electric bulb shone straight into his eyes and he closed them at once.

"Why?" Daru repeated, standing beside the bed.

The Arab opened his eyes under the blinding light and looked at him, trying not to blink. "Come with us," he said.

In the middle of the night, Daru was still not asleep. He had gone to bed after undressing completely; he generally slept naked. But when he suddenly realized that he had nothing on, he wondered. He felt vulnerable and the temptation came to him to put his clothes back on. Then he shrugged his shoulders; after all, he wasn't a child, and, if it came to that, he could break his adversary in two. From his bed, he could observe him lying on his back, still motionless, his eyes closed under the harsh light. When Daru turned out the light, the darkness seemed to congeal all of a sudden. Little by little, the night came back to life in the window where the starless sky was stirring gently. The schoolmaster soon made out the body lying at his feet. The Arab was still motionless but his eyes seemed open. A faint wind was prowling about the schoolhouse. Perhaps it would drive away the clouds and the sun would reappear.

During the night the wind increased. The hens fluttered a little and then were silent. The Arab turned over on his side with his back to Daru, who thought he heard him moan. Then he listened for his guest's breathing, which had become heavier and more regular. He listened to that breathing so close to him and mused without being able to go to sleep. In the room where he had been sleeping alone for a year, this presence bothered him. But it bothered him also because it imposed on him a sort of brotherhood he refused to accept in the present circumstances; yet he was familiar with it. Men who share the same rooms, soldiers or prisoners, develop a strange alliance as if, having cast off their armor with their clothing, they fraternized every evening, over and above their differences, in the ancient community of dream and fatigue. But Daru shook himself; he didn't like such musings, and it was essential for him to sleep.

A little later, however, when the Arab stirred slightly, the schoolmaster was still not asleep. When the prisoner made a second move, he stiffened, on the alert. The Arab was lifting himself slowly on his arms with almost the motion of a sleepwalker. Seated upright in bed, he waited motionless without turning his head toward Daru, as if he were listening attentively. Daru did not stir; it had just occurred to him that the revolver was still in the drawer of his desk. It was better to act at once. Yet he continued to observe the prisoner, who, with the same slithery motion, put his feet on the ground, waited again, then stood up slowly. Daru was about to call out to him when the Arab began to walk, in a quite natural but extraordinarily silent way. He was heading toward the door at the end of the room that opened into the shed. He lifted the latch with precaution and went out, pushing the door behind him but without shutting it.

Daru had not stirred. "He is running away," he merely thought. "Good riddance!" Yet he listened attentively. The hens were not fluttering; the guest must be on the plateau. A faint sound of water reached him, and he didn't know what it was until the Arab again stood framed in the doorway, closed the door carefully, and came back to bed without a sound. Then

Daru turned his back on him and fell asleep. Still later he seemed, from the depths of his sleep, to hear furtive steps around the schoolhouse. "I'm dreaming! I'm dreaming!" he repeated to himself. And he went on sleeping.

When he awoke, the sky was clear; the loose window let in a cold, pure air. The Arab was asleep, hunched up under the blankets now, his mouth open, utterly relaxed. But when Daru shook him he started dreadfully, staring at Daru with wild eyes as if he had never seen him and with such a frightened expression that the schoolmaster stepped back. "Don't be afraid. It is I. You must eat." The Arab nodded his head and said yes. Calm had returned to his face, but his expression was vacant and listless.

The coffee was ready. They drank it seated together on the cot as they munched their pieces of the cake. Then Daru led the Arab under the shed and showed him the faucet where he washed. He went back into the room, folded the blankets on the cot, made his own bed, and put the room in order. Then he went through the classroom and out onto the terrace. The sun was already rising in the blue sky; a soft, bright light enveloped the deserted plateau. On the ridge the snow was melting in spots. The stones were about to reappear. Crouched on the edge of the plateau, the schoolmaster looked at the deserted expanse. He thought of Balducci. He had hurt him, for he had sent him off as though he didn't want to be associated with him. He could still hear the gendarme's farewell and, without knowing why, he felt strangely empty and vulnerable.

At that moment, from the other side of the schoolhouse, the prisoner coughed. Daru listened to him almost despite himself and then, furious, threw a pebble that whistled through the air before sinking into the snow. That man's stupid crime revolted him, but to hand him over was contrary to honor; just thinking of it made him boil with humiliation. He simultaneously cursed his own people who had sent him this Arab and the Arab who had dared to kill and not managed to get away. Daru got up, walked in a circle on the terrace, waited motionless, and then went back into the schoolhouse.

The Arab, leaning over the cement floor of the shed, was washing his teeth with two fingers. Daru looked at him and said, "Come." He went back into the room ahead of the prisoner. He slipped a hunting jacket on over his sweater and put on walking shoes. Standing, he waited until the Arab had put on his *chèche* and sandals. They went into the classroom, and the schoolmaster pointed to the exit saying, "Go ahead." The fellow didn't budge. "I'm coming," said Daru. The Arab went out. Daru went back into the room and made a package with pieces of rusk, dates, and sugar in it. In the classroom, before going out, he hesitated a second in front of his desk, then crossed the threshold and locked the door. "That's the way," he said. He started toward the east, followed by the prisoner. But a short distance from the schoolhouse he thought he heard a slight sound behind him. He retraced his steps and examined the surroundings of the house; there was no one there. The Arab watched him without seeming to understand. "Come on," said Daru.

They walked for an hour and rested beside a sharp needle of limestone. The snow was melting faster and faster and the sun was drinking up the puddles just as quickly, rapidly cleaning the plateau, which gradually dried and vibrated like the air itself. When they resumed walking, the ground rang under their feet. From time to time a bird rent the space in front of them with a joyful cry. Daru felt a sort of rapture before the vast familiar expanse, now almost entirely yellow under its dome of blue sky. They walked an hour more, descending toward the south. They reached a sort of flattened elevation made up of crumbly rocks. From there on, the plateau sloped down—eastward toward a low plain on which could be made out a few spindly trees, and to the south toward outcroppings of rock that gave the landscape a chaotic look.

Daru surveyed the two directions. Not a man could be seen. He turned toward the Arab, who was looking at him blankly. Daru offered the package to him. "Take it," he said. "There are dates, bread, and sugar. You can hold out for two days. Here are a thousand francs too."

The Arab took the package and the money but kept his full hands at chest level as if he didn't know what to do with what was being given him.

"Now look," the schoolmaster said as he pointed in the direction of the east, "there's the way to Tinguit. You have a two-hour walk. At Tinguit are the administration and the police. They are expecting you."

The Arab looked toward the east, still holding the package and the money against his chest. Daru took his elbow and turned him rather roughly toward the south. At the foot of the elevation on which they stood could be seen a faint path. "That's the trail across the plateau. In a day's walk from here you'll find pasturelands and the first nomads. They'll take you in and shelter you according to their law."

The Arab had now turned toward Daru, and a sort of panic was visible in his expression. "Listen," he said.

Daru shook his head. "No, be quiet. Now I'm leaving you." He turned his back on him, took two long steps in the direction of the school, looked hesitantly at the motionless Arab, and started off again. For a few minutes he heard nothing but his own step resounding on the cold ground, and he did not turn his head. A moment later, however, he turned around. The Arab was still there on the edge of the hill, his arms hanging now, and he was looking at the schoolmaster. Daru felt something rise in his throat. But he swore with impatience, waved vaguely, and started off again. He had already gone a distance when he again stopped and looked. There was no longer anyone on the hill.

Daru hesitated. The sun was now rather high in the sky and beginning to beat down on his head. The schoolmaster retraced his steps, at first somewhat uncertainly, then with decision. When he reached the little hill, he was bathed in sweat. He climbed it as fast as he could and stopped, out of breath, on the top. The rock fields to the south stood out sharply against the blue sky, but on the plain to the east a steamy heat was rising. And in that slight haze, Daru, with heavy heart, made out the Arab walking slowly on the road to prison.

A little later, standing before the window of the classroom, the schoolmaster was watching the clear light bathing the whole surface of the plateau. Behind him on the blackboard, among the winding French rivers, sprawled the clumsily chalked up words he had just read: "You handed over our brother. You will pay for this." Daru looked at the sky, the plateau, and, beyond, the invisible lands stretching all the way to the sea. In this vast landscape he had loved so much, he was alone.

Questions and Assignments

1. How does the setting of this story—the school, the weather, the land, the times—contribute to the mood and, eventually, to the meaning of the story?

2. Describe Daru's character. What particular facts are revealed of his background and present circumstances? What qualities are most important in his character?

3. Explain these statements: "Daru felt a sudden wrath against the man, against all men with their rotten spite, their tireless hates, their blood lusts." "You always have been a little cracked. That's why I like you; my son was like that." Why does Daru not keep a gun handy and why does he leave the pistol in the drawer?

4. Is Balducci a sympathetic, unsympathetic, or neutral character? What does Camus tell us about him to make us like or dislike him? How is he similar to Daru, how different?

5. Why does Daru encourage the Arab to escape? Why does the Arab not escape? What is the meaning and relevance of the words chalked on the board? What is the significance of the title?

6. Examine in detail the conflict which is central to the story. Write an argument about the solution Camus gives to the conflict.

7. What is Camus' intention in regard to Daru? Write an essay about whether he is a villainous, heroic, confused, lukewarm, or kind-hearted character. Or write a similar essay on the character of the Arab.

INDEX

Aging Is Living